Date Due

DEC 8 2001			
SEP 24 2002			
1/6/02			

BRODART, CO.   Cat. No. 23-233-003   Printed in U.S.A.

CISCO ROUTER HANDBOOK

Cisco Router Handbook

George C. Sackett

McGraw-Hill
New York • San Francisco • Washington, D.C. • Auckland
Bogotá • Caracas • Lisbon • London • Madrid • Mexico City
Milan • Montreal • New Delhi • San Juan • Singapore
Sydney • Tokyo • Toronto

McGraw-Hill

A Division of The McGraw·Hill Companies

1 2 3 4 5 6 7 8 9 0   DOC/DOC   0 5 4 3 2 1 0

ISBN 0-07-212756-2

*The executive editor for this book was Steven Elliot and the production manager was
Clare Stanley. It was set in Century Schoolbook by MacAllister Publishing Services, LLC.*

Printed and bound by R. R. Donnelley & Sons Company.

McGraw-Hill books are available at special quantity discounts to use as
premiums and sales promotions, or for use in corporate training programs.
For more information, please write to Director of Special Sales, McGraw-Hill,
Two Penn Plaza, New York, NY 10121. Or contact your local bookstore.
Throughout this book, trademarked names are used. Rather than put a trademark symbol
after every occurrence of a trademarked name, we use names in an editorial fashion only,
and to the benefit of the trademark owner, with no intention of infringement of the trademark. Where such designations appear in this book, they have been printed with initial
caps.

This study guide and/or material is not sponsored by, endorsed by or affiliated with Cisco
Systems, Inc., Cisco®, Cisco Systems®, CCDA™, CCNA™, CCDP™, CCNP™, CCIE™, CCSI™,
the Cisco Systems logo and the CCIE logo are trademarks or registered trademarks of
Cisco Systems, Inc. in the United States and certain other countries. All other trademarks
are trademarks of their respective owners. Rather than put a trademark symbol after
every occurrence of a trademarked name, we use names in an editorial fashion only, and
to the benefit of the trademark owner, with no intention of infringement of the trademark. Where such designations appear in this book, they have been printed with initial
caps.

This book is printed on recycled, acid-free paper containing a minimum of 50
percent recycled de-inked fiber.

DEDICATION

This book is dedicated to my wife Nancy, without whom I would not have realized the meaning of "true love," nor understood the meaning behind dedication and commitment. With all my heart and soul I dedicate and commit to you, Nancy, my deepest love.

George Sackett

ACKNOWLEDGMENTS

First and foremost I must thank my wife Nancy for her incredible support on this time-consuming and lengthy project. She is the best. Secondly, I must extend my appreciation to Steve Elliot, Executive Editor at McGraw-Hill, who throughout this project was able to keep me driven, focused and excited about the handbook. I would also like to acknowledge Tony Costa CCIE#4140, Andrew Cassera, John Mairs, Gil Held, and Robert Caputo CCIE #1332, for their contributions to making this book timely and up-to-date with the newer technologies supported by Cisco Systems routers. I would also like to thank Gary Stewart, Technical Illustrator with Cisco Systems Icons Document Resource Connection department for providing the latest icon illustrations on this project. Not to be forgotten are the talented people who have made Cisco Systems the definitive networking company. Their insight, dedication, and fortitude have not only created a multibillion-dollar company but have forged cultural and social change not seen since the availability of the automobile to the masses. All their efforts are greatly appreciated. Finally, I must thank all my children, Chelsea, Pamela, James, Meredith, and Abigail for accepting my absence and irritability after many sleepless nights, and for the many times they have made me smile.

George Sackett

CONTENTS

Contents

Contents

Contents

Contents

Contents

Contents

About the Author

George C. Sackett is Managing Director of NetworX Corporation, a Cisco Systems Premier Certified Reseller and an AT&T Alliance Partner that develops corporate data networks for the communications, entertainment, medical, financial, manufacturing, and transportation industries. The author of other titles on Internetworking, including ATM & Multiprotocol Networking (Osborne-McGraw-Hill) and Internetworking with Cisco Solutions (Cisco Press), he has more than 18 years of technical and managerial experience with corporate data networks.

Technical Reviewer

As the leading publisher of technical books for more than 100 years, McGraw-Hill prides itself on bringing you the most authoritative and up-to-date information available. To ensure that our books meet the highest standards of accuracy, we have asked a top professional and technical expert to review the accuracy of the material you are about to read.

We take great pleasure in thanking the following technical reviewer for his insights:

Ashish M. Bakshi (A+, MCP+I, MCSE, MCT, CCNP, CCDP) is an independent networking and training consultant. He has passed his CCIE written and is currently preparing for the CCIE lab.

About the Contributors

John L. Mairs lives and works in San Francisco. He has his CCNA and CCDA certifications from Cisco Systems and his MCSE and MCP+I certifications from Microsoft. He is currently working for GE Capital IT Solutions as a Systems Engineer.

I would like to dedicate this to Dwight and Cathy Needham for their love and support through a critical time in my life. I miss you and Aunt Cathy.

John Mairs

First I would like to thank my children Nicole, Jessica, and Jake for putting up with the only dad in the world who makes his kids read Cisco manuals to him while he drives instead of getting to listen to the radio like normal children. I would like to thank Sean Manly and Arlene Uyemura for losing sleep to help me with this and finally I would like to thank George for the opportunity to work on this with him and to Steve Elliot for moral support and patience.

John Mairs

Gil Held is an award-winning author and lecturer who specializes in the application of computer and communications technology. He is the author of more than 40 books covering personal computers and data communications. Mr. Held was selected by Federal Computer World as one of the top 100 persons in government, industry, and academia who have made a difference in the acquisition and use of computer systems.

CHAPTER **1**

Cisco IOS
Software

We have all heard the saying, "It's what's inside that counts." In the world of networking, Cisco's Internetwork Operating Systems (IOS) has taken that saying to heart. The very core of Cisco Systems' phenomenal success is the breadth of services provided by the Cisco IOS software.

No two networks are exactly alike. Connectivity requirements differ between healthcare and manufacturing, entertainment and shipping, finance and telecommunications—each of which has different security issues. Each requires the capability to scale with reliability and manageability. The Cisco IOS software has proven to meet these criteria and to build on new requirements due to its flexibility in meeting the rapidly changing network requirements of all businesses.

Benefits

Cisco IOS software provides a foundation for meeting all the current and future networking requirements found in today's complex services-driven business environments. Businesses rely heavily on generating income from their network infrastructure. Cisco IOS software has the broadest set of networking features primarily based on international standards allowing Cisco products to interoperate with disparate media and devices across an enterprise network. Most importantly, Cisco IOS software enables corporations to deliver mission-critical applications seamlessly between various computing and networking systems.

Scalability

The network infrastructure for every corporation must be flexible to meet all the current and future internetworking requirements. Cisco IOS software uses some proprietary but also adheres to international standards for congestion avoidance using scalable routing protocols. These routing protocols allow a network using Cisco IOS to overcome network protocol limitations and deficiencies inherent in the protocols' architectures. Additional features in scaling an efficient use of bandwidth and resources include the ability of the IOS software in detailed packet filtering for reducing "chatty" protocol traffic as well as reducing network broadcasts through timers and helper addresses. All these features and more are available with the goal of reducing network traffic overhead, thereby maintaining an efficient yet effective network infrastructure.

Adaptiveness

Network outages occur frequently in corporate networks. However, these outages do not often affect the flow of business due to the reliability and adaptiveness of the policy-based IOS software routing features. Using routing protocols, each Cisco router can dynamically decide on the best route for delivering packets through the network around outages, thereby providing reliable delivery of information. The prioritization of packets and services enables Cisco routers to adapt to bandwidth constraints due to outages or high bandwidth utilization. IOS software load-balances traffic throughput over various network connections, preserving bandwidth and maintaining network performance.

The concept of virtual local area networks (LANs) has become a reality for many corporate networks. Cisco routers have the capability to participate in these virtual LANs using emulated LAN functions for physical LAN extensions and ATM LAN Emulation (LANE) services. These are just two of the many newer networking technologies incorporated into the IOS software feature set, enabling networks to implement newer technologies without the added expense of new hardware.

Access Support

The Cisco IOS software access support encompasses remote access and protocol translation services. These services provide connectivity to

- Terminals
- Modems
- Computers
- Printers
- Workstations

Various network configurations exist for connecting these network resources over LANs and wide area networks (WANs). LAN terminal service support is as follows:

- TCP/IP support for Telnet and rlogin connections to IP hosts.
- TN3270 connections to IBM hosts.
- LAT connections to DEC hosts.

For WANs, Cisco IOS software supports four flavors of server operations:

- Connectivity over a dial-up connection supporting

  - AppleTalk Remote Access (ARA)

  - Serial Line Internet Protocol (SLIP)

  - Compressed SLIP (CSLIP)

  - Point-to-Point Protocol (PPP)

  - Xremote, Network Computing Device's (NCD) X Window System terminal protocol

- Asynchronous terminal connectivity to a LAN or WAN using network and terminal emulation software supporting Telnet, rlogin, DEC's Local Area Transport (LAT) protocol, and IBM TN3270 terminal protocol.

- Conversion of a virtual terminal protocol into another protocol, such as LAT-TCP or TCP-LAT communication between a terminal and a host computer over the network.

- Support for full Internet Protocol (IP), Novell Internet Packet Exchange (IPX), and AppleTalk routing over dial-up asynchronous connections.

Performance Optimization

Optimizing networks requires network equipment to dynamically make decisions on routing packets in a cost-effective manner over the network. Cisco IOS software has two features that can greatly enhance bandwidth management, recovery, and routing in the network. These two features are dial-on-demand access (DDA) and dial-on-demand routing (DDR).

DDA is useful in several scenarios. These are

- Dial backup

- Dynamic bandwidth

In many instances, connectivity to a location fails because of a modem, DSU/CSU failure, or the main telecommunications line to the office is disrupted in some way. A good network design has a backup solution for this type of outage. Using DDA, a router can sense the line outage and perform a dial backup connection over a switched serial, ISDN, T1, or frame relay. In this manner, the office maintains connectivity to the WAN with minimal downtime. The DDA function monitors the primary line for activation and can cut back to the primary connection automatically if so desired.

DDA features the capability to determine a low and high bandwidth watermark on the permanent lines. This feature allows the addition of a temporary bandwidth to another location to meet throughput and performance criteria. The IOS monitors the permanent line for high bandwidth utilization. If the bandwidth reaches the defined threshold, DDA is enabled to add extra bandwidth to the remote location of the permanent line. IOS continues to monitor the bandwidth for utilization to fall under the threshold for a period of time. Once the low watermark is reached, IOS disconnects the DDA line. Using DDA in this fashion enables the IOS to maintain performance criteria between the two locations.

DDR allows Cisco routers to create temporary WAN connections based on interesting packets. IP, Novell IPX, X.25, Frame Relay, and SMDS destination addresses can be specified under DDR as interesting packets. Once the router interprets the packet and determines it is an interesting packet, it performs the dialup connection to the destination network specified in the packet that corresponds to the DDR configuration. In this way, connectivity to remote locations is provided on a temporary basis, thereby saving network connectivity costs.

Management

Cisco IOS software supports the following protocols:

- The two versions of Simple Network Management Protocol (SNMP) for IP-based network management systems
- The Common Management Interface Protocol (CMIP)/Common Management Interface Service (CMIS) for OSI-based network management systems
- IBM Network Management Vector Transport (NMVT) for SNA-based network management systems

These management protocols are pertinent to the type of network supported by the Cisco router. The IOS itself has the capability to perform configuration management services as well as monitoring and diagnostics services using the IOS command interface.

Cisco Systems has a suite of network management tools under the name of CiscoWorks. CiscoWorks works with Cisco IOS for change, configuration, accounting, performance, and fault management disciplines.

Security

Cisco IOS software supports many different types of security capabilities. Some of these, such as filtering, are not usually thought of as a security feature. Filtering, for example, was actually the first means of creating the now infamous firewall techniques for corporate connectivity on the Internet, prior to actual commercial offerings.

Secondly, filtering can be used to partition networks and prohibit access to high-security server networks. The IOS has the capability to encrypt passwords, authenticate dial-in access, require permissions on changing configurations, and provide accounting and logging to identify unauthorized access.

The IOS supports standard authentication packages for access to the router. These are RADIUS and TACACS+. Each security package requires unique user identification for access to the router. These security packages offer multilevel access to IOS command interface functions.

Packaging

The ordering of Cisco IOS software has been streamlined into feature sets. Prior to IOS Version 11.2, the IOS software was built based on the router requirements. A second enhancement to the delivery of IOS software is the use of feature packs. Feature packs allow you to order the IOS software images and a Windows 95 utility to load the image on the router.

Feature Sets

Each feature set contains a standard offering. However, options are provided to enable the IOS software to meet more specific needs. Each hardware platform has a feature set. For the most part, all the routers share the same feature sets. The sets are broken down into three categories:

- Basic: The basic feature set for the platform.
- Plus: The basic feature set plus added features depending on the platform.
- Encryption: 40-bit (Plus 40) or 56-bit (Plus 56) data encryption feature sets with the basic or plus feature set.

The list of features and feature sets and the platforms supporting them are found in Appendix A.

Feature Packs

IOS Release 11.2 introduced software feature packs, which offer a means for receiving all materials including software images, loading utilities, and manuals on CD-ROMs. Each feature pack contains two CD-ROMs. The software CD-ROM contains

- IOS software images
- AS5200 modem software images
- Windows 95 software installer program

A second CD-ROM is included, providing the Cisco IOS software documentation reference library. The remaining documentation provided by the feature pack includes an instruction manual for using the Windows 95 software installer program, release notes for the IOS release included on the software CD-ROM, and the software license.

Features Supported

All the features found in the matrices of Appendix A are applicable to each router and access server platform. These features cover a wide range of services and functions to take into account old, current, and future network configurations.

Protocols

Cisco IOS supports a wide array of networking protocols. Of these protocols, Transmission Control Protocol/Internet Protocol (TCP/IP) is by far the most widely used.

TCP/IP   Cisco IOS software supports the following TCP/IP features:

- IP access lists
- IP Security Option (IPSO)

- IP accounting
- Simple Network Management Protocol (SNMP)
- Serial Line Interface Protocol (SLIP)
- Address Resolution Protocol (ARP)
- Reverse Address Resolution Protocol (RARP)
- Domain Name System (DNS) support
- Internet Common Message Protocol (ICMP)
- Internet Group Management Protocol (IGMP)
- User Datagram Protocol (UDP)
- Telnet
- TN3270
- Trivial File Transfer Protocol (TFTP)

Release 10 and 10.3 of IOS introduced new features to already existing standards that have given Cisco routers the capability to provide higher levels of security, greater availability, and increased network scalability. Among these features are

- Hot Standby Router Protocol (HSRP) and Multigroup HSRP
- Next Hop Resolution Protocol (NHRP)
- Department of Defense Intelligence Information System Network Security for Information Exchange (DNSIX) extended IPSO
- Type of Service (TOS) queuing
- Cisco Discovery Protocol (CDP)
- Border Gateway Protocol (BGP) Communities

With the introduction of Release 11 and 11.1, the Cisco IOS software enhances router functionality in the areas of security, performance, and routing services. The major enhancements for these releases are

- Route Authentication with Message Digest 5 (MD5) encryption algorithm
- IP Access Control List (ACL) Violation Logging
- Policy-based routing
- Weighted fair queuing
- NHRP on IPX
- Fast Install for Static Routers

- Fast Switched GRE
- RIPV2

Release 11.2 implements more routing protocol enhancements, IP address translation features, and access control list usability. The major features introduced are

- On-Demand Routing (ODR) for stub routers
- OSPF On-Demand Circuit (RFC1793)
- OSPF Not-So-Stubby-Area (NSSA)
- BGP4 enhancements
  - Soft Configuration
  - Multipath
  - Prefix filtering with inbound route maps
- Network Address Translation (NAT)
- Named IP access control list
- Integrated routing and bridging (IRB)

ISO CLNS　The Open Systems Interconnection (OSI) reference model implements the International Organization for Standardization's (ISO) Connectionless Network Service (CLNS) as the network layer protocol. Cisco IOS fully supports the forwarding and routing of ISO CLNS. The ISO standards and Cisco implemented features supported by Cisco IOS are

- ISO 9542 End System-to-Intermediate System (ESIS) routing protocol
- ISO 8473 Connectionless Network Protocol (CLNP)
- ISO 8348/Ad2 Network Service Access Points (NSAP)
- ISO 10589 Intermediate System-to-Intermediate System (IS-IS) routing protocol
- DDR for OSI/CLNS
- Connection-Mode Network Service (CMNS) for X.25 using NSAP

DECnet Phase IV and Phase V　Cisco routers have supported DECnet for some time. IOS software has full functional support of local and wide area DECnet Phase IV and Phase V routing on all media types. Currently, Cisco IOS supports these enhanced DECnet features:

■ DECnet dial-on-demand (DDR)

■ Dynamic DECnet Route Advertisements

■ DECnet Host Name-to-Address Mapping

■ Target Address Resolution Protocol (TARP) support over SONET

Novell IPX   Since IOS Release 10.0, Cisco IOS provides complete IPX support. Beginning with Release 10.3, IOS enhancements for Novell have centered on performance, management, security, and usability. These enhancements are

■ Novell Link State Protocol (NLSP)

■ IPXWAN 2.0

■ IPX floating static routes

■ SPX spoofing

■ Enhanced IGRP to NLSP route redistribution

■ Input access lists

■ Per-host load-balancing

■ NLSP route aggregation

■ Raw FDDI IPX encapsulation

■ IPX header compression

■ Display SAP by name

■ IPX ACL violation logging

■ Plain English IPX access lists

AppleTalk Phase 1 and Phase 2   AppleTalk has been a long-standing supported protocol on Cisco IOS software. Extended and non-extended networks under AppleTalk Phase 2 are supported. Cisco IOS routes AppleTalk packets over all media types. The AppleTalk features implemented by Cisco IOS are

■ MacIP

■ IPTalk

■ SNMP over AppleTalk

■ Routing Table Maintenance Protocol (RTMP)

■ AppleTalk Update-Based Routing Protocol (AURP)

■ AppleTalk over enhanced IGRP

- Inter-enterprise routing
- AppleTalk Name Binding Protocol (NBP) filtering
- AppleTalk floating static routes
- Simple multicast routing protocol (SMRP)
- AppleTalk load-balancing
- SMRP fast switching

Banyan VINES   Banyan's Virtual Integrated Network Service (VINES) is supported on all media types with Cisco IOS software. The VINES routing protocol itself automatically determines a metric for delivering routing updates. This metric is based on the delay set for the interface. Cisco IOS enhances this metric by allowing you to customize the value for the metric. Other enhancements and features supported on Banyan VINES using Cisco IOS are

- Address resolution in response to address requests and broadcast propagation
- MAC-level echo support to Ethernet, IEEE 802.2, Token Ring, and FDDI
- Name to address mapping for VINES host names
- Access list filtering of packets to or from specific networks
- Routing Table Protocol (RTP)
- Sequenced Routing Update Protocol (SRTP)
- VINES DDR
- Floating static routes

Xerox Network System (XNS)   XNS is the foundation for the Novell IPX protocol. As such, Cisco IOS supports an XNS-routing protocol subset of the XNS protocol stack. XNS is supported on

- Ethernet
- FDDI
- Token Ring
- Point-to-point serial lines using HDLC
- Link Access Procedure Balanced (LAPB)
- X.25 Frame relay
- SMDS networks

Apollo Domain   Apollo workstations use the Apollo Domain routing protocol. Cisco IOS supports packet forward and routing of this protocol on

- Ethernet
- FDDI
- HDLC
- X.25 encapsulation

HP Probe   HP Probe is a protocol used by HP devices that provide machine name resolution to the physical IEEE 802.3 address. Cisco routers acting as HP Probe Proxy servers on IEEE 802.3 LANs allow the router to resolve the machine name to the IEEE 802.3 address, eliminating the need for a separate server on each IEEE 802.3 LAN and saving corporate resources.

Multiring   Cisco IOS supports the framing of Layer 3 protocol packets in Source Route Bridging packets using the Multiring protocol. Multiring is primarily used for Token Ring networks.

Management

Cisco IOS software supports the three network management schemas:

- SNMP
- CMIP/CMIS
- IBM NMVT

These network management schemas used by network management applications execute on workstations, minicomputers, or mainframes. For the most part, they use a client/server type of architecture between the router and the management system.

IOS Release 11.2 introduced the capability to manage Cisco routers using HyperText Transfer Protocol (HTTP) from Web browsers. HTTP utilizes HyperText Markup Language (HTML) for navigating Web pages from a browser. All Cisco routers in Release 11.2 or higher have the capability of presenting a home page to a Web browser. The default home page allows you to use IOS command line interface commands through Web-like hot links. This home page is modifiable to meet the needs of any router or organization.

Web-based interfaces have been available for the Cisco 700, 1000, and 1600 access routers since IOS Release 11.0. This Web-based application on the Cisco access product line is called ClickStart. The ClickStart interface presents at installation an initial setup form, guiding the operator through router configuration. Once the router is configured and connected to the network, it is manageable from any central location.

Multimedia and QoS

The advent of higher bandwidth and technologies enabling the integration of audio, video, and data on the same network medium have given rise to the need for supporting multimedia applications with guaranteed service. Cisco IOS Release 11.2 meets the quality of service (QoS) requirement of the following multimedia applications:

- Resource Reservation Protocol (RSVP)
- Random Early Detection (RED)
- Generic Traffic Shaping.

RSVP is an IETF standard that enables applications to dynamically reserve network resources (bandwidth, in other words) from end-to-end. Video or audio feeds over the network can now coexist with data traffic without the need for parallel networks. Each router or networking device used on the path between the two end resources requiring RSVP participates in delivering the QoS demanded by the multimedia application.

Network congestion is monitored and managed through the implementation of Random Early Detection (RED). During peak traffic loads, transmission volume can lead to network congestion. RED works in concert with RSVP to maintain end-to-end QoS during these peak loads by selectively dropping traffic at the source using TCP slowstart characteristics. Thus, the source stations feeding into the network slow down their feed until the network metrics defined for the low watermark against RED are met.

Generic traffic shaping works in a similar fashion to RED. However, generic traffic shaping, also called interface-independent traffic shaping, reduces the flow of outbound traffic to the network backbone. This takes effect when a router connecting to a network backbone composed of Frame Relay, SMDS, or Ethernet receives Layer 2-type congestion packets from downstream network transport devices. Generic traffic shaping throttles back the outbound traffic entering the backbone network at the source of entry.

Packet Classification and QoS

The notion of prioritizing packets based on the type of data being delivered can find its roots in IBM Systems Network Architecture (SNA) where it is called Class of Service (CoS). Cisco IOS is enabled to support packet classification through the use of traffic descriptors that are adhered to by the source device of the packet. Network devices agreeing to deliver traffic based on traffic descriptors providing a network quality of service (QoS). The classification of packets is possible by setting the appropriate bits in assigned headers of Layer 2, 3 and 4. In some instances the data within the packet itself is used to determine the class of service. The classification of packets is set by using the IP Precedence bits within the IP header. Cisco IOS QoS feature set supports many different ways of classifying traffic. Among these are:

- Policy-Based Routing
- QoS Policy Propagation via BGP
- Committed Access Rate
- Differential Service (diff-serv)
- Extended Access Control Lists
- Distributed Weighted Random early Detection (DWRED)
- Weighted Random Early Detection
- Weighted Fair Queuing

Secure Data Transmission

Security, privacy, and confidentiality over public or untrusted IP networks are paramount for using Virtual Private Networks (VPN). Cisco IOS Release 11.2 reduces the exposure by enabling the capability to provide router authentication and network–layer encryption. Router authentication enables two routers to exchange a two-way Digital Signature Standard (DSS) public key before transmitting encrypted traffic over VPNs using generic routing encapsulation (GRE). The exchange is performed once to authenticate the routers by comparing the hash signature of the keys.

Network-layer encryption uses Diffie-Hellman keys for security. These keys form a Data Encryption Standard (DES) 40- or 56-bit session key and triple-DES (3DES) which is 56-bit DES performed three times yielding a 168-bit encryption key. The keys are configurable and set a "cryptomap" that use extended IP access lists to define network, subnet, host, and/or protocol pairs requiring encryption between routers.

Security, Protection and Detection

Release 12.0 of Cisco IOS has incorporated a firewall feature set named Cisco Secure Integrated Software. The Cisco Secure Integrated Software (IS) feature set is comprised on access control list enhancements, some new open security standards, the use of address translation, port mapping and the inclusion of a previously stand-alone product called NetSonar which has been repackaged under Cisco IOS as Cisco Secure Intrusion Detection System (IDS). The Cisco Secure IS suite is comprised of the following features:

- Standard Access Lists and Static Extended Access Lists
- Lock-and-Key (Dynamic Access Lists)
- Reflexive Access Lists
- TCP Intercept
- Context-based Access Control
- Cisco Secure Integrated Software Intrusion Detection System
- Authentication Proxy
- Port to Application Mapping
- Security Server Support
- Network Address Translation
- IPSec Network Security
- Neighbor Router Authentication
- Event Logging

- User Authentication and Authorization

These features along with security design and practices provide a robust secure network environment.

IP Routing Protocols

Cisco IOS supports a variety of routing protocols. Two of these are Cisco developed and therefore are considered proprietary. All other routing protocols are international standards. The two Cisco routing protocols are Interior Gateway Protocol (IGRP) and Enhanced (IGRP).

IGRP supports IP and ISO CLNS networks. IGRP has its roots in distance-vector-transport-routing schemas with enhancements for determining the best route based on a four-part composite metric that includes bandwidth, delay, load, and reliability. In this decision process, IGRP assumes that the route with the highest aggregate should be the preferred route. However, it does not take into account bandwidth utilization and can therefore itself overload a route and cause congestion. Enhanced IGRP utilizes the Diffusing Update Algorithm (DUAL) along with its roots in link-state-routing protocols to determine the best path between two points. Enhanced IGRP merges the best of distance vector and link-state-routing algorithms to provide greater route decision making control. Enhanced IGRP has support for routing IP, AppleTalk, and IPX natively.

The following list provides the remaining open standard routing protocols available for use on Cisco routers:

- Routing Information Protocol (RIP)
- RIP2
- Exterior Gateway Protocol (EGP)
- Border Gateway Protocol (BGP)
- BGP4
- Protocol Independent Multicast (PIM)
- Intermediate System-Intermediate System (IS-IS)
- Next Hop Routing Protocol (NHRP)

Bridging

Independent Local Area Networks (LANs) have traditionally been bridged together to expand their size and reach. There are two bridging techniques that all others are based on: Transparent and Source Route. A transparent bridge is also known as a learning bridge. This type of bridge is the type typically found bridging Ethernet LANs. Cisco IOS supports the following Transparent bridging features:

- IEEE 802.1(d) Spanning-Tree Protocol
- IEEE 802.10 virtual LANs
- DEC spanning tree
- Bridging over X.25 and Frame Relay networks
- Remote bridging over synchronous serial lines

Source Route bridging provides the path between session partners within the frame itself. Transparent bridging has been coupled with Source Route bridging to allow both techniques to be operable on the same interface. This bridging technique is known as Source Route Transparent (SRT) bridging. Another type of bridging that enables the passing of LAN frames from an Ethernet to a Token Ring LAN is called Source Route/Translational Bridging (SR/TLB). This bridging technique enables SNA devices on an Ethernet, for example, to communicate with the mainframe off of a Token ring LAN.

Packet Switching

Packet switching has its foundation in X.25 networks. Today the most widespread use of packet switching is considered to be frame relay. Cisco provides packet switching for frame relay, SMDS, and X.25 for corporate network support. The most comprehensive of these is frame relay. Cisco IOS supports the following functions and enhancements to frame relay networking:

- Virtual subinterface
- TCP/IP header compression
- Broadcast queue
- Frame Relay switching
- RFC 1490—multiprotocol encapsulation
- RFC 1293—Frame Relay Inverse ARP for IP, IPX, AppleTalk, and DECnet
- Discard eligible (DE) or tagged traffic bit support
- LMI, ANSI Annex D, and CCITT Annex A support
- Dial backup
- Frame Relay over ISDN
- Autoinstall over Frame Relay
- RFC 1490—Transparent bridging
- Frame Relay dial backup per DLCI
- Fast Switched Frame Relay bridging
- DLCI Prioritization
- Frame Relay Switched Virtual Circuit (SVC) support
- Dynamic modification of network topologies with any-to-any connectivity

- Dynamic network bandwidth allocation or bandwidth-on-demand
- Backup for PVC backbones
- Resources allocated only when the connection is required to transfer data in private networks
- Traffic shaping over Frame Relay
- Rate enforcement on a per-VC basis
- Per-VC backward explicit congestion notification (BECN) support
- VC-level priority/custom/weighted-fair queuing (PQ/CQ/WFQ) support

NetFlow Switching

Details of session flows through the router network used to be an elusive quest for the network management team. Cisco IOS NetFlow Switching provides "call detail recording" of traffic through the network on both the network and transport layers. This allows Cisco IOS to manage traffic on a per-user, per-application basis. It does this using a connection-oriented model of the end-to-end flows, applying relevant services to the flow of data. What makes NetFlow even more attainable, it is accomplished in software without added hardware features on the Cisco 7500 and 7000 series routers using Route Switch Processor (RSP) or Versatile Interface Processor (VIP) boards.

Tag Switching – MPLS

Multiprotocol Label Switching (MPLS) is an open standard that is based on Cisco Tag Switching protocol. MPLS enables Layer 3 functionalities on Layer 2. MPLS is used predominantly by Internet Service Providers (ISPs). MPLS is a label swapping mechanism that enables Layer 2 networks like frame relay and ATM to perform Layer 3 functionality. The first time a device sends a packet that enters an MPLS device the IP addresses are placed into a tag information base (TIB) where the IP address is associated with a tag value. The tag is placed into the Layer 2 header. MPLS devices transmit the TIB between them. The TIB also contain information on the bandwidth, delay, classification and other metrics that describe the packet. The TIB is communicated to all other MPLS devices and each then updates their own TIB. The TIB is used to determine the most direct "shortest path" route to the destination IP address. Using MPLS the frame relay or ATM switch is viewed as a router by the sending edge router. Because of this the edge router views the entire network as a fully meshed topology. Cisco IOS builds on the layer2/3 overlay model by using engineering techniques as follows:

- Label-switched path tunnels in combination with RSVP establishing an LSP or IOS tunnel interface for a configured destination with unidirectional transmission.
- Link-state interior gateway protocols (IGP) (for example OSPF) with extensions to support automatic routing on LPS tunnels.
- Traffic calculation module to assist in determining paths used for LSP tunnels.
- Label switching forwarding enabling traffic to pass across multiple hops
- Dynamic creation of multiple tunnels between given ingress and egress resources to allow load sharing.

ATM

Cisco IOS is fully compliant with all the ATM standards. Cisco itself is very active in establishing the ATM standards and, as such, has a complete feature set. Cisco IOS supports all the ATM standards, including the following:

- ATM point-to-multipoint signaling
- ATM Interim Local Management Interface (ILMI)
- RFC 1577—classical IP and ARP over ATM
- SVC Idle Disconnect
- Bridged ELANs
- LANE (LAN Emulation) MIBs
- SSRP (Simple Server Redundancy Protocol) for LANE
- HSRP for LANE
- DECnet-routing support for LANE
- UNI 3.1 signaling
- Rate queues for SVCs per subinterface
- AToM MIB

Dial-on-demand Routing

As mentioned earlier, Cisco supports dial-on-demand (DDR) services that enhance the availability and performance of internetworks. DDR uses switched circuit connections through public telephone networks. Using these switched circuits allows Cisco routers to provide reliable backup and bandwidth optimization between locations. The features supported by Cisco DDR include

- POTS via an external modem
- SW56 via an external CSU
- ISDN (BRI and PRI) via integrated ISDN interfaces or external terminal adapters
- Dial backup
- Supplementary bandwidth
- Bandwidth-on-demand
- Snapshot routing
- Multiprotocol routing and transparent bridging over switched circuits
- ISDN fast switching
- Asynchronous ISDN access

Access Server

Cisco routers that function primarily as devices for remote users to access the network are referred to as access servers. These access servers support all the features of DDR with enhancements to support terminal types, connection protocols, security, management, and virtual private networks over the Internet. Access servers provide the following services and features:

- Asynchronous terminal services that include X.25 packet assembler/disassembler (PAD), TN3270, Telnet, and rlogin
- Remote node access over a telephone network using Point-to-Point Protocol (PPP, IPCP, and IPXCP), Xremote, SLIP, and compressed SLIP (CSLIP), AppleTalk Remote Access (ARA) protocol versions 1 and 2, and MacIP
- Multichassis Multilink PPP (MMP)—an aggregate methodology for sharing B channels transparently across multiple routers or access servers

- Asynchronous routing—IP, IPX, and AppleTalk routing
- TN3270 enhancements
- PPP/SLIP on protocol translator virtual terminals
- TACACS+
- TACACS+ single connection
- TACACS+ SENDAUTH function
- ATCP for PPP
- Asynchronous mobility, which connects users to private networks through public networks such as the Internet
- Asynchronous callback, in which a router recognizes a callback request and initiates the callback to the caller
- Asynchronous master interfaces, which are templates of standard interface configurations for multiple asynchronous interfaces on the access server
- ARAP and IPX on virtual asynchronous interfaces
- Local IP Pooling, a pool of reusable IP addresses assigned arbitrarily to asynchronous interfaces
- Remote node NetBEUI, which uses PPP Network Control Protocol (NCP) for NetBEUI over PPP NetBIOS Frames Control Protocol (NBFCP)
- Modem auto-configuring, which is auto-discovery and auto-identification of attached modems, allowing for automatic modem configuration
- NASI (Novell Asynchronous Services Interface)
- RFC 1413 Ident
- RADIUS (Remote Authentication Dial-In User Service)
- Virtual Private Dial-up Network (VPDN)
- Dialer profiles
- Combinet Packet Protocol (CPP)
- Half bridge/half router for CPP and PPP

LAN Extension

Cisco central-site routers, like the 7x00 series, can extend their LAN connectivity over a WAN link using Cisco IOS LAN Extension. The central site router configures LAN Extension services to a multilayer switch at the remote site in a hub-and-spoke configuration. This connection provides a logical extension of the central sites LAN to the remote.

The LAN extension is a practical use of Cisco's CiscoFusion architecture. CiscoFusion describes the combined use of Layer 2 switching or bridging with Layer 3 switching or routing. This combination provides transparent connectivity under the LAN extension supporting

- IP
- IPX
- AppleTalk
- DECnet
- VINES
- XNS protocols.

Since LAN extension supports functions of Layer 2 and 3, MAC address and protocol filtering and priority queuing are accomplished over the WAN links for efficient use of bandwidth.

Voice and data integration

The integration of voice and data onto the same network is a focus of many corporations. Cisco IOS and hardware has enabled the transmission of voice traffic over traditional data communication lines. Cisco solutions support voice in the following manner:

- Voice over IP (VoIP)
- Voice over Frame Relay (VoFR)
- Voice over ATM (VoATM)

The sensitivity of delay and dropped packets in a voice connection is evident. Voice transmission is ensured through the various QoS features implemented in Cisco IOS. The transporting voice over data lines saves corporations communications costs and can extend the functionality of the PBX. This enables a corporation to avoid costly toil charges between offices or to clients by setting up calls to clients that reside in the area code and exchanges of the a corporate office through the data network.

Virtual Private Network (VPN)

Virtual private networking is a means of establishing private communications between two IP devices through the public network. VPN connectivity is software based and therefore does not require hardware upgrades. This makes the use of VPNs a cost-effective solution. Because security is inherent in a VPN connection many companies have seized this capability to architect remote access service to mobile and telecommuters through the many free internet service providers. VPNs are enabled in three methods:

- Access VPN—connecting mobile or telecommuters to the corporate intranet or extranet through a public dial-up IP network with private network policies and security.

- Intranet VPN—connects corporate offices over public IP networks using dedicated links.

- Extranet VPN—connecting communities of interest to a corporate intranet over dedicated links through the public Internet to a corporate internet.

CHAPTER 2

CISCO ROUTER NETWORK DESIGN

The hierarchical structure of the Cisco router network design model is based on the type of services provided at each layer. The notion of using layers creates a modular architecture, enabling growth and flexibility for new technologies at each layer. The Cisco hierarchical design model consists of three layers. Figure 2-1 diagrams the Cisco hierarchical design model.

Figure 2-1
The Cisco Hierarchical Design Model

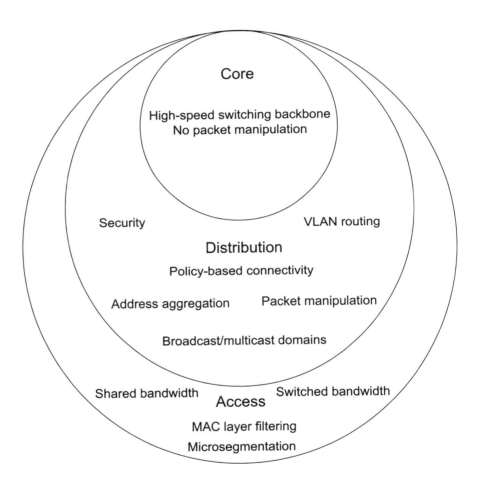

The core layer provides the high-speed backbone for moving data between the other layers. This layer is geared towards the delivery of packets and not packet inspection or manipulation.

The distribution layer provides policy-based networking between the core and access layer. The distribution layer provides boundaries to the network topology and provides several services. These services are

- Address or area aggregation
- Departmental or workgroup access
- Broadcast/multicast domain definition
- *Virtual LAN* (VLAN) routing
- Any media transitions that need to occur
- Security

The access layer is the edge of the network. Being on the edge, the access layer is the entry point to the network for the end user community. Devices participating in the access layer can perform the following functions:

- Shared bandwidth
- Switched bandwidth
- MAC layer filtering
- Microsegmentation

It is important to remember that the Cisco hierarchical design model addresses the functional services of a network. The different layers described can be found in routers or switches, and each device can partake in the functions of more than one layer. Separation of functional layers is not mandatory, however. Maintaining a hierarchical design fosters a network optimized for performance and management.

The Cisco router product line has three flavors. Cisco routers are available as modular, fixed, or combination configurations. Along with full-router configuration, Cisco offers router platforms on personal computer (PC) card formats. Additionally, Cisco combines routers and small hubs into one device suitable for small office installations. The key to a successful implementation of Cisco routers in a networking environment is proper placement and configuration of the router. Each Cisco router offering is suited for a specific function. These functions are depicted in Figure 2-2 as core, distribution, and access. These functional characteristics make up Cisco's router internetwork architecture.

Cisco Router Network Hierarchy

Early on in the development of internetworks, an architecture emerged. This architecture for deploying routers was incorporated into a hierarchical architecture that Cisco employs and preaches to its customer base. The architecture relies on the capability of the processor in the router and its need for processing routes, filters, and physical connections. It places the larger Cisco 7x00 series and 12000 series routers at the center or core of the network. The 4x00 series routers are at the net layer of the network architecture called the distribution layer. Finally, the 25xx, 100x, and 7x0 series routers constitute the access layer of the architecture.

Although these assignments to the three different layers of the architecture make sense, it does not mean that 7x00 series routers cannot be used as a distribution or access router. Likewise, in some cases, the 4500 and 4700 series router platforms can be used as a core or access router. However, the smaller fixed and combination routers are most suited for the access layer and will not perform the physical or logical requirements of the core or distribution routers.

Core

The routers that comprise the core layer of the architecture are often referred to as the backbone routers. These routers connect to other core routers, providing multiple paths over the backbone between destinations. These routers carry the bulk of WAN traffic between the distribution routers. Core routers are usually configured with several high-speed interfaces, as shown in Figure 2-3.

However, due to the introduction of ATM and interface cards that provide up to OC-12 speeds (622 Mbps), core routers may only require two physical interfaces. However, as the section on ATM configuration will reveal, multiple subinterfaces are allowed on each physical interface. The need for the core router to manage many high-speed interfaces is still a requirement, even with only two physical ATM interfaces.

Figure 2-2
Cisco router
hierarchical network.

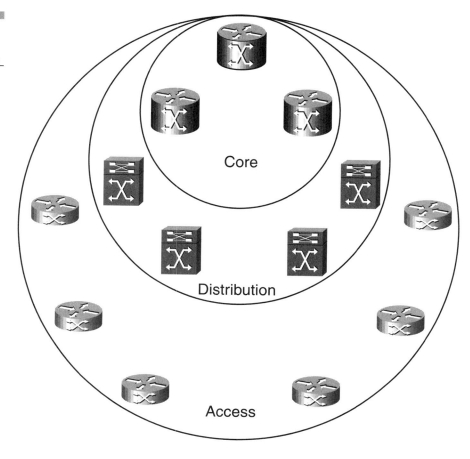

Figure 2-3
Core router
bandwidth and line
network
configuration.

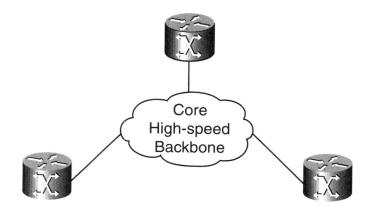

The use of Packet over SONET is another alternative to providing a high-speed core using Cisco routers. In large wide area networks (WANs) and metropolitan area networks (MANs), it is common to have the backbone built on synchronous optical network (SONET) rings with OC-3, OC-12, and OC-48 connections. Packet over SONET allows for the transmission of IP directly over the SONET network without the use of ATM. This provides a great incentive to corporations that have yet to embrace ATM but have a need for high speed and bandwidth over their backbone. Using Packet over SONET as the backbone transport requires an investment in only routers versus ATM, which requires investments in routers and switches.

Distribution

The distribution router functions as the main conduit for a location back to the core. As an example, in Figure 2-4, the distribution router acts as a core router for a campus environment but as a distribution router for a building. Or the distribution router may act solely as a distribution router for a region or campus, managing only the transmission of data between the core and the access layers.

Access

The outer layer of the architecture is the access layer. It is at this layer that end users gain access to the network resources connected by the routers. A typical example for using access routers is in large buildings or campuses. As depicted in Figure 2-5, access routers connect workgroups and/or floor segments within a building to the distribution router. Access routers also provide remote dial-up connectivity for temporary connections.

The Network Infrastructure Lifecycle

Every corporation has a network infrastructure in place as the framework supporting the business processes. Just as applications and systems have lifecycles, so does a network infrastructure. This section highlights a network infrastructure lifecycle that can be used as a general guideline for designing and implementing Cisco-based networks.

Figure 2-4
Distribution router network configuration.

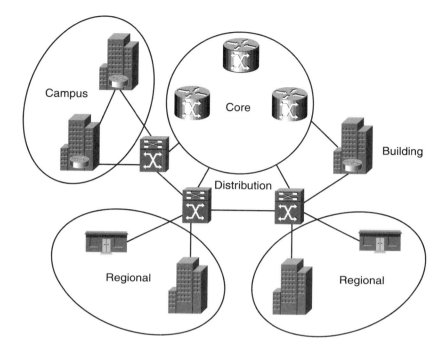

Figure 2-5
Access router network configuration.

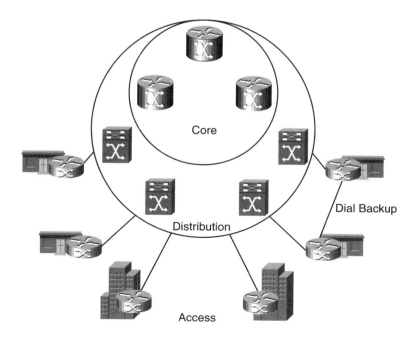

Executive Corporate Vision

Corporate organizational restructuring through regional consolidation or through business group integration will certainly have an effect on the network infrastructure. Aligning the corporate vision with the business directives builds the foundation for the network infrastructure.

Gather Network Infrastructure Information

This involves research and discovery of the current network WAN topology as well as corporate and branch office LAN topologies. A full understanding of end-to-end network configuration is required. Additionally, bandwidth allocations and usage costs must be determined to provide the complete picture.

Determine Current Network Requirements

Communication protocols, client/server architectures, e-mail, distributed processing, Internet and intranet, voice and video, each has its own unique characteristics and can place demands on the network. These demands have to be recognized and understood for planning an enterprise-wide solution. The result from this study is a network profile for each business process and the network itself.

Assess Current Network Operational Processes

Network operational processes involve not just daily troubleshooting, but the other disciplines of network management: inventory, change, configuration, fault, security, capacity/performance, and accounting. Documenting the processes in place today will assist in evaluating the current baseline of service provided and identify areas that may need reengineering to meet the changing business requirements.

Research Plans for New Applications

The effect of new applications on network characteristics must be discovered prior to business groups moving into development, testing, and production. Desktop video conferencing and voice communications along with data traffic require up-front knowledge to reengineer a network. Business group surveys and interviews, along with each group's strategic plan, will provide input to creating a requirements matrix.

Identify Networking Technologies

The selection of the appropriate technologies and how they can be of use in meeting current and future networking requirements relies on vendor offerings and their support structure. Paramount to this success is the partnership with and management of the vendors through an agreed-on working relationship.

Define a Flexible Strategic/Tactical Plan

The strategic plan in today's fast-paced changing technology environment requires flexibility. A successful strategic plan requires business continuity through tactical choices. The strategic plan must demonstrate networking needs in relation to business processes, both current and future.

Developing an Implementation Plan

This is the most visible of all the previous objectives. The planning and research performed prior to this can be for naught if the implementation does not protect current business processes from unscheduled outages. This must meet current business requirements and demands while migrating the network infrastructure to the strategic/tactical design. The perception to the business community must be business as usual.

Management and Review

The effectiveness of the new infrastructure is achieved through management and review. Reports highlighting the network health measured against expected service levels based on the strategic/tactical plan and design reflect the ability of the network to meet business objectives. The tools and analysis used here provide the basis for future network infrastructures.

Design Criteria

In planning for your network design, many criteria must be considered. These criteria are based on the current network design and performance requirements, as measured against the business direction compared to internetworking design trends. The trends of internetworking design affect the four distinct components of an enterprise internetwork:

Local area networks (LANs):   These are networks within a single location that connect local end users to the services provided by the entire enterprise network.

Campus networks: These are networks within a small geographic area, interconnecting the buildings that make up the corporate or business entity for the area.

Wide area networks (WANs):   These networks span large geographic areas and interconnect campus networks.

Remote networks: These types of networks connect branch offices, mobile users, or telecommuters to a campus or the Internet.

Figure 2-6 illustrates today's typical enterprise-wide corporate network topology.

The Current LAN/Campus Network Trend

LANs and campus networks are grouped together for the simple reason that they share many of the same networking issues and requirements. Depending on the technologies used, a LAN can be focused within a building or span buildings. The spanning of a LAN makes up the campus network. Figure 2-7 diagrams a LAN/campus network topology.

Campus networks are a hybrid of LANs and WANs. From LAN/WAN technologies, campus networks use

- Ethernet
- Token Ring
- Fiber Distributed Data Interface (FDDI)
- Fast Ethernet
- Gigabit Ethernet
- Asynchronous Transfer Mode (ATM)
- T1/T3 networks
- Frame Relay

Figure 2-6
The enterprise-wide
internetwork
components

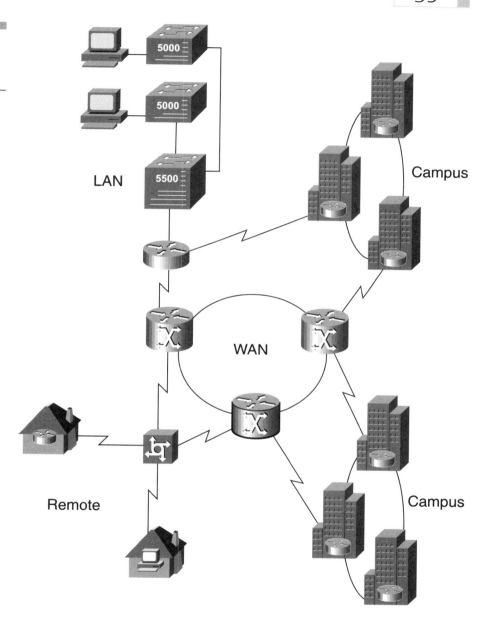

Two LAN technologies that serve to increase throughput and flexibility for LAN design are Layer 2 and Layer 3 switching. In short, Layer 2 switching occurs at the data link layer of the OSI Reference model and Layer 3 switching occurs at the Network layer of the OSI Reference model. Both switching algorithms increase performance by providing higher bandwidth

Figure 2-7
LAN/Campus
Network Topology

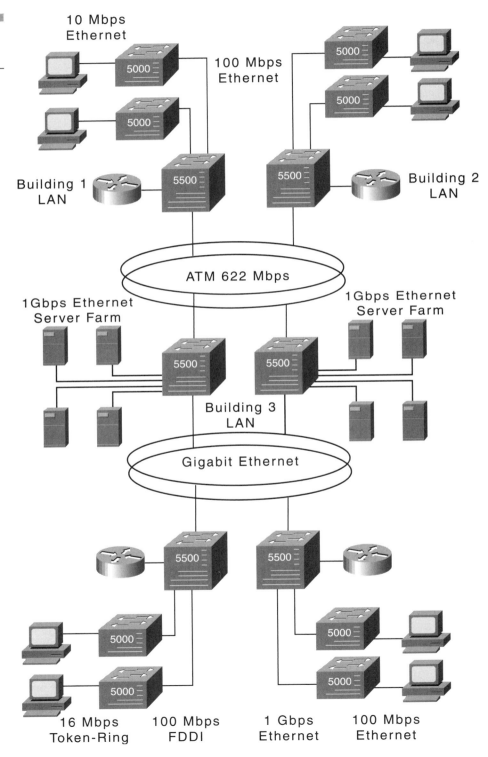

to attached workgroups, local servers, and workstations. The switches replace LAN hubs and concentrators in the wiring closets of the building.

The ability to switch end user traffic between ports on the device has enabled the concept of *Virtual LANs* (VLANs). Defining VLANs on the physical LAN enables logical groupings of end user segments or workstations. This enables traffic specific to this VLAN grouping to remain on this virtual LAN, rather than use bandwidth on LAN segments that are not interested in the grouped traffic. For example, the Finance VLAN traffic does not affect the Engineering VLAN traffic. Table 2-1 lists the important technologies affecting LAN and Campus network design.

WAN Design Trends

Routers are typically the connection points to WANs. Being at this juncture, the routers have become an important decision point for the delivery of traffic. With the advent of switching, the routers are slowly moving away from being the WAN device. The WAN services are now being handled by switches with three types of switching technologies:

- circuit switching
- packet switching
- cell switching

Table 2-1

Key LAN and Campus Network Technologies

Routing technologies	Routing has long been the basis for creating internetworks. For use in a LAN/campus environment, routing can be combined with Layer 3 switching, which may also replace the entire function of a router.
LAN switching technologies	
Ethernet switching	Ethernet switching is Layer 2 switching, which can enable improved performance through dedicated Ethernet segments for each connection.
Token Ring switching	Token Ring switching is also Layer 2 switching. Switching Token Ring segments offers the same functionality as Ethernet switching. Token Ring switching operates as either a transparent bridge or a source-route bridge.
ATM switching technologies	ATM switching offers high-speed switching technology that integrates voice, video, and data. Its operation is similar to LAN-switching technologies for data operations.

Circuit switching provides dedicated bandwidth, while packet switching enables the efficient use of bandwidth with flexibility to service multiple requirements. Cell switching combines the best of both circuit- and packet-switched networks. ATM is the leading cell-switched technology used in WANs today.

Because the WAN links end up servicing all traffic from one location to another, it is important that the bandwidth and performance be optimized. The optimization is due in part to the explosive growth of remote site connectivity, enhanced application architectures such as client/server and intranets, and the recent development of consolidating servers to a centralized location to ease administration and management. These factors have reversed the rules for traffic profiles from that of 80 percent LAN and 20 percent WAN to 80 percent WAN and 20 percent LAN.

This flip-flop of traffic characteristics has not only increased the requirement for WAN traffic optimization, but also for path redundancy, dial backup, and *quality of service* (QoS) to ensure application service levels over the WAN. The technologies available today that enable the effective and efficient use of WANs are summarized in Table 2-2. *Digital Subscriber Line* (DSL), Etherloop, *Low-Earth Orbit* (LEO) satellites, and advanced wireless technologies are making great strides in displacing traditional WANs.

Remote Network Trends

Branch offices, telecommuters, and mobile users constitute remote networks. Some of these may use dial-up solutions with ISDN or analog modems. Others may require dedicated lines, allowing access to the WAN 24 hours a day, seven days a week (24x7). A study of the user's business requirements will dictate the type of connection for these remote locations.

Using ISDN and vendor functionality, a remote location can be serviced with 128 Kbps of bandwidth to the WAN only when traffic is destined out of the remote location. Analysis of the ISDN dial-up cost, based on uptime to the WAN as compared to the cost of a dedicated line to the WAN, must be determined for each location. This analysis will provide a break-even point on temporary versus dedicated WAN connectivity. Any of the various technologies discussed for the WAN may be well suited for remote network connectivity.

Table 2-2

WAN Technologies and Use

WAN Technology	Typical Uses
Analog modem	These are typically used for temporary dial-up connections or for backup of another type of link. The bandwidth is typically 9.6 Kbps to 56 Kbps.
Leased line	Leased lines have been the traditional technology for implementing WANs. These are links "leased" from communications services companies for exclusive use by your corporation.
Integrated Services Digital Network (ISDN)	An ISDN is a dial-up solution for temporary access to the WAN but adds the advantage of supporting voice/video/fax on the same physical connection. As a WAN technology, ISDN is typically used for dial-backup support at 56, 64, or 128 Kbps bandwidth.
Frame Relay	This is a distance-insensitive telco charge, thereby making it very cost-effective. It is used in both private and carrier-provided networks and most recently is being used to carry voice/video/fax/data.
Switched Multimegabit Data Service (SMDS)	SMDS provides high-speed, high-performance connections across public data networks. It can also be deployed in Metropolitan Area Networks (MANs). It is typically run at 45 Mbps bandwidth.
X.25	X.25 can provide a reliable WAN circuit, but it does not provide the high bandwidth requirements as a backbone technology.
WAN ATM	This is used as the high-bandwidth backbone for supporting multiservice requirements. The ATM architecture supports multiple QoS classes for differing application requirements, delay and loss.
Packet over SONET (POS)	POS is an oncoming technology that transports IP packets encapsulated in SONET or SDH frames. POS meets the high bandwidth capabilities of ATM and through vendor implementations supports QoS.

Application Availability Versus Cost-Effectiveness

It is the job of the network to connect end users with their applications. If the network is not available, then the end users are not working and the company loses money. Application availability is driven by the importance of the application to the business. This factor is then compared against the cost of providing application availability using the following:

- Redundant lines for alternate paths
- Dial-backup connectivity
- Redundant devices with redundant power supplies for connecting the end users
- Onsite or remote technical support
- Network management reach into the network for troubleshooting
- Disaster recovery connectivity of remote locations to the disaster recovery center

Designing an internetwork therefore has the main objective of providing availability and service balanced with acceptable costs for providing the service. The costs are generally dominated by three elements of supporting a network infrastructure:

- The number and location of hosts, servers, terminals, and other devices accessing the network; the traffic generated by these devices and the service levels required to meet the business needs.
- The reliability of the network infrastructure and traffic throughput that inherently affects availability and performance, thereby placing constraints on meeting the service levels required.
- The capability of the network equipment to interoperate, the topology of the network, the capacity of the LAN and WAN media, and the service required by the packets all affect the cost and availability factor.

The ultimate goal is to minimize the cost of these elements while at the same time delivering higher availability. The *total cost of ownership* (TCO), however, is dependent on understanding the application profiles.

Application Profile

Each application that drives a business network has a profile. Some profiles are based on corporate department requirements and others may be a directive for the entire company. A full understanding of the underlying architecture of the application and its use of the network is required for creating an application profile. Three basic components drive a network profile:

- Response time
- Throughput
- Reliability

Response time is a perceived result by the end user and a measured function of the network engineer. From a user standpoint, it is the reduced "think-time" of interactive applications that mandates acceptable response time. However, a network design that improves response time is relative to what the end user has perceived as normal response time.

A network engineer will break down the components that make up the response time into the following components:

- host time

- network time

The difference between the two is that host time is application processing, be this disk access to retrieve data or analysis of data. Network time is the transit time, as measured from leaving the host to the network interface of the end user device. Host time is then again computed on the workstation. Typically, host time on a workstation is based on presentation to the end user. Online interactive applications require low response times. These applications are usually referred to as time-sensitive applications.

Applications that rely on the delivery of large amounts of data are termed throughput-intensive applications. Typically, these applications perform file transfers. They require efficient throughput, yet many of these applications also depend on the delivery of the data within a time window. This is where they can adversely affect interactive application response times due to their throughput.

Reliability is often referred to as uptime. Applications requiring a high reliability inherently require high accessibility and availability. This in turn requires hardware and topology redundancy not only on the network side, but also on the application host or server side. The importance of the function served by the application is weighed against the cost of downtime incurred by the business. The higher the cost of downtime, the higher the requirement for reliability.

Creating an application becomes paramount in understanding the needs of a network design. Application profiles are assessed through exercising some or all of the following methods:

- *Profile the user community:* Determine corporate versus departmental internetworking requirements by separating common applications from specific applications for each community. If possible, develop the application flow from the end user to the host/server for each common and specific application. Using network management tools, gather network traffic profiles to parallel the user community.

- *Interviews, focus groups, and surveys:* Using these methods, insights into current perceptions and planned requirements are discovered.

This process is key for developing the current baseline of the network, in addition to coalescing information about planned requirements shared by independent departments. Data gathered here in combination with the community profiles is used for developing the new network design.

■ *Design testing*: This is the proof-of-concept stage for the resulting design. Using simulated testing methods or real-time lab environments, the design is measured against the requirements for response-time, throughput, and reliability.

Cost-Efficiency

The network is now an asset to all corporations. As such, investment into the network must be viewed as a *total cost of ownership* (TCO). These costs are not only equipment investments but also include the following:

■ *Total cost of equipment:* This includes not only hardware, but software, installation costs, maintenance costs, and upgrade costs.

■ *Cost of performance:* This is a variable which measures improved network performance and reliability against the increase of business conducted. The ratio between the two determines the effectiveness of the investment.

■ *Installation cost:* The physical cabling infrastructure to support the new design becomes a large one-time investment cost. A physical cabling infrastructure should be implemented to meet current and future networking technology requirements.

■ *Growth costs:* These costs can be reduced by implementing technologies today that can follow the direction of technologies tomorrow.

■ *Administrative and Support:* These limit the complexity of the internetwork design. The more complicated they are, the higher the costs for training, administration, management, and maintenance.

■ *Cost of downtime:* Analyze the cost of limited, reduced, or inaccessible application hosts, servers, and databases. A high downtime cost may require a redundant design.

■ *Opportunity costs:* Network design proposals should provide a minimum of two designs with a list of pros and cons to each design. Opportunity costs are the costs that may be realized by not choosing a design option. These costs are measured more in a negative way; not moving to a new technology may result in competitive disadvantage, higher productivity costs, and poor performance.

■ *Investment protection:*   The current network infrastructure is often salvaged due to the large investment in cabling, network equipment, hosts, and servers. However, for most networks, investment costs are recovered within three years. Understand the cycle of cost recovery at your corporation. Apply this understanding to the design as a corporate advantage in the design proposal.

Keep in mind that the objective of any network design is the delicate balance of meeting business and application requirements while minimizing the cost to meet the objective.

Network Devices and Capabilities

The phenomenal growth to internetworks has predicated the move from bridges to routers and now to switches. Four basic devices are used in building an internetwork. Understanding the functions of each is important in determining the network design. These four devices are

■ Hubs

■ Bridges

■ Routers

■ Switches

Hubs are often called concentrators and made centralized LAN topologies possible. All the LAN devices are connected to the hub. The hub essentially regenerates the signal received from one port to another acting as a repeater. These devices operate at the physical layer (Layer 1) of the OSI Reference Model.

Bridges connect autonomous LAN segments together as a single network and operate at the data link layer (Layer 2) of the OSI Reference Model. These devices use the *Media Access Control* (MAC) address of the end station for making a decision forwarding the packet. Bridges are protocol-independent.

Routers performing a routing function and operate at the network layer (Layer 3) of the OSI Reference Model. These devices connect different networks and separate broadcast domains. Routers are protocol-dependent.

Switches were at first advanced multiport bridges with the capability to isolate collision domains. Layer 2 switches that enhance performance and functionality through virtual LANs have replaced hubs. The second incarnation of switches enables them to perform Layer 3 routing decisions, thereby performing the function of a router.

Bridging and Routing

Bridging for this discussion is concerned with transparent bridging. This is opposed to *source-route bridging* (SRB), which is closer to routing than bridging. Bridging occurs at the MAC sublayer of the IEEE 802.3/802 .5 standard applied to the data link layer of the OSI Reference Model. Routing takes place at the Network layer of the OSI Reference Model. Bridging views the network as a single logical network with one hop to reach the destination. Routing enables multiple hops to and between multiple networks. This leads to four distinct differences between the routing and bridging:

- The data-link packet header does not contain the same information fields as network layer packets.
- Bridges do not use handshaking protocols to establish connections, while network layer devices do utilize them.
- Bridges do not reorder packets from the same source, while network layer protocols expect reordering due to fragmentation.
- Bridges use MAC addresses for end node identification. Network layer devices, such as routers, use a network layer address associated with the wire to which the device is attached.

Although these differences exist between bridging and routing, bridging occasionally may be required or preferred over routing and vice versa. The advantages of bridging over routing are as follows:

- Transparent bridges are self-learning and therefore require minimal, if any, configuration. Routers require definitions for each interface for the assignment of a network address. These network addresses must be unique within the network.
- Bridging has less overhead for handling packets than does routing.
- Bridging is protocol-independent, while routing is protocol-dependent.
- Bridging will forward all LAN protocols. Routing uses network layer information only, and therefore can only route packets.

In contrast, routing has the following advantage over bridging:

- Routing allows the best path to be chosen between source and destination. Bridging is limited to a specific path.

- Routing is a result of keeping updated, complete network topology information in routing tables on every routing node. Bridging maintains a table of devices connecting through the interface. This causes bridges to learn the network slower than routing, thereby enabling routing to provide a higher level of service.

- Routing uses network layer addressing, which enables a routing device to group the addresses into areas or domains, creating a hierarchical address structure. This leads to an unlimited amount of supported end nodes. Bridging devices maintain data link layer MAC addresses; therefore, they cannot be grouped and result in a limited number of supported end nodes.

- Routing devices will block broadcast storms from being propagated to all interfaces. Bridging spans the physical LAN segment to multiple segments and therefore forwards a broadcast to all attached LAN segments.

- Routing devices will fragment large packets to the smallest packet size for the selected route and then reassemble the packet to the original size for delivery to the end device. Bridges drop packets that are too large to send on the LAN segment without notification to the sending device.

- Routing devices notify transmitting end stations to slow down the transmission of data (congestion feedback) when the network itself becomes congested. Bridging devices do not possess that capability.

The general rule of thumb in deciding to route or bridge is to bridge only when needed. Route whenever possible.

Switching

The process of switching is the movement of packets from the receiving interface to a destination interface. Layer 2 switching uses the MAC address found within the frame. Layer 3 switching uses the network address found within the frame.

Layer 2 switching is essentially transparent bridging. A table is kept within the switching device for mapping the MAC address to the associated interface. The table is built by examining the source MAC address of each frame as it enters the interface. The switching function occurs when the destination MAC address is examined and compared against the switching table. If a match is found, the frame is sent out of the corresponding interface. A frame that contains a destination MAC address not found in the switching table is broadcast out to all interfaces on the switching device. The returned frame will allow the switching device to learn the interface and therefore place the MAC address in the switching table.

MAC addresses are predetermined by the manufacturers of the *network interface cards* (NICs). These cards have unique manufacturer codes assigned by the IEEE with a unique identifier assigned by the manufacturer. This method virtually ensures unique MAC addresses. These manufacturer addresses are often referred to as *burned-in addresses* (BIA) or *universally administered addresses* (UAA). Some vendors, however, allow the UAA to be overridden with a *locally administered address* (LAA). Layer 2 switched networks are inherently considered flat networks.

In contrast, Layer 3 switching is essentially the function of a router. Layer 3 switching devices build a table similar to the Layer 2 switching table. Except in the case of the Layer 3 switching table, the entries are mapping network-layer addresses to interfaces. Since the network-layer addresses are based on assigning a logical connection to the physical network, a hierarchical topology is created with Layer 3 switching. As packets enter an interface on a Layer 3 switch, the source network-layer address is stored in a table that cross-references the network-layer address with the interface. Layer 3 switches carry with them the function of separating broadcast domains and network topology tables for determining optimal paths.

Combining Layer 2 and Layer 3 switching within a single device reduces the burden on a router to route the packet from one location to another, as shown in Figure 2-8. Switching therefore increases throughput due to the

Figure 2-8

Combined Layer 2 and Layer 3 switching and the Cisco router

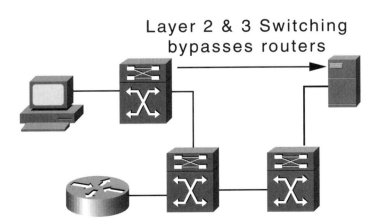

Layer 2 & 3 Switching
bypasses routers

decisions being done in silicon, reduces central processing unit (CPU) overhead on the router, and eliminates hops between the source and destination device.

Backbone Considerations

The network backbone is the core of the three layer hierarchical model. Many factors affect the performance of the backbone:

- Path optimization
- Traffic prioritization
- Load balancing
- Alternate paths
- Switched access
- Encapsulation (Tunneling)

Path optimization is generally a function of a router that occurs using the routing table created by the network layer protocols. Cisco routers support all of the widely implemented IP routing protocols. These include

- *Open Shortest Path First* (OSPF)
- RIP
- IGRP
- EIGRP
- *Border Gateway Protocol* (BGP)
- *Exterior Gateway Protocol* (EGP)
- HELLO

Each of these routing protocols calculates the optimal path from the information provided within the routing tables. The calculation is based on metrics such as bandwidth, delay, load, and hops. When changes occur in the network, the routing tables are updated throughout all the routers within the network. The process of all the routers updating their tables and recalculating the optimal paths is called convergence. With each new generation of IP routing protocols, the convergence time is reduced. Currently, the IP routing calls with the smallest convergence times are Cisco proprietary routing protocols, IGRP and EIGRP.

Traffic prioritization enables the router to prioritize packets on the interface queue for delivery. This allows time-sensitive and mission-critical traffic to take precedence over throughput-sensitive traffic. Cisco routers employ three types of traffic prioritization:

- Priority queuing
- Custom queuing
- Weighted-fair queuing

Priority queuing is the simplest form of traffic prioritization. It is designed primary for low-speed links. The traffic under priority queuing is classified based on criteria that includes protocol and subprotocol types. The criteria profile is then assigned to a one-of-four output queuing. These queues are high, medium, normal, and low. In IP-based networks, the IP *type of service* (TOS) feature and Cisco IOS software capability to prioritize IBM logical unit traffic enable priority queuing for intraprotocol prioritization.

Custom queuing answers a fairness problem that arises with priority queuing. With priority queuing, low-priority queues may receive minimal service, if any. Custom queuing addresses this problem by reserving bandwidth for a particular type of traffic. Cisco custom queuing therefore allows the prioritization of multiprotocol traffic over a single link. For example, the greater the reserved bandwidth for a particular protocol, the more service is received. This provides a minimal level of service to all traffic over a shared media. The exception to this is underutilization of the reserved bandwidth. If traffic is not consuming the reserved bandwidth percentage, then the remaining percentage of reserved bandwidth will be shared by the other protocols. Custom queuing can use up to 16 queues, which are serviced sequentially until the configured byte count has been sent or the queue is empty.

Weighted-fair queuing uses an algorithm similar to time-division multiplexing. Each session over an interface is placed into a queue and allocated a slice of time for transmitting over the shared media. The process occurs in a round-robin fashion. Allowing each session to default to the same weighting parameters ensures that each session will receive a fair share of the bandwidth. This use of weighting protects time-sensitive traffic by ensuring available bandwidth and therefore consistent response times during heavy traffic loads.

The weighted-fair algorithm identifies the data streams over an interface dynamically. Because the algorithm is based on separating the data streams into logical queues, it cannot discern the requirements of different conversations that may occur over the session. This is an important point when considering queuing methods for protecting IBM SNA traffic.

Weighted-fair queuing becomes a disadvantage for SNA traffic when the SNA traffic is encapsulated in DLSw+ or RSRB.

The differences between the three queuing methods are dependent on the needs of the network. However, from an administrative point of view, weighted-fair queuing is far easier due to it being a dynamically-built queue versus priority and custom queuing, which both require the definitions of access lists, pre-allocated bandwidth, and predefined priorities.

Load balancing for IP traffic occurs with two to four paths to the destination network. It is not necessary for these paths to be of equal cost. The load balancing of IP traffic may occur on a per-packet basis or a per-destination basis. Bridged traffic over multiple serial links becomes balanced by employing a Cisco IOS software feature called circuit groups. This feature logically groups the multiple links as a single link.

Redundancy is a major design criterion for mission-critical processes. The use of alternate paths not only requires alternate links but requires terminating these links in different routers. Alternate paths are only valuable when a single point of failure is avoided.

Recovery of dedicated leased connections is mandatory for ensuring availability and service. This function is often termed switch access or switched connection; however, it does not relate to the Layer 2 or Layer 3 switching function. Switched access calls for the instantaneous recovery of WAN connectivity due to an outage on the dedicated leased line.

Switched access is also used to supplement bandwidth requirements using a Cisco IOS software feature called *bandwidth on demand* (BOD), which uses *dial-on-demand routing* (DDR). Using DDR along with the dedicated leased WAN connection, a remote location can send large mounts of traffic in a smaller time frame.

Encapsulation techniques are used for transporting non-routable protocols. IBM's SNA is a non-routable protocol. Encapsulation techniques are also used when the design calls for a single protocol backbone. These techniques are also referred to as tunneling.

Distributed Services

Within the router network, services can be distributed for maximizing bandwidth utilization, routing domains, and policy networking. The Cisco IOS software supports these distributed services through the following:

▪ Effective backbone bandwidth management

▪ Area and service filtering

- Policy-based distribution
- Gateway services
- Route redistribution
- Media translation

Preserving valuable backbone bandwidth is accomplished using the following features of Cisco IOS software:

- Adjusting priority output queue lengths, so overflows are minimized.
- Adjust routing metrics such as bandwidth and delay to facilitate control over path selection.
- Terminate local polling, acknowledgment, and discovery frames at the router using proxy services to minimize the high volume of small-packet traffic over the WAN.

Traffic filtering provides policy-based access control into the backbone from the distribution layer. The access control is based on area or service. Typically, we see the use of service access controls as a means for limiting an application service to a particular segment on the router. Traffic filtering is based on Cisco IOS software access control lists. These access control lists can affect inbound and outbound traffic of a specific interface or interfaces by being either permitted or denied.

Policy-based networking is a set of rules that determine the end-to-end distribution of traffic to the backbone. Policies can be defined to affect a specific department, protocol, or corporate policy for bandwidth management. The CiscoAssure initiative is a policy-based direction that enables the various network equipment to work together to ensure end-to-end policies.

Gateway functions of the router enable different versions of the same networking protocol to the internetwork. An example of this is connecting a DECnet Phase V network with a DECnet Phase IV network. These DECnet versions have implemented different addressing schemes. Cisco IOS within the router performs as an *address translation gateway* (ATG) for transporting the traffic between the two networks. Another example is AppleTalk's translational routing between different versions of AppleTalk. Route redistribution enables multiple IP routing protocols to interoperate through the redistribution of routing tables between the two IP routing protocols within the same router.

There are times in corporate networks when communication between different media is a requirement. This is seen more and more with the expansion of networks and newer technologies. For the most part, media translation occurs between Ethernet frames and Token Ring frames. The translation is not a one-for-one since an Ethernet frame does not use many of the fields used in a Token Ring frame. An additional translation that can be observed is one from IBM SDLC to Logical Link Control 2 (LLC2) frames. This enables serial-attached IBM SDLC connections to access LAN attached devices.

Local Services

At the local access layer of the three-layer model, features provided by the Cisco IOS within the router provide added management and control over access to the distribution layer. These features are

- Value-added network addressing
- Network segmentation
- Broadcast and multicast capabilities
- Naming, proxy, and local cache capabilities
- Media access security
- Router discovery

The discovery of servers and other services may sometimes cause broadcasts within the LAN. A feature of Cisco IOS software directs these requests to specific network-layer addresses. This feature is called helper addressing. Using this feature limits the broadcast to only segments of the helper addresses defined for that service. This is best used when protocols such as Novell IPX or DHCP typically search the entire network for a server using broadcast messages. Helper addresses thereby preserve bandwidth on segments that do not connect the server requested.

Network congestion is typically a result of a poorly designed network. Congestion is manageable by segmenting networks into smaller, more manageable pieces. Using multiple IP subnets, DECnet areas and AppleTalk zones further segment the network so that traffic belonging to the segment remains on the segment. Virtual LANs further enhance this concept by spanning the segmentation between network equipment.

Although routers control data link (MAC address) broadcasts, they allow network layer (Layer 3) broadcasts. Layer 3 broadcasts are often used for locating servers and services required by the host. The advent of video broadcasts has proliferated the use of multicast packets over a network. Cisco IOS does its best in reducing broadcast packets over IP networks through directed broadcasts to specific networks, rather than the entire network.

In addition, the Cisco IOS employs a spanning-tree technique when flooded broadcasts are recognized, minimizing excessive traffic but enabling the delivery of the broadcast to all networks. IP multicast traffic moves from a single source to multiple destinations. IP multicast is supported by a router running Cisco IOS with the *Internet Group Management Protocol* (IGMP) implemented. Using IGMP, the router can serve as a multicast distribution point, delivering packets to only segments that are members of the multicast group, ensuring loop-free paths, and eliminating duplicate multicast packets.

The Cisco IOS software contains many features for further reducing bandwidth utilization using naming, proxy, and local cache functions. The function drastically reduces discovery, polling, and searching characteristics of many of the popular protocols from the backbone. The following is a list of the features available with Cisco IOS that limits these types of traffic from the backbone:

- *Name services:* NetBIOS, DNS, and AppleTalk Name Binding Protocol
- *Proxy services:* NetBIOS, SNA XID/Test, polling, IP ARP, Novell ARP, AppleTalk NBP
- *Local Caching:* SRB RIF, IP ARP, DECnet, Novell IPX

Selecting Routing Protocol

Routing protocols are the transport of IP-based networks. The following are examples of routing protocols:

- *Routing Information Protocol* (RIP)
- *Routing Information Protocol 2* (RIP2)
- *Interior Gateway Routing Protocol* (IGRP)
- *Enhanced Interior Gateway Routing Protocol* (EIGRP)
- *Open Shortest Path First* (OSPF)
- *Intermediate System-Intermediate System* (IS-IS)

In selecting a routing protocol for the network, the characteristics of the application protocols and services must be taken into consideration. Network designs enabling a single routing protocol are best for network performance, maintenance, and troubleshooting. Six characteristics of a network must be considered when selecting a routing protocol:

- Network topology
- Addressing and route summarization
- Route selection
- Convergence
- Network scalability
- Security

Network Topology

Routing protocols view the network topology in two ways: flat or hierarchical. The physical network topology consists of the connections of all the routers within the network. Flat routing topologies use network addressing to segregate the physical network into smaller interconnected flat networks. Examples of routing protocols that use a non-hierarchical flat logical topology are RIP, RIP2, IGRP, and EIGRP.

OSPF and IS-IS routing networks are hierarchical in design. As shown in Figure 2-9, hierarchical routing networks assign routers to a routing area or domain. The common area is considered the top of the hierarchy, which the other routing areas communicate through. Hierarchical routing topologies assign routers to areas. These areas are the routing network addresses, used for delivering data from one subnet to another. The areas are a logical grouping of contiguous networks and hosts. Each router maintains a topology map of its own area, but not of the whole network.

Addressing and Route Summarization

Some of the IP routing protocols have the capability to automatically summarize the routing information. Using summarization, the route table updates that flow between routers, which are greatly reduced, thereby saving bandwidth, router memory, and router CPU utilization. As shown in Figure 2-10, a network of 1,000 subnets must have 1,000 routes. Each of the routers within the network must therefore maintain a 1,000-route table. If we assume that the network is using a Class B addressing scheme with a subnet mask of 255.255.255.0, summarization reduces the number of routes within each router to 253. Three routes in each of the routers describe the

Figure 2-9
Flat versus
hierarchical routing
topologies.

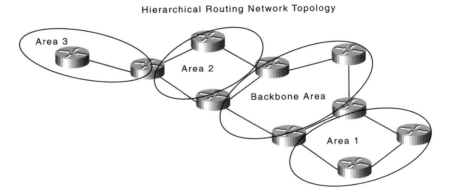

Flat Routing Network Topology

Hierarchical Routing Network Topology

path to the other subnets on the other routers, and 250 routes describe the subnets connected to each router.

Route Selection

In networks where high availability and redundancy are a requirement, the route selection algorithm of the routing protocol becomes an important factor in maintaining acceptable availability. Each of the routing protocols uses some type of metric to determine the best path between the source and the destination of a packet. The available metrics are combined to produce a "weight" or "cost" on the efficiency of the route.

Depending on the routing protocol in use, multiple paths of equal cost

Figure 2-10
The effect of route
summarization.

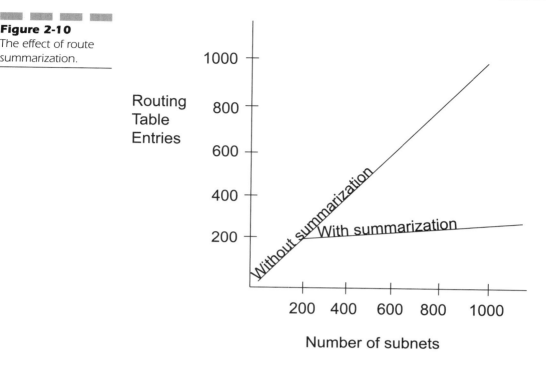

may provide load balancing between the source and destination, thereby spreading the load across the network. some protocols like EIGRP can use unequal cost paths to load balance. This capability to load balance further improves the management of network bandwidth.

Load balancing over multiple paths is performed on a per-packet or per-destination basis. Per-packet distributes the load across the possible paths in proportion to the routing metrics of the paths. For equal cost paths, this results in a round-robin distribution. There is, however, the potential in a per-packet load balancing technique for the packets to be received out of order. Per-destination load balancing distributes the packets based on the destination over the multiple paths to the destination. For instance, as shown in Figure 2-11, packets destined for subnets attached to router R2 from router R1 use a round-robin technique based on the destination. Packets destined for subnet 1 flow over link 20, while packets destined for subnet 2 flow over link 21 versus the per-packet basis of alternating the packets for subnet 1 and subnet 2 over the two links.

Figure 2-11
Packet distribution using a round-robin technique

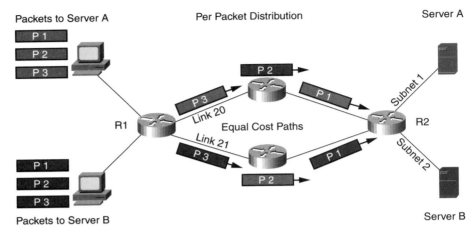

The Concept of Convergence

Convergence is the time it takes a router to recognize a network topology change, calculate the change within its own table, and then distribute the table to adjacent routers. The adjacent routers then perform the same functions. The total time it takes for the routers to begin using the new calculated route is called the convergence time. The time for convergence is critical for time-sensitive traffic. If a router takes too long to detect, recalculate, and then distribute the new route, the time-sensitive traffic may experience poor performance or the end nodes of the connection may drop.

In general, the concern with convergence is not with the addition of new links or subnets in the network. The concern is the failure of connectivity to the network. Routers recognize physical connection losses rapidly. The issue of long convergence time is the failure to detect poor connections within a reasonable amount of time. Poor connections caused by line errors, high collision rates, and other reasons require some customization of the router for detecting these types of problems faster.

Network Scalability

The capability of routing protocols to scale to a growing network is not so much a weakness of the protocol, but the critical resources of the router hardware. Routers require memory, CPU, and adequate bandwidth to properly service the network.

Routing tables and network topology are stored in router memory. Using a route summarization technique, as described earlier, reduces the memory requirement. In addition, routing protocols that use areas or domains in a hierarchical topology require the network design to use small areas, rather than large ones, to help in reducing the memory consumption.

Calculation of the routes is a CPU-intensive process. Through route summarization and the use of link-state routing protocols, the CPU utilization is greatly reduced since the number of routes needing re-computing is reduced.

Bandwidth on the connections to each router becomes a factor in not only scaling the network, but in convergence time. Routing protocols find information on neighbor routers for the purpose of receiving and sending routing table updates. The type of routing protocol in use will determine its affect on the bandwidth.

Distance-vector routing protocols such as RIP and IGRP send their routing tables at regular intervals. The distance-vector routing protocol waits for the time interval before sending its update, even when a network change has occurred. In stable networks, this type of updating mechanism wastes bandwidth yet protects the bandwidth from an excessive routing update load when a change has occurred. However, due to the periodic update mechanism, distance vector protocols tend to have a slow convergence time.

Link-state IP routing protocols such as OSPF and IS-IS address the bandwidth wastefulness of distance-vector routing protocols and slow convergence times. Due to the complexity of providing this enhancement, however, link-state protocols are CPU-intensive and require higher memory utilization and bandwidth during convergence.

During network stability, link-state protocols take up minimal network bandwidth. After start-up and initial convergence, updates are sent to neighbors only when the network topology changes. During a recognized topology change, the router will flood its neighbors with the updates. This may cause excessive load on the bandwidth, CPU, and memory of each router. However, convergence time is lower than that of a distance-vector protocol.

Cisco's proprietary routing protocol, EIGRP, is an advanced version of a distance-vector protocol with properties of a link-state protocol. EIGRP has taken many of the metrics for route calculation from the distance-vector protocols. The advantages of link-state protocols are used for sending routing updates only when changes occur. Although EIGRP preserves CPU, memory, and bandwidth during a stable network environment, it does have high CPU, memory, and bandwidth requirements during convergence.

Table 2-3

Recommended
Number of Neigh-
bors per Router
with IP Routing
Protocols

Routing Protocol	Neighbors per Router
Distance vector (RIP, IGRP)	50
Link state (OSPF, IS-IS)	30
Advanced distance vector (EIGRP)	30

The convergence capability of the routing protocols and their effect on CPU, memory, and bandwidth has resulted in guidelines from Cisco on the number of neighbors that can effectively be supported. Table 2-3 lists the suggested neighbors for each protocol.

Security

Routing protocols can be used to provide a minimal level of security. Some of the security functions available on routing protocols are

- Filtering route advertisements
- Authentication

Using filtering, routing protocols can prohibit the advertisements of routes to neighbors, thereby protecting certain parts of the network. Some of the routing protocols authenticate their neighbor prior to engaging in routing table updates. Although this is protocol-specific and generally a weak form of security, it does protect unwanted connectivity from other networks using the same routing protocol.

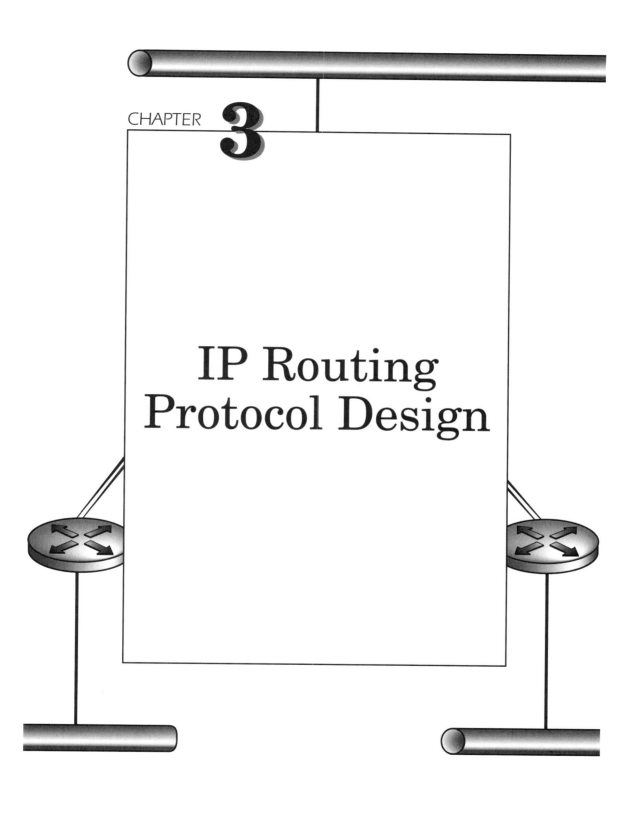

CHAPTER **3**

IP Routing
Protocol Design

Routing is the process of moving packets from one network to another. A routing decision takes place at the source network device, which is a router. The decision is made based on metrics used for a particular routing protocol. Routing protocols can use some or all of the following metrics in determining the best route to a destination network:

- Path length
- Reliability
- Delay
- Bandwidth
- Load
- Communication cost

Path length is a measure of either a cost or a hop count. In link-state routing protocols, the cost is the sum of the costs associated with each link in the path. Distance-vector routing protocols assign a hop count to the path length, which measures the number of routers a packet traverses between the source and destination.

Reliability is typically the bit-error rate of a link connecting this router to a source or destination resource. For most of the routing protocols, the reliability of a link is assigned by the network engineer. Since it is arbitrary, it can be used to influence and create paths that are favorable over other paths.

The delay metric is an overall measurement of the time it takes for a packet to move through all the internetworked devices, links, and queues of each router. In addition, network congestion and the overall distance traveled between the source and destination are taken into consideration in evaluating the delay metric value. Because the delay value takes into account many different variables, it is an influential metric on the optimal path calculation.

Using bandwidth as a metric in optimal path calculations can be misleading. Although a bandwidth of 1.544 Mbps is greater than 56 Kbps, it may not be optimal due to the current utilization of the link or the load on the device on the receiving end of the link.

The load is a metric that assigns a value to a network resource based on the resource's overall utilization. This value is a composite of CPU utilization, the packets processed per second, and the disassembly or reassembly of packets, among other things. The monitoring of the device resources itself is an intensive process.

In some cases, communication lines are charged based on usage versus a flat monthly fee for public networks. For example, ISDN lines are charged based on usage time and the amount of data transmitted during that time.

In these instances, communication cost becomes an important factor in determining the optimal route.

In designing a routing protocol-based network, the routing algorithm should have the following characteristics built into the design:

- *Optimality:*   This concerns using some or all of the metrics available for a routing protocol in order to calculate the optimal route. Different routing protocols may apply one metric as having a higher weight to the optimal route calculation than another. An understanding of this behavior is important in choosing the routing protocol.

- *Simplicity:*   Although routing protocols themselves may be complicated, their implementation and operational support must be simplistic. Router overhead and the efficient use of router resources is important in maintaining a stable and reliable network.

- *Robustness:*   Choose a routing algorithm that meets the requirements of the network design. In some cases, such as with small networks, a simplistic distance-vector routing protocol is sufficient. Large networks that require a hierarchical design require the capability of the routing protocol to scale to the size of the network without itself becoming a hindrance on the network.

- *Rapid Convergence*:   The convergence time to recalculate and then use a new optimal path between a source and destination resource is paramount in meeting availability and service level requirements of a network.

- *Flexibility:*   The algorithms employed by the selected routing protocol must be flexible and adapt to the changing dynamics of network resources and the network as a whole.

RIP, RIP2, and IGRP Network Design

RIP, RIP2, and IGRP are distance-vector-based routing protocols. Such routing protocols base the optimal route on the number of hops (devices, in other words) a packet must pass through to reach a destination.

Routing Information Protocol (RIP) was the first routing protocol algorithm for distributing, calculating, and managing available routes within a network. *Interior Gateway Routing Protocol* (IGRP) is a Cisco proprietary routing protocol algorithm using enhanced optimal route calculation. IGRP calculates optimal routes based on bandwidth, delay, reliability, and load. RIP2 is the second generation of RIP. RIP2 supports the Internet Protocol

Version 6 specification for 128-bit addressing, *variable-length subnet masks* (VLSM), and route summarization.

RIP, RIP2, and IGRP Topology

Distance-vector routing protocols use a flat network topology, as shown in Figure 3-1. Since these protocols are distance-vector-based routing algorithms, it is beneficial to minimize the number of hops between two destinations. This requires careful planning of the core, distribution, and access topology layers in planning the hierarchical service model. For most cases, when deploying distance-vector-based routing protocols, the service functions of the core, distribution, and access layers typically commingle within a single router.

RIP, RIP2, and IGRP Addressing and Summarization

In RIP and IGRP networks, the IP 16-bit addressing scheme of IP version 4 is supported. RIP2 supports both the IP version 4 16-bit and IP version 6

Figure 3-1
Flat topology of a distance-vector-based router network

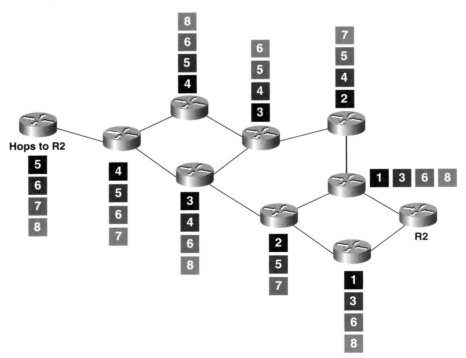

128-bit addressing scheme. Additionally, RIP and IGRP support fixed sub-net masks for a network. Every subnet address used in the RIP or IGRP network must use the same subnet masking. RIP2 using VLSM and the 128-bit addressing scheme allows for varied subnet masks of the router interface. This is because the RIP2 routing packet includes the subnet mask of the source and destination IP address. Summarization reduces the memory requirements on the router by keeping the routing table to a minimum.

RIP, RIP2, and IGRP Route Selection and Convergence

Both RIP and RIP2 base the optimal route selection on the number of hops. IGRP enhances this by incorporating bandwidth, delay, reliability, and load. Figure 3-2 illustrates the route selection difference between RIP, RIP2, and IGRP. RIP and IGRP use the first route within their routing tables as the optimal route for a destination network or subnet. Because IGRP uses bandwidth as a metric, the IGRP optimal route in the figure has more hops than the RIP optimal route. The Cisco IOS implementation of RIP provides for up to six entries on which the router can load-balance to a destination. IGRP will load-balance packets over equal-cost paths to a destination network or subnet. This load balancing occurs in a round-robin fashion.

Figure 3-2
Route selection differences between RIP, RIP2, and IGRP

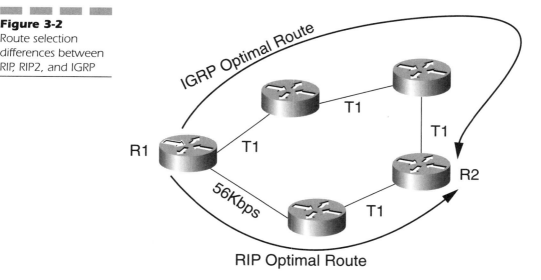

Both RIP and IGRP build their tables and then transmit the entire routing table to adjacent routers. Each router in turn recalculates its table based on the information received from the sending router. Once this is completed, the router forwards its new table to adjacent routers.

Both RIP and IGRP also periodically send their routing tables to adjacent routers. RIP defaults to a 30-second interval for sending the routing table to adjacent routers. IGRP defaults to a 90-second interval for sending the routing table to adjacent routers. Both RIP and IGRP recalculate routing entries once recognizing a link outage or timeout to an adjacent router. The recalculated routing table is not forwarded to adjacent routers, however, until the update interval has been reached. The periodic updating of neighbor routers for topology changes causes excessive convergence time for the network to learn new optimal routes.

RIP2, however, addresses the periodic update problem by sending only the updated route entry at the time of the recalculation. Although this sounds much like a link-state protocol update, RIP2 still sends the entire table on a periodic basis. The capability of RIP2 to send an update at the time it is recalculated reduces the convergence time. RIP2 sends the entire routing table on a periodic basis, just as RIP and IGRP. However, the table is smaller due to the use of VLSM and route summarization. RIP2 will load-balance packets to a destination network or subnet over equal-cost paths.

RIP, RIP2, and IGRP Network Scalability

Time for the convergence of RIP, IGRP, and RIP2 networks is the single inhibitor to scaling these protocols to large networks. Convergence is not just a time factor, but also a CPU and memory issue on each router. These protocols recalculate the entire table during convergence, as opposed to just the affected route. Therefore, convergence becomes a CPU-intensive process, thereby reducing the capability of a router to provide service levels during convergence. Since these protocols send the entire table in a periodic time frame, they consume bandwidth, causing bandwidth constraints on an ongoing basis.

EIGRP Network Design

Enhanced Interior Gateway Protocol (EIGRP) is a proprietary routing protocol of Cisco Systems. EIGRP merges the best of distance-vector protocol characteristics with advantages of link-state protocol characteristics. In addition, EIGRP uses *Diffusing Update Algorithm* (DUAL) for fast convergence and the further reduction of possible routing loops within the network. An advantage to using EIGRP over other routing protocols is its capability to support not only IP, but also Novell NetWare IPX and AppleTalk, thus simplifying network design and troubleshooting.

EIGRP Topology

EIGRP uses a non-hierarchical flat networking topology. It automatically summarizes subnet routers for networks directly connected to the router using the network number as the boundary. It has been found that the automatic summarization is sufficient for most IP networks.

EIGRP Addressing and Summarization

EIGRP supports *variable-length subnet masking* (VLSM). Defining an address space for use by an EIGRP is a primary step in developing the routing architecture. EIGRP support for VLSM is made possible by including the subnet mask assigned to the router interface in the EIGRP routing messages. VLSM is essentially the subnetting of a subnet (or a sub-subnet).

Using an appropriate addressing scheme, the size of the routing tables and convergence time can drastically be reduced through route summarization. EIGRP automatically summarizes the routes at network number boundaries. Figure 3-3 diagrams the use of route summarization.

The network engineer can configure route summarization at the interface level, however, using any bit-boundary of the address to further summarize the routing entries. The metric used in route summarization is the best route found for the routes used to determine the summarized route. The summary points to the NULL interface of the summarizing router. This makes the metric the cost of reaching the summarizing router.

EIGRP Route Selection

EIGRP uses the same metrics as IGRP. These values are bandwidth, delay, reliability, and load. The metric placed on a route using EIGRP defaults to the minimum bandwidth of each hop, plus a media-specific delay for each hop. The value for the metrics used in EIGRP are determined as follows:

- *Bandwidth:* EIGRP uses the default value for each interface to the value specified by the bandwidth interface command.

■ *Delay:* The inherent delay associated with an interface. The delay metric can also be defined on an interface using the delay interface command.

■ *Reliability:* A dynamically computed value averaged over five seconds. The reliability metric changes with each new weighted average.

■ *Load:* A dynamically computed weighted average over five seconds. The load metric changes with each new weighted average.

EIGRP Convergence

EIGRP employs a *diffusing update algorithm* (DUAL) for calculating route computations. DUAL uses distance vector algorithms to determine loop-free efficient paths, selecting the best path for insertion into the routing table. DUAL, however, also determines the second-best optimal route for each entry; this route is termed a feasible successor. The feasible successor entry is used when the primary route becomes unavailable. Figure 3-4 illustrates the use of the feasible successor. Using this methodology of successor routes avoids a recalculation and therefore minimizes convergence time. Along with primary routes, EIGRP distributes the feasible successor entries to the neighboring routers.

Figure 3-3
EIGRP route summarization using VLSM

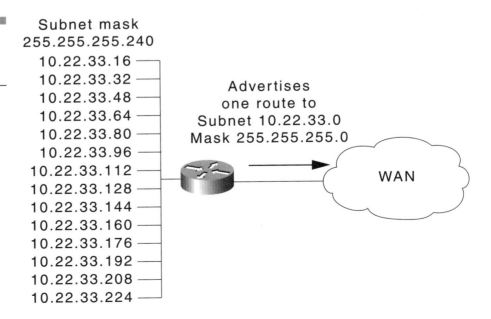

Figure 3-4
EIGRP use of
a feasible successor

Stable Network

( ) Link cost
⟶ Cost to Subnet 8

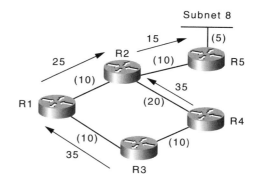

Successor Discovery

( ) Link cost
⟶ Cost to Subnet 8

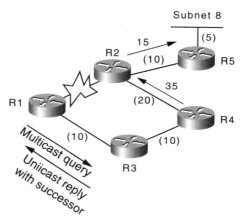

Stable Network

( ) Link cost
⟶ Cost to Subnet 8

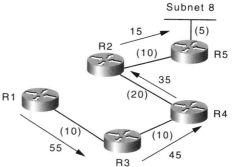

EIGRP Scalability

Scalability is a function of memory, CPU, and bandwidth efficiencies. EIGRP is designed for optimizing these resources. Through route summarization, the routes advertised by neighbors are stored with minimal memory required. This enables an EIGRP network to expand without routing issues. Since EIGRP uses DUAL only, routes that are affected by a change are recomputed, and since EIGRP is based on the same metrics as IGRP, the computation CPU requirements are minimal. Because EIGPR only sends updates due to topology changes, bandwidth is preserved. Steady-state bandwidth utilization of EIGRP is minimal due to the use of EIGRP's HELLO protocol for maintaining adjacencies between neighbors.

EIGRP Security

Since EIGRP is a Cisco IOS proprietary routing protocol, it is available only on Cisco routers. Additionally, route filters and authentication can be specified to further limit accidental or malicious routing disruptions from unknown routers connecting to the network.

OSPF Network Design

Open Shortest Path First (OSPF) is a standards-based link-state routing protocol defined by the *Internet Engineering Task Force* (IETF) OSPF workgroup and published in *Request for Comment* (RFC) 1247. OSPF is based on an *autonomous system* (AS), which is defined by OSPF as a group of routers exchanging routing information using link-state protocol. OSPF is based on using a hierarchical networking topology. Defining the hierarchy requires planning to define boundaries that denote an OSPF area and address assignment.

OSPF Topology

OSPF defines its hierarchy based on areas. Figure 3-5 illustrates the OSPF hierarchy and various areas used to build and connect the OSPF network. An area is a common grouping of routers and their interfaces. OSPF has one single common area through which all other areas communicate. Due to the use of the OSPF algorithm and its demand on router resources, it is

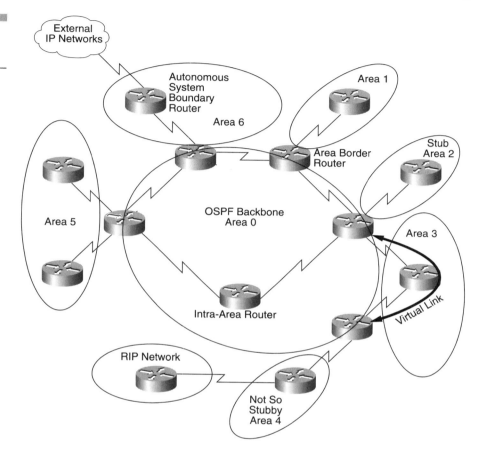

Figure 3-5
OSPF network
hierarchy and areas

necessary to keep the number of routers at 50 or below per OSPF area. Areas with unreliable links will therefore require many recalculations and are best suited to operate within small areas.

The OSPF algorithm using a flooding technique for notifying neighbors of topology must change. The greater number of neighbors, the more CPU-intensive the topology becomes since the new route must be recalculated and forwarded to all attached neighbors. Cisco studies have resulted in a recommendation of no more than 60 neighbors per OSPF router.

The OSPF link-state algorithm calculates a change for each specified area defined on the router. Area routers are usually also *area border routers* (ABR). That is, they maintain and support OSPF routing tables for two OSPF areas. In general, there is a minimum of two areas for an ABR: the backbone area and one non-backbone area. The recommendation for OSPF is to limit the number of supported areas in a router to three. This minimizes resources utilization for the calculation and distribution of link-state updates.

OSPF uses a designated router as the keeper of all the OSPF routes within a LAN. This reduces routing updates over a LAN, thereby preserving LAN media bandwidth. OSPF routers attached to the same LAN as the designated router request a route only if their own table does not have an entry for the destination resource. A backup designated router is also used for availability and redundancy. The recommendation is to have a designated and backup designated router supporting only one LAN. In addition, the designated and backup designated router should be the least CPU-intensive router on the LAN.

The OSPF backbone must be designed for stability and redundancy. A link failure that partitions the backbone will result in application outages, which leads to poor availability. The size of the backbone should be no more than 50 routers.

Routers within the OSPF backbone must be contiguous. This follows the concept of the hierarchy and maintains the traffic for backbone updates within the backbone area routers. However, OSPF offers the use of a virtual link for connecting two non-contiguous routers through a non-native area router. Using a virtual link, a partitioned backbone can be circumvented until the link failure causing the outage is corrected. Finally, reserve the media used for the OSPF backbone for routers to avoid instability and unrelated routing protocol traffic.

As with backbone areas, each OSPF area must be contiguous, and not only contiguous in design, but contiguous in the network address space. Using a contiguous address space makes route summarization possible. The routers of an area connecting the area to the OSPF backbone area are termed *area border routers* (ABR). For availability, it is deemed appropriate to have more than one ABR connecting the area to the backbone area.

Designing large-scale OSPF networks requires a review of the physical connectivity map between routers and the density of resources. Designing the network into geographic areas can be beneficial for simplifying implementation and operations but may not be beneficial for availability or performance. In general, smaller OSPF areas generate better performance and higher levels of availability than large OSPF areas.

OSPF Addressing and Summarization

Maximizing the address space in OSPF networks assists in reducing resource utilization and maximizes route summarization. A hierarchical addressing scheme is the most effective means of designing an OSPF network. OSPF supports VLSM that lends itself to a hierarchical network address space specification. Using VLSM, route summarization is maximized at the backbone and ABR routers. Guidelines for defining an OSPF network for optimized route summarization are as follows:

- Define the network address scheme in subnet ranges for use in each contiguous area.
- Use VLSM addressing to maximize address space.
- Define the network address space for future growth to allow the splitting of an area.
- Design the network with the intention of adding new OSPF routers in the future.

Route summarization increases the stability of an OSPF network and keeps route changes within an area. Route summarization must be explicitly specified when working with OSPF networks on Cisco routers. The specification of router summarization requires the following information:

- Determine route information needed by the backbone about each area.
- Determine route information needed by an area for the backbone and other areas.

OSPF route summarization occurs in area border routers. Using VLSM, bit-boundary summarization is possible on network or subnet addresses within the area. Since OSPF route summarization is explicit, the network design must incorporate summarization definitions for each OSPF area border router.

OSPF areas offer four types of routing information:

Default: A default route for packets whose destination IP network or subnet cannot be found in the routing tables.

Intra-area routes: These are routes for network or subnets within a given area.

Interarea routes: This information provides areas with explicit network or subnet routers for networks or subnets within the OSPF autonomous system, but not within the area.

External routes: These are routes learned from the exchange of routing information between autonomous systems. This results in routes that are external to the OSPF autonomous system.

OSPF route information provides information on three types of OSPF areas: non-stub areas, stub areas, and stub areas without summaries. Stub areas are OSPF areas that connect only to one other area and therefore are considered a stub off the hierarchy. A non-stub area is an OSPF area that provides connectivity to more than one OSPF area.

Non-stub area characteristics include the following:

- They store default routes, static routes, intra-area routes, interarea routes, and external routes.
- They have OSPF inter-area connectivity.
- Autonomous system border routers are used.
- Virtual links require non-stub areas.
- They are the most resource-intensive type of area.

Stub area characteristics are as follows:

- They build default, intra-area, and inter-area routes.
- They are most useful in areas containing one ABR.
- They may contain multiple area border routers to the same area.
- Virtual links cannot connect through stub areas.
- They cannot use autonomous system border routers.

Stub areas without summaries have the following characteristics:

- They serve as default and intra-area routers.
- They are recommended for single router connections to the backbone.

Table 3-1 lists the OSPF area types along with the routing information supported.

Table 3-1

OSPF Area Type and Support for Routing Information

Routing Information Type

Area Type	Default	Intra-area	Interarea	External
Nonstub	Yes	Yes	Yes	Yes
Stub	Yes	Yes	Yes	No
Stub without summaries	Yes	Yes	No	No

OSPF Route Selection

OSPF defaults route selection to the bandwidth metric. Under OSPF, the bandwidth metric is determined by the type of media being used and the cost is measured on the outgoing interface only. The bandwidth metric for a link is the inverse of the bandwidth supported by the media used for the link. The bandwidth metric is calibrated based on a metric of 1 for FDDI media. Figure 3-6 depicts an OSPF network and the applied bandwidth metric.

The total metric for a given route is the sum of all the bandwidth metric values of all the links used for the route. Media that support bandwidth greater than FDDI 100 Mbps default to the FDDI metric value of one. In a configuration where media types connecting the router are faster than FDDI, a manual cost greater than one must be applied to the FDDI link in order to favor the higher-speed media type. OSPF route summarization uses the metric of the best route found within the summarized routes as a metric value for the summarized entry.

OSPF external routes are defined as being either a type 1 or type 2 route. The metric for a type 1 external route is the sum of the internal OSPF metric and the external route metric. Type 2 external routes use only the metric of the external route. Type 1 external route metrics are more favorable in providing a truer metric for connecting to the external resource.

For single ABR OSPF areas, all traffic leaving the area flows through the single ABR. This is done by having the ABR exchange a default route with the other routers of the area. In multiple ABR OSPF areas, the traffic can leave either through the ABR closest to the source of the traffic or the ABR closest to the destination of the traffic. In this case, the ABRs exchange summarized routes with the other routers of the area.

Figure 3-6

OSPF route selection using bandwidth metrics

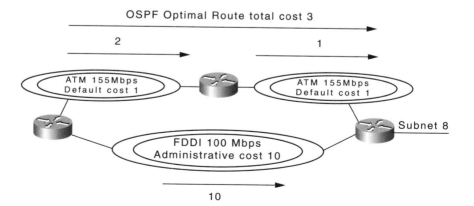

High-availability network design requires redundant paths and routers. Redundancy is useful when employing equal-cost paths to take advantage of load balancing. Cisco routers will load-balance over a maximum of four equal-cost paths between a source and destination using either per-destination or per-packet load balancing when using OSPF. The default of per-destination is based on connectivity bandwidth at 56 Kbps or greater.

OSPF Convergence

Since OSPF is a link-state-based routing protocol, it adapts quickly to network topology changes. OSPF detects topology changes based on the interface status or the failure to receive a response to an OSPF HELLO packet of an attached neighbor within a given amount of time. OSPF has a default timer of 40 seconds in broadcast networks (such as LANs) and two minutes in non-broadcast networks (such as WANs).

The routes are recalculated by the router recognizing the failed link and sends a link-state packet to all the routers within the area. Each router then recalculates all the routes within its routing table.

OSPF Scalability

The addressing scheme, number of areas, and number of links within the OSPF network all affect the scalability of an OSPF network. Routers use memory for storing all the link states for each area to which a router belongs. The more areas attached to a router, the larger the table. Scaling OSPF therefore depends on the effective use of route summarization and stub areas to reduce memory requirements. The larger the link-state database, the more CPU cycles are required during the recalculation of the shortest-path-first algorithm.

Minimizing the size of an OSPF area and the number of links within the area, along with route summarization, enables OSPF to scale to large networks. OSPF only sends small HELLO packets and link-state updates when a topology change occurs or at startup. This is a great benefit for preserving bandwidth utilization, as compared to distance-vector routing protocols such as RIP or IGRP.

OSPF Security

OPSF can use an authentication field to verify that a router connecting as a neighbor is indeed a router that belongs within the network. OSPF routers by their very nature do not allow the filtering of routes, since all OSPF routers must have the same routing information within an area. Using authentication, an OSPF router can verify that it should exchange topology information with a new router that has joined the network. In this way, not only does OSPF provide some protection from unwanted access, it assists in keeping a stable network.

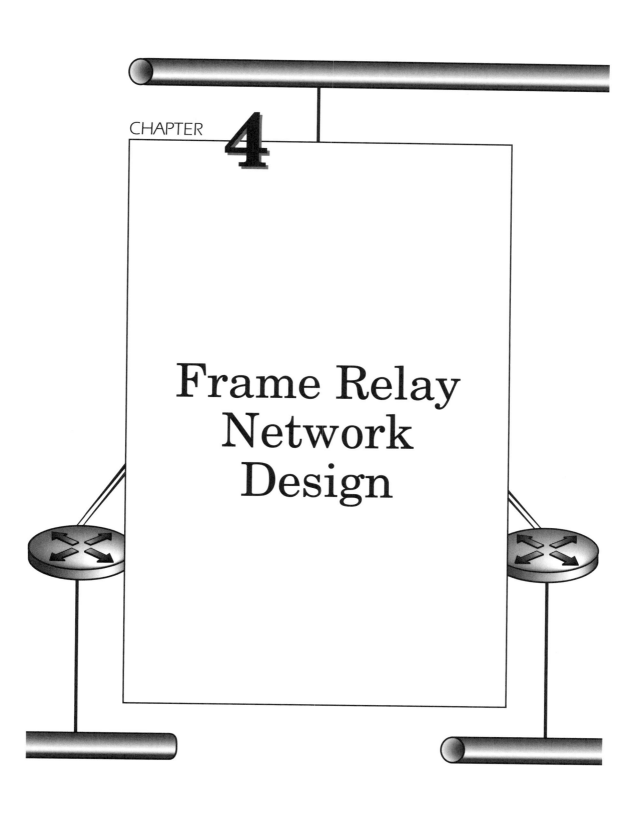

4

Frame Relay Network Design

Frame Relay is based on a packet-switched data network. The differential of Frame Relay to previous packet-switched networks like X.25 is that Frame Relay switches a frame versus a packet. Frame Relay has considerable low overhead and its speed through the network is in part due to not ensuring the delivery of data. Frame Relay as a WAN network solution has grown because of its low cost for acceptable performance, as compared to leased-line WAN solutions. An optimal Frame Relay network design is based on the following:

- Balancing the cost savings of using a public network with the business performance requirements
- A scalable WAN design founded in a manageable environment
- Utilizes a hierarchical design

Main concerns for implementing a Frame Relay design is the ability of the design to scale to not only topology growth but to traffic growth. Components for creating a scalable Frame Relay network designs are as follows:

- The adherence to the three-layer router model of core, distribution, and access layers
- Overall hierarchical design
- Implementing various mesh topology design
- Addressing protocol broadcast issues
- Addressing performance concerns

Meeting these guidelines results in providing a scalable, high-availability, and low-cost Frame Relay network design.

Hierarchical Design of Frame Relay Internetworks

Frame Relay design is based on *permanent virtual connections* (PVCs). A PVC is identified using a *Data Link Connection Identifier* (DLCI) number. Multiple PVCs are possible over a single physical communication link. Using this capability, a single link can communicate with multiple locations. This function is shown in Figure 4-1 where router R1 using two PVCs communicates with two other routers over the public Frame Relay network.

Figure 4-1

Frame Relay PVCs
connecting a single
router to two routers

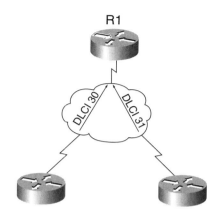

Figure 4-1

Frame Relay PVCs
connecting a single
router to two routers

A PVC can be assigned a bandwidth. The total bandwidth of all defined PVCs can equal the actual bandwidth of the physical communication link. In a sense, Frame Relay acts as a *time-division multiplexer* (TDM) over a public network.

Due to the nature of Frame Relay services through PVCs, hierarchical designs are more logical than physical in definition. Each PVC may be guaranteed two bandwidth parameters, the *committed information rate* (CIR) and *excessive burst* limits (Be). The CIR is an agreement with the Frame Relay provider for a minimum throughput for the PVC. The excessive burst limit is an agreement with the Frame Relay provider for the available bandwidth for use by the PVC over and above the PVC bandwidth to the maximum available on the physical link. These two variables greatly influence the cost and therefore the design of the Frame Relay network.

Frame Relay Scalability

Scalability is achieved in Frame Relay network design through the implementation of a hierarchy. Using a hierarchy enables incremental growth. The hierarchical approach, however, must follow the three-layer routing model in order for meeting high-availability, acceptable performance, and low-cost requirements. These requirements can be met through careful planning of actual performance requirements at remote locations, the degree of high-availability service, and minimizing the complexity of the hierarchy.

Frame Relay Management

Managing a hierarchical network is minimized through the partitioning of the network into smaller elements. By simplifying the network into manageable modules, troubleshooting is eased. The partitioning also provides protection against broadcast storms and routing loops. A hierarchical design inherently provides a flexible network topology, allowing the inclusion of other technologies into the network design. This leads to a hybrid approach for the overall network infrastructure. Although hybrid network design may enable greater service, it does make network management a bit more complex. Finally, router management in hierarchical Frame Relay networks is reduced due to fewer network connections based on the hierarchy.

Frame Relay Performance

Hierarchical network design lends itself to protecting networks from broadcast and multicast traffic issues. A regional hierarchy with smaller areas enables the Frame Relay network to maintain overall network performance requirements. Limiting the number of routers within an area or layer minimizes the chances of traffic bottlenecks due to broadcast traffic.

Frame Relay Network Topology

The network topology design chosen for implementing Frame Relay networks is dependent on many variables. Among these are the types of protocols supported and the actual traffic characteristics and patterns generated by applications using the network. It is recommended that an optimal Frame Relay network design support anywhere from a maximum of 10 to 50 PVCs per physical interface. Consider the following factors in determining the number of PVCs to support:

- Broadcast-intensive protocols constrain the number of PVCs. Segregating the protocols into their own PVC for better management requires more PVCs in multiprotocol networks.

- Broadcast updates due to routing protocols may consume bandwidth. The number, type, and frequency of the routing protocol updates will dictate the number of PVCs required to meet service levels.

- The available bandwidth of the physical Frame Relay connection as measured against the amount of broadcast traffic may dictate higher-bandwidth PVCs with higher CIRs and excess burst limits. Because each PVC has more bandwidth, however, the number of PVCs is reduced.

- Static routes can either eliminate or reduce the amount of broadcasts, thereby enabling more PVCs per physical connection.

- Large networks tend to create large routing protocol updates. Large updates and frequencies require higher bandwidth, thereby reducing the number of available PVCs per physical link.

The topology of a Frame Relay network is comprised of different design formats. Each format has its advantageous and disadvantageous. The network requirements along with the considerations outlined above on the number of PVCs required in a design need to be addressed in using the various topology layouts.

Frame Relay Star Topology

A Frame Relay star topology is depicted in Figure 4-2. The configuration is referred to as a star due to the single connection by all remote sites to a central location. Star topologies minimize the number of PVCs and result in a low-cost design. Due to its design, however, bandwidth at the central site becomes an issue since it becomes limited due to the number of remote locations connecting over the physical connection. Likewise, high-availability through alternate paths and rerouting of data from the remote locations is non-existent since there is only one path from the remote location to the rest of the network.

An advantage to a star topology is its ease of management, but its disadvantages make it a poor choice for basing a foundation on its network design. These drawbacks include the core or hub router as a single point of failure, performance problems of the backbone due to the single core router connection, and the inability of a star topology to scale.

Figure 4-2
Frame Relay
star topology

Public Frame Relay
Star Topology

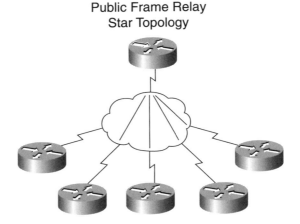

Frame Relay Fully Meshed Topology

A fully meshed Frame Relay network provides a very high degree of availability. As shown in Figure 4-3, a fully meshed network uses PVCs connecting all Frame Relay points on the network. Disadvantageous to using a fully meshed network is the number of PVCs required. A PVC is required for logically connecting to each router on the network. A fully meshed topology requires $[n(n-1)]/2$ PVCs, where n is the number of routers being connected to the Frame Relay network. For example, a fully meshed network of five routers requires $[5(5-1)]/2$, which equals 10 PVCs.

Although Frame Relay networks are *non-broadcast multi-access* (NBMA) networks, a router sends a broadcast over each active PVC. This replication process leads to excessive CPU and bandwidth requirements for routing updates, spanning tree updates and SAP updates.

In small Frame Relay networks, a fully meshed topology is a reasonable design. The issues that make a fully meshed network for large networks a poor design are as follows:

- A large number of PVCs
- CPU and bandwidth overhead due to packet and broadcast replication
- Management complexity

Figure 4-3
Frame Relay fully
meshed topology

Public Frame Relay
Full Mesh Topology

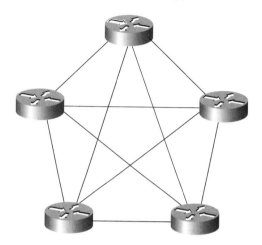

Frame Relay Partially Meshed Topology

Merging the ease of design and management using a star topology with the high-availability feature provided by a fully meshed topology results in a requirements-balanced partially meshed topology. Seen in Figure 4-4, a partially meshed topology consists of two star topologies being supported by remote locations. Partially meshed topologies are ideal for regional implementation. Their advantages are as follows:

- High-availability
- Relatively low cost, as compared to fully meshed
- Minimum number of PVCs required
- Acceptable performance at a reasonable cost

   Data must flow through one of the core routers for communication between locations of a partially meshed topology without a direct PVC.

Figure 4-4
Frame Relay partial
mesh topology

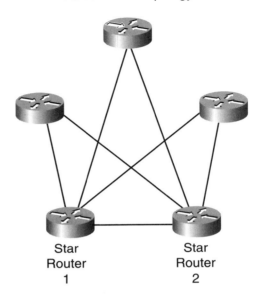

Public Frame Relay
Partial Mesh Topology

Star
Router
1

Star
Router
2

Frame Relay Fully Meshed
Hierarchical Topology

Applying the fully meshed topology to an overall hierarchy for the three layers of the routing layer model results in a design that scales and localizes
traffic due to the creation of manageable segments. The modularity of the
design enables the network as a whole to scale well. As shown in Figure 4-5,
the hierarchy is based on the strategic connections made across the routing
layer model.

Although, again, this topology provides high redundancy and modularity,
it continues to have the packet-broadcast replication problem. The balance
of service to cost is also lost due to the extra number of routers, physical
links, and PVCs required.

Figure 4-5
Frame Relay fully
meshed hierarchical
topology

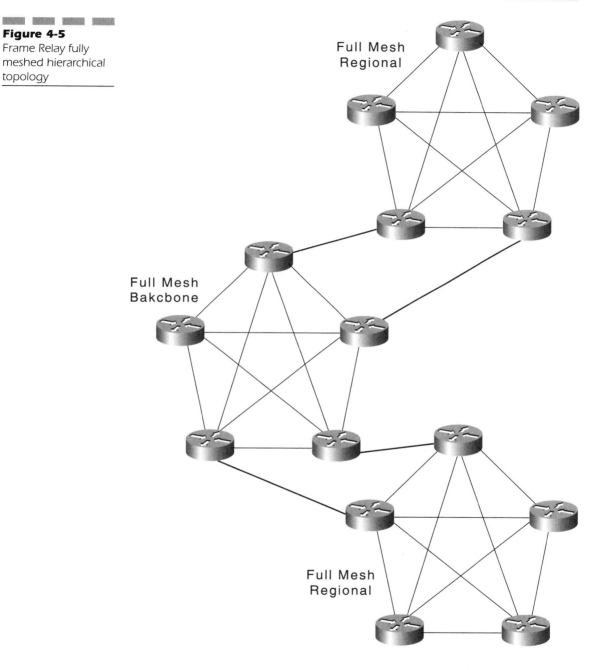

Full Mesh
Regional

Full Mesh
Bakcbone

Full Mesh
Regional

Frame Relay Hybrid Meshed Hierarchical Topology

Managing the balance between core backbone performance and maintaining a low-cost network design results in a hybrid hierarchical Frame Relay network. A hybrid hierarchical network, as depicted in Figure 4-6, uses private leased lines for creating a fully meshed backbone and partially or fully meshed Frame Relay networks for connection to the regional network.

In Figure 4-6, we see the use of an ATM core backbone feeding a leased line distribution network. The distribution layer then provides network connectivity using a partially meshed topology. This topology provides high-availability, great bandwidth for the backbone, network segmentation, and simplified router configuration management.

Broadcast Traffic Issues

Broadcasts are typically used for routing protocols to update network devices on selecting the best path between two destinations on the network. Many routing protocols update their neighbors or peers on a periodic basis. Routers replicate a broadcast to every active PVC defined on the router for transmission to the partner node at the other end of the PVC. Figure 4-7 illustrates this point.

In managing the broadcasts of routing protocols, it is important to understand the time requirement for topology changes. In stable networks, the timers that manage the broadcast updates for individual routing protocols can be extended, which helps router and bandwidth overhead in supporting the routing protocol updates.

Another alternative is to include efficient routing protocols, such as EIGRP, in the design in order to reduce the routing protocol broadcast updates over the Frame Relay network. Managing the replication of broadcasts and packets is of paramount concern. Fully meshed networks actually increase the overall cost of a network and increase the overall load on the network. Table 4-1 lists the relative traffic levels as they relate to broadcast traffic generated by routing protocols.

Figure 4-6
Use of private leased
lines and regional
Frame Relay
networks

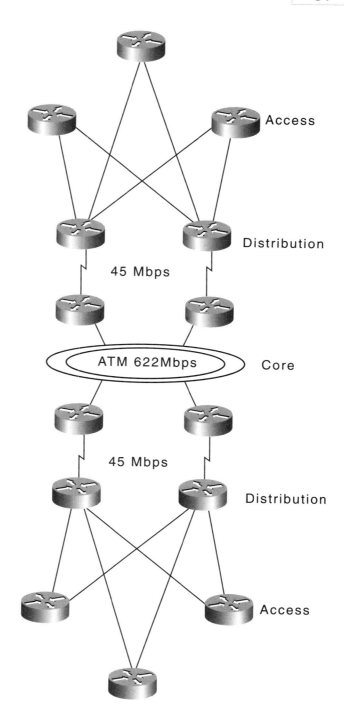

Figure 4-7
Broadcast replication
over Frame Relay
PVCs

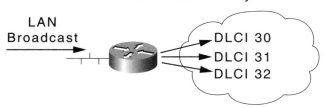

Broadcast Replication
over Frame Relay

LAN
Broadcast

DLCI 30
DLCI 31
DLCI 32

Table 4-1

Relative Broadcast
Traffic Generated
by Popular Routing
Protocols

Network Protocol	Routing Protocol	Relative Broadcast Traffic Level
AppleTalk	Routing Table Maintenance Protocol (RTMP)	High
	Enhanced Interior Gateway Routing Protocol (EIGRP)	Low
Novell Internetwork Packet Exchange (IPX)	Routing Information Protocol (RIP)	High
	Service Advertisement Protocol (SAP)	High
	Enhanced Interior Gateway Routing Protocol (EIGRP)	Low
Internet Protocol (IP)	Routing Information Protocol (RIP)	High
	Interior Gateway Protocol (IGRP)	High
	Open Shortest Path First (OSPF)	Low
	Intermediate System -Intermediate System (IS-IS)	Low
	Enhanced Interior Gateway Protocol (EIGRP)	Low
	Border Gateway Protocol (BGP)	None
	Exterior Gateway Protocol (EGP)	None
DECnet Phase IV	DECnet Routing	High
DECnet Phase V	IS-IS	Low
International Organization for Standardization (ISO) Connectionless Network Service (CLNS)	IS-IS ISO-IGRP	Low High
Xerox Network Systems (XNS)	RIP	High
Banyan Virtual Integrated Network Service (VINES)	Routing Table Protocol (RTP) Sequenced RTP	High Low

Performance Considerations

Several factors affect the performance of Frame Relay networks. We have already discussed the effect of broadcasts on the network. Broadcasts are the primary concern for designing the bandwidth and number of PVCs necessary for a viable Frame Relay network. During the planning stage of developing the Frame Relay network design, the following must be considered:

- Maximum rate requirements
- CIR
- Management of multiprotocol traffic

Determining Maximum rate

The Frame Relay provider uses several metrics to determine the billing of the Frame Relay connections. Therefore, it is important to fully understand the bandwidth and number of PVCs required to meet business service levels. The metrics used for determining the Frame Relay network configuration are

Committed burst (Bc): The number of bits committed to accept and transmit at the CIR

Excess burst (Be): The number of bits to transmit after reaching the Bc value

Committed Information Rate (CIR): The maximum permitted traffic level for each PVC

Maximum data rate (MaxR): Calculated value measured in bits per second; (Bc + Be)/Bc * CIR

Determination of the CIR, Bc, and Be is predicated on the actual speed of the physical line. The maximum values cannot extend past the maximum speed of the link. In addition, the application profiles will influence the metrics based on the type of service, transport mechanisms, and usage of each application using the PVCs.

Committed Information Rate (CIR)

The CIR is the guaranteed bandwidth the Frame Relay service provides for each PVC on the physical link. For example, a CIR of 19.2 Kbps on a 128 Kbps physical link commits the Frame Relay network to provide 19.2 Kbps of throughput for the PVC between source and destination. CIR is the metric most influencial on the capability to meet the service levels for the applications. Failure to properly calculate the appropriate CIR level results in poor performance and failure to meet service levels.

Underestimating the CIR results in *discard-eligible* (DE) frames. The DE bit value is activated by a Frame Relay switch when the bandwidth used on the PVC begins to exceed the CIR. Frame Relay switches inspect the DE bit value within the frame. If the DE bit is on, the frame may be discarded based on the switches resource constraints, network congestion, and available bandwidth.

FECN/BECN Congestion Protocol

Frame Relay institutes a congestion protocol to protect network resources from overuse, known as FECN/BECN. *Forward Explicit Congestion Notification* (FECN) is a Frame Relay message used to notify a receiving device that there is a congestion problem. B*ackward Explicit Congestion Notification* (BECN) is a Frame Relay message used to notify a sending device that there is a congestion problem. These messages enable the network devices to throttle the traffic onto the network. Cisco routers support the use of FECN and BECN.

Virtual Subinterface and Multiprotocol Management

Support for multiple protocols over Frame Relay connections requires some thought on traffic management. Cisco IOS enables the use of subinterfaces on physical interfaces. This capability to create virtual interfaces, diagrammed in Figure 4-8, enables a network designer to use all the tuning, reporting, and management functions of the Cisco IOS interface commands for each individual PVC.

Using this feature of virtual interfaces also creates unique buffers on the output queues for each PVC, versus one output buffer queue for the entire physical connection. The result is better performance and management using virtual subinterfaces.

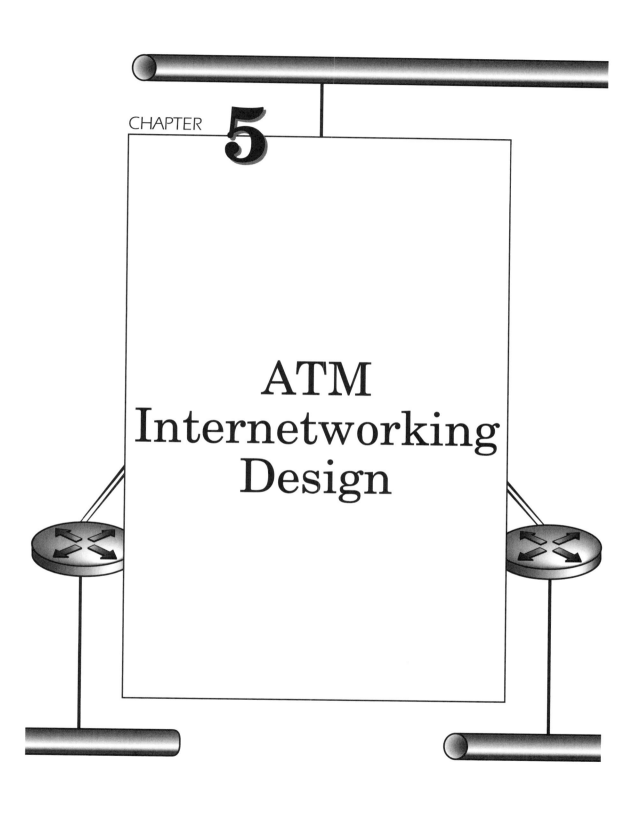

ATM
Internetworking
Design

Asynchronous Transfer Mode (ATM) is the first networking architecture developed specifically for supporting multiple services. ATM networks are capable of supporting audio (voice), video, and data simultaneously. ATM is currently able to support up to 2.5 Gbps of bandwidth. Data networks immediately get a performance enhancement when moving to ATM due to the increased memory. Voice networks realize a cost savings, due in part to sharing the same network with data and through voice compression, silence compression, repetitive pattern suppression, and dynamic bandwidth allocation. The ATM fixed-size 53-byte cell enables ATM to support the isochronicity of a *time-division multiplexed* (TDM) private network with the efficiencies of *public switched data networks* (PDSN).

Most network designers are first challenged by the integration of ATM with the data network. Data network integration requires legacy network protocols to traverse a cell-based switched network. ATM can accomplish this in several ways. The first of these is LAN emulation.

LAN Emulation (LANE)

ATM employs a standards-based specification for enabling the installed base of legacy LANs and the legacy network protocols used on these LANs to communicate over an ATM network. This standard is known as *LAN emulation* (LANE). LANE uses the *Media Access Control* (MAC) sublayer of the OSI data link control Layer 2. Using MAC encapsulation techniques enables ATM to address the majority of Layer 2 and Layer 3 networking protocols. ATM LANE logically extends the appearance of a LAN, thereby providing legacy protocols with equivalent performance characteristics, as are found in traditional LAN environments. Figure 5-1 illustrates a typical ATM topology with LANE support.

LANE uses ATM's *emulated LANs* (ELANs). Using ELANs, a LAN in one location is logically connected to a LAN in another location. This allows a network designer to extend a LAN over an ATM WAN, avoiding the need for routing packets between the two locations. LANE services can be employed by ATM-attached servers or workstations, edge devices such as switches, and routers when routing between ELANs is required.

ATM LANE uses four components to establish end-to-end connectivity for legacy protocols and devices:

- LAN Emulation Client
- *LAN Emulation Configuration Server* (LECS)

Figure 5-1
ATM LANE topology

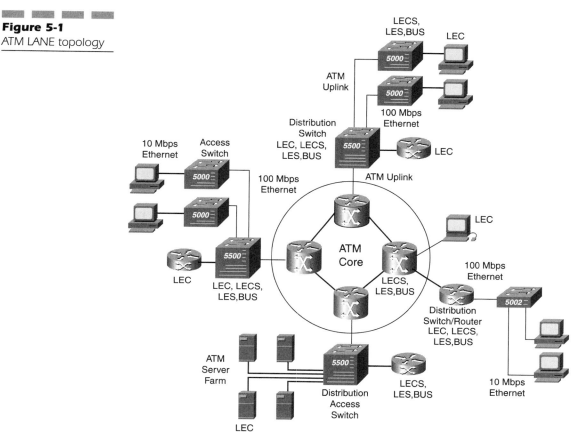

- *LAN Emulation Server* (LES)
- *Broadcast and Unknown Server* (BUS)

LAN Emulation Client (LEC)

Any end system that connects using ATM requires a *LAN emulation Client* (LEC). The LEC performs the emulation necessary in support of the legacy LAN. An LEC performs the following functions:

- Data forwarding
- Address resolution
- Registering MAC addresses with the LANE server

- Communication with other LECs using ATM *virtual channel connections* (VCCs)

  End systems that support the LEC functions act as

- ATM-attached workstations
- ATM-attached servers
- ATM LAN switches (Cisco Catalyst family)
- ATM attached routers (Cisco 12000, 7500, 7000, 4700, 4500, and 4000 series)

LAN Emulation Configuration Server (LECS)

The ELAN database is maintained by the *LAN emulation configuration server* (LECS) and is manually updated by the router administrator. In addition, the LECS builds and maintains an ATM address database of *LAN Emulation Servers* (LES). The LECS maps an ELAN name to a LES ATM address. The LECS performs the following LANE functions:

- It accepts queries from a LEC.
- It responds to a LEC query with an ATM address of the LES for the ELAN.
- It serves multiple ELANs.
- It is manually defined and maintained.

The LECS assigns individual clients to a ELAN by directing them to the LES that corresponds to the ELAN.

LAN Emulation Server (LES)

LECs are controlled from a central control point called a *LAN Emulation Server* (LES). LECs communicate with the LES using a Control Direct *Virtual Channel Connection* (VCC). The Control Direct VCC is used for forwarding registration and control information. The LES uses a Control Distribute VCC, a point-to-multipoint VCC, enabling the LES to forward control information to all the LECs. The LES services the LAN *Emulation Address Resolution Protocol* (LE_ARP) request, which it uses to build and maintain a list of LAN destination MAC addresses.

Broadcast Unknown Server (BUS)

ATM is based on the notion that the network is point-to-point. Therefore, there is no inherent support for broadcast or any-to-any services. LANE provides this type of support over ATM by centralizing broadcast and multicast functions on a *Broadcast And Unknown Server* (BUS). Each LEC communicates with the BUS using a Multicast Send VCC. The BUS communicates with all LECs using point-multipoint VCC, known as the Multicast Forward VCC. A BUS reassembles received cells on each Multicast Send VCC in sequence to create the complete frame. Once a frame is complete, it is then sent to all the LECs on a Multicast Forward VCC. This ensures the proper sequence of data between LECs.

LANE Design Considerations

The following are guidelines for designing LANE services on Cisco routers:

- The Cisco AIP has a bidirectional limit of 60 thousand packets per second (pps).
- The ATM interface on a Cisco router has the capability of supporting up to 255 subinterfaces.
- Only one active LECS can support all the ELANs. Other LECS operate in backup mode.
- Each ELAN has one LES/BUS pair and one or more LECs.
- LES and BUS must be defined on the same subinterface of the router AIP.
- Only one LES/BUS pair per ELAN is permitted.
- Only one active LES/BUS pair per subinterface is allowed.
- The LANE Phase 1 standard does not provide for LES/BUS redundancy.
- The LECS can reside on a different router than the LES/BUS pair.
- VCCs are supported over *switched virtual circuits* (SVCs) or *permanent virtual circuits* (PVCs).
- A subinterface supports only one LEC.
- Protocols such as AppleTalk, IP, and IPX are routable over a LEC if they are defined on the AIP subinterface.
- An ELAN should be in only one subnet for IP.

Network Support

The LANE support in Cisco IOS enables legacy LAN protocols to utilize ATM as the transport mechanism for inter-LAN communications. The following features highlight the Cisco IOS support for LANE:

- Support for Ethernet-emulated LANs only. There is currently no Token Ring LAN emulation support.
- Support for routing between ELANs using IP, IPX, or AppleTalk
- Support for bridging between ELANs
- Support for bridging between ELANs and LANs
- LANE server redundancy support through *simple server redundancy protocol* (SSRP)
- IP gateway redundancy support using *Hot Standby Routing Protocol* (HSRP)
- DECnet, Banyan VINES, and XNS-routed protocols

Addressing

LANE requires MAC addressing for every client. LANE clients defined on the same interface or subinterface automatically have the same MAC address. This MAC address is used as the *end system identifier* (ESI) value of the ATM address. Although the MAC address is duplicated, the resulting ATM address representing each LANE client is unique. All ATM addresses must be unique for proper ATM operations. Each LANE services component has an ATM address unique from all other ATM addresses.

LANE ATM Addresses

LANE uses the NSAP ATM address syntax. The address format used by LANE is as follows:

- A 13-byte prefix that includes the following fields defined by the ATM Forum:
    - An *Authority and Format Identifier* (AFI) field (one byte)

    - A *Data Country Code* (DCC) or *International Code Designator* (ICD) field (two bytes)

- A *Domain Specific Part Format Identifier* (DFI field) (one byte)
- An Administrative Authority field (three bytes)
- A Reserved field (two bytes)
- A Routing Domain field (two bytes)
- An Area field (two bytes)
- A six-byte *end-system identifier* (ESI)
- A one-byte selector field

Cisco's Method of Automatically Assigning ATM Addresses

The Cisco IOS supports an automated function of defining ATM and MAC addresses, which are used in the LECS database. The automation process uses a pool of eight MAC addresses that are assigned to each router ATM interface. The Cisco IOS applies the addresses to the LANE components using the following methodology:

- All LANE components on the router use the same prefix value, which identifies a switch and must be defined within the switch.
- The first address in the MAC address pool becomes the ESI field value for every LANE client on the interface.
- The second address in the MAC address pool becomes the ESI field value for every LANE server on the interface.
- The third address in the MAC address pool becomes the ESI field value for the LANE broadcast-and-unknown server on the interface.
- The fourth address in the MAC address pool becomes the ESI field value for the LANE configuration server on the interface.
- The selector field for the LANE configuration server is set to a 0 value. All other components use the subinterface number of interface to which they are defined as the selector field.

The requirement that the LANE components be defined on different subinterfaces of an ATM interface results in a unique ATM address, due to the use of the selector field value being set to the subinterface number.

Using ATM Address Templates

ATM address definitions are greatly simplified through the use of address templates. However, these templates are not supported for the E.164 ATM address format. The address templates used for LANE ATM addressing can use either an asterisk (*) or an ellipsis (…) character. An asterisk is used for matching any single character, while an ellipsis is used for matching leading or trailing characters. Table 5-1 lists the address template value determination.

The ATM address templates can be either a prefix or an ESI template. When using a prefix template, the first 13 bytes match the defined prefix for the switch but use wildcards for the ESI and selector fields. An ESI template matches the ESI field but uses wildcards for the prefix and selector fields.

Rules for Assigning Components to Interfaces and Subinterfaces

The LANE components can be assigned to the primary ATM interface as well as the subinterfaces. The following are guidelines for applying LANE components on a Cisco router ATM interface:

- The LECS always runs on the primary interface.
- Assigning a component to the primary interface falls through to the subinterface 0 definition.
- The LES and LEC of the same emulated LAN can be configured on the same subinterface in a router.

Table 5-1

Determining ATM Address Template Values

Unspecified Digits In	Resulting Value Is
Prefix (First 13 bytes)	Obtained from ATM switch via Interim Local Management Interface (ILMI)
ESI (Next six bytes)	Filled using the first MAC address of the MAC address pool plus 0-LANE client 1-LANE server 2-LANE broadcast-and-unknown server 3-LANE configuration server
Selector field (last byte)	Subinterface number, in the range 0 through 255.

- LECs of two different emulated LANs must be defined on a different subinterface in a router.
- LESs of two different emulated LANs must be defined on a different subinterface in a router.

Redundancy in LANE Environments

The ATM LANE V 1.0 specification does not provide for redundancy of the LANE components. High availability is always a goal for network designers and the single point of failure in the LANE specification requires a technique for redundancy. Cisco IOS supports LANE redundancy through the implementation of Simple Server Replication Protocol (SSRP).

SSRP supports the redundancy of LECS and LES/BUS services. LECS redundancy is provided by configuring multiple LECS addresses in the ATM switches. Each defined LECS is defined with a rank, which is the index (the number of the entry in the LECS address table) of the LECS address in the table.

At initialization the LECS requests the LECS address table from the ATM switch. The requesting LECS on receipt of the LECS address table tries to connect to all the LECSs with a lower rank. In this way, the LECS learns of its role in the redundancy hierarchy. A LECS that connects with a LECS whose rank is higher places itself in a backup mode. The LECS that connects to all other LECS and does not find a ranking higher than its own assumes the responsibility of the primary LECS.

In this hierarchy, as shown in Figure 5-2, the failure of a primary LECS does not result in a LANE failure. Rather, the second-highest ranking LECS assumes the primary LECS role. Loss of the VCC between the primary and highest ranking secondary signals the highest secondary ranking LECS that it is now the primary LECS.

In theory, any number of LECS can be designed using SSRP. Cisco recommends, however, that no more than three LECS be designed into SSRP. This recommendation is based on adding a degree of complexity to the network design, which can lead to an increase in the time it takes for resolving problems.

LES/BUS redundancy using SSRP is similar in that it uses a primary-secondary hierarchy; however, the primary LES/BUS pair is assigned by the primary LECS. The LECS determines the primary LES/BUS pair by determining the LES/BUS pair having the highest priority with an open VCC to the primary LECS. The LES/BUS pair priority is assigned during configuration into the LECS database.

Figure 5-2
SSRP configuration
for LECS redundancy

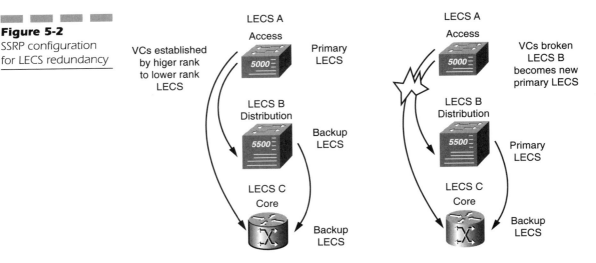

The following guidelines are highly recommended for designing the LECS redundancy scheme and ensuring a properly running SSRP configuration:

- Each LECS must maintain the same ELAN database.
- Configure the LECS addresses in the LECS address table in the same order on each ATM switch in the network.
- Do not define two LECSs on the same ATM switch when using the Well Known Address. Only one of the LECS will register the Well Known Address with the switch, which can lead to initialization problems.

A second type of redundancy mechanism used in LANE is specific to ELANS using IP protocol. The *Host Standby Router Protocol* (HSRP), developed for traditional IP LAN topologies, enables two routers to share a common virtual IP address using a virtual MAC address assigned to the resulting virtual interface. This enables two routers to respond as the single IP gateway address for IP end stations. Figure 5-3 illustrates the use of HSRP with LANE.

The primary and secondary router interface is determined by the definition of HSRP on the interface or subinterface. HSRP exchanges definition information between the two routers to determine which interface is the primary gateway address. The secondary then sends HELLO messages to the primary to determine its viability. When the secondary does not receive a HELLO message from the primary HSRP router, it assumes the primary role.

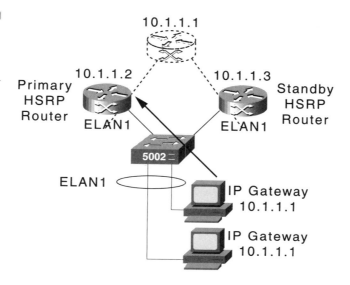

Figure 5-3
HSRP configuration
for IP redundancy of
LANE clients

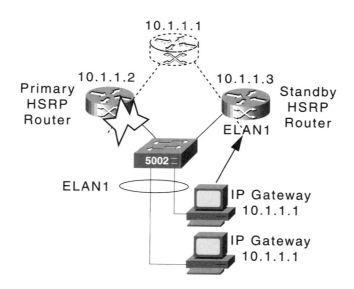

Data Exchange Interface (DXI)

ATM networks connect to serial-attached routers by implementing the ATM *data exchange interface* (DXI) specification. The DXI specification enables ATM *user-network interface* (UNI) connectivity between a Cisco router with only a serial interface to the ATM network. This is accomplished using an ATM *Data Service Unit* (ADSU).

As shown in Figure 5-4, router R1 connects to the ADSU using a *High Speed Serial Interface* (HSSI) connection. The ADSU receives data from the router in the ATM DXI format. The ADSU then converts the data into ATM cells and forwards them to the ATM network. The ADSU performs the opposite function for data going to the router.

Supported Modes

Although ATM DXI comes in three modes, the Cisco IOS supports only mode 1a. The three modes are

- Mode 1a, which supports AAL5 only, a 9232-octet maximum, and a 16-bit FCS, with up to 1,023 virtual circuits.
- Mode 1b, which supports AAL3/4 and AAL5, a 9224-octet maximum, and a 16-bit FCS. AAL5 supports up to 1,023 virtual circuits and AAL3/4 is supported on one virtual circuit.
- Mode 2, which supports AAL3/4 and AAL5 with 16,777,215 virtual circuits, a 65535-octet maximum, and a 32-bit FCS.

Figure 5-4
ATM DXI connectivity
for Cisco routers

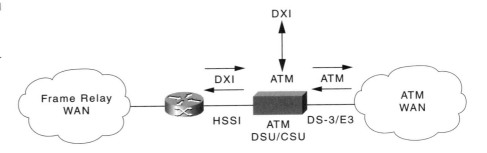

DXI Addressing

DXI addressing uses a value that is equivalent to a Frame Relay data link connection identifier. In DXI, this field is called a DFA. The ADSU maps the DFA to the appropriate ATM *Virtual Path Identifier* (VPI) and *Virtual Connection Identifier* (VCI). Figure 5-5 illustrates the bytes and position mapping of the DXI DFA address to the ATM cell VPI and VCI values.

Classical IP

Cisco routers are configurable as both an IP client and an IP server in support of Classical IP. Classical IP enables the routers to view the ATM network as a *Logical IP Subnet* (LIS). Configuring the routers as an ATM ARP server enables Classical IP networks to communicate over an ATM network. The benefit to this is a simplified configuration. Classical IP support using an ATM ARP server alleviates the need to define the IP network address and ATM address of each end device connecting through the router in the router configuration.

ATM uses PVCs and SVCs and the ATM ARP server feature of Classical IP is SVC-specific. Using the ATM ARP server feature, each end device only configures its own ATM address and the address of the ATM ARP server. Since RFC 1577 allows for only one ATM ARP server address, no redundancy is available in Classical IP.

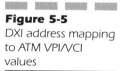

Figure 5-5
DXI address mapping to ATM VPI/VCI values

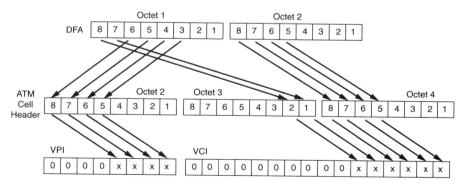

As shown in Figure 5-6, the ATM ARP server address can point to a Cisco router. IP clients using Classical IP make a connection to the ATM ARP server address defined in their configuration. The server then sends an ATM *Inverse ARP* (InARP) request to the client. The client responds with its IP network address and ATM address. The ATM ARP server places these addresses in its cache, which is used to resolve ATM ARP requests from IP clients. The IP client establishes a connection to the IP-ATM address provided in the ATM ARP server reply.

Multiprotocol over ATM (MPOA)

MPOA provides a single solution for transporting all protocols through an ATM network. MPOA V1.0, in concert with LANE *User-to-Network Interface* (UNI) V2.0, allows routers and other ATM networking devices to fully exploit VLANs, QoS, and high-availability. These network enhancements enable designers to add services while relieving traffic congestion and flexibility to the network. The key benefits to MPOA are as follows:

- Inter-VLAN "cut-through," which maximizes bandwidth and network segmentation.
- Robust Layer 3 QoS features to support packetized traffic, such as video or voice, while ensuring data service levels.
- A software-only upgrade, which minimizes the cost and simplifies implementation.

The MPOA specification is built on four components:

- *MPOA Client* (MPC)
- *MPOA Server* (MPS)
- *Next Hop Resolution Protocol* (NHRP)
- *LAN Emulation* (LANE)

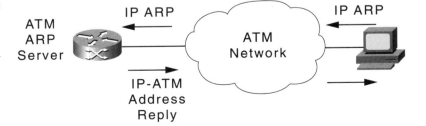

Figure 5-6
Classical IP support on Cisco routers

ATM ARP Server

IP ARP

IP-ATM Address Reply

ATM Network

IP ARP

Both MPC and MPS functions are supported on Cisco routers. MPOA uses a direct *virtual channel connection* (VCC) between the ingress (inbound) and egress (outbound) edge or host device. Direct VCCs are also termed shortcut VCCs. The direct VCC enables the forwarding of Layer 3 packets, normally routed through intermediate routers, between the source and destination host, thereby increasing performance and reducing latency.

Figure 5-7 illustrates the use of MCP, MPS, and NHRP for establishing a direct VCC between two edge devices servicing two end stations.

Multiprotocol Client (MPC)

Typically, the *Multiprotocol client* (MPC) will reside on an ATM edge device, such as a Cisco Catalyst family of switches. However, a Cisco router can perform the functions of an MPC or MPS. An MPC provides the following functions:

- Ingress/egress cache management
- ATM data-plane and control-plane VCC management

Figure 5-7
The MPOA flow for establishing a direct VCC between end stations

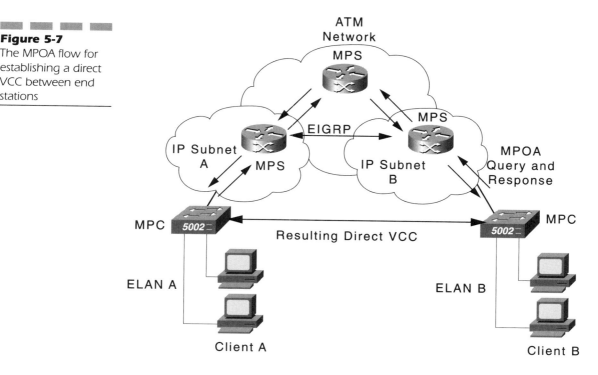

Chapter 6

- MPOA frame-processing
- MPOA protocol and flow detection
- Identification of packets sent to an MPOA-capable router
- Establishes a direct VCC with the egress MPC

Multiprotocol Server (MPS)

The *Multiprotocol server* (MPS) provides the forwarding information used by the MPCs. The MPS maintains the information by using *Next Hop Resolution Protocol* (NHRP). MPS interacts with the NHRP module running in the router. MPS interacts with NHRP in the following manner:

1. The MPS converts the MPOA resolution request to a NHRP request. The MPS then sends the NHRP request to either the Next Hop MPS or the *Next Hop Server* (NHS) based on the results from the next hop information search through the MPS tables. MPS ensures that the correct encapsulation is used depending on the NHS type.

2. If the next hop is determined to be on a LANE cloud, the NHS sends resolution requests to the MPS. Likewise, the NHS sends resolution requests when the destination of the packet is unknown. The MPS can also request the NHS to terminate the request or discard the packet.

3. If the replies terminate in the router or the next hop interface uses LANE, resolution replies are sent from the NHS to the MPS.

4. Upon receiving resolution replies from the NHS, the MPS sends a MPOA resolution reply to the MPC.

MPS uses a network ID. The default network ID for all MPSs is one. Using different network IDs allows the network designer to segregate traffic. This enables the designer to permit direct VCCs between groups of LECs and deny direct VCCs between others. The network ID of an MPS and NHRP on the same router must be the same in order for requests, replies, and shortcuts to be transmitted across the MPS and NHRP.

MPOA Guidelines

The following is a list of guidelines for designing MPOA:

- An ELAN identifier must be defined for each ELAN.
- An MPC/MPS can serve as a single LEC or multiple LECs.
- A LEC can associate with any MPC/MPS.
- A LEC can attach to only one MPC and one MPS at a time.
- A LEC must break its attachment to the current MPC or MPS before attaching another MPC or MPS.
- A primary ATM interface can have multiple MPCs or MPSs defined with different control ATM addresses.
- Multiple MPCs or MPSs can be attached to the same interface.
- The interface attached to the MPC or MPS must be reachable through the ATM network by all LECs that bind to it.

Bandwidth Support on Routers

ATM is supported on the Cisco 7500 and 7000 series routers using the *ATM Interface Processor* (AIP). In designing the ATM internetwork in support of LANE, the total ATM bandwidth support for the entire router should not exceed 200 Mbps in full-duplex mode. This results in the following possible hardware configurations:

- Two *Transparent Asynchronous Transmitter / Receiver Interface* (TAXI) connections
- An OC–3 *Synchronous Optical Network* (SONET) and a E3 connection
- An OC–3 SONET and a low-use OC–3 SONET connection
- Five E3 connections

Chapter 5

Configurable Traffic Parameters

The AIP provides the capability to shape various traffic. It supports up to eight rate queues. Each queue is programmed for a different peak rate. The ATM virtual circuits can be assigned to one of the eight rate queues. A virtual circuit can have an average rate and a burst size defined. The AIP supports the following configurable traffic rate parameters:

- Forward peak cell rate
- Backward peak cell rate
- Forward sustainable cell rate
- Backward sustainable cell rate
- Forward maximum burst
- Backward maximum burst

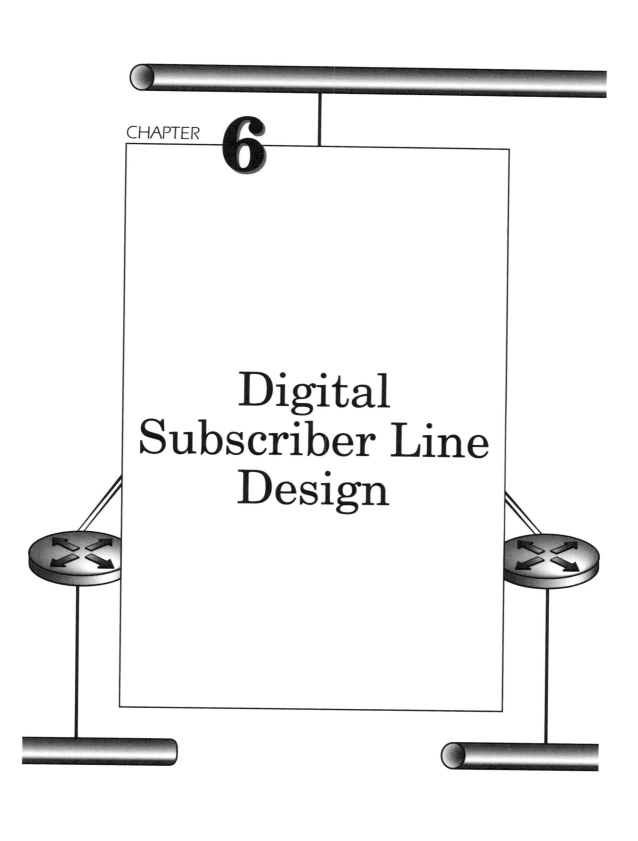

Digital Subscriber Line Design

An estimated 700 million two-wire twisted-pair copper wire connections exist worldwide. These connections comprise the worldwide telephone network infrastructure, also known as the *Public Switched Telephone Network* (PSTN). This well-established infrastructure is the basis for connectivity of corporations and the Internet.

The advent of the Internet and its promise has led to the use of a technology named *Digital Subscriber Line* (DSL). DSL is actually a service, not a line. DSL uses the existing telephone copper wire from a telephone provider's central office to the customer location. The origin of DSL comes from a communication service offering called T1.

T1 Background

T1 is a four-wire, two-pair unshielded cable used for a high-speed digital network (1.544 Mbps) developed by AT&T Bell Labs in 1957 and implemented in the early 1960s to support long-haul *pulse-code modulation* (PCM) voice transmission. The primary innovation of T1 was to introduce "digitized" voice and to create a network fully capable of digitally representing what was up until then, a fully analog telephone system. The T1 service developed a system that would digitize an analog voice signal into a *digital signal* (DS) 64 Kbps data stream. This signaling is termed DS-0. The data stream is transmitted using 8,000 voltage samples per second with each sample expressed in eight bits. Each 64 Kbps data stream is referred to as a channel. These 64 Kbps data streams were organized into groups of 24 creating a framed data stream. This resulted in an equivalent data rate of 1.544 Mbps, that is, 1.536 Mbps of payload (data) and frame overhead. With each frame is a synchronizing frame bit, from which an extra 8,000 bits are transmitted. The resulting 1.544 Mbps digital signal was named *digital signal-1* (DS-1). Traditional high-speed communication of 1.544 Mbps is delivered on a service from the telecommunication companies, known as *Terrestrial-1* (T1) service. The European equivalent of this service provides 30 64 Kbps data streams resulting in a 2.048 Mbps per second framed data stream and is called E1 service.

The signaling hierarchy created from the 64 Kbps data stream, also called a "trunk," is built based on the aggregation of these trunks. Shown in Table 6-1, the bundling of 24 64 Kbps trunks together is the foundation of the T1. Two T1s can be grouped into a T1C (C means concatenated). Grouping two T1Cs results in a circuit named T2, with a 6.312 Mbps data rate. The T2 was implemented in support of the Picturephone trials in the early

Table 6-1

Relative Data Rates Available with the Digital Signal Pulse-Code Modulation

Sig. Lvl	Carrier	# of T1s	# 64 Kbps Channels	Speed Mbps
DS-0	—	1/24	1	.064
DS-1	T1	1	24	1.544
DS-1C	T1C	2	24	3.152
DS-2	T2	4	96	6.312
DS-3	T3	28	672	44.736
DS-4	T4	168	4032	274.760

1970s. The grouping of seven T2s results in T3 circuits, which is now the most abundant connection used by *Internet Service Providers* (ISPs) to connect to the Internet. A final configure called T4 is six T3s grouped together resulting in a data rate of 274.760 Mbps, which is more than the OC-3 carrier rate but rarely used.

The traditional scheme used for transmitting the signal on a T1 is self-clocking *Alternate Mark Inverse* (AMI) code. The AMI code is bipolar. This means that a plus voltage (0.5+), a zero voltage, and a minus voltage (0.5−) are important to the coding of the signal. As illustrated in Figure 6-1, this means that if a 1 or Mark is coded as a positive voltage, the very next 1 must be a minus voltage or the result will be a *Bipolar Violation* (BPV). T1 digital service using an AMI coding scheme modulates the analog waveform on the copper wire loop as a digital bit representation of 1s and 0s. Therefore, AMI coding schemes are based on 1-bit per baud. A baud is one cycle of the sinusoidal waveform. It is this waveform that is modulated to represent a digital 1 or 0. The number of cycles within one second is referred to as the frequency in Hertz. AMI uses 1Hz per bit, the spectrum required to send 1.544 Mbps is 1.544Mhz. The high-frequency requirement for transmission using AMI coding created a distance limitation. Maintaining the high frequency requirement of AMI coding requires a repeater of at least 3,000 feet from the central office and then 6,000 feet between repeaters on 22 gauge copper wire. The use of the repeaters for providing T1 service with AMI coding led to the term of "conditioned" circuit. Use of the repeaters to provide T1 service led to the high cost of T1s.

In the 1980s, a driving force in the development of DSL was the delivery of T1 services without the use of repeaters. The high-frequency requirement of 1.544 Mbps or higher and the need to keep costs low

Figure 6-1
AMI sequence for
bipolar signaling

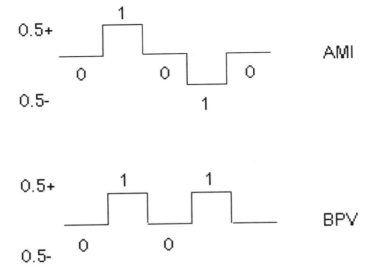

required a new type of technology to meet the application. Bellcore (the original AT&T Bell Labs) devised a method for transmitting high-bandwidth networks over two pair of unconditioned wires by placing transceivers on each end. The resulting technology was called *High bit-rate DSL* (HDSL).

High Bit-Rate Digital Subscriber Line (HDSL)

HDSL is the most mature of the DSL technology. HDSL is based on a signal processing and line coding modulation that effectively double the AMI coding technique. This newer coding technique is based on sending two bits of information during each analog waveform or baud cycle resulting in less frequency required. The line code is called *2 Binary, 1 Quaternary* (2B1Q). The 2B1Q line code technique is implemented on Basic Rate ISDN using frequencies from 0 to 80 KHz enabling the length of the cable to reach 18,000 feet. Basic Rate ISDN allows for only two 64 Kbps channels and a 16 Kbps channel (totaling 144 Kbps). HDSL operates in the 80 KHz to 240 KHz frequency spectrum enabling a data rate up to 1.544 Mbps without the use of repeaters on the line at a distance of 12,000 to 15,000 feet on 24-gauge wire (9,000 feet, 26-gauge wire) from the central office.

HDSL achieves the traditional T1 data rate by splitting the 1.544 Mbps service between the two twisted-pair wires. As shown in Figure 6-2, each pair operates at 784 Kbps. The splitting of the bandwidth between the pairs increases the bits per baud and the per-line speed, and results in the lower frequency range of 80 KHz to 240 KHz over the four wires, as compared to T1 frequency requirement of 1.544 MHz.

The telecommunication companies have applied HDSL as a means of connecting central offices, digital loop carriers, and remote terminal locations, as well as private branch exchanges within the central offices. The tariffing of using HDSL in the 1980s enabled the telecommunication companies to offer T1 bandwidth and service at affordable rates to corporations for WAN connections from their offices to the central office.

Figure 6-2

HDSL and T1 standards compared

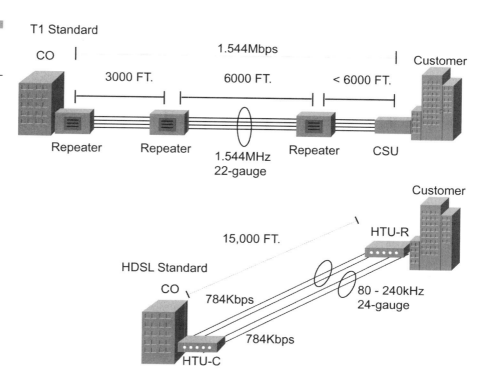

HDSL is currently being modified in standards committees to support a single twisted pair direct to the customer premise. However, this limits the bandwidth to 784 KHz because it was designed to handle half of a traditional T1. The new standard is being dubbed HDSL-2.

The HDSL transmission is symmetrical in nature. Bandwidth to the customer premise (downstream) is the same as the bandwidth away from the customer premise (upstream). However, the need for more bandwidth without the use of repeaters became a requirement during the late 1980s when *video-on-demand* (VoD) was seen as the next big market to the mass consumer market for telecommunication companies. VoD is an application that requires asymmetric data rates. This potential consumer service gave rise to the currently popular DSL service called *Asymmetric DSL* (ADSL).

Asymmetric DSL

Though the markets for VoD did not come to fruition in the 1990s, the resulting technology to deliver the service has thrived. ADSL is the most prolific DSL offering due to the ability to deliver broadband over traditional *plain old telephone service* (POTS) twisted-pair wire. At 18,000 feet, ADSL provides up to 1.544 Mbps transmission rates for downstream and 64 Kbps upstream. The reduction in the footage between the customer premise and the central office increases the transmission rate. At distances of 9,000 feet or less, ADSL can provide 9 Mbps downstream and 640 Kbps upstream. ADSL accomplishes high transmission rates over POTS lines through the use of two modulation techniques.

ADSL Modulation Techniques

One line coding, *Discrete Multi-Tone* (DMT), is established as the ANSI and ETSI standard; another, *Carrierless Amplitude and Phase* (CAP) modulation is widely implemented and being pushed by certain proponents as a side-by-side standard with DMT. Just to keep things interesting, some companies are advancing the use of *Quadrature Amplitude Modulation* (QAM), a line-coding scheme similar to CAP.

Simply put, DMT divides the 1 MHz spectrum offered by a phone line into 256 4 KHz channels. It then varies the bit densities on each of these channels to overcome noise and interference that may be present in sections of that spectrum. Proponents argue that DMT is better on noisy lines because of the ability to maximize throughput on good channels and minimize throughput on channels with heavy interference. Figure 6-3 graphically highlights DMT line coding used for ADSL.

In contrast, CAP relies on a single carrier and uses techniques similar to the QAM used in V.34 (28.8 Kbps) modems to make the most of phone lines.

Despite the ratification of the DMT standard, modems utilizing both methods are being used in networks globally in order to gauge cost of deployment and performance attributes. Both encoding algorithms have elicited positive responses from a performance standpoint. If both perform similarly, cost and manageability is likely to be the deciding factor between the two. CAP currently leads DMT in cost and size, but DMT offers greater flexibility. Over time, both will trend towards one another, creating more options for vendors. The method that will be preferred in carrier networks remains to be seen, and most consumers will not know which is implemented in their modems.

From a technical standpoint, both the DMT and CAP approaches place an ADSL modem on each end of a twisted-pair telephone line, creating three information channels: a high-speed downstream channel, a medium-speed duplex channel, and a POTS channel. The POTS channel is split off from the digital modem by filters, thus isolating the voice circuit so a traditional phone line can power it. This guarantees uninterrupted POTS connections, even if the ADSL connection or outside power fails.

Voice service on POTS lines uses the lowest 4 KHz bandwidth. This leaves the remaining bandwidth available for data services. The voice POTS connection can still exist on the same line as DSL enabling non-disruption of POTS service even if the ADSL modem loses power. The POTS voice connection is filtered out using a POTS splitter either at the central office or within the customer premises. Another variant on this is the use of a microfilter on the wire that connects each telephone in the customer premise to the POTS

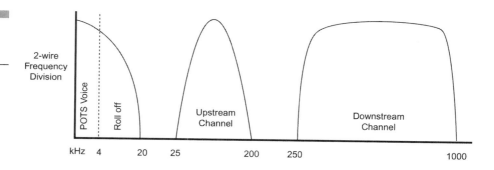

Figure 6-3
ADSL frequency spectrum

line. The microfilter enables only the bottom 4 KHz frequency to pass through to the phone. In this way, the microfilter enables each phone line to make and receive phone calls while the customer is using the same line for data.

Rate-Adaptive DSL (R-ADSL)

ADSL maintains a constant transmission rate even if the wire conditions are not favorable. R-ADSL was developed to dynamically determine the best rate at the time of connection. R-ADSL operates in the same frequency as ADSL. During power on, the R-ADSL modem synchs up with the central office and negotiates the optimal speed for the connection. This negotiation usually takes place in 20 seconds. The negotiation can also take place during the connection or as a result of a signal from the central office.

ADSL Lite

ADSL Lite is a lower speed version of ADSL eliminating the need to install a POTS splitter for voice calls. ADSL Lite senses that an analog telephone handset has gone off-hook. Sensing the new power level used to modulate the line, the ADSL Lite modem enters into a fast-retrain procedure to establish the proper power levels for data transmission. This retraining is usually completed in one to two seconds. When the analog service is back on hook, the ADSL Lite modem retrains service back to its maximum speed. Because the ADSL Lite modem senses the change in the line, no splitters or microfilter are required, hence using customer installation and reducing implementation costs to the customer.

Single-Line Digital Subscriber Line (SDSL)

SDSL is actually successor to HDSL-2. Though it is loosely based on HDSL, SDSL provides variable-rate data along with voice without the use of splitters. SDSL has an adaptable rate of 2 Mbps maximum. It is sometimes referred to as symmetric DSL and is often the DSL used for what is marketed as Business DSL service.

ISDN DSL

ISDN DSL (IDSL) is actually ISDN without the dial connection. It transmits full-duplex data at a rate of 128 Kbps up to 18,000 feet. IDSL uses a 2B1Q line code enabling connection to the ISDN U interface. Because this is DSL, the connection does not use the voice switch network. The limitation to using IDSL is the fact that ISDN signaling and voice services over the same line are no longer available.

Very High Data Rate DSL (VDSL)

VDSL uses sophisticated digital signal processors to channel the bandwidth into 2048 4 KHz bands as compared with ADSL 256 4 KHz bands. VDSL uses the 300 KHz to 300 MHz bandwidth on the 24-gauge wire. This protects the POTS/ISDN service, which is still possible using a splitter. The data rates available range from 2 Mbps upstream up to 51.84 Mbps downstream. The fast data rates are possible by extending the service from the central office over fiber optics to an *Optical Network Unit* (ONU) near the subscribers. The distances measured for VDSL are based on length from the ONU, not the central office. The viable distance is 1,000 feet for the higher bandwidth to 5,000 feet for lower bandwidths.

Network Components

The basic components of a DSL network are comprised of a *DSL Access Multiplexer* (DSLAM) at a *central office* (CO). Within the DSLAM is an *ADSL Central Transceiver Unit* (ATU-C). The customer location has a *DSL Remote Transceiver Unit* (ATU-R).

A transport system, as depicted in Figure 6-4, is the component that provides the backbone connection for the DSLAM in central office. The backbone is typically T1/E1, T3/E3, OC-1, OC-3, STS-1, and STS-3.

The local access network provides the infrastructure foundation through inter-CO connections. This enables connectivity between multiple service providers and multiple services. Typically, the local access network may be comprised of Frame Relay switches, ATM switches, and routers. The majority of these local access networks are now being built with ATM.

Figure 6-4
Integrating DSL
service with the
traditional voice
network

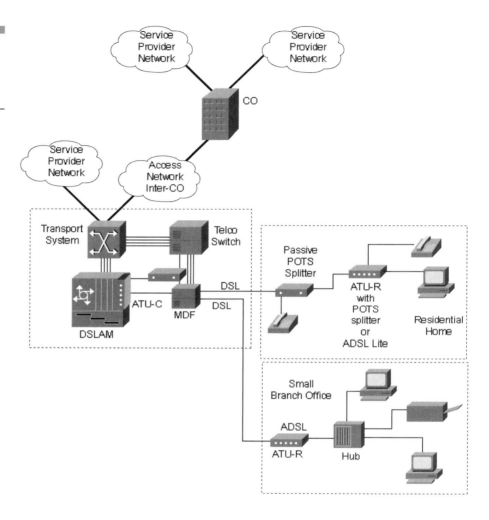

DSLAMs provide a wide array of functionality. The main focus of the DSLAM is to concentrate data traffic from multiple DSL loops onto a backbone network connection. The primary functions of a DSLAM are

- Multiservice support enabling varied services and applications through the DSLAM.
- Provide a point for concentrating the ATU-C interfaces.
- Multiplex the traffic from ATU-C interfaces to a backbone circuit.
- Demultiplex traffic form the backbone connection to the correct ATU-C.
- Negotiate the line speed.

- Support multiple line codes for use on the line.
- Serve as the central management platform for DSL network management.
- Cause ATM termination for packets mode traffic delivered to the ATU-R.

The ATU-R resides at the customer premise or endpoint of the DSL loop. The ATU-R connection is typically 10Base-T but can support V.35, ATM-25, or T1/E1. Many product offerings support a voice, data, and/or video connection. Many of the ATU-R devices available today support the functions of bridging, routing TDM multiplexing, or ATM multiplexing. The most desirable features of the ATU-R are

- Provision of Layer 1 and 2 management statistics.
- Providing Layer 3 SNMP/MIB statistics.
- Remote management capabilities.
- Remote maintenance capabilities.

Enabling voice or fax communication over the DSL connection requires a POTS splitter or filter. The splitter is installed at the CO and customer location. A POTS splitter has two configurations. The first is a single splitter used at the customer location. The second is the multiple-splitter used to terminate the split signal at the CO. POTS splitters are either passive or active. If using an active POTS splitter, an external power source for voice and DSL is required. Passive POTS splitters require no power and consequently enable power to the telephone in case the DSLAM or ATU-R loses power. The importance of voice calls without power is critical for enabling a customer to make emergency phone calls.

Network Design

The DSLAM is the key component to providing DSL services to the public networks (such as PSTN and Internet). Placement of the DSLAM is dependent on the provider. Typically if the provider is a *Regional Bell Operating Company* (RBOC) or an *independent local exchange carrier* (ILEC), then the DSLAM is located within the central office. RBOCs and ILECs are commonly termed *network access providers* (NAPs). However, because of the Telecommunications Act of 1996, anyone can provide telecommunication services as long as they meet certain requirements. *Network service providers* (NSPs) must situate their DSLAM within 12,000 to 18,000 feet of the user service base in support of ADSL. The NSPs are also known as *Competitive Local Exchange Carriers* (CLECs). Four basic options for the locations of the DSLAM are as follows:

Central Office

The RBOCs and ILECs have an advantage here. Placing DLSAM in the central office is not a great added expense for these types of *local exchange carriers* (LECs). For the CLEC, however, they must negotiate co-location services with the RBOC or ILEC to gain a presence within the central office. CLECs can either provide the installation and maintenance of their own DSLAM and other networking equipment used by the CLEC, or they can outsource the installation and maintenance of their DSLAM to the RBOC or ILEC, thereby creating a virtual co-location.

Adjacent to the Central Office

To reduce provisioning issues with the RBOCs or ILECs, CLECs can opt to locate their own facility near the central office of the servicing area. While this adds a degree of independence for the CLEC, it may end up being more costly. The cost is due to the fact that the CLEC must now acquire space suitable for emulating a central office. In addition, each DSL line to be serviced must be extended from the RBOC or ILEC CO to the CLEC CO. This added distance must be taken into consideration when determining the length of the complete copper loop. The total DSL loop from the user premise to the ILEC CO to the CLEC CO to the DSLAM must be within the 12,000 to 18,000 feet limits. Factors determining whether the CLEC should use the adjacent office location are whether the ILEC CO has adequate space for initial and future growth, whether the business relationship with the ILEC will enhance the CLEC ability to provide services, and finally, the charges incurred for co-locating at the ILEC CO versus the CLEC CO.

Remote Terminal

Because DSL services are subject to loop length restrictions, furthering the reach of DSL from a CO can be accomplished through the installation of a DSLAM at a remote terminal location. Installing a DSLAM at a remote terminal location outside the 12,000- to 18,000-feet limitation and connecting the DSLAM to a digital backbone connection enables a DSL provider to increase the service area. The problem with remote terminal locations is that typically, they are extremely small and may not have adequate environments for the DSLAM. Finally, space and co-locating at a remote terminal is not usually available to the CLECs. However, it is a very viable opportunity for the owning RBOC or ILEC to implement.

Customer Premise

Locating a DSLAM at the customer premise is ideal for *multidwelling units* (MDUs), commercial parks, and other "campus" type topologies. A campus, for our purposes, can be any entity that owns or controls its copper wire infrastructure. This includes high-rise office and residential buildings, universities, corporate and government campuses. This type of implementation is similar to the remote terminal installation described above. The DSLAM is located at the *campus demarcation* (dmarc) where the campus copper loop is aggregated. In this way, the distance limitations of DSL are factored from the DSLAM to the distance within a building or campus, generally less than 18,000 feet. The DSLAM is connected to the NSP through a traditional ILEC broadband service. Many NSPs have latched on to this configuration to provide high-speed Internet for large buildings or campus environments. These types of NSPs are termed *Building-LECs* (BLECs).

HDSL Providing T1/E1 Services

Because traditional T1/E1 services using AMI line code are costly, carriers have increasingly begun to use HDSL. As a result, HDSL is currently the most widely implemented DSL technology to date.

The extension of T1/E1 services from the CO to the *customer premise* (CP) is a main use of HDSL by the LECs. As shown in Figure 6-5, an HDSL line replaces the traditional T1 service from a CO to the CP. In this scenario, the CO shoots the HDSL nest containing the HDSL line cards. Each HDSL line card terminates the two HDSL lines, each of which transmits 784 Kbps for T1 and 1.168 Kbps for E1 from the CO. The HDSL lines are converted to either E1 or T1 interfaces for connecting to a DACS or other CO switching equipment.

At the CP HDSL standalone line, units are configured to support either a V.35 port or a native T1/E1 port, (G.703/704 for E1 or DSX-1 for T1). When configured as a V.35 port the HDSL unit connects to a router or other type

Figure 6-5
HDSL for T1/E1
connectivity to the
CO

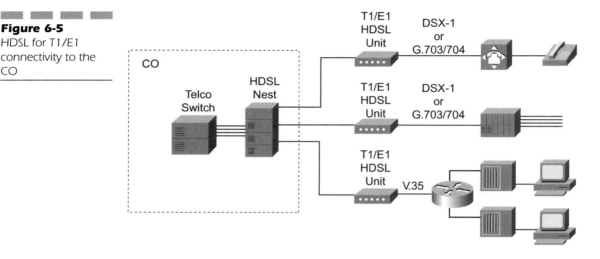

of data equipment supporting the V.35 interface. The native port configuration connects the HDSL line unit to either a digital PBX, multiplexer, or some other CPE capable of supporting native T1/E1 interfaces.

HDSL is also a valid service for use by the cellular communication companies. As shown in Figure 6-6, HDSL service provides the broadband service from the *Mobile Telephone Switching Office* (MTSO) to the actual cell sites. The HDSL standalone line unit is configured for native T1/E1 interfaces to receive the cell transmission for delivery to the HDSL nest within the MTSO using HDSL from the cell site.

SDSL is also a viable service for delivering the broadband requirement in these scenarios. SDSL provides an added benefit in that costs are reduced because SDSL requires only two wires instead of the four wires required by HDSL. The reduction in wire requirement further enables a carrier to support more bandwidth on the binder groups.

As depicted in Figure 6-7, a DSLAM connecting to a channelized T1 can further reduce costs of connecting end users using DSL. Here again the DSLAM with a *Time-Division Multiplexing* (TDM) feature can direct individual channels of the T1 to multiple DSL connections. The connection from the DSLAM to the WAN can be made either direct, if the DSLAM provides routing functionality, or through a channel bank, voice switch, or traditional multiplexer device.

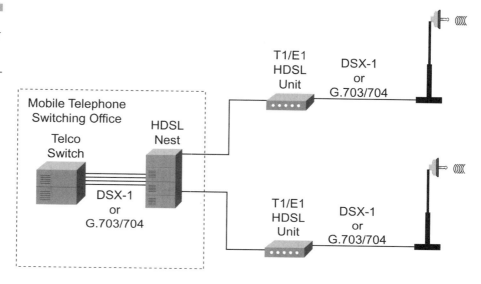

Figure 6-6
HDSL connectivity for cell tower connections

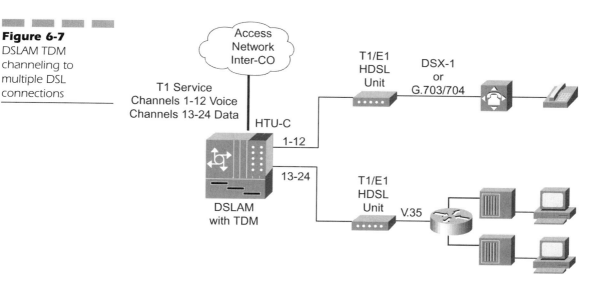

Figure 6-7
DSLAM TDM channeling to multiple DSL connections

Remote LAN Access

Telecommuting and access to corporate LANs has become a necessity since the early to mid-1990s. The requirement for employees to remain in contact with their company information has created increased demand on higher throughput. The traditional methods of dial-up analog access or ISDN switched connectivity no longer provide the necessary bandwidth required by remote access users. Using traditional remote access technologies provide at best 128 Kbps bandwidth but at a cost that can no longer be justified for a small branch office or a telecommuter. The cost is not only in the connection to the remote access user but also in the building of a dial-up infrastructure at the corporate data centers.

DSL technology as a replacement for the traditional dial-up analog connections can now provide the high-speed data rates more cost effectively. In addition, the remote access user can now utilize *Virtual Private Network* (VPN) technologies to provide a secured connection to the corporate network infrastructure. For example, in Figure 6-8, a remote access user accesses the corporate network through an ADSL service to a local *Internet*

Figure 6-8
Remote LAN access
for telecommuter

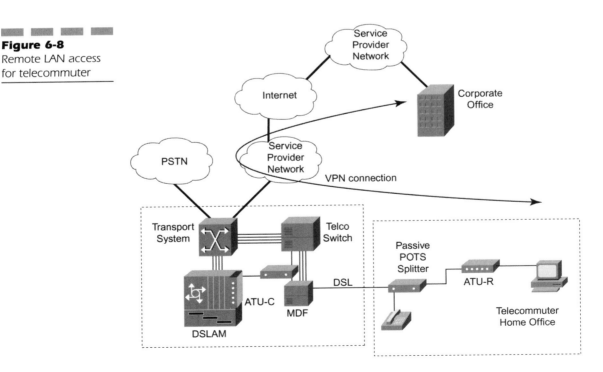

Service Provider (ISP). The connection is using the traditional POTS line to their home office with a POTS splitter enabling data and voice transmission simultaneously.

Some DSL providers are offering a VPN DSL service whereby the network connecting remote offices all use the DSL service for communicating between the corporate offices and the remote access users.

IP LAN Services

The support for IP/LAN services using DSL as the technology for this is enabled using one of three types of models:

- IP/LAN services on Layer 2
- IP/LAN services on Layer 3
- IP/LAN services with ATM

In the Layer 2 model, *Point-to-Point Protocol* (PPP) is used for the transport of IP data between the ATU-R and the DSLAM. This is illustrated in Figure 6-9. In this model, the DSLAM performs Layer 2 MAC address switching. The delivered data is funneled onto a specific Frame Relay PVC or ATM PVC to the access network. Note that Layer 3 policing, forwarding, and authentication still take place within the DSLAM to enforce security policies and dynamic IP address assignments using *Dynamic Host Configuration Protocol* (DHCP).

Figure 6-9

Remote LAN access using Layer 2 PPP over DSL

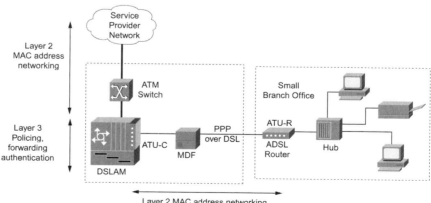

This type of architecture is highly scalable and enables efficient use of WAN resources. When using traditional Frame Relay networks, this type of architecture requires a single PVC per DSLAM in the entire network multiplied by the number of service providers.

In the second model, Layer 3 functions are used for delivering the traffic from DSL connections. This is accomplished by implementing router functions within the DSLAM and/or the access network. In the model depicted by Figure 6-10 the DSLAM still performs Layer 3 policing, forwarding, and authentication services. The advantage here is the reduction in PVCs required to make a connection to all the DSLAMs through the access network. Each DSLAM provides a connection to the hub router (for example, Frame Relay, ATM, T1). The hub router using *Multiprotocol Label Switching* (MPLS) connects to all other resources in the network using a single PVC connection. This requires a single PVC from the DSLAM to connect all access and service providers.

A concern exists on behalf of the NAPs and NSPs when using the Layer 3 model. The routing functions within the single hub router are managed by only one entity. The selection of the NAP and NSP for the network will direct which model, Layer 2 or 3, is used. When the NAP and NSP are separate providers, the Layer 2 is the preferred model. If the NAP and the NSP are the same provider, the Layer 3 model is preferred and provides greater advantages over the Layer 2 model.

The ATM model for providing IP/LAN services extends the ATM PVC through the DSLAM over the DSL connection to the end user ATU-R. Shown in Figure 6-11 the cell/packet internetworking functions take place at the ATU-R. A PPP session is created and uses *ATM Adaptation Layer 5*

Figure 6-10

Remote LAN access for Layer 3 PPP over DSL

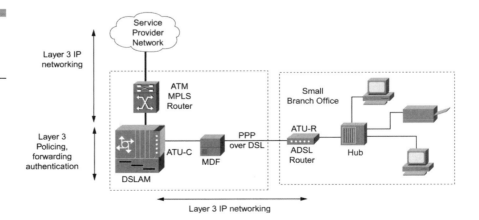

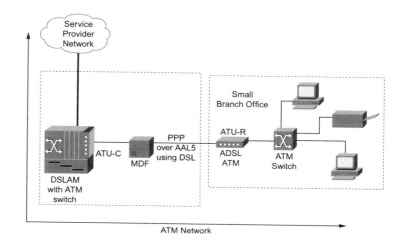

Figure 6-11
Remote LAN access
using Layer 2 PPP
over ATM AAL5 with
DSL

(AAL5). The PPP session is terminated at the backbone edge device using a PPP server that has an ATM interface.

The other option for using ATM is to have ATM service all the way to the end user workstation. In this type of scenario, the ATU-R functions as an ATM switch without routing functionality. The advantages in implementing the ATM model are as follows:

- Only Layer 2 is used under the ATM model to connect to the access network, thereby alleviating the concern of having routers within the access network. Because it is based on ATM multimedia applications, ATM QoS features are inherent.

- Using PPP for the session connection enables authentication and security.

Using ATM over DSL occurs in the developmental stage. Some disadvantages must be noted:

- Extensions to the IETF PPP standard must be created to accommodate the use of PPP to connect a LAN rather than a single workstation.

- The IETF is still completing the standard for PPP over AAL5.

- PPP, being a session layer-type protocol, is CPU intensive. PPP services must be developed to become scalable in support of LAN connectivity.

- ATM PVC per user is required. This requires large amounts of memory in an ATM switch to support thousands of PVCs. However, this may be reduced through the use of SVCs, and SVCs would place overhead on the ATM switch CPU. This is obviously an undaunting challenge.

The type of transceiver used for supporting IP/LAN services is dependent on the traffic characteristics. Careful analysis is required in order to determine whether ADSL, RADSL, SDSL, or HDSL is the best DSL service for the networking requirement.

Frame Relay Connectivity with DSL

Traditionally, corporate offices access the Frame Relay network through dedicated access lines of 56 Kbps or Fractional T1 or full T1 connections. In Figure 6-12, DSL connects a small branch office to the DSLAM, which connects to the Frame Relay switch that provides access to the corporate Frame Relay WAN.

The benefits of using DSL to connect to the Frame Relay networks are as follows:

■ DSL reduces the local access portion for the end user subscribing to the Frame Relay service.

Figure 6-12
Using Frame Relay
WAN connectivity
with DSL

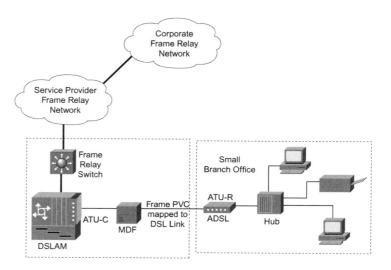

■ DSL eliminates the need for expensive repeater and setup fees for connections over 56 Kbps.

■ DSL brings the access point closer to the end user.

From a Frame Relay provider point of view, the DSLAM residing in the CO can aggregate multiple Frame Relay subscribers using the DSLAM providing another cost savings to the provider and lower Frame Relay costs to the subscriber.

The ATU-R is Frame Relay aware. Frame relay protocols are carried across the DSL connection to the DSLAM. The backbone is connected to the DSLAM using a Frame Relay T1 connection to the backbone Frame Relay switch. The DSL connection is mapped within the DSLAM to a Frame Relay PVC providing security, access control, and connectivity to only the corporate Frame Relay network. Because Frame Relay connections are typically used for interconnecting LANs upstream and downstream, flows are expected to be equal, requiring a symmetric DSL service. The preferred DSL method for connecting to the Frame Relay network is using one of the symmetric services, SDSL, HDSL, or RADSL in symmetric mode.

Campus and Private Networks with DSL

DSL is capable of high data transfer rates for determined distances over a single copper-wire pair at multimegabit speed at 10,000 feet. In addition, this same copper wire can concurrently provide standard telephone services. Comparing DSL to other traditional campus models proves the cost effectiveness of DSL. Traditionally, campus/private networks utilize Category 5 wiring or fiber-optic cable for getting high-speed connectivity to the campus environment. The problem is that Category 5 cable, although it can now support 1Gbps using Cat5E, it requires installation and is limited to 300 feet. Fiber optic on the other hand can support over 2Gbps up to 20 miles and is still too expensive to install. These two concerns for traditional wiring are what give DSL the edge in a campus environment.

The challenge in the campus environment is the extension of LANs between the campus buildings. Just recently, fixed wireless technology has come on the scene providing 11 Mbps connectivity between buildings with line of site offering campus complexes a relatively simple solution. However, the capital expense for the wireless equipment is still more than the DSL transceiver units.

Typically, campus complexes have a telephone-wiring infrastructure in place using a star or distributed-star topology. Shown in Figure 6-13, the standard telephone copper wiring connects all the buildings with the campus environment. This telephone wiring can be used by DSL transceivers for inexpensive LAN-to-LAN connectivity. The DSL transceiver is connected to a single twisted pair of telephone wire and mapped to the same pair at the other building. In the second building, the same DSL transceiver type is connected to the telephone wire pair. The transceivers in each building are connected to the LAN through a router, bridge, or LAN switch.

In another example, DSL can provide a clear advantage to connect multidwelling buildings for high-speed data access while maintaining voice connection via POTS lines. In Figure 6-14, a DSLAM is installed in the telecommunication room of the multiunit dwelling. The DSLAM is connected to a campus backbone or to an NSP through a T3 or OC-3 type connection. By leveraging the telephone wire infrastructure, the DSLAM can provide multimegabit connectivity to each apartment within the building using the existing copper wire that carries the voice network. In each room with a unique phone line, a DSL transceiver unit is installed with a POTS splitter to enable both voice and data transmission over the same wire. The

Figure 6-13

Using existing telephone wiring to extend LANs in a campus environment

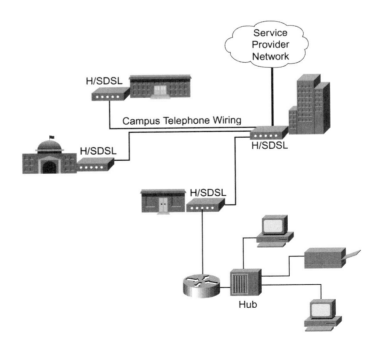

use of more than one computer within the room is possible through the use of an ADSL transceiver with multiple connections for Cat5 device connections or by connecting the TU itself to a hub. Connecting multiunit dwellings in this manner eliminates the dial-up solution issues of capacity within the PBX, low throughput, and speed.

Figure 6-14
Leveraging DSL in
multiunit dwellings

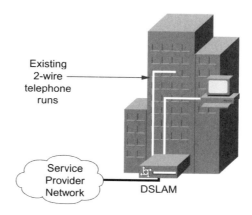

Existing
2-wire
telephone
runs

Service
Provider
Network

DSLAM

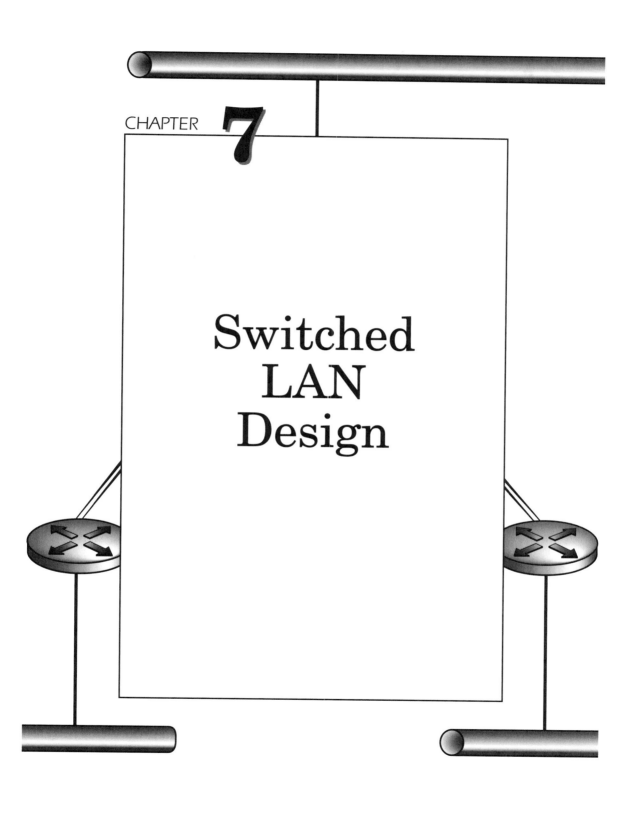

Switched LAN Design

Local area networks (LANs) were initially developed to enable communities to share computing resources. As LANs grew in popularity, it became evident that the sharing of resources also mandated higher performance requirements. Higher performance is gained by dedicating what was once a shared medium used by many resources to a single network device. The dedication of a shared medium to a single device required the development of a networking hub that could itself become the shared medium, enabling the network devices to continue to share networking resources. LAN switching is the resulting technology.

As shown in Figure 7-1, a shared Ethernet hub connects multiple users to a router. The hub emulates the broadcast topology of an Ethernet and sends each Ethernet frame to all connected resources. In a switching environment, only Ethernet frames destined for the attached resource flow on the media. This is accomplished by the LAN switch, which uses OSI Layer 2 addressing. The *medium access control* (MAC) address is used for making the decision. In essence, the switch is a high-speed multiport bridge. This type of switching is called Layer 2 switching.

Enhancements to the switching technology paradigm have moved up the OSI Reference Model to the network layer. The network layer, Layer 3, supports routing protocols such as IP, Novell IPX, and AppleTalk. The switching intelligence now includes the capability to direct frames based on the Layer 3 addressing, versus the Layer 2 addressing.

In a shared hub environment, all devices attached to the shared media connection of the hub must be on the same IP subnet or network. A switched LAN environment enables multiple IP subnets or networks to coexist on the same switching medium. Communication between the IP subnets or networks is accomplished using Layer 3 switching, which is, in essence, the function of a router.

Switched LAN Factors

Many of the same issues that pertain to router networks are found in the switching networks. Because switching networks are based on the concept of bridging broadcast storms, offnet traffic and administration become factors in designing a viable switched network topology.

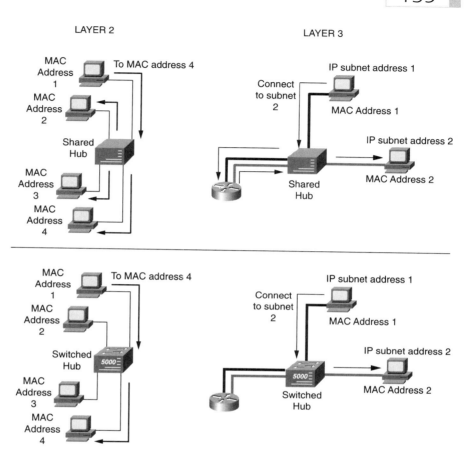

Figure 7-1
Shared LAN
compared to
switched LAN

Broadcast Radiation

Switching, though faster than routing, must still address the issue of broadcast storms or broadcast radiation. As is the theme with maintaining peak performance on the network, switching designs must minimize the affect of broadcasts. The use of *virtual LANs* (VLANs) in a switched network design helps to minimize the affect of broadcasts, but this results in scaling the number of hosts that can be supported on a VLAN. Using routers, a VLAN can be subsegmented based on traffic patterns, enabling a scalable network design. In such a design, multiple routers are required to avoid overutilization, due to the amount of VLAN traffic serviced by the router.

Well-behaved VLANs

VLANs were introduced at a time when the 80/20 rule was still in effect. The term "well-behaved VLAN" is used to characterize a VLAN that has 80 percent or more of its traffic local to the VLAN. Designing a "well-behaved VLAN" requires segmentation of services as well as devices. That is, client-server application database servers, e-mail servers, and file and print servers should all be dedicated to each VLAN. Although this type of design bodes well for network performance, management, and troubleshooting, it causes a strain on the network budgeting process. Since the term "well-behaved VLAN" was coined, we have seen a reversal of the 80/20 rule, where now clearly 80 percent of the VLAN traffic is destined outside the VLAN due to service consolidation.

Inter-VLAN Available Bandwidth

Routers are required to transport traffic between VLANs. A switched LAN design must account for the new 20/80 paradigm of traffic going off the VLAN. Therefore, the bandwidth connecting the various networking resources between the source and destination VLAN must be enough to handle the traffic load to meet service-level requirements.

Administrative Boundaries

In defining the switched network design, administrative boundaries must be given consideration. This is because switching tends to have a flattening affect on the operation of a network. Switching outside of the administrative boundary may affect the network within the administrative boundary, thereby causing poor performance or possibly disruption of service.

Cisco VLAN Implementation Support

VLANs are a logical grouping of devices. Typically, these devices are grouped either by function, department, floor, or for segmenting the LAN. Figure 7-2 illustrates a typical VLAN implementation and identifies six workstations on different ports of different switches on different floors.

VLAN1 logically defines a "broadcast domain" on the switches with Stations A, D, and G. Likewise, the other stations should follow suit. The router in Figure 7-2 connects to all the VLANs, enabling VLAN-VLAN communication.

The first inception of VLANs is based on the OSI Layer 2 bridging and multiplexing mechanisms. The design of one host per port provides both high bandwidth for the attached host and ease of VLAN configuration.

Since switching relegates a network topology to a flat network, scalability and management of broadcast storms is made possible through the implementation of VLANs and routers. Combining the two realizes the following advantages:

- VLANs further refine the isolation of collision domains provided by a switching environment by only forwarding traffic within the VLAN. This contains broadcast and multicast traffic within the bridging domain created by the VLAN.

- VLANs enhance security since the logical groupings disallow Layer 2 inter-VLAN communication and require a router for Layer 3 VLAN communication. Inter-VLAN communication through the router allows a network engineer to employ the security features of the Cisco router by filtering appropriate packets from reaching other VLANs.

Figure 7-2
VLAN topology

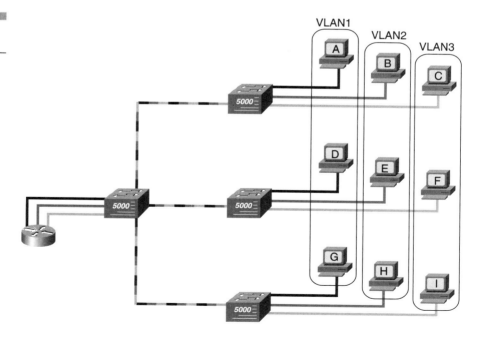

- Logically grouping high-bandwidth end users together on a VLAN provides improved performance for devices requiring less bandwidth. This segregation of users enables performance design to meet service levels.

- The logical grouping of users on VLANs enables the moves, additions, and changes that frequently occur on a network to take place almost dynamically, rather than waiting for the altering of the actual infrastructure.

There are three types of methods for grouping devices on switches when defining VLANs:

- *Port-based VLANs*: Logically grouping VLANs based on the physical ports is known as segment-based VLANs. Only one VLAN is defined for a port and multiple VLANs are available for assignment on a switch. Intra-VLAN traffic within a switching hub is switched and must first be passed to a router, which then routes the traffic to the destined VLAN. Since port-based VLANs do not recognize Layer 3 addressing, all VLANs supporting Layer 3 traffic, such as IP, IPX, or AppleTalk, must be defined on the same network within the same VLAN.

- *Protocol-based VLANs*: The use of Layer 3 addressing enables a VLAN to differentiate between different network protocols. This type of VLAN is called a virtual subnet VLAN. Using network Layer 3 addressing as the scheme for defining VLANs enables more than one VLAN per port.

- *User-defined values*: This type of VLAN enables the network engineer to design a VLAN based on any field value within a packet. This provides the most flexibility along with granularity in defining VLANs. VLANs can be defined based on the type of service being requested or advertised.

Cisco VLAN implementation supports the following standards:

- IEEE 802.10
- IEEE 802.1d
- ATM LANE
- Cisco's own *Inter-Switch Link* (ISL)

These functions enable the design to handle multiple, disjointed, and overlaid broadcast groups on a flat network. Cisco currently employs port-based VLANs.

IEEE 802.10

The IEEE 802.10 standard defines two strategies for bridging the VLANs over a *metropolitan area network* (MAN) or *wide area network* (WAN) backbone in support of intra-VLAN communications. These strategies provide VLAN support for switching and routing.

The IEEE 802.10 standard implements a VLAN ID between the source MAC address and the *Link Service Access Point* (LSAP) fields of an FDDI frame prior to leaving the switch. The VLAN ID is a four-byte value within this header. The receiving switch examines the header to determine if the VLAN ID exists on the switch. If it does, it removes the IEEE 802.10 header and forwards the frame to the interfaces that match the VLAN ID. Only one VLAN ID is allowed per end user interface. The interface connecting to the MAN or WAN FDDI network is considered a VLAN trunk and supports multiple VLAN IDs.

In Figure 7-3, we see three switches connected over a MAN FDDI backbone. VLAN1 is defined on switch A, B, and C. The VLAN ID is 10. Switch A and B has VLAN2 with VLAN ID 20. Switch A and C has VLAN3 with VLAN ID 30. Using IEEE 802.10, the switches are able to forward packets between them, connecting the virtual LANs over the MAN or WAN.

In a routing scenario, IEEE 802.10 enables a split network by "gluing" the network together using a bridged path between the routers. This must include the enforcement of a same network addressing scheme for the VLANs being glued. Figure 7-4 illustrates the IEEE 802.10 routing configuration.

Some design considerations for using IEEE 802.10 include the following:

- Cisco routers use fast-switching mechanisms with IEEE 802.10.

- VLANs should be designed without splitting between locations over the backbone:

  - If subnets are split, they need to be "glued" by a bridged path.

  - VLANs must adhere to normal routing behavior in order for inter-VLAN communications to take place.

Table 7-1 lists the pros and cons of IEEE 802.10 switching and routing.

Figure 7-3
IEEE 802.10
connections for a
switched VLAN
environment

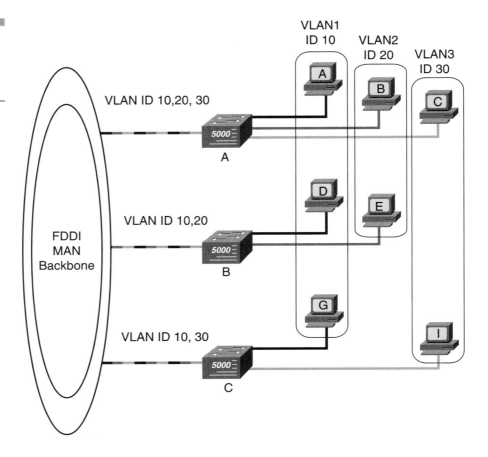

Table 7-1

Advantages and
Disadvantages of
Switching and
Routing when
Employing IEEE
802.10 VLANs

Switched Backbone		Routed Backbone	
Advantages	**Disadvantages**	**Advantages**	**Disadvantages**
Propagates VLAN ID information across the network	Backbone is running bridging.	No bridging in backbone	VLAN ID information is not propagated across backbone and must be configured manually.
Extends bridging domains, thereby enabling greater scaling	Broadcast traffic is high on the backbone.	Easily integrates into an existing network	Split subnets communicate using a bridged path between switches.
		Can run native protocols in the backbone	

Figure 7-4
IEEE 802.10
connections for a
routed VLAN
environment

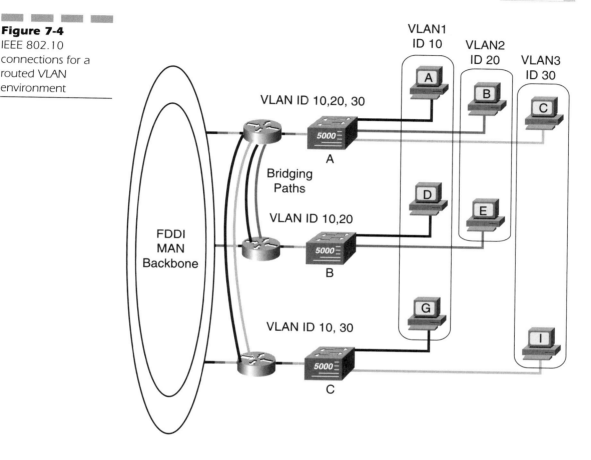

Figure 7-4
IEEE 802.10 connections for a routed VLAN environment

IEEE 802.1d

In high-availability designs, such as that shown in Figure 7-5, loops are possible, due to the replication of packets. As shown in the figure, switch A and B provide redundancy for a VLAN segment. Station A sends a packet to station B. Due to the high-availability design, the packet is looped back to segment A from switch B. The IEEE 802.1d standard prevents looping by employing the spanning tree protocol and placing ports in blocking mode, allowing a loop-free topology. Routers inherently prevent loops by using optimal paths.

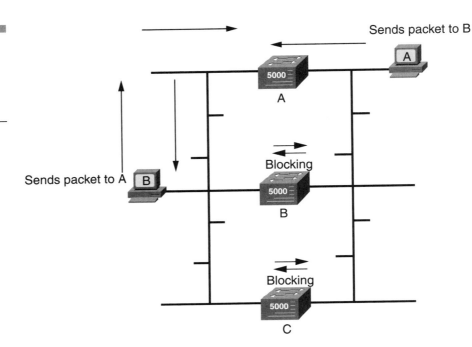

Inter-Switch Link (ISL)

Cisco has taken the IEEE 802.10 specification and applied it to 100-Mbps Ethernet links between switches and routers. This proprietary specification is called the *Inter-Switch Link* (ISL) protocol. Shown in Figure 7-6, 100-Mbps Fast Ethernet links connect switch A to switch B, and then switch B to router C and switch D. Station A on switch A sends a packet to station D on switch D. Switch A determines the destination as being destined for a different switch for the same VLAN. ISL sends a 30-byte header to the Ethernet frame, which contains a two-byte VLAN ID field, prior to sending the packet over the Fast Ethernet link to switch B. Switch B interprets the ISL header and forwards the packet to the router C, which analyzes the ISL header and forwards the packet to switch D. At this point, switch D determines that the packet is for a station on a VLAN defined to it and forwards the packet over the appropriate port.

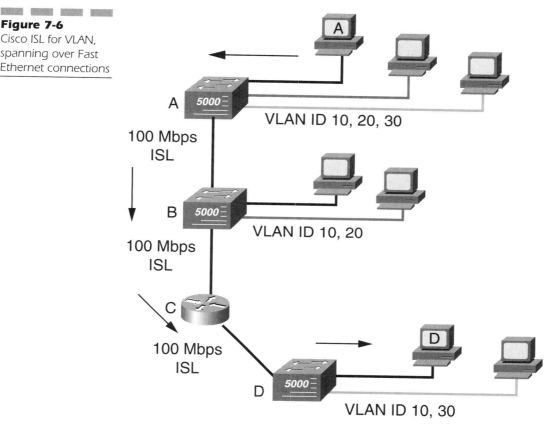

LAN Emulation

Using ATM LANE specifications, VLANs can be mapped to an ELAN, enabling switches and routers to handle the majority of Layer 3 protocols over VLANs. Routers are used for inter-ELAN communications, which map to inter-VLAN communications. An ATM switch handles intra-ELAN communications.

Virtual Multi-homed Servers

Every network supports servers for corporate-wide access that are typically Web or e-mail servers. The mapping of VLANs to ATM ELANs enables multi-homed servers, thereby eliminating the need for routing packets to the server. ATM NICs allow up to eight ELAN and VLAN definitions. The advantage here is that all packets of a VLAN defined to the end user domain and the server pass from switch to switch without the use of the router. The disadvantage is that the server ends up receiving all the broadcasts and multicasts of each ELAN defined to the NIC of the server. This may cause excessive overhead on the server, outside of providing services to the end user domain.

Figure 7-7 illustrates a multi-homed ATM server configuration. For non-ATM network topologies, the server must support multiple NICs for connecting to multiple VLANs or NICs supporting the backbone VLAN-trunking technology, IEEE 802.10 or ISL.

Switched LAN Topologies

Switched LAN topologies have quickly become the current network topology of choice. The switching topology designs fall into three generic categories:

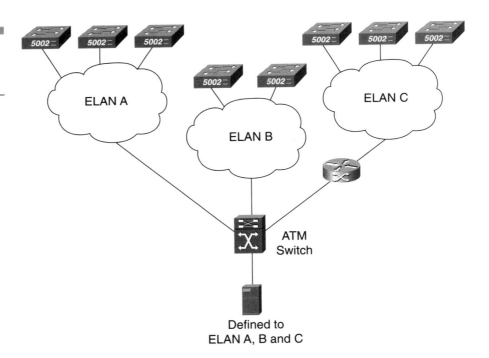

Figure 7-7
Multi-home server configuration using ATM LANE topology

- Scaled
- Large switching/minimal routing
- Distributed routing/switching

Each of these designs follows the three-layer hierarchical structure of a core, distribution, and access layer.

Scaled Switching

Scaled switching is the simplest for configuring in a small campus environment. Each switch is part of a single broadcast domain and therefore uses the same addressing scheme for each connection. Expanding a scaled switching environment is possible through the use of VLANs to segment the network into multiple broadcast domains. Implementing VLANs, however, will require the use of a router for inter-VLAN communications. Figure 7-8 diagrams a scaled switching topology.

Large Switching/Minimal Routing

The large switching/minimal routing topology employs LAN switching at the access layer and either ATM switching or LAN switching at the distribution and core layers. In Figure 7-9, the ATM switching topology requires the following for proper deployment:

- LANE support on all routers and switches.
- Support for ATM UNI 3.x or higher signaling, using point-to-point and point-to-multipoint.

If using LAN switching in the distribution layer, VLAN trunking (IEEE 802.10 or ISL) must be supported in all devices. Additionally, the switches must be running spanning-tree protocol, which inhibits load balancing.

Scaling the large switched/minimal routing topology requires a hierarchical design built on VLANs. The VLAN design should be one that enables the 80/20 rule over the VLANs. This minimizes the use of the routers in the distribution layer.

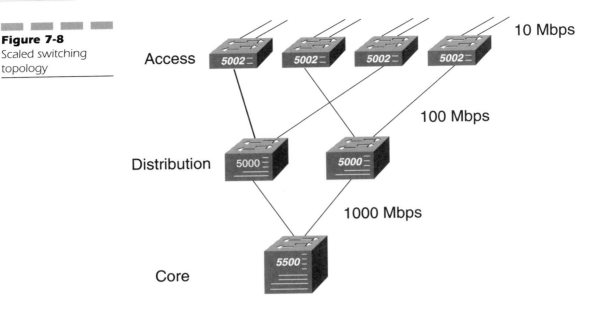

Figure 7-8
Scaled switching
topology

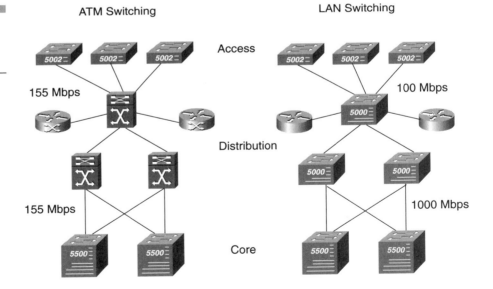

Figure 7-9
Large switching/
minimal routing
topology

Figure 7-10
Distributed routing
topology

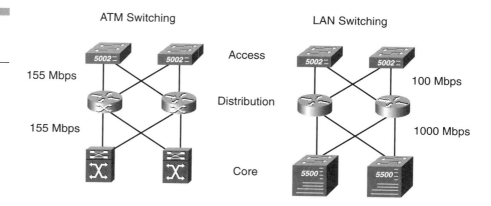

Distributed Routing/Switching

In this topology, the distribution layer is populated with routers only. In either the ATM or LAN switching configuration, shown in Figure 7-10, the routers become the focus of decision making.

This switching topology design follows the classic hierarchical network model. The routers distribute the traffic between the core and the access layers. The use of routers actually serves the new $^{20}/_{80}$ rule well. The consolidation of services at a central location is also served well by this design.

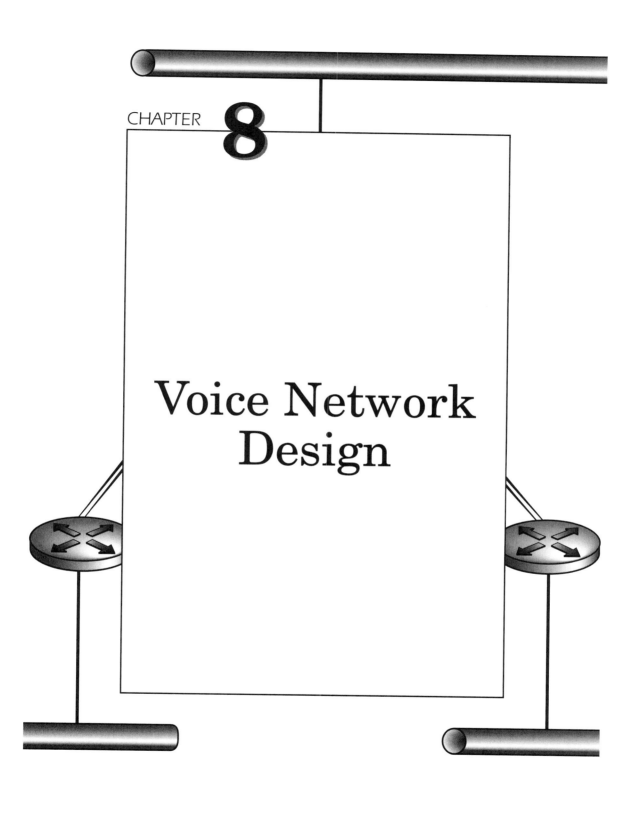

CHAPTER **8**

Voice Network Design

This chapter introduces concepts for developing an integrated voice network from the ground up. The process begins with an analysis of preliminary requirements and continues with selecting equipment and a network design.

Analyzing Requirements

Before building anything, it is appropriate to figure out just what needs to be built and what tasks it must perform. The concepts in voice networking are similar to those in designing a data network. The only thing that changes is the type of equipment with which the network interfaces. In fact, an argument could be made that voice networking is somewhat simpler because the interfaces and protocols are fewer and better defined. Also, the characteristics of the application and its network requirements are well defined and understood, which is in stark contrast to data networking where all too often a lot of guess work is performed because application characteristics are poorly documented.

Information Gathering

The first step in analyzing requirements is to figure out the physical logistics associated with the project. Divide the project into sites and, within each site, identify the types of systems that must be connected and how many of them will be needed. Then, per device, identify the specific requirements. This section contains templates that can provide a starting point for this process.

Site Listing   Administrative information should be collected for each site or department that the network is divided into. Figure 8-1 provides a template that can be used to organize your site's administrative information.

Identification of Telephony Equipment   Once the individual sites are organized, the next step is to gather information on the telephony equipment that will connect to the voice-enabled router at each site. First, identify all phone systems that will connect to the router. Often this is a single *Private Branch Exchange* (PBX) or key system. Figure 8-2 provides a template as an aid in this process.

▬▬ ▬▬ ▬▬ ▬▬
Figure 8-1
*Site administrative
information*

Site/Department

Name: Address:

City/State: Approximate Number of Phones:

Location of Phone Closet: Site Code:

Contact Information   Office   Pager   Email   Other

Administrative

Telecom

Datacom

Additional Information:

▬▬ ▬▬ ▬▬ ▬▬
Figure 8-2
*Telephony
equipment summary*

Type of System: PBX / Key System / Analog phone / FAX machine

Vendor: Model:

Location in Building: Approx. # of Station Ports:

Connection to PSTN: Analog / T1-CAS / T1-PRI

Type of connection to voice-enabled router: Analog / T1-CAS / T1-PRI

Number of connections to voice-enabled router:

Additional Information:

    Based on the type of connection you have to the voice-enabled router, which would be either analog or digital, you can fill out the appropriate worksheet, as shown in Figures 8-3 and 8-4.

Existing Data Networking Environment   Once the telephony equipment is identified, the next step is to identify the data-networking environment at each site. The goal of this step is to establish the type of network

Figure 8-3
Analog port
information

Connection Type: Trunk / Tie-Line / PLAR

Signaling Type: FXS / FXO / E&M

E&M-Specific   Type: I / II / III / V   E&M implementation: 2-wire / 4-wire

Off-hook Signaling: Loop Start / Ground Start / Immediate / Delay-dial / Wink

Additional Information:

Figure 8-4
Digital port
information

Type of Interface: T1 / E1   Line Coding: AMI / B8ZS

Framing: SF(D4) / ESF   Number of Channels:

Clocking Source: Internal / External Companding: (u-law / a-law

Type of Signaling: CAS / PRI

CAS specific   Signaling type: E&M Feature Group B / E&M Feature Group D /

                                  FXS-Loop Start / FXS-Ground Start

PRI specific   Switch-type: 5ESS / 4ESS / DMS100 / NI1

traffic with which the voice traffic will be mixed. Only information relative to the voice traffic flow is important. To quantify this, think of the path that the *voice over IP* (VoIP) traffic will take from the site to its destination. Figure 8-5 is a template for a router configuration summary and should be filled out for the relevant router(s). For each relevant *Wide Area Network* (WAN) interface, a template like Figure 8-6 should be filled out.

Voice Traffic Flow Analysis

After the tedious component information-gathering process, the next step is to profile the desired voice traffic flow. This can be done in many ways,

Figure 8-5
Router summary

Relevant Routers (hostnames):
Vendor: Model: Software Version:
Relevant Interfaces:
Protocols Configured on Router:
Protocols Running on Relevant Interfaces:
Console Password: Enable Password:
TELNET Password: Out-of-Band Password:
Main IP Address:
Additional Information:

Figure 8-6
Router WAN interface
summary

Interface Name: Queuing: FIFO / WFQ / WRED / Custom / Priority
WAN Technology: 56 kbps / T1 / T3 / Packet over SONET
Fractional T1 rate: Fractional T3 rate:
Frame Relay-specific   Port Speed: LMI-type: ANSI / Cisco / Other
Per-PVC   DLCI: CIR: Protocols Enabled:
DLCI: CIR: Protocols Enabled:
DLCI: CIR: Protocols Enabled:
DLCI: CIR: Protocols Enabled:
ATM: T1 / T3 / OC-3c
Per-PVC   VPI/VCI: QoS Type: CBR / rt-VBR / nrt-VBR / UBR / ABR
Traffic Rate: Protocols Enabled:
VPI/VCI: QoS Type: CBR / rt-VBR / nrt-VBR / UBR / ABR
Traffic Rate: Protocols Enabled:
VPI/VCI: QoS Type: CBR / rt-VBR / nrt-VBR / UBR / ABR
Traffic Rate: Protocols Enabled:
Additional Information:

ranging from a thorough analysis to a best guess. Performing a traffic analysis is done in four steps:

1. Gather traffic data.
2. Profile traffic.
3. Determine trunking requirements.
4. Match network trunk links with bandwidth requirements.

Gathering the Data If the existing systems communicate with each other through the public network, then traffic can be profiled using the call-detail reports from the phone systems and/or telco bills. If the existing systems communicate with each other through leased-line circuits, then the call-detail reports are probably the only source of traffic information. The pertinent variables to be gathered are the time of day, the date, the length of call, and the destination. If the systems do not currently communicate or, for that matter, don't exist, then some educated guesses will be required.

Processing the Data The call-detail reports and/or telco bills should be analyzed and broken down into hour-long increments, ideally over one or more months' time. The information should then be placed into a spreadsheet identifying the 1-h interval in which the call was made, the destination of the call, and its duration in minutes. The spreadsheet should then be manipulated to provide totals for each destination in terms of the number of calls per hour/day/month, the average call length per hour/day/month, and the total number of call minutes per hour/day/month.

Profiling the Data The pertinent information should then be used to determine the network's peak traffic flow. Call-flow rates are determined by multiplying the number of calls per hour by the average call duration during that time. This information is used to identify the busy hour for the voice network. Several complex methods exist for busy-hour calculations that involve statistical analysis, probability theories, and extensive computations. Luckily, a simple method is available that yields reasonable results. The simple method consists of the following steps:

1. Use the traffic data to compute the call-flow rate for each 1-h interval. The equation is A = C 3 T, where A equals the call-flow rate, C equals the number of calls initiated during the time interval, and T equals the average call duration during the interval.

2. Sum the call-flow rates from each hour interval across all days in the analysis. That is, add the call-flow rate for day 1, 9 am to 10 am, to the call-flow rate from day 2, 9 am to 10 am, and so on.

3. Identify the time interval with the largest aggregate call-flow rate.

4. Determine the average-flow rate during the sample period (divide the sum by the number of days data were collected for).

Determining Trunking Requirements   Using the output from the spreadsheet, the trunking requirements for each site and between each site can be determined. The call-flow rate for the busy hour can be translated to approximate data-network bandwidth requirements. In order to determine the trunking requirements, the busy hour call flow must be converted to a traffic measurement called an *erlang*. An erlang is equivalent to the amount of traffic that can be handled by a single trunk in one hour. To convert the busy hour calculation to erlangs, divide the 1-h call-flow rate by 60 minutes and multiply by 15 percent. The 15 percent is added to compensate for call setup and teardown overhead. This is depicted in the following equation:

$$\text{Busy hour} = (A/60 \text{ min}) \times 1.15 = \text{erlangs}$$

This leaves a dimensionless quantity for the busy hour. The final step is to determine what is called the *grade of service* (GoS). GoS is essentially an estimate of the number of calls that will be blocked. Typical design goals fall between 0.01 and 0.05, which translates to between one and five out of 100 calls being dropped. Luckily, the telecommunications industry has provided guidelines for trunk selection, which are based on busy-hour traffic and GoS. These charts are derived using complex statistical analyses of call distributions and arrival rates. Table 8-1 provides a guideline for trunk selection. You may find it helpful to document the trunk requirements in a simple chart such as Table 8-2.

NOTE: *The number of trunks required should always be rounded up to the largest integer. This number needs to be calculated for each remote destination with which the site will communicate.*

Determining Network Bandwidth Requirements   Once the trunking requirements are determined, the final step is to convert the number of

Table 8-1

Trunking
Requirements
Based upon Busy
Hour and Grade of
Service

Number of Trunks	Grade of Service					
	.01	.02	.03	.05	.07	.10
1	0.01	0.02	0.03	0.05	0.07	0.11
2	0.15	0.21	0.27	0.35	0.43	0.53
3	0.44	0.56	0.66	0.82	0.94	1.10
4	0.82	1.01	1.15	1.36	1.53	1.74
5	1.28	1.53	1.71	1.97	2.18	2.43
6	1.79	2.09	2.30	2.61	2.86	3.14
7	2.33	2.68	2.92	3.28	3.56	3.89
8	2.92	3.31	3.58	3.97	4.28	4.67
9	3.50	3.94	4.25	4.69	5.03	5.44
10	4.14	4.61	4.94	5.42	5.78	6.22
11	4.78	5.31	5.67	6.17	6.56	7.03
12	5.42	6.00	6.39	6.92	7.33	7.83
13	6.11	6.69	7.11	7.69	8.11	8.64
14	6.78	7.42	7.86	8.47	8.92	9.47
15	7.47	8.14	8.61	9.25	9.72	10.31
16	8.19	8.89	9.36	10.03	10.53	11.14
17	8.89	9.64	10.14	10.83	11.36	11.97

Table 8-2

Voice Trunking
Requirements

Source	Destination	No. of Trunks
Site A	Site B	2
Site A	Site C	3
Site A	Site D	1
Site B	Site C	1
Site C	Site D	1

trunks to bandwidth requirements for intersite links. This is straightforward and requires the trunking information and the bandwidth per voice call. The formula is as follows:

$$\text{Bandwidth} = \text{no. of trunks 3 CODEC bandwidth}$$

For G.729 traffic using the *Compressed Real-Time Protocol* (CRTP), the formula becomes the following:

$$\text{Bandwidth} = \text{no. of trunks 3 11.2 kbps}$$

The bandwidth requirements are then used to assist in the data-network design and *Quality of Service* (QoS) selection.

QoS Determinations

One of the most difficult tasks in setting up VoIP networks is determining which type of QoS mechanism should be used and where it should be applied. This determination requires that a lot of information be gathered from multiple sources. The key determining factors are as follows:

- Path for voice calls
- Voice-encoding algorithm
- Router models deployed in the network
- Relative processor utilization on routers
- Packet-switching mode employed on the routers
- Layer 2 WAN transports
- Voice design issues
- Existing QoS and queuing models
- Router software versions

Each of these factors and their effect on the decision process is described in the following subsections.

Path for Voice Calls

Determining the path through the data network that the packetized voice calls will take is important because it identifies the individual routers and links that are required to complete the call. Once identified, the individual routers and links are then further analyzed to determine which QoS techniques should be applied. This process serves to identify the critical components that will support voice traffic. Also, if the entire path is not under control of the administrator because it is the Internet, an outsourced WAN, an IP *virtual private network* (VPN), or under control of another department, these conditions must be identified so appropriate measures can be taken. Policy-based routing and/or other techniques can be used to direct traffic over the desired links. The process of evaluating the individual routers and links is described in forthcoming sections.

Voice-Encoding Algorithm

The voice-encoding algorithm in use determines the bandwidth, variability, and latency requirements for the voice calls. These are all important factors when determining the appropriate QoS technique to apply. Tables 8-3 and 8-4 show the characteristics of each voice-encoding algorithm.

This information, along with the voice traffic profiling, helps to determine the amount of bandwidth required to support the voice traffic. Bandwidth requirements are determined by multiplying the expected number of concurrent calls by the bandwidth consumed by each call. This influences decisions over whether or not to use CRTP, as well as rate-limiting QoS features such as Frame Relay traffic shaping, generic traffic shaping, *Resource Reservation Setup Protocol* (RSVP), and the *committed access rate* (CAR). Delay characteristics influence prioritization and link-efficiency mechanisms, such as a multilink *point-to-point protocol* (PPP) with link fragmentation and interleaving or FRF.12 Frame Relay fragmentation. Table 8-5 provides rudimentary guidelines for applying CODEC information to QoS techniques.

Table 8-3

Bandwidth Characteristics of Voice-Encoding Algorithms

Algorithm	Bandwidth (voice stream in kbs)	Bandwidth (packetized in kbs)	Bandwidth (w/CRTP in kbs)
PCM - G.711	64	82	67
CS-ACELP - G.729	8	26	11.2
MP-MLQ - G.723.1	6.3	20	10

Table 8-4

Delay Characteristic of Voice-Encoding Algorithms

Algorithm	Algorithm Delay, ms	Playout Buffer Delay, ms	VAD Delay, ms	Packet Size (best), bytes
PCM - G.711	.75	5	5	168
CS-ACELP - G.729	10	5	5	28
MP-MLQ - G.723.1	30	5	5	38

Table 8-5

LFI and FRF.12 Segmentation Suggestions

Link Speed or CIR	Efficiency Mechanism	Bandwidth Reservation/Maximum Recommended Fragment Size/Maximum No. of Calls		
		G.711	G.729/G.729a	G.723.1
32 kbps	LFI	Insufficient bandwidth	12 kbps/15 ms/1	11 kbps/15 ms/1
	FRF.12	Insufficient bandwidth	12 kbps/60 bytes/1	12 kbps/60 bytes/1
56 kbps	LFI	Insufficient bandwidth	24 kbps/20 ms/2	33 kbps/20 ms/3
	FRF.12	Insufficient bandwidth	24 kbps/140 bytes/2	33 kbps/140 bytes/3
128 kbps	LFI	70 kbps/20 ms/1	60 kbps/20 ms/5	66 kbps/20 ms/6
	FRF.12	70 kbps/320 bytes/1	60 kbps/320 bytes/5	66 kbps/320 bytes/6
256 kbps	LFI	140 kbps/20 ms/2	156 kbps/20 ms/13	154 kbps/20 ms/14
	FRF.12	140 kbps/640 bytes/2	156 kbps/640 bytes/13	154 kbps/640 bytes/14
512 kbps	LFI	280 kbps/20 ms/4	264 kbps/20 ms/22	264 kbps/20 ms/24
	FRF.12	280 kbps/1280 bytes/4	264 kbps/1280 bytes/22	264 kbps/1280 bytes/24
768 kbps	LFI	384 kbps/20 ms/6	384 kbps/20 ms/32	385 kbps/20 ms/35
	FRF.12	384 kbps/1600 bytes/6	384 kbps/1600 bytes/32	385 kbps/1600 bytes/32
1.544 Mbps	LFI	Not required	Not required	Not required
	FRF.12	Not required	Not required	Not required

Router Models

The specific router model number determines a number of factors including the processing power, the feature availability, the interface functionality, the switching modes supported, the ability to offload processing, and memory availability/performance. It is important to understand which routers the voice traffic will pass through and which capabilities they support. A summary of Cisco router designs is provided in this section.

Shared Memory   The router models here include Cisco 800, 1400, 1600, 1720, 2500, 3800, 4x00, and AS5x00. Shared-memory-based routers use a shared memory pool to process packets. The *Central Processing Unit* (CPU) is responsible for most packet-processing and memory-transfer functions. Packet and system memory are partitioned either through software or physically distinct memory banks. The following notes are some important points to keep in mind when dealing with the shared memory router design:

- Interface *Application-Specific Integrated Circuits* (ASICs) can be utilized to offload low-level packet processing functions.
- The CPU is required to process, queue, classify, and forward all packets.
- The CPU is responsible for all system functions as well as packet functions.
- Router performance is usually CPU-bound, but it can be memory-bound.
- The forwarding capability is bound by the CPU and memory transfer rates.
- 4500/4700/AS5300 supports significantly higher data rates for process-intensive tasks.

  The QoS implications are as follows:

- QoS functions directly affect system performance.
- CPU performance limits QoS support.
- Heavy QoS functions are limited to lower-speed interfaces.
- Not all QoS functions are supported.

Versatile Interface Processor (VIP) Architecture with a Peripheral Component Interconnect (PCI) Interface Bus   The router models here include the Cisco 2600 and 3600 series. The system architecture is based on the *Versatile Interface Processor* (VIP) design used in the 7500 series. The *Peripheral Component Interconnect* (PCI) interface for network modules provides sufficient bandwidth for interface rates up to OC-3. Here are some points to be aware of:

■ VIP's benefits include enhanced data flow, processing, and memory access.

■ This design offers more processing power than base-shared memory routers.

■ The PCI interface is flexible (9.6 kbps async through OC-3c *Asynchronous Transfer Mode* (ATM), voice, hard disk, compression, and encryption).

■ VIP-based features are more easily ported.

The QoS implications are as follows:

■ More processing power enables QoS functions to run at higher rates on more interfaces.

■ Optimized data paths provide improved QoS performance.

Distributed Forwarding/Processing   The router models here include 7200 (for processing only) and 7500. The routing tables are computed by the main processor and then are distributed to line cards, which make forwarding decisions independent of the main processor. The distributed processing can offload CPU-intensive tasks from the main processor. The following are some important points to keep in mind when using this router design:

■ It is capable of offloading QoS functions to line modules, such as *Weighted Random Early Detection* (WRED), *Weighted Fair Queuing* (WFQ), IP/ATM CoS, RSVP to ATM interworking, CAR, *Frame Relay Traffic Shaping* (FRTS), and *Generic Traffic Shaping* (GTS).

■ It is capable of offloading packet forwarding from RSVP.

The QoS implications are as follows:

■ This design is the most scalable QoS implementation.

■ The 7500 series supports Cisco's full suite of QoS techniques.

■ This design requires a careful selection of features.

ASIC-Based Forwarding   The router models in use here are Cisco 70x0, Catalyst 8500 CSR, Catalyst 6500 with a MSM, Catalyst 5x00 with a *Rate Switch Model* (RSM), and NFFC. Routers with ASIC-based forwarding mechanisms rely upon the main CPU for routing protocol operations, route computations, table maintenance, console access, and other system functions. Packet forwarding is performed by customized ASICs that are optimized for that function. Here are some points to be aware of:

- The 70x0 and Catalyst 5x00 with RSM and NFFC implement cache-based forwarding mechanisms. Initial packets, sometimes called candidate packets, are forwarded through the central routing function. The central route processor then develops a cache entry and updates the ASIC-based caching mechanism that performs subsequent packet forwarding.
- The 8500 and 6500 with MSM perform cacheless forwarding and require that the central route processor develop a complete forwarding table for access by the forwarding ASICs.
- Enhanced functions such as security, queuing, or statistics are often lacking and, if possible, require a significant development to implement within the ASICs.
- Extremely high forwarding rates are achieved, but enhanced services often suffer.

The QoS implications are as follows:

- The 70x0 is now obsolete and has minimal support for QoS.
- The 5x00, with RSM and NFFC, provides some flow-based QoS using the RSM, but not the NetFlow ASICs, thereby limiting performance.
- The 8500 and 6500 MSM implement a limited QoS set that includes *per-flow queuing* (PFQ) and *weighted round robin* (WRR) scheduling based on IP precedence.
- The 8500 and 6500 do not offer FRTS, GTS, RSVP, WFQ, WRED, or CAR today.
- Daughter cards may offer the capability to classify traffic using the access lists.

Processor Utilization

Most QoS functions require a significant amount of router processing power to implement. For this reason, it is important to quantify the relative processor utilization both before and after implementing a QoS function. Routers that consistently run at a high utilization (over 80 percent) are subject to reduced packet-forwarding rates as well as lost packets and other anomalies. If processor utilization rates are relatively high (greater than 50 percent), an extremely lightweight QoS mechanism, like IP-precedence tagging at the source and WFQ or WRED, should be chosen.

Packet-Switching Mode

Cisco routers forward packets using a number of different mechanisms and/or algorithms. It is important to identify which forwarding mechanism is in place before implementing any QoS technique. Certain QoS techniques require one form of switching or another. The impact of changing the switching mode in conjunction with a QoS technique should be evaluated before implementing any changes. Tables 8-6 and 8-7 summarize the different packet-switching modes and the implications of QoS functions on them.

Layer 2 WAN Transports

Identifying the pertinent layer 2 WAN transport facilities and their access rates is important because it directly affects the type of QoS mechanism to

Table 8-6

Router Packet Switching Modes

Switching Mode	Description	Platforms
Process switching	Traditional routing, the CPU processes all layers	All except GSR, 8500, 6500 MSM
Fast switching	Cache-based forwarding, runs at an interrupt level, resulting in better performance and greater efficiency	All except GSR, 8500, 6500 MSM
NetFlow switching	Similar to fast switching; creates cache entries based upon flows, expedites statistics collection	4500, 4700, 7200, 7500, RSM/NFFC
Optimum switching	Uses optimized cache and lookup algorithm for fastest possible cache-based switching	7200, 7500
Cisco Express Forwarding (CEF)	Cacheless routing using expedited route lookup mechanism	All
Distributed switching	Independent VIP2-based packet forwarding; may use fast or optimum switching as well as CEF	7500, 8500, 12000

Table 8-7

QoS Functions and Packet-Switching Modes

	CAR	RSVP	PQ/CQ	WFQ	Policy	WRED	FRTS	GTS	MLPPP	CRTP
Process switching		X	X	X	X	X	X	X	X	X
Fast switching		X	X	X	X	X				
NetFlow switching		X		X	X	X				
Optimum switching				X	X	X				
Cisco express forwarding (CEF)	X		X			X				
Distributed switching	X	X	X	X[1,2,3,4]	X	X[1,2,3,4]	X	X		

1. All non-IP traffic is placed in a single queue.

2. Not supported on subinterfaces.

3. Not supported on Fast EtherChannel or Tunnel interfaces.

4. Incompatible with RSP-based priority queuing, custom queuing, or WFQ.

be deployed. Point-to-point and point-to-multipoint links face similar challenges. A generic approach to these challenges is presented below.

Point-to-Point   Point-to-point links have predictable bandwidth characteristics and place the routers in a good position to control transmission rates and variability. The main challenges for point-to-point links and some of their resolutions are presented in Table 8-8.

Point-to-Multipoint Circuits   Point-to-multipoint links face similar challenges, but their operation is complicated by the multiple-access nature of the facility and network queuing delays. Also, it is common for multiaccess networks to be implemented with a central or hub site running at significantly faster data rates than each of the remote or spoke sites. This provides a challenge in that the hub site is capable of overwhelming one or more of the remote sites with traffic. Another unique challenge for point-to-

Table 8-8

QoS Challenges for Point-to-Point Circuits

Challenge	Interface Speed	
	Low Speed	High Speed
Bandwidth Access	CRTP, VAD, RSVP	VAD (GTS, CAR, RSVP—only if required)
Voice-packet rate variability	MLPPP with LFI, WFQ—IP precedence	N/A—given proper prioritization
Serialization delay	MLPPP with LFI	N/A
Prioritization of voice traffic	WFQ—IP precedence, WRED, RSVP, PQ, CQ	WFQ—IP precedence, WRED, RSVP

Table 8-9

QoS Challenges for Point-to-Multipoint Circuits

Challenge	Interface Speed	
	Low Speed	High Speed
Bandwidth access	CRTP, VAD	VAD
Voice-packet rate variability	Reduced MTU size, FRF.12 fragmentation	N/A—given proper prioritization
Serialization delay	FRF.12	N/A
Prioritization of voice traffic	WFQ—IP precedence, PQ, CQ, DE-lists	WFQ—IP precedence, RSVP (ATM only), IP/ATM CoS, policy routing/tag switching, RSVP-ATM interworking
Network queuing delays	FRTS, GTS	FRTS
Central site—remote site speed mismatch	FRTS, GTS, FRF.12	FRTS, GTS, FRF.12
PVC isolation	FRTS, GTS	FRTS, GTS, IP/ATM CoS
Packet loss within the carrier network	FRTS, GTS—each with no bursting	FRTS, GTS—each with no bursting

multipoint circuits is isolating the voice-carrying *Permanent Virtual Circuit* (PVC) from the ill effects of another PVC on the same physical port. Table 8-9 lists the QoS challenges for this type of circuit.

NOTE: *The techniques described previously should be applied to the WAN links that will support voice traffic. Table 8-9 will help determine the appropriate low- or high-speed technique, depending upon the router involved and the interface rate.*

Outsourced WAN In the event that all or part of the intermediary network is not under one administering control, additional considerations must be made to ensure acceptable voice quality. These concerns include prioritization through the external WAN, control over network latency, and network goodput. Several techniques can be applied and are discussed below.

Prioritization Given Cisco's dominance in the ISP and backbone-routing environments, Cisco routers are probably used in part or all of the transit network. Setting the precedence bits capitalizes on the fact that Cisco's WFQ implementation automatically considers the precedence bits when prioritizing flows. In many cases, you may be able to gain a preferential transport through the network without the provider even being aware and therefore not charging you for preferential service. Also, some providers may implement random early detection on their core routers to manage congestion, but they may not actively inspect or modify precedence bits. As with WFQ, Cisco's implementation of random early detection automatically prioritizes traffic based on precedence bits, so preferential access can be achieved. This does not guarantee that all network providers will support this, nor does it guarantee that an ISP will not reset these bits. However, it does provide a better probability than simple best effort traffic.

Latency Network latency is hard to control when an external party controls the intermediary network. Not knowing or being able to control the traffic and links with which your traffic will be intermixed renders most packet-based latency controls ineffective. The best option is to limit the amount of high-latency effects caused by your own traffic. This can be done by lowering the IP MTU for links connecting to an IP VPN or by using FRF.12 if the intermediary network offers a Frame Relay connection.

Network Goodput Many network providers and even ISPs are offering *service-level agreements* (SLAs) that promise throughput levels through their own network. In order to maximize goodput, traffic offered to the outsourced network should not exceed the guaranteed throughput levels. This can be performed using traffic-shaping tools at the network edge.

IP Precedence Setting the precedence level within the appropriate dial-peer statements provides the flexibility for configuring priorities for only the appropriate sessions and/or offering preferential service on a per-session basis. In environments where nonvoice traffic may be using precedence bits or where all voice-enabled routers cannot be modified to set the precedence bits, it may be appropriate to use policy-based routing or a CAR at the network edge to control which packets are prioritized. Policy-based routing is recommended unless a CAR is already in use.

Others All the other techniques discussed should be applied at the network edge that interfaces with the external network. FRF.12 is only applicable when an outsourced WAN is nothing more than a Frame Relay network where the nodes communicate with each other over predefined PVCs. If the intermediary network terminates any of the PVCs along the way, FRF.12 does not work unless the intermediary router agrees to run FRF.12 as well. Table 8-10 summarizes the QoS types that can be applied for each type of outsourced WAN.

Voice Quality Design Issues

The integration of voice into a packet-based network represents a challenge for network designers and *Local Area Network* (LAN) administrators. In a conventional voice network, a 64 Kbps time slot is reserved to transport digitized voice. That time slot is based upon the use of *Pulse Code Modulation* (PCM) as the voice digitization method. Although PCM is considered to

Table 8-10

QoS Options for Externally Controlled WANs

	Outsourced WAN	WAN Group	IP-VPN	Internet
Prioritization	IP precedence	IP precedence	IP precedence	IP precedence
Latency	Latency SLA IP precedence FRF.12 if frame relay	IP precedence	Latency SLA Reduced IP mtu IP precedence	Latency SLA within ISP network IP precedence
Goodput	Throughput SLA and GTS or CAR		Throughput SLA and GTS or CAR	Throughput SLA and GTS or CAR

represent toll-quality voice, its use is inefficient. More modern voice-coding methods, which include a family of hybrid coders based on a modified linear prediction technique originally developed during the 1970s, permit near toll-quality communications at data rates under 16 Kbps. Considering that human speech is normally half-duplex, the reservation of 64 Kbps time slots to transport digitized voice is inefficient in an era of packet networks.

This section focuses on voice quality design. When considering the integration of voice into a packet network, you must carefully consider the manner by which packets flow through the network. Because real-time voice is delay-sensitive, it is transported by a *User Datagram Protocol* (UDP) in an IP network environment. This means an errored packet is not retransmitted and is simply dropped. Your first inclination probably would be to carefully consider the error rate associated with the use of communications carrier transmission facilities. In actuality, modern communication circuits have a relatively low error rate, and the human ear has a relatively slow sound absorption capacity. This means that the periodic dropping of small pieces of a digitized conversation will have a negligible effect upon the understanding of a conversation. Instead, the delay or latency of packets as they flow through a packet network has a major effect upon the ability of a person to understand a conversation. Thus, voice quality design is primarily a latency minimization effort, and this chapter's discussion of voice quality design will be focused on the methods to use to determine if VoIP is practical prior to implementing this application.

Unlike the weather that people like to talk about but have minimum control over, many tools and techniques can be used to insure that a VoIP application has a good potential for success. The reason the term "good" is used is because a public IP network, such as the Internet, is currently incapable of reserving bandwidth. This means that the random process of packet flow can turn a viable solution today into an impractical one tomorrow. However, by using some well-known TCP/IP application tools and a handful of logical networking techniques, you can literally stack the deck in your favor and enhance the chance of a successful VoIP implementation.

Latency Is the Key

The ability to implement a VoIP solution depends upon the one-way latency or delay between the originator and recipient of the call. This delay, as you will soon note, is variable. It depends upon several parameters, some of which will be under your control, although others, when using a public network, are not.

Table 8-11 lists the major components associated with the end-to-end, analog-to-digital coding, transmission, and conversion back to the voice of a packet carrying a digitized portion of a conversation. Note that the fixed and variable delays associated with the end-to-end transmission of a packet can generally range between approximately 60 and 289 milliseconds (ms). To put this time in perspective, you should note that a typical human ear can accept up to 250 ms of delay every once in a while prior to the conversation becoming annoying. Although a full-duplex transmission is desirable for most data applications, it is not useful and, in fact, creates problems when voice is carried over a network. This is because people do not have a conversation in which both parties are talking at the same time. Instead, one person waits for the other to finish talking before responding. If the latency or delay begins to exceed a quarter of a second for significant portions of a conversation, the conversation will begin to resemble a CB-radio conversation, with each party having to say "over" to inform the other party it is OK to talk. Otherwise, the delay results in one party periodically thinking the other has finished talking when he or she has not, resulting in a full-duplex conversation that requires one party to stop and the other party to begin anew. In fact, the *International Telecommunications Union* (ITU) standard for one-way delays in a voice call requires a maximum latency of 150 ms, which ensures that the call does not turn into a full-duplex conversation. For most organizations, a maximum latency of 200 ms and a mean latency approaching or under 150 ms should be sufficient to provide a good -quality reconstructed voice.

Table 8-11

Packet Network
Delays

	Fixed and Variable Delays (ms)
Compression (voice coding)	10-45
Inter-process (origin)	10
Network access at origin	.25-7
Network transmission delay	20-200
Network egress at destination	.25-7
Buffer (configurable)	10
Decompression	10
Total fixed and variable delays	60.50-289

If you are curious about the latency associated with a *Public Switched Telephone Network* (PSTN), it can be considered almost negligible. That is, telephone company switches introduce delays measured in microseconds (s), one thousandth of a ms. Similarly, PCM and the *Adaptive Differential Pulse Code Modulation* (ADPCM) have a coding delay of a few (s, which, as you will shortly note, represents a thousandth of the delay associated with the use of low-bit, voice-encoding methods.

Now that you have an appreciation for the amount of one-way delay a VoIP application can tolerate, let's examine the delay component listed in Table 8-11. In doing so, techniques that you can use to modify or adjust certain delays will also be discussed.

Compression

You can select numerous low bit rate compression or coding methods. In fact, most equipment vendors, including Cisco Systems, typically support between four and six voice-coding methods. Most of these methods are members of the *Code Excited Linear Prediction* (CELP) family of voice coders. The original CELP voice coder was a hybrid, incorporating both waveform coding similar to PCM, ADPCM, and linear predictive coding. Although the first CELP voice coder operated at a relatively low bit rate in comparison to PCM and ADPCM, its coding delay was relatively high, approaching 60 ms. Since the first CELP voice coder was introduced, numerous variations have been developed, with approximately half a dozen now standardized by the ITU. Two of the most popular members of the CELP family are the *low delay* (LD) CELP (G.723) that operates at 16 Kbps but has a delay of 10 ms, and the G.729.1 multicoder that operates at both 5.3 and 6.3 Kbps. The G.729.1 multicoder also has a coding delay of approximately 30 ms. Other coders have delays up to 45 ms.

If you carefully examine the specification sheets associated with different voice-coding techniques, you will note that normally a direct relationship exists between the coder bit rate and its *Mean Optimum Score* (MOS), the latter a measurement of voice quality. That is, the higher the bit rate, the higher the MOS. Also, an inverse relationship takes place between the coder's bit rate and its coding delay. That is, the higher the resulting bit rate produced by the coder, the lower the coding delay. Thus, a technique you can use to make a VoIP application work when too much latency exists is to change the voice-coding method. In general, changing the coder from one that operates at 5.3/6.3 Kbps to 8 Kbps reduces the coding delay by approximately 10 ms. If you change the coder to an LD-CELP coder, you can remove an additional 10 ms of delay. Although 20 ms is not earth-shattering, it may be enough to ensure that the quality of reconstructed voice is acceptable for your VoIP application. In addition, if you save a few ms with other techniques, the cumulative effect of these savings will really add up. The effect of changing these settings may be sufficient to provide an acceptable level of reconstructed voice that might otherwise preclude your organization from implementing a VoIP application.

Interprocessing Delay

The interprocessing delay represents the time required to form an IP datagram from each segment of digitized voice produced by a voice coder and then routes the resulting datagram to a router connected to the IP network. The total interprocessing delay is approximately 10 ms and represents a series of delays that can vary due to the fact that the utilization level of the LAN, which connects the voice gateway to the router, governs the gateway-to-router delay. In addition to the gateway-to-router delay, the gateway itself has some processing delay as it forms an IP datagram. Similarly, the router must process each datagram prior to sending it on its way towards its destination. Although this author used 10 ms for the total interprocess delay at the origin, it is possible to slightly reduce this time. To do so, you can consider obtaining a faster processor for the voice gateway.

Most voice gateways are modular devices, with voice-processing boards that are inserted into a PC. Although each voice-processing board contains its own processor that enables support for different voice-coding methods and actually performs the analog-to-digital conversion, the formation and movement of datagrams through the gateway is a function of its main processor. This means that a Pentium III 700 MHz system will have less delay and support the faster movement of datagrams through the gateway and onto the LAN than a Pentium III 500 MHz-based system. From tests performed by this author, the replacement of the gateway system with a faster processor can be expected to shave one ms for every extra 100 MHz of processor power.

A second method you can consider using to reduce the interprocess delay is to upgrade the LAN if it is operating at a utilization level beyond 50 percent. Based upon this author's experience, replacing an Ethernet LAN operating at slightly over a 50-percent utilization level with a Fast Ethernet network reduces delay by approximately one ms. Thus, by upgrading the gateway process from a 500 MHz system to a 700 MHz system, and replacing an Ethernet network that connects the gateway to the router with a

Fast Ethernet network, you may be able to shave approximately three ms off the end-to-end delay.

Network Access at Origin

A digitized voice conversation consists of a stream of small datagrams in order to reduce the impact of one or more being lost. If the router is connected to the Internet at 56 Kbps and the average datagram length is 49 bytes, then the network access delay at the origin becomes 7.0 ms (49 bytes * 8 bits/byte) ÷ 56 Kbps.

Of the 49 bytes in a typical datagram, 20 represent the IP header and eight represent the UDP header, resulting in 21 actual bytes transporting digitized voice. Although you may encounter references to TCP and UDP being used to transport voice, in actuality TCP is used for the connection setup, while UDP is used for the actual transport of digitized voice. Because you cannot retransmit lost or erroneous datagrams, UDP is used to transport digitized voice because it is a connectionless, best-effort protocol. Because it is extremely important to insure that call setup information such as the number dialed is received correctly, TCP, which is a connection-oriented error free protocol, is used to transport call setup information.

If the access line is upgraded to a T1 line operating at 1.544 Mbps, then the network access delay becomes 0.25 ms (49 bytes * 8 bits/byte) ÷ 1.536 Mbps. Note that a divisor of 1.536 Mbps is used instead of 1.544 Mbps for the T1 line because 8 Kbps is used for framing and is not available for data transfer.

If you examine the network access delay at the origin, it is possible to reduce the latency associated with moving datagrams from the local network into the Internet by upgrading the access line. As shown in the previous computations, moving from a 56 Kbps access line to a T1 access line can reduce latency by almost seven ms. If the cost of a T1 is prohibitive, you can consider different types of *fractional T1* (FT1) access lines that operate between 56 Kbps and 1.544 Mbps. Such lines could be used to reduce network access delays.

When transmitting from the edge of a network, you should carefully consider the use of a routing protocol. When a router is an edge device, normally you'll have little reason to use a routing protocol that results in a periodic exchange of routing table updates. Instead, the use of static routing avoids table update exchanges and can eliminate periodic latency shifts by a digitized voice segment transported via a packet being delayed by a routing table update. Although the use of static routing has a minimal gain when employed on a high-speed communications link, when applied using a relatively low-speed communications link, such as a 64 Kbps circuit, its use can considerably reduce latency.

Network Transmission Delay

Because VoIP is rarely used in intra-city communications, you can assume that the IP network will route data between dissimilar geographical areas. Because at least two backbone routers will be involved in the routing process, you can expect a minimum delay of 20 ms. Most network transmission delays are under 200 ms, so the range of delays listed in Table 8-11 are from 20 to 200 ms. Two key tools can be used to determine network delay: Ping and Traceroute.

Ping   One of the key tools you can use ahead of time to determine the viability of a VoIP application is the Ping utility program. Figure 8-7 illustrates the basic format of Ping implemented under different versions of Microsoft Windows. Although you can also use Ping from a Cisco router, doing so provides round-trip latency from the router to the target device. Because VoIP packets flow over a network to the router, a more accurate determination of latency is to use Ping from a workstation on the LAN where a voice gateway resides, because this enables all network delays to be observed. Note that you can simply enter Ping with a host name or IP address, or you can enter one or more of the options listed in Figure 8-7. Although the primary use of Ping

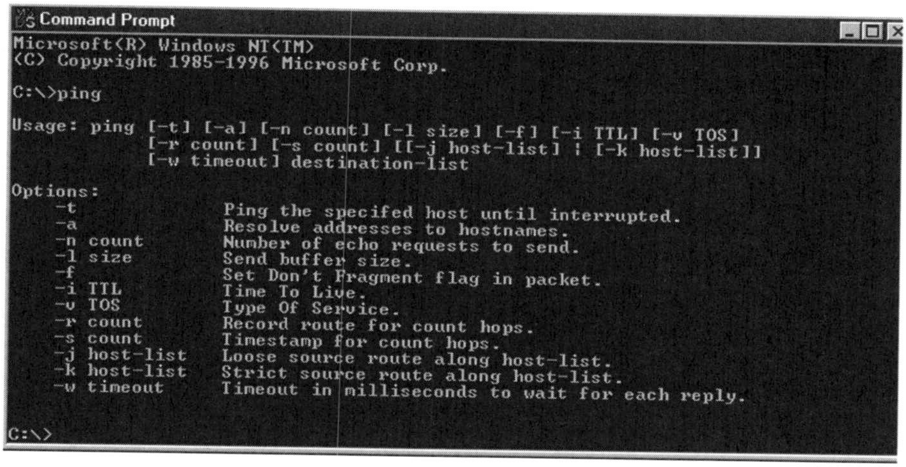

Figure 8-7

You can display the format of Ping by entering the command without any options

```
Command Prompt                                                    _ □ x
Microsoft(R) Windows NT(TM)
(C) Copyright 1985-1996 Microsoft Corp.

C:\>ping

Usage: ping [-t] [-a] [-n count] [-l size] [-f] [-i TTL] [-v TOS]
            [-r count] [-s count] [[-j host-list] : [-k host-list]]
            [-w timeout] destination-list

Options:
    -t              Ping the specified host until interrupted.
    -a              Resolve addresses to hostnames.
    -n count        Number of echo requests to send.
    -l size         Send buffer size.
    -f              Set Don't Fragment flag in packet.
    -i TTL          Time To Live.
    -v TOS          Type Of Service.
    -r count        Record route for count hops.
    -s count        Timestamp for count hops.
    -j host-list    Loose source route along host-list.
    -k host-list    Strict source route along host-list.
    -w timeout      Timeout in milliseconds to wait for each reply.

C:\>
```

is to determine the operational status of the target host or address, it also provides you with the round-trip delay from the originator to the destination.

Figure 8-8 illustrates the use of the Ping utility to determine the round-trip delay time between the author's computer and the Web server operated by Yale University. In examining Figure 8-8, note that the Microsoft implementation of Ping results in the transmission of a sequence of four echo-request packets to the target. The target responds with an echo-reply to each echo-request, with the originating station computing the round-trip delay. If a response is not received within 250 ms, which is the default time-out value, the originating station considers its request to have timed out and generates its next echo request.

In examining Figure 8-8, note that the initial round-trip delay is 156 ms, while the second and fourth round-trip delays are computed to be 125 ms and 110 ms, respectively. One of the most common mistakes many people make when using Ping is to use the first round-trip delay time. In actuality, if you enter a host name that was not previously resolved, the resolution of the host name into an IP address results in the first round-trip delay being longer than subsequent delays. The only exception to this is when traffic or processing at a router reaches the point where it results in significant delays that cause Ping to time out. The third line illustrates this after the Pinging message in Figure 8-8.

Thus, when using Ping to determine the round-trip delay through a network, you should always discard the first delay because it can include time for a host-to-IP-address resolution. In addition, you should consider running Ping throughout the day to determine if one or more periods of time

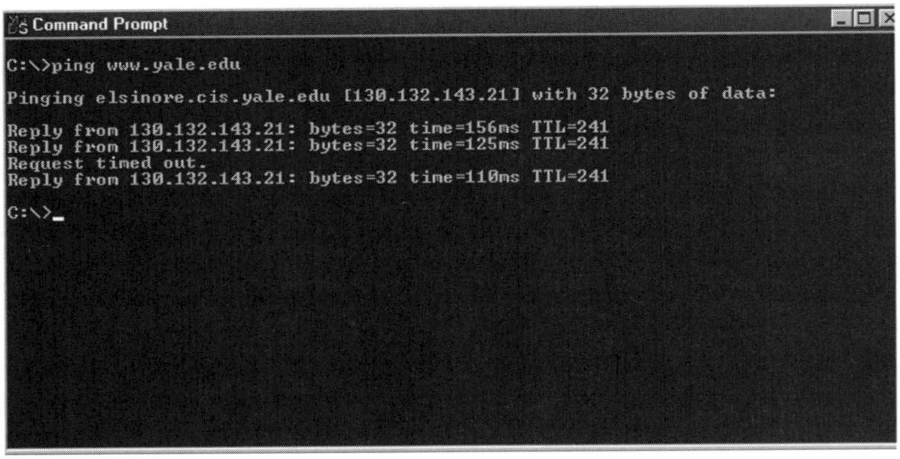

Figure 8-8
Pinging the Web
server at Yale
University

```
Command Prompt                                                    _ □ X

C:\>ping www.yale.edu

Pinging elsinore.cis.yale.edu [130.132.143.21] with 32 bytes of data:

Reply from 130.132.143.21: bytes=32 time=156ms TTL=241
Reply from 130.132.143.21: bytes=32 time=125ms TTL=241
Request timed out.
Reply from 130.132.143.21: bytes=32 time=110ms TTL=241

C:\>_
```

occur when delays escalate. You can either write a script to run Ping at different times or you can use the -t option to run it continuously during the day. If you pipe the results to a file, you can then read the file into a spreadsheet and easily determine the mean, peak, and average values, as well as other statistics about round-trip delay. For example, the following DOS command would run Ping on the target www.yale.edu continuously and pipe its output to the file test:

```
Ping -t www.yale.edu >test
```

If the response to a series of Pings issued over a period of time indicates that the network delay is too great to enable a VoIP application to have an overall delay under 200 ms, many would be tempted to give up on the application. Instead, you should consider the use of a second TCP/IP application tool built into Windows and other operating systems. Such a tool is the traceroute application, which is called tracert under Windows.

Tracert   Tracert operates by initially transmitting a series of packets with the *Time to Live* (TTL) field value set to one. Routers automatically decrement the TTL field value. If its value equals zero, the packet is discarded and the router returns an error message to the originator along with the IP address of the router, information about the router, and information about its network connection. The originator then transmits a new series of packets with the TTL field value incremented by one to two. The packets flow through the first router on the path to the destination, where the TTL field value in each packet is decremented by one to one. Thus, the second router in the packet to the destination discards the series of packets and returns error messages to the originator. This process continues until a sequence of packets either reaches their destination or the maximum default TTL value is reached. Under Windows, the default maximum TTL value is 30 hops.

Figure 8-9 illustrates the format of Microsoft Windows' tracert. Note that you can change the maximum number of hops in your search for the route to a target via the use of the -h option.

Because we used Ping to determine the round-trip delay to the Web server at Yale University, let's use tracert to trace the path to the Web server. Figure 8-10 illustrates the resulting display from tracert. Note that a total of 15 hops is required to reach the destination. Also note that tracert issues a sequence of three packets for each TTL value used, resulting in three round-trip delay computations. On the twelfth hop, the second packet has a response time that exceeds 250 ms, resulting in an asterisk (*) being displayed to indicate a timeout condition.

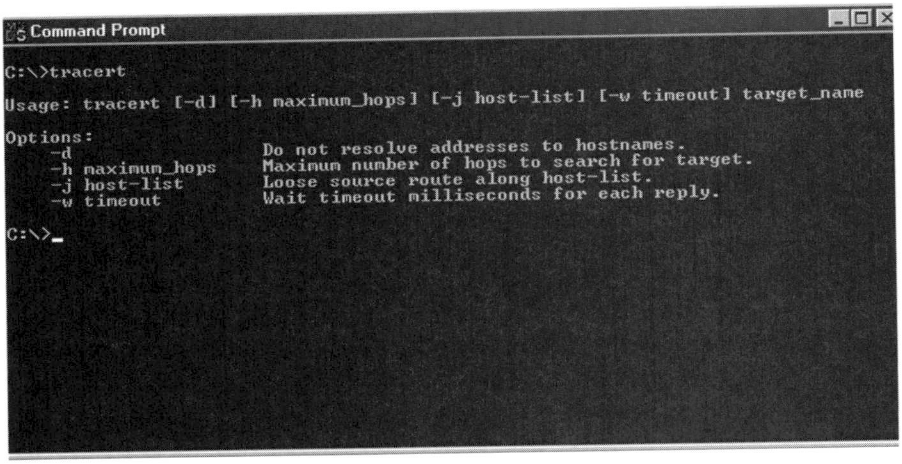

Figure 8-9
The format of tracert

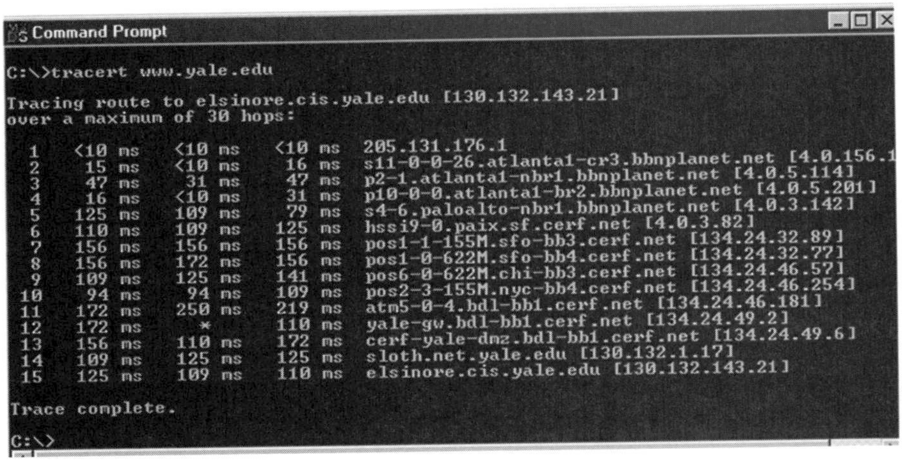

```
Command Prompt                                                    _ □ ×

C:\>tracert

Usage: tracert [-d] [-h maximum_hops] [-j host-list] [-w timeout] target_name

Options:
    -d                  Do not resolve addresses to hostnames.
    -h maximum_hops     Maximum number of hops to search for target.
    -j host-list        Loose source route along host-list.
    -w timeout          Wait timeout milliseconds for each reply.

C:\>_
```

Figure 8-10
Tracing the route to
the Yale University
Web server

```
Command Prompt                                                    _ □ ×

C:\>tracert www.yale.edu

Tracing route to elsinore.cis.yale.edu [130.132.143.21]
over a maximum of 30 hops:

  1    <10 ms    <10 ms    <10 ms   205.131.176.1
  2     15 ms    <10 ms     16 ms   s11-0-0-26.atlanta1-cr3.bbnplanet.net [4.0.156.1
  3     47 ms     31 ms     47 ms   p2-1.atlanta1-nbr1.bbnplanet.net [4.0.5.114]
  4     16 ms    <10 ms     31 ms   p10-0-0.atlanta1-br2.bbnplanet.net [4.0.5.201]
  5    125 ms    109 ms     79 ms   s4-6.paloalto-nbr1.bbnplanet.net [4.0.3.142]
  6    110 ms    109 ms    125 ms   hssi9-0.paix.sf.cerf.net [4.0.3.82]
  7    156 ms    156 ms    156 ms   pos1-1-155M.sfo-bb3.cerf.net [134.24.32.89]
  8    156 ms    172 ms    156 ms   pos1-0-622M.sfo-bb4.cerf.net [134.24.32.77]
  9    109 ms    125 ms    141 ms   pos6-0-622M.chi-bb3.cerf.net [134.24.46.57]
 10     94 ms     94 ms    109 ms   pos2-3-155M.nyc-bb4.cerf.net [134.24.46.254]
 11    172 ms    250 ms    219 ms   atm5-0-4.bdl-bb1.cerf.net [134.24.46.181]
 12    172 ms       *       110 ms   yale-gw.bdl-bb1.cerf.net [134.24.49.2]
 13    156 ms    110 ms    172 ms   cerf-yale-dmz.bdl-bb1.cerf.net [134.24.49.6]
 14    109 ms    125 ms    125 ms   sloth.net.yale.edu [130.132.1.17]
 15    125 ms    109 ms    110 ms   elsinore.cis.yale.edu [130.132.143.21]

Trace complete.

C:\>
```

If the use of Ping indicates a periodic delay that exceeds the amount of latency required for a VoIP application to work, you can use tracert to determine if one or more routers is abnormally contributing to the delay. If so, it may be possible to request that your ISP reroute the path your packets must take or perhaps they might be willing to upgrade or replace a router that acts as a bottleneck. If your organization operates an internal TCP/IP network, you can use the results of tracert to determine if an internal router upgrade is required. If you carefully examine Figure 8-10, you will note that the routers at hops 11, 12, and 13 represent bottlenecks. If this author were planning a VoIP application to the Yale campus, he would certainly bring this to the attention of his ISP.

Network Egress at Destination

Returning to Table 8-11, note that the latency or delay for datagrams flowing from the Internet is shown to be between .25 ms and 7 ms. Once again, this range represents the variance in delay resulting from the use of a T1 access line (.25 ms) and a 56 Kbps access line (7 ms). Thus, by upgrading one or both access lines, it becomes possible to reduce end-to-end delay.

Buffer

As we talk, a voice coder produces a series of datagrams with a uniform time delay between each datagram. As the datagrams flow through the Internet, they experience random delays at each node in the network based on the flow of traffic to the router as well as the state of its queues. By the time the datagrams exit the Internet and flow towards the destination gateway, the gaps between datagrams have random delays. If these datagrams were directly used to reconstruct voice, the result would be awkward-sounding gaps between each small segment of voice. Thus, instead of being directly converted back to analog voice, the datagrams are first moved into a jitter buffer. Then they are removed in order with a uniform time delay between extractions, resulting in a natural sounding voice when the contents of the datagrams are converted back into analog voice.

Most jitter buffers can be set from 0 (disabled) to a maximum of 255 ms. Because you need to reduce the random delays between received datagrams, the jitter buffer should never be set to a value of 0. Similarly, because the human ear can only tolerate 200 ms of delay and many other delays must be considered, the jitter buffer should never be configured anywhere near its maximum value. Instead, a good rule of thumb is to initially set its value to a delay of 10 ms. If the total delay to include the jitter buffer delay is well under 200 ms, you can then experiment and gradually increase the jitter buffer delay to determine if doing so makes reconstructed voice sound better.

Decompression

Unlike voice coding delays that can significantly vary based on the coding technique, decompression is relatively fixed at approximately 10 ms, regardless of the method used. Thus, although minor differences in decompression time can be found between voice-coding methods, a good rule of thumb is to use a 10 ms delay for compression.

Recommended Course of Action

Seven major components are associated with the end-to-end delay or latency of datagrams transporting voice. Although some components are relatively fixed and little can be gained by altering their parameters, other delay components are quite variable and several techniques exist for altering their contribution to overall delay. In addition, through the use of Ping and tracert, you obtain the tools to examine the major contributing factor to end-to-end delay: network transmission delay. By carefully examining each component of delay and using applicable tools, it becomes possible to successfully implement VoIP applications that otherwise might never become a reality.

Existing QoS and Queuing Models

Although many data networks do not currently support QoS, some may have already implemented QoS techniques within the routed network. At a minimum, most networks implement WFQ, as it is the default on all interfaces running at less than 2 Mbps. Before designing and implementing a QoS strategy for voice networking, it is important to identify any and all existing QoS implementations. This can be done by scanning the existing router configurations for each of the QoS techniques and documenting their locations. Each implementation must be analyzed to determine the effect that voice traffic will have on it, as well as the implications of switching to a different QoS technique. The important questions to ask are as follows:

- Why is this technique being applied?
- What traffic does it support? Neglect?
- What systems and/or applications does it affect?
- How do the newer QoS techniques interact with it?
- What are the effects of making voice traffic a higher priority within the existing scheme?
- If a different technique is required, how can the new technique emulate the service provided by the older one?
- If WFQ is enabled, will transmitting voice at a higher priority (when the IP precedence equals 5) significantly affect existing traffic?

The answers to these questions should provide some direction toward resolving any conflicts with the existing QoS configurations. As with any network configuration change, time and resources must be dedicated to planning and testing the change before putting it into production.

Router Software Versions

The voice-enabled routers will most likely be running up-to-date software due to the currency of the voice hardware and software. However, the existing network environment may not be running the latest software. In order to implement many of the QoS techniques mandated by VoIP, IOS versions 11.3 and 12.0 are required. The software versions for all routers that will be involved in transporting voice traffic must be gathered and reviewed. At times, these routers may not be able to be upgraded due to hardware support, interface compatibility, *Dynamic Random Access Memory* (DRAM) and Flash memory sizes, corporate policy, or other political and/or business requirements. These issues must be considered when developing a networkwide QoS policy.

QoS Configuration Guidelines   Tables 8-12a and 8-12b provide relative guidelines for implementing the QoS techniques discussed. They serve as references for planning and should not be used as absolute metrics. Further information on QoS is found in Chapter 11, "Quality of Service."

WARNING: *These tables are only guidelines! The actual implementation results may vary greatly depending upon several factors including, but not limited to, protocol mix, interface traffic rates, traffic mix, router software versions, configuration and implementation issues, network design and topology, and additional processes running on the router. Proper planning and testing should be conducted before implementing QoS techniques or any network configuration change.*

Dial Plan Creation

After the initial information has been gathered and a direction has been set for QoS application, the next step is to develop the dial plan. Typically, the same dialing plan that has been implemented on the voice PBX network can be used in the routers. For a discussion of dial plan, see Chapter 25, "Defining Voice Networks."

Table 8-12a

QoS Feature and
Router Model
Support Matrix

QoS Class	Classification and Prioritization						Traffic Shaping	
	CAR (H)	RSVP (H)	PQ/CQ (M)	WFQ (L)	Policy Routing (L)	WRED (L)	FRTS (H)	GTS (H)
1600	No	11.2P	11.2P	11.2P	11.2P	11.2P	11.2P	11.2P
2500	No	11.2	9.14	11.2	11.0	11.2	11.2	11.2
2600	12.0	12.0	12.0	12.0	12.0	12.0	12.0	12.0
3600	12.0	11.2	11.3	11.2	11.2	11.2	11.2	11.2
3810	No	11.3	11.3	11.3	11.3	11.3	11.3	11.3
4500	12.0	11.2	11.2	11.2	11.0	11.2	11.2	11.2
4700	12.0	11.2	11.2	11.2	11.0	11.2	11.2	11.2
AS5300	No	11.2P	11.2P	11.2P	11.2P	11.3	No	11.2P
7200	11.1 CC	11.2	11.1	11.2	11.0	11.2	11.2	11.2
7500	11.1 CC	11.2	11.1	11.2	11.0	11.2	11.2	11.2
RSM	12.0	11.2	11.2	11.2	11.2	No	11.2	11.2
8500	No	No	No	No/WRR	12.0	No/WRR	No	No
6500 MSM	No	No	No	No/WRR	12.0	No/WRR	No	No

H = heavy, M = medium, and L = light weighting; CAR = committed access rate; PQ/CQ = priority queuing and custom queuing; WFQ = weighted fair queuing; WRED = weighted random early detection; FRTS = frame-relay traffic shaping; GTS = generic traffic shaping; MLPPP with LFI = multilink PPP with link fragment interleaving; CRTP = compressed real-time protocol; WRR = weighted round robin scheduling.

Network Integration

This section discusses some of the issues associated with integrating VoIP into an existing IP network. It is not intended to provide detailed configuration information for building the IP network from scratch, but rather information to help augment the IP network to better support VoIP traffic.

Security Filters

Packet filters are often used to control traffic in IP networks. Cisco's access list structure offers the capability to deny, permit, or log traffic based on a

Table 8-12b

QoS Feature and
Router-Model
Support Matrix

| QoS Class | Link Efficiency | | Enhanced Integration | | QoS Policy Propagation via BGP (H) | Tag Switching/ MPLS (H) |
	MLPPP with LFI (M)	CRTP (M)	RSVP-ATM Interworking (H)	IP to ATM CoS (H)		
1600	11.3	11.3	No	No	No	No
2500	11.3	11.3	No	No	No	No
2600	12.0	12.0	No	No	No	No
3600	11.3	11.3	No	No	No	No
3810	11.3	11.3	No	No	No	No
4500	11.3	11.3	No	No	No	No
4700	11.3	11.3	No	No	No	No
AS5300	11.3	11.3	No	No	No	No
7200	11.3	11.3	12.0	12.0	11.1 CC	12.0
7500	11.3	11.3	12.0	11.1 CC	11.1 CC	12.0
RSM	No	No	No	No	No	No
8500	No	No	No	No	No	12.0
6500 MSM	No	No	No	No	No	Planned

wide range of criteria. When modifying an access list to permit voice traffic, a few parameters must be considered:

- The destination IP address of all VoIP dial peers
- The number of voice channels in each voice-enabled router
- The source address used to reach all dial peers

Extracting the session targets from all the VoIP dial peers in the configuration easily identifies the first parameter.

The number of voice channels supported by the router is also easy to identify, and this value determines the range of UDP ports that will be used for voice calls. The UDP ports allocated begin with port 16384 and end with 16384 1 (4 * N), where N is the number of voice channels in the router. For example, an AS5300 supporting 24 voice channels would use a UDP port range of 16384 through 16480.

The third parameter may seem strange but must be given consideration. When a router initiates a call, the source IP address for the call is that of the interface used as the exit path toward the destination. If Serial 0/0 is the output interface, then Serial 0/0's IP address is used. This can be confusing if the remote router's dial peers point to the Ethernet interface's IP address instead of the serial interface's address. It may cause problems if packets are filtered by both the source and destination IP addresses.

Rerouting

Many IP networks are designed to provide enhanced fault tolerance through the use of multiple routers and links. Routing protocols are then used to establish loop-free paths through the network. It is important to be cognizant of the traffic flows and paths during failure conditions. This affects dial-peer session target assignments, security filters, and interface-bound QoS functions.

In fault-tolerant WAN environments, avoid using serial-port IP addresses as the session target for VoIP dial peers. Serial port IP addresses become unavailable when the WAN link they are connected to goes down. This leads to the undesirable effect of not being able to route voice calls to a remote router, even though connectivity to the router is available through a backup or secondary WAN link. A possible workaround for this is to use IP-unnumbered for WAN links, in which case the same IP address is assigned to all WAN links and therefore is reachable in most rerouting scenarios. Loopback interface definitions thus have a clear advantage. Because loopback interfaces are always considered up and active, they are always available as the dial peer target.

Security filters and QoS functions that are applied to specific interfaces must also be considered. More to the point, the application of these same functions must be applied to the backup paths as well as the primary paths.

Network Address Translation

Network Address Translation (NAT) is increasingly being used within corporate networks to overcome address space limitations and to increase security and networking issues created due to corporate mergers. *Port address translation* (PAT) offers the capability to translate multiple IP addresses to a single external IP address by multiplexing TCP or UDP port numbers. Both NAT and PAT present challenges for VoIP networking.

NAT's use of dynamic address pools is incompatible with VoIP's need to map sessions to a consistent IP address. PAT's changing of source UDP ports is incompatible with how the VoIP software establishes sessions and passes session responsibility for H.245 to RTCP. For these reasons, static translations must be used to support VoIP calls across NAT boundaries.

Summary

Implementing voice networks requires thorough planning for both the telephony aspects and their impact on the data network infrastructure. Voice traffic engineering requirements must also be mapped to data networking requirements. This process fuels the implementation of QoS functions within the equipment, and it influences network design, product selection, and software configuration. Careful evaluation of these criteria provides the basis for building high-performance integrated voice and data networks.

Designing
Security and
Firewalls

This chapter discusses the two important subjects of security and firewalls. Understand that these two subjects are related but are by no means the same. Security is a state of being, and firewalls are devices or, more commonly, a group of devices that assist you in achieving this state of security.

Security

Let's take an example of security where it matters most. Everyone can identify with the concept of security at home. The saying "A man's home is his castle" provides a good example. Castles or homes rely on layers of security. Castles have moats, drawbridges, gates with huge locks, stairways to different floors, doors to rooms, and . . . well, you get the idea as to the layers involved in castle security.

All of these ideas are, to all outward appearances, good ways of implementing security at different levels, but everything has its vulnerabilities. A finely placed fire arrow into the ropes holding the drawbridge up could quickly eliminate that barrier. The gates with huge locks might have small hinge pins that could be knocked out, and so on.

Whenever you talk about security, you must consider your risks. You need to identify what you have and why you are protecting it. You must also identify the threats and your vulnerability to those threats. If you have a company that sells shoes, your concerns that people might break into your store and steal catalogs or even shoes would be less than that of a banking firm's concern that customer accounts could be altered and cash stolen.

The bottom line of security rests with policy. After identifying what you have and what the threats are, you need to decide on a security policy. A network security policy should include, but is not limited to, the following issues:

- **Authentication**: Who is allowed access to the network?
- **Authorization**: What do they have permission to do once they are logged on to the network?
- **Administration**: Who should give the permissions?
- **Data Integrity**: How will we protect our data, for example, encryption, backup, or storage methods?
- **Auditing/Intrusion Detection**: Who is using what resources and when? How will we learn of unauthorized use?
- **Accountability**: What will we do when policies are not followed?

- **Response and Recovery**: What will we do when data is lost, stolen, altered, or eavesdropped?
- **Prevention**: How will we make sure the same problem or vulnerability does not happen again?

These are critical areas that must be addressed. You may have other areas that need addressing based on your given situation, but these provide a good foundation for any network security policy.

You must understand the tradeoffs involved in implementing this security. The issues surrounding these tradeoffs are cost, convenience, availability, productivity, and performance to name a few.

Cost

The costs involved with implementing a strong security policy can be considerable. Firewalls and their related products are expensive. The personnel necessary to implement, audit, and maintain the security policies are not only hard to find, but they are even more expensive.

Convenience

Strong security policies are more inconvenient than lax or no security policies. People don't like using hard-to-remember passwords, nor do they like to change them frequently. Firewalls can make certain services on the Internet unavailable. Things like external email, audio and video files, as well as Internet chat or meeting services are just some of the examples of the packets that firewalls may disallow.

Availability

Firewalls can introduce what are known as single points of failure. The nature of firewalls is that they examine every packet coming in and leaving the network. Should the firewall fail for whatever reason, communications could be brought to a halt. Redundancy is complicated and even more expensive.

In computer security, three basic things need to be considered:

1. Keeping private the contents of your data.
2. Making sure you maintain the integrity of your data.
3. Making sure that your data and network remain accessible.

These three should be combined and integrated so that the characteristics of one of these subjects does not interfere with the others. For example, if others are prevented from accessing our data, both integrity and privacy are preserved. If the network remains accessible, integrity is also insured. Part of maintaining accessibility is by preventing malicious hackers from destroying its usefulness, such as with a virus or a *denial of service* (Dos) attack.

Productivity/Performance

People like to use the path with the least resistance. If security policies make logging in remotely from home or travel difficult, people might be less likely to log in and work when they are away. Firewalls can slow transmissions considerably depending on how granular the filtering methods are.

The Tools for Security

The tools that help you achieve this state of security are firewalls. Firewalls provide for all of the previously mentioned issues. Before going into what firewalls are, it is important to describe the principles of layering and describe in more detail the inner workings of TCP/IP. This will help you gain a better understanding of exactly what these firewalls do. It will also explain how one goes about deciding who can access your network and what a user can do on your network. You can learn how to keep malicious hackers from not only breaking in, but also how to make sure that a hacker can't damage or deny access to your network.

Protocol Layering

One of the most important tenets of security is to know how your enemies plan to attack you. The way they will attack is through the many friendly and unsophisticated protocols of the TCP/IP suite. When the Internet was established, it was not done with security in mind. In order to understand how firewalls work and where security needs to be applied, you must have a basic understanding of the protocols used and the methods most likely used to subvert them. Networking protocols are based on a principle called layering. Attacks can come at any one of these layers, so in this section we talk about each of these layers and how an attack might be pursued. We'll start with the OSI model.

International Standards Organization - Open Systems Interconnect Reference Model (ISO-OSI)

As LANs became more and more popular, people made attempts to connect these different networks. These attempts were unsuccessful as each company marketing their own network created and used their own standards of communication over the network. In 1984, in an effort to solve this problem, the *International Standards Organization* (ISO) proposed a seven-layer model that provided a common basis for developing standards that would enable different systems to be connected. This is more of a guideline than a strict set of rules that must be adhered to. This model is called the Open Systems Interconnection model. The ISO-OSI reference model defines seven layers, and they are listed in Figure 9-1.

Figure 9-1

The OSI reference model

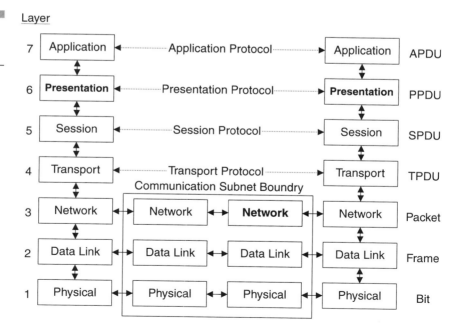

Layering Principles

Approaching any problem works best when approached in layers. Whether it is something as simple as cleaning your house or as complicated as the Federal Income Tax system, layering makes the task more achievable. It helps reduce the complexities of large tasks. This facilitates standardization because when programmers are writing protocols, they need only worry about the details of the specific layer for which the protocol is intended. This makes updates or changes easier as well because modifications to a certain layer will not affect the whole stack. Prior to the use of layered protocols, simple changes, such as adding one terminal type to the list of those supported by an architecture often required changes to all of the software in the protocol stack.

When talking about any given layers, you usually refer to them as the N layer. This is because each N layer provides services to the higher layer above (referred to as N+1) and uses the services provided by the lower layer underneath (referred to as N−1) as illustrated in Figure 9-2.

These N layers communicate with each other through what are called *Service Access Points* (SAPs). So, an *N Service Access Point* (N-SAP) is where an N service is provided to an N+1 entity by the N service provider. The N service data is the packet of data exchanged at an N-SAP. *N Service Data Units* (N-SDUs) are the individual units of data that are exchanged at an N-SAP. Therefore, N service data is made up of N-SDUs. Figure 9-3 illustrates this concept.

Figure 9-2
Illustration depicting the layers of a protocol

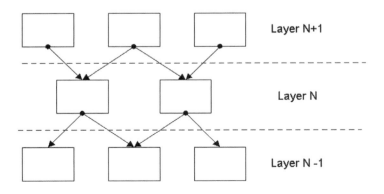

Layer N+1

Layer N

Layer N -1

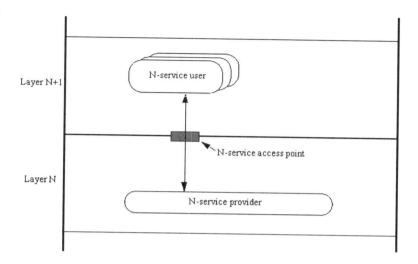

Figure 9-3
A SAP connection
between layers

Layer N+1

N-service user

N-service access point

Layer N

N-service provider

Layer Communication Dynamics

Many functions need to be performed by the protocols in each layer. These range from the specification of connectors, addresses of the network nodes, identification of interfaces, options, flow control, reliability, error reporting, synchronization, and so on. Because of the many different actions that need to take place in communications, protocol suites were designed to do these complex tasks. These protocols are designed together to form a layered design also known as a protocol stack. Each layer in the protocol suite handles one specific aspect of the communication. All major network architectures currently used or being developed use a layered approach for their protocol architectures. Outgoing data passes down through each layer and incoming data passes up through each layer, making the design of protocol software in each layer much simpler as one only needs to concern themselves with the data from the layer above and the layer below. The individual adjacent layers communicate with each other through *Service Data Units* (SDUs). By appending *Protocol Control Information* (PCI) to the SDU you get a *Protocol Data Unit* (PDU). The peer layers on each end of a communication session communicate using PDUs. So in essence, two protocols on the Application layer communicate via APDUs. The Presentation layer communicates via PPDUs and so on. You can see this at work in the

Network Architecture figure in OSI reference model section. The components of the PDU are diagramed in Figure 9-4.

Encapsulation Mechanics

To elaborate further, an SDU is a piece of information passed by a layer above it (the N+1 Layer in Figure 9-5) to the current layer (the N Layer) for transmission using the service of that layer. To transport the SDU, the current layer encapsulates the SDU by appending a Protocol Control Header, which is part of PCI. The combined PCI and SDU is known as the PDU occupying that N layer. This then becomes the SDU of the N-1 layer below. This process is known as encapsulation. Figure 9-5 illustrates the process during transmission of data. Upon arrival, the receiving station on the network reverses the process as seen in Figure 9-6.

If you look at Figure 9-7, you see the headers associated with each of the seven layers of the OSI reference model. Once the application process passes a unit of data to the application, it is then processed. It then adds its

Figure 9-4
PDU format

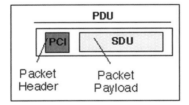

Figure 9-5
PDU flow down the protocol stack

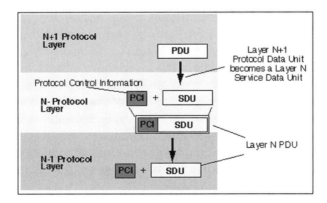

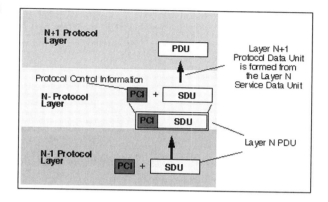

Figure 9-6
PDU flow up the
protocol stack

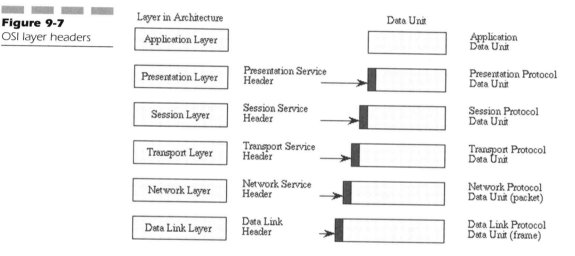

Figure 9-7
OSI layer headers

protocol header and passes the packet along with the header to the layer below. This layer in turn processes the data and adds its own header. Each layer treats the unit of information from higher layers as data, and does not concern itself with the contents therein. This process continues until the packet reaches the physical layer.

It is the physical layer that then converts the Data Link PDU into a series of bits encoded by changes in voltage states and sends it across the transmission medium (such as a wire) to its intended receiver. At the receiver, the remote system reassembles the series of bits to form a packet and forwards the packet for processing by the data link layer. Then the data link header is removed and passed to the network layer. This process continues until the original packet's data unit is sent to the remote application program.

The Application Layer (Layer 7)

The application layer interacts directly with and issues requests to the presentation layer through *Presentation Service Access Point* (PSAP). It differs from the other layers in that it does not provide services to any of the other OSI layers, but rather to application processes above the OSI model. The application layer identifies and establishes the availability of intended communication partners, synchronizes cooperating applications, and establishes agreement on procedures for error recovery and control of data integrity. The application layer also determines whether sufficient resources for the intended communication exist. Examples of protocols that occupy this layer are *File Transfer Protocol* (FTP), Web browser *Hyper-text Transfer Protocol* (HTTP), Telnet, *Network File System* (NFS), *Simple Mail Transfer Protocol* (SMTP), *Simple Network Management Protocol* (SNMP), and *File Transfer Access Management* (FTAM), to name a few.

The Presentation Layer (Layer 6)

The job of the presentation layer is to make sure that information passed down from the application layer of one system will be readable by the application layer of the system to which it is transmitting. Other responsibilities of the presentation layer are data encryption, data compression, and character conversion between disparate systems such as *American Standard Code for Information Interchange* (ASCII) to IBM's *Extended Binary Coded Decimal Interchange Code* (EBCDIC). It also handles common graphics compression. Examples of protocols that occupy this layer are *Graphics Interchange Format* (GIF), *Joint Photographic Experts Group* (JPEG), *Tagged Image File Format* (TIFF), PICT, ASCII, EBCDIC, encryption, *Moving Picture Experts Group* (MPEG), *Musical Instrument Digital Interface* (MIDI), and *HyperText Markup Language* (HTML).

The Session Layer (Layer 5)

The session layer controls the setting up and tearing down of the connections established between two machines. While the connection is being maintained, the machines might communicate either uni-directionally known as half duplex, or bi-directionally, known as full duplex. A session between two users or machines might include events like remote login and remote file transfer sessions. This involves dialogue control, token management, and synchronization, sometimes referred to as the port layer because computer services communicate with each other through ports. A good example is HTTP, which occupies the well-known port 80. It is one way a firewall or packet filter restricts or enables certain protocols based on the protocol port numbers. Examples of protocols that occupy this layer are *Remote Procedure Call* (RPC), *Structured Query Language* (SQL), NetBios names, and *AppleTalk Session Protocol* (ASP).

The Transport Layer (Layer 4)

The transport layer separates the complexities of the network from the layers above it, and concerns itself with reliable end-to-end communication. The messages transported are called segments, and the transport layer implements reliable internetwork data transport services that are transparent to the upper layers. Transport layer services generally involve flow control, multiplexing, error checking, and recovery. Flow control manages data transmission between devices, making sure that the receiving device is not overwhelmed with more data than it can handle at any given time. Multiplexing alternates or interleaves segments from multiple applications, enabling what appears to the upper levels as simultaneous transmission over a single interface. Error checking involves implementing methods to detect transmission errors while they occur. Recovery involves methods that can resolve such errors as requesting the retransmission of lost segments.

The transport layer provides services for both connection-oriented and connectionless transmissions. Messages that are sent on a best effort status are considered connectionless. A common form of this is email. Connection-oriented means that a stream of messages is delivered in sequence end to end without any loss or failure, an example of which is file transfer using the FTP protocol. You might be asking yourself why anyone would use anything but a connection-oriented protocol, because it guarantees delivery. The answer lies in overhead. Connectionless protocols are far more efficient and require much less bandwidth. Also, some services can't make use of retransmission and error correction because they occur in real time. Examples of protocols that occupy this layer are *Transmission Control Protocol* (TCP), U*ser Datagram Protocol* (UDP), and *Sequence Packet Exchange* (SPX).

The Network Layer (Layer 3)

The network layer concerns itself with delivery of a message from end to end, and it deals with logical addressing as opposed to physical addressing. As an example, when you buy an airline ticket from San Francisco to New York City, you (like the network layer) are only concerned that you get from point A to point B. The airline, however, must concern itself with stopovers in Phoenix and Dallas, plane changes, seat numbers, and so on. The network layer also supports both connection-oriented and connectionless service from higher layer protocols. Message units in this layer are generally referred to as packets or datagrams. Examples of protocols that occupy this layer are the *Internet Protocol* (IP), *Internetwork Packet Exchange* (IPX), *Border Gateway Protocol* (BGP), *Open Shortest Path First* (OSPF), and *Routing Information Protocol* (RIP).

The Data Link Layer (Layer 2)

The data link layer concerns itself with the delivery of packets on a given wire segment. Unlike the network layer, it deals with physical addressing. To use the airline example, it is from the point of view of the pilot as opposed to the passenger. The pilot's job is concerned with getting the plane from San Francisco to Phoenix. He is not concerned whether or not his passengers continue on to Dallas, New York, Chicago, or London, for that matter. The data link layer also defines how devices are to be physically connected, such as in a bus, star, or a ring topology. Data link error control involves alerting upper layer protocols that a transmission error has occurred. Data link frame sequencing takes frames that are transmitted out of sequence and rearranges them into their proper order. The data link layer also deals with flow control, making sure that the receiving device is not overwhelmed with more data than it can handle at any given time. Message units in the data link layer are generally referred to as frames. Examples of protocols that occupy this layer are Frame Relay, *High-Level Data Link Control* (HDLC), *Point to Point Protocol* (PPP), *Fiber Distributed Data Interface* (FDDI), Automatic teller mach . . . .sorry, *Asynchronous Transfer Mode* (ATM) IEEE 802.3 (Ethernet), and IEEE 802.5 (Token Ring).

The Physical Layer (Layer 1)

The physical layer deals with the physical characteristics of the data transmission medium. Connectors, pins, use of pins, electrical currents, voltage specifications, encoding schemes, and light modulation are all part of different physical layer specifications. Many specifications can be combined to define the components of the physical layer; for example, the RJ-45 defines the shape of the connector and number of wires in the cable as well as the specific pinouts for the connector being used. Ethernet and 802.3 define the use of wires to pins 1,2,3, and 6, and specifications exist for choosing Category 3 cable for 10baseT or Category 5 for use with 100baseT. These are combinations of different physical layer specifications for use with a twisted pair Ethernet scheme. Examples of specifications that occupy this layer are EIA/TIA-232, EIA/TIA-449, V.35, V.24, RJ-45, Ethernet, 802.3, 802.5, FDDI, NRZI, NRZ, and B8ZS.

As discussed earlier, the OSI model is viewed currently as a model or framework from which to base networking protocols rather than a strict adherence to rules. The original intent was to build a protocol stack that conforms strictly to this structure; however, TCP/IP eventually won out over this stack. Many protocols can perform services that encompass two, three or more layers at once. In the next section, you can compare the TCP/IP protocol stack as it applies to the OSI reference model.

TCP/IP Protocol Stack

In the early 1980s, specifications were released for the TCP/IP protocol stack. They are the building blocks of the Internet. The Internet has grown from a small network connecting a small community of researchers, schools, and government agencies into a global network connecting people of all types. The Internet has evolved from a specialized project to what could be argued as a basic necessity of modern life. However, the growth of the Internet has created problems with security. The problems revolve around the fact these protocols were designed when the Internet was small, and users generally trusted each other. The protocols lack many features that are currently needed to keep a network secure.

Look at TCP/IP as it relates to the OSI model. The OSI Reference Model is a seven-layer architecture, and TCP/IP is a layered architecture as well, comprised of four layers. The TCP/IP protocols themselves occupy only three of the four. As you will see, they do not correspond one-to-one with the OSI model. You can overlay the TCP/IP protocols on this model to give you a rough idea of where all the TCP/IP layers reside. Figure 9-8 is a diagram of how the two protocol stacks relate to each other.

TCP/IP does not concern itself with the bottom two layers of the OSI model (data link and physical) but begins in the network layer, where the IP resides. In the transport layer, the TCP and UDP are involved. Above this, the utilities and protocols that make up the rest of the TCP/IP suite are built using the TCP or UDP and IP layers for their communications system. Figure 9-9 shows how this stacks up.

Modern routers are programmable devices that enable *Access Control Lists* (ACLs) and access control through tables. You can make rules that determine who is allowed to send protocols through the router.

Filtration can be based on various criteria:

- Protocol type (TCP/UDP/ICMP)
- Whether traffic is incoming or outgoing

Figure 9-8

Comparison of OSI and IP protocol stack

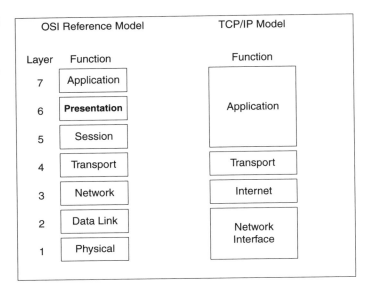

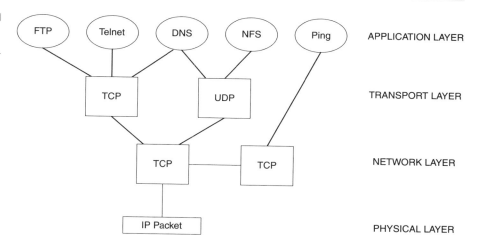

Figure 9-9
Author: need caption

- IP address (Source or destination)
- Port number (Source or destination)
- SYN flag in the TCP header (refer to the following Protocol Descriptions section)

To understand more about these topics, you need to review some basic facts about TCP/IP, which will be outlined in detail in the next section.

Protocol Descriptions

Discussing the individual protocols in more detail is important because if you are going to protect your network, you need to know what is being attacked in these protocols and where their weaknesses lie. Dissect network layer protocols first, starting with IP, which is the backbone upon which the majority of the world's traffic rides.

TCP/IP Network Layer Protocols

The TCP/IP network layer protocols include the *Internet Protocol* (IP), the *Address Resolution Protocol/Reverse Address Resolution Protocol* (ARP/RARP), and the *Internet Control Message Protocol* (ICMP).

Internet Protocol (IP)

The IP occupies the network layer of the OSI model as well as the TCP/IP model. IP is a connectionless service. That means no virtual circuit is nailed up during the transmission. The packets are simply sent on a best effort basis. The job of IP is to route and send a packet from its origin to its destination. IP provides no guarantee for the packets being sent.

IP packets are also referred to as datagrams. If the packet or datagram originates on a network other than its own, then the datagrams have to go through a series of routers before they can reach their destination. At each router along the way, the packet is sent up the protocol stack only as high as the network layer where the router can examine the logical address and determine the physical address of the next hop. Because the network is dynamic, it is possible that two datagrams from the same source take different paths to make it to the destination. Because the network has variable delays, it is not guaranteed that the datagrams will be received in sequence. Since IP only tries for a best effort delivery, it does not concern itself with lost packets; this responsibility is left to the higher layer protocols. No connection state is maintained between the two locations, which is why it is considered to be connectionless. Figure 9-10 diagrams the steps in the layering process that the packet must follow.

IP Packet   Now you are going to dissect the IP packet in depth. The reason for this is because this is what routers do as well as the people that

Figure 9-10
Packet layering
process

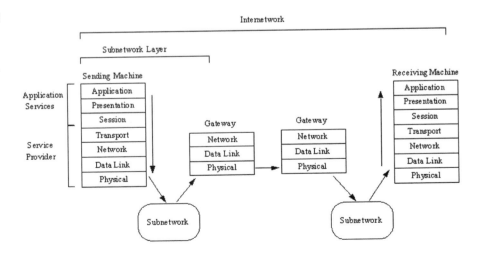

want to break into your network. The high level format of an IP datagram is shown in Figure 9-11.

IP Header A typical IP header is usually 20 bytes long, if it has no options set. If any options exist, the IP header can be as large as 24 bytes. Figure 9-12 diagrams the IP header portion of the IP datagram. How to populate the mandatory fields is explained in the following pages.

Version Field The 4-bit version field dictates which IP version number of the protocol is being used. The version number is necessary so that the receiving device knows how to decode the rest of the header. The version field is almost always set to version 4; however, several systems are now testing IPv6 or IPng (next generation). The Internet and most LANs do not support IP version 6 yet, but the change is inevitable.

Header Length Field The 4-bit header length field specifies the length of the IP packet header in 32-bit words. The minimum value for a valid header is 5 words (20 bytes) or, with use of optional fields, can increase the header size to its maximum of 6 words (24 bytes). The field exists because in order to properly decode the header, IP must know where the IP header ends and the data begins.

Type of Service (ToS) Field The 8-bit *Type of Service* (ToS) field tells IP how to process the datagram properly. The precedence portion of the field was an early attempt at *Quality of Service* (QoS). The first three bits

Figure 9-11
High level format of
IP datagram

IP Header	IP Payload

Figure 9-12
IP datagram format

0	1	2	3	4	5	6	7	8	9	10	11	12	13	14	15	16	17	18	19	20	21	22	23	24	25	26	27	28	29	30	31
Version				Hdr. Length				Type of Service (TOS)								Total length															
Identification																Flags			Fragment Offset												
Time To Live (TTL)								Protocol								Header checksum															
Source IP address																															
Destination IP address																															
Options (If Any)																								Padding							
...Data																															

indicate the datagram's precedence, which increases proportionally to the value. That value can range anywhere from 0 (normal) through 7 (network control). However, most current implementations of TCP/IP and practically all hardware that uses TCP/IP ignores this field, treating all datagrams with the same priority. The next three bits are 1-bit flags that control the delay, throughput, reliability, and monetary cost of the datagram. If the bit is set to 0, the setting is normal. A bit set to 1 implies low delay, high throughput, high reliability, and low monetary cost for their respective flags. The last bit of the field is not used and set to 0. For most purposes, the values of all the bits in the type of service field are set to 0 because differences in precedence, delay, throughput, reliability, and monetary cost between machines are virtually nonexistent unless a special network has been installed. Figure 9-13 shows how the ToS byte in the header breaks down into bits.

Total Length Field   This 16-bit field indicates the total length of the datagram, including the header, in bytes. The length of the data area itself can be computed by subtracting the header length from this value. The size of the total datagram length field is 16 bits, which obviously means that the entire packet cannot exceed 65,535 bytes, including the header. This field is used to determine the length value to be passed to the transport protocol in order to set the total frame length.

Identification Field   The 16-bit identification field contains a value that is a unique identifier created by the sending device. This number is necessary for the reassembly of fragmented messages to make sure that the fragments of one message are not mixed in with others. Each unit of data received by the IP layer from a higher protocol layer is assigned one of these unique identifiers when the data arrives. If a datagram is fragmented, each fragment has the same unique identifier. The sending device numbers each packet, incrementing the value after each packet is sent. This value doesn't necessarily have to start at zero and also doesn't necessarily increment by one on all IP implementations.

Flags Field   The flags field is a 3-bit field. The first bit is reserved and should always be set to 0. The other two bits are called the *Don't Fragment* (DF) and the *More Fragment* (MF). When the DF flag is set to 1, the data-

Figure 9-13

ToS byte in IP header of IP datagram

0	1	2	3	4	5	6	7
Precedence			D	T	R	M	0

gram cannot be fragmented under any circumstances. If this bit is set to 1, then the datagram is discarded and an error message sent back to the sending device. When the MF flag is set to 1, it means that the current datagram are to be followed by more packets or sub-packets. Then these packets need to be reassembled in order to re-create the original message. When a series of packets have their DF bits set for fragmentation, then the last fragment sent will have its MF flag set to 0 so that the receiving device knows the final fragment has been received and can then reassemble the rest of the fragments. Because the fragments may not arrive in the order in which they were sent, the MF flag is used in conjunction with the fragment offset field (the next field in the IP header) to tell to the receiving machine the full extent of the message. Figure 9-14 shows how the flags field in the header breaks down into bits.

Fragment Offset Field   If the MF flag bit is set to 1, meaning that these are the fragment of a larger datagram, the 13-bit fragment offset field identifies the position in the chain of fragments that is occupied within the current datagram. This enables IP to reassemble the fragments in the right sequence. These offsets are relative to the beginning of the message. These offsets are calculated in units of 8 bytes, corresponding to the maximum packet length of 65,535 bytes. The IP layer on the receiving machine uses the identification number, which indicates the message the transmitted datagram belongs with, to reassemble the complete message.

Time to Live (TTL) Field   *Time to Live* (TTL) is an 8-bit field that indicates the amount of time, in seconds, that a datagram can remain on the network before being discarded. The sending device sets this value. The TTL field is generally set at 32 or 64. The value of the TTL field is decreased by no less than one second for each device through which the packet travels. When the packet is processed by a router, the arrival time is noted so that should the datagram have to wait in the queue, the TTL can be decremented accordingly. If that router is overloaded significantly, the packet can actually die in the queue. Once the TTL value reaches 0, it is immediately discarded. When this happens an *Internet Control Message Protocol* (ICMP) message is sent to notify the original sending device to which the packet was discarded so that the device can retransmit the datagram. The purpose of TTL field is to prevent IP packets from circulating through networks forever.

Figure 9-14
Breakout of the flags field

0	1	2
R	DF	MF

Protocols Field This 8-bit field is an identification number of the transport protocol in the IP payload. Obviously, this allows for a maximum of 256. Table 9-1 lists the more common numbers you are likely to encounter.

Table 9-1

Most Common
Transport Protocol
Identification
Numbers

Value	Protocol
0	IPv6 Hop-by-Hop Option
1	ICMP, Internet Control Message Protocol
2	IGMP, Internet Group Multicast Protocol
3	GGP, Gateway to Gateway Protocol
4	IP in IP Encapsulation
6	TCP, Transmission Control Protocol
8	EGP, Exterior Gateway Protocol
9	IGRP
17	UDP, User Datagram Protocol
18	Multiplexing
27	RDP, Reliable Data Protocol
28	IRTP, Internet Reliable Transaction Protocol
33	Sequential Exchange Protocol
35	IDPRP, Inter-Domain Policy Routing Protocol
37	Datagram Delivery Protocol
42	SDRP, Source Demand Routing Protocol
43	IPv6 Routing header
44	IPv6 Fragment header
45	IDRP, Inter-Domain Routing Protocol
46	RSVP, Reservation Protocol
47	GRE, General Routing Encapsulation
50	ESP, Encapsulating Security Payload
51	AH, Authentication Header
53	IP with Encryption
57	SKIP
83	VINES
88	EIGRP
89	OSPF, Open Shortest Path First Routing Protocol
92	MTP, Multicast Transport Protocol
94	IP-within-IP Encapsulation Protocol
108	IPPCP, IP Payload Compression Protocol
111	IPX in IP
112	VRRP, Virtual Router Redundancy Protocol
115	L2TP, Level 2 Tunneling Protocol

Header Checksum Field This 16-bit field is a checksum for the protocol header field only in order to enable faster processing. Because the TTL field is decremented at each device, the checksum too changes with every device that the datagram passes through. The checksum algorithm takes the ones-complement of the 16-bit sum of all 16-bit words. This is a fast algorithm, but it can miss unusual errors like the loss of an entire 16-bit word that contains only 0s. Because the data checksums used by both TCP and UDP cover the entire packet, these types of errors usually can be caught as the frame is being assembled for the network transport.

Source IPAddress Field This 32-bit field contains the logical source IP addresses of the sending device and is not altered at any time along the way to its destination.

Destination IP Address Field This 32-bit field contains the logical destination IP addresses of the receiving device and is not altered at any time along the way to its destination.

Options Field This is a variable length field that includes several codes of variable length. More than one option can be used in the datagram. If more than one option is used, they are listed consecutively in the IP header. Figure 9-15 illustrates the options field.

All the options are controlled by a single byte that is usually divided into three fields:

- 1-bit copy flag
- 2-bit option class
- 5-bit option number

The copy field of this byte is used to stipulate how the option is handled when fragmentation is necessary in a gateway. When the bit is set to 0, the option should be copied to the first datagram but not subsequent ones. If the bit is set to 1, the option is copied to all the datagrams.

The option class field in this byte indicates the type of option. When the value is 0, the option applies to datagram or network control. A value of 2 means the option is for debugging or measurement purposes. The values 1 and 3 are currently reserved for future use.

The options field in this byte includes options that enable the routing and timestamps to be recorded. These are used to provide a record of a

Figure 9-15
Options field

0	1	2	3	4	5	6	7
C	Class		Options				

datagram's passage across the internetwork, which can be useful for diagnostic purposes. Both these options add information to a list contained within the datagram.

Two kinds of source routing are indicated within the options field. Loose source routing provides a series of IP addresses that the machine must pass through, but it enables any route to be used to get to each of these addresses. Strict source routing enables no deviations from the specified route. If the route can't be followed, the datagram is abandoned. Strict routing is frequently used for testing routes but rarely for transmission of user datagrams because of the higher chances of the datagram being lost or abandoned. Both of these settings are highly suspect in today's security-conscious networks and are almost always denied at any router or firewall because of the obvious damage that can be caused when anyone can control the paths of packets. Table 9-2 lists the options and the IETF *Request for Comments* (RFCs) that refer to them.

Padding Field The value of the padding area depends on the options selected. The padding is used to make sure that the datagram header ends on and that the data starts on a 32-bit boundary.

Address Resolution Protocol/Reverse Address Resolution Protocol (ARP/RARP)

A device uses the ARP protocol to find the hardware or physical address of another device on the same network by broadcasting an ARP request. The request includes the IP address of the device whose physical address is being requested. By virtue of it being a broadcast, all of the devices on the network process the packet, but only the device whose IP address is in the packet responds with a directed transmission to the device requesting the physical address. The RARP protocol does the reverse of this process as the name suggests. Their packets are identical and shown in Figure 9-16.

Figure 9-16
ARP/RARP format

0	1	2	3	4	5	6	7	8	9	10	11	12	13	14	15	16	17	18	19	20	21	22	23	24	25	26	27	28	29	30	31
Hardware type																Protocol type															
Hardware address length								Protocol address length								Option code															
Source hardware (MAC) address																															
Source IP address																															
Destination hardware (MAC) address																															
Destination IP address:																															

Table 9-2

Options and
Referenced RFCs

Option	Copy	Class	Value	Length	Description	References
0	0	0	0	1	End of Options List	RFC 791
1	0	0	1	1	No Option (used for padding)	RFC 791
2	1	0	130	11	Security (military purposes only)	RFC 791, RFC 1108
3	1	0	131	variable	Loose Source Route	RFC 791
4	0	2	68	variable	Time Stamp (adds fields)	RFC 781, RFC 791
5	1	0	133	3 .. ?	Extended Security	RFC 1108
6	1	0	134		Commercial Security	
7	0	0	7	variable	Record Route (adds fields)	RFC 791
8	1	0	136	4	Stream ID	RFC 791, RFC 1122
9	1	0	137	variable	Strict Source Route	RFC 791
10	0	0	10		Experimental Measurement	
11	0	0	11		Maximum Transmission Unit (MTU) Probe	RFC 1063
12	0	0	12		Maximum Transmission Unit (MTU) Reply	RFC 1063
13	1	2	205		Experimental Flow Control	
14	1	0	142		Experimental Access Control	
15	0	0	15			
16	1	0	144		IMI Traffic Descriptor	
17	1	0	145		Extended Internet Protocol	
18	0	2	82		Traceroute	RFC1393
19	1	0	147		Address Extension	RFC 1475
20	1	0	148	4	Router Alert	RFC 2113
21	1	0	149	variable	Selective Directed Broadcast Mode	RFC 1770
22	1	0	150		NSAP Addresses	
23	1	0	151		Dynamic Packet State	
24	1	0	152		Upstream Multicast Packet	

Internet Control Message Protocol (ICMP)

This *Internet Control Message Protocol* (ICMP) is exploited often when malicious hackers attack a network. The reason lies in the name of the protocol itself. The ICMP carries a lot of weight in the IP stack. It can control how computers and routers behave when messages are received, and nothing in the protocol enables checking the credibility of the message. It is similar to you unconditionally trusting my word when I tell you that Highway 101 is closed so that you take a street through a bad part of town to get to work. While you are on that street you are subject to many dangers, just as packets that are redirected from their proper path through a malicious network where the packet can be examined even before it is sent on its way.

ICMP messages are generated for several reasons. When a datagram cannot reach its destination, when the router does not have the buffering capacity to forward a datagram, and when the router can direct the host to send traffic on a shorter route, messages appear. IP was not designed to be reliable, and the purpose of ICMP is to provide information about problems in the communication path. No guarantee exists that a datagram will be delivered or that a control message will be returned. Some datagrams may be undelivered without any report of their loss. It is up to the higher layer protocols to implement their own reliability procedures. No ICMP messages are sent concerning the fates of other ICMP messages. Figure 9-17 diagrams the fields of an ICMP header and message.

The ICMP Header   The 8-bit message type field in the ICMP header contains the type of message being sent. Table 9-3 lists the most common instances of this value.

The 8-bit code field expands on the message type, providing a little more information for the receiving machine

The checksum in the ICMP header is calculated in the same manner as the normal IP header checksum.

The ICMP Message   The many different types of ICMP messages that can be sent are listed in Figure 9-18.

Figure 9-17
Format of the ICMP message

0 1 2 3 4 5 6 7	8 9 10 11 12 13 14 15	16 17 18 19 20 21 22 23 24 25 26 27 28 29 30 31
Type	Code	ICMP header checksum
ICMP message		

Table 9-3

ICMP Common
Message Types

Value	Description
0	Echo Reply
3	Destination Not Reachable
4	Source Quench
5	Redirection Required
8	Echo Request
11	Time to Live Exceeded
12	Parameter Problem
13	Timestamp Request
14	Timestamp Reply
15	Information Request (now obsolete)
16	Information Reply (now obsolete)
17	Address Mask Request
18	Address Mask Reply

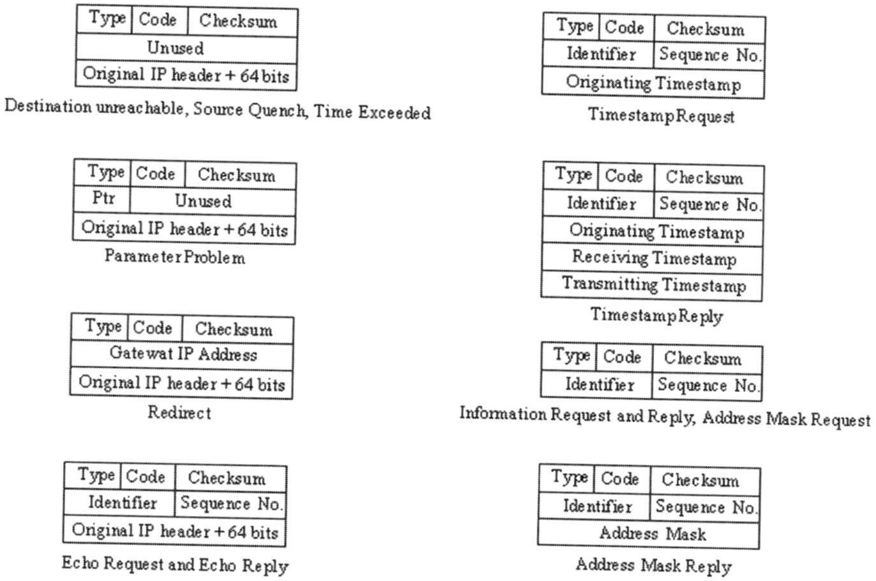

Figure 9-18
The various ICMP
type messages

Type	Code	Checksum
Unused		
Original IP header + 64 bits		

Destination unreachable, Source Quench, Time Exceeded

Type	Code	Checksum
Ptr	Unused	
Original IP header + 64 bits		

Parameter Problem

Type	Code	Checksum
Gatewat IP Address		
Original IP header + 64 bits		

Redirect

Type	Code	Checksum
Identifier	Sequence No.	
Original IP header + 64 bits		

Echo Request and Echo Reply

Type	Code	Checksum
Identifier	Sequence No.	
Originating Timestamp		

Timestamp Request

Type	Code	Checksum
Identifier	Sequence No.	
Originating Timestamp		
Receiving Timestamp		
Transmitting Timestamp		

Timestamp Reply

Type	Code	Checksum
Identifier	Sequence No.	

Information Request and Reply, Address Mask Request

Type	Code	Checksum
Identifier	Sequence No.	
Address Mask		

Address Mask Reply

The Destination Unreachable and Time Exceeded messages are not only used for the obvious reasons but in other instances as well, such as when a datagram must be fragmented but the DF flag is set.

Source Quench ICMP messages are used for flow control. When a device receives a Source Quench message it slowly reduces the transmission until it stops receiving Source Quench messages. When a given device's buffer is full, it sends a Source Quench message for each datagram that it discards.

ICMP Redirect messages are sent to a device when a better route is known. When a router receives datagram and sees that it has a "better" route, it sends an ICMP Redirect message to the source of the datagram with the IP address of what it considers to be the better route. When a Redirection message is sent, a value is placed in the code field of the header to indicate the conditions for which the new route applies. A value of 0 means that datagrams for any device on the destination network should be redirected. A value of 1 indicates that only datagrams for the specific device should take the new route. A value of 2 implies that only datagrams for the network with the same ToS, read from one of the IP header fields, should take the new route. A value of 3 will only reroute for the host with the same ToS.

Parameter Problem messages are used whenever a syntax is detected in the IP header. When a Parameter Problem message is sent back to the sending device, the parameter field in the ICMP error message contains a pointer to the byte in the IP header where the error was detected.

ICMP Echo Request and Echo Reply messages, also referred to as *Packet InterNet Groper* packets (PING), are easily the most common forms of IP troubleshooting used today and probably in the future. The PING command sends a series of Echo Requests and waits for Echo Replies. Whenever an Echo Request is sent, a device or router down the path sends an Echo Reply back to the requesting device.

Timestamp Requests and Replies can be used to measure the amount of time a packet takes to cross a given distance in a network. When combined with strict source routing, it can identify bottlenecks.

Address Mask Requests and Replies are used for testing within the parameters of a specific network or subnet.

TCP/IP Transport Layer Protocols

Now we move into the transport layer where upper layer protocols are spared the complexities of the network layer and where the protocols tell packets which applications will use its contents. The two players in this field are UDP and TCP. Before talking about UDP and TCP, it is important that you understand the concepts behind ports and sockets.

Ports and Sockets

When one process wants to communicate with another process, it first identifies its upper layer protocols by what are known as ports. A port is a 16-bit number; mathematically this means it must be in a range from 1 to 65535. The transport layer protocols such as UDP and TCP use these ports to identify which upper layer protocol or application program (process) to which the incoming messages are to be delivered. Many protocols such as TELNET, FTP, and SMTP use the same port number in all TCP/IP implementations. These ports have been assigned to these protocols by the *Internet Assigned Numbers Authority* (IANA) and are referred to as well-known ports and the standard applications are referred to as well-known services. The assigned well-known ports occupy the port numbers in the range of 0 to 1023. The ports with numbers in the range 1024-65535 are not controlled by the IANA, and on most systems, can be used by ordinary user-developed programs. These days, however, it is usually agreed that the ports from 1024 to 49151 are better left to standard uses and are generally referred to as *registered ports*. The ports ranging from 49152 to 65535 are considered to be public and anybody can use them. These are referred to as *ephemeral ports*. Until recently the registered ports were only up to 5000 and above that they were ephemeral. The explosive growth of Internet applications soon expanded this number. It is important to keep aware of these port numbers when setting up filters on your routers and firewalls. Usually port 0 is used as a wild card and also for requesting the kernel to find a port for users.

Every network connection going into and out of a host's port is uniquely identified by a combination of 2 numbers: the IP address of the machine and the port number in use, which together, loosely translated, make up a socket. Because at least two computers are involved in any connection, sockets are put on both the sending and receiving ends of the connection. And because both the IP addresses and the ports are unique to each machine, the sockets are also unique. This is how applications talk to each other across the network—communication is based entirely on the socket number. Both machines on the connection maintain port lists that list all active ports, and the two machines involved have reversed entries for each session between them. This process is called binding. For example, if one machine has a source port at 23 and the destination at 25, the other machine will have a source port at 25 and a destination at 23.

Two kinds of sockets have been developed. The first is called a stream socket, which is connection-oriented in nature and relates to TCP. The other is called a datagram socket, which is connectionless in nature and relates to UDP.

UDP

UDP does very little as transport protocols are concerned. Apart from multiplexing and simple error checking, it really adds nothing to IP. Should the application developer choose UDP over TCP, the application ends up communicating almost directly with the IP protocol. UDP takes messages from application processes, attaches source and destination port number fields for the multiplexing service, adds length and checksum fields, and then passes the resulting segment to the network layer. The network layer encapsulates the segment into an IP datagram and then makes a best-effort attempt to deliver the segment to the receiving host. If the segment arrives at the receiving host, UDP uses the port numbers and the IP source and destination addresses to deliver the data in the segment to the correct application process. With UDP, no handshaking occurs between sending and receiving transport-layer entities before sending a segment. This is why UDP is considered to be a connectionless protocol. Figure 9-19 is a diagram of a UDP segment.

Source Port   Populating the 16-bit source port field is optional. If it is not used, it is set to 0. Otherwise, it specifies the port of the sender.

Destination Port   This 16-bit field indicates the port on the destination machine.

Length   This 16-bit field specifies the length in bytes of the UDP header and the encapsulated data. The minimum value for this field is 8.

Figure 9-19
Diagram of the UDP segment

0	1	2	3	4	5	6	7	8	9	10	11	12	13	14	15	16	17	18	19	20	21	22	23	24	25	26	27	28	29	30	31
Source Port																Destination Port															
Length																Checksum															

Checksum   Checksum is computed as the 16-bit 1's complement of the 1's complement sum of a pseudo header of information from the IP header, the UDP header, and the data, padded as needed with zero bytes at the end to make a multiple of two bytes. Wow! That's a mouthful (but not a very important one, go ahead and spit that out if you want. OK, you can rinse now.)

TCP

TCP provides connection-oriented, acknowledged services to the IP layer and the upper layer protocols, which enables an application to be sure that datagrams sent out over the network are received in the order sent and in their entirety. Unlike UDP, TCP provides for reliable communications. If a datagram is damaged or lost, TCP handles the retransmission, rather than the applications in the higher layers. It does this by sequencing the segments with a forward acknowledgment value that tells the destination which segment the source expects to receive next. If an acknowledgement is not received within a given period of time, then those segments are retransmitted. The reliability mechanism of TCP makes it possible to handle missing, delayed, duplicate, or damaged packets. A timeout mechanism enables devices to detect lost packets and request retransmission.

Many people think that because it is mentioned in the same breath as TCP/IP that it somehow relies on or is tied to the IP protocol. This is not the case. TCP is a completely independent protocol capable of being used with almost any underlying protocol. TCP is used in the *File Transfer Protocol* (FTP) and the *Simple Mail Transfer Protocol* (SMTP), neither of which use or rely on the IP protocol. This protocol is typically used by applications that require guaranteed delivery.

Sliding Window   TCP uses a sliding window algorithm to provide a method for efficient segment transfers as well as for handling both timeouts and retransmissions. The byte stream is transferred in segments. The window size determines the number of bytes of data that can be sent before an acknowledgement from the destination device is received. Figure 9-20 displays the sliding window.

TCP establishes a full duplex virtual connection between the two endpoints. Each endpoint is defined by an IP address and a TCP port number that defines its state. Because the connection state resides entirely in the two end systems and not in the intermediate network elements, such as routers, the intermediate network elements do not maintain the TCP connection states. Instead, the intermediate routers are completely oblivious to

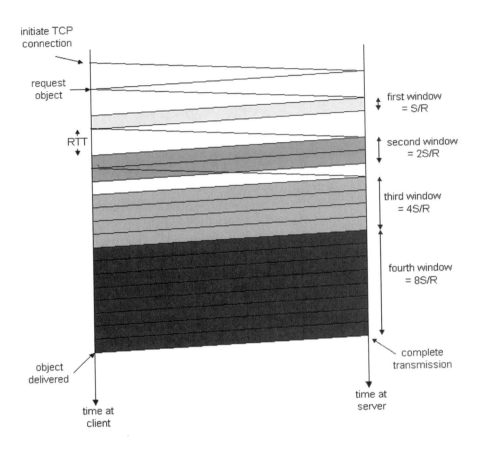

the TCP connections; they see only datagrams, not connections. Communications begin with what is known as a *three-way handshake*. The three-way handshake is a connection establishment procedure. The procedure synchronizes both ends of a connection by enabling both sides to agree upon initial sequence numbers. This procedure also guarantees that both sides are ready to transmit and receive data. This is necessary so that this data is not transmitted or retransmitted during session establishment or after the session is finished.

Three-Way Handshake   When host A wants to open a connection to host B, A sends an initial segment to B. The initial segment has the *Initial Sequence Number* (ISN) that B needs to use to send data to A. This initial segment is identified by the SYN bit set to 1 in the TCP header. If the SYN bit is set, the 32-bit sequence number in the header is interpreted as the ISN. In all other cases (when the SYN bit is not set), the 32-bit sequence number identifies the sequence number of the first data byte contained in that segment. When B receives the SYN from A, it has to respond with another SYN, as well as acknowledge the SYN sent by A. This is indicated by SYN+ACK in Figure 9-21.

When B receives the SYN from A, it must respond with another SYN and acknowledge the SYN sent by A.

When closing a connection, the three-way process is repeated. Connection release uses the FIN in place of the SYN as shown in Figure 9-22.

TCP Segment Header   To learn more about connection establishment procedure, the elements of the TCP segment header are examined in this section. Figure 9-23 diagrams this header.

Figure 9-21
State machine
diagram

Figure 9-22
Repeating the three-
way process

Figure 9-23
The TCP segment
header format

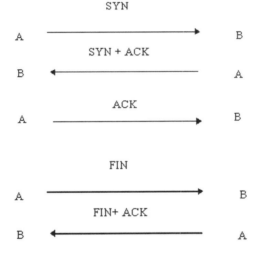

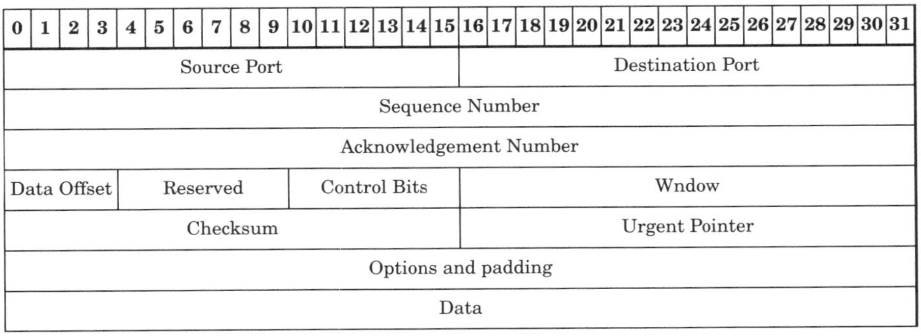

Source Port   The source port is a 16-bit field that identifies the local TCP user, and is usually an upper-layer application program.

Destination Port   The destination port is a 16-bit field that identifies the remote machine's TCP user.

Sequence Number   The 32-bit sequence number field represents the sequence number of the first data byte in this segment. If the SYN bit is set, the sequence number is the initial sequence number and the first data byte is initial sequence number + 1.

Acknowledgment Number   If the ACK bit is set, this 32-bit field contains the value of the next sequence number that the sender of the segment is expecting to receive. Once a connection is established, this is always sent.

Data Offset   The 4-bit Data Offset field represents the number of 32-bit words in the TCP header. This indicates where the data begins. The length of the TCP header is always a multiple of 32 bits.

Reserved   A 6-bit field is reserved for future use. The six bits must be set to 0.

Control Bits   The six control bits are shown in Figure 9-24 and are outlined in the following bulleted list.

- **U, URG**: The significant urgent pointer field.
- **A, ACK**: The significant acknowledgment field.
- **P, PSH**: The push function field.
- **R, RST**: The reset connection field.
- **S, SYN**: The synchronization sequence number field. This indicates that the sequence numbers are to be synchronized. This flag is used when a connection is being established.
- **F, FIN**: The end of data field. This indicates that the sender has no more data to send. This is the equivalent of an end-of-transmission marker.

Figure 9-24
Control bits

0	1	2	3	4	5
U	A	P	R	S	F

Window   The 16-bit window field represents the number of data bytes beginning with the one indicated in the acknowledgment field which the sender of this segment is willing to accept.

Checksum   This is computed as the 16-bit 1's complement of the 1's complement sum of a pseudo header of information from the IP header, the TCP header, and the data, padded as needed with zero bytes at the end to make a multiple of two bytes. The pseudo header contains the following fields:

Urgent Pointer   This 16-bit field is used if the URG flag was set; it indicates the portion of the data message that is urgent by specifying the offset from the sequence number in the header. No specific action is taken by TCP with respect to urgent data; the action is determined by the application.

Options   Similar to the IP header option field, this is used for specifying TCP options. Each option consists of an option number (one byte), the number of bytes in the option, and the option values. Only three options are currently defined for TCP:

- **0:** End of option list
- **1:** No operation
- **2:** Maximum segment size

Padding   Padding is used to make sure that the header is a 32-bit multiple.

TCP/IP Application Layer Protocols

In this section some of the application layer protocols will be discussed, concentrating on the protocols most likely to be attacked. This is where you can apply what you learned in the Ports and Sockets section. DNS will be examined first.

Domain Name System (DNS)

Domain Name System (DNS) is a distributed database system used to map hard-to-remember IP addresses into easy-to-remember common names. A good example is something like a phone directory. When you want to call someone, you know their name, and look up their number. When you want to connect to a certain type of Web site, all you need to remember is the URL. However, the computer needs the numerical IP address in order to communicate with this Web site, and that's where DNS comes in.

The domain name server keeps a table of hosts and their IP addresses. When a computer needs to resolve a name to an IP address, it does what is known as a lookup, which is basically sending the name to the *domain name server* (DNS) and the DNS server responds with the IP address. It does this by sending either UDP or TCP (depending on whether it is a request or a zone transfer) but most of the time it will be UDP packets to port 53. The message has a fixed 12-byte header and four variable length fields, which you can see in Figure 9-25. The earlier sections covered protocols in depth, but in this section you don't need such intimate security details are not needed. However, you should be aware that this is one of the most vulnerable and attack-prone protocols.

The reason that DNS servers are so attractive to malicious hackers is because once a DNS server has been compromised, it can be fooled into redirecting. A client makes use of this server directly to and through the hackers computer. Because of this impersonation, man-in-the-middle attacks are easy to perform. If you don't harden your DNS servers against false zone transfer packets, then false information can be fed to it, and then the hacker will be in charge of your name space. That is not what you want to happen, trust me.

Chargen Chargen is generally used as a troubleshooting tool. It works by sending out a continuous stream of ASCII characters. It is useful for testing network applications. Although intrinsically not a danger to your system, it can be used to annoy or overload systems that are vulnerable to

Figure 9-25
Format of the DNS lookup segment

0	1	2	3	4	5	6	7	8	9	10	11	12	13	14	15	16	17	18	19	20	21	22	23	24	25	26	27	28	29	30	31
Identification																QR	Opcode				AA	TC	RD	RA	0			Rcode			
Total Questions																Total Answer Resource Records															
Total Authority Resource Records																Total Additional Resource Records															
Questions																															
Answer Resource Records																															
Authority Resource Records																															
Additional Resource Records																															

a continuous flood of ASCII characters in a weak kind of DoS attack. It uses UDP and TCP port 19. It is a data only packet that uses no headers.

Echo   This is another tool that is useful in testing networks. It essentially repeats to a client whatever the client sends to it. Again it is not a threat to your system in terms of being able to take control, but it is a popular protocol to use in DoS attacks. It uses UDP port 7. It is a data only packet that uses no headers.

Finger   The finger service is a tool that is used to help people discover things such as the last time a user checked their email, as well as things like office hours, telephone numbers, projects, and other personal data. This information is essential to malicious hackers trying to glean usernames and password possibilities. Again, this probing does not cause much damage to the network system itself, but should be blocked. It is rarely used anymore for obvious reasons. It used TCP port 79. It is a data only packet that uses no headers.

FTP

FTP is a protocol used for just what it says: file transfers. It is very popular and also can be used to remotely update Web content on Web servers. Its usefulness makes it tough to block completely and it usually has a way through the firewall. The way it works is that a client will open a connection to the FTP control port (TCP port 21) of an FTP server. To ensure that the server will later be able to send data back to the client machine, a second FTP data port (TCP port 20) connection must be opened between the server and the client. To make this second connection, the client sends a PORT command to the server machine. This command includes parameters that tell the server to which IP address to connect and which port to open at that address, which in most cases is intended to be an arbitrary higher numbered port on the client machine. The server then opens that connection, with the source of the connection being port 20 on the server and the destination being the arbitrary higher numbered port specified in the PORT command parameters. If you are not careful, a malicious hacker could use the nature of this process to bypass a firewall or filtering router in certain network configurations. For example, assume that a site has its FTP server behind the firewall. Using any number of port scanning techniques, our malicious hacker can determine that an internal Web server at that site is available on port 8080, a port normally blocked by a firewall. By connecting to the public FTP server at the site, the malicious hacker can initiate a further connection between the FTP server and an arbitrary port on a non-public machine at that site (for instance the internal Web server at port 8080). As a result, the attacker establishes a connection to a machine that would otherwise be protected by the firewall. Hopefully now you can start to see how hackers can use ports and sockets to circumvent lax security.

HTTP

HTTP is a connectionless protocol, running over a TCP communications stream. An HTTP client sends a *Uniform Resource Locator* (URL), which contains a hostname and path portion (although the hostname can also include a port number for Web servers that do not necessarily have to use the standard of TCP port 80), to an HTTP server to establish a TCP stream connection. Even though it was stated that the client establishes a connection with a server, the protocol is called connectionless because once the server has responded to the client's request, the connection between client and server is dropped and forgotten. Memory ceases between client connections. HTTP server implementations treat every request as if it were brand new. Other protocols typically keep the connection open such as in an FTP session where you can move around in remote directories, and the server can keep track of who and where you are.

An HTTP connection generally consists of a header followed by an empty line and some data. The header specifies things such as the action expected of the server, the type of data being returned, or a status code. The use of header fields sent in HTTP transactions gives the protocol a lot of flexibility. These fields allow descriptive information to be sent in the transaction, enabling authentication, encryption, and/or user identification. The header is a block of data preceding the actual data and is often referred to as meta-information. Meta simply means something about something. Basically, meta-information is simply information about more information. HTTP is a complex protocol, which is why it is a favorite of malicious hackers. The more complex something is, the harder it is to protect. Because HTTP is not dynamic, many add-ons such as ActiveX and Java make this a very big security risk indeed and in both directions. This means sites exist that are just as malicious as individuals trying to get into your site. Once an ActiveX control has been downloaded and run onto a client computer in your network, it can assume the same degree of privilege as any program running on that machine. All of this happens behind your firewall and without your knowledge. You must take great care when setting up a firewall to screen for all of these things.

NetBIOS

Meet the malicious hacker's best friend in the world. Windows is easily the most ubiquitous operating system in the world and is a favorite of the least sophisticated users. That is a bad combination. Don't misunderstand; Net-BIOS itself is not the danger, although it can be when you leave all of the ports and features open. The problem is that unsophisticated users don't know that they should, or how, to turn them off. The first rule of network security is to block incoming access to TCP ports 135, 137, and 138, as well as UDP port 139 on your router. These ports are used by the NetBIOS over the TCP/IP protocol stack.

Network File System (NFS)

Meet the UNIX equivalent of NetBIOS. NFS is not secure because the protocol was not designed with security in mind. NFS sends all file data over the network in clear text. Even if a malicious hacker is unable to get your server to send him a sensitive file, he or she can just wait until a legitimate user accesses it, and then can pick it up as it goes by on the network. NFS uses UDP and TCP port 2049. You should always block this port as well.

Remote Procedure Call (RPC)

The *Remote Procedure Call* (RPC) protocol is one that enables two devices to coordinate the execution of software routines. A program on one device will use RPC to transfer the execution of a sub-routine to another computer and have the result returned back to this same device via RPC. RPC can be dangerous and you should not let RPC traffic through any firewall.

Simple Mail Transport Protocol (SMTP)

Simple Mail Transfer Protocol (SMTP) is the protocol by which mail clients, and other user agents, send mail messages over the Internet. SMTP transactions take place over a TCP communications stream, usually on TCP port

25. SMTP is used solely for sending mail. You obviously need to allow this protocol, but it is important that you know which port it uses.

Simple Network Management Protocol (SNMP)

The *Simple Network Management Protocol* (SNMP) is a protocol that enables the exchange of management information between network devices. SNMP enables network administrators to manage network performance, find and solve network problems, and plan for network growth. This protocol can be dangerous because it can do just as the name implies; it can manage devices. Computers by their nature are very trusting and can't wait to do what you tell them. Many versions of this protocol have no way of authenticating the source of the command. You should always block SNMP at your firewall. It uses UDP port 161.

Telnet

Telnet is simply a remote login protocol that enables a user on one host to establish a connection with a remote host and interact as if the user was physically present at his terminal. The problem from a security standpoint is that none of the traffic is encrypted and when you are logging on, both your username and password can be read by any device listening on the network. Telnet uses TCP port 23 and you should always consider blocking this port on your firewall.

Security Issues

Packet Sniffing

One of the most common ways to glean information from your network is by using what is called a packet sniffer or network analyzer. Many of these programs are completely free and easy to use. Once a host has been compromised, the sniffer software can be loaded onto it and then can listen on the Ethernet port for things such as "Password," "Login," and "su" in the packet stream as well as the traffic that follows it. This way, attackers can find out passwords for systems they are not even attempting to break into.

Clear text passwords are very vulnerable to this attack. This can be done even easier by people internally. They can load the software themselves and do the same thing. Remember, most malicious activity on computer networks occurs from inside the organization.

IP Spoofing

IP spoofing is when one machine pretends to be another machine. The spoofing machine does this by convincing a server that its source address is that of a machine with which it originally intended to communicate. Machines that transmit data to one another do so by providing source and destination addresses in the IP packet. If you forge these at just the right time, you can convince another computer that you are the intended source and recipient. This technique can be used to find out user accounts, passwords, and other damaging information. Another way is by using IP source routing; an attacker's host can impersonate a trusted host or client. IP source routing is an option that can be used to specify a direct route to a destination as well as the return path back to where it originated. The route can literally mandate and can involve the use of other routers or hosts that normally would not be used to forward packets to the destination. You could do this by masquerading as a trusted client of a given server in the following manner:

1. First, the attacker could change his machine's IP address to be the same as a trusted client machine.

2. Then this attacker would create a source route to the server by specifying the exact path that the IP packets should take to the server and from the server back to the attacker's machine, using the trusted client as the last hop in the route to the server.

3. A client request is sent by the attacker to the server using this source route.

4. The client request is then accepted by the server just as though it came directly from the trusted client and then returns the reply to the trusted client.

5. The trusted client, using the source route, forwards the packet on to the attacker's host.

Another way to spoof a client, which is even easier, is to simply wait until his machine is turned off and *then* impersonate the client's machine. One way to do this would be to use NFS to obtain access to server directories and files (NFS uses IP addresses only to authenticate clients). Then, after hours, simply configure a machine with the same name and IP address and then initiate connections to the server as if it were the "real" client.

Denial of Service

Denial of Service (DoS) is an attack designed to render a computer or network useless and incapable of providing normal services. The most common DoS attacks will target network bandwidth or connectivity. Bandwidth attacks flood the network with so much traffic, that all of the network resources are consumed, making it impossible for normal users to get through. Connectivity attacks flood a computer with so many connection requests, that all available operating system resources are consumed, and the computer can no longer process normal user requests. Another kind of DoS attack variant is called a *Distributed Denial of Service* (DDoS) attack. This uses multiple computers to launch a synchronized DoS attack against one or more targets. Using client/server technology, the attacker is able to multiply, also known as amplifying, the effectiveness of the DoS significantly by using the resources of multiple unwitting accomplice machines as distributed attack platforms. Here are some of the more common methods used for DoS attacks:

- **SYN Flood** - SYN flooding is a network DoS attack. It takes advantage of the way TCP connections are created. A SYN flood attack simply sends TCP connection requests faster than a machine can process them.

    1. First, the attacker creates a random source address for each packet.
    2. Then, the SYN flag set in each packet is a request to open a new connection to the server from the spoofed IP address.
    3. The victim then responds to the spoofed IP address and waits for confirmation that never arrives (usually about 3 minutes).
    4. This causes the victim's connection table to fill up while waiting for these replies.
    5. Once the table is full, all new connections are ignored.
    6. A SYN flood can be used for other types of attacks, such as disabling one side of a TCP connection in preparation for a session hijacking attack or by preventing authentication or logging between servers.

- **Land Attack** - The Land Attack uses IP spoofing in combination with an initial TCP connection. It sends a packet where the SYN flag in the header is set during the opening of a TCP connection. Then, the IP addresses in the underlying IP packet are altered. In a Land Attack, both the source and destination IP addresses are modified to be identical in the address of the destination host. Once the destination host receives the packet, it answers to the SYN request. When answering, the destination host first creates a packet with the ACK flag set, and then changes the destination address to the source address and vice versa. So, if both addresses are identical, then the machine obviously starts sending the packet back to itself. Now the machine is in an ACK war against itself, which continues creating a DoS situation.

- **ICMP Flood** - This DoS attack sends such a large amount of ICMP echo request packets to the target machine that it cannot respond quickly enough to handle the amount of traffic on the network. First the attacker will spoof his source IP, otherwise, his machine would be a victim of its own attack because it would not only use resources to send the packet but also to receive packet responses. Now it just continues to send packets, while the target has to use resources to receive *and* reply to the packets. Multiply this by a distributed attack across multiple machines, and the target will easily be brought down. *Intrusion detection system* (IDS) services on routers and firewalls can be programmed to limit ICMP echo requests or drop them entirely from entering the subnet.

- **Ping of Death** - The Ping of Death attack sends ICMP echo request packets (pings) that are larger than the operating system's data structures storing this information can hold because sending a single, large ping packet to many systems will cause them to hang or even crash.

- **Smurf Attack** - The Smurf attack is one that takes advantage of a feature in the IP stack known as directed broadcasts. A Smurf attack will flood your router with ICMP echo request packets (pings). Because the destination IP address of each packet is the broadcast address of your network, your router will broadcast the ICMP echo request packet to all hosts on the network. The more machines connected to the network, the more ICMP echo request and response traffic that will be generated. Should the attacker choose to spoof the source IP address of the ICMP echo request packet, the resulting ICMP traffic will not only clog up your network (the "intermediary" network) but will also congest the network of the spoofed source IP address known as the "victim" network by sending ICMP echo reply packets. To prevent a network from becoming an intermediary, you would want to turn off broadcast addressing on any network routers that enable it or configure the firewall to filter the ICMP echo requests. To avoid becoming the victim of the attack itself, set the firewall or routers to filter ICMP echo replies or limit echo traffic to a small percentage of overall network traffic.

- **UDP Flood** - The *User Datagram Protocol* (UDP) is a connectionless protocol. It does not need to establish a connection to transfer data. Because no connection setup is required before data is transferred, it is difficult to bring a host down by flooding the host with just UDP packets. A UDP Flood DoS attack is created when the agent host sends a packet to a random port on the target machine. When the target host receives a UDP packet, it will determine what is listening on the destination port. If nothing is listening, then it will return an ICMP packet to the forged source IP address notifying that the destination port is unreachable. If enough UDP packets are sent to dead ports on the target host, not only will the target host go down, but computers on the same segment will also be disabled because of the amount of traffic.

- **TearDrop Attack** - Most networks have a maximum packet size that they can handle. This packet size is called the *Maximum Transfer Unit* (MTU). If the underlying network cannot transport a given packet because it is too large, the packet has to be broken up into smaller pieces. This is called fragmentation. Once the packet fragments have reached their final destination, the packet is reassembled from the fragments. Both fragmentation and reassembly are done in TCP/IP by the IP layer. When the IP layer receives an IP packet, it typically does the following:

  1. First, it verifies that the packet is at least as long as the IP header and makes sure that the header is contiguous.
  2. Then, it runs a checksum on the header of the packet to check for any errors. If errors are present, the packet will be dropped.
  3. It then verifies that the packet is at least as long as the header indicates. If it is not, the packet will be dropped.
  4. Then it processes the IP options if any exist.
  5. It checks to see if the packet is for this machine. If it is, it will continue processing the packet. If it is not, it will either forward it or drop it.
  6. If the packet has been fragmented, it will keep the fragment in a queue until all other fragments have been received.
  7. Finally, it passes the packet to the upper levels.

TearDrop attacks exploit these procedures by trusting the information in the packet headers of the fragments. If you overlap these fragment offsets, then you can cause the system to crash, causing a DoS.

Password Attacks

Password Attacks can happen in any number of ways:

- **Network sniffing** - A malicious hacker could use a network sniffer to view all data transmitted over a network. As the password is transmitted across the network, the hacker could capture it and store it for later use.

- **Trojan Horse** - Some Trojan Horse programs can capture passwords as they are typed in at the user's keyboard.

- **Brute Force** - In a brute force attack, a specially designed computer program tries to guess your password by trying every single combination of characters until your password is found.

- **Dictionary Attack** - Instead of trying to guess your password by trying every single possible combination of characters as in a brute force attack, the attacker may use the dictionary attack and try every word in a dictionary or multiple-dictionaries until your password is found. This method is popular because it is well-known that many people use common words as passwords.

- **Social Engineering** - Social engineering is the easiest and most successful form of them all. Social engineering is a way of tricking and conning people into providing information to help you unwittingly.

Application Layer Attacks

Application layer attacks can be implemented using several different methods. One of the most common methods is exploiting well-known weaknesses in software commonly found in the stack. Examples of the services in the TCP/IP stack that are commonly exploited are as follows:

- **File Transfer Protocol (FTP)** performs stateful, basic interactive file transfers between hosts.

- **Telnet** enables users to execute terminal sessions remotely.

- **Simple Mail Transfer Protocol (SMTP)** is a very basic message delivery service.

- **HyperText Transfer Protocol (HTTP)** is a stateless, connection-oriented and object-oriented protocol with simple commands that select and transport objects between the client and the server.

- **Domain Name Service (DNS),** also called *name service,* is an application that maps IP addresses to the names assigned to network devices.

- **Routing Information Protocol (RIP)** is central to the way TCP/IP works. RIP is used by network devices to exchange routing information.

- **Simple Network Management Protocol (SNMP)** is used to collect management information or MIB's from different network devices.

- **Network File System (NFS),** a system developed by Sun Microsystems, enables computers to operate drives on remote hosts as if they were local drives.

By exploiting these weaknesses, attackers can gain access to a computer with the permissions of the account running the application, which usually has permissions that can do a lot of damage.

One of the newest forms of application layer attacks exploits the openness of several new technologies used commonly on the Web today. Examples include new HTML specifications, Web browser functions, and other popular protocols such as *Internet Relay Chat* (IRC). These attacks, which include Java applets and ActiveX controls, involve passing harmful programs over the Internet and into your network by loading them through the victim's browser.

Firewalls

Now that you have been given some background on protocol, packets, layers, ports, and sockets you can get an idea of what firewalls are and how they work to secure your network from the data itself. Remember the biggest obstacle in network security isn't errant data—it is people. Firewalls are synonymous with locks and keys in the real world. The saying, "locks keep honest people honest" carries the same meaning when it comes to firewalls. You could have the most sophisticated firewalls, DMZ, and perimeter security in the world and one simple modem attached to some employee's PC inside your network can bring the whole system to its knees, without your or your employee's knowledge. Always keep this fact in mind. That being said, let's talk about firewalls.

Firewalls or gateways are tools consisting of three types that provide for security. They can be used as standalone items or in concert with some or all of the other types. The design you choose depends on the resources available to you, the level of security you require, the degree of convenience you wish to maintain, and any number of the other factors unique to your situation. The three types discussed are:

- Packet-filtering gateways
- Circuit-level gateways
- Application-level gateways

We will be discussing them in this order, so let's begin with packet-filtering.

Packet-Filtering Gateways

Packet-filtering gateways are the most rudimentary form of firewalls. They work by examining packets as they come into and leave your network. You will also hear terms like ingress and egress. Those terms, respectively, refer to packets entering and leaving the network, which is a standard feature of any good router. The router inspects the contents of the packet's headers to see the source IP address, the destination, the protocol, and so on to decide whether to let it pass or to drop it. Most packet-filter implementations are done at what are called border routers. The reason for the name is because they tend to sit at the border between your internal network and the outside world. Most packet-filters are stateless.

Stateless and Stateful

You will hear the terms stateful and stateless when packet-filters are discussed. Most router based firewalls are stateless. This means that each packet is evaluated on its own merit and on a packet-by-packet basis. Stateless (also known as static) packet-filters do not maintain call setup information between client and server. You will recall in the Protocols Description section an explanation of connection-oriented protocols like TCP and the applications that use them, such as FTP. In FTP, the client would send a PORT command to the server machine. This command would include parameters to tell the server which socket (IP address to connect to and port to open at that address) to connect to, which would be some arbitrary, higher numbered port on the client machine. This is what creates a "state" of communications. If we wanted to keep track of the state of this connection, then the outgoing PORT command of an FTP session would have to be remembered so that an incoming FTP data connection can be verified against it. Stateless packet filters don't do this. A client requests information on one TCP port, causing the server to return data at some arbitrary TCP port above the well-known range. In this scenario, which is typical of FTP, all ports above 1,023 must be opened. This enables a malicious hacker to create Trojan horses that wait for packets entering at ports above 1,023 and ride in on top of them.

Stateful packet filters will listen to all communications and store these conversations in memory so that responses are returned on expected ports from expected IP addresses. Ports will be opened only if the stateful device determines that these packets are part of a conversation from a machine originating the request. If the packet matches a conversation stored in memory, it lets it pass through. When the conversation is completed, the port closes so that should a packet be returned without the expected response, the packet will be dropped.

How Packet Filtering Works

A packet-filtering router inspects every packet and determines where to deliver it based on the source, destination, and port addresses. A packet filter is a software feature set on the router that lets you control IP addresses, protocol types, TCP/UDP ports, and source routing information. You then use the packet-filtering software to configure what the router passes or drops and defines which devices users can access inside or outside the firewall from specific servers at a given TCP or UDP port. This filtering may be performed as the packets enter the router, exit the router, or a combination of the two. As a rule, Cisco routers will let everything through by default. However, once you tell the router that you wish for it to inspect these ACL packets, the router becomes very literal indeed. This means that once you tell the router to let all packets with source address 192.10.15.20 through, then the router says to let all packets from that address through and promptly drops everything on the planet that doesn't come from that address. This is known as the implicit deny. This characteristic is always in place whether or not you specify it at the end of every access list. It is also very literal in terms of the order of the request you make. If you tell it to let all packets through but to deny 192.10.15.20, it will perform the first command before moving on to the next request (the deny). So it is important that you make a request in logical order that the router can interpret directly. Figure 9-26 is a representation of where packet-filtering gateways relate to the OSI reference model.

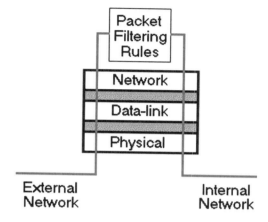

Figure 9-26
How packet-filtering gateways relate to the OSI reference model

Apart from filtering by source and destination addresses, you can also filter protocols or port numbers. You can either do it by filtering entire suites of protocols such as UDP, ICMP, TCP, and so on, but this tends to be a bit too general. As a rule, packet-filters are used to filter data based on the following criteria:

- The physical network interface on which the packet arrives
- Source address from where the data is (supposedly) coming (source IP address)
- Destination address to where the data is going (destination IP address)
- The type of transport layer (TCP, UDP, ICMP)
- The transport layer source port
- The transport layer destination port
- Whether this packet is a start of a connection request or not

You can, for example, decide to set up a policy blocking the SMTP mail port number 25. Although port 25 is indeed the normal mail port, it is not possible to control the use of that port on an outside host. A malicious hacker could easily access any internal machine and port by originating his call from port 25 on the outside machine. A better policy would be to permit outgoing calls to port 25. That is, you want to permit your hosts to make calls to someone else's port 25 so that you can be sure that it is in fact mail delivery that is taking place.

A TCP conversation consists of packets flowing in two directions. Even if all of the data is flowing one way, acknowledgement packets and control packets must flow the other way. You can accomplish what you want by paying attention to the direction of the packet and by looking at some of the control fields. In particular, an initial open request packet in TCP does not have the ACK bit set in the header, like all other TCP packets do. So, packets with the ACK bit set are part of an ongoing conversation. Packets without the ACK bit set represent connection establishment messages, which you permit only from hosts inside your network. The idea is that an outsider cannot initiate a connection, but can continue one.

ICMP is a different story in that the ICMP protocol layer does not utilize port numbers for its needs, so it is difficult for packet filters to apply any kind of real security policy to this form of network traffic. In order to apply an effective security policy to ICMP, the packet filter must maintain state tables to ensure that an ICMP reply message was recently requested from an internal host. This requires stateful packet-filtering capabilities. Since most packet filters are implemented in the network layer, they generally do not understand how to process state information in the higher-level protocols, such as FTP. Some of the more sophisticated packet filters are able to detect IP, TCP, UDP, and ICMP. Using a packet filter that includes the TCP/UDP port filtering capability enables you to permit certain types of connections to be made to specific computers while prohibiting other types of connections to those computers and similar connections to other computers.

Headers also contain other information deeper inside the packet for options like source routing. Source routing and fragmentation are a favorite technique of malicious hackers. The problem is that source routing makes address spoofing, which is pretending to be from an address that is not yours, very easy. Once the malicious hacker can spoof a source IP address, then he can do whatever that address has been authorized to do. Source routing overrides any normal routing tables. Normally you can easily send random TCP packets with a bogus source address, and normally you won't see the reply. Although that's not a perfect defense against attacks, it does make them much more difficult. With source routing, however, the malicious hacker will manually specify the hops that the packet should take on its way back to him. What's worse is that when a TCP packet arrives via source-routing, the destination host is supposed to turn the route around for response packets, making it so that all of the reply packets will arrive at the malicious hackers machine. This is not what you want, trust me.

The upside to stateless packet filters is that they work at close-to-wire speeds, which means that it is not very processor intensive. For Cisco routers in particular, it has to do with whether or not you choose to do extended ACLs over standard ACLs when it comes to processor usage. Generally, the best solution is a combination of packet-filtering routers used in conjunction with true firewalls and/or proxy devices, which are covered later in the chapter.

One thing to always keep in mind is that packet filtering is not limited to just routers and firewalls. Most operating systems come with some form of packet-filtering capabilities that can be implemented at the host level, which can provide a lot more protection. This is also known as end-system filtering because it is the last stop for the packet. Remember a lot of your biggest threats come from within, so it is good policy to have this last line of defense. Think of it as a backup firewall should your perimeter security be compromised.

Circuit-Level Gateways

All that circuit-level gateways do is relay TCP connections. When an outside user tries to connects to a TCP port on a given system, it first connects to the port on the circuit-level gateway, which then connects to the destination on the internal network. During the conversation, the circuit-level gateway simply copies the bytes from the outside system to the destination system and vice versa. The circuit-level gateway acts like a wire or pipe, copying bytes between the inside connection and the outside connection. However, because the connection appears to originate from the gateway itself, it conceals information about the protected network. A circuit-level gateway monitors TCP handshaking between packets from trusted clients or servers to foreign hosts and vice versa to determine whether a requested session is legitimate. Figure 9-27 is a representation of where circuit-level gateways relate to the OSI reference model.

How Circuit-Level Translation Works

To see whether or not a requested session is legitimate, a circuit-level gateway goes through a series of steps. The following is an example (referring to the Protocol Description section might help clarify some of these steps):

1. A trusted client requests a service, and the gateway accepts this request, assuming that the client meets basic filtering criteria (such as whether DNS can locate the client's IP address and associated name).

2. Next, acting on behalf of the client, the gateway opens a connection to the requested foreign host and then closely monitors the TCP

Figure 9-27
Circuit-level gateway
relationship in OSI

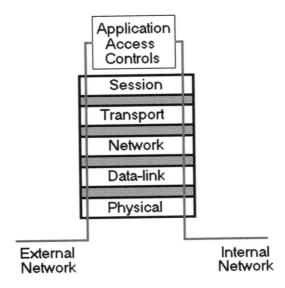

handshaking process that follows the connection. This handshaking process involves the exchange of TCP packets that have their SYN or ACK bits set. These packet types are legitimate only at certain points during the session.

3. The first packet of a TCP session has the SYN bit set, indicating a request to open a session. This packet contains a random initial sequence number. For example, the trusted client might transmit a SYN packet with 1000 as the initial sequence number. Then the return packet from the foreign host will have the ACK bit set, acknowledging the receipt of the client's SYN packet. In this example, the foreign host would transmit an ACK packet numbered 1001, which is the next number in the sequence established by the trusted client.

4. Now the foreign host also transmits a packet with an initial sequence number, such as SYN 2000, for its side of the connection. The trusted client then transmits an ACK 2001 packet, which is the next number in the sequence, acknowledging receipt of the foreign host's SYN packet and marking the end of the TCP handshaking.

A circuit-level gateway determines that a requested session is legitimate only if the SYN and ACK bits are set, and that the sequence numbers involved in the TCP handshaking process between the trusted client and the foreign host are logical and legitimate. Once a circuit-level gateway determines that the trusted client and the foreign host are authorized to participate in a TCP session and verifies the legitimacy of this session, the gateway enables establishment of the connection. From this point on, the circuit-level gateway simply copies and forwards packets back and forth. It no longer needs to filter them.

The circuit-level gateway maintains a table of established connections, enabling data to pass when session information matches an entry in the table. When the session is completed, the gateway then removes that particular entry in the table and closes the circuit for that session. So with a circuit-level gateway, all outgoing packets appear to have originated from that gateway, preventing direct contact between the trusted network and the foreign host. The circuit-level gateway's IP address is the only active IP address and the only IP address that the foreign host is aware of. This helps to protect trusted networks from spoofing attacks by foreign hosts.

Circuit-Level Weaknesses

A circuit-level gateway isn't perfect and has vulnerabilities. For example, once a circuit-level gateway establishes a connection, any application can run on top of that connection because a circuit-level gateway filters packets at the session layer of the OSI model only. This means that a circuit-level gateway cannot examine the application-level content of the packets it relays between a trusted network and a foreign network. Because a circuit-level gateway does not filter individual packets but instead just relays packets back and forth across established connections, a malicious hacker on a foreign network could possibly slip malicious packets past the gateway. The malicious hacker could then deal directly with an internal server. As long as the initial TCP packets exchanged between the trusted internal server and the foreign host meet the handshaking criteria, the gateway establishes a connection and copies and forwards subsequent packets regardless of their content. To filter the application-level content of individual packets generated by particular services, you need an application-level gateway.

Application-Level Gateways

Like a circuit-level gateway, an application-level gateway intercepts incoming and outgoing packets, copies and forwards information across the gateway, and functions as a go-between or proxy, which prevents any direct connection between a trusted server or client and a foreign host. However, the proxy service that an application-level gateway offers differs from the proxy services in two important ways offered by circuit-level gateway:

- The proxy is application specific.
- The proxy can filter packets at the application layer of the OSI model.

Application-level gateways only accept packets generated by services they are designed to copy, forward, and filter. For example, only a Telnet proxy can copy, forward, and filter Telnet traffic. If a network relies only on an application-level gateway, incoming and outgoing packets cannot access services without a proxy. For example, if an application-level gateway ran FTP and Telnet proxies, only packets generated by these services could pass through the firewall. All other services are blocked. Unlike a circuit-level gateway, an application-level gateway examines and filters individual packets, rather than simply copying them and blindly forwarding them across the gateway. Application-specific proxies check each packet that passes through the gateway, verifying the contents of the packet up through the application layer of the OSI reference model. Application-level gateways can filter particular kinds of commands or information in the application protocols they are designed to copy, forward, and filter. For example, you can be as specific as preventing users from using the FTP PUT command. This PUT command enables anyone who can access an FTP server to write to it. Many network administrators prohibit use of the PUT command to limit the risk of someone altering or damaging information stored on an FTP server. Figure 9-28 is a representation of where application-level gateways relate to the OSI reference model.

Another key benefit is that most application-level gateways log activities and note significant events, intrusion detection, and other anomalies by sounding alarms, sending pages, emails, and so on. It maintains logs that record the source and destination addresses of packets associated with attempted or successful entries into your system, the time these attempts were made, and the protocol used.

Drawbacks

An application-level gateway is one of the most secure firewalls available and takes away from the transparency and speed provided by other gateway types. Ideally, an application-level gateway would be as transparent as it is secure. Users on the trusted network would not notice that they were accessing Internet services through a firewall. The reality, however, is that

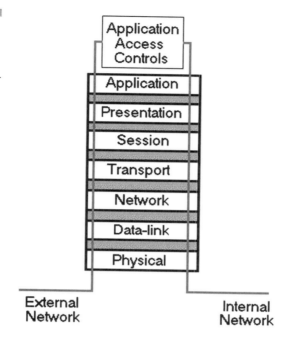

Figure 9-28
Application-level
gateway relationship
to OSI

users will often experience delays or need to login several times before they
are connected to the Internet or an intranet via an application-level gateway. Another common problem is that you get timeouts when trying to
access virtually anything on the Internet. This goes back to deciding how
granular you wish your security to be when compared to the inconvenience
and lack of productivity that can be a consequence of such granularity.

Designing Intrusion Detection Systems (IDS)

Intrusion detection systems (IDSs) are designed to know when your system
is being probed or attacked. It generally collects information from different
sources at strategic vantage points in the network, analyzes the information and sends alarms, drops data or entire segments, implements counter-
measures, and performs any number of other responses. It is not entirely
passive in that it doesn't just wait for something to happen. It probes itself
for weaknesses and looks for any statistical anomalies in the data it cap-

tures. Most intrusion detection operates by examination of three areas: misuse detection, anomaly detection, and signature recognition.

Misuse Detection

Misuse detection involves encoding information about specific behaviors known to be indicators of intrusion and then filtering this data for these indicators.

Misuse detection involves the following:

- A good understanding of what "misuse" is
- A reliable record and baseline of user activity
- A reliable way for analyzing these records

Misuse detection is best used for detecting known use patterns. One of its weaknesses is that you can only detect about what you know. You can, however, use your knowledg to spot new exploits of old problems.

Anomaly Detection

Sometimes referred to as statistical analysis, this method involves finding deviations from normal patterns of behavior, hence the term anomaly. The most common way people approach network intrusion detection is to detect these statistical anomalies. The idea behind this approach is to measure a baseline of CPU utilization, disk activity, user logins, file activity, and so on. Averages in frequency and variability are then calculated. Then, the system can trigger alarms when a deviation from this baseline occurs. The benefit of this approach is that it can detect the anomalies without having to understand the underlying cause behind the anomalies.

For example, you monitor the traffic from individual workstations. Then, the system notes that at 2 a.m., a lot of these workstations start logging into the servers and carrying out tasks. This is something interesting to note and possibly take action on.

Signature Recognition

Most products are based upon examining the traffic looking for well-known patterns of attack. This means that for every known hacker technique, a signature for this technique is then programmed into the system.

This can be as simple as a pattern matching or character string matching. One classic example of this is to example every packet on the wire for the pattern /cgi-bin/phf?, which might indicate somebody attempting to access this vulnerable CGI script on a Web server. Some IDS systems are built from large databases that contain hundreds (or thousands) of such strings. They sniff the network and trigger alarms and/or logs events for every packet they see that contains one of these strings.

Integrity Analysis

Integrity analysis generally focuses on file or object specifics and patterns, not unlike some virus protection schemes that look for attempts to change file size or location and duplication. Other methods include file attributes, directory structures, as well as content and data streams. Most of this can be accomplished using one-way hash algorithms such as MD5 and others.

Assessment Architectures

The following section outlines a couple of dependable assessment plans: host-based assessments and network-based assessments.

Host-Based Assessment

Host-based systems generally involve passive, non-invasive techniques that monitor system settings, system software and hardware configurations, file permissions, file ownership, software updates, and patches and system resources. To monitor system resource activity, agents are loaded on each machine and monitor disk space, RAM, CPU time, application use, and system audit trails. The collected information will then be compared to some given set of rules to determine if a security incident has indeed taken place.

These agents can be internal. In this arrangement, alarms and events are sent to the device itself. These agents can be managed remotely. Alarms and events would be sent through periodic updates and security information or polled individually. Some host-based systems include centralized management that make upgrades and new signature installation much easier. These systems are best suited for a limited number of devices that are not likely to change profoundly, as these implementations do not scale very well. They tend to work best when combined with a network-based IDS. Figure 9-29 is an example of a host-based architecture.

Network-Based Assessment

Unlike host-based systems, network-based systems use active, invasive monitoring techniques to detect possible vulnerabilities. A database of attack scenarios is available to run against target systems within the network. System analysis determines whether or not weaknesses or holes exist that can be exploited. Cisco's NetSonar is an example of such an implementation. Regular port scanning techniques are run on a regular basis to not only check for weaknesses but whether proper auditing and logging are up to par. Network-based systems are usually dedicated platforms involving two components: a sensor, for analyzing network traffic, and some kind of management device such as Cisco's NetRanger Director.

The sensors in a network-based IDS capture traffic on the network being monitored and analyze the traffic using configured parameters. The sensors analyze packet headers to determine source and destination addresses, type of protocol being used, and the packet payload. Once the sensor sees a violation, it can take a number of actions such as sending alarms, logging the event, resetting the data connection, or dropping any future traffic from that host or network. An example of a network-based system can be seen in Figure 9-30.

Figure 9-29
Host-based IDS
topology

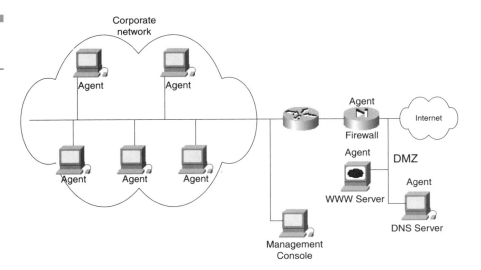

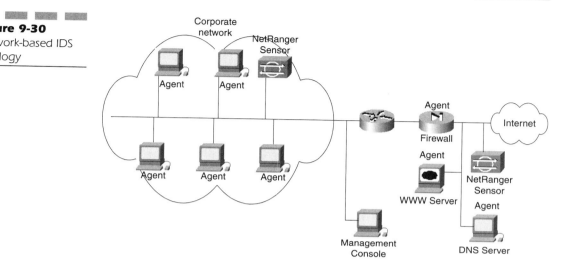

Figure 9-30
Network-based IDS topology

Cisco's IDS Components

Cisco offers a number of products that are all designed to work independently and in concert. Cisco's centralized management system is NetRanger Director. NetRanger can obtain and process alarm and event data from its other devices. NetRanger can work in combination with dedicated NetRanger Sensor devices, ACLs, and the Cisco IOS IDS feature of the IOS Firewall feature set for a comprehensive IDS solution. NetSonar is Cisco's active intrusion device software that can actively scan and probe for weaknesses. Figure 9-31 is a representation of a typical package and its components.

The NetRanger Director/Sensor Combination

NetRanger sensors can monitor almost any type of TCP/IP network, ranging from Internet connections, LAN segments, and the network side of dial-in modem pools as well as with business partners. A typical high-level diagram of sensor placement can be seen in Figure 9-32.

The sensor contains NetRanger real-time intrusion detection, which examines each individual packet, including its header and payload, as well as its relationship to adjacent and related packets in the data stream. Immediately after the sensor detects a policy violation, it sends an alarm to the centralized NetRanger director console.

Figure 9-31
Cisco IDS
components

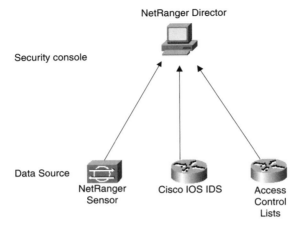

NetRanger Director

Security console

Data Source

NetRanger
Sensor

Cisco IOS IDS

Access
Control
Lists

Figure 9-32
High-level diagram of
sensor placement

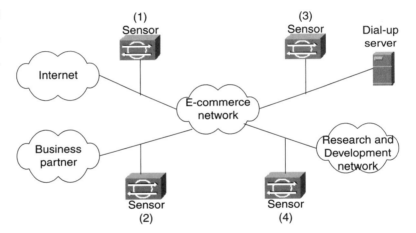

(1)
Sensor

(3)
Sensor

Dial-up
server

Internet

E-commerce
network

Business
partner

Research and
Development
network

Sensor
(2)

Sensor
(4)

Sensor installation requires seven addressing parameters and no special training. Once the sensor is installed, it immediately begins monitoring as a promiscuous mode device in the network. The NetRanger director then can be configured to find the sensor and begin receiving alarms. The sensors are self-contained devices that can be moved around the network at will.

The NetRanger sensor's uses a three-tier attack detection scheme that provides for comprehensive and effective intrusion detection capabilities that include the following:

■ **Name Attacks** are those with specific names such as Land, Smurf, and PHF.

- **General Category Attacks** are name attacks with many variations, such as Out-of-Band Data (Teardrop) or IP fragmented packets. This simplifies signature management and provides perpetual protection against new attack variations that would otherwise go undetected.

- **Extraordinary Attacks** have extremely complex signatures such as Simplex-Mode TCP hijacking or email Spam.

The NetRanger system can be configured to automatically shun or eliminate specific connections by actually changing ACLs on Cisco routers. This feature can be temporary or permanent. The rest of the network traffic functions normally; only the unauthorized traffic from internal users or external intruders is removed.

You can create custom security string-matching signatures and update the sensors when new attacks are discovered. This also enables you to search for evidence of misuse that is unique to your specific environment such as scanning for unique words in the data stream like proprietary or confidential and deal with them accordingly.

The NetRanger sensor comes with a comprehensive default configuration that can be set to whatever specification is required for any given environment. For example, if a user consistently receives ping sweep alarms from a network management system that is trusted, the user can program the sensor to ignore that specific alarm from that specific network address. All other alarms from that address would be recognized. It also has a hierarchical reporting architecture that can be configured to deliver different alarm levels to different NetRanger Directors. For example, multiple ping sweeps could constitute major alarm to a local NetRanger Director, but may only constitute a low-level alarm on the NetRanger Director in the central network operations center. NetRanger is not limited to just the Sensor/Director combination but can also work in conjunction with NetRanger Post Office and Cisco IOS Firewall Intrusion Detection.

NetRanger Post Office

The NetRanger post office is simply a communications infrastructure that enables sensors and directors to communicate with each other. The post office also enables for the transfer of configuration files and log files between other NetRanger devices. You can see an example of this in Figure 9-33.

Figure 9-33
Topology with the
NetRanger post office

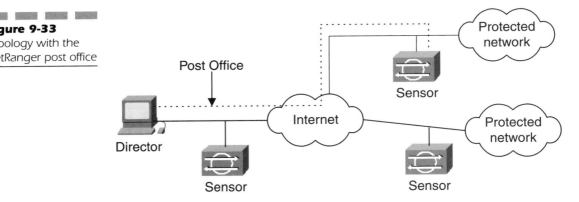

Cisco IOS Firewall Intrusion Detection

The Cisco IOS IDS feature of the IOS Firewall feature set is an option for Cisco routers to be used as a limited perimeter IDS but can work in conjunction with the NetRanger sensor/director combination. Cisco IOS IDS contains only a subset of signatures found on the NetRanger sensor. It was not designed to detect all attacks, but when combined with strong ACLs and a firewall, it can work as a very robust intrusion detection option. A high level view of a possible implementation can be seen in Figure 9-34.

The Cisco IOS IDS uses signatures to identify some of the more common attacks and can protect the network using three basic methods:

- Sending an alarm to a syslog or NetRanger director console
- Dropping the offending packet
- Resetting the TCP connection

Cisco IOS IDS signatures can be deployed alongside or independent of other Cisco IOS Firewall feature set options. Unlike the NetRanger sensor, the IOS version cannot dynamically configure an access list or ignore a specific host or network and cannot be configured by the NetRanger director. It uses ACLs bound to actual interface ports to either permit or deny packets over those same interface ports. Each numbered or named ACL contains permit and deny conditions that apply to IP addresses or types of traffic and then checks these conditions in the access list one at a time. The packets are accepted or rejected once a match is found. This is also used as a signal to stop testing conditions, making the order of these

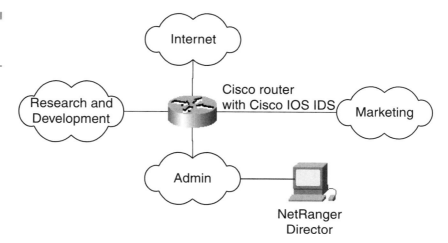

entries paramount. Before an ACL can send syslog data back to a NetRanger director, it must be configured to trap all log information. Each ACL deny rule must have the word "log" appended to the end of the line so that all policy violations that fail the ACL test will be reported to the NetRanger director.

CHAPTER 10

Designing Cisco VPN Solutions

When combined with Cisco *Internet protocol security* (IPSec) technology, the Cisco IOS Firewall feature set provides integrated *Virtual Private Network* (VPN) functionality. VPNs are developing rapidly to provide secure data transfer over public networks and the Internet. The obvious reason is that VPNs reduce the need for expensive leased lines. They also reduce the need for expensive IT personnel and avoid complex management.

The Cisco IOS Firewall feature set operates with Cisco IOS software encryption, tunneling, and *Quality of Service* (QoS) features to make these VPNs very secure. Network Layer encryption capability prevents monitoring sensitive data. One way hash functions eliminate tampering of data and guarantee authenticity and non-repudiation during transmission. The Cisco IOS Firewall feature set encrypts data for private communications over untrusted networks using the IPSec encryption standards with both 56-bit (DES) and 168-bit (3DES) varieties.

Cisco IOS software works with many tunneling protocol standards such as *Generic Routing Encapsulation* (GRE), *Layer 2 Forwarding* (L2F), and the *Layer 2 Tunneling Protocol* (L2TP). It also supports multiple QoS functions which are used to classify traffic, manage congestion, and prioritize traffic with fine granularity as needed.

The Cisco IOS Firewall feature set can be used with many Cisco VPN capable devices, such as the Cisco 1720, 2600, 3600, and 7100 series routers. These solutions extend an existing network to not only normal routing functions but VPNs as well all in the same box. The Cisco IOS Firewall, combined with a 7100 series router can provide scalable encrypted tunnels, while integrating strong perimeter security, advanced bandwidth management, and intrusion detection. The Cisco IOS Firewall authentication proxy feature also provides for user authentication and authorization on all Cisco VPN client software. Cisco makes three different kinds of VPNs:

- Access VPN
- Intranet VPN
- Extranet VPN

Cisco Access VPN

Access VPNs are used to provide remote access to corporate intranet or extranet over a shared infrastructure. Access VPNs can use analog, ISDN, xDSL, mobile IP, and cable technologies to provide secure access for mobile users, telecommuters, and branch offices. Two types of Access VPNs are available to implement: client-initiated and NAS-initiated.

■ **Client-initiated access VPNs**

In a client-initiated model, the encrypted tunnel is established at the client using IPSec, L2TP, or *Point-to-Point Tunneling Protocol* (PPTP), thereby making the service provider network solely a means of transport to the corporate network. An advantage of a client-initiated model is that VPN intelligence resides in the *customer premise equipment* (CPE), enabling VPN functionality to be delivered over any network infrastructure, including the Internet. Furthermore, in the client-initiated model, the "last mile" service provider access network used for dialing to the *point-of-presence* (POP) is secured. An additional consideration in the client-initiated model is whether or not to use common native security software, such as PPTP, or a more secure client software such as the Cisco Secure VPN client. While software installed on the client offers more security, it still involves installing and maintaining this software on each client accessing the remote access VPN. Figure 10-1 illustrates the client-initiated model.

■ **NAS-initiated access VPNs**

In a NAS-initiated VPN, the need for client software is eliminated. A remote user can simply dial into his local ISP using a PPP or SLIP connection. All authentication is handled by the service provider where upon the ISP initiates the secure tunnel to the corporate network using L2TP or L2F, which is then authenticated by the enterprise. With a NAS-initiated solution, VPN intelligence resides in the ISPs network so it is not necessary for the remote user to have a special client software installed, eliminating any client management issues. One thing to consider, however, is the lack of security on the local

Figure 10-1

Client-initiated model

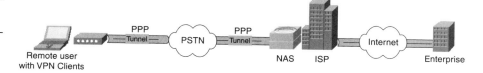

access dial network connecting the client to the service provider network and the required use of a single service provider end to end. Figure 10-2 illustrates the *Network Acces Server* NAS-initiated model.

Cisco Intranet and Extranet

Intranet and Extranet VPN services link remote offices, suppliers, partners, customers, and *communities of interest* (COINs) over a shared infrastructure with the same policies as a private network, as shown in Figure 10-3. Cisco include a range of ATM- and IP-based choices for large scale Intranet and Extranet VPN requirements. Here are some examples:

- IP tunnels based on IPsec, GRE, or mobile IP for wireless communication
- *Virtual circuits* (VCs) based on ATM or Frame-Relay technology
- *Multiprotocol Label Switching* (MPLS) whose QoS characteristics enable secure, time sensitive application VPNs

In all these cases, Intranet and Extranet VPN services create secure tunnels across an IP network. They take advantage of industry standards to establish secure, point-to-point connections in a mesh topology that utilizes

Figure 10-2
NAS-initiated model

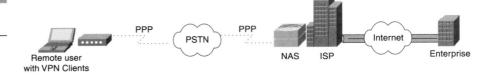

Figure 10-3
Intranet VPN

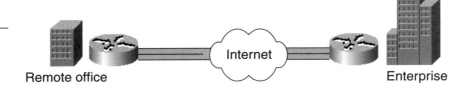

the service provider's trusted IP network or even the Internet. IPsec archi-tectures also include standards based IP based encryption, creating encrypted tunnels from the remote user to the intranet or extranet.

Just like Cisco's Access VPNs, Intranet and Extranet VPNs can use either the CPE-based or network-based models (see Figure 10-4). When IPsec is used, these Cisco devices can ensure the security of any data transmitted over the service provider's network.

Service providers can also set up very large scale intranet and extranet VPN services using a Cisco MPLS VPN solution. MPLS is protocol that is based on Cisco Tag Switching.

MPLS makes scalability and flexibility across any IP, IP+ATM, or mul-tivendor backbone possible. MPLS forwards packets using labels for VPN-based identifier. The VPN identifier in the label isolates traffic to a specific VPN. MPLS VPNs use connectionless routing within each VPN community. This enables service providers to scale their services to support thousands of VPNs on the same infrastructure that include all of the full QoS benefits enjoyed on IP and ATM environments.

Cisco IPsec Solutions

In an access VPN environment, the first important aspect of security revolves around identifying a user as a member of an approved customer

Figure 10-4
Extranet VPN

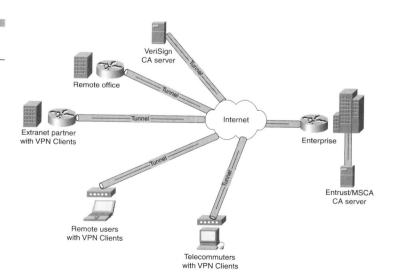

company and establishing a VPN session, often called a tunnel, to the customer network, typically through a VPN concentrator. The VPN concentrator handles per user authentication, security policy enforcement, and accounting. Authentication is based on a combination of user names and passwords, often using *one-time password* (OTP) products or digital certificates for businesses employing the emerging *public key infrastructure* (PKI) technologies. User authentication is a vital characteristic of an access VPN. Authentication has two stages: First, a client establishes communication with the ISP through a local POP. Then the client establishes a connection with the corporate network. The client initiates the VPN connection through the access provider network, usually using PPP or L2TP, and is then authenticated using a protocol such as *Password Authentication Protocol* (PAP), *Challenge Handshake Authentication Protocol* (CHAP), or *Remote Access Dial-In User Service* (RADIUS). The access provider gateway maintains a relationship with an *access control server* (ACS), also known as an *authentication, authorization,* and *accounting* (AAA or triple-A) server to authenticate the user. When the remote user is authenticated and has an IP connection, the VPN tunnel is created by using the policies stored in the VPN concentrator. This is done either at the customer network edge, on the CPE or as an additional service in the service-provider network.

Now that you have an idea of what is involved, we will now go over in detail exactly what takes place during the creation of these VPNs.

What is a VPN?

VPN is simply an acronym for Virtual Private Network. You also may have seen it represented as a *Virtual Private Dial-up Network* (VPDN). So much for the acronyms. To define what these acronyms mean you must first understand what took place prior to their "invention." This chapter begins with a brief discussion about the "olden days," when companies used private networks.

Prior to the Internet, companies that had geographically dispersed locations created *Wide Area Networks* (WANs) to tie their *Local Area Networks* (LANs) together by leasing private lines from public telephone carriers. These might have included T carriers (T1/T3), *Asynchronous Transfer Modes* (ATMs), Frame Relay, *Integrated Services Digital Networks* (ISDNs), and even X.25s or *Public Switched Telephone Networks* (PSTNs). Mobile users used the PSTN, or possibly an ISDN connection, to dial in to access servers maintained by these companies at given locations around the world. These networks were considered private because they were, for all practical purposes, the only ones using these leased lines.

With the advent of the Internet (you've probably heard of this recent phenomenon), the rules changed. Companies had many compelling reasons for having a presence on this new information super-highway by connecting themselves to *Internet Service Providers* (ISPs) that had direct connections to the Internet. This posed some interesting new problems, namely, privacy. Having their private WANs connected to the Internet exposed their networks to anyone and everyone on this new Internet, thus creating the need for firewalls.

Today this need can be met with a VPN. A VPN is a virtual network that is kept private by tunneling this private data through the underlying infrastructure of the public Internet. A VPN uses the Internet or other public network service as all or part of its WAN backbone. In a VPN, PSTN or ISDN dial-up connections for remote users, as well as expensive leased lines such as ATM or Frame Relay connections for LANs at remote sites, are replaced with inexpensive local connections to an ISP. A VPN also enables a private intranet to be tunneled securely through the Internet, making secure e-commerce and extranet connections possible with other business partners, suppliers, and customers. Tunneling enables two corporate sites to connect in a secure manner by using the infrastructure of the Internet transparently as what appears to be its own private network in just a single hop. The security is accomplished by using end-to-end authentication and encryption, thus saving money by replacing long-haul links with local links and reducing the cost of maintaining and constantly upgrading their *Customer Premise Equipment* (CPE) telecommunications devices.

This chapter discusses each of the many different types of tunneling, but first we'll start off with a brief overview of the basics. Tunneling is a technology that enables one network to send its data over another network's connections. It works by encapsulating a network protocol within packets carried by the second network, which involves taking this data and encapsulating it inside a protocol that is understood at the entry and exit points of this other network. These entry and exit points are the end points of the tunnel. The system at the entry point encapsulates the data, while the system at the exit point removes this data from the encapsulation. To clarify, tunneling creates circuit-like connections across the packet-oriented Internet. Instead of using a packet-oriented protocol such as the *Internet protocol* (IP), which might send packets across a variety of different routes before they reach their common destination, a tunnel represents a dedicated virtual circuit between two endpoints. However, because it works across a shared-network infrastructure, tunneling gives enterprises a cost-effective solution between packet and leased-line communications.

To create the virtual circuit, a special tunneling protocol must encapsulate each source network packet into a new packet that contains the connection management intelligence necessary to set up, tear down, and manage the tunnel. The great thing about this is that it doesn't matter *what* kind of protocol is carried. It could be AppleTalk, Novell *Internetwork Packet Exchange* (IPX), DECnet, *Systems Network Architecture* (SNA), *NetBIOS Extended User Interface* (NetBEUI), anything, routable or not! You could even use non-Internet, routable, reserved IP addresses set aside in RFC 1918 (10.0.0.0, 172.16.0.0, 192.168.0.0, and so forth) internally, obviating the need for *Network Address Translation* (NAT). Now if that's not a deal, I don't know what is. This is a big factor in what makes VPN so secure. The following sections detail the special tunneling protocols that one can choose from.

A Tunnel from the Past

To help grasp the concept of tunneling, it is helpful to understand some recent history in the development of the tunneling protocols being used today. In the mid-nineties, it was becoming apparent that the concept of VPNs had the potential of becoming a very lucrative market. At that time, a couple of small companies that you have probably never heard of (Cisco and Microsoft) were working on two different tunneling protocols. Microsoft (for the most part) was developing the PPTP, an OSI layer 2 protocol that encapsulates PPP packets into IP packets.

Cisco, on the other hand, was busy working on the L2F protocol that would, unlike PPTP, use typical data link protocols such as ATM, Frame Relay, and so on. I was actually hoping *you* might be able to extract which OSI layer the L2F protocol occupies (feel free to email me should you get stuck here.) Then, considering the size of these two behemoths, they realized that perhaps the best thing to do would be to combine these two protocols into the L2TP and again emails are still welcome. These protocols are generally considered to be best for host-to-host tunnels as opposed to LAN-to-LAN.

To address this problem and to avoid the problems that come with proprietary solutions, a working group of the *Internet Engineering Task Force*

(IETF) set about finding a way to make the IP protocol itself more secure. This Layer 3 solution was known as Secure IP or IPSec. IPSec defines two headers in IP packets to handle authentication and encryption. The IP *Authentication Header* (AH) is for authentication, while the *Encapsulating Security Payload* (ESP) is for encryption purposes. These, in conjunction with other technologies that will be touched on, such as the *Generic Routing Encapsulation* (GRE) protocol, are the most common methods used in tunneling today.

Another alternative that has been making progress is SOCKS. This is a session layer (layer 5) protocol that supports all IP transported applications, including the *Transmission Control Protocol* (TCP) and *User Datagram Protocol* (UDP). Because it is a session layer protocol, it operates independent of any application. It has been in development since about 1990 and is now an IETF standard (RFC 1928). SOCKS does not encapsulate traffic, and therefore does not compete with standard tunneling protocols. However, SOCKS does brings other benefits to VPN environments using these protocols such as user-level authentication and encryption, continuous access control for any existing connections, uni-directional security, and application-specific security. Version 5 includes encryption negotiation. Any firewall can be configured to pass SOCKS traffic transparently.

As protocols such as IPSEC, L2TP, and SOCKS mature, tunnels will interconnect much easier. All of these technologies can now be used in conjunction with each other to increase compatibility between systems, to help create transparency for the user, and to make VPNs extremely secure.

Tunneling Protocols

Before discussing the actual tunneling protocols, it is important to understand the kinds of tunnels that are created with these protocols. The two types of tunnels are as follows:

- **Voluntary tunnels:** This is where the remote PC initiates the tunnel. This is also known as a *client-initiated tunnel*. It is called a voluntary tunnel because the end device is in control of the tunnel creation. In this situation, the remote PC is the tunnel endpoint.

- **Compulsory tunnels:** This involves an intermediate device, which is usually a NAS, located at some ISP POP that is VPN-aware. Any client can dial in with a non-VPN protocol, usually PPP, and connect to the ISP NAS. At this point, the NAS creates a compulsory tunnel with some host VPN server. With a compulsory tunnel, the remote PC is not the tunnel endpoint. The ISP NAS that sits between the remote PC and the host VPN server is the tunnel endpoint and acts as the tunnel client. This is also referred to as a *NAS-initiated tunnel*.

As a rule, voluntary tunnels tend to be the most popular type. However, sometimes a combination of the two is best (L2TP is a good choice), because not all the computers that you will allow to access your VPN will always have the required VPN client software necessary for a pure voluntary tunnel. It is important to understand that the terms mentioned previously are completely synonymous (that is, voluntary/client-initiated and compulsory/NAS-initiated). This point must be reiterated because different companies use these terms interchangeably (as will we!) depending on their marketing approach. If you take a look at Figure 10-5, you can get an idea of what takes place and the tunneling protocols that are used in each type.

Voluntary Tunnels

Voluntary tunnels are those created by a remote PC initiating a secure connection with a host VPN. This means that an appropriate *and* compatible tunneling protocol must be installed on the remote PC or client computer. Voluntary tunnels must also have some kind of an IP connection. It can be

Figure 10-5
Tunneling protocols

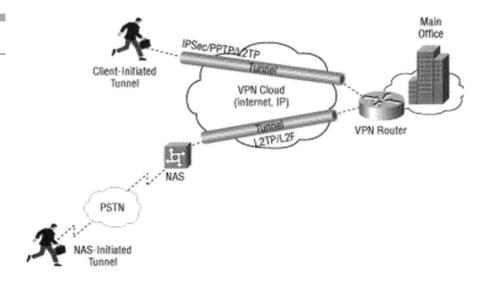

a dial-up connection or even be directly attached to the LAN locally. Here are two possible situations:

- Let's say you are dialing in to the network. First, you must establish a dial-up connection to the internetwork before the computer can set up a tunnel. This is the most common situation. A good example of this is the dial-up Internet user, who must dial an ISP and obtain an Internet connection before a tunnel over the Internet can be created.

- For a LAN-attached PC, the client already has a connection to the internetwork that can provide routing of encapsulated payloads to the chosen LAN tunnel server. This would be the case for a client on a corporate LAN that initiates a tunnel to reach a private or hidden subnet on that same LAN for a Human Resource department, for example.

All that is required is some form of IP connection. Some clients use dial-up connections to the Internet to establish the IP connection. This is a preliminary step in preparing to create a tunnel and is not part of the tunnel protocol itself.

Compulsory Tunnels

A number of ISPs' network access servers are able to create a tunnel on behalf of a dial-up client. The computer or network device providing the tunnel for the client computer is variously known as a *Front End Processor* (FEP) in PPTP, an *L2TP Access Concentrator* (LAC) in L2TP, or an IP Security Gateway in IPSec. For the rest of this section, the term LAC will be used because it is the most common. However, what the device is usually called depends on the tunneling protocol being used on the NAS. Generally what happens is that a corporation has an agreement with an ISP to deploy a nationwide set of LACs that establish tunnels across the Internet to a host VPN server connected to the corporation's private LAN. This enables calls from geographically dispersed locations to go through a single Internet connection located at the corporate network. The reason it is called a compulsory tunnel is that the client is compelled to use the tunnel created by the LAC. After the connection is made by the remote PC, all the network traffic to and from the remote PC is automatically sent through the tunnel that sits between the LAC and the corporate host VPN server. Any LAC can be configured to tunnel all dial-up clients to a specific tunnel server or even tunnel individual clients based on the user name or destination.

Unlike the separate tunnels created for each voluntary client, multiple dial-up clients can share a tunnel between the LAC and the host VPN server. If a second client dials into the NAS to reach a destination for which a tunnel already exists, there is no need to create a new instance of the tunnel between the LAC and the host VPN server because all of the data from the new client is sent over the existing tunnel. Whenever multiple clients are connected over a single tunnel, the tunnel is not terminated or "torn down" until the last user of the tunnel disconnects.

Point to Point Tunneling Protocol (PPTP)

Now let's get into some of the mechanics of PPTP. PPTP is a protocol that encapsulates other common LAN protocols, such as NetBEUI, IPX/SPX (Novell), TCP/IP, and so on, into an IP packet. The nice thing about this is that you can route any of these protocols over an IP-only network (such as the Internet) in a manner that is completely transparent to the user. From the user's perspective as well as the machine's, even though they might be a thousand miles away, it still appears as though they are directly connected to the LAN in their office that might be running Novell exclusively.

PPTP is generally viewed as a remote access solution. It was originally designed by Microsoft to allow a user to connect to a corporate access server by using the Internet as opposed to dialing directly into the corporate access server over a standard PSTN line. This can be accomplished in a couple of ways, depending on whether or not the ISP being used to access the Internet has hardware that is PPTP-aware. The variations differ only slightly in that, should the ISP NAS be PPTP-aware, then the remote user need only initiate a standard PPP connection, at which point the PPTP-aware NAS creates the PPTP tunnel directly to the user's corporate access server. If the ISP NAS is not PPTP-aware, then after the user has connected to the ISP NAS via a PPP connection, he or she needs to initiate a second PPTP connection, over the existing connection, straight through to the corporate access server.

Data sent using this second connection is in the form of IP datagrams that contain PPP packets, referred to as encapsulated PPP packets. Now the tunnel extends all the way from the corporate access server in the office to his or her remote PC, as opposed to the tunnel only extending from the office to the ISP NAS the user dialed into initially. Another benefit is that at this point the corporate access server can dynamically assign either a unique global IP address from the pool it has registered or any number of non-routable IP addresses defined in RFC 1918 (10.0.0.0, 172.16.0.0, 192.168.0.0, and so on) covered earlier.

The PPTP protocol consists of two communications channels between the client and the server. The first one is a control channel over which link management information is passed. The second is a data channel over which private network traffic gets carried. The control channel that is set up then uses a standard TCP connection to well-known port number 1723 on the corporate access server. The data channel, carrying the private network traffic, uses IP protocol type 47 or the GRE protocol. Basically, PPP packets are encapsulated in GRE and tunneled on top of IP. They are similar in some respects to TCP segments. They both may carry a sequence and acknowledgement number. GRE also uses a sliding window to avoid congestion. The transparent transmission of data over the data channel is achieved by negotiating a standard PPP connection over it, just as if the remote PC were dialing directly into the corporate access server. PPTP simply makes it possible to tunnel PPP packets over the TCP/IP protocol. PPP can use any layer 2 frames running across a point-to-point link. What PPTP does is emulate this point to point layer 2 functionality on top of TCP (a layer 4 protocol), fooling PPP into thinking it is riding a normal layer 2 link.

L2F Protocol

L2F was designed by Cisco as a transmission protocol that enables dial-up network access servers to wrap dial-up traffic inside of PPP packets and transmit them over WAN links to an L2F server, which is usually a VPN-capable router. The L2F server then unwraps the packets and places them on the internal network. Unlike PPTP and L2TP, L2F has no defined client and is used with compulsory tunnels only. This protocol was later merged with PPTP to create the L2TP protocol.

L2TP

This protocol incorporates the best features of PPTP and L2F. In L2TP terminology, the NAS at the ISP is the L2TP client and is, as stated earlier, called a LAC. The device at the corporate LAN is the server and is called an *L2TP Network Server* (LNS). A tunnel exists between the LAC and the LNS. A LAC forwards packets and generally has the PSTN connection. The LNS negotiates PPP but does not necessarily have a PSTN connection. Obviously, the LAC and the LNS must have access to the Internet, and both are referred to as the L2TP endpoints. After call connection, the user and the LNS negotiate PPP in exactly the same fashion as a direct connection. However, instead of connecting through a physical device (such as an ISDN), the LNS is talking through an L2TP tunnel, which is a logical connection. Here is an example of the process:

1. The remote user dials into the ISP, which collects logon information from the client. A PPP connection using a modem or a native ISDN connection is established between the client (remote PC) and the ISP.

2. The ISP checks the username in the logon process and determines whether or not a VPN connection is required. The ISP maintains a database known as an endpoint table that associates the username with a specific endpoint or the corporate LNS.

3. The ISP establishes a tunnel by contacting the corporate LNS.

4. Any authentication information that was initially collected from the remote PC is forwarded to the corporate LNS. Then the remote user is authenticated by the corporate LNS.

At this point, the connection between the remote PC and the corporate LAN is like any PPP connection. When the ISP receives frames from the remote PC over the PPP link, they are encapsulated in L2TP and forwarded over the tunnel to the LNS. The corporate LNS takes the frames, strips the L2TP header, and processes them as normal incoming PPP frames.

When comparing PPTP to L2TP, they are similar in that they use PPP to provide the initial envelope for the data and then append additional headers for transport through the internetwork. PPTP and L2TP differ in the following points:

- PPTP requires that the internetwork be an IP internetwork. L2TP requires only that the tunnel media access method use a packet-oriented, point-to-point connection. L2TP can be used over IP (using UDP), Frame-Relay *permanent virtual circuits* (PVC), X.25 *virtual circuits* (VC), or ATM VCs.

- PPTP can only support a single tunnel between end points, while L2TP enables the use of multiple tunnels between end points. With L2TP, you can create different tunnels for different *qualities of service* (QoS).

- L2TP provides for header compression and when it is enabled, L2TP has only four bytes of overhead, as compared to six bytes for PPTP.

- L2TP enables tunnel authentication, while PPTP does not. However, when either protocol is used over IPSec, the actual tunnel authentication is done by IPSec, so obviously layer 2 tunnel authentication is not necessary.

IPSec

IPSec is actually a suite of protocols that can be used to protect the data, authenticate communications, control access, and provide for non-repudiation. It was designed by the IETF as an end-to-end mechanism for ensuring data security in IP communications. IPSec has been published in a series of RFCs (1825 through 1827) that define its overall architecture. This includes an *Authentication Header* (AH) to verify the data integrity and an ESP that has provisions for both data integrity and data encryption, as well as a method of key exchange. IPSec uses an AH to provide for source authentication and integrity *without* encryption and it uses the ESP to provide for authentication and integrity *with* data encryption. With IPSec, only the sender and recipient know the security key. If the authentication data is valid, the recipient of this data knows that the communication actually came from the sender and that it has not been tampered with.

Think of IPSec as a layer below the TCP/IP stack. This layer is controlled by a security policy on each machine and a negotiated *security association* (SA) between the sender and receiver. The policy consists of a set of filters and associated security behaviors. Once the packet's IP address, protocol, and port number matches the filter criteria, the packet is subject to SA negotiation.

Security Association (SA)

Now that the packet has made it through the filter, it triggers a negotiation of an SA between the sender and receiver. ISAKMP/Oakley is the protocol used for this negotiation. This is also known as *key management*. During an ISAKMP/Oakley key exchange, the two machines agree on authentication and data security methods, perform mutual authentication, and generate a shared key for subsequent data encryption. Once the SA has been established, all data transmission can proceed for any machine that applies this data security to the packets being transmitted. This method guarantees the integrity of the transmitted packets, or depending on the protocols used, can encrypt the packets as well. The protocol choices are AH or ESP. These protocols can be used alone or in combination with each other.

Authentication Header (AH)

Data integrity and data authentication for IP payloads can be provided by the AH that is located between the IP header and the transport header. The AH includes authentication data and a sequence number. When used together, they can verify the sender, ensure that the message has not been tampered with in transit, and prevent a replay attack. The IPSec authentication header does not do data encryption; it simply guarantees that the data originated from a specific user and that it was not modified in transit.

Encapsulation Security Payload (ESP)

The ESP provides for encryption IP payload as well as some of the services provided by the AH. ESP authentication capabilities are limited compared to AH because ESP does not include the IP header information in its authentication process. The two protocols can be used together if a more comprehensive solution is required. Another powerful feature of ESP is payload padding. With this, you can conceal the actual size of the packet, making it even harder to determine the contents within.

IPSec Tunnel Mode

In addition to its definition of encryption mechanisms for IP traffic, IPSec also provides for an IP-over-IP tunnel mode, generally referred to as IPSec Tunnel Mode. An IPSec tunnel consists of the client and a host VPN server that both need to be configured using IPSec tunneling and a negotiated encryption mechanism. IPSec Tunnel Mode can use a negotiated SA to encapsulate and encrypt all of the IP packets for secure transfer across a private or public IP internetwork. The encrypted payload is then encapsulated again with a plain text IP header and sent on the internetwork for delivery to the host VPN server. Upon receipt of this datagram, the host VPN server first removes the plain text IP header and decrypts the contents to get the original payload IP packet. The payload IP packet is then processed normally and routed to its destination on the internal LAN.

Components of VPN Design

The components of a good VPN should include authentication, encryption, encapsulation, and, in certain cases, some kind of policy-based filtering. This section discusses each of these items in some detail.

Authentication

A distinct difference exists between authentication and encryption, although a lot of confusion tends to crop up between these two because they both involve the use of cryptography, which will be discussed later.

One of the problems when connecting with a system remotely is that the computer needs a way to find out that you are who you say you are. Once a user has identified him- or herself to the computer, the computer has to decide whether or not that user is authentic. This process is known as authentication.

Essentially, you can accomplish this with a computer in three different ways. To prove to someone that you are who you say you are is to provide something you know, something you have, or something you are.

By far, the most common form of authentication is by providing something you know. Everyone is familiar with the almost everyday exercise of entering passwords to log on to a computer, entering a *personal identification number* (PIN) into an automated teller, or retrieving messages from a voicemail system. This is generally referred to as password or user name/password authentication. This is the method used most commonly on the Internet. In order to authenticate yourself, you simply provide the site you are visiting with something you know, such as a user name and password.

Some of you might even have experienced the extension of the something-you-know method. Let's say you forget your password. You may have been asked to answer a whole series of questions that were agreed upon when you signed up to use this site, such as your mother's maiden name, the name of a pet, and so on. Once you answer any or all of these questions, you are either permitted to create a new password or have your original password emailed to you. Unfortunately, this form of authentication is considered to be the least secure because a lot of this is predictable and it is information that another person could find.

Because of this, another authentication variation that is growing in popularity is that of allowing the registrant to make up a couple of questions and answers of their own. For example, you might choose to provide the name of your first dog, the name of your first girlfriend's brother, or maybe the name of your math teacher in high school. Although this may virtually eliminate public research of these facts, the problem that remains is the nature of the password itself. These passwords are usually words that exist in any standard dictionary. The average human knows about 8,000 words, while the average vocabulary of an educated (and I use this term loosely) college graduate is about 15,000. To a computer, trying all the variations of these common English words is utter child's play. So what if you pepper it with a number or symbol here and there? You might even juxtapose a word or two. Now the poor computer has to worry about hundreds of thousands or even hundreds of millions of permutations. Does the acronym MIPS ring any bells (it stands for millions of instructions per second)? This is how all computers' *central processing units* (CPUs) are rated these days. Do the math, people (because you know the computer sure will). Most of these passwords would be deciphered in no time.

Now we move on to being authenticated by something you have. Almost all of us are familiar with this concept because we all have ATM cards. The card is useless without the PIN, and the PIN is useless without the card. On the Internet, organizations often issue what are generally called tokens, which are categorized into soft tokens and hard tokens. This technology creates what are known as *one-time passwords* (OTPs). A soft token is a piece of software that emulates a hard token that a given organization has you install on your home computer. This software creates a secure channel between your computer and the organization by using this OTP to authenticate you. Although soft tokens provide fairly good authentication, the problem is that software can, if it falls into the wrong hands, be replicated. Another limitation of soft token authentication is that it isn't very mobile. Often, the software that you are sent can only be installed on one computer, or it could be that if you try to install it on your computer at work, it might not function through your network firewall. This, of course, reduces mobility, as you can only perform your transactions from one computer.

The other type of token is a hard token. A hard token could be a smart card that you run through a computer with a card reader, or it might be a USB device or a *Personal Memory Card International Association* (PCM-CIA) card that you plug into a given port on a computer. The benefit of a hard-token authentication system is greater security because they require users to present a physical element (something you have) in addition to an ID and password (something you know) to provide an added layer of protection against hackers. A good example of this would be the key-fob hard-token device. This piece of hardware, which looks like a tiny calculator display face, works by using number combinations that are time-synchronized between the server being accessed and the key fob itself. The numbers on the display change every 30 seconds or so and at the moment that you want to log in, you key in the number that appears on the key-fob display along with a password and/or PIN. This provides a high degree of authentication, mainly because the numbers change constantly and provide excellent mobility.

This brings us to "something you are." Don't ask me what protocol or layer this is, but I have been told that I am an S.O.B. I can think of absolutely no instance where this has been used to grant me access to anything. However, it has gotten me kicked out of a few places. Now there does exist something called *Biometrics*. This "something you are" is considered to be the most secure type of authentication. This can include thumbprints, fingerprints, voiceprints, retinal scans, handprints, and even a person's signature. Although very mobile and, even though they are very secure and almost impossible to duplicate, they do present a problem and that is change. Personal traits can change dramatically. A woman's retina changes when she is pregnant. Retinas can also change when cholesterol levels rise or lower dramatically. Thumbprints and fingerprints are also a problem because all you have to do is cut your thumb and it will no longer match the print on the file. Your voice can be affected by illness and aging, as can your signature. As important as it is to keep impersonators from accessing a computer, it is equally important that legitimate people be allowed to access these computers.

Obviously, you need to decide how much you are willing to spend, how important the data being accessed is, and how much people will put up with to maintain any level of productivity. The best solution is to use a combination of these. Remember when you were in school and a friend would say, "I'll flip you for it," at which point you agreed, only to find it didn't fall your way. You would then immediately suggest, "OK, best two out of three" (or until *you* would win). Because biometrics are subject to change and passwords can easily be beaten, using a combination of all of them, such as a best three-out-of-five series or whatever combination you choose, might work best.

Sometimes it is just as important that the computers themselves be authenticated, as opposed to users being authenticated to computers. I mean, fair is fair. Have you ever downloaded software from a Web site before? Maybe you have downloaded updates for your operating system from Microsoft. I hope this is the case for your sake, but then again, there might only be five or 10 people in the entire world that own a Microsoft product anyway, although I could be off just a bit; your figures may vary.

You might have software that updates itself without any intervention from you at all. Well, it is just these very instances where computer authentication is important. We are all aware of the damage that can occur, on an unimaginable scale, from viruses, worms, and Trojan horses. This is where digital signatures and certificates come in. The difference between them is that you can check the authenticity of a certificate with a *Certificate of Authority* (CA). These topics will be examined in more depth later on, but this is a perfect example of *you* authenticating a computer.

Encryption

Encryption deals with the business of taking meaningful data like "the rain in Spain lies mainly on the plain" and converting it into something meaningless like "lkk3$#54rjk#j9&*&^09978kljh" (I hope I spelled that right, please correct me if you catch any errors in that last quote). The original message is called plaintext or clear text. The scrambled message is called cipher-text. Encryption involves any procedure that converts this plaintext or clear text into cipher-text, while decryption involves any procedure that converts this cipher-text into plaintext. This is done mathematically via a cryptographic algorithm. An algorithm is nothing more than a given set of instructions. A recipe is a good example of an algorithm. A cryptosystem is usually a whole collection of algorithms that are labeled. The labels are called keys.

Three different encryption methods are available: hash algorithms (also known as one-way functions, message digests, fingerprints or trapdoors), private key (or symmetric) algorithms, and finally public key (or asymmetric) algorithms. Encryption can be exploited in a number of ways, such as encrypting communications, file storage, user and computer authentication, and password or key exchanges. The latter two work by using the inverse procedure of the same type of algorithm. Huh? This will all be discussed in the Cryptography section, but suffice it to say, this is essentially how the authentication and encryption of data differ.

Encapsulation

Data that travels across the Internet does so in IP packets. These IP packets contain all kinds of information, such as spreadsheet data, audio and video data, and program files, which is carried in the IP payload portion of the packet. The IP payload varies in sizes ranging from eight bytes up to 65,515 bytes, depending on the size of the header. An IP packet also contains an IP header that can also vary in size from as few as 20 bytes up to 60 bytes. This always includes a source IP address and a destination IP address that is used for routing across the Internet over several different networks. It also includes a protocol field, which is very important as it is used to indicate the type of protocol that is contained in the IP payload portion (also referred to simply as the data portion). It is this very protocol type field that enables us to encapsulate virtually anything we want inside the data portion, even another IP packet containing the same items and formats that have been described.

You may recall back in the PPTP section where I referred to "IP Protocol Type 47." This protocol type is the protocol or the GRE protocol, the very protocol that enables us to encapsulate an IP packet inside of another IP packet. Now you might ask yourself, "why would I want to encapsulate one IP packet inside of another?" The answer is that this is what makes VPN possible. This can make two distant networks or hosts appear as though they are on the same network, even though they might be separated by a bunch of different networks using completely different addressing schemes traveling over several Internet routers. Different methods, some more secure than others, are available that can accomplish this type of encapsulation, such as IPSec, which you can read about in the Protocols section.

Policy-Based Filtering

Policy-based filtering is not a mandatory requirement for implementing a VPN solution, but it significantly increases the security of the network itself as well as the integrity of the data being transported across the Internet. This is accomplished through the use of a firewall or router. It can either be a dedicated firewall or a perimeter router with a firewall feature set used in parallel with a VPN device. You can also use VPN capable firewalls by themselves.

The basic idea of policy-based filtering is to give you the ability to enforce the flow of certain types of network traffic on a per-packet basis. What this enables you to do is control who can and can't use specific network resources. Filtering can be used in several different ways to block connections to or from specific hosts and/or networks. You can even block connections to specific ports and from certain addresses, such as from hosts or networks that you consider hostile or untrustworthy. You might even choose to block connections from *all* addresses external to your network with the exception of a specific few.

Adding TCP or UDP port filtering to address filtering can give you even more flexibility. Services, such as Telnet, reside (unless specifically changed) at specific ports, referred to as well-known ports. For example, Telnet resides at well-known port 23. If you set policies to block TCP or UDP connections to or from specific ports, then you can implement policies that call for certain types of connections to be made to some hosts, but not others. You may want to allow only specific services, such as the *Simple Mail Transfer Protocol* (SMTP) for one system and Telnet or *File Transfer Protocol* (FTP) connections to another system. With filtering on TCP or UDP ports, this policy can be easily implemented in a firewall, a packet filtering router, or by specific hosts with packet-filtering capabilities. Now you can start to see just how granular you can set the requirements for access to your network.

Cryptography

The underlying technology that even makes VPNs a viable solution in today's public networks, including but by no means limited to the Internet, is cryptography. It is not only the single most important factor in secure communications of any kind, but it is also very interesting once you get beneath the surface to actually see what is taking place.

Some Cryptographic Background

What is cryptography anyway? How did it come to be? Cryptography is the art and science of taking an original legible message, know as plaintext, and converting it through some agreed-upon procedure into any form that is unreadable, known as ciphertext. That agreed-upon procedure is an algorithm. The product of that algorithm is called a key. The art and science of analyzing and undoing that procedure to recreate the original message is known as cryptanalysis.

To understand how it came to be, one must go back to about 100 BC when a certain Roman emperor named Julius Caesar began to distrust his own messengers that carried sensitive items to those he actually trusted. History clearly shows, however, that the messengers would end up being the least of his problems as far as trust was concerned. This first recorded cipher was an algorithm that replaced each character in the Roman alphabet with a character three positions ahead of it. This algorithm is still used commonly even to this day. Perhaps you may have run across an email or newsgroup message that has a bunch of random characters with <rot13> at the top of this message. The rot stands for rotate and the 13 indicates by how many. The 13 in this case is lucky, when you consider the amount of letters in the English alphabet (OK, stop counting, it's 26), because it enables you to rotate the characters in either direction. This algorithm is known as a *substitution cipher*.

Another similar algorithm is the *transposition cipher*. Instead of substituting each letter, you rearrange them. Let's say you have some graph paper that has 10 rows and 10 columns. You could place the letters of the message in each box left to right on one paper and on another paper transpose them in a top-to-bottom order, backwards, diagonally, or any way you choose. A cipher is something that protects a message modifying or altering the actual components of that message. The components in the previous cases would be the letters themselves. This gives one the ability to encrypt virtually any message regardless of content.

Now let us examine a cousin of the cipher, the code. On the surface, they might seem the same, but the difference lies in the method. Although ciphers alter the contents of a message to encrypt it, a code alters its meaning. You have probably heard of codebooks used in clandestine operations throughout history. This means that in order for each party to be able to unscramble a coded message, they each must have a codebook, as opposed to a cipher where each party need only know the method or how to unscramble a message. Let's say I want to send my brother in England a message that only we would be able to understand. I could tell him to rotate the letters by 13 (a cipher), but that is easy to break considering the consistency and repetitive nature of written language. If you have ever watched Wheel of Fortune, you may have noticed that when contestants are asked to pick five letters to help them solve the puzzle they always say, "OK Pat, I'll take R, S, T, L, N." That is because these are the most common consonants in the English language. The letter E is by far the most common letter of all. So a pattern could quickly be observed and eventually figured out with some ease.

A codebook is a different story. You might ask "oh swell, all I have to do is make a codebook and send it to my brother." Not so, we could speak on the phone and decide that each of us buy a 1985, third-edition *Webster's* paperback dictionary and for every *word* we use, substitute the word located 13 definitions in front of it. Now you would need to know the method *and* have the codebook. Trust me when I say that the ability to find a pattern here would be less than that of a 13-letter rotation. Patterns are a cryptographer's nightmare and a cryptanalyst's dream.

This brings us to the subject of *randomness*. The most effective weapon against patterns is randomness. Having to perform the task of encrypting and decrypting messages manually would certainly become quite tedious and unproductive. That is why machines are perfect for this kind of activity. Have you ever heard of the enigma machine? It was a three-rotor substitution machine. In World War II, the allies sure heard of it, and it is a good thing they did. Otherwise, you could very well be reading the German version of this text. It was because of this very device that most governments now classify cryptographic methods literally as weapons. This is the reason you may have heard the terms 128-bit domestic versions and 40-bit export versions of certain types of software.

Thus, clearly the best possible device we can use for these repetitive and complex tasks is the modern computer. However, even though it is a fast and powerful tool for implementing all the cryptographic algorithms being used today, it does pose an interesting problem. When executing an algorithm to generate a cryptographic key, the single most import element in this procedure is *randomness*. The key that is produced by any cryptographic protocol depends completely on the unpredictability of this key. The minute you can predict a key's value, or even narrow down the number of keys that need to be tried, then that key can be broken with much less effort than if a completely random number, known as a *seed value*, had been used in the algorithm to create that key. Consequently, it is of the utmost importance that this key be generated from the seed value of a truly unpredictable random number source.

The problem that exists is that computers by their very nature are extremely predictable and deterministic. It wouldn't do us much good to have a calculator that managed to produce a completely random number every time we entered the equation $2 + 2$. We depend on the fact that a computer will operate exactly the same way every single time it runs any given algorithm. So, by definition, it is impossible for a computer to generate a *truly* random number of any kind. The only source of true randomness exists in nature.

For example, if you were to take some graph paper that was 20 feet square and place it on the ground while it was raining, and you used the coordinates of the location of each raindrop that fell at 30-second intervals, *that* would be truly random. The best a computer can hope to do is what is known as a *Pseudo-Random Number Generator* (PNRG). A PNRG can use any available source of randomness for its initial seed value. Then it repeatedly scrambles this seed. Usually, the seed is a short, random number that the PRNG expands into a longer, random-looking number. Some PNRGs use a multiple of this seed with the number of seconds that have passed from a given date. Another method is for the computer to take a random measurement of time between the keystrokes of a user at any given moment (this one is actually quite good).

Steganography

The word *steganography* literally means *covered writing,* as derived from Greek. This is not only clever, but formidable as well. Think of steganography as a sort of digital "Where's Waldo?" If you have never seen a Where's Waldo? picture, it is generally a drawing of hundreds of similar-looking characters that, if the question wasn't posed, you would never even begin to look for this single Waldo character. Steganography is the digital equivalent.

One thing about cryptography is that the output is so nonsensical that it is painfully obvious that someone is trying to hide something. This triggers the human nature in us to automatically want to find out why someone would want to hide this item and, even more, now want to know what it is. If you were to combine steganography with cryptography, you would have yourself one formidable and rather sneaky solution. For example, in very high-color graphic images, the low-order bits that describe each pixel, when altered, do not make a distinguishable difference in the original quality of the image. This is just one of many way that steganography can be implemented in computer communications.

Now that you have been given some background on the workings of cryptography, let's examine some current algorithm categories that are currently being used by VPNs.

Cryptographic Algorithms

Before discussing some of the specific algorithms, you should be reminded of the three main categories that these algorithms fall into: hash algorithms, private key algorithms, and finally public key algorithms.

At certain points in this section, certain algorithms will be discussed in a series of numbered steps. To do this, different individuals will be used to describe these algorithms' steps. Please refer back to this point for the cast of characters being used, as their function in these steps will remain consistent:

Alice: The first participant in all the algorithms (in keeping with cryptographic tradition)

Bob: The second participant in all the algorithms (in keeping with cryptographic tradition)

Malcolm: The one that is malicious or *in the middle* (in keeping with a current television show)

Ted: A trusted third party (because you can't spell trusted without Ted)

Hash Algorithms

One of the more interesting and impressive cryptographic subjects is the hash algorithm. What makes it so elegant is that the product of a hash algorithm is so *easy* to calculate in one direction and just plain *awful* to try and calculate in the reverse direction. Along with being a very powerful tool, it is also very compact. They also are often referred to as one-way hash functions. You will also hear them interchanged with terms such as message digests (MD4, MD5, and so on), fingerprints, or even trapdoors, but for the most part, they all do the same thing. The main characteristic of a hash is that it's easy to compute, ridiculously hard to reverse, and extremely unlikely to repeat. To fully appreciate this, the following scenario is a basic idea of what happens in a hash function:

Enter spy number one, Yuri. He has been ordered by his boss to send sensitive messages to the mother country via the post office and told that the contents of these messages can never be revealed to the capitalist enemy. Now there is spy number two, John. Through diligent intelligence work, John has discovered the actual post office that Yuri's country uses to mail these messages. John's boss says, "Good work, John! I want you to apply for a job at this post office, intercept these messages, and inform me of the contents therein." This should be a cakewalk for John, he just needs to retrieve the message from the outgoing mailbag, copy the message, and bring it to his boss.

Yuri has an idea. He decides that he is going to take this message, convert the words of this message into a numeric value, divide that value into the numeric equivalent of that day's date and write down the number that occupies the second position (or digit) of the remainder. He calls his comrade in the mother country and informs him of this exact procedure. Let's just say the words in the message calculate into the number 512 (how he did this is not important). It is October 31, 2000. Written numerically, this works out to be (10312000). He takes out a pencil and a piece of scrap paper and divides 512 into 10312000. As it turns out, the second digit of the remainder is the number 2. This little procedure takes him maybe a minute and a half. Yuri then takes out a nice new sheet of stationary and writes the number 2 on it. He then places this in an envelope and drops it into the mail slot at his local post office. Night has fallen and John painstakingly sifts through hundreds of envelopes and Bingo! He finds the envelope. With great enthusiasm he returns to his boss, opens the envelope, and plunks down a piece of paper with the number 2 written on it. John's boss replies, "So, you have intercepted a 2. Just go ahead and reverse whatever steps they took to arrive at that number and get back to me with the original message."

I can tell you this for free. I wouldn't want to apply for that job! Even though this is a simplistic view of the one-way hash process, it is not all that different from what actually takes place. In a hash function, the method used is known as modular arithmetic or modulo math. Let's look at how it works and why it is virtually impossible to undo. When we say 5 mod 3 = 2, the way we arrive at 2 is quite simple. 5 mod 3 = x means divide 5 by 3 and the remainder will be x. Thus, 5 divided by 3 is 1 with a remainder of x, which is 2. The number that we use to divide by (3, in this example) is called the modulus. The reason this is virtually impossible to undo is that 17 mod 3 = 2, as does 8 mod 3 = 2, and 10 mod 8, and so on. So, if like our friend, spy number two (John), you discover this 2, how can you possibly determine which mod was performed on which set of numbers? I'll tell you how. *You can't*, that's how! Computers will use extremely large prime and almost-prime numbers that will always, regardless of their original size, mod to 0, 1, 2 . . . you get the idea.

Where hashes excel is when you want to check whether or not a message is valid or if any kind of tampering has occurred. What happens is when a one-way hash function is used to compute a hash value, any change to the message produces a different hash value when the same hash function is used after the message is received. Another common use is to check a password. This is the method used by Windows NT. Instead of maintaining a plaintext list of the passwords being used by all authorized users, Windows NT saves a one-way hashed value of the password.

The benefits here are twofold. For one, it means if someone were to obtain the "password" list file, all they would have on their hands would be a bunch of very small numbers. And two, the list becomes very compact because instead of saving hundreds or thousands of ASCII characters, it saves a very small numeric hash value. Of the two types of hash functions, one is called a *Message Authentication Code* (MAC) hash that uses a secret key (sometimes called a keyed hash). The other is known as a *Manipulation Detection Code* (MDC) hash and does not involve a key. Their uses are pretty self-explanatory. With a MAC hash, it is impossible to compute the hash value without knowledge of the secret key. For an MDC hash, it need only be a one-way function whose purpose is making sure that the data has not been manipulated or tampered with. Hash functions can be used to protect the authenticity of large quantities of data with a short secret key MAC hash, or to protect the integrity of a short string MDC hash. Sometimes an MDC hash is used in conjunction with encryption and can guarantee both confidentiality and authenticity. The following is a comprehensive list of some of the more common hash algorithms being used today. You are very likely to run across many of these when working with VPNs and you should be familiar with them.

MD5 and MD4 (Message Digests)   MD5 and MD4 are secure hash algorithms developed by Ron Rivest from MIT and RSA Security, Inc. The MD5 algorithm takes a message of any given length and produces a 128-bit fingerprint or message digest. It is virtually impossible to produce two messages that will have the same message digest. It is also impossible to produce any message having a pre-specified target hash value. The MD5 algorithm is generally used for digital signature applications, where a large file must be "compressed" in a secure manner before being encrypted with a private key before being signed with an RSA public-key type of cryptosystem. You can read a more in-depth description in RFC 1321 for MD5 and RFC 1320 for MD4. Although MD4 may be a bit quicker, it is less secure and generally not recommended. A better choice might be the RIPE Message Digest.

Secure Hash Algorithm (SHA)   Also known as the *Secure Hash Standard* (SHS), this is a cryptographic hash algorithm published by the U.S. Government. It produces a 160-bit hash value from an arbitrary-length string. This and the RIPE 160-bit Message Digest are considered to be better than MDx series.

RACE Integrity Primitives Evaluation Message Digest (RIPEMD-160)   This hash algorithm is relatively new. It is a 160-bit cryptographic hash function that was designed to replace the MDx series of message digests. It produces a digest of 20 bytes that can supposedly run at up to 40

Mb/s on just a 90-MHz Pentium computer and has been placed in the public domain by its designers.

Private Key (Symmetric) Algorithms

Private key algorithms are very simple in principle. You use the same key to encrypt a message as you do to decrypt a message. This is why it is called a symmetric key algorithm. The benefit of using private key or symmetric algorithms is that it doesn't require nearly as much computing power when compared to public-key or asymmetric algorithms, in some cases a 1,000 times less than public key algorithms. When sending vast amounts of information, this becomes a huge factor, especially when using WAN links, whose bandwidth is limited anyway. The drawback comes from finding a way to exchange this key without it being disclosed over a public network. One way to overcome this dilemma is to use a hybrid system (this will be explained in the Diffie-Hellman section). That is, use a public-key algorithm to encrypt the actual symmetric keys first and then use those keys to encrypt the rest of the data. The most important factor in symmetric key encryption is key length. The longer the key, the harder it is to crack.

The same principle applies to passwords. A chain is only as strong as its weakest link. Therefore, if you use the password "dog" and encrypt it with even a 128-bit key, you weaken its strength profoundly. This means that if you scramble the letters d, o, and g, chances are good that you can rearrange them back into the word dog without much effort. Even if you were not sure if it was god or dog, you wouldn't have to waste a very big portion of your day to try them both. The private key approach is well suited to situations where one location requires secure interaction with relatively few other applications or users.

The following are some of the more common symmetric key algorithms. Again, these are listed because you are very likely to run across many of them and it is better that you have at least some understanding of what they are when you do. Figure 10-6 illustrates a basic idea of what takes place.

Figure 10-6
High-level view of the data encryption.

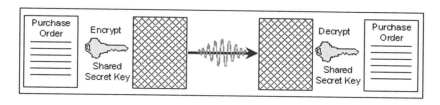

Data Encryption Standard (DES)   The *Data Encryption Standard* (DES) is an algorithm that was developed in the 1970s in an arrangement with IBM and the *National Security Agency* (NSA). It was made a standard by the U.S. government and has also been adopted by several other governments worldwide. Its use is extremely common, especially in the financial industry. Virtually all ATMs use DES to protect the data that is transmitted from the ATM to the transaction processing location.

DES is a symmetric *block cipher* that uses 64-bit block size. A *block cipher* operates on blocks of data where several bytes are put together prior to encryption. A *stream cipher* encrypts the bytes or bits individually, but block ciphers are the more common of the two. DES uses 56-bit keys; this is because the last eight bits of the 64 are used for parity checking. It was designed to be resistant to differential cryptanalysis, but it is still somewhat susceptible to linear cryptanalysis. DES, for the most part, is strong enough to keep most hackers and individuals out, but it can be cracked easily with today's computers.

Triple DES (3DES)   A derivative of DES, *Triple-DES* (3DES) is an iterative block cipher. An iterative block cipher encrypts the input multiple times. The 3DES uses the same key length as the standard DES key, 56-bits, but now it encrypts the plaintext three times with three different keys. There are different ways of encrypting the data with each key. The most common methods are as follows:

- *DES-EEE3*: Triple DES encryption using three completely different keys
- *DES-EDE3*: Triple DES operations using an encrypt-decrypt-encrypt method with three different keys
- *DES-EEE2* and *DES-EDE2*: Triple DES operations using an encrypt-decrypt-encrypt method also, but using the same key during the first and third operations

All that the EEE and EDE, which were appended to the DES, refer to is the method, simply "encrypt-encrypt-encrypt" and "encrypt-decrypt-encrypt," respectively. The most secure form of this is 3DES using the three different keys, which is considered to be much safer than using just plain DES.

International Data Encryption Algorithm (IDEA)   The *International Data Encryption Algorithm* (IDEA) is a symmetric block cipher algorithm with a 64-bit block length and a 128-bit key, which is twice as long as for that of DES. IDEA is immune from not only differential cryptanalysis, but linear cryptanalysis as well. It has patents in the U.S. as well as Europe.

Blowfish Algorithm   Blowfish is a 64-bit symmetric block cipher that was invented by Bruce Schneier in 1993. It can be used as a replacement for DES or IDEA, which are both patented. The data is encrypted and decrypted in 64-bit chunks. It can have a key length that varies anywhere from 32 to 448 bits. The algorithm uses 16 rounds, or iterations, of the main algorithm. The number of rounds is exponentially proportional to the amount of time required to find a key using a brute-force attack. This means that as the number of rounds increase, the security of the algorithm increases exponentially. It too is immune from both differential and linear cryptanalysis. Blowfish was placed in the public domain so that there would be no restrictions on the use or distribution of the algorithm. It has been extensively analyzed publicly, and no real weaknesses have been found. Thus, Blowfish has yet to be broken.

RCx Algorithms (RC2, RC4, and RC5)   The RC is sometimes referred to as Rivest Cipher or Ron's Code. These ciphers were developed by Professor Ron Rivest of the Massachusetts Institute of Technology (MIT) and RSA Security. RC2 is a 64-bit *block cipher*. It uses a variable key size and can be made more or less secure than DES by varying the key size. It is anywhere from two to three times faster than DES. RC4 is a *stream cipher* that also uses a variable key length size. RC5 is a *block cipher,* which is an algorithm that not only has a variable block size, but also a variable key size, and a variable number of rounds (you can consider this cipher to be variable). The block size can be 32, 64, or 128 bits long. The key size can be anywhere from 0 (not very big) all the way up to 2,048 bits (you won't be breaking this cipher with an abacus!). The number of rounds can range from 0 to 255.

Skipjack Algorithm   The Skipjack algorithm, developed by the NSA, was first called Clipper and then Capstone. It requires a hardware-based chip scheme that incorporates the Skipjack algorithm (which is classified) using a 64-bit block size and an 80-bit key. This key is used in combination with an escrow key (or keys) used by the government or some other kind of escrow agency. These keys are used so that law enforcement agencies can decrypt messages if they have reason to believe laws are being broken. Because the algorithm is classified, it is not subject to public scrutiny, therefore making it impossible to test its security fully. This one is not very popular for obvious reasons.

Public Key (Asymmetric) Algorithms

Public key algorithms not only solve the problem of how two people can exchange a secret key over a public medium, but they also, by their very nature, provide some very powerful services other than encryption. These protocols also allow for digital signatures, secure private key exchange, authentication, and for some, all of the above. Now you might ask, "Well, if they are so good, why even bother with using anything else?" The answer lies in speed. These protocols require a lot more processing power and can take, as was mentioned before, a thousand times longer to encrypt the same amount of data, as does a symmetric protocol. Before examining some of the individual protocols, the following examples discuss the basics of how a public-key protocol actually works.

Most everyone has been to a post office at one time or another and seen the many rows of P.O. boxes with locks and numbers on them. For this example, let's use the same P.O. boxes but arrange them a little differently. Picture the post office with all of these P.O. boxes filling up one whole side of the room. Instead of each person getting one box, imagine each person having a column of mailboxes from floor to ceiling, with each name printed at the top. At the foot sits a container of identical keys with the person's name inscribed, open to the public and free for the taking. Every individual P.O. box has two locks side by side. The lock on the left will *lock* the mailbox and the lock on the right will *unlock* the mailbox. The container full of keys has one thing in common, they can only lock the P.O. Boxes.

Now one and *only* one key has been hand delivered to the owners of the P.O. boxes. Prior to being issued this key, fingerprints, driver's licenses, and birth certificates had to be verified by the company that made the keys. The owners were instructed to keep this key *privately* secured.

Assume that this post office is open 24 hours a day, that everyone using this post office knows one another, and that there may even be friends and enemies among this group. You also want to invite four of these friends to a dinner party but don't want all of your other friends to find out because it might hurt their feelings. You take these invitations to put in the P.O. boxes of these friends: Sean, Carlyn, Justin, and Arlene. You go to the Sean column, reach down, and pick up one of his *public* keys, place the invitation in one of his open P.O. boxes, turn the key, and lock it shut. You then toss this public key back into the container at the bottom. You go to the other columns and repeat the same procedure.

You notice that some of your other friends and even enemies are at the post office. They have all witnessed this event. This doesn't worry you in the least because you know that the invitations have been locked away and that only Sean, Carlyn, Justin, and Arlene can retrieve them with the respective *private* keys that were issued to them.

This is exactly how public-key encryption works over the Internet, with the only difference being that the public key is used to *encrypt* the invitation instead of lock the P.O. Box. The private key is used to *decrypt* the invitation rather than unlock the P.O. box. Now what if someone at the post office that didn't like you somehow discovered that you were throwing this party and would like nothing better than to ruin it? Well, it is a public, 24-hour post office, right? What would stop them from going into the post office late at night and, using the exact same procedure, put "sorry, party cancelled" notices, ostensibly from you, into each of these four friends other, open P.O. boxes? What could be done to make sure that not only could they not pretend to send something from you, but also provide a way to let your four friends be absolutely sure that the original invitations were from you in the first place? Go back to your post office example and find out.

You get a call from the company that originally gave you the private key to your P.O. box. They inform you of a new item they are planning to distribute to everyone in this post office. Once again, your fingerprints, driver's license, and birth certificate have to be verified. They deliver a big case of lock-boxes with your name printed on them that are just small enough to fit inside the existing P.O. boxes in the post office. You notice that they are very similar to your P.O. boxes. They each have two locks on them, side by side. The difference is that now your private key is used to lock this box. Any of your public keys in the post office can be used to unlock this box.

It dawns on you that a person who doesn't like you has just seen you put invitations into your four friends' P.O. boxes, and that this person is just the type to put "party cancelled" notices in their other P.O. boxes. You make up four new invitations, put one in each of your new lock-boxes, lock it shut with your private key, and go to the post office. You then place these lock-boxes into each of your four friend's remaining open P.O. boxes. You reach down and take a public key out of their containers and lock their respective P.O. boxes shut with them.

The next day your friends arrive at the post office, open their respective P.O. boxes with their private keys and extract the locked box, with your name on it, which is inside. They each walk over to your column of P.O boxes, reach down into the container and use one of your public keys to unlock this box, and retrieve their invitations.

This is exactly how public-key algorithms are used to digitally sign a message and guarantee its integrity. To take this a step further, you can consider the manufacturer of these boxes and keys as the *issuing authority* or a *trusted third party* seeing as how they make the lock-boxes, check identities, and fill up the containers in the post office with public keys whenever they run out. Later you will see the significance of the issuing authority in the Certificates section, but more importantly this arrangement has now left you sure that your invitation is encrypted, digitally signed, and positive that the integrity of its contents is tamper-free. You also take comfort in knowing that your friends are just as sure the invitation is legitimate and from you as well. Pretty neat, yes? That should give you a pretty good feel for what is happening when public-key algorithms are used. The next section discusses the different specific protocols that use this public-key method so that when you run across them while designing VPNs in the future, they will make some sense.

Diffie-Hellman Algorithm In 1976, Martin Hellman, a professor at Stanford University, and two graduate students who worked with him at the time, Ralph Merkle and Whitfield Diffie, came up with a solution that would allow two people in different locations to safely communicate a secret key over a public medium. This was the birth of public-key cryptography. The Diffie-Hellman algorithm also helps us with another problem. Public-key encryption methods are processor-intensive and extremely slow when compared to private-key methods. Why not combine their strengths and reap the benefits of both? This is where Diffie-Hellman shines.

Diffie-Hellman is not used to encrypt data per se. This algorithm is designed to exchange symmetric (private) keys securely and very quickly. Once the symmetric keys have been safely exchanged, then encryption can begin with a thousand times less overhead. This is also what is referred to as a hybrid method. Here is an example of how this hybrid works:

1. Alice sends Bob her public key unprotected over the Internet (Bob could have the key already or even get it from a trusted third party).

2. Bob decides on a secret key to be used with a symmetric algorithm (like DES or IDEA), encrypts this symmetric key using Alice's public key, and sends this key back to Alice.

3. Alice now decrypts, with her private key, the symmetric key that will be used for the duration of the encrypted communication session. (This is where you may hear the term *session key*.)

4. Alice and Bob now communicate with confidence knowing that all subsequent data is fully encrypted.

Diffie-Hellman is susceptible to one drawback and that is a man-in-the-middle attack. It is *extremely* hard to pull off in practice, but in theory the danger exists. Here is an example of how this unlikely event could occur:

1. Alice sends Bob her public key unprotected over the Internet (Bob could have the key already or even get it from a trusted third party).

2. Malcolm (who is in the middle) intercepts Alice's public key and sends Bob a copy of his own public key disguised as Alice's.

3. Bob decides on a secret key to be used with a symmetric algorithm (such as DES or IDEA), encrypts this symmetric key using Malcom's public key (he thinks this is Alice's public key), and send this symmetric key back to Alice.

4. Malcolm intercepts Bob's message containing this secret symmetric key. Malcolm now takes this secret key, encrypts it with Alice's public key and sends it to Alice.

5. Alice now decrypts this secret symmetric key using her private key.

6. Malcolm can now create the illusion that Bob and Alice are communicating with each other when, in fact, it is really Malcolm intercepting the messages midway, subverting the messages and resending them to each party.

One way around this subversion using a public-key system such as Diffie-Hellman is to first send messages *already* encrypted with the symmetric key system and then *afterwards* send that symmetric key necessary to read the message using the normal Diffie-Hellman method. It would work something like this:

1. Alice sends Bob her public key unprotected over the Internet (Bob could have the key already or even get it from a trusted third party).

2. Bob sends Alice his public key unprotected over the Internet (Alice could have the key already or even get it from a trusted third party).

3. Alice decides on a secret key to be used with a symmetric algorithm (such as DES or IDEA), encrypts the message first using this symmetric, and sends it off to Bob. Bob cannot read the message (yet), but more importantly neither can Malcolm.

4. Bob decides on a secret key to be used with a symmetric algorithm (such as DES or IDEA), encrypts the message first using this symmetric, and sends it off to Alice. Alice cannot read the message either (yet), but again, neither can Malcolm.

5. Alice encrypts her secret symmetric key using Bob's public key and sends it off to Bob. Now Bob can read the original message.

6. Bob encrypts his secret symmetric key using Alice's public key and sends it off to Alice. Now Alice can read the original message.

7. Using the secret key that they now both have in their possession, Bob and Alice can continue to communicate.

This won't necessarily stop Malcolm from reading the message eventually, but it will remove his ability to subvert the message and fool them into thinking they are communicating with each other unmolested. By using digital signatures and/or public-key certificates, Malcolm cannot do either. Those topics will be covered shortly.

RSA Algorithms   About a year after our friends at Stanford came up with this new public key concept, three professors from MIT, Ron Rivest, Adi Shamir, and Len Adleman, used this underlying technology to come up with RSA, the most popular asymmetric cipher in use today. The way their algorithm works is really quite clever. RSA is a block cipher that encrypts data in large blocks using the product of two large prime numbers. Their method is also extremely secure.

The algorithm performs what is called a one-way trap door function. It simply multiplies two prime numbers together to get a product that is used to create the key. The whole basis of their method revolves around how computationally easy it is to multiply two *prime* numbers (factors) to get a product and how immensely difficult it is, computationally, to find the two factors (numbers multiplied by each other to get a product) of a *very* large number, consisting of only two numbers in its equation, both of which are *prime* (numbers that, when they are divided, are only the number itself and 1). When using any cryptographic algorithm, the longer the key is, the harder it is to crack.

For example, let's say I multiplied 7×11 to get 77 (a two-digit key) and the only information I gave you was that I used two prime numbers to calculate this. You would probably be able to figure out that I used 7 and 11 to arrive at this without much trouble. If I then gave you the number 7,387 (a four-digit key), you almost certainly would be there a while longer. A popular key size for RSA (which is variable) uses a 140-digit key. It took almost 200 computers and a team of cryptographic experts 11 solid weeks to crack this key. This included about 125 Silicon Graphics and Sun workstations running at 175 MHz on average, and 60 Pentium class PCs running at 300 MHz on average. The total amount of CPU time spent on the process equaled 8.9 CPU years. (I think it is safe to say we all have friends of this caliber and access to resources like these). Let's say you were paranoid and decided to use a 617-digit key. That would involve using the most efficient numeric sieve known to man (something that creates what amounts to a very large spreadsheet), creating a matrix with 10^{150} cells. You might be saying, "so what—is that a big number?" Well, current estimates of the total number of atoms in the entire universe range between 10^{78} and 10^{100} atoms. Both estimates pale in comparison to our 617-digit key-derived matrix. Hopefully now you have some idea of just how hard a procedure this is (if you don't, then, boy, are you hard to impress!).

Without using a hybrid method, the following is a pure public-key example (see Figure 10-7):

1. Alice sends Bob her public key unprotected over the Internet (Bob could have the key already or even get it from a trusted third party).

2. Bob sends Alice his public key unprotected over the Internet (Alice could also have the key already or get it from a trusted third party).

3. Alice uses Bob's public key to encrypt all of the plaintext in her message that will be used during this communication session and sends it to Bob.

4. Bob decrypts Alice's message using his private key and now reads the message in plaintext form.

5. Bob uses Alice's public key to encrypt all of the plaintext in his message that will be used during this communication session and sends it to Alice.

6. Alice decrypts Bob's message using her private key and now reads the message in plaintext form.

This is an excellent man-in-the-middle way of communicating securely, but it is theoretically possible, although very difficult, for a man-in-the-middle attack. But, fear not, because this hypothetical malfeasance can be stopped. The method used to avoid this activity is called the Interlock protocol.

Interlock Protocol   The Interlock protocol was invented by Ron Rivest and Adi Shamir. Their method of defending against the attack begins with both parties exchanging their respective public keys. Then each in turn

Figure 10-7

A depiction of public encryption key usage

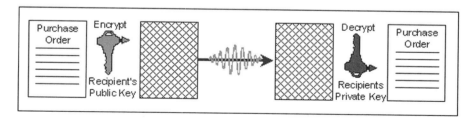

sends the first half of an already encrypted message. After which, each party sends the second half of their already encrypted message, as follows:

1. Alice sends Bob her public key.

2. Bob sends Alice his public key.

3. Alice encrypts her message using Bob's public key. She sends the first half of the resulting encrypted text to Bob.

4. Bob encrypts his message to Alice with Alice's public key. He now sends the first half of the resulting encrypted text to Alice.

5. Alice sends Bob the second half of her encrypted text.

6. Bob puts the two halves together and recovers the plain text of Alice's message.

7. Bob sends Alice the second half of his encrypted text.

8. Alice puts the two halves together and recovers the plain text of Bob's message.

Here's why this protocol causes a problem for Malcolm. Let's say he is again sitting in the middle of this conversation and is trying to replace the original messages with subverted ones. He will again replace the two public keys with his own public key. Then he receives the first half of Alice's message to Bob. He has no way to read the contents of this first half of the message without the second half. Well, he has to send Bob something; otherwise, the communication stops. Malcolm has to make up a message, completely from the scratch, encrypt it with Bob's public key, and send it to Bob. True to the form of the Interlock protocol, Bob sends Alice the first half of his message. Malcolm is in the same boat. He has to make up a completely new message and send its first encrypted half to Alice. Alice sends out the second half of her message to Bob, which is intercepted by Malcolm. Now Malcolm can read the contents of the Alice's message, but he cannot adapt the message to Bob's anymore, because he has sent Bob the first half already. Well, isn't that a shame? I never liked that Malcolm anyway.

For this protocol to work, the first half of the encrypted message must not be able to be decrypted without the second half of that same message. This is very easy to achieve using an algorithm that encrypts blocks of text. Because the RSA algorithm is a block cipher and encrypts the data in large blocks, nothing can be done with just half the digits from a given block of a completely encrypted message. Again, this protocol does not protect Alice and Bob from Malcolm reading the message, but it protects them from receiving subverted messages. All of this could be taken care of using digital signatures and/or public-key certificates.

Digital Signatures Remember our post office example? What good is keeping something secret if you can't be sure of who sent you this secret something? A digital signature is proof that a certain message was really written by Alice, for example. You will probably hear the term *Digital Signature Algorithm* (DSA). DSA's also have the added ability to guarantee that a message has not been tampered with. A one-way hash function is used to compute a hash value. Any change to the message produces a different hash value when the same hash function is used. Using one-way hash functions and public key encryption, a DSA can, for example, be issued as follows:

1. Alice first runs some one-way function over the document she is signing (checksum).

2. Alice now encrypts this checksum using her secret key.

3. She then appends this encrypted checksum to the end of her document.

Now, anybody that has or obtains her public key, can verify that it was Alice who wrote the document. Using Alice's public key, Bob is now able to recover the checksum. He then calculates the checksum created from the one-way hash of the document he received and compares it with the checksum that was appended to the end of the document. If the two checksums are identical, he knows for sure that Alice's public key matches the private key that was used to create the digital signature for this document, thereby proving it was, in fact, Alice (see Figure 10-8).

Two major versions of DSAs are currently being used. The first is *Digital Signature Standard* (DSS) also referred to as FIPS-186 (an acronym for *Federal Information Processing Standard*). The other is the RSA version of a DSA. RSA is generally considered to be the best.

Certificates A *certificate* is a digitally signed statement that provides independent confirmation of a person's public key. Certificates are issued by

Figure 10-8

A checksum of public key encryption

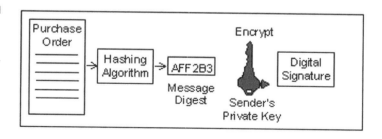

trusted third parties such as governments or financial institutions or companies that specialize in certificates such as VeriSign.® These trusted third parties are referred to as *certificate authorities* (CAs). The certificate generally includes, at minimum, the following items (it can contain much more information and with more detail, depending on the class rating):

1. The name of the CA
2. The name and attributes of the person who owns the public key
3. The actual public key of the person represented by the CA
4. A digital signature of the CA at the end of the certificate itself

Recall in the public key section that issuing authorities were mentioned during the discussion about CAs. In the post office example, issuing authorities were the companies that distributed and replenished public keys to anyone who needed, and they also verified the identities of the individuals beforehand. Figure 10-9 illustrates a visual representation of what takes place when a sender generates a digitally signed document with a certificate prior to transmission.

Figure 10-9

The representation of a digitally signed document with a certificate prior to transmission

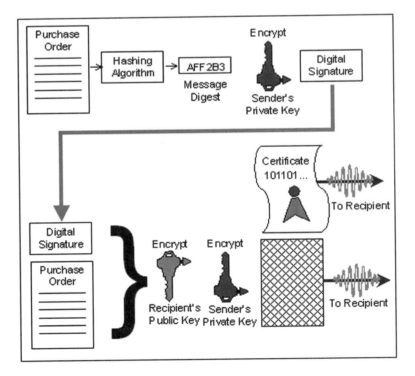

After transmission, the recipient does the following, as shown in Figure 10-10.

As far as man-in-the-middle attacks go, this eliminates Malcolm's ability to intercept and forge public keys because Alice and Bob would be getting these keys from a trusted third party, a CA. These certificates would be digitally signed by the CA as well. Thus, the middle, with regard to key exchange, has been removed from the picture. Pretend for a moment that a guy named Ted is the world's most famous CA and your trusted third party. Let's see how Malcolm deals with this example:

1. Alice emails Bob asking for his public key and certificate.

2. Bob sends Alice his public key and certificate and digitally signs it.

3. Alice emails Ted asking for Bob's public key and certificate.

4. Ted sends Alice Bob's public key and certificate and digitally signs it.

5. Alice compares Ted's version of the certificate with Bob's version and they match perfectly.

6. Alice encrypts a secret symmetric key using Bob's public key and sends it along with her public key and certificate digitally signed by her.

7. Bob emails Ted asking for Alice's public key and certificate.

8. Ted sends Bob Alice's public key and certificate and digitally signs it.

9. Bob compares Ted's version of the certificate with Alice's version and they match perfectly.

10. Alice and Bob communicate very securely.

11. Malcolm sees that his future in being a cryptographic middleman is starting to fade and now sets his sights on becoming an attorney where his future as a middleman is very bright indeed.

Figure 10-10
Action taken on receipt of the digital certificate

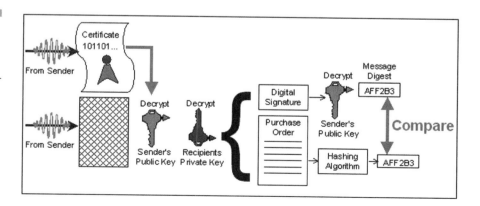

The next sections discuss the two most common protocols used by CAs. By far, the most common and widely recognized certificate in the world is the X.509 version 3, as put forth by the *International Standard Organization* (ISO). The other is *Lightweight Directory Access Protocol* (LDAP).

X.509 Digital Certificates   The X.509 standard defines what information can go into a certificate and it describes how to write it down (the data format). All X.509 certificates have the following data, in addition to the signature:

- *Version*: This identifies which version of the X.509 the certificate represents. This includes the kind of information contained within. Three versions currently exist.

- *Serial Number*: Whoever creates a certificate is responsible for assigning a serial number to it. You need some way tell them apart. This is the information used when publishing the expiration date of the certificate. When it is revoked, the serial number is published in a *Certificate Revocation List* (CRL).

- *Signature ID*: This is to identify the algorithm used by the CA to sign the certificate.

- *Issuer Name*: The X.500 name of the authority that signed the certificate.

- *Validity Period*: Usually a certificate is valid only for a limited amount of time. This includes a start time and date, as well as an end time and date. This can be anywhere from a few seconds to several years. The validity period is the expected period when entities can rely on the public value if the associated private key has not been compromised.

- *Subject Name*: The name of the person whose public key the certificate represents. This name uses the X.500 standard that divides names into distinct groups that make it unique across the Internet. This is known as the *Distinguished Name* (DN) of the person:

  - *Common Name* (CN): Private John Doe
  - *Organizational Unit* (OU): U.S. Army
  - *Organization* (O): U.S. Military
  - *Country* (C): United States of America

- *Public-key info*: This is the actual public key of the person named in the certificate. This includes the algorithm the person is using and which kind of public-key system this key is to be used with, as well as any associated key parameters.

All the information in the certificate is encoded using two related standards: *Abstract Syntax Notation 1* (ASN.1), which is used to describe the data and the *Definite Encoding Rules* (DER), which describe how the data is to be stored and how to transfer that data.

Lightweight Directory Access Protocol (LDAP)   The LDAP is pretty similar to the X.509 in that it uses the X.500 naming convention, but it is smaller and easier to implement. Generally, the way it works is when a server gets a request from a client, it asks for the client's certificate before proceeding. The client then sends its certificate to the server. The server then takes the CA listed in the certificate and tries to match it to a trusted CA that is listed on that server. If there isn't a match, some servers end the connection and some perform a different operation based on the failed match. After the server checks that the certificate's CA is trusted, then the server performs the following steps to map the certificate to an LDAP entry:

1. It maps the user's DN from the user's certificate to a branch point in the LDAP directory.

2. It searches the LDAP directory for an entry that matches the information about the user of the certificate.

3. It then verifies the user's certificate with one in the LDAP entry that maps to the DN.

4. After the server finds a matching entry and certificate in the LDAP directory, it uses that information to process whatever transaction is being requested.

Cryptographic Attacks

As important as it is to know how to defend yourself from an enemy, it is also important that you find out the methods that they will use to attack you. Keep one thing in mind as well. The faster and more powerful computers become to help us implement newer and better cryptographic algorithms, the faster and more powerful they become to crack those algorithms. Cryptographers develop encryption algorithms. Cryptanalysts find ways to break them, well, cryptanalysts and a few pale, pimply teenagers. The attacks are broken down into types because, as in any investigation, it all depends on how much evidence you have to start with. Two main types of categories exist that you should be aware of, which are crypt-analysis and protocol subversion. Think of cryptanalysis as a kind of encryption forensics and protocol subversion as the equivalent of what a con artist does, but to data instead of people. We'll start with cryptanalysis methods first.

Cryptanalysis Methods

This section covers four cryptanalysis methods: ciphertext-only attacks, known-plaintext attacks (also known as linear cryptanalysis), chosen-plain-text attacks (also known as differential cryptanalysis) and chosen-cipher-text attacks.

Ciphertext-Only Attacks

In this type of attack, the cryptanalyst has no idea what the message contains; all he has is garbage the algorithm produces. In this method, the cryptanalyst tries to gather as much of the ciphertext as possible in order to look for patterns. The ultimate goal is to try to figure out the key being used so that it may be used to decipher future messages. This is the most difficult attack because you haven't much to work with. This is also what is known as the *brute force* method because it involves trying the entire key-space. This is not as "out of the question" as it might seem. If you look back to the RSA algorithms section and recall the description of how the 140-digit key was cracked, you will notice that it took 8.9 CPU years, which translates into only 11 weeks. By using many computers at once or, in cases where you don't own that many computers, you could use the spare CPU cycles of someone else's computers to accomplish the same thing without them even knowing you are doing it. There are several known instances of this happening since the Internet came into being.

Known-plaintext Attack

What happens here is that the cryptanalyst has samples of both the cipher-text and the plaintext. He either has some of the plaintext or tries to guess what that plaintext might be. Many documents begin in a very predictable way. In business letters, you may have your "to whom it may concern"s and "sincerely"s to work with. If you know the name of the company sending the document, you could even use the letterhead as a constant in your search for the key. The more you have to work with, the better your chances are of using these items to discover the key, thereby deciphering any future correspondence.

Chosen-plaintext Attack

In this case, the cryptanalyst not only has the ciphertext and plaintext, but he or she also has the ability to send any other text through the algorithm to produce more ciphertext to work with. The cryptanalyst can now have any text he or she wants encrypted with the unknown key. Each time he or she does this, more clues are necessary to reveal the key. This is a popular method of attacking many of the RSA algorithms.

Chosen-ciphertext Attacks

This is a situation where the cryptanalyst might actually have access to whatever means were used to decrypt the ciphertext, but he or she is unable to extract the actual decryption key.

Protocol Subversion

Protocol subversion is another method that can cause problems for your network. Obviously, it is very important to use a good encryption technique, but without using the proper combination, you are vulnerable to subversion methods. Recall the example in the Diffie-Hellman section where Malcolm intercepts packets between Alice and Bob and fools them into thinking they are speaking to each other when, in fact, Malcolm is substituting his own packets in place of theirs. This is exactly how protocol subversion works. Another clever way of protocol subversion would be in the form of a denial of service attack being used prior to another man-in-the-middle attack.

Denial of Service

Computers use numbers to communicate with each other. Humans on the other hand are a different story. We need to use names because numbers are not familiar to us and we would quickly lose track of all the different numbers that represent the computers we communicate with regularly. The way around this is by using a *Domain Naming System* (DNS) server. The job of this server is to resolve familiar human names to unfamiliar numeric addresses. Many of the current DNS versions are not very bright. A malicious hacker could run a denial of service attack on the DNS server you use and, knowing that your computer was waiting for some kind of resolution, he could convince your computer that the hacker's DNS server was the one it should use. He would then redirect or subvert your email or any other packets for that matter to wherever he likes and read it at will. Similar subversion techniques can be used on border routers as well. By sending bogus routing table updates to these routers, he could subvert all of your packets through his router before sending them on their way to a final destination and again be in a position to examine or alter the contents. These are just a couple of examples. Sometimes, to malicious hackers, rendering your network useless is just as good as breaking into it.

VPN Architectures

The following section discusses the three kinds of VPN architectures that are used most commonly today. These are known as access VPNs, intranet VPNs, and extranet VPNs. Access VPNs differ in many ways from intranet and extranet VPNs. The differences lie in the tunneling methods used by these architectures. We'll start with access VPNs.

Access VPN

Access VPNs are sometimes referred to as remote access VPNs or *Virtual Private Dial-up Networks* (VPDN). These are generally created for individual users who want to access the corporate network from a remote location such as their home, a satellite office, or anywhere in the world for that matter. As was mentioned before, in order for remote users to access the corporate network prior to VPN technology, they would have to use the *Public Switched Telephone Network* (PSTN). They would dial in to access servers using long-distance charges. This also required individual modem connections and phone numbers that had to be maintained locally on the corporate campus by internal IT staff. Remote Access VPNs obviate the need for all of these things. With the advent of the Internet, ISPs maintain local access numbers virtually everywhere. This means that the remote user as well as the corporate campus need only make what amounts to local phone calls to access the Internet over which these VPN tunnels are created. What's more is that they are no longer locked into these slow analog phone lines. Virtually any technology can now be used, including high-speed xDSL, ISDN, and cable technologies, in addition to analog connections. Even wireless technologies can be used. Basically, two kinds of access VPNs exist. The client-initiated access VPN and the NAS-initiated Access VPN.

The client-initiated VPNs create a tunnel all the way from the corporate access server to the remote client itself. This will require the remote user to have some kind of VPN client software installed that is compatible with whatever VPN technology is being used by the corporate Access Server. This is a two-step process. The client must first access the local ISP NAS using PPP to connect to the Internet. Once this connection has been established, the user (client) using PPTP or L2TP creates a tunnel all the way through to the corporate access server. When using this method, all communication between the corporate network and the remote client is completely encrypted from end to end. Figure 10-11 shows a client initiated VPN.

The NAS-initiated VPN is where the remote client simply dials into the local ISP NAS over a standard PPP connection, at which point the ISP NAS creates the encrypted tunnel with the corporate access server. All communication over the Internet infrastructure to the corporate access server is encrypted; however, the connection from the remote client PC to the local ISP NAS is not. The difference here is that no special client software is required on any of the remote clients. The connection over the PSTN is far less vulnerable than the actual Internet, but technically is still a liability. Figure 10-12 illustrates the use of NAS-initiated connections.

Figure 10-11
Client initiated VPN

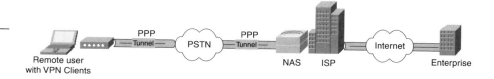

Figure 10-12
NAS initiated VPN connection

Intranet VPN

Intranet VPNs, also known as router-to-router or site-to-site VPNs, essentially provide the same type of function. These VPNs use the Internet to replace traditional WANs used in connecting LANs at remote sites. These types of VPNs can be built using the Internet, or even over a part of the ISP's private IP infrastructure. For example, global companies tend to have offices around the world. Traditionally, they would provision expensive leased line technologies such as Frame Relay, T1 or T3, or even ATM provided by public exchange carriers. Intranet VPNs avoid this by setting up secure tunnels at the border routers of each of these locations. These IPSec or GRE tunnels actually pass through the public Internet transparently via the local ISPs. Many categories exist, from *small office / home office* (SOHO) sites, branch office-to-main office, enterprise, or a combination of all of these. New technologies such as DSL, cable, and wireless can now provide high-speed access at extremely low rates. Some ISPs are starting to provide a complete routing service where the corporate intranet tunnels are maintained by the ISPs completely. This would obviate the need for complex router configurations at the corporate sites so that these companies need not maintain extensive IT staffing at the smaller branch offices.

The things that need to be taken into consideration revolve around QoS. This has to do with prioritizing certain types of traffic such as SNA or even voice, which require little or no delay, over standard email or file transfer communications. The nature of the Internet is geared toward packet-switching technologies that are connectionless and can't always guarantee this QoS, as opposed to circuit-switching technologies that are connection oriented. However, these problems can be solved using priority-queuing techniques, tag-switching, and *Multi-Protocol Label Switching* (MPLS). Traditional WAN carriers can offer a VPN service similar to a Frame-Relay service with QoS, based on the *Committed Information Rate* (CIR). Figure 10-13 illustrates a basic representation of a simple router-to-router VPN.

Figure 10-13
Intranet VPN

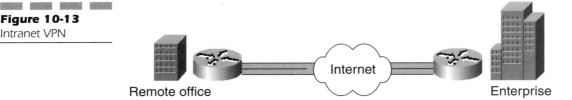

Remote office

Internet

Enterprise

Extranet VPN

Extranet VPNs use many of the same technologies as Intranet VPNs but differ from intranets in that they enable access to remote users or business partners outside of their company's corporate internal network. These kinds of VPNs link customers, suppliers, partners, or *communities of interest* (COINs) to the company's corporate intranet using a shared infrastructure over dedicated connections. Extranets could also be thought of as intranets that provide limited access to these customers, suppliers, and partners while simultaneously allowing authorized access for telecommuters and remote offices. This is a powerful tool in business-to-business relationships. Figure 10-14 shows the Cisco implementation of an extranet VPN design. By using digital certificates, clients establish a secure tunnel over the Internet to the enterprise. A CA issues a digital certificate to each client for device authentication. VPN Clients may either use static IP addressing with manual configuration or dynamic IP addressing with *Internet Key Exchange* (IKE) protocols or configurations. The CA checks the identity of remote users and then authorizes these remote users to provide access to the corporate network.

Figure 10-14
Extranet VPN
topology

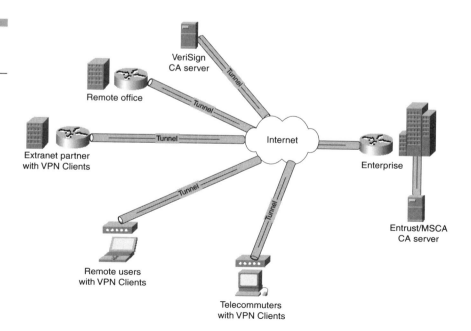

Types of VPNs

Implementing a VPN can be done in four different ways. The type you use will vary, depending on the situation. Most of the time the complete solution will involve a combination of one or more of these types. All of them support remote access and some can also support intranets and extranets too.

Hardware-Based VPN

Hardware-based VPNs involve the use of routers or dedicated VPN devices that are commonly referred to as VPN appliances. These products must be capable of authentication, encryption, filtering, and encapsulation. Almost all Cisco products have these capabilities depending on the version of IOS being used. This type of VPN usually provides the best performance due to the dedicated chipsets and architecture that are designed to handle some or all of these functions internally. Because they have been designed from the ground up, they are generally easier to manage as well. By virtue of using hardware-based encryption, and in some cases proprietary real-time operating systems, they tend to be much harder to crack than software-based VPNs. Some hardware based VPN solutions use external servers to handle authentication, authorization, and auditing. This can help enable VPN access to be integrated into the existing authentication, authorization, and auditing system that may make implementation less complicated.

Software-Based VPN

Software-based VPNs involve running some kind of VPN software on a server. Many software-based VPNs can enable tunneling based on addressing or by protocol. This can help when there are different types of traffic at the remote locations that can include both VPN and non-VPN traffic. This might be a good solution for remote users connecting over the PSTN. Software-based VPNs are slower and more difficult to manage than hardware-based VPNs, but they are usually less expensive.

Firewall-Based VPN

Firewall-based VPNs include some kind of software; however, they are usually just modules that are added to whatever firewall system you are running. Firewall-based VPNS also usually have a lot of functions required for VPN implementation such as *network address translation* (NAT), as well as authentication, authorization, and auditing with real-time alarms and extensive logging capabilities, which can make it easier to monitor what is going on. Firewall-based VPNs also harden the host operating system by disabling or removing unnecessary services that are prone to attack. Most have an another interface known as a *demilitarized zone* (DMZ) interface with its own access controls. The DMZ enables controlled access to Web servers, proxies, and other services in an environment that can be compromised without affecting the security of the internal network. As most firewalls run on hosts operating systems, they tend to have user-friendly interfaces, which make the VPN and security installation easier. Firewall-based VPNs are the best choice for intranet-based VPNs requiring limited remote access. They can also be used to provide extranet connections to business partners, suppliers, and customers. When implementing large-scale remote access or intranet VPNs, you should use a combination of these types of VPNs in order to handle the throughput and performance. Firewall-based VPNs usually require an external router for connection to the Internet.

ISP-Based VPN

A lot of ISPs provide managed VPN services for all of the VPN architectures such as access, intranet, and extranet VPNs. This is usually done on a combination of hardware based and firewall-based VPNs that are owned, operated, and managed by the ISP itself. The major consideration here is whether or not you want the ISP involved in handling and/or managing your security infrastructure.

Other Considerations

It is important to consider which type of protocol that you will use as well as the authentication and encryption methods.

Protocols

Protocols that must be considered include the type of end-user protocols that the VPN can handle as well as the method they use to encapsulate or tunnel across the VPN. Although most VPN solutions focus on IP only, some can handle other protocols such as IPX or SNA either natively or by encapsulation within IP. Each of these methods relies on tunneling to transport the information across the VPN. Tunneling protocols include layer 2 protocols such as PPTP, L2F, L2TP, and layer three tunneling protocols such as IPSec.

Authentication and Encryption

A lot of VPN solutions use their own authentication servers. They could also use other common authentication methods such as *Remote Authentication Dial-In User Server* (RADIUS) and *Terminal Access Controller Access System* (TACACS). The advantage of using these authentication methods is that they can be centralized and scale to large numbers of users better.

CHAPTER **11**

Quality of
Service Design

If you pick up a trade publication, it is difficult not to encounter the term *Quality of Service* (QoS). That term references the capability of a network to provide a set of characteristics that tailors the delivery of data to user requirements and is the focus of this chapter. This chapter is designed to give you an appreciation for what the term QoS really means. This discussion will detail the metrics by which QoS can be specified and why some metrics are more suitable than others for different types of applications, as well as examine various networking architecture components that support QoS. Because there truly is no free lunch in networking, the discussion also will cover one of the key issues that may hamper the ability to obtain QoS on an inter-network basis: charging for the service.

Overview

When you pick up a telephone and call a distant party, you obtain a quality of service that makes a voice conversation both possible and practical. The practicality of the call results from the basic design of the telephone company network infrastructure. That infrastructure digitizes voice conversations into a 64 Kbps data stream and routes the digitized conversation through a fixed path, established over the network infrastructure. For the entire path, 64 Kbps of bandwidth is allocated on an end-to-end basis to the call. The fixed path is established through a process called circuit switching.

Under circuit switching, a 64 Kbps time slot is allocated from the entry (ingress) point into the telephone network, through the network, to an exit (egress) point. The 64 Kbps time slot is commonly referred to as a *Digital Signal* (DS) *level 0* (DS0), and the path through which the DS0 signal is allocated occurs by switches reserving 64 Kbps slices of bandwidth.

As voice is digitized at the ingress point into the telephone company network, a slight delay of a few milliseconds occurs. As each switch performs a cross-connection operation, permitting digitized voice to flow from a DS0 contained in one circuit connected to the switch onto a DS0 channel on another circuit connected to the switch, a path is formed through the network and another delay occurs. Although each cross-connection introduces a slight delay to the flow of digitized voice, the switch delay is minimal, typically a fraction of a millisecond or less. Thus, the total end-to-end delay experienced by digitized voice as it flows through a telephone network can be considered as minimal.

Another characteristic of the digitized voice flow through the telephone network infrastructure concerns the variability or latency differences between each digitized voice sample. Although voice digitization and circuit-switching processes add latency to each voice sample, that delay is uniform. Thus, the telephone network can be characterized as a low delay, uniform or near-uniform delay transmission system. Those two qualities—low delay and uniform or near-uniform delay—represent two key Quality of Service metrics.

The two metrics are important considerations for obtaining the ability to transmit real-time data, such as voice and video. However, the telephone company infrastructure also provides a third key QoS metric, which is equally important. That metric is a uniform, dedicated, 64 Kbps bandwidth allocated to each voice conversation. Because that bandwidth is dedicated on an end-to-end basis, you can view it as being similar to providing an expressway that allows a stream of cars to travel from one location to another, while prohibiting other cars destined to other locations to share the highway.

A fourth QoS characteristic provided by the telephone company infrastructure is the fact that digitized voice flows end-to-end essentially lossless. That is, there is no planned dropping of voice samples during periods of traffic congestion. Instead, when the volume of calls exceeds the capacity of the network, such as on Mother's Day or Christmas Eve, new calls are temporarily blocked and the subscriber encounters a "fast" busy signal when dialing. Table 11-1 provides a summary of commonly used QoS metrics and their normal method of representation.

Although the telephone company network infrastructure provides the QoS necessary to support real-time communications, its design is relatively inefficient. This inefficiency results from the fact that unless humans shout at one another, a conversation is normally half duplex; this results in half of the bandwidth utilization being wasted. Also, unless we talk non-stop, like the man in the Federal Express commercial that was popular a few years ago, we periodically pause as we converse. Because 64 Kbps of bandwidth is allocated for the duration of the call, bandwidth utilization is far from optimal.

Table 11-1

Common QoS Metrics

Metric Representation	Normal
Dedicated bandwidth	bps, Kbps, or Mbps
Latency (delay)	msec
Variation (jitter)	msec
Data Loss	percent of frames or packets transmitted

Packet Network

Compared to a circuit-switched network, where bandwidth use is dedicated to a user, packet networks allow multiple users to share network bandwidth. Although this increases the efficiency level of network utilization, it introduces several new problems. For an overview of those problems, this section examines the operation of a generic packet network; this could be a TCP/IP network such as the Internet, a corporate intranet, or even a frame-relay network.

Figure 11-1 illustrates the flow of data from two different locations over a common backbone packet network infrastructure. In this example, two organizations—labeled 1 and 2—share access via packet network node A to the packet network. Assume that packets destined from organization 1 flow to the network address Z connected to mode E, while packets from organization 2 flow to location Y, which is also connected to packet network mode E.

Figure 11-1
Data flow via a packet network

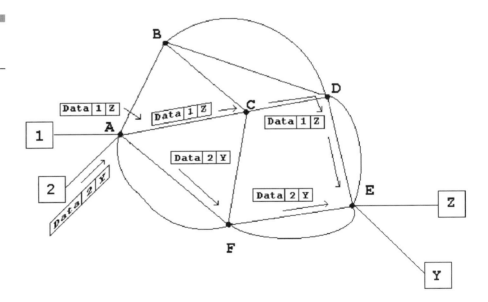

In Figure 11-1, packets could flow over different backbone routes; however, their ingress and egress locations are shown to be in common. Assuming that location 2 is transmitting real-time information to location Y, what happens when, periodically, a packet from location 1 arrives at mode A ahead of the packet from location 2? When this situation occurs, the packet from location 1 delays the processing of the packet arriving from location 2.

Suppose data sources connected to nodes B, C, and D all require access to devices connected to node A. The device at node A may be literally swamped with packets beyond its processing capability and the network device at node A may be forced to drop packets. Although applications such as a file transfer could simply retransmit a dropped packet without a user being aware of it, if real-time data such as voice or video was being transmitted, too many packet drops would become noticeable. They cannot be compensated for by retransmission that further delays real-time information.

Consider what happens when the packet from location 2 is serviced at node A. If other packets require routing to node F, packets from location 2 could be further delayed. After packets from location 2 are forwarded onto the circuit between nodes A and F, they will be processed by node F. At this location, packets arriving from nodes C and E could delay the ability of node F to forward packets destined to node E. Next, packets are forwarded on towards node E for delivery to address Y. For the previously described data flow, several variable delays will be introduced, each adversely affecting the flow of packets from location 2 to address Y. In addition, once a packet reaches mode E, it could be delayed by the need to process other packets. Examples include the one arriving from location 1 and destined to address Z.

Another characteristic of a packet network is that when a node becomes overloaded, it will send some packets to the great bit bucket in the sky. This is a normal characteristic of packet networks and, in fact, a frame-relay performance metric involves discard rate for such packets. Based on the preceding examination of data flow in a packet network, note that there is no guarantee that packets will arrive at all, with minimal delay, or with a set amount of variation between packets. Because this situation makes it difficult, if not impossible, to transport real-time data over a packet network, various techniques were developed in an attempt to provide a QoS capability to packet networks.

Those techniques can be categorized into three general areas, which include expediting traffic at the ingress point into the network, expediting traffic through the network, and expediting delivery of traffic at the destination or egress point out of the network. For each area, different hardware and software vendors support several techniques to provide QoS capability.

Some techniques are standardized, while others will be standardized in the near future.

The manner by which an organization connects equipment to the ingress and egress points on a packet network have a bearing upon whether or not additional QoS tools and techniques are required; they provide an end-to-end transmission capability within certain limits for delay, jitter, and obtainable bandwidth. Keeping this in mind, attention is turned to the ingress point of a packet network and examining the flow of traffic from a LAN to the ingress point. For lack of a better term, this is called the LAN egress location.

LAN Egress and the IEEE 802.1p Standard

A *local area network* (LAN) can be connected to a packet network through several methods. Although it is quite common to connect a LAN to a packet network using a router, numerous network configurations can reside behind the router and represent the structure of the corporate LAN or even an intranet.

Because this chapter is concerned with QoS, this section turns your attention to a network configuration that allows traffic from several LAN and non-LAN–based sources to be differentiated from one another as the data is passed to a router. The key to this capability is the IEEE 802.1p standard.

The IEEE 802.1p standard represents a Layer 2 (data link layer) signaling technique that permits network traffic to be prioritized. This standard is implemented by relatively recently manufactured Layer 2-compliant switches and routers, which can classify traffic into eight priority levels. By using IEEE 802.1p-compliant equipment, it becomes possible for time-critical applications on a LAN to receive preferential treatment over non-time–critical applications. It is important to note that the IEEE 802.1p standard is a Layer 2 standard. This means that a priority tag added to LAN frames to differentiate traffic is removed at the Layer 2-to-Layer 3 conversion point, when LAN frames are converted to packets for transmission over a WAN. Thus, the IEEE 802.1p standard is applicable only to expedite traffic on a LAN.

Figure 11-2 illustrates an example of the use of the IEEE 802.1p standard use. In this example, a PBX is shown connected to a voice gateway, which in turn is connected to a port on a Layer 2 LAN switch. Other switch connections include support for several LAN and server connections, as well as a connection to a router, with the latter providing connectivity to a packet network.

▰▰ ▰▰ ▰▰ ▰▰

Figure 11-2
The IEEE 802.1p
standard supports
the ability to provide
preferential treatment
for time-critical
applications

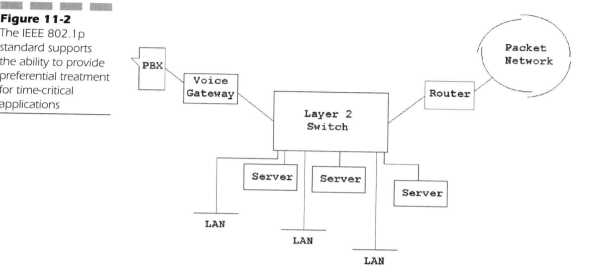

A non-IEEE 802.1p-compliant switch treats all flow requests equally. If a user on one LAN requires access to the router at approximately the same time as a user on another LAN, the second request received is queued behind the first. This is the classic *first-in, first-out* (FIFO) queuing method.

Under the IEEE 802.1p standard, traffic can be placed into different queues, based upon the level of priority. Thus, voice calls digitized by the voice gateway could be assigned a high level of priority, enabling the switch to service frames generated by the voice gateway and destined to the router, prior to frames originated from other connections destined to the router.

Router Egress

Although only one connection from the Layer 2 switch to the router is shown in Figure 11-2, a router actually can have several LAN side and WAN side connections. Because a heavily utilized router can add a significant delay to real-time traffic, Cisco added several techniques to expedite the flow of traffic through their products. Some of those techniques represent compliance with industry standards, while other techniques are proprietary features incorporated into their products.

Router Queuing Methods

Router manufacturers support several queuing methods beyond FIFO queuing. Some of those additional queuing methods include priority queuing, custom queuing, and weighted fair queuing.

Priority queuing permits users to prioritize traffic based upon network protocol, incoming interface, packet size and source, and destination address. Because digitized voice traffic is transported in relatively short packets, you could use priority queuing to expedite digitized voice ahead of file transfers and other types of traffic carried in relatively long packets.

Under custom queuing, you can share bandwidth among applications. Thus, you could use it to ensure that a voice or video application obtains a guaranteed portion of bandwidth at an entry point into a WAN. Under weighted fair-queuing, interactive traffic is assigned to the front of a queue to reduce response time; the remaining bandwidth is shared among high-bandwidth traffic flow. The Cisco IOS statements applicable to configuring different queuing methods will be covered later in this chapter.

Traffic Expediting

Within the IP header is a field labeled Type of Service, which is also referred to as the Service Type field. This eight-bit field was intended to enable applications to indicate the preferred type of routing path, such as low delay, high throughput, and high reliability for a real-time application. Although a great idea, this field is rarely used and is usually set to a value of 0.

A second traffic-expediting method recognizes the limited use of the Service Type field and involves both renamed and reassigned values to the field. This method reuses the Service Type field as a DiffServ (Differentiated Services) field. Under DiffServ, traffic definitions are assigned to denote the manner by which data flows are handled by routers. Currently, Assured Service and Preferred Service (each with slightly different definitions of service) have been defined by the *Internet Engineering Task Force* (IETF).

A third traffic-expediting method involves mapping a flow of traffic between two locations and adding a label to packets. The goal behind this label method is to avoid searching through each router's address table to find the relevant port to output a packet. Because a router could have thousands of entries in its address tables, bypassing the address search expedites the flow of traffic. Cisco originally referred to this technique as tag-switching. It was standardized by the IETF as *Multi-protocol Label Switching* (MPLS).

Link Efficiency

Because any technique that reduces the number of bytes of traffic increases the efficiency of a *wide area network* (WAN), several compression methods are now standardized. Two of these techniques include TCP header compression and *Real-Time Transport Protocol* (RTP) header compression. RTP represents a standard for time-stamping packets, which allows a receiving device to use a jitter buffer to remove timing discrepancies or variations between packets. Although RTP is a key for ensuring that digitized voice is reconstructed in an acceptable manner conducive for a listener, it has a 40-byte header that is relatively high in proportion to the typical 40- to 120-byte payload of an IP datagram. Thus, both TCP header and RTP header compression can be used to reduce the volume of traffic required to flow through a WAN.

Reserving Bandwidth

In the Overview section, it was noted that the key to the telephone company circuit switching network's QoS capability is the 64 Kbps of bandwidth allocated to each voice call for the duration of the call. In the wonderful world of IP, the *Resource ReserVation Protocol* (RSVP) was standardized by the IETF to provide QoS by allowing applications to dynamically reserve network bandwidth. Although RSVP can be used on small to medium size intranets, it does not scale to a network the size of the Internet. In addition, as bandwidth allocations cross ISP boundaries, there is no present method to bill for the allocation of bandwidth. Although some ISPs may support RSVP within their network portion of the Internet, it is doubtful that the use of RSVP will cross ISP boundaries in the foreseeable future.

WAN Egress

Once traffic flows through a packet network, it must be delivered to its recipient. For real-time traffic that requires a high QoS capability, the flow of packets from the packet network egress point to the recipient must be expedited. To do so, routers can use different types of priority queuing and the destination LAN can employ IEEE 802.1p priority switching. Thus, both ingress and egress to and from the packet network can involve several methods to expedite the flow of Layer 2 traffic. Now that this chapter has covered the different aspects of QoS, it will focus on specifics. In doing so, it will start with an examination at Layer 2 in the ISO Reference Model.

Layer 2 Quality of Service

In the *International Standards Organization* (ISO) *Open System Interconnection* (OSI) Reference Model, Layer 2 represents the data link layer. That layer is responsible for the creation of frames to include applicable addressing and the computation of a cyclic redundancy check, as well as the transmission of such frames. Other functions performed at Layer 2 include error detection and correction, as well as the use of positive and negative acknowledgments to indicate whether or not the destination received error-free frames. One function omitted from the original OSI Reference Model for Layer 2 operations is the topic of this chapter, QoS.

Although the OSI Reference Model does not define QoS as a Layer 2 function, the efforts of the *Institute of Electrical and Electronic Engineers* (IEEE) resulted in the development of a traffic expediting standard for Layer 2 operations.

Overview of Standards

Many years ago, the IEEE was given the task of developing LAN-related standards by the *American National Standards Institute* (ANSI). Although the series of Ethernet (IEEE 802.3) and Token Ring (IEEE 802.5) standards are well known, the IEEE also developed many additional standards since then that are equally important. Some of these standards include the use of the spanning tree algorithm for bridging, flow control as a mechanism to regulate the flow of data devices, virtual LANs, and traffic expediting.

Conventional LAN Data Flow

You can appreciate the problems associated with obtaining QoS on a LAN by examining the data flow on a conventional, shared-media LAN. Figure 11-3 illustrates a shared-media Ethernet LAN used in this section to examine data flow.

Figure 11-3
Data flow on a
shared-media LAN

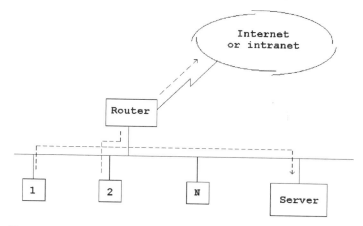

On a shared media network each station has an equal probability of
access, precluding true quality of service from being achieved.

Assume that station 1 is performing a file transfer to the local server,
while station 2 is in the process of conducting a *Voice over IP* (VoIP) call via
the router to a destination on the Internet or on a corporate intranet.
Because the LAN is a shared-media network, each station must contend for
access to the media. If station 1 just began transmitting, when station 2 "lis-
tens" to the LAN, it will note that the network is busy and will wait. In this
example, the wait will more than likely represent the time required to
transmit a frame with a maximum length Information field of 1500 bytes,
because we assumed station 1 was performing a file transfer operation.
That type of operation uses a maximum length Information field for all
frames but the last. Note that there is no method to prioritize gaining
access to the media among stations in this example. Thus, this precludes
the ability to obtain a true quality of service that would require bandwidth
to be allocated on a shared-media network.

In actuality, the preceding is true for shared-media Ethernet networks.
In a Token Ring networking environment, the Control field of a frame contains three priority bits, which enable certain types of applications to gain
access to the media ahead of other types of applications. Although the priority scheme expedites traffic and forms the basis for subsequent efforts by
the IEEE, the priority scheme does not reserve bandwidth and represents
a limitation carried over into the LAN switch environment. However,
although the Token Ring standard does not define the mapping of frames
with different priority values into queues, the IEEE 802.1p standard does,

and can be considered a more sophisticated evolution resulting from the Token Ring effort.

LAN Switching

In an Ethernet shared-media environment, it is not possible to favor access to the media. Recognizing this limitation, the IEEE focused its traffic-expediting efforts upon the LAN switch environment.

A LAN switch can be considered to represent a contention device similar to a telephone switch. When two people dial the same number, one will receive a busy signal, while the other will make a connection through the switch, allowing the dialed phone to ring. Viewing a LAN switch as making connections on a frame-by-frame basis, a similar analogy can be made, with frames routed towards the same destination and causing blockage. However, unlike a telephone company switch that does not hold calls, a LAN switch includes buffer storage that can be used to temporarily hold frames when two or more input ports have data destined to the same output port.

Figure 11-4 illustrates the general flow of data through a Layer 2 LAN switch when two input port data sources contend for access to the same destination port. In this example, two clients are shown attempting to access a switch port connected to a server. Because many Layer 2 switches allocate buffer storage for queuing frames destined to a common output port, the switch contention example shown in Figure 11-4 shows two frames in a

Figure 11-4

Data flow through a switch to the same destination results in frames being queued in memory

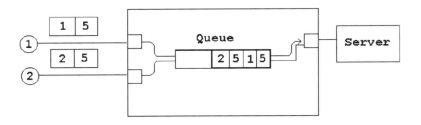

Legend: Frame format (no data shown)

source address	destination address

queue in memory, with one frame in the process of exiting the queue, while new frames are shown flowing towards the queue.

The queue shown in Figure 11-4 is technically referred to as a *first-in, first-out* (FIFO) queue. Thus, frames that reach the queue are processed in the order in which they arrive. Also note that if the queue becomes full, succeeding frames that reach the queue are dropped. Therefore, a single FIFO queue has no mechanism to distinguish the needs of different applications concerning their ability to flow through a switch with minimal delay or delay variation.

Although FIFO queuing was simple to implement and equitable in the allocation of switch resources, it failed the differentiation test, being incapable of distinguishing different application requirements. Although some switch vendors began to develop proprietary priority queuing techniques, the IEEE was in the process of developing virtual LAN standards and recognized the need to provide a common traffic expediting method. The initial IEEE effort, referred to as 802.1Q, was oriented towards developing a standard for *virtual LANs* (VLANs). Here the term references a broadcast domain. The goal behind VLANs was to enable network administrators to position switches based upon organization, application, network protocol, or other criteria that enabled users to be grouped dynamically into a broadcast domain. Because one domain does not "hear" the broadcasts associated with other domains, using VLANs can boost switch performance while providing administrative flexibility.

As part of the IEEE 802.1Q effort, a tag was added to the Layer 2 MAC frame as it entered a VLAN-compliant switch. The 32-bit tag is inserted after the frame's normal Destination and Source Address fields, as illustrated in Figure 11-5. In examining Figure 11-5, note that the IEEE "killed two birds with one frame modification" by defining three bits within the 32-bit header as a priority field.

As indicated in Figure 11-5, the three priority field bits provide the ability to specify eight levels of priority per frame, with the default priority set to a value of 000. The two-byte *Tag Protocol Identifier* (TPID) identifies the frame as a tagged frame. The two-byte *Tag Control Information* (TCI) field contains three subfields to include the previously mentioned three-bit user priority field, a one-bit Token Ring encapsulation flag, and a *VLAN Identifier* (VID). The Token Ring encapsulation flag indicates whether the encapsulated frame is in a native Token Ring (802.5) format. The VID uniquely identifies the VLAN to which the frame belongs and also is referred to as the VLAN tag.

In the priority subfield shown in Figure 11-5, note that priority levels range from 7 (highest priority) to 0 (lowest priority). As part of a revised 802.1D bridging standard, the IEEE ratified its 802.1p specification, which

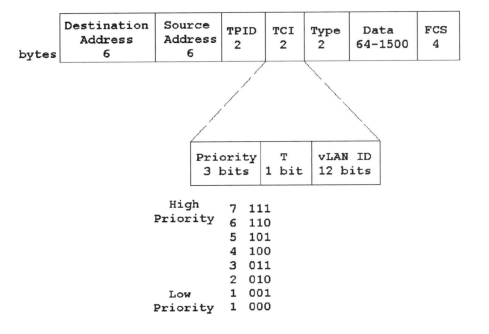

Figure 11-5
IEEE traffic prioritization uses three bits in the two-byte TCI field, which represents half of the four-byte VLAN frame extension

provides a mechanism for Layer 2 switches to prioritize traffic. Although network managers must determine actual mappings, the IEEE has made broad recommendations concerning priority settings. The following mini-table indicates those broad recommendations.

111 (7) Network Critical

110 (6) Interactive Voice

101 (5) Interactive Multimedia

100 (4) Streaming Multimedia

011 (3) Business Critical

010 (2) Standard

001 (1) Background

000 (0) Best Effort (Default)

In the previous table entries, network critical traffic could represent *Routing Information Protocol* (RIP) and *Open Shortest Path First* (OSPF) table updates. Priority six could be used for VoIP applications, while priorities five and four would represent different multimedia applications. Business critical traffic could include *Service Advertising Protocol* (SAP) traffic, while a zero value is used as a best-effort default. That is, if an application does not set the priority subfield, its default value is set to zero.

The priority bits are within the 802.1Q frame. Desktop clients, servers, routers, and switches can set those bits. In desktop clients and servers, 802.1p-compliant network adapter cards can form 802.1Q frames, as well as set the bits in the priority subfield. The actual setting of the priority bits is commonly invoked by monitoring the network socket. Here the term socket references the IP address and upper layer port that identifies the application.

As 802.1Q frames reach switches and routers that are designed to act upon traffic priorities, such devices employ multiple queues. In fact, the 802.1p specification provides recommendations concerning how eight traffic classes can be assigned with 2, 3, 4, or more queues per port. As you might expect, higher priority frames are automatically assigned to highest priority queues, while lower priority frames are assigned to lower priority queues. Once a frame is in a queue, it will be selected for transmission only if the higher traffic class queue(s) supported by the port is empty at the time the selection process occurs.

To illustrate an example of the use of the 802.1p traffic expediting standard, assume your organization uses 802.1p-compliant switches in a tier or hierarchical structure, as illustrated in Figure 11-6. In this example, assume client 1 is performing a file transfer to the server attached to switch 3 (shown as a sequence of x's), while client 2 is in the process of transferring a file via switches 1 and 2 to a distant location on the Internet or a corporate intranet (shown as a series of dots . . .). At the same time the preceding activity is occurring, client 3 is conducting a videoconference via switches 3 and 2 to a distant party on the Internet or corporate intranet (shown as a sequence of dashes - - -).

Although the flow of data from clients 2 and 3 flow over a common path from switch 2 to the router, and then to the Internet or corporate intranet, the actual exiting of frame out of switch 2 to the router occurs based upon the priority bit settings of the applications forming the data flow from clients 2 and 3. That is, during periods of congestion when frames from both sources arrive at the switch destined for the same output port, the priority queuing scheme governs which frames gain access to exiting the port.

Figure 11-6
Priority traffic-control
example

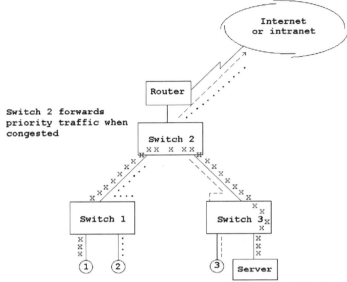

Assuming switch 2 is 802.1p compliant, it places traffic from Client 2 (dots ...) and traffic from client 3 (dashes ---) into different queues and extracts frames from client 3 for transmission to the router prior to extracting frames from the client 2 queue.

For example, assume frames from client 2 have a default priority setting of 0, while frames from client 3 have a priority setting of 6. When frames from clients 2 and 3 contend for output via switch 2 to the router, they would flow into different queues. The switch would empty frames from the high-priority queue prior to extracting frames from the lower-priority queue, providing a traffic-expediting capability to the VoIP application being conducted by client 3.

Limitations

Although the 802.1p specification provides a method to expedite traffic, it has several key limitations. They include its Layer 2 operation, tagging method, and need for mapping to obtain an end-to-end QoS capability. As you will see shortly, by itself, 802.1p represents one piece of the QoS puzzle instead of a complete solution.

The first limitation of the 802.1p specification is that it is restricted to Layer 2 operations. This means that when frames cross a router boundary and are converted into network packets, they lose their priority tags. Thus, the 802.1p specification does not address true end-to-end network performance.

A second limitation associated with the 802.1p specification is that the 802.1Q VLAN tag extends the MAC frame. When placed on the media, the maximum frame length is four bytes more than the 1526 associated with a maximum-length Ethernet frame. Although 802.1Q-compliant equipment has no problem recognizing the extended frame, it is quite possible that "legacy" Ethernet equipment could treat such frames as jumbo frames, sending them to the great bit bucket in the sky. Thus, you need to examine the compatibility of equipment with respect to extended frames and possibly replace some of it if such equipment is not compatible with extended frames.

Another problem related to VLAN tags is the manner by which tagged and non-tagged frames are handled. Under the IEEE 802.1Q and 802.1p specifications, non-tagged frames are treated the same as frames tagged with a 0 user priority level. That is, the non-tagged frame is treated on a best-effort basis, which may not be your intention.

The third limitation associated with the 802.1p specification is related to the first limitation. Because the 802.1p specification is limited to Layer 2 operations, one or more additional QoS mechanisms are required to provide QoS on an end-to-end basis. Those mechanisms can include the use of Differential Service (DiffServ), if communications via the router are over a TCP/IP-based network, or mapping applicable frames into *Constant Bit Rate* (CBR) cells, if the router is connected to an ATM-based network. If DiffServ is not supported by the TCP/IP network and it is impractical or not cost-effective to use an ATM infrastructure, it may be possible to prioritize traffic through an existing router-based TCP/IP network infrastructure. This is discussed in the next section.

QoS into the Network

You can consider several methods for expediting the flow of traffic into a network. Those methods include the use of router queues, the ToS byte, and its revision as the DiffServ byte. This section will address each of these topics.

Router Queues

Cisco's IOS current supports four different queuing algorithms: FIFO, priority queuing, custom queuing, and weighted fair queuing. As you might expect, and will see shortly, certain advantages and disadvantages are associated with each queuing method.

FIFO

The first, simplest, and the default queuing method for interfaces operating above 2 Mbps is FIFO. The term FIFO is descriptive of both the manner by which accountants can compute the cost of goods sold and the flow of data when there is no method available to differentiate traffic. FIFO queuing was previously illustrated in Figure 11-4. As indicated, packets are forwarded out of a router's interface in the order in which they arrive.

The key advantage of FIFO is that it requires the least amount of router resources. However, the simplistic nature of FIFO queuing is also its key disadvantage. That is, because packets are output to the interface in their order of arrival, it is possible neither to prioritize traffic nor to prevent an application or user from unfairly over-utilizing available bandwidth.

Priority Queuing

A second type of queuing supported by Cisco routers is referred to as priority queuing. Under priority queuing, traffic can be directed into up to four queues: high, medium, normal, and low. Traffic in the highest priority queue is serviced prior to traffic in lower priority queues. Through priority queuing you can configure a router to place traffic that is relatively intolerant to delay into an appropriate queue that favors its extraction onto a WAN.

In a Cisco router environment, several methods are available for both identifying traffic to be prioritized as well as for placing identified traffic into appropriate queues. Although it is possible to use the IOS priority-list command by itself to assign traffic to predefined queues, it also can associate an access list with a priority list. This adds the considerable flexibility that access lists provide in filtering data as a mechanism to control the flow of traffic into priority queues.

To illustrate an example of priority queuing, as well as obtain a basis for describing some of the limitations of this queuing technique, assume that traffic from a file transfer and voice gateway's digitized voice packets are flowing into a router. Both data sources are destined to locations beyond the router, resulting in a requirement for each type of traffic to flow over a common WAN link. Now assume priority queuing is enabled so that the use of the queues might be configured such that file transfer packets are directed into the low priority queue, while digitized voice packets are directed into the high priority queue. An example of this packet direction based upon priority queuing is shown in Figure 11-7, where voice gateway-generated packets are directed into the high priority queue and file transfer packets flow into the low priority queue.

The assignment of traffic to priority queues is accomplished by using the priority-list command. It can be used by itself or in conjunction with an access-list command to direct traffic to applicable queues. When used by itself, the format of the priority-list command is as follows:

```
priority-list list-number protocol protocol-name
[high|medium|normal|low] keyword keyword-value
```

Here the list-number is in the range 1 to 10 and identifies the priority list created by a user. The protocol-name identifies the protocol type, such as IP, IPX, and similar Layer 3 protocols. Next, select one of the four priority

Figure 11-7
Priority queuing

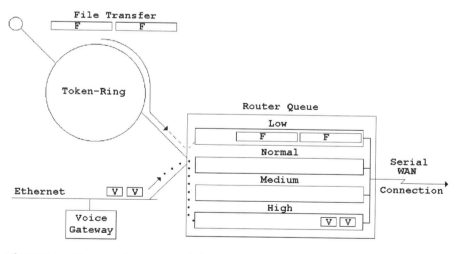

When priority queuing is used in a Cisco router environment you can direct traffic into up to four distinct queues.

queue levels. This is followed by a keyword that can further define the protocol by specifying a transport protocol carried by the network protocol, such as TCP or UDP. Then specify a keyword-value that can be used to identify a specific TCP or UDP port or range of ports.

A second version of the priority-list command can be used to reference an access list. That version of the command has the following format:

```
priority-list list-number protocol protocol-name
{high|medium|normal|low} list list number
```

When using the second version of the priority-list command, the list-number variable references an extended access-list number.

Because digitized voice is transported via UDP without the use of a standardized port, assume that in the example shown in Figure 11-7, UDP port 3210 is used. Because FTP uses TCP port 21, the priority-list statements in a Cisco router environment required to configure priority queuing for the two data sources are as follows:

```
priority-list 1 protocol ip low tcp 21
priority-list 1 protocol ip high udp 3210
```

To affect the filtering of traffic into applicable ports you use a priority group command that assigns the specified priority list to the router WAN interface. Assuming the IP address of the serial port connected to the WAN is 198.78.46.1, the applicable set of commands is as follows:

```
interface serial 0
ip address 198.78.46.1 255.255.255.0
priority-group 1
!
priority-list 1 protocol ip low tcp 21
priority-list 1 protocol ip high udp 3210
```

Although only two types of traffic are assigned to queues, it should be noted that any traffic that does not match the priority list entries is automatically, by default, placed in the normal queue. To use access lists to differentiate traffic, you could associate separate access lists to a common priority list. An example of this is shown below:

```
interface serial 0
ip address 198.78.46.1 255.255.255.0
priority-group 1
!
access-list 100 permit tcp any any eq 3210
access-list 101 permit udp any any eq 21
priority-list 1 protocol ip low tcp 101
priority-list 1 protocol ip high udp 100
!
```

One of the disadvantages of priority queuing is that it is possible to literally starve the ability of certain applications to obtain access to an interface, such as the WAN shown in Figure 11-7. The reason for this is that any time packets are in the high-priority queue, they will be extracted first.

Therefore, if the voice gateway is heavily utilized and generates a sustained, heavy flow of traffic to the router, it is quite possible to exclude the servicing of traffic entering other queues. In this type of situation, the other queues could fill to capacity, resulting in packets flowing to those queues being dropped. This, in turn, could result in the retransmission of packets until a threshold is reached that terminates the application. Perhaps recognizing the previously described limitation of priority queuing, Cisco added support for two additional queuing methods to its router platforms. One of those methods is custom queuing.

Custom Queuing

Custom queuing provides a mechanism to allocate the bandwidth of a transmission facility based upon specifying a byte count in a series of queue-list commands. By defining the number of bytes to be extracted from a queue prior to having the router process the next queue, you obtain the capability to indirectly allocate bandwidth. For example, assume that you want to allocate 60 percent of the bandwidth of the WAN connection previously shown in Figure 11-7 to the voice application, 30 percent to file transfers, and the remaining 10 percent to all other traffic. To do so, you would use the queue-list command to classify traffic and assign the byte counts in order to specify the maximum quantity of data to be extracted from each queue prior to the next queue being serviced.

You could use two versions of the queue-list command. One version established queuing priority based upon the protocol type, while the second version designates the byte size serviced per queue. The format of the queue-list command used to establish queuing priority is shown next:

```
queue-list list number protocol protocol-name queue-number keyword
keyword-value
```

The first four entries in the queue-list command function in the same manner as the first four entries in the priority-list command. The fifth entry, queue-number, is an integer between 1 and 16, and represents the number of the queue. The keyword and keyword values function in the same manner as their counterparts in the priority-list command.

The second version of the queue-list command you could use is the queue-list-byte-count command. The format of this command is shown in the following line:

```
queue-list list-number queue queue-number byte-count byte-count-
number
```

In this version of the queue-list command, the list-number and queue-number continue as identifiers for the number of the queue list and number of the queue, respectively. The key change is the addition of the keyword "byte-count." This is followed by the byte-count-number, which specifies the normal lower boundary concerning the number of bytes that can be extracted from a designated queue during a particular extraction cycle. Note that the queue extraction process proceeds in a round-robin order and up to 16 distinct queues can be specified under custom queuing. Once you use the queue and queue-list-byte-count commands, you would then use the custom-queue-list command to associate the queue list with an interface.

In the Figure 11-7 example, the custom queuing entries, assuming the same serial port and IP address, would be as follows:

```
interface serial 0
ip address 198.78.46.1 255.255.255.0
custom-queue-list 1
!
queue-list 1 protocol ip 1 udp 3210
queue-list 1 protocol ip 2 tcp 21
queue-list 1 default 3
queue-list 1 queue 1 byte count 3000
queue-list 1 queue 2 byte count 1500
queue-list 1 queue 3 byte count 500
```

In the preceding example, custom queuing was configured to accept 3,000 bytes from the UDP queue, 1,500 bytes from the FTP queue, and 500 bytes from the default queue. Note that this allocates the percentage of available bandwidth as 60, 30, and 10 percent to queues 1, 2, and 3, respectively. Also note that during the round-robin queue extraction process, if less than the defined number of bytes is in a queue, the other queues can use the extra bandwidth. That use will continue until the number of bytes in the queue equals or exceeds the specified byte count for the queue.

Although the byte count plays a significant role in the allocation of bandwidth when custom queuing is used, you should carefully consider the length of each frame to obtain the desired allocation. This is due to the manner by which TCP operates, as well as how queuing extraction works. Concerning the former, if you are using a TCP application where the window size for a protocol is set to 1, then that protocol will not transmit another frame into the queue until the transmitting station receives an acknowledgment. Therefore, if your byte count for the queue was set to 1500 and the frame size is 512 bytes, then only approximately one-third of the expected bandwidth will be obtained because 512 bytes will be extracted from the queue. Concerning frame extraction, entire frames are extracted regardless of the byte count value for a queue. This means that if you set the byte count to 512 but the frame size of the protocol assigned to the queue is 1024 bytes, then each time the queue is serviced, 1,024 bytes will be extracted. Thus, this would double the bandwidth used by this particular protocol each time there was a frame in an applicable queue when the round-robin process selected the queue. You must carefully consider each protocol's frame size when determining the byte count to be assigned to a queue.

Although custom queuing can prevent the potential starvation of lower-priority queues, the actual allocation of bandwidth may not actually reach your desired metric. Another limitation of custom queuing is that processing byte counts for up to 16 queues uses more processing power than the previously described queuing methods. Perhaps recognizing the first problem, Cisco provided another method that can be used to achieve a level of fairness in allocating bandwidth. That method is referred to as *weighted fair queuing* (WFQ).

Weighted Fair Queuing (WFQ)

WFQ represents an automated method to obtain a level of fairness in allocating bandwidth. Under WFQ, all traffic is monitored and conversations are subdivided into two categories—those requiring large amounts of bandwidth and those requiring relatively small amounts of bandwidth. This subdivision results in packets queued by flow, with a flow based upon packets having the same source IP address, destination IP address, source TCP or UDP port, or destination TCP or UDP port. The goal of WFQ is to ensure that low-bandwidth conversations receive preferential treatment in gaining access to an interface, while permitting the large bandwidth conversations to use the remaining bandwidth in proportion to their weights.

Under WFQ, response times for interactive query-response and the egress of small digitized voice packets can be improved when they are sharing access to a WAN with such high-bandwidth applications as HTTP and FTP. For example, without WFQ, a query to a corporate Web server residing on a LAN behind a router could result in a large sequence of lengthy HTTP packets flowing onto the WAN link that precede a short digitized voice packet in the interface's FIFO queue. This would cause the digitized voice packet to wait for placement onto the WAN that could induce an unacceptable amount of delay, which would adversely affect the ability to reconstruct a portion of the conversation being delayed. When WFQ is enabled, the digitized voice frame would be automatically identified and scheduled for transmission between HTTP frames, which would considerably reduce its egress time onto the WAN. A second advantage of WFQ is that it requires no configuration commands. It is simply enabled by the use of the following interface command:

```
fair-queue
```

Under WFQ, traffic from high-priority queues is always forwarded during an absence of low-priority traffic. Because WFQ makes efficient use of available bandwidth for high-priority traffic and is enabled with a minimal configuration effort, it is the default queuing mode on most serial interfaces configured to operate at or below the E1 data rate of 2.048 Mbps.

Although WFQ does not require any configuration commands, the fair-queue command has three options that can be used to tailor its operation. To better understand those options, focus on the basic manner by which traffic is classified under WFQ, illustrated in Figure 11-8.

Note in Figure 11-8 that the WFQ classifier automatically classifies frames by protocol, source and destination address, session layer protocol, source/destination port, and IP Precedence value in the Service Type byte. One other classification, RSVP flow, is a mnemonic for Resource ReSerVation Protocol, which represents a standard for allocating bandwidth across IP networks and is described later in this chapter.

Configurable options in the fair-queue command include the congestive discard threshold, the number of dynamic queues available to hold distinct conversations, and the number of queues that can be reserved by RSVP. The

Figure 11-8
Weighted fair queuing

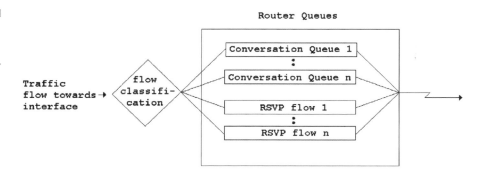

congestive discard threshold specifies how many packets may be queued in each flow's queue. The default is 64, which can be adjusted in powers of 2, from 2 through 4096 (2^{16}). The dynamic queue value controls the maximum number of conversations a router will monitor. The default value is 256. The reservable-queues option defines the number of queues RSVP can reserve. The default value is 0; however, enabling RSVP on your router automatically results in WFQ reserving 1000 queues for RSVP.

Although WFQ is a good queuing method when you have a mixture of data, in its present incarnation it cannot tell the difference between a 64-byte telnet packet and a 64-byte packet transporting digitized voice. WFQ treats both equally, ahead of longer packets transporting files, which may not be your actual preference. In addition to a lack of control, WFQ consumes more router resources, which may or may not be a problem, depending upon the level of utilization of your router.

Another type of WFQ that warrants a brief discussion is *Class-Based WFQ* (CB-WFQ). Class-based weighted fair queuing allows users to create traffic classes and to assign weights to each class. CB-WFQ represents a powerful tool for backbone network connections within a Layer 3 network. The next section examines the Type of Service byte in the IP header.

The ToS Byte

Within the 20-byte IP header is an eight-bit byte, commonly referred to as the ToS field. The function of this byte is to denote the importance of the datagram, as well as the datagram's requirements with respect to delay, throughput, and reliability.

Figure 11-9 illustrates the format of the ToS byte. Note that the first three bit positions can be used to assign a precedence to a datagram. Although eight levels of precedence are available, the highest two values are normally reserved for internal network utilization, enabling the ToS byte to provide a mechanism for partitioning traffic in up to six classes of service.

The setting of a precedence value is normally a function of an application. Although the original intention of the ToS byte was to provide a mechanism for both specifying precedence and the reliability, throughput, delay, and cost requirements of a datagram, like many good intentions its use never approached its goal. In fact, a popular joke is that, by default, IP traffic is unreliable, slow, and costly, which perhaps explains why applications did not turn on any of the relevant ToS bits. However, if you obtain an

Figure 11-9
The IPv4 ToS byte

```
    0    1    2    3    4    5    6    7

  ┌──────────────┬────┬────┬────┬────┬──────────┐
  │  PRECEDENCE  │ D  │ T  │ R  │ C  │  UNUSED  │
  └──────────────┴────┴────┴────┴────┴──────────┘
```

```
bits 0-2 define precedence

    111   Network control
    110   Internetwork control
    101   Critic
    100   Flash override
    011   Flash
    010   Immediate
    001   Priority
    000   Routine

bit 3   Delay          0 = normal, 1 = low delay

bit 4   Throughput     0 = normal, 1 = high

bit 5   Reliability    0 = normal, 1 = high

bit 6   Cost           0 = normal, 1 = low
```

application that can be configured to turn on an applicable precedence bit, you can use a Cisco extended-IP access list in conjunction with a priority-list command to associate traffic with an applicable precedence bit setting into a predefined queue.

Although Cisco and other router manufacturers provide a mechanism for traffic differentiation based upon the setting of the ToS precedence bits, it will more than likely be a warm day in Antarctica before its use becomes popular. Recognizing the low level of utilization of the ToS byte, the Internet Engineering Task Force worked on a series of *Requests for Comments* (RFCs) that redefined the use of that byte. Under the revision, the byte is used to provide *differentiated services* (DiffServ) information to routers. That is the topic of the next section.

Differentiated Services (DiffServ)

DiffServ can be considered to represent a set of technologies that permits network service providers to offer different categories of QoS to different customer traffic streams. The use of Differentiated Services requires the establishment of a *Service Level Agreement* (SLA). The SLA is established between the service provider and the customer prior to the use of Differentiated Services. The SLA can specify the manner by which packets are handled based upon one or more metrics. Those metrics can include the expected throughput obtained, the probability of a packet being dropped, the delay or latency resulting from packets flowing through a network, and the variation in the flow of packets received when a stream is presented to the network (commonly referred to as jitter).

A network operator uses the SLA to define how packets are handled, based on the composition of the DiffServ byte. Here handling is a loose term that refers to the forwarding service customers will receive for a particular packet class or set of classes. Once the SLA is established, the customer submits packets with applicable DiffServ bit settings to indicate the service desired. The service provider then becomes responsible for assuring that routers are configured with applicable forwarding policies to provide the QoS specified in the SLA for each packet class.

Instead of taking the traditional approach to QoS in which routers along the path from source to destination reserve bandwidth for a traffic stream, DiffServ simply assigns a value to a byte in the IP header that allows all routers on a path to forward traffic according to the byte setting. This action eliminates the necessity to convey separate signaling information between routers. By eliminating the need for separate signaling information, DiffServ avoids the high overhead associated with RSVP that made it impractical for use on the Internet.

Another advantage associated with DiffServ is that many traffic streams can be aggregated to one of a small number of *behavior aggregates* (BAs). That is, all traffic with the same DiffServ byte settings are treated in the same manner by each DiffServ compatible router, regardless of source, destination, or composition of a packet. It is possible for a voice conversation and a near–real-time application between pairs of dissimilar addresses to be treated in the same manner as their packets flow through a network. The BA traffic streams are forwarded by each DiffServ compatible router based upon one of a limited number of *per hop behaviors* (PHBs), further simplifying data flow as well as minimizing the processing effort of routers.

Operation

Differentiated Services represents a service provided by network service providers to customers. This service requires negotiation between the two parties ahead of time so that customer traffic can be processed through the network based upon the manner by which the DiffServ byte is marked or classified in each packet at the edge of the network.

The DiffServ byte is based upon the use of the ToS field in the IPv4 header and the Traffic Class field in the IPv6 header. However, it maintains backward compatibility with the RFC 791 IPv4 specification that defined the original use of the bit positions in the ToS field. To obtain backward compatibility, the DiffServ byte uses bit positions 0, 1, and 2 for priority settings that provide a general mapping to the Precedence field in the ToS byte. Thus, routers that use the Precedence field in the ToS byte will not choke on the DiffServ byte. Instead, such routers will provide a priority flow similar to that provided to a packet where the IPv4 header uses a ToS byte.

The DiffServ byte both reorganized and renamed the first three bit positions of the IPv4 ToS byte. Table 11-2 lists the eight precedence levels now defined under DiffServ.

Note in Table 11-2 that precedence levels 6 and 7 remain the same because they are still assigned to network operations such as routing protocols and keep alive signals. Collectively, Classes 1 through 4 are referred to as Assured Forwarding (AF) and are used in conjunction with bit positions 3 and 4 of the DiffServ byte. By setting bits 3 and 4, it becomes possible to specify the forward percentage of packets for each class of traffic.

Table 11-2

DiffServ Byte
Precedence Levels

Precedence Level	Bit Settings	Meaning
7	111	Network
6	110	Network
5	101	Express forwarding
4	100	Class 4
3	011	Class 3
2	010	Class 2
1	001	Class 1
0	000	Best effort

Collectively, bits 3 and 4 of the DiffServ byte are referred to as the *Diff-Serv Code Point* (DSCP). Table 11-3 illustrates the use of the DSCP codes that enable traffic to be differentiated within a class. Note that the reason six bit positions are shown for each drop percentage in each class is because bit 5 is always assigned a value of zero.

Although bits 3 and 4 represent the DSCP bits, in some literature, the first six bits in the DiffServ byte are referred to as the DS codepoint. That codepoint takes the following form to indicate a drop percentage for each of the four traffic classes:

xxxyy0

where xxx represents a zero or 1 and is the revised ToS precedence level, while yy represents the DSCP bit values, with a trailing 0 in the sixth position of the byte.

Two other codepoint bit compositions included in RFC 2474 that define the DiffServ byte are xxxx11 and xxxx01, with x again representing either a binary 0 or 1. The first format is currently reserved for experimentation. The second format is also reserved for experimentation; however, it can be allocated for future use by a subsequent DiffServ specification. Last but not least, a DSCP value of all zeros (000000) represents a default packet class best effort forwarding request. This means that packets marked with this value are forwarded in the order they are received whenever bandwidth is available.

Also note that under this router forwarding mechanism, the forwarding action that occurs based upon the setting of bits 3 and 4 is not standardized. That is, no precise definition of low, medium, and high drop percentages exists. Because not every router will initially be DiffServ-compliant and recognize bit positions 3 and 4, its previously mentioned backward compatibility with the precedence field in the ToS byte permits routers to forward packets based upon a lower level of granularity by only considering a packet precedence value.

Table 11-3

The DSCP Bits Provide the Mechanism That Enables Packets within a Class to Be Differentiated

Drop Percentage	Traffic class			
	Class 1	Class 2	Class 3	Class 4
Low	001010	010010	011010	100010
Medium	001100	010100	011100	100100
High	001110	010110	011110	100110

Additionally, note that instead of including a granular capability for a precedence value of 5, the use of expedited forwarding provides a higher level of service that enables service providers to guarantee a minimum service level. To do so, a service provider could use a queuing method that results in packets with a DiffServ precedence of 5 receiving a minimum amount of bandwidth. This would compensate for the situation where a severely congested circuit could result in poor performance for classes 1 through 4.

DiffServ Code Point (DSCP) Processing

Once a packet's DSCP bits are set at the entry to a network, all routers within the network examine them. Because the Internet represents a network of interconnected networks, the term "domain" is used to reference an administrative entity, such as an *Internet Service Provider* (ISP). Within a domain, packets receive a consistent level of service based upon the setting of the DSCPs, which enables the service provider to negotiate SLAs with their customers. A customer can be a user organization or another domain. When customer is another domain, the home domain will attempt to forward packets to the foreign domain requesting appropriate service to match the original requested level of service. Unfortunately, there is no standard billing mechanism or available metering software that examines DiffServ traffic classes, which means that the practicality of interdomain DiffServ communications may take some time to occur.

Routers within a domain can be classified as either boundary nodes or interior nodes. Interior node routers perform forwarding based upon the composition of the bits in the DiffServ byte. This forwarding treatment is referred to as PHB. In comparison, boundary routers are responsible for the classification of packets. With this in mind, the next section focuses on the functions performed at the edge of the network, which provides the information used by the interior nodes within a domain.

Ingress Functions

As data from a host enters a DiffServ compatible router at the edge of a network, a traffic conditioning process will occur. That process is based upon four QoS control functions. First, each message will be classified based upon a set of rules, resulting in the name "classifier" associated with this function. A second function involves measuring submitted traffic to determine whether it conforms to the negotiated SLA. This function is referred to as metering. A third function involves performing one or more actions applicable to the classification of the packet. One action is applying a policy or set of policies to traffic by changing the assignment of codepoints, a technique referred to as marking. Another action, referred to as traffic shaping, results in traffic being delayed to ensure it does not exceed the traffic rate specified for a particular class. This control function alters the flow rate. A third action, called dropping, results in the discard of packets when their rate exceeds that of the rate specified for their class and the flow cannot be delayed via traffic shaping. Finally, the fourth QoS control function involves the queuing of traffic for output in an appropriate queue based upon its DSCP bit settings.

The relationships of the four previously described DiffServ control functions are illustrated in Figure 11-10. Note that all packets are first classified. Once classified, the resource utilization of a sequence of packets that represent a flow must be measured. This measurement occurs by the metering function measuring the volume of packets in the flow over a predefined time interval. It permits the compliance of the flow with the SLA to be determined and an applicable action to occur. As previously noted, available actions include marking, traffic shaping, and dropping. However, there is a fourth action that is not shown in Figure 11-10. That action, or inaction, is to do nothing and simply pass the classified packet to the queuing control function.

Classifier Operation

A classifier can be considered to represent a logical 1:N fan-out device. Although it forwards packets in a serial stream, to the marker it generates N logically separate traffic streams as output. The simplest type of classifier

Figure 11-10

Relationship between DiffServ control functions at the igress point of a domain

is a *behavior aggregate* (BA) classifier. The BA classifier uses only the DSCP in the IP packet header to determine an appropriate output stream to which the packet should be directed. A more complex classifier would be a multi-field classifier. This type of classifier is based on using one or more fields plus the DSCP field. One common multi-field classifier is represented by using the Destination Address, Source Address, and IP Protocol Type fields in the IP header, along with the source and destination ports in the UDP or TCP header following an IP header. Because the preceding field values are used in conjunction with the DSCP, this multi-field classifier is also referred to as a sextuple classifier.

Metering

Metering also represents a logical 1:N fan-out operation, with the rate of traffic flow compared to SLA thresholds to determine the flow's conformance to a particular SLA. Three levels of conformance can be referred to as "colorful" due to the use of different color terms. A green level of conformance indicates that a flow conforms to its associated SLA. In comparison, yellow indicates particular conformance, while red indicates nonconformance. These three levels of conformance can trigger an applicable action, such as marking or dropping, or can be used to trigger a particular type of queuing.

Action

Figure 11-10 illustrated three action elements and described a fourth, which is to do nothing. This is called a null action. Because there is probably no free lunch, service providers can charge different fees or surcharges for the flow of packets within different traffic classes. Due to this, another potential action is counting. Counting represents a passive action, with respect to traffic that could be used for billing. In addition, this action could provide a mechanism for service verification, as well as provide the service provider with qualitative information useful for network engineering purposes.

Because DiffServ was only recently standardized via a series of RFCs, great effort is needed to both implement the technology and make it effective. Concerning the latter, suppose your organization entered into an SLA with a service provider and wanted to verify the level of service obtained. Although you might trust your service provider to furnish packet counting in different classes, the ability to use SNMP to directly query counters might be a more suitable method. However, it may be quite some time until customers obtain this capability because it cannot be expected to represent a vendor implementation priority.

Routing

As briefly mentioned earlier in this section, the routing or forwarding of packets within a domain is referred to as PHB. Because an edge router is responsible for classifying, metering, and performing several action elements, interior routers are normally relieved of those functions. Thus, an interior router will normally have its DiffServ operations focused upon examining the DSCP bit settings in inbound packets and transferring the packet to an appropriate queue based on the previously mentioned bit settings. PHB is expected to be supported over various underlying technologies, such as the mapping of the DSCP byte to a *Multi Protocol Label Switch* (MPLS) label value, or via ATM. In fact, the ATM Forum is working on defining a new VC call setup information element to transport PHB ID codes between ATM switches.

Another area being considered by various committees is the development of an optional QoS agent that could provide either active or passive support for the RSVP. Here, possible support would result in the agent snooping through RSVP messages to learn how to classify traffic without having to participate as an RSVP protocol peer. In comparison, under active support, the QoS agent could participate in a per-flow-aggregate signaling of QoS requirements. A DiffServ-compliant router could then accept or reject RSVP admission requests to provide a mechanism of admission control to DiffServ-based services.

Operational Problems

In the "Traffic Expediting" section, it was noted that DiffServ divides transmission into a small number of classes. Routers then apply a standardized set of behaviors to each class of traffic, which is referred to as a per-hop behavior. Because DiffServ-aware routers perform their operation without the need to know the path of traffic or information about other routers in the network, the technology avoids the need for conveying signaling information—other than the bit composition of the revised ToS byte. Although this is a key advantage of DiffServ, it also results in the need to carefully consider, as well as control, the arrival rate of one or more types of traffic classes.

For example, consider the use of *expedited forwarding* (EF), which represents a simple per-hop behavior that informs routers that packets marked for EF status should be forwarded with minimal delay and loss. The only way that a network operator can guarantee minimal delay and loss at each hop to all packets marked for expedited forwarding is to limit the arrival rate of such packets to less than the rate at which routers can forward EF packets. Although this task may appear simple, in actuality this method of flow control can be quite complex (see Figure 11-11).

Examining Figure 11-11, assume routers 1 and 2 are connected via a T1 circuit in the middle of a network, while router 1 has connections via circuits labeled A, B, and C to three other devices. This means that the network operator needs to limit the aggregate arrival rate of EF marked packets via circuits A, B, and C destined to router 2 via router 1 to less than 1.544 Mbps.

Figure 11-11
The difficulty of DiffServ

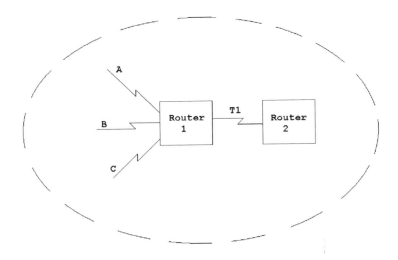

The arrival rate for all ingress ports at a router must be kept under the egress rate of the traffic class for each route outbound from the router.

In actuality, the network operator must also consider other traffic classes and control the aggregate arrival rate of EF marked packets to a rate significantly under 1.544 Mbps to enable router 1 to transfer other traffic to router 2. Because routers connected to circuits A, B, and C may have one or more inputs that will flow from router 1 to router 2, EF marked packets at another hierarchy in the network must also be considered. As a network increases in complexity, it becomes harder for the network operator to configure devices at the edge of the network to mark packets that allow routers within the network to guarantee a consistent handling of the packets as they flow through the network. For this reason, an alternate approach to provide a QoS capability through a network may be desirable. One such method is based upon what is referred to as *Integrated Services* (IntServ).

Integrated Services (IntServ)

IntServ references a suite of evolving standards intended to provide a QoS transport capability over IP-based networks. IntServ dates to the work of the IEFT during the mid-1990s and is defined in RFC 1633.

The basic design issued covered by IntServ concerns sharing available bandwidth during times of congestion. Under IntServ, congestion management consists of the following:

- an admission control that is invoked by a reservation protocol to determine if resources are available for the flow at the requested QoS

- a routing algorithm, which maintains a routing database that provides next hop information for each destination address

- a queuing algorithm that controls the flow of traffic through a router

- a discard policy, which provides a uniform mechanism that denotes the conditions under which packets are sent to the great bit bucket in the sky

Although IntServ includes an admission control function, it does not define the method of control to be used. However, when discussing admission control, many people incorrectly associate RSVP with IntServ. RSVP can be used under IntServ, but is not a required member of the architecture. Because RSVP is currently the only mechanism that can be employed to deliver guaranteed bandwidth within an IP network, the next section focuses on the basics of this signaling protocol.

Resource ReServation Protocol (RSVP)

RSVP represents a signaling protocol, which enables applications that require guaranteed bandwidth to request such bandwidth from a network. In doing so, RSVP provides an admission control capability on an end-to-end basis because the availability of required bandwidth determines whether or not the application gains access to the network.

Unlike most protocols that are sender-driven, RSVP is receiver-driven. The rationale for this change is based upon the need to accommodate different members of a multicast group that can have different resource requirements. For example, one member of a multicast group could be connected to an IP network via a 56 Kbps digital circuit, while a second member is connected via a corporate LAN connection using a T1 line operating at 1.544 Mbps.

Under RSVP, a sender will transmit a Path message downstream towards all receivers. The Path message includes information on the traffic characteristics of the data stream that will be generated. Each receiver requests a specific QoS from the network by responding to the Path message with a *reservation* (Resv) message. As the Resv message flows towards the originator, each router in the path checks to determine whether sufficient resources are available. If so, a reservation is established and the Resv message is forwarded to the next upstream router. Otherwise, the reservation fails and an error message is returned to the receiver.

To reduce signaling requirements, a sequence of packets from a common address with a common destination are treated as a *flow specification* (flowspec). The flowspec describes the service requirements in terms of a desired QoS or reservation request and can include such information as a service class defined by the application and a *reservation specification* (Rspec), which defines the bandwidth required.

Each RSVP-compliant router includes a packet classifier and packet scheduler. The classifier determines the route of the packet, while the scheduler is responsible for servicing and forwarding decisions required to achieve the requested QoS.

Another integral part of each RSVP-compliant router is a *filter specification* (filterspec). The filterspec specifies packets that will be serviced and the manner that they will be serviced based upon the flowspec. An example of the relationship between the filterspec and flowspec is shown in Figure 11-12. Note that the packet classifier aggregates a series of packets that flow to a common destination. The filterspec specifies packets that will be

Figure 11-12
The relationship between RSVP filterspec and flowspec

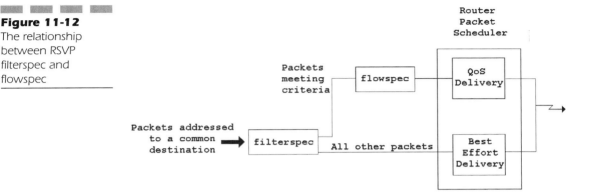

Under RSVP the filter specification (filterspec) defines the packets that will be serviced by the flow specification (flowspec).

serviced by the flowspec, while the flowspec parameters are used by the router to place packets into applicable QoS delivery queues.

Both Resv and Path messages have timeout values that are used by routers and switches to set their internal timers. If those timers expire, the reservation and routing information associated with the reservation are turned down. This limits the seizure of resources by the failure of a receiver to terminate an RSVP session.

Although RSVP is several years young, its implementation is commonly restricted to intranets whose sizes are but a small fraction of the Internet. The reason for its limited use is primarily due to the signaling overhead associated with the protocol, the need for all routers in a network to be RSVP-compliant, and the inability to negotiate the cost of bandwidth when a QoS traffic flow crosses an Internet service provider boundary. The simplicity of allocating bandwidth to an application does not mean that it is easy to bill for the bandwidth. This is because allocated bandwidth can be temporarily de-allocated when the application is quiescent, permitting a router to use previously allocated bandwidth until the application needs it. Thus, an interesting issue is how, for example, would one ISP bill another for an application that required 8 Kbps of bandwidth that was available for use by the host ISP 60 percent of the time?

Although billing issues between ISPs may take a while to resolve, many carriers are taking another look at RSVP for internal use to include its proposed extension to support label distribution and explicit routing, which is referred to as RSVP-TE (traffic engineering.) Because this requires knowledge of label distribution, the next section discusses this topic in the form of Internet draft documents that describe *multiprotocol label switching* (MPLS).

Multiprotocol Label Switching (MPLS)

MPLS represents a switching architecture where packets entering a network are assigned a label. Then, instead of forwarding packets based upon searching their routing table, a router uses the label as a forwarding criteria. Because there can be tens of thousands of entries in a routing table while label entries are associated with device interfaces, it is much faster for the router to make its forwarding decision based upon the contents of the label.

The original goal of MPLS was to provide the efficiency of Layer 2 switching to Layer 3 networking. Although the manufacture of *application-specific integrated circuit* (ASIC)-based routers permits relatively fast router table lookup operations that negates the original goal of MPLS, other benefits are associated with label switching. Those benefits include the ability to define paths for different types of traffic through a network, which is referred to as traffic engineering, and the creation of IP tunnels through a network that facilitates the creation of *virtual private networks* (VPNs).

The MPLS Label

The MPLS label is 32 bits in length and consists of four fields as indicated below:

```
|-20 bits Label-|-3 bits CoS-|-1 bit stack-|-8 bits TTL-|
```

The 20-bit label field contains the actual value of the MPLS label and has local significance in the same manner as a *Frame Relay Data Link Control Identifier* (DLCI) is used to convey path information. The *Class of Service* (CoS) field permits packets to be placed into one of eight classes that can affect queuing and discard algorithms applied to the packet as it flows through each router in a network. The third field in the label is the Stack (S) field. This one-bit field is used to indicate a hierarchical label stack and is referred to as a label stack. This means that it becomes possible for a packet to have multiple paths with the value of the label stack identifying a particular path to be taken.

The fourth field, *time to live* (TTL), consists of eight bits that provide the functionality of the conventional IP TTL field in the MPLS header. That is, it prevents a labeled packet from endlessly wandering through a network.

The MPLS label is inserted after the Layer 2 header, resulting in it preceding the IP header. The specific path through an MPLS network is referred to as a *label switch path* (LSP). The LSP is provisioned via the use of a *label distribution protocol* (LDP), which both establishes a path through an MPLS network, as well as reserves resources required to satisfy the pre-defined service requirements for the data path. One pending LDP is the previously mentioned extension to RSVP to support label distribution and explicit routing referred to as RSVP-TE. Although one group of vendors including Cisco and Juniper Networks supports the extension of RSVP, a second group of vendors including GDC and Nortel are backing a second signaling mechanism referred to as CR-LDP. Although both proposed signaling protocols have many similarities, they are not interoperable and the IETF's MPLS working group has its work cut out in attempting to select one. If you point your browser to www.mplsrc.com, the home page of the MPLS Resource Center—a Web site that functions as a clearinghouse for information on the IETF's Multiprotocol Label Switching standard—you can determine whether a selection between the two signaling protocols was made, as well as access a wealth of MPLS-related information.

Other QoS Techniques

Although DiffServ, MPLS, and other techniques are considered to be representations of traffic-expediting methods, end-users can employ other techniques that also affect QoS. Those techniques generally can be classified as efficiency methods that facilitate the flow of data through a network. One example of an efficiency method is the use of *Real-Time Transport Protocol* (RTP) header compression.

RTP represents a protocol that adds time stamping and data sequencing information to a packet. In a voice-over IP environment, an RTP header consisting of 12 bytes is used to prefix an eight-byte UDP header. The RTP and UDP headers are in turn prefixed with a 20-byte IP header. If RTP is employed with an 8 Kbps voice digitization method that results in 20 ms portions of speech being encoded, then the payload of the UDP segment will be 160 bits or 20 bytes. Therefore, the total length of the IP datagram conveying the digitized voice sample is 60 bytes, of which only 20 represent the actual payload. Through the use of RTP header compression, it becomes possible to reduce the IP/RTP/UDP header from 40 bytes to between two to five bytes, with the actual reduction dependent upon the susceptibility of the header's contents to compression.

RTP compression is currently defined in an IETF draft appropriately titled *Compressed RTP (CRTP)*. Several vendors including Cisco Systems have implemented RTP header compression to enhance communications on serial lines using frame relay, HDLC, *Point to Point Protocol* (PPP) encapsulation, or via an ISDN interface. Because there is literally no free lunch in communications, it is important to note that there is a relationship between router processing time required to perform header compression and the speed at which compressed data is provided to a router's interface. In general, the higher the data rate, the higher the processing time required. Thus, RTP header compression is commonly recommended for use on slower links operating up to 512 Kbps where RTP header compression can reduce overhead without adversely affecting the processing capability of the router.

Another QoS technique that can be protocol-independent is setting router queues to prioritize traffic, based upon packet length. Because digitized voice and interactive queries are normally transported in relatively short-length packets, it becomes possible to favor such applications over other types of traffic transported in lengthy frames, such as Web pages and graphics.

If we focus our attention upon a particular communications transport protocol, it may be possible to control one or more transmission parameters in conjunction with a *service level agreement* (SLA) initiated with a carrier. For example, in the wonderful world of frame-relay networking, you can use an SLA governing the delivery rate of frames with and without their *discard eligibility* (DE) bit set, as well as a maximum latency time through the network to provide a QoS capability to traffic.

The QoS puzzle has many parts to it. Unlike telephone company-provided QoS in the form of reserved 64 Kbps time slots, the ability to provide QoS to packet networks is significantly more complex. However, the fact that packet networks dynamically allocate bandwidth makes their transport efficiency much greater than the use of reserved time slots, resulting in an economic reward for these efforts. Although it may be quite some time until all the pieces of the QoS puzzle come together in an orderly and manageable manner, it doesn't take a rocket scientist to note the future.

With communications carriers installing tens of thousands of fiber miles each year, while the migration from single channel to *wavelength division multiplexing* (WDM) and *dense WDM* (DWDM) continues to add significant networking bandwidth orders of a magnitude beyond what was available less than a decade ago, it is quite possible that another approach to QoS will evolve. That approach is for carriers to provide sufficient bandwidth to overcome any potential bottlenecks. In the interim, as we plan for the vast migration onto packet networks, we need to periodically check the progress of various standards, examine SLA offerings, and be aware of the techniques available for expediting traffic flow through the networks we directly control. Who said the life of a network manager or LAN administrator is boring?

CHAPTER 12

ISDN and DDR Design

Integrated Services Digital Network (ISDN) was created with the idea of being able to digitize all forms of communication for transport over telephone networks. Router implementation of ISDN has been in the areas of providing temporary extra bandwidth, temporary casual remote access, and as a high-speed switched backup connection for recovering remote locations after a dedicated line outage.

Dial-on-demand routing (DDR) enables Cisco routers to communicate over temporary public-switched telephone networks (PSTN) for on-demand services. DDR is functional using any of the switched interface connections available to a Cisco router platform. DDR can be used for providing a switched backup connection to support outages in a dedicated WAN link topology or it can be used as a means of providing temporary connectivity based on "interesting" packets that flow through the router interfaces.

Site Options

The Cisco Systems products offer many varied solutions for both remote and centralized ISDN connections. The more popular Cisco router ISDN solutions are listed in Table 12-1.

Table 12-1

Sample ISDN Offerings on Cisco Router Platforms

Cisco Router Platform	ISDN Interfaces
Cisco 700 series	One BRI
AccessPro PC card	One BRI
Cisco 1003/4	One BRI
Cisco 2503/4	One BRI
Cisco 2516/17	One BRI
Cisco 3600 series router (per NPM)	Four or eight BRIs per NPM, one or two PRI per NPM
Cisco 4000 series router (per NPM)	Four or eight BRIs per NPM, one PRI per NPM
Cisco 7000 series/Cisco 7500 series	One or two PRIs per MIP

For a complete description of these platforms and the ISDN offerings on each, consult Chapter 2, "Cisco Router Hardware," or the appropriate Cisco systems product catalog. Of the Cisco router platforms listed, the 3600, 4000, and 7000 series routers are traditionally used at the central site, which acts as the hub of a larger hub and spoke topology, offering one or two ISDN PRI lines for connection to the dialer cloud.

Central Office Switch Considerations

In preparing for designing the ISDN network, it is imperative that the capabilities of the provider central office switches be discovered early on in the design effort. Telephone companies may use a wide variety of ISDN switches that are based on the standard but have been modified by the manufacturer. Knowing the type of switch being used by the telephone company for central and remote connections will ease your implementation process.

The predominant ISDN switches used in North America are the AT&T 5ESS and the Nortel DMS-100. Prior to the release of the National ISDN-1 software standard for ISDN, calls from an AT&T ISDN phone would fail when connecting to a Nortel DMS-100. Likewise, a Nortel ISDN phone set would fail on connecting to an AT&T 5ESS ISDN switch. Both the AT&T 5ESS and Nortel DMNS-100 ISDN switch support up to 100,000 local loop connections. The switches are geared towards either PRI or BRI line configurations. Table 12-2 lists the various North American switches and their keyword definitions within the Cisco IOS router definitions.

ISDN networks are now available around the world. In countries outside of North America, however, other ISDN switches may be deployed in the central offices that are not AT&T 5ESS or Nortel DMS-100. The possible switch types used on other countries of the world are listed in Table 12-3.

In some cases, the switch being used deactivates the Layer 2 functions of the D channel on a BRI connection when no calls are active. In this case, the router must perform a Terminal Equipment Identification (TEI) negotiation when a call is first made, rather than when a router powers-up and activates the BRI interface.

Table 12-2

AT&T 5ESS and
Nortel DMS-100
Switch Specifica-
tion for Router Def-
initions

ISDN Switch Type	Router Keyword
AT&T basic rate switch	Basic-5ESS
Nortel DMS-100 basic rate switch	Basic-DMS100
National ISDN-1 switch	Basic-NI1
AT&T 4ESS (ISDN PRI only)	Primary-4ESS
AT&T 5ESS (ISDN PRI only)	Primary-5ESS
Nortel DMS-100 (ISDN PRI only)	Primary-DMS100

Table 12-3

ISDN Switch Types
Used in Other
Countries and the
Router Configura-
tion Keyword

Country	Switch Type	Router Keyword
Australia	TS013 BRI switch, TS014 PRI switch	Basic-TS013, primary-TS014
France	VN2 ISDN switch, VN3 ISDN switch	VN2, VN3
Germany	1TR6 ISDN switch	Basic-1TR6
Japan	NTT ISDN switch, ISDN PRI switch	NTT, primary-NTT
New Zealand	NET3 ISDN switch	Basic-NZNET3
Norway	NET3 ISDN switch (phase one only)	Basic-NWNET3
United Kingdom	NET3 BRI switch, NET5 PRI switch	Basic-NET3, primary-NET5

ISDN connections are established through the use of service profile identifiers (SPIDs). SPIDs are assigned by the ISDN provider to identify the
line configuration of the BRI service. Using SPIDs, voice, data, video, and
fax can share the local loop. The DMS-100 and National ISDN-1-supported
switches require a SPID. The AT&T 5ESS does not always require a SPID,
but specifying a SPID will not be detrimental as long as the carrier provides
the correct corresponding SPID.

An AT&T 5ESS switch can support up to eight SPIDs per BRI, while the
DMS-100 and National ISDN-1 switches support only up to two SPIDs per
BRI. The capability of the AT&T 5ESS to support multiple SPIDs per BRI
B channel allows multiple services simultaneously over the same B chan-
nel. The DMS-100 and National-ISDN-1 allows only one SPID per BRI
channel, and hence only one service at a time over each of the channels.

There is no standard for the SPID number; however, many ISDN providers implement the standard seven-digit telephone number format as the SPID number.

ISDN call setups are highly dependent on the type of switches and services provided by the carrier's central office. The United States primarily uses the Signaling System 7 (SS7) switch in the central offices. The SS7 inter-office communication is at 64 Kbps. Prior to the SS7 switch, the inter-office communication was at 56 Kbps. If the ISDN connection is specified to an office without an SS7 switch, the router must be configured to use 56 Kbps when placing a call and have the bandwidth of the ISDN interface manually configured to 56 Kbps.

Another case a designer must be aware of is when calls are made at 56 Kbps, but the receiving end clocks at 64 Kbps. This incompatibility of the line speeds can cause data corruption and the ISDN setup to fail. The Cisco routers can be configured to handle this change in line speeds of a completed call by automatically clocking the line at the line speed received on the incoming call.

Using some of the advanced services provided by the carriers, a router can perform some connection time security using caller ID. The central office switch must support the caller ID feature, and the router must have the screening ISDN security feature enabled. When a call is received, the router interprets the called ID provided in the setup message. The caller ID is matched against configured incoming caller ID values. If the incoming caller ID does not match, the router rejects the call.

PRI and BRI

The ISDN primary rate interface (PRI) and basic rate interface (BRI) provide the physical connection to the ISDN network. Each PRI and BRI bundles B and D channels. The bearer (B) channel is rated at 56 or 64 Kbps for data or voice services. The D channel provides the signaling and controls of the services for ISDN end-to-end connectivity establishment. In some instances, the D channel is used as a low-bandwidth data channel and operates at 16 Kbps.

The BRI ISDN connection provides two 64-Kbps B channels and one 16-Kbps D channel. This is also referred to as a 2B+D line. The two 64 Kbps B channels can establish connections to different locations, one can be used for data and the other for voice, or they can be "bonded" to act as a full 128-Kbps data connection between two points.

The PRI ISDN service is provided over T1- or E1-leased lines from the customer premise equipment (CPE) to the ISDN switch at the carrier central office. The T1-based PRI provides 23 B channels and one D channel. The D channel on a PRI-based T1 is the 24th channel on the circuit. The E1-based PRI service, mostly found outside North America, provides 30 B channels and a 64-Kbps D channel (30B+D). The D channel on a E1-based PRI service is the 16th channel on the E1 connection.

DDR Model

Cisco DDR uses a design stack for providing DDR services that is comprised of five layers (see Figure 12-1). Although DDR is not an actual networking architecture, the use of a design model enables network designers and engineers to build scalable and fault-tolerant DDR internetworks while meeting performance, service, and cost requirements.

Figure 12-1
DDR design model.

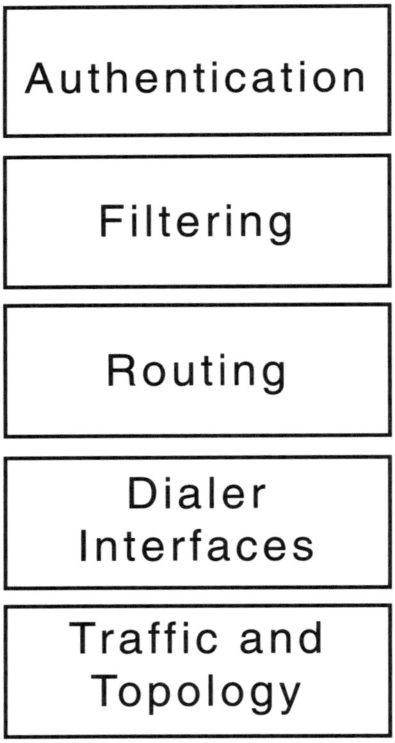

Authentication

Filtering

Routing

Dialer Interfaces

Traffic and Topology

DDR Dialer Cloud

Cisco DDR supports switched circuit connections over the following interface types:

- Integrated Services Digital Network (ISDN) interfaces using BRI and PRI
- ISDN terminal adapters (TAs)
- Asynchronous serial interfaces available on the auxiliary port on Cisco routers
- V.25bis and DTR dialing for switched 56 CSU/DSUs
- Synchronous modems

The switched circuit connections use one of the following protocols or encapsulation techniques to establish end-to-end transport:

- PPP
- HDLC
- X.25
- SLIP

The type of dial-interface and protocol used depends on the DDR services required. Establishing the services is based on the dialer cloud created by the DDR internetwork design.

The dialer cloud is the network formed by the interconnection of DDR devices. A dialer cloud is a network concept that is collectively the potential interconnections and the current active point-to-point connections. The active connections have the characteristics of a non-broadcast multi-access (NBMA) media network akin to frame relay networks. The outbound connections used to establish the dialer cloud and the router must map the network protocol address to a directory number indicating the partner(s) of the dial-out process. The inactive DDR connections are "spoofed" by the router, so as to allow them to appear in the routing tables exchanged over the WAN dedicated links.

The dialer cloud is directly affected by the design of the DDR internetwork. Therefore, it is important to understand the different topologies, traffic, protocol addressing in use, routing structure, and the mechanisms used for triggering the DDR connection.

IP Addressing

Since a dialer cloud provides network communication between locations, an addressing scheme must be established for the various protocols that will be mapped to the dialer cloud. The router configuration maps protocols to the dialer interface used as the DDR connection. The two methods used for assigning the networking addresses to the dialer interfaces are subnet and unnumbered.

Subnet allocation to the dialer cloud amounts to a unique address shared by all the DDR routers that enter the DDR dialer cloud. This type of addressing is really no different than that used now in a LAN or multipoint WAN, or an NBMA networking environment. The addressing scheme used by one interface must be followed through on all the other dialer interfaces used in the dialer cloud.

Using unnumbered interfaces is similar to the unnumbered addressing implemented on Cisco WAN interfaces. Unnumbered addressing uses the address of another interface as the address of the dialer interface. This is possible, due to the fact that the routing table will point to the dialer interface and a next-hop address, which is represented by the dialer interface mapping.

Topology

The design of the DDR internetwork is closely related to the traffic requirements and the number of sites supported on the dialer cloud. In determining the type of topology to plan for, a network designer must discover the frequency of traffic required between DDR locations. The traffic analysis applied here will also assist the network designer in determining which DDR site is to initiate the DDR connection. The three basic topologies used for DDR are point-to-point, hub and spoke or star, or a fully meshed topology.

Point-to-Point

The simplest of DDR topologies is the point-to-point configuration, shown in Figure 12-2. Each site has defined a dialer interface that maps the remote sites address to a telephone number. For instances when extra bandwidth can be the impedance of a DDR connection, multiple DDR connections can be established where the connections use Multilink PPP to aggregate the total bandwidth as a single link between the sites.

Hub and Spoke

A hub and spoke or start topology is built on the notion of DDR connections occurring on a central site that manages every remote DDR connection. This is typically found when DDR is used as a backup topology for routers that have lost their primary dedicated WAN link. The central site or hub of the configuration is often the corporate telecommunications data center. Figure 12-3 illustrates this scenario.

The hub and spoke topology provides for centralized management of the DDR cloud and therefore is easier to configure on the routers at the remote locations. Any-to-any connectivity between the remote locations occurs via traditional routing functions, rather than establishing a new DDR connection to the remote location.

Figure 12-2
DDR point-to-point
topology.

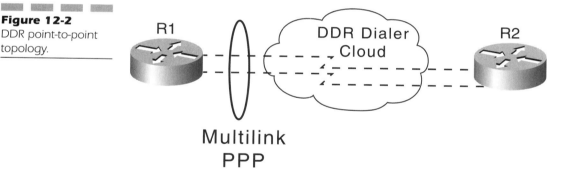

Figure 12-3
Hub and spoke
topology for DDR
internetworks.

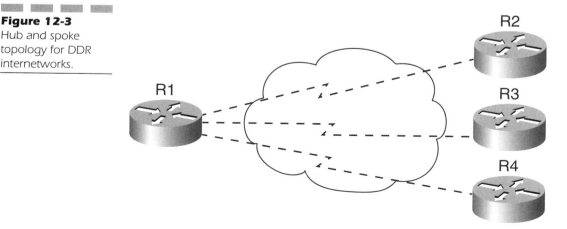

Fully Meshed

Fully meshed configurations, as shown in Figure 12-4, lend themselves to providing direct any-to-any connections, yet they increase the complexity and cost of implementation. Each DDR router must have the complete dialer mapping for connecting to all the other remote DDR routers. Providing this capability means careful coordination between switched circuit providers and adequate dialer interfaces to support the potential for all remote DDR routers connecting at the same time to any other DDR router.

Dial Service Considerations

The media used for the DDR connection is accessed using the Cisco IOS dialer interface feature. The Cisco router platforms support ISDN B channels, synchronous serial interfaces, and asynchronous interfaces as dialer interfaces.

Data Encapsulation

The transported data between two DDR routers must be encapsulated in accordance with the media type used for the connections. DDR supports the following encapsulation techniques:

PPP: Point-to-point protocol (PPP) supports multiple protocols and is available on all the various supported DDR media. PPP also negotiates addressing and provides authentication. Since it is an open standard, it is interoperable between vendors.

HDLC: High-level Data Link Control is supported on synchronous serial and ISDN interfaces. HDLC supports the transport of multiple protocols however it does not have an authentication capability.

SLIP: is only supported by IP protocol on asynchronous interfaces. The addresses used must be manually configured. SLIP does not support authentication.

X.25:   supports both synchronous serial lines and single ISDN B channels.

Of these different interface types, the most widely used is ISDN and PPP for the transport of data between the two DDR routers.

Figure 12-4
Fully meshed DDR
network topology.

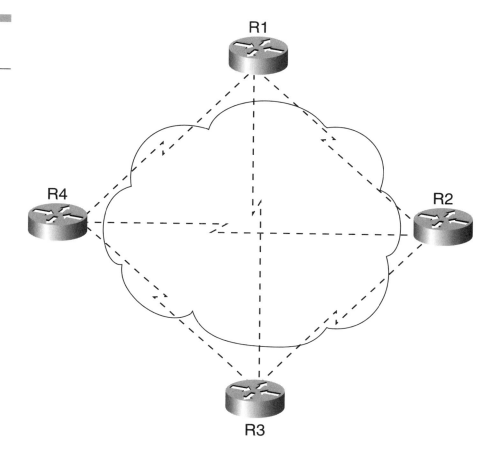

Synchronous Lines

Synchronous serial interfaces support the dialer feature by using V.25bis dialing or DTR dialing. V.25bis uses in-band dialing, which uses the same bandwidth that carries the data between the connecting locations. The V.25bis standard is used with a synchronous modem, ISDN terminal adapters (TAs), and switched 56 DSU/CSUs. The DTR dialing option is used for only connecting out. If the interface is defined for DTR, connect-in attempts will fail. The DTR signal raised on the physical interface causes the attached device to dial a number. Synchronous serial interfaces can use PPP, HDLC, or X.25 datagram encapsulation techniques.

Asynchronous

Asynchronous DDR connections are made through communications servers or by using the auxiliary port on the router. DDR connection setup using asynchronous connections takes longer and requires a chat script to initiate the modem dialing and login commands sent to the remote device. Asynchronous connectivity supports outbound calls and, depending on the design criteria, may provide a cost-effective solution for low-bandwidth-switched connections.

ISDN

The ISDN interfaces on a Cisco router are either ISDN BRI or PRI. Typically, BRI is used at remote locations and PRI is used in situations for consolidating BRI access to the DDR dialer cloud. In the hub and spoke configuration, for example, the central site router employs an ISDN PRI interface to support multiple ISDN BRI connections. The two B channels available on a BRI can be aggregated when using Multilink PPP. This doubles the bandwidth of the configured ISDN BRI connection. ISDN interfaces are automatically configured as dialer in-band interfaces capable of connecting out or connecting in. ISDN with DDR supports PPP, HDLC, X.25, and V.120 encapsulation. PPP is the more widely used encapsulation technique for ISDN interfaces.

Dialer Rotary Groups

Multiple DDR interfaces can be grouped together to form a dialer rotary group. The hub-and-spoke or fully meshed topologies can take advantage of this feature. The physical interfaces inherit their configuration from the corresponding dialer interface definition. DDR automatically groups ISDN B channels of a BRI or PRI into a rotary group. Cisco DDR supports dialer groups of multiple physical interfaces, enabling one physical interface to be busy and a second physical interface defined in the rotary group to place or receive a connection.

Dialer Profiles

Cisco IOS 11.2 introduced the feature of dialer profiles. Using these profiles, the dialer logical definition is decoupled from a physical dialer interface, thereby adding design flexibility. This feature allows multiple interfaces to use the profile simultaneously, enabling the capability to bridge multiple sites over ISDN.

Dialer Maps

Mapping the protocol address to a telephone number is the core of DDR. This function is called dialer map. The network address is mapped to a telephone number on a DDR dialer interface. Setting up DDR between more than two sites necessitates the use of PPP authentication. Using authentication facilities protocol address mapping to user names, thereby authenticating the connection.

When planning for DDR, it is always good practice to create a table listing the location, protocols needed for dial-in, and the phone number used for making a connection. Using such a table enables the designer to understand the actual connectivity requirements and hence the features required in support of DDR at each location. Using the table, a designer can also quickly note if a location is a dial-in only location, therefore not requiring the dial-out feature support. For dial-in only DDR configurations, the telephone (directory) numbers are not a requirement and are best left out to avoid accidental dialing. Dial-in DDR routers use the PPP authentication name mapping for protocol addresses, ensuring outbound packet placement on the correct PPP connection.

Recent enhancements to Cisco IOS allow dynamic dialer maps using IPCP address negotiation for IP protocol and IPXCP address negotiation for IPX protocol on DDR routers configured as dial-in only.

Routing Packets

The type of routing protocol in use and the frequency of the DDR connection may create an unstable routing environment. To avoid this, DDR routes and directory service tables must be maintained, even during idle time. This is accomplished using the static, dynamic, and snapshot routing techniques.

In addition, default routing and remote node spoofing can be combined with the routing techniques to simplify and stabilize the routing design of the DDR dial cloud.

Static Routing

Static routes defined for connecting the DDR dialer cloud routers are entered manually on each DDR router. Using static routes eliminates the need for DDR routers to broadcast routing updates and tables over the DDR connection. Because static routes are not broadcast, we typically redistribute the static routes, defining the path to the DDR router connection into the dynamic routing protocol used for the router-dedicated backbone. Redistributing these routers ensures DDR route awareness for all the routers of the enterprise-wide network.

Dynamic Routing

Dynamic routing protocols are RIP, RIP2, EIGRP, IGRP, and OSPF. When using these protocols, routing updates flow between the DDR routers once the DDR connection is made. Typically, only the distance vector routing protocols of the dynamic routing protocols are used for dynamic routing in a DDR dialer cloud. This is because link-state routing protocols like OSPF end up performing convergence every time a DDR connection is established or broken. To alleviate this problem, OSPF has an on-demand circuit feature to take care of the DDR connection.

Using Passive Interfaces

The Cisco IOS feature called passive interface prohibits the selected dynamic routing protocol from sending route table updates over an interface. Making the DDR dialer interface passive prevents the router from making a DDR connection based on route table updates. Note that if the DDR is made active, routing updates are still prohibited from traversing connection; however, the router receives route table updates on the DDR connection.

The exception to this is EIGRP and OSPF, which do not accept routing updates when an interface is specified as passive. This type of scenario can be useful in a hub-and-spoke topology when the remote locations are set to passive and the central DDR router advertises routes over the DDR connection.

Split Horizons

For DDR connections that support two or more B channel connections over a single physical interface, the split horizons function should be enabled. Split horizon is a function of the router used with distance vector routing protocols to reduce routing loops. Enabling split horizons on the DDR connection prohibits the router from advertising routes learned on an interface back onto that interface.

Enabling split horizon in a hub-and-spoke configuration will prohibit remote locations from communicating with each other through the hub. In such a case, split horizon should be disabled on the single physical interface. Cisco has subinterface features, however, that can be applied to ISDN PRI lines that enable each BRI channel used on the PRI to be represented as a unique physical interface, allowing split horizon without affecting remote-to-remote communications.

Dynamically Connected Routes

There are two possible methods for having dynamic connected routers: per-user and PPP peer routers. Per-user AAA-installed routers are defined on AAA servers and are associated with users defined in the AAA server. Using per-user AAA provides a means of authenticity and protection. PPP peer routers use IPCP address negotiation by defining the full host address as a subnet mask for the remote peer. This route is then propagated to the rest of the network through normal routing protocol convergence.

Snapshot Routing

In conjunction with dynamic routing, snapshot routing, or using a client-server model, controls the routing table updates between the DDR routers. Shown in Figure 12-5, when using a hub-and-spoke configuration, the hub is defined as the snapshot server and one or more DDR connecting routers are defined as snapshot clients. Snapshot routing works with the following distance vector routing protocols:

- Routing Information Protocol (RIP) for IP
- Interior Gateway Routing Protocol (IGRP) for IP
- Routing Information Protocol (RIP) and Service Advertisement Protocol (SAP) for Novell Internet Packet Exchange (IPX)
- Routing Table Maintenance Protocol (RTMP) for AppleTalk
- Routing Table Protocol (RTP) for Banyan VINES

During DDR connection, the client and server exchange routing tables and then go into a quiet period. At the end of the defined quiet period, the client and server again exchange routing tables. This type of routing table update mechanism preserves valuable bandwidth since it is common that distance vector routing protocols transmit their entire routing table in 10- to 60-second intervals. Snapshot routing therefore protects the DDR bandwidth from being overutilized every 10 to 60 seconds for routing updates.

Snapshot is very useful in networks that have few topology changes and a stable physical topology. In networks that use OSPF or EIGRP as the backbone routing protocol, standard route redistribution can be used to propagate the updates between the routing protocols.

The snapshot client router ISDN interface configuration specifies the key variables for enabling snapshot routing:

- The length of the active period (which must match the length specified on the central router)
- The length of the quiet period, which can be specified up to 100,000 minutes or 69 days
- Whether the router can dial the central router to exchange routing updates in the absence of regular traffic
- Whether connections that are established to exchange user data can be used to exchange routing updates

Employing snapshot routing is a good way for periodic testing of the ISDN backup line. Setting the snapshot parameters and DDR triggers properly enables management to address any DDR line problems before they are needed in a backup situation. Although snapshot is used primarily for keeping remote location DDR router table updates in synch with the backbone network, it can be used during active backup purposes as a means of reducing bandwidth consumption during backup and recovery.

████ ████ ████ ████

Figure 12-5
*Snapshot-routing
client-server model.*

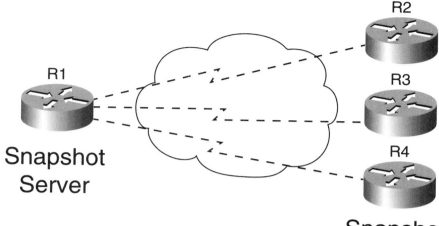

DDR as Dial Backup

DDR used as a dial-backup mechanism for dedicated WAN links requires planning for the use of floating static routes or backup interfaces. Typically, the network designer must address the total number of backup lines to support at any given time and plan the appropriate router interface support. Usually, a hub-and-spoke configuration is useful for DDR as a dial backup. In such scenarios, the hub is setup as dial-in only and the remotes are set up as dial-out only. In this way, contention avoidance is achieved during recovery.

Connection Triggering

The DDR connection established by the router can be triggered by various set parameters. In some instances, a load threshold can be set to establish a second DDR connection between two routers for extra bandwidth. In other scenarios, packets can be identified as "interesting," which will be interpreted to establish a DDR connection to another DDR router for a period of time.

Bandwidth

DDR enables a utilization threshold to be specified on a DDR connection. If this utilization is met, a second DDR connection is established to the remote DDR router, thus meeting performance requirements. This load-threshold parameter is calculated based on the bandwidth value defined for the dialer interface being used. The load is calculated dynamically.

If the specified threshold is met, DDR then establishes a second DDR connection to that remote router. The Cisco router distributes packets over multiple DDR links between two DDR routers based on the queue depth. The link with the shortest queue receives the next packet for sending. If a scenario arises in which the load-threshold value is met for a period of time, the router establishes a second DDR connection to meet the performance requirements.

Using this technique with a low load-threshold specified may result, however, in a single DDR connection being used for transport, since there is no longer a queue depth, but costs are incurred for establishing the second link for the duration of the DDR session. This can occur on BRI connections using the two B channels, as a DDR link is between two routers, and PRI lines use a round-robin technique, ensuring that multiple DDR connections are used. Idle secondary DDR connections are avoided by ensuring that the load-threshold value is not set too low. It is recommended that 50 to 70 percent of the line utilization be set as the trigger for a second DDR connection.

Interesting Packets

Packets are defined as interesting or uninteresting, and interesting packets trigger DDR connections. Uninteresting packets are those that are not destined for active interfaces on the router and will not trigger a DDR connection. The router therefore drops uninteresting packets, while interesting packets are those that have a destination outside the router active interfaces and will trigger a DDR connection. Packets are defined as interesting packets by using a permit access list, while uninteresting packets are defined using a deny access list. The following list outlines the decision process.

1. If a packet is uninteresting and there is no active DDR connection, the packet is dropped.

2. If a packet is uninteresting and there is an active DDR connection to the specified destination of the uninteresting packet, the packet is sent over the DDR connection.

3. If the packet is interesting and there is no active DDR connection to the destination of the interesting packet, a DDDR connection will attempt to be made.

4. If an active DDR connection exists for a destination specified within an interesting packet, the packet is sent and an idle timer is then reset.

Controlling Routing Updates as Triggers

A router for any routing protocol supported on the router after waiting a period of time typically sends routing updates. Distance vector routing protocols send their entire routing table periodically. Link-state and advanced routing distance routing protocols (such as Enhance IGRP) send hello messages to verify the connection to another router using the same protocol. Table 12-4 lists the various default periods for periodic routing update cycles of IP networks.

In the case of OSPF, IS-IS, and Enhanced IGRP, the DDR connection for the destination of the hello messages keeps the DDR connection up all the time. This is not only costly but also a waste of router resources. For distance vector protocols like RIP and IGRP, the DDR connection will "flap" between connected and disconnected, causing excessive route convergence on the partner DDR routers and any routers connected to them. It is for this reason that it is recommended to apply a deny access list to the above routing messages listed in the table.

Table 12-4

Periodic IP Routing Protocol Messages

IP Routing Protocol	Update Period
Enhanced IGRP	Five seconds (Hello)
IGRP	90 seconds
RIP	30 seconds
OSPF	10 seconds (Hello, depends on link type)
IS-IS	10 seconds (Hello)

Note that once a DDR is active, these routing messages are not filtered and flow through to the destination DDR routers. In this way, it is the application requirements of the location that dictate whether the DDR connection is made and not the inherent network protocol requirements that trigger the DDR connection. Once a DDR connection is made, however, the inherent network protocol mechanisms are used to establish routes to the destinations.

Novell IPX networks characteristically generate many different types of packets on a periodic basis. These too should also be reviewed and marked as uninteresting to avoid the flapping of DDR connections and the costs in router CPU cycles and connection times. The packets that should be reviewed along with their default update time are listed in Table 12-5.

The watchdog packet is used by a server to verify that a previously established client is still on the network and is maintaining a session with the server. This packet is sent out approximately every five minutes. Instead of using an access list filter to deny this packet, the Cisco IOS employs a spoofing technique. Using the watchdog-spoofing technique, a router replies back to the server on behalf of the destination IP workstation. In this way, the DDR connection is not established for this keepalive packet between the server and the client.

Access Lists

Cisco IOS access lists are used in IP network environments to trigger the DDR connection for any type of IP application. The access list used can define a specific IP host or it can be granular in support of a TCP or UDP port number for activating the DDR link. A generic access list can be created that can be used for all the DDR connections, instead of a unique access-list for each interface. In this way, the access list can be applied to any interface, as it is required. Similarly, access lists to deny or permit on Novell packet types can be defined for generic denial and granular permits.

Table 12-5

Novell IPX Packet Types Requiring Attention Using DDR

Novell Packet Type	Update Period
RIP	60 seconds
SAP	60 seconds
Serialization	66 seconds
Watchdog	Five minutes

Security

Security for switched connections is a great concern. Many corporate networks have been compromised due to a lack of authentication by a connecting resource. Cisco has two basic front-line authentication features available for ISDN implementation, callback and screening. This section briefly discusses each of these options.

Callback

Using the callback feature, a router receiving a call from another location is requested to callback the calling router. Typically, a central site router receives a call from a remote location and calls back to the remote location using PPP along with AAA authentication.

Screening

If caller ID is supported by the central office ISDN switch, a router receiving an incoming call can be screened. Using the caller ID found in the setup message, the router can determine if the calling number is a valid participant for making connections to this router. If it is, the call setup continues. If the caller ID presented by the ISDN switch is not found, the receiving router disconnects the call.

CHAPTER 13

Preparing the Cisco Router

This chapter discusses the basics of router installation and the core parameters that reflect loading the IOS code, configuring the router, loading microcode, and managing the files.

Determining the Proper IOS Code

The Cisco IOS system image distribution system is quite extensive and at times confusing. Prior to deciding on what image is required for each router, it is important to understand the services required at each location. The quick checklist needed to answer these questions follows:

- Which network protocols are required to facilitate business processes at each location?
- Which, if any, network protocols are unique for site-to-site location?
- Is temporary connectivity required?
- What is the addressing plan for each network protocol?
- Which routing protocol(s) will be in use to facilitate connectivity?
- What are the WAN protocols needed for each interface?

Once you have answers to these questions, you must match them with the different feature sets available for the hardware platform. The feature sets are categorized into the following:

- *Basic:* The basic feature set for the hardware platform.
- *Plus:* The basic feature set plus additional features, depending on the hardware platform selected.
- *Encryption:* The addition of 40-bit (Plus40) or 56-bit (Plus56) data encryption feature sets to either a basic or plus feature set.

The Cisco IOS releases vary and fluctuate with code fixes almost weekly. Table 13-1 is included to assist you in understanding the position in the release lifecycle of a Cisco IOS release.

Two types of images can be found on Cisco routers. The system image is the complete Cisco IOS software that loads into the router RAM and is used to operate the router. The second type of image is the boot image. The boot image is a subset of the Cisco IOS software and is used to load the complete Cisco IOS software image on the router at start-up or on execution of the Cisco enable configuration command BOOT. For all Cisco router platforms except those specified in Table 13-2, the images are located in Flash memory.

Table 13-1

Table Listing Cisco IOS Release Generations

Release Type	Description	Timing	Numbering Example
Major release—Functionally Complete Software (FCS)	Introduces significant features, functionality, and/or platforms on a stability-oriented release vehicle	As needed to support customer needs	12.0(1)
Major release—Scheduled maintenance updates	Periodic revisions to major releases: fully regression-tested, incorporates the most recent bug fixes, and no new platforms or features—focused on stability	Regular maintenance cycles	12.0(3)
Major release—Interim builds	Working builds, usually not regression-tested, and not intended for customer use except in unusual circumstances	Weekly	12.0(4.2)
General deployment (GD)	A major release that is appropriate for general, unconstrained use in customers' networks	When stability of release has been proven internally by Cisco and externally by customers	12.0(8) and all subsequent maintenance updates of 12.0 [12.0(9), 12.0(10), etc.]
Early deployment (ED)—FCS	Introduces significant new features, functionality, and/or platforms on a feature-oriented release vehicle: based on a major release and will not achieve general deployment	As needed to provide support for newly emerging technologies	12.0(1)T
Early deployment—Scheduled maintenance updates	Periodic revisions to ED releases: fully regression-tested, incorporates the most recent bug fixes including those from Major Release, and usually delivers new platforms and/or features	Regular maintenance cycles	12.0(3)T
Early deployment—Interim builds	Working builds—usually not regression-tested and not intended for customer use except in unusual circumstances	Generally weekly, though some ED Releases may follow a different policy	12.0(4.2)T

Table 13-2

System and Boot
Image File Loca-
tions for the Cisco
7000, 3600, and
1600 Series
Routers

Router	Flash (flash:)	Bootflash (bootflash:)	First PCMCIA Slot (slot0:)	Second PCMCIA Slot (slot1:)
Cisco 7000 family	-	yes	yes	yes
Cisco 3600 series	yes	-	yes	yes
Cisco 1600 series	yes	-	-	-

The image name format identifies the router platform, features, and the type of area on the router from which the image executes. The image name is formatted as *platform-features-type*.

Table 13-3 provides a sample listing of the platform variable of the IOS naming convention.

The feature variable identifies the feature sets included in the image. Table 13-4 lists some examples of the feature variable used in the IOS naming convention. If more than one feature set is included, the features are listed in the variable by alphabetical sequence.

The *type* field identifies the location of the running image in the router.

Table 13-3

Sample Platform
Variables for IOS
Image Name

Cisco Router Platform	*platform* Value in IOS Name
Cisco 7000 series with RSP7000	rsp
Cisco 7500 series	rsp
Cisco 4500/4700 series	c4500
Cisco 4000 series	c4000
Cisco 3600 series	c3600
Cisco 2600 series	c2600
Cisco 2500 series	c2500
Cisco 1600 series	c1600
Cisco 1005 series	c1005

Table 13-4

Sample Feature Variable Values for IOS Naming Convention

Variable	*feature* Value in IOS name
APPN	a
ATM	a2
Desktop subset (SNMP, IP, Bridging, WAN, Remote Node, Terminal Services, IPX, Atalk, ARAP) (11.2—Decnet)	d
Reduced desktop subset (SNMP, IP, IPX, ATALK, ARAP)	d2
IPeXchange (no longer used in 11.3 and later) StarPipes DB2 Access enables Cisco IOS to act as a "gateway" to all IBM DB2 products for downstream clients/servers in 11.3T	e
FRAD subset (SNMP, FR, PPP, SDLLC, STUN)	f
ISDN subset (SNMP, IP, Bridging, ISDN, PPP, IPX, Atalk)	g
Enterprise subset (formerly bpx, includes protocol translation), *not used until 10.3*	j
kitchen sink (enterprise for high-end) (same as bx) (Not used after 10.3)	k

This *type* field can be one of the following values:

- *f:* The image runs from Flash memory.
- *m:* The image runs from RAM.
- *r:* The image runs from ROM.
- *l:* The image is relocatable.
- *z:* The image is zip-compressed.
- *x:* The image is mzip-compressed.

Locate IOS Using Cisco Connection Online (CCO)

The Cisco IOS software image selected for the router can be accessed directly from the Cisco Systems Web site named Cisco Connection Online (CCO). The CCO Web page is at http://www.cisco.com and the Cisco

IOS software images are found at `http://www.cisco.com/kobayashi/ sw-center/sw-ios.shtml`. Here the supported and available Cisco IOS release levels are listed. Drilling further down by selecting a release level, the specific router model and feature sets are selected.

CCO Software Center

Authorized users with a user ID and password access the CCO software center. Typically, these are provided after you have purchased a maintenance agreement with Cisco Systems. To locate the release, you must follow the following path through the software center. In this example, we are locating a major release of Cisco IOS 12.0:

```
http://www.cisco.com/
```

Enter the following in the browser:

```
http://www.cisco.com/kobayashi/library/12.0/index.shtml
    http://www.cisco.com/cgi-bin/iosplanner/iosplanner.cgi?major-
    Rel=12.0
LOGIN to CCO
```

From here, select the hardware platform of the Cisco router being prepared for upgrading. After selecting the router platform, select the feature set required, based on your answers from the previous questions. At this point, CCO Software Center will require you to verify the agreement for downloading the software and then display the name of the Cisco IOS software image to be downloaded to your computer. Upon selecting the software image, a software license agreement appears to which you must answer yes to obtain the IOS software image. The image name is then shown with three options for downloading to your location:

- FTP directly to your computer
- Use HTTP to download the image
- Receive an e-mail message with an attached file

If these approaches do not work for any reason, the same IOS software image can be obtained by executing a FTP connection to `http://www.cisco.com` and logging in with the registered CCO user ID and password. In this case, the image name found from the previous CCO software center steps outlined above are entered using the FTP "get" command. For the example we used, the FTP command will be entered as:

```
get /cisco/ios/12.0/12.0.1a/7500/rsp-jsv-mz.120-1a.bin
```

In either case, be sure to specify a directory on your computer that has enough storage space to handle the IOS software image.

Downloading IOS to the TFTP Server

Typically, the IOS software image retrieved from CCO is stored on the UNIX computer or a Windows 95/98/NT workstation that executed the download. Cisco routers, in a corporate environment, are typically updated using Trivial File Transfer Protocol (TFTP). Using any number of free TFTP server offerings on the Internet for a Windows 95/98/NT workstation, you can download the IOS software image to the target router.

The following steps must be followed with either a UNIX or Windows platform:

1. Start the TFTP server application on the UNIX computer or Windows workstation.
2. Ensure the correct IOS image is placed in the TFTP directory.
3. Be sure to use the exact IOS image name, as found on the TFTP server.

The last step is important because some browsers and/or operating systems may change the name of a .bin extension to a .exe extension on the file name. Once these steps have been verified, the IOS can be transferred to the target router.

Loading IOS on the Router

The IOS image stored on a TFTP server must be written to the target router. Although the router supports alternative methods for transferring a system image, TFTP is the most widely used. FTP transfer of the IOS image is available, starting with Release 12.0 of Cisco IOS. A Cisco router arrives with an onboard Cisco IOS system image for initial start-up. Typically, routers are ordered with flash memory to allow the storage of new IOS software images. Access to the contents of the flash memory requires the end user to be in privileged mode.

Figure 13-1
File transfer of Cisco
IOS image to and
from a TFTP or FTP
server.

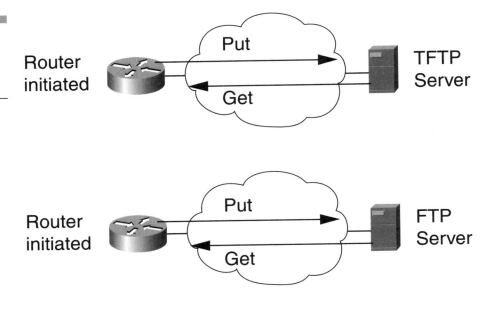

NOTE: *Cisco routers do not support remote file transfer initiation. All transfers of files on a router must be initiated from the router.*

Enter Privileged Mode on the Terminal Interface

Privileged mode on a Cisco router allows the end user to access system-level commands that can affect router or network performance as well as configuration mode commands. Entering privileged mode is accomplished by entering the EXEC mode command:
enable

The router prompts for a privileged password at this point. If this router is starting up for the first time, just entering the enable EXEC mode command will allow the end user to enter the privileged mode.

Once the end user has entered privileged mode, the IOS copy command can be executed to either get an IOS image from a server or to put an IOS image on a file server.

Issue Copy to/from a TFTP Server

Before loading a new IOS on an existing Cisco router, it is prudent to write the previous IOS image used on the router to a server. Existing routers typically have the onboard system image that came with the router and a system image in the flash memory of the router.

Copying an IOS image from a 7000, 7200, or 7500 series router to a TFTP server requires the use of the following command:

copy *device:filename* **tftp**:[[[*///location*]/*directory*]/*filename*]

The *device:filename* variable is the value of the flash memory location on the 7000, 7200, or 7500 series router. An example of a resolved *device:filename* variable is slot1:ios12.0-1, which indicates that the file named ios12.0-1 on the flash PCMCIA memory card, located in slot1 of the primary RSP card on a 7500 series router, is the file to copy. The location, directory, and filename positional optional variables of the **tftp** keyword specify the TFTP host name or IP address, the directory tree to use on the TFTP server, and the name of the file to be written on the TFTP server.

For example, copying an image from a 7000 router to a TFTP server using the image found on the internal flash of the 7000 router is entered as

```
copy flash:ios12.0-1 tftp://tftpserver/ciscoimages/7000/ios12.0-1
```

Optionally, this command can be abbreviated and the router can prompt you for the variable inputs. For instance, the above command can be entered as

```
copy flash: tftp:
```

and the router will prompt the end user with the following questions:

```
IP address of remote host [255.255.255.255]?
filename to write on TFTP host?
```

The router administrator must provide the IP address of the TFTP server or the DNS name of the TFTP server, and then the IOS image name found (in this case) in the flash memory location. In this instance, the router writes the IOS image specified to the TFTP server default directory.

NOTE: *When writing files to a server, the process must have the capability to create a new file. If not, the copy will fail. To avoid this, either set the processes with the authority to create files or have a predefined file with the same name already on the server.*

The value for the *device* parameter of the *device:filename* variable is listed in Table 13-5 with a description for each variable.

On routers that support multiple flash memory locations, the change directory (cd) command must be entered, pointing to the flash location. This is similar to the change directory command for any UNIX or Windows command. For example, specifying cd slot0: changes the working directory from flash to the PCMCIA memory card installed in memory slot0 of the router. In the case of a Cisco router with multiple flash memory locations, the command points the copy command to the correct location just by specifying copy.

Some routers, like the 3600 series, allow the partition of flash memory. In this case, the copy command must be entered by specifying *device:partition:filename* to point to the appropriate flash memory location. For example, writing an image from a 3600 series router to a TFTP server can be accomplished using the following **copy** command:

```
copy slost0:2:c3600-ios tftp:
```

In this example, the flash memory card in slot0 is accessed and the file c3600-ios is found in partition 2 of the flash memory card installed in slot0 of the router. The router will prompt for the destination TFTP server and then verify the write command.

Table 13-5

The Device Parameter Values Available for the **device:filename** Variable for Copying IOS Images to a TFTP Server

device Parameter Value	Description
flash	Internal flash memory on the router
bootflash	Internal flash memory specific to the 7200/7500 series routers
slot0	PCMCIA flash memory card in the first or only slot on the router
slot1	PCMCIA flash memory card in the second slot on the router
nvram	Internal non-volatile RAM on the router
slavebootflash	Internal flash on the 7507/7513 slave RSP card configured for high availability
slaveslot0	First PCMCIA flash memory card on the 7507/7513 slave RSP card configured for high availability
slaveslot1	Second PCMCIA flash memory card on the 7507/7513 slave RSP card configured for high availability
slavenvram	Internal non-volatile RAM on the slave RSP card of a 7507/7513 configured for high availability.

Copying an IOS image to the flash of a router is similar in structure. The **copy** command is used, but in this case the format is changed to

copy tftp:[[[*///location*]/*directory*]/*filename*] *device*:[*filename*]

The location, directory, and filename positional variables are the same as that found for the **copy** *device:filename* command. The *device* value is the same as found in Table 13-5; however, the *filename* variable is optional on the command. In using the **copy tftp**: command for loading am IOS image on the router flash memory, the router will prompt for a name if one is not specified on the command line.

In the following example, the IOS image rsp-11.3 is written from a TFTP server named TFTPSERVER to flash memory located in slot0 of a Cisco 7513 series router.

```
Router# copy tftp://tftpserver/tftpboot/cisco/7500/rsp-11.3 slot0:
Destination filename [rsp-11.3]?
Accessing tftp://tftpserver/tftpboot/cisco/7500/rsp-
11.3...Translating
"tftpserver"...domain server (192.168.32.1) [OK]

Loading tftpboot/cisco/7500/rsp-11.3 from 192.168.32.1 (via
Ethernet0/0):
!!!!!!!!!!!!!!!!!!!!!!!!!!!!!!!!!!!!!!!!!!!!!!!!!!!!!!!!!!!!!!!!!!!!!!!!
!!!!!!!!!!!!!!!!!!!!!!!!!!!!!!!!!!!!!!!!!!!!!!!!!!!!!!!!!!!!!!!!!!!!!!!!
!!!!!!!!!!!!!!!!!!!!!!!!!!!!!!!!!!!!!!!!!!!!!!!!!!!!!!!!!!!!!!!!!!!!!!!!
!!!!!!!!!!!!!!!!!!!!!!!!!!!!!!!!!!!!!!!!!!!!!!!!!!!!!!!!!!!!!!!!!!!!!!!!
!!!!!!!!!!!!!!!!!!!!!!!!!!!!!!!!!!!!!!!!!!!!!!!!!!!!!!!!!!!!!!!!!!!!!!!!
!!!!!!!!!!!!!!!!!!!!!!!!!!!!!!!!!!!!!!!!!!!!!!!!!!!!!!!!!!!!!!!!!!!!!!!!
!!!!!!!!!!!!!!!!!!!!!!!!!!!!!!!!!!!!!!!!!!!!!!!!!!!!!!!!!!!!!!!!!!!!!!!!
!!!!!!!!!!!!!!!!!!!!!!!!!!!!!!!!!!!!!!!!!!!!!!!!!!!!!!!!!!!!!!!!!!!!!!!!
!!!!!!!!!!!!!!!!!!!!!!!!!!!!!!!!!!!!!!!!!!!!!!!!!!!!!!!!!!!!!!!!!!!!!!!!
!!!!!!!!!!!!!!!!!!!!!!!!!!!!!!!!!!!!!!!!!!!!!!!!!!!!!!!!!!!!!!!!!!!!!!!!
!!!!!!!!!!!!!!!!!!!!!!!!!!!!!!!!!!!!!!!!!!!!!!!!!!!!!!!!!!!!!!!!!!!!!!!!
!!!!!!!!!!!!!!!!!!!!!!!!!!!!!!!!!!!!!!!!!!!!!!!!!!!!!!!!!!!!!!!!!!!!!!!!
!!!!!!!!!!!!!!!!!!!!!!!!!!!!!!!!!!!!!!!!!!!!!!!!!!!!!!!!!!!!!!!!!!!!!!!!
!!!!!
[OK - 4823492/9646080 bytes]

4823492 bytes copied in 264.312 secs (18270 bytes/sec)
```

The exclamation point (!) in the example means that 10 packets have been transferred successfully. The router first requested the address of the system named tftpserver by querying the DNS server at 192.168.32.1, prior to establishing the TFTP request. If the fully qualified file name had not been specified, the TFTP process would search only the tftpboot directory or the default directory specified for the tftp process on the workstation. This would result in a failed TFTP request.

Issue Copy to/from the FTP Server

The FTP for transferring files between the router and a server was introduced with Release 12.0 of Cisco IOS. Since FTP is a connection-oriented application using TCP/IP, it provides better throughput and a higher rate of success than does TFTP, which is a connectionless oriented applications using UDP/IP for delivery services.

Being a connection-oriented application, FTP requires the use of a login and password prior to transferring the IOS image. Establishing the username for the login and the password presented by the router to the FTP server is accomplished using the configuration operation of the privileged mode on the router. The following sequence is used to again provide this information to the router IOS in preparation of using FTP to transfer an IOS image.

```
enable
Enter password: xxxxxx
configure terminal
ip ftp username login-name
ip ftp password login-password
end
write memory
```

As with TFTP, the **enable** command, followed by the privileged password, allows the operator to gain access to privileged mode commands. The **configure terminal** command executes the configuration mode of the router. In this mode, any and all options and definitions can be entered to modify, add, or delete the router running configuration. The FTP username associated with a login name on the target FTP server is provided to the router IOS by the **ip ftp username** command. The **ip ftp username** login-name variable defines the default user login name used by the router if a login name is not specified on the **copy ftp**: command.

The *login-name* variable is a valid user name on the target FTP server. The **ip ftp password** command is the default password associated with the specified *login-name* on the target FTP server. The **end** command exits the configuration mode.

After executing these commands, the router IOS configuration has the FTP parameters necessary to connect to a FTP server. The **write memory** command at the end of the statements saves the running configuration in the router to the router's NVRAM for permanent storage. Saving the running configuration to memory saves the just entered configuration information between power-on reset and router reloads.

Backing up the current IOS image to an FTP server is accomplished by entering the following command:

copy *device:filename* **ftp:**[[[//[*login-name*[:*login-password*]@]*location*]/ *directory*]/*filename*]

Using this command, the router administrator specifies the flash location of the router using the device parameter of the *device:filename* variable and the name of the image using the *filename* parameter. The *device* parameter can be any value specified in Table 13-5 and the *filename* is an image name found on the flash device.

The *login-name* and the *login-password* values may be the values set by the **ip ftp username** and **the ip ftp password** commands. However, remember that these commands are used only for default. If the commands were never entered, the FTP server prompts the router administrator for the user name and password. The remaining variables of location, directory, and filename are defined the same as with TFTP copy.

For example, to transfer an image from flash memory to an FTP server at the server name FTPSERVER, the router administrator enters the following command:

```
copy flash:ios-image ftp://joev:jandj@FTPSERVER/cisco/image/ios-image
```

The image named ios-image is copied to the directory //cisco/image/ in relation to the directory structure assigned to the FTP server authorized user named joev. The IP address of the server named FTPSERVER is determined by the router performing a DNS query to the specified DNS server found in the router configuration file.

Transferring a new image file to the router is performed using the following copy ftp: command:

copy **ftp:**[[[//[*login-name*[:*login-password*]@]*location*]/*directory*]/*filename*] *device***:**[*filename*]

The **copy ftp:** command uses all the same variables as previously discussed. In using the command, you need only specify the following:

```
copy ftp: slot1:
```

Using this abbreviated format of the command, the default *login-name* and default *login-password* are passed to the FTP server. If the router does not have the defaults specified, the FTP server prompts for the login name and the login password. The FTP connection is treated like any other and the router administrator then enters the *filename* of the file to retrieve. Note that, in this instance, the default directory structure associated with the login name must have the requested *filename* to retrieve. The requested file will be saved on the flash memory card specified as slot1 in this example.

The Cisco IOS uses a default mechanism for providing the FTP *login-name* and *login-password* values. For the *login-name,* the IOS will use the following criteria:

1. The *login-name* specified with the **copy** command, if a *login-name* is specified.
3. The *login-name* set by the **ip ftp username** command, if the command is configured.
3. The default FTP login name of anonymous.

The password is determined by the following:

1. The *login-password* specified in the **copy** command, if a *login-password* is specified.
2. The *login-password* set by the **ip ftp password** command, if the command is configured.
3. The router forms a *login-password login-name@routername.domain.* The variable *login-name* is the login name associated with the current session, *routername* is the configured host name of the router, and *domain* is the domain name of the router.

NOTE: *Copy operations can be interrupted by pressing **Ctrl-^** or **Ctrl-Shift-6**. This terminates the current copy operation, but the partially copied file remains in flash memory until erased.*

Loading CIP or CPA Microcode on a Cisco 7000/7200/7500 Router

The process of transferring CIP/CPA microcode to the 7000/7200/7500 (7K) series routers uses the same mechanisms as that of transferring IOS system images. Either copy tftp: or copy ftp: commands can be entered to retrieve the CIP/CPA microcode. The CIP/CPA microcode images once copying begins are self-exploding images. During a copy operation, the following output occurs on the terminal:

```
routername#copy tftp slot0:
Enter source file name: cip22-25.exe
6843800 bytes available on device slot0, proceed? [confirm]
```

```
Address or name of remote host [tftp.domain.com]? 10.16.47.72
Accessing file "cip22-25.exe" on 10.16.47.72 ...FOUND
Loading cip22-25.exe from 10.16.47.72 (via Ethernet2/2): !
-- expanding multi-segment file --
slot0:cip22-25.exe_kernel_hw4 size = 257888
!!!!!!!!!!!!!!!!!!!!!!!!!!!!!!!!!!!!!!!!!!!!!!!!!!!!!!CCCCCCC
-- expanding multi-segment file --
slot0:cip22-25.exe_kernel_hw5 size = 256914
!!!!!!!!!!!!!!!!!!!!!!!!!!!!!!!!!!!!!!!!!!!!!!!!!!!!CCCCCCC
-- expanding multi-segment file --
slot0:cip22-25.exe_seg_802 size = 233792
!!!!!!!!!!!!!!!!!!!!!!!!!!!!!!!!!!!!!!!!!!!!!!!!!!!CCCCCCC
-- expanding multi-segment file --
slot0:cip22-25.exe_seg_csna size = 85896
!!!!!!!!!!!!!!!!!!!!CC
-- expanding multi-segment file --
slot0:cip22-25.exe_seg_eca size = 461408
!!!!!!!!!!!!!!!!!!!!!!!!!!!!!!!!!!!!!!!!!!!!!!!!!!!!!!!!!!!!!!!
!!!!!!!!!!!!!!!!!!!!!!!!!!!!!!!!!!!!CCCCCCCCCCCCCCC
-- expanding multi-segment file --
slot0:cip22-25.exe_seg_offload size = 64656
!!!!!!!!!!!!!!C
-- expanding multi-segment file --
slot0:cip22-25.exe_seg_pca size = 69360
!!!!!!!!!!!!!!!CC
-- expanding multi-segment file --
slot0:cip22-25.exe_seg_push size = 13752
!!!
-- expanding multi-segment file --
slot0:cip22-25.exe_seg_tcpip size = 182032
!!!!!!!!!!!!!!!!!!!!!!!!!!!!!!!!!!!!!!!!CCCCC
-- expanding multi-segment file -
slot0:cip22-25.exe_seg_tn3270 size = 542392
!!!!!!!!!!!!!!!!!!!!!!!!!!!!!!!!!!!!!!!!!!!!!!!!!!!!!!!!!!!!!
!!!!!!!!!!!!!!!!!!!!!!!!!!!!!!!!!!!!!!!!!!!!!!!!CCCCCCCCCCCCCCCCCC
```

In this output, the CIP microcode named cip22-25.exe is transferred from a TFTP server named tftp.domain.com to the router using the **copy tftp**: command. The command specifies that the PCMCIA flash memory card installed in slot0 of the router is the destination for the CIP microcode. As you can see from the example, the CIP microcode is expanded during the transfer process.

Locating CIP/CPA Microcode on the CCO Software Center

In a process similar to locating the IOS image for a Cisco router, the CIP/CPA microcode image is determined. A similar path is followed, as outlined below, to locate the CIP microcode for a 7500 series router using Release 12.0(1) Cisco IOS:

```
http://www.cisco.com
    LOGIN to CCO
```

```
http://www.cisco.com/public/sw-center
http://www.cisco.com/public/sw-center/sw-ios.shtml
http://www.cisco.com/kobayashi/sw-center/interworks/cip
```

The location on CCO for the CIP/CPA microcode from the Cisco Web site is specific to the IOS release level. For example, the microcode for Release 11.3 of Cisco IOS is located at

```
http://www.cisco.com/cgi-bin/tablebuild.pl/cip113
```

Release 12.0 of Cisco IOS CIP microcode is found at

```
http://www.cisco.com/cgi-bin/tablebuild.pl/cip120
```

At these URLs, the list of available microcode releases and the supported platform can be found. From here, select the appropriate CIP/CPA code for the router platform being prepared for upgrading. The CIP code is for the Cisco 7000 and 7500 series routers, while the CPA code is for the Cisco 7200 series routers.

After selecting the router platform, select the feature set required, based on your answers from the previous questions. At this point, the CCO Software Center will require that you verify the agreement for downloading the software and then display the name of the Cisco IOS software image to be downloaded to your computer.

After selecting the image, a software license agreement appears to which you must answer yes to obtain the IOS software image. The image name is then shown with three options for downloading to your location:

- FTP directly to your computer
- Use HTTP to download the image
- Receive an e-mail message with an attached file

If these approaches do not work for any reason, the same CIP/CPA image can be obtained by executing a FTP connection to http://www.cisco.com and logging in with the registered CCO user ID and password. In this case, the image name found from the previous CCO software center steps outlined above are entered using the FTP "get" command. For example, the FTP command is entered as

```
get /cisco/core/cip/12.0/cip26-4.bin
```

In either case, be sure to specify a directory on your computer that has enough storage space to handle the IOS software image.

Enter config Parameters to Load Microcode

The router configuration file must have a pointer to the CIP microcode name and location. This is accomplished by entering the configuration mode on the router and entering the microcode configuration command:

microcode *interface*[*device*:*filename* [*slot*] | **system** [*slot*] | **rom** [*slot*]]

The *interface* variable of the microcode command identifies the interface processor board type being addressed in the **microcode** command. Again, the *device* parameter is the flash memory location where the microcode identified by the *filename* parameter is found. The *slot* parameter identifies the slot location of the interface processor type being addressed by the **microcode** command if more than one board of the same interface type is present. Using the *slot* parameter allows you to load different microcode releases into different processors. For example, to specify the loading of CIP microcode CIP22-25.exe, found on flash memory slot0 on the CIP board located at slot 2 on the router, the following command is issued under configuration mode:

```
microcode CIP flash slot0:cip22-25.exe 2
```

This command sets the router configuration to load the CIP card installed on the router with the microcode cip22-25.exe.

After entering this **microcode** command, exit the configuration mode by entering the **end** command. Follow this with the **write memory** or **copy running-config start-config** command to save the new microcode definition in the startup configuration file.

The CIP and CPA interface processors are the only offerings with microcode outside the IOS image. All other processors obtain their microcode from the IOS image used at load time on the router. Table 13-6 lists the possible values for the interface variable on the **microcode** command.

Microcode for interface processors other than the CIP/CPA cards obtain their microcode from the IOS image currently running in the system. Typically, Cisco routers run using the IOS image found in flash memory. The microcode for all processor boards other than CIP/CPA are loaded from this code. The system keyword on the microcode command indicates that the specified interface type should be loaded from the system IOS microcode level.

Loading the microcode is accomplished by issuing the following command under configuration mode:

microcode reload

This command immediately has the IOS reload all the interface processors installed that have microcode running. The **microcode reload** command reloads the interface processors based on the microcode commands entered in the running configuration.

The microcode reload command need only be executed to refresh interface processors or to initially prime an interface processor for the first time. Normal microcode load processing occurs in the following manner:

Table 13-6

The **Interface** Variable Values Available for the **Microcode** Command

Microcode *interface* Variable	Interface Type
AIP	ATM Interface Processor
CIP	Channel Interface Processor
EIP	Ethernet Interface Processor
FEIP	Fast Ethernet Interface Processor
FIP	FDDI Interface Processor
FSIP	Fast Serial Interface Processor
HIP	HSSI Interface Processor
MIP	Multi-Channel Interface Processor
POSIP	Packet over Sonet Interface Processor
SIP	Serial Interface Processor
SP	Switch Processor
SSP	Silicon Switch Processor
TRIP	Token Ring Interface Processor
VIP	Versatile Interface Processor
VIP2	Versatile Interface Processor 2

1. The system is booted.
2. A card is inserted or removed.
3. The configuration command **microcode reload** is issued.

Loading the microcode on Cisco 12000 GSR routers is the same as loading images on the Cisco 7500 series routers. In addition, however, each line card on the 12000 series router has a complete copy of the Cisco IOS image. Each line card gets the IOS image after the image is loaded into the GRP of the 12000 series router. The GRP then automatically distributes the image to each line card.

Instances may occur that necessitate upgrading a line card without upgrading the GRP due to temporary fixes that affect the specific function of the line card. To do this, follow the procedures already outlined for the using TFTP or FTP to download an IOS image to a Cisco router. After the download has taken place, the following command is used to load the new image on a specific GSR line card:

microcode {oc12-atm | oc12-pos | oc3-pos-4} flash *file-id slot-number*

The first keywords identify the interface type being addressed by the **microcode** command. The *file-id* variable following the flash keyword identifies the IOS image name being used for the load. The *slot-number* variable is the position of the line card on the GSR. By omitting the *slot-number* variable, the IOS image is loaded into all line cards.

The line card is reloaded with the new IOS image by specifying the following command under configuration mode:

microcode reload *slot-number*

The **slot-number** variable is the position of the line card affected by this reload command. If the *slot-number* variable is omitted, all the line cards are reloaded.

Router Basic Configuration and IOS Commands

A few basic IOS commands should be specified within a router for minimal operation. This section discusses these commands and the most commonly used parameters of each command.

Setting up EXEC and Privileged Mode Access

During a first time installation of a router, the router administrator can connect to the router using the console port or the auxiliary port with a personal computer, laptop, or notebook PC. During a first-time installation, the router does not have a password for the privileged mode of the router. In this case, the router administrator simply enters the EXEC mode command **enable** to access privileged mode.

In a previously configured router with a privileged password defined, the router administrator must enter the privileged-password for gaining access to privileged mode. The authorization of the mode allows three attempts. After the failed third attempt, the router administrator falls back to EXEC mode.

Once gaining access to privileged mode, router configuration parameters can be altered. To alter the router configuration, the router administrator must gain access to the configuration mode. Entering the **configuration terminal** command under privileged mode does this.

In first-time installations, it is best to immediately address basic security issues for remote users gaining access to the router. The first of these defenses is the use of a password at the EXEC mode of the router. The EXEC mode is the operational mode presented to all Telnet users and direct serial attached users. Defining this access is performed by using the following basic line commands:

```
line con 0
    exec-timeout 15 0
    password RTRPSWD
    login
line aux 0
    transport input all
    exec-timeout 15 0
    password RTRPSWD
    login
line vty 0 4
    exec-timeout 15 0
    password RTRPSWD
    login
```

Using these configuration commands, three means of access are defined through the console and auxiliary ports and the virtual terminals (vty). The **line con 0** command identifies that the router console port is available for direct access to the router. The **exec-timeout** command following this specifies that the connection will timeout within 15 minutes if data is not transmitted between the router and the end user workstation. The password for EXEC mode access is RTRPSWD and login password authorization is required, meaning that the router administrator gains EXEC mode access using the console port by providing the password.

The **line aux 0** command defines the use of the auxiliary port for access to the router. Typically, this port is used for remote dial-up access to the router in case the router WAN links or LAN connections are down. The auxiliary port in the example uses the same time restrictions, password, and login parameters to authorize remote access to the router. The added parameter **transport input all** enables all possible protocols supported by the auxiliary to communicate with the router. These protocols are shown in Table 13-7.

Table 13-7

The Supported Protocols for the Auxiliary Line on a Cisco Router

Supported Protocol Value	Auxiliary Port-Supported Protocols
lat	DEC LAT protocol
mop	DEC MOP remote console protocol
nasi	NASI protocol
none	No protocols
pad	X.3 PAD
rlogin	Unix rlogin protocol
telnet	TCP/IP Telnet protocol
v120	Async over ISDN

The final line command is the **line vty 0 4,** which defines five virtual terminal connections. Each terminal connection is used when Telnet connections are established to the router via the LAN/WAN network. All five connections use the same EXEC mode password RTRPSWD to gain access to the basic router operational commands. Each connection will timeout after 15 minutes of idleness.

NOTE: *The **line console** and **line auxiliary** commands allow for only one connection, hence the 0 value following the **con** and **aux** keywords.*

The next time a router administrator accesses the router through any of these connections, the router will prompt for the EXEC mode password. The router administrator has three attempts to enter the newly assigned password RTRPSWD and the router disconnects the Telnet connection after the failed third attempt.

The assignment of a password to the privileged mode is possible using two methods. The first is the use of the **enable password** command. This can be used for providing a hidden password during the printing of the configuration. The **enable password** command is the first stage of a second tier of authorization on the router for gaining privileged access. However, the execution of the **show config**, **show running-config,** or **show startup-config** displays the privileged password on the terminal screen.

Anyone looking over the router administrator's shoulder could easily get the privileged password.

Encrypting the password for display or print requires the inclusion of the **service password-encryption** global configuration command as well as the **enable secret** global configuration command. Using this command in the following format will result in a displayed encrypted command:

```
service password-encryption
enable secret RTRPsWD
```

Using the **enable secret** command, the router encrypts the password RTRPsWD to protect its anonymity. The lower case "s" is used here to demonstrate that the Cisco IOS uses upper and lower case, as well as special characters such as ^, ~, or ` as viable characters for the password. The resulting display from a **show running-config** or **show config** command is

```
enable secret 5 $1$7bcf$LTYfEFUTGj.nrhsG76RBe0
```

The 5 in the resulting display indicates that the encrypted password is shown. In this manner, the displayed configuration on the terminal screen and in print is encrypted.

BOOT SYSTEM List

While in configuration mode, the best practice for insuring the successful loading of a router is through the use of a fault-tolerant booting strategy. A fault-tolerant booting strategy provides a sequential list for the IOS boot strap to locate and successfully load a working IOS image. Using this method, multiple locations can be searched for loading a viable IOS image into the router. The fault-tolerant method can be outlined as follows:

1. Boot the system from flash.

2. Boot the system from a network server.

3. Boot the system from ROM (BOOTFLASH on Cisco 7500).

For example, a fault-tolerant list on a router that has on-board flash and two PCMCIA flash memory cards, along with support for using an FTP server to get the IOS image, would look like the following:

```
Router# configure terminal
Router(config)# boot system flash rsp-IOS
Router(config)# boot system flash slot0:rsp-IOS
Router(config)# boot system flash slot1:rsp-IOS
Router(config)# boot system FTP rsp-IOS 10.6.1.11
```

```
Router(config)# boot system rom
Router(config)# config-register 0x010F
Router(config)# end
Router# copy running-config startup-config
Router# reload
```

Using the above fault-tolerant method, the router uses the list provided based on the boot register value of 0x010F, specified by the **config-register** command. This value indicates that the system will find the IOS image for loading based on the definitions found in the configuration file. The **boot system FTP** command is dependent on the requirements of the FTP server used and whether the **ip ftp username** and **ip ftp password** commands were previously defined in the configuration file. A TFTP server could also have been specified that would not require the login name and an associated password. Because the boot system ftp and boot system tftp commands do not provide a fully qualified file name structure for locating the IOS image, the image must reside in the default directory assigned to the username profile on the server.

Prior to loading the router using the reload command or by executing a power-on reset, the configuration changes made must be copied to the NVRAM of the router in order for the config-register value to take effect. Reloading without performing this step will result in the router performing the locate of the IOS image based on the previous config-register setting.

NOTE: *This text assumes that at the end of all configuration changes a* ***write memory*** *or* ***copy running-config startup-config*** *command is executed to save the configuration changes in non-volatile memory.*

BOOT CONFIG List

Many Cisco router shops have standardized the configuration files such that many of the standard base parameters are the same on all routers. This type of configuration file is known as the network configuration.

Typically, in a network configuration, you will find standardized definitions for routing, bridging, DNS, SNMP, terminal lines, login banners, logging, and possibly access lists. The network configuration file can be merged with a host-specific configuration file. The host configuration file has information specific to a host (router) that is information unique to the individual router. For instance, unique information pertains to interface definitions, access-lists, and host names.

The provision of a configuration list is one that allows for the centralized management of network-wide and router-specific configuration files. For example, the following commands at startup or reload provide a router with the locations for the configuration files specific for the router:

```
Router# configure terminal
Router(config)# boot host tftp://10.16.1.1/tftpboot/hostfile1
Router(config)# boot network tftp://10.16.1.1/tftpboot/networkfile1
Router(config)# service config
Router(config)# end
Router# copy running-config startup-config
```

In the example, the boot host tftp and boot network tftp commands attempt to retrieve the configuration file from the TFTP server at IP address 10.16.1.1 using the fully qualified file name of /tftpboot/hostfile1 and /tftpboot/networkfile1 for the respective commands. If the first attempt does not succeed, the router continues to try every 10 seconds.

The service-config command enables the router to use the boot host and boot network commands to locate the configuration file. If the service config command is omitted, the configuration file found in the NVRAM startup-config location is used. If the startup-config is corrupted and the boot host and boot network commands are present, however, the service config command is automatically enabled to allow the retrieval of a working configuration.

The final step in the procedure saves the running configuration to the NVRAM startup-config location. At this point, the router can be reloaded using the **reload** command or a power-on reset.

The format of the boot host and boot tftp are listed below. The variable parameters follow the guidelines discussed earlier in this chapter. Both of the boot host and boot network are not necessarily required. Either can be used to load a working configuration for this router at startup.

boot host | network {**ftp:**[[[//[*login-name*[*:login-password*]**]@]** *location*]/*directory*]/*filename*] | **tftp:**[[[//*location*]/*directory*]/*filename*]}

Again, the FTP login name and login password must match a user profile on the FTP server, if specified.

Managing configuration files is akin to managing the IOS image files. The copy commands previously discussed can assist in moving files from the router to a server or from a server to the router. The only change is the device location of the running and startup configuration files.

In the following example, we protect the current startup config from being changed by first copying it to a flash card on the router. Then we issue a copy of the running-config to the startup-config location in NVRAM:

```
copy startup-config slot0:old-config
copy running-config startup-config
```

Using this method, we can always manually reboot the configuration pointing at the saved old-config on the flash memory card at slot0, should the new configuration fail. We can do this by issuing a copy of the saved old-config into the running-config location. This will be acted upon as if the commands were being entered on the router in configuration mode.

```
copy slot0:old-config system:running-config
```

Doing this command will restore the router to the previous running configuration.

Assigning a Name to the Router

The router name is very important. Not only does it give the router an entity, its name is used in providing default configuration file names and login names. The router name is defined using the following command:

```
hostname
```

The *name* parameter is the name of the router. It is referred to as the host name. It can be used as the entry in the Domain Name System (DNS) server. As we will see later on in the book, a router can have a virtual interface defined that is always considered active. The virtual interface is defined using the **interface loopback 0** command and is accessible from any available LAN/WAN connection that is active on the router. By assigning an IP address to the virtual interface and registering the fully-qualified host name in a DNS with the virtual interface IP address, the router is easily accessible, using the host name for a Telnet connection.

A descriptive name is preferred, one that can provide you with some type of knowledge as to the location of the router. For example, examine the following command:

```
hostname c1r2Lndn
```

The router name of c1r2Lndn can denote that this router is in the second row in cabinet 1 of the London office. Using a naming convention leads to a simpler troubleshooting solution.

Enabling a DNS Search and Assigning a Domain

The router has Telnet capabilities for accessing other router- or other Telnet-capable hosts. Many times the router administrator may know the name of the host but not the IP address. To facilitate this type of function, the Cisco IOS allows the entry of a domain name and a pointer to the DNS server used by the network for resolving names to IP addresses. The commands are

ip domain-name *name*
ip name-server *ip-address*

The *name* variable of the **ip domain-name** command is the fully qualified domain name assigned to the network. The *ip-address* variable of the **ip name-server** command is the IP address of a DNS server for resolving host names to IP addresses. Multiple **ip name-server** commands can be entered to provide multiple DNS servers for resolving the host name to an IP address. Here is a sample of these two commands at work:

```
host c1r2Lndn
ip domain-name networxcorp.com
ip name-server 10.10.10.10
ip name-server 10.10.10.11
```

In this example, the router's fully qualified name is c1r2Lndn.networxcorp.com and the DNS servers that the router will use for resolving host names are found at 10.10.10.10 and 10.10.10.11 IP-addressed host computers. The importance of the **ip name-server** command is not only for Telnet connectivity, but for resolving host names entered on any IOS operational command that may use an IP address. Instead of the IP address, a host name can be used that is then resolved using the DNS servers specified with the **ip name-server** command.

Specifying SNMP for Router Management

Router management is extremely important, especially in large router-based networks. The primary means for managing Cisco routers is through the use of Simple Network Management Protocol (SNMP).

SNMP is a network management application layer protocol used for managing IP-based devices. The SNMP architecture requires an SNMP manager and an SNMP agent. An SNMP manager receives messages from an SNMP agent or sends messages to an agent. The messages sent between the SNMP manager and agent are termed traps. These traps contain a tree-structure that identifies occurrence and resources triggering the trap. The tree-structure is called a Management Information Base (MIB), which is an international standard for formatting SNMP messages. Today, all IP devices provide an SNMP agent.

The SNMP messages contain the SNMP MIB; however, a trap notification does not guarantee that the SNMP manager has received the notification message. An inform message will retry sending the message if the

SNMP manager does not positively reply to the inform message with an SNMMP response PDU message.

Cisco IOS supports SNMP Version 1 and SNMP Version 2 C. The differences between Cisco IOS release 12.0 and 11.3 are outlined below.

Cisco IOS Release 12.0 supports

- **SNMPv1**, the Simple Network Management Protocol version 1, as specified in IETF RFC 1157.

- **SNMPv2C,** which consists of the following:
  - **SNMPv2**: Version 2 of the Simple Network Management Protocol, an IETF draft defined in RFCs 1902 through 1907.
  - **SNMPv2C**: The Community-based Administrative Framework for SNMPv2, an experimental IP defined in RFC 1901.

Cisco IOS Release 11.3 removed support for the following version of SNMP:

- **SNMPv2Classic**: The IETF-Proposed Internet Standard of version 2 of the SNMP, defined in RFCs 1441 through 1451.

All other Cisco IOS releases support SNMPv1.

The **snmp-server community** command is used for enabling the SNMP agent function on the router. The format of the command is as follows:

snmp-server community *string* [**view** *view-name*] [**ro** | **rw**] [*number*]

The *string* variable is the access character-string used for identifying the SNMP management community that will be monitoring the router using SNMP. The optional keyword **view** and its variable *view-name* is used to restrict the SNMP information available to the SNMP managers using the community string. The **ro** keyword denotes read-only and the **rw** keyword denotes read-write capabilities for this community. The *number* optional variable is a number relating to an IP access list that can further restrict which SNMP managers use the provided community string for obtaining information from/to the router.

The **view** keyword *view-name* variable value must match a previously defined view if it is included. The format for defining the view is

snmp-server view *view-name oid-tree* {**included** | **excluded**}

The *view-name* is a label given to the view being defined. The *oid-tree* variable is an object identifier that follows the ASN.1 subtree standard. The value can either be the subtree string of numbers, such as 1.3.6.2.4, or a word that defines a hierarchy of the ANS.1 subtree string, such as system. You can also use a wild card "*" character in the numeric string to specify a complete subtree family. The **include exclude** keywords are used to define the scope of the view.

For example, the command defines a view for all MIB-II system group objects with the exception of sysService (System 7):

```
snmp-server view sys system included
snmp-server view sys system.7 excluded
snmp-server view sys cisco included
```

The following commands provide information that can be obtained by an SNMP manager and are useful for troubleshooting:

snmp-server contact *text*
snmp-server location *text*
snmp-server chassis-id *number*

Using these commands, the name of the contact for supporting the router, the location of the router, and the serial number of the router can be provided and queried at any time by an SNMP manager. The *text* variable is a free-form character string that can be used for any reason to convey information to a network operator responsible for managing the router. The *number* variable of the **snmp-server chassis-id** command is typically used for the serial number of the router but can also contain the router name.

For optimal use of the SNMP agent on the router, the default traps and specific traps must be sent to a specific SNMP manager by using the **snmp-server host** command. The default traps, such as interfaces becoming active or inactive, router reloads, or configuration changes, do not need to be enabled. All other supported traps, however, must be enabled using the **snmp-server enable traps** command.

The formats of these two commands are as follows:

snmp-server host *host* [**version** {**1** | **2c**}] *community-string* [**udp-port** *port*] [*notification-type*]
snmp-server enable traps [notification-type] [notification-option]

The *host* variable is the IP name of the SNMP manager or the IP address of the SNMP manager. The *community-string* variable is the community string associated with the SNMP manager. The *port* variable of the **udp-port** keyword allows you to modify the UDP port number from the default UDP port number 162. The *notification-type* variable of the **snmp-server enable traps** command indicates the specific type of trap to send to the SNMP manager. Not specifying the *notification-type* variable results in all types of traps being sent. Table 13-8 lists the possible *notification-type* variable values.

The *notification-option* is used to enable specific notification-types for the **envmon, isdn, repeater**, or **snmp** notification types that are selected. Table 13-9 lists the variable for the notification-option variable.

You can stop traps from being sent on interfaces that are expected to become active or inactive by using the **no snmp trap link-status** interface command. For instance, in order to stop traps/informs on ISDN dial-up connections, the following can be entered on the ISDN interface definitions:

```
interface BRIO
  no snmp-trap link-status
```

Using this configuration on the ISDN interface definition, the SNMP agent does not send traps/informs to the SNMP manager when the ISDN line becomes active and goes inactive.

For a more reliable method of sending notification messages to an SNMP message, the **snmp-server host** command is used as

Table 13-8	*notification-type* **value**	**Description of** *notification-type*
The notification-type Values for Use with the **snmp-server Traps** and **snmp-server Informs** Commands	**bgp**	Sends Border Gateway Protocol (BGP) state change notifications.
	config	Sends configuration notifications.
	entity	Sends Entity MIB modification notifications.
	envmon	Sends Cisco enterprise-specific environmental monitor notifications when an environmental threshold is exceeded. When the **envmon** keyword is used, you can specify a notification-option value.
	frame-relay	Sends Frame Relay notifications.
	isdn	Sends Integrated Services Digital Network (ISDN) notifications. When the **isdn** keyword is used on Cisco 1600 series routers, you can specify a notification-option value.
	repeater	Sends Ethernet hub repeater notifications. When the **repeater** keyword is selected, you can specify a notification-option value.
	rtr	Sends response time reporter (RTR) notifications.
	snmp	Sends Simple Network Management Protocol (SNMP) notifications. When the **snmp** keyword is used, you can specify a *notification-option* value.
	syslog	Sends error message notifications (Cisco Syslog MIB) and specifies the level of messages to be sent with the **logging history level** command.

notification-type Values	Possible *notification-option*
envmon	**voltage | shutdown | supply | fan | temperature**
isdn	**call-information**—enables an SNMP ISDN call-information notification for the ISDN MIB subsystem.
	isdnu-interface—enables an SNMP ISDN U interface notification for the ISDN U interface MIB subsystem.
repeater	**health**—enables IETF Repeater Hub MIB (RFC 1516) health notification.
	reset—enables IETF Repeater Hub MIB (RFC 1516) reset notification.
snmp	**authentication**—enables SNMP Authentication Failure notifications.

>>>If no notification-option is coded, then all traps/informs are sent for the notification-type.<<<

snmp-server host *host* **informs** [version {1 | 2c}] *community-string* [**udp-port** *port*] [*notification-type*]

The parameters are used in the same fashion as those specified for the trap version of the command. The **snmp-server enable traps** command with any specified *notification-type* and *notification-option* specified is also required to denote the types of inform requests sent to the SNMP manager.

The *notification-type* on the **snmp-server host traps|informs** command are listed in Table 13-10.

Because inform requests provide a reliable delivery of the notification message, the resending parameters can be defined to meet the networks expectation. The format of specifying the resend operational parameters for using inform request messages is

snmp-server informs [**retries** *retries*] [**timeout** *seconds*] [**pending** *pending*]

The *retries* variable is the number of times the inform request process used by this SNMP agent will attempt to send the notification message to the SNMP manager before aborting the send process. The *seconds* variable is the amount of time the SNMP agent will wait between retries. The *pending* variable is the total number of outstanding acknowledgments of inform

Table 13-10

The notification-type Values for Use with the **snmp-server host traps|informs** Command

notification-type values	Description of *notification-types*
bgp	Sends Border Gateway Protocol (BGP) state change notifications.
config	Sends configuration notifications.
dspu	Sends downstream physical unit (DSPU) notifications.
entity	Sends Entity MIB modification notifications.
envmon	Sends Cisco enterprise-specific environmental monitor notifications when an environmental threshold is exceeded.
frame-relay	Sends Frame Relay notifications.
isdn	Sends Integrated Services Digital Network (ISDN) notifications.
llc2	Sends Logical Link Control type 2 (LLC2) notifications.
rptr	Sends standard repeater (hub) notifications.
rsrb	Sends remote source-route bridging (RSRB) notifications.
rtr	Sends response time reporter (RTR) notifications.
sdlc	Sends Synchronous Data Link Control (SDLC) notifications.
sdllc	Sends SDLLC notifications.
snmp	Sends Simple Network Management Protocol (SNMP) notifications defined in RFC 1157.
stun	Sends serial tunnel (STUN) notifications.
syslog	Sends error message notifications (Cisco Syslog MIB). The level of messages to be sent can be specified with the **logging history level** command.
tty	Sends Cisco enterprise-specific notifications when a Transmission Control Protocol (TCP) connection closes.
x25	Sends X.25 event notifications.

requests sent to the SNMP manager. Once the *pending* value is reached, the oldest outstanding unacknowledged inform requests are discarded.

A final SNMP command useful on the router is the **snmp-server trap-**

source command. The format of this command is

snmp-server trap-source *interface*

The *interface* variable is the name of any active interface on the router. Using a defined interface, loopback 0 is an optimal choice to be the source address for the SNMP agent since it is always considered to be active.

NOTE: *SNMP managers use a basic IP PING command to determine if a router is reachable on the network. Using the IP address of the interface loopback 0 virtual interface enables the SNMP manager PING to reach the router on any available active network interface on the router.*

An example of enabling an SNMP agent on a router is as follows:

```
snmp-server community allmgrs
snmp-server trap-source loopback0
snmp-server chassis-id 7000-234-5654
snmp-server contact Network Operations
snmp-server location 1770 Orchard Lane, Atlanta, GA
snmp-server enable traps
snmp-server host Prisnmp netmgrs snmp
snmp-server host Secsnmp netmgrs snmp
```

In this example, the SNMP community string used by all SNMP managers for reading or writing to this router must use the allmgrs string. All traps and inform requests sent from this router will have the IP address of interface loopback0. Two SNMP managers, Prisnmp and Secsnmp, will be receiving all SNMP traps and inform requests.

Using the Banner Command

A final command that can be useful for displaying information to the router administrators is the banner command. It enables the display of information at various entrance points to the establishment of a successful connection:

```
banner exec   ^
**************************************************
*                                                *
*    ROUTER NAME: c1r2LNDN SN 77778888           *
*    LOCATION:    10 Downing St.                 *
*          Newark, NJ                            *
*    CONTACT:    Sam Samson                      *
*          201-222-2222                          *
*    CONTACT PAGE: 800-888-8888                  *
*    Cisco TAC:  800-553-2447                    *
```

```
*     Cisco ACCT:   1111111                              *
******************************************************^
banner motd ^
WARNING: The unauthorized use of devices or the tampering with
access
            to this network and its resources are CRIMINAL offenses.
            *** ALL VIOLATORS ARE SUBJECT TO PROSECUTION *** ^C
```

In this example, the **banner** command is used for displaying a warning message for unauthorized use of the router. This is done using the **motd** (message of the day) keyword of the **banner** command. The ^ character marks the beginning and end of the text to be displayed. The **motd** banner is displayed before any operational router access is attempted, including anything prior to the login password prompt.

The **banner exec** command displays the banner once the router administrator has gained access to the EXEC mode on the router. We use this banner for our example to denote the location of the router, contact phone numbers, and the Cisco Systems maintenance contract code along the router serial number.

The other points of banner displays are listed in Table 13-11.

Table 13-11

The Banner Command Display Points Parameters

Banner Display Point	Description of Point
exec	Sets EXEC process creation banner
incoming	Sets incoming terminal line banner
login	Sets login banner
motd	Sets message of the day banner

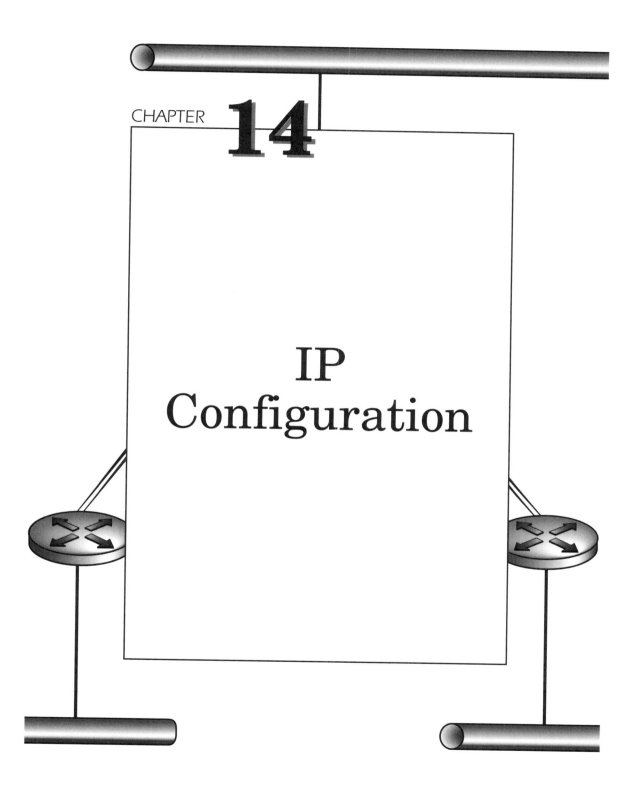

IP
Configuration

The basis for building routed networks lies in defining IP subnets to the interfaces on a router that connect LANs and WANs. This chapter focuses on the definition of IP protocol and service provided by the implementation of the IP protocol on Cisco routers.

Defining Subnets on the Router Interfaces

The definition of IP subnets on a router interface enables that interface to transport IP-based application traffic. Defining the IP addresses on an interface requires a planned implementation of the IP subnet space. The space refers to the projected number of networks and hosts needed to be supported on the corporate-wide network. For each physical interface on a router, a new IP network or IP subnet is required, which is a basic IP network-addressing requirement. If a network has 100 individual LANs, for instance, then it is possible that there is a need for a minimum of 100 networks or subnets. Since it is not possible for any one corporation to attain 100 IP networks from the Inernet Assigned Numbers Authority (IANA), a single IP network is used and this network is subnetted.

Within each subnet, the number of supported hosts must be determined. A router interface is represented as a host on the IP subnet being defined. Table 14-1 reviews the list of IP address class and the available range of IP networks within each class.

In addition to the IP networks identified in Table 14-1, the IETF has reserved address space for any network to use. The requirement is that the IP addresses are not advertised on the Internet. This is because the following addresses are not registered with the IANA and therefore are not unique, which creates the potential of routing problems. These "open" IP network addresses are defined in the Internet Engineering Task Force's (IETF) RFC 1918, which describes their general use for any IP network.

In planning your IP address schema, it is prudent to define a network addressing standard. For instance, the host address of the IP address assigned to an interface is always 1, IP addresses assigned to Windows NT servers fall within a range of consecutive host numbers, and send user workstations fall within a range of consecutive host numbers. Diligence in planning the IP address allocation facilitates the ease of assignment and simplifies initial troubleshooting analysis.

Table 14-1

IP Address Class Address Ranges and Their Associated Statuses

IP Address Class	IP Address or Range	Status
A	0.0.0.0	Reserved
	1.0.0.0 to 126.0.0.0	Available
	127.0.0.0	Reserved
B	128.0.0.0 to 191.254.0.0	Available
	191.255.0.0	Reserved
C	192.0.0.0	Reserved
	192.0.1.0 to 223.255.254	Available
	223.255.255.0	Reserved
D	224.0.0.0 to 239.255.255.255	Multicast group addresses
E	240.0.0.0 to 255.255.255.254	Reserved
	255.255.255.255	Broadcast

Table 14-2

RFC 1918 Non-registered IP Network Address Ranges for Any IP Network

RFC 1918 IP Address Class	RFC 1918 IP Address or Range	Status
A	10.0.0.0	The entire address space available for use.
B	172.16.0.0–172.31.0.0	The entire address space available for use.
C	192.168.0.0	The entire address space available for use.

Assigning an IP address to a router interface is performed while under interface configuration mode. Recall that to enter configuration mode the router administrator must first access the privileged command line interface (CLI) function of the router. Once in configuration mode, the router administrator enters the name of the interface type to which the IP address is being applied. Using Figure 14-1 as an example, we can assign IP addresses to the routers and interfaces shown.

Figure 14-1

Sample network
configuration for
assigning IP
addresses to router
LAN interfaces.

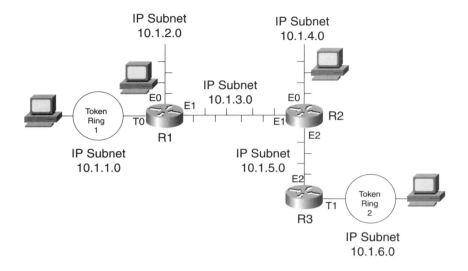

Assume that, outside of the configuration shown, each router is reachable over the corporate network. The router administrator Telnets to the already active IP interface on each router. Once in each router, the router administrator access configuration mode. The procedure for this on each router is

```
routername> enable
password: xxxxxxx
routername#> configuration terminal
routername(config)#>interface etherent 0
```

At this point, the router administrator enters the interface type (interface Ethernet 0) being given an IP address. Assigning the IP address is performed by issuing the following command:

ip address *ip-address mask*

The *ip-address* positional variable value is the complete IP address being assigned to the interface. The positional *mask* variable value defines the bits used against the address to determine the IP subnet and host value used to access the interface with IP. Cisco IOS only supports masks using contiguous bits flushed left in the addressing. For example, a mask of 255.255.255.0 against a Class B address is represented in bit notation as

```
Class B Network number  | subnetwork  | host number
1111 1111 . 1111 1111 . | 1111 1111 . | 0000 0000
```

If this example is based on a Class B address, then the third octet is masking the value as a subnet of the network. For instance, 172.16.8.0 is a different subnet than 172.16.9.0 using the above mask. If we applied a network mask using the following decimal representation of 255.255.252.0, however, the mask is as follows:

```
Class B Network            | subnet  | host number
1111 1111 . 1111 1111 .    | 1111 11 | 00 . 0000 0000
```

If this is the applied mask to the sample 172.16.8.0 subnet, then the 172.16.9.0 addressing is also found in the same subnet. The use of the consecutive bits to the left in the mask has increased the number of host addresses and decreased the number of possible networks. In this example, the actual complete subnet range is 172.16.8.0–172.16.11.255. This subnetting provides 1,022 host addresses and 62 subnet addresses. This subnetting range follows IETF RFC 950. Cisco IOS, however, enables the full range of an IP network to be used for addressing, as we will see further on, by allowing the use of subnet 0 within an address space.

NOTE: *An IP subnet can be defined to only one active router interface at any given time. Router interfaces in shutdown (inactive) mode can have the same subnet or, for that matter, the same IP address assigned. It is strongly suggested to not do this, however, as it can lead to confusion during troubleshooting.*

Using the following configuration commands, the routers shown in Figure 14-1 are assigned IP addresses. The Ethernet interfaces are represented in the figure using an E and the Token Ring interface are represented in the figure using a T. The number following each interface is the port used on the interface processor for connecting to the network. Router R1 Configuration:

```
interface Ethernet 0
 ip address 10.1.2.1 255.255.255.0
interface Ethernet 1
 ip address 10.1.3.1 255.255.255.0
interface Tokenring 0
 ip address 10.1.1.1 255.255.255.0
end
```

Router R2 Configuration:

```
interface Ethernet 0
 ip address 10.1.4.1 255.255.255.0
interface Ethernet 1
 ip address 10.1.3.2 255.255.255.0
```

```
interface Ethernet 2
 ip address 10.1.5.1 255.255.255.0
end
```

Router 3 Configuration:

```
interface Ethernet 2
 ip address 10.1.5.2 255.255.255.0
interface Tokenring 1
 ip address 10.1.6.1 255.255.255.0
end
```

The IP addresses assigned in the sample configuration are referred to as the primary IP address for each interface. In the sample configurations, we see that the mask 255.255.255.0 is applied to a Class A IP address of 10.0.0.0. The subnet mask is actually 0.255.255.0 since the IP address is a Class A network address. On the interface configuration command **ip address,** however, the *mask* variable value is expressed as all the bits used for denoting the network and the subnet of the IP address assigned. A mask of this nature is also referred to as a 24-bit mask.

In the sample configuration, the Ethernet LAN attaching router R1 to R2 requires that the interfaces on each of these routers use a unique host number in the IP address. The same requirement goes for the definitions of the Ethernet interfaces connecting R2 with R3.

When to Assign Multiple IP Addresses to an Interface

Cisco IOS allows for multiple IP addresses on a single router interface. The IP addresses assigned to an interface that are not the primary router interface are termed secondary IP addresses. There is no restriction on the number of secondary IP addresses that can be defined to a router interface. Typically, multiple IP addresses are assigned to a router interface in one of the following situations:

- Host address allocation has become insufficient to support the number of IP addressed devices on a single physical network.

- For supporting the migration from a bridged IP network to a routed IP network.

- For connecting two subnets of a single network that are currently connected through another network.

Suppose the network has the topology shown in Figure 14-2. Here we see that on router R1 Ethernet 0 all 253 host addresses have been allocated. Seven new workstations are being added to the Ethernet segment to support the expansion of the department. The router administrator can accommodate the expansion by adding a secondary IP address that specifies another subnet to be associated with Ethernet 0. The router administrator performs the following commands in configuration mode on router R1:
Router R1 Configuration:

```
interface Ethernet 0
ip address 10.1.7.1 255.255.255.0 secondary
end
```

The router administrator has added a secondary subnet to Ethernet 0 on router R1 that provides another 253 possible host addresses for connecting IP hosts to the network. It is the addition of the **secondary** keyword to the **ip address** command that denotes as additional IP address assignment on the interface being configured. The resulting configuration for Ethernet 0 on router R1 looks like the following:
Router R1 Configuration:

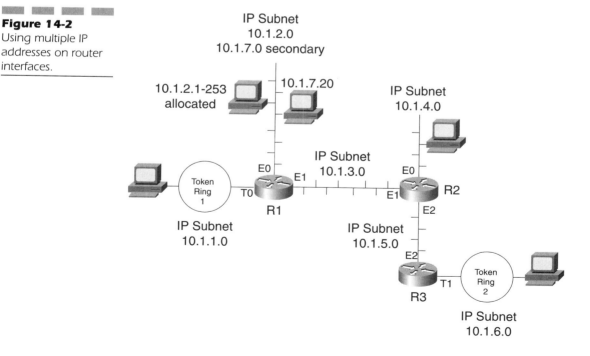

Figure 14-2
Using multiple IP addresses on router interfaces.

```
interface Ethernet 0
  ip address 10.1.2.1 255.255.255.0
  ip address 10.1.7.1 255.255.255.0 secondary
interface Ethernet 1
  ip address 10.1.3.1 255.255.255.0
interface Tokenring 0
  ip address 10.1.1.1 255.255.255.0
```

From the configuration sample for router R1, we can see that the configuration for Ethernet 0 uses 10.1.2.1 as the primary IP address and 10.1.7.1 becomes the secondary IP address, thus providing a second subnet to the Ethernet LAN. Now the LAN, assuming traffic load does not cause performance problems, can support up to 506 connected IP devices through the Ethernet 0 interface of router R1.

NOTE: *All routers connecting to the same LAN must define the same IP subnet address in order to participate in delivering IP traffic for the LAN. Each router on the same LAN, however, must use a different host number within the same IP subnet. Try using Hot Standby Routing Protocol (HSRP) to allow multiple routers the capability to respond to the same IP address.*

Maximizing Network Address Space Using Subnet Zero

The total number of networks available in any given subnet is the decimal value of the bits used in defining the mask for the IP address range minus one. For example, a Class B address (172.16.0.0) with a mask of 255.255.255.0 (0.0.255.0) has the potential for 255 subnets. However, the all-zeroes subnet, 172.16.0.0, is reserved in the RFC 791 specifications to denote the network address. The all-ones subnet, 172.16.255.0, though it can be explicitly defined, is discouraged from use. The format for specifying the use of subnet zero as a viable addressable subnet is as follows:

ip subnet-zero

This command is a global command and enables the use of subnet zero on all the routers' interfaces. The feature is disabled if not specified. Be aware that if employing the subnet zero feature, the 172.16.0.0 network address in our example, subnetted using 255.255.255.0, is written exactly the same and hence is distributed by the routers as both a network and a subnet.

Routing Same Network Packets Without a Routing Table Entry

At times a router may encounter a packet that is to be sent to a subnet within its own network, but the routing table within the router does not have a route to the destination subnet. In such a case, the router throws the packet of the unknown destination subnet away. Since the destination subnet is within the major network addressing of the overall IP network, however, a route should be available to the destination. Cisco IOS provides such a method using IP classless routing.

For example, in Figure 14-3, a workstation sends a packet with 10.8.1.0 as the destination. The local router receives the packet and inspects its routing table. In doing so, the router determines that a specific route to the destination does not exist. Using the IP classless routing feature, however, the router sends the packet out an interface that meets the network addressing portion of the destination. Specifying the global configuration command **ip classless** under configuration mode enables this feature. Once this command is specified, it applies to all routing protocols used by the router.

The following lists some instances when the classless feature is used:

- For multiple routing protocols within a network.

- When using the passive keyword on a router's only interface to the WAN.

- When static choose to save the IP address space by not assigning an IP address to the WAN serial interfaces. The reasoning behind this is that many subnets are utilized for two host addresses: one serial interface on one router and the serial interface on another router. This means that a subnet supporting 254 host addresses wastes 252 addresses needlessly. To avoid the waste of addresses but maintain the capability of the serial interface to carry IP traffic, the Cisco IOS employs a feature called IP unnumbered.

The command for specifying IP unnumbered has the following format:

ip unnumbered *type number*

The *type* positional variable value is an active interface on the router with a valid IP address. The *number* variable denotes the specific port on the interface type being used as the source IP address of the packets, leaving the router over the serial interface.

Figure 14-3
Use of the IP classless
feature to route
unknown subnets to
the best supernet
interface.

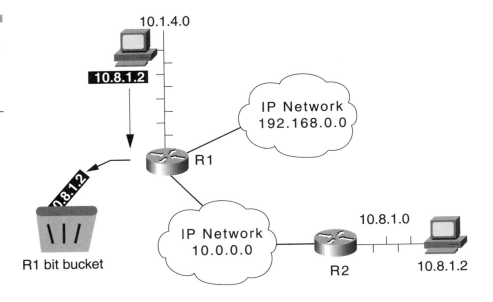

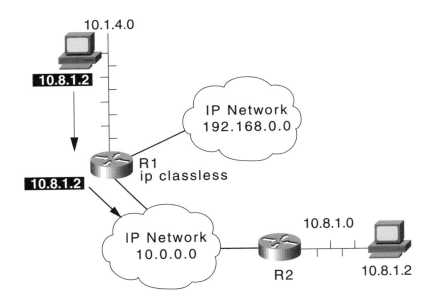

The command is specified under the interface configuration mode for the serial interface being assigned the unnumbered feature. The following is an example of such a configuration:

```
interface loopback 0
 ip address 10.10.10.1 255.255.255.0
interface serial 4/1
 ip unnumbered loopback 0
```

Using this configuration, the router sends all packets from interface serial 4/1 with the IP address 10.10.10.1 as the source of the packet. This technique can save IP address space. The command can be applied to HDLC, PPP, LAPB, Frame Relay, ATM, SLIP, and tunnel interfaces. It cannot be applied to SMDS or X.25 interfaces.

Because the IP address is "borrowed" from another active interface, an SNMP manager cannot determine if the interface is up or down by pinging the borrowed IP address. The SNMP manager, however, can receive traps or informs from the router on the status of the interface. Likewise, you cannot ping the actual interface, perform a netboot over the interface, or support IP security options on an unnumbered serial interface.

In the configuration example, the loopback interface was chosen since the router always interprets this interface as being active and connected to the network.

IP Address Mapping

Part of the role of the router is to resolve IP addresses. The router resolves IP addresses through a mapping process using various protocols. These are:

Address Resolution Protocol (ARP): Known IP-address mapping to a 48-bit MAC address

Proxy ARP: A process in which the router places its own MAC address in the outbound packet

Reverse ARP: Known 48-bit MAC-address mapping to an IP address

ARP is a request sent by an IP host to determine the Layer 2 MAC address of the destination IP host device. Seen in Figure 14-4, the requesting ARP is sent into the network using the MAC broadcast address 0x'FFFFFFFFFFFF'. Each IP device receives the ARP packet and inspects the packet as to whether the target IP address specified is indeed its own IP address. If the IP address does not match, the IP host discards the packet. If the IP address does match, the matching IP host places its own MAC address in the target MAC field of the ARP reply packet and sends the ARP reply back to the original requesting IP host.

Routers assist an IP host in mapping the target IP address to a MAC address by using proxy ARP. Shown in Figure 14-5, the proxy ARP function

Figure 14-4
ARP process for determining the MAC address of the destination IP host.

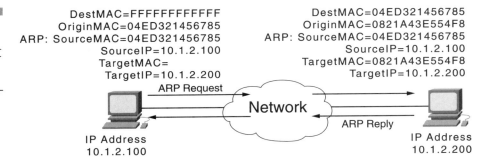

DestMAC=FFFFFFFFFFFF
OriginMAC=04ED321456785
ARP: SourceMAC=04ED321456785
SourceIP=10.1.2.100
TargetMAC=
TargetIP=10.1.2.200

DestMAC=04ED321456785
OriginMAC=0821A43E554F8
ARP: SourceMAC=04ED321456785
SourceIP=10.1.2.100
TargetMAC=0821A43E554F8
TargetIP=10.1.2.200

ARP Request

Network

ARP Reply

IP Address
10.1.2.100

IP Address
10.1.2.200

of the router replies back to the requesting ARP workstation on behalf of the actual destination IP host. This is possible because of the router building an ARP table based on all the packets that traverse the interfaces of the router and the use of the routing table.

Upon receiving the ARP request, the router determines if it has IP address to MAC address mapping already completed for the target IP address in the ARP. This is done by searching the ARP table (ARP cache) built by the router. If it finds a match of the IP address and has a valid route to the subnet of the matching IP address, the router performs the reply but uses its own MAC address, instead of the MAC address of the true target device.

The proxy ARP function is enabled by default on a Cisco router. It is on by default because any time an IP host tries to communicate with another IP host that is not in its local ARP cache, the origin IP host must send an ARP. Having the Cisco router act as an ARP server using proxy ARP functionality eliminates unproductive packet delivery throughout the network.

Reverse ARP, as illustrated in Figure 14-6, works in the same manner as ARP. The difference is the discovery of the IP address of the requesting host, instead of the MAC address of a target IP host. A RARP server is required on the network to perform this function. Since the purpose of RARP is to provide an IP address for the requesting IP host, it is often associated with diskless workstations that normally do not store their network configuration between power-on resets. Cisco IOS can be configured on a router to support a RARP server function for RARP requests when a static IP to MAC address mapping has been defined for the requesting device. The router can also forward the RARP requests directly to a known RARP server.

The dynamic ARP cache entries built by the router have a default timeout of four hours. The timeout ARP cache entries can be changed by using the global or interface configuration command

arp timeout *seconds*

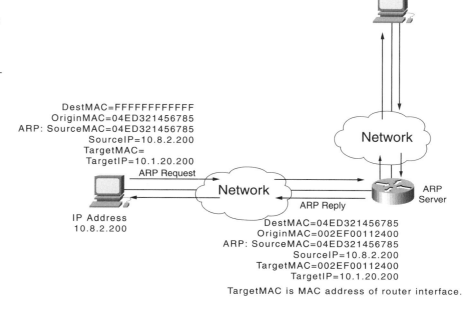

Figure 14-5

The proxy ARP process for reducing unproductive packets to resolve MAC addresses of destination IP hosts.

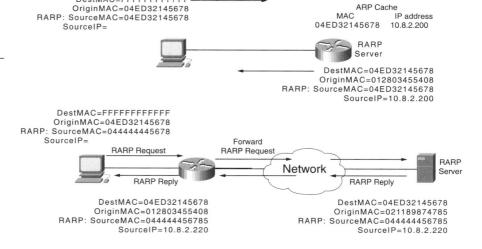

Figure 14-6

RARP process for determining IP address of a host.

where *seconds* can be from 0 to 14400. A value of 0 indicates that the entries never have a timeout.

Define a Static ARP Cache

Routers perform ARP caching by default, but in some cases a static ARP entry may be needed, such as in supplying an IP address for a RARP request from a diskless workstation. In this case, the following global configuration command must be entered to define static ARP cache entries:

arp *ip-address hardware-address type***[alias]**

The **arp** global command;commands;arp allows the router administrator to map an IP address (*ip-address*) of a host that is found through any directly attached interface defined on the router with a MAC address (*hardware-address*). The *type* variable identifies the encapsulation type being used for the mapping. The type can be **arpa**, **snap,** or **probe**. The **arpa** value is the default and supports all Ethernet resources, **snap** is used for FDDI and Token Ring resources, and **probe** is a Hewlett-Packard-specific protocol (HP-Probe) that can be used on any interface type for resources supporting the HP-Probe protocol. The HP-Probe is not greatly used. The alias keyword directs the Cisco IOS to respond to the ARP request with its own hardware address as though the router were the owner of the IP address.

For example, to define an ARP cache entry for the diskless workstation in Figure 14-6, the following definition was provided on the router:

```
arp 10.8.2.200 04ED.3214.5678
interface ethernet 0
 ip address 10.8.2.1 255.255.255.0
 ip rarp-server 10.8.2.1
```

Using this definition, the *type* variable of the **arp** command is defaulting to **arpa**. This indicates to us that the workstation using the 04ED.3214.5678 MAC address resides on an Ethernet LAN segment. Using this entry, the router replies back with the 10.8.2.200 IP address to an RARP request from the 04ED.3214.5678 MAC address. The **ip rarp-server** interface configuration command enables the router to act as a RARP server. The **ip rarp-server** command identifies the 10.8.2.1 IP address as the source address in the RARP reply.

Supporting Multiple ARP Encapsulation Types on an Interface

The ARP encapsulation type supported on any interface can be modified to support more than just the default arapa encapsulation. When working with the **arp** interface configuration command, one or more encapsulation techniques can be used. The following describes the three different types supported and how they are specified for the interface:

> **arp arpa**: IEEE 802.3 Ethernet, as described with RFC 826 (the default value)
>
> **arp probe**: HP-Probe protocol for IEEE 802.3 networks
>
> **arp snap**: ARP packets in support of RFC 1402 for FDDI and Token Ring networks

Disable Proxy ARP

Cisco IOS has a proxy ARP function enabled by default. Disabling it forces the router to deliver the Layer 2 broadcast packet along the supported route for the IP subnet specified in the ARP request. Entering the following global configuration command disables the proxy ARP function:

```
no ip proxy-arp
```

To reenable the proxy ARP function after it has been disabled, enter the global configuration command

```
ip proxy-arp
```

NOTE: *All Cisco IOS commands have their definitions or functions negated by entering a "no" in front of the enabling command under configuration mode.*

Enabling the Use of IP Host Names in Cisco IOS Commands

Cisco IOS has several commands that support the use of a host name within the command, instead of an IP address. Examples of the commands are connect, telnet, ping, write network, and configuration network. The IP address to IP host name mapping within the Cisco router is enabled by defining specific IP host names and their IP addresses and/or by implementing Domain Naming System (DNS) services.

Static Definition of IP Host Names and IP

Addresses

Manual definition of an IP address to a IP host name enters a static mapping in the host name table of the router. The format of the global configuration command for this static mapping is

ip host *name* [*tcp-port-number*] *address1* [*address2...address8*]

The *name* positional variable is the name assigned by this router for the IP address (*address1*) defined on the command. The optional *tcp-port-number* positional variable is the TCP port used for connecting to the IP host being defined. The optional variables *address2...address8* provide up to a total of eight IP addresses that are bound to the host name defined with the command.

NOTE: *The DNS standards allow multiple host names to an IP address but not multiple IP addresses to a single host name.*

Using this command, suppose a server has four Ethernet attachments on four different subnets. Using the ip host command, we can define the router to four IP addresses that attempt to connect to the desired host. For example, in the following code

```
ip host backbone-router 10.1.1.1 10.2.2.2 10.3.3.3 10.4.4.4
```

the router attempts to connect to the IP host names backbone-router by trying each address in sequence. Using static IP host to address mapping provides for a fast IP address resolution.

Enable the Use of DNS Services

Cisco IOS can try to resolve IP host names by using DNS services. Entering an IP host name for a remote host can be resolved if the following global configuration command has been entered on the router:

ip domain-lookup

Having domain lookup enabled allows the Cisco IOS to query the network DNS servers for an IP address. The router sends the fully qualified name and the Cisco IOS performs the name qualification based on the use of the following global configuration command:

ip domain-name *name*

The *name* variable is the domain name used by this router to resolve the host-to-address mapping. For example, entering

```
ip domain-name networxcorp.com
```

qualifies the host name of corpmail in a ping command to corpmail.networxcorp.com as the qualified name presented to the DNS server for IP address resolution. Multiple domain names can be entered by using multiple **ip domain-list** commands to assist in resolving host names with fully qualified alias domain names. The ip domain-list command has the same command format as the **ip domain-name** command. The domain name(s) specified with the **ip domain-list** take precedence, in sequential order, over the default domain name defined by the use of the **ip domain-name** command.

The DNS servers used to resolve the queries are defined using the **ip name-server** global configuration command. For example, entering

```
ip name-server 10.10.10.200 10.10.20.200 10.10.30.200
```

causes the router to send DNS queries to the three IP addresses specified on the ip name-server command. The first response received is the IP address used for the router command that caused the query. The ip name-server command supports up to six DNS server addresses.

NOTE: Although the DNS server's IP addresses can be specified on a single ip name-server command, they are written in the configuration file as separate ip name-server commands. For instance, the example shown is written as

```
ip name-server 10.10.10.200
ip name-server 10.10.20.200
ip name-server 10.10.30.200
```

To complete the DNS services example, the configuration file is written as

```
ip domain-lookup
ip domain-name networxcorp.com
ip name-server 10.10.10.200
ip name-server 10.10.20.200
ip name-server 10.10.30.200
```

Disable IP Routing

Cisco IOS software enables IP routing once an IP address is specified on a router interface and an IP routing protocol is defined for use by the router. If bridging IP is a requirement for connecting the router to a network, IP routing must be disabled. This affects the entire operation of the router. The **no ip routing** global command disables the routing function on the entire router. Disabling IP routing causes the router to act as an IP end host, and it can be reenabled by specifying the **ip routing** global configuration command.

Routing Assistance When IP Routing Is Disabled

With IP routing is disabled, Cisco IOS can still learn of IP routes to other networks acting as IP host computers. The three methods used by a Cisco router to learn IP routes when IP routing is disabled are

- Proxy ARP
- Defining a default gateway
- ICMP Router Discovery Protocol (IRDP)

As described earlier, the Cisco IOS software enables the proxy ARP function by default. Using just proxy ARP, a router can provide a route to an IP host based on the ARP cache table. As a request enters the router, the router searches the ARP cache for a matching IP address and, when found, it forwards the packet on the interface.

NOTE: *If IP routing is disabled and the router is now relying on the proxy ARP function for routing packets, it is beneficial to specify a shorter ARP cache entry timeout on the router interface definitions to ensure the validity of the route.*

The second method of defining a default-gateway (router) IP address specifies to the Cisco IOS software that all packets with IP networks that are not defined on any interface specific to the router will forward the non-local packet to a specified IP address. Using the following global configuration command, a default gateway address is defined for a Cisco router:

ip default-gateway *ip-address*

The *ip-address* variable of the **ip default-gateway** global configuration command must be the IP address of a router that has a routing table and is attached to a network known by the router being defined. Cisco IOS supports only one ip default-gateway definition. For example, by specifying

```
no ip routing
ip default-gateway 10.1.1.2
interface Ethernet 0
 ip address 10.1.1.1 255.255.255.0
```

the default gateway router is reachable via the Ethernet 0 interface of the router. Any packets received by the router from attached networks with destination networks not directly connected to the router are forwarded on the Ethernet 0 interface to the IP address 10.1.1.2 for routing of the packet. The router specified as the default gateway can either route the packet based on its routing table or reply back to the original router with an IP Control Message Protocol (ICMP) redirect message that indicates another attached router can provide a better path to the destination.

The router with IP routing disabled then caches the redirected route and uses this route for future requests to the cached IP address. This process is depicted in Figure 14-7. Using the default-gateway works is not always reliable, however, since the status of the default-gateway router is not available.

The final method employs RFC 1256 ICMP Router Discovery Protocol (IRDP). The Cisco IOS software dynamically learns of available potential default gateways by employing IRDP. It is the preferred method of the three methods discussed because IRDP can determine the availability of a default gateway and enable multiple default gateways. Cisco's implementation of IRDP is enhanced to "wire tap" an interface for RIP and IGRP routing updates. The Cisco IOS software adds the sending IP address of a RIP- or IGRP-routing update packet to the IRDP eligible default-gateway cache. Using this in addition to the sending and receiving or IRDP packets, a Cisco router can route to non-local networks with great success. Enabling

Figure 14-7

Using default-gateway and ICMP redirect messages for routing packets on a router with IP routing disabled.

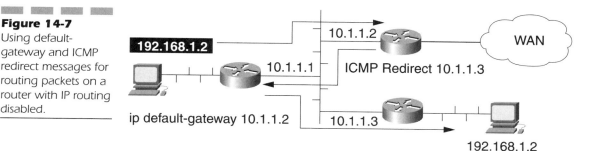

IRDP is made possible by including the following interface configuration command:

ip irdp [**multicast** | **holdtime** *seconds* | **maxadvertinterval** *seconds* | **minadvertinterval** *seconds* | **preference** *number* | **address** *address* [*number*]]

Specifying **ip irdp** for an interface causes the Cisco IOS to broadcast IRDP advertisements with a maximum interval between advertisements of 600 seconds and a minimum advertisement interval of (600 x .075) seconds. Specifying **multicast** enables IRDP to be used with Sun Solaris systems, which respond to the multicast IP address of 224.0.0.1, instead of the all ones, or 255.255.255.255, IP broadcast address.

Using **holdtime** on the **ip irdp** command defines the length of time an IRDP advertisement is considered valid. After the **holdtime** expires, the advertisement is flushed from the IRDP table. The **holdtime** default is three times the **maxadvertinterval** value. If specified, **holdtime** must be greater than **maxadvertinterval** up to 9,000 seconds. The **maxadvertinterval** is the maximum number of seconds between sending IRDP advertisements; its default is 600 seconds. The **minadvertinterval** default is 0.75 times the **maxadvertinerval** value.

NOTE: *The* **holdtime** *and* **minadvertinterval** *values will default based on the value of* **maxadvertinterval**. *Therefore, it is recommended that the* **maxadvertinerval** *be changed prior to modifying the* **holdtime** *or* **minadvertineterval** *values.*

The **preference** keyword variable *number* value defines the use of this router's interface as a preferred default gateway for any other IRDP router receiving the IRDP advertisement from this router. The default value is 0 and can range anywhere from -2^{31} to 2^{31}. The higher the value, the greater the preference.

The **address** keyword allows the router administrator to specify the IP address of a known IRDP router and a *preference* value for using that router within its IRDP advertisement. In this manner, a preferred IRDP-determined default gateway can be used for all IRDP routers.

In the following example, interface Ethernet 0 enables the use of IRDP, sets its own preference to a value of 50, and advertises a second IRDP router address of 10.1.1.95 with a higher preference value of 100 as a preferred default gateway.

```
no ip routing
interface ethernet 0
  ip address 10.1.1.90 255.255.255.0
```

```
ip irdp
ip irdp preference 50
ip irdp address 10.1.1.95 100
```

Using any of the above methods, or a combination of them, enables the routing of IP packets when IP routing has been disabled.

Bridging IP, Instead of Routing IP

IP is based on using a routing protocol; however, it can be bridged as well as routed at the same time. To transparently bridge IP and disable the routing of IP, the following commands must be entered into the router configuration:

no ip routing
interface *type number*
bridge-group *group*
bridge *number* **protocol** [**ieee** | **dec**]

Specifying the global configuration command, **no ip routing,** disables the routing of IP traffic on the router. The interface configuration command directs the configuration mode to the specified interface *type* and port *number* or slot/port *number* of the interface being configured.

The **bridge-group** *group* interface command defines the common bridge-group number applied to the interface for building a transparent bridge network. The global configuration command bridge protocol is required to identify the type of spanning tree protocol in use for a specific bridge-group. The number variable of the bridge protocol command ranges from 1 to 63 and identifies the bridge-group number that will use the specified spanning tree protocol. The spanning tree protocol available is either **ieee** or **dec**. For example,

```
no ip routing
!
interface Ethernet 0
 ip address 10.1.1.1 255.255.255.0
 bridge-group 1
!
interface Ethernet 1
 ip address 10.1.1.2 255.255.255.0
 bridge-group 1
!
bridge 1 protocol ieee
```

The value of the bridge-group command can be anywhere from 1 to 63. In the example, IP and all other protocol traffic between Ethernet 0 and Ethernet 1 LAN segments is bridged, instead of routed. The **bridge** global configuration command at the end of the example defines the use of the IEEE bridging encapsulation standard for packets bridged on the interfaces joined to this bridging group. The DEC encapsulation technique can also be used by specifying the **dec** keyword at the end of the bridge global configuration command. Bridging is supported in the following instances:

- Ethernet
- Token Ring
- FDDI
- ATM
- X.25 (HDLC)
- Frame Relay (HDLC)
- ISDN

NOTE: *When defining the bridge-group command on an active Token Ring or on FDDI interfaces, or when you are adding new interfaces to an existing bridge-group that contains Token Ring or FDDI interfaces, all Token Ring and FDDI interfaces of the bridge-group are immediately reinitialized, disrupting connectivity.*

Controlling and Managing Broadcast Packets

Broadcast packets are used by several important Internet protocols. Because broadcast messages have the potential to overload a network, control of these packets is essential to the health of an IP network. Two types of broadcast packets are supported with Cisco IOS software. The first is a directed broadcast.

A directed broadcast is an IP address that uses the network and or subnet field of the IP address. For example, the 172.16.0.0 network can have a directed broadcast of 172.16.255.255 to which all hosts will respond. Let's assume that the subnet mask, 255.255.255.0, is applied to this Class B address. Applying this mask to the third octet of the IP address is the subnet field. Now the 172.16.30.255 address becomes a broadcast address for all hosts on the 172.16.30.0 subnetwork. Upon recognizing this IP address as a directed broadcast, the router will re-encapsulate the packet in a frame with a broadcast destination MAC address of x'FFFF.FFFF.FFFF', causing all devices to access the frame for processing.

Contrast this to flooding, (also known as local broadcast) the second type of supported broadcast. A flooding broadcast is answered by all devices on all networks. A flooding broadcast is defined by the destination IP address being all ones, or 255.255.255.255 in decimal notation. Sending a broadcast of this nature can cause serious overload on the network, known as a broadcast storm. Routers by default will not forward an all ones IP destination address, thereby keeping the broadcast on the local network.

Enable Directed Broadcast-to-Physical Broadcast Translation

Directed broadcasts are enabled per interface. Prior to Cisco IOS 12.0, directed broadcast translation to a physical broadcast would default as enabled and thereby forward directed broadcasts using a MAC broadcast address. With Release 12.0 of Cisco IOS, this directed broadcast is disabled by default. This is due in large part to the myriad of broadcast storms created by deviants on the Internet using attacks called "smurf" and "fraggle." These attacks place a known IP address within the broadcast as the source of the packet, even though the true source is outside on the Internet. Therefore, in Release 12.0 of Cisco IOS software, directed broadcasts must be explicitly defined on any interface that requires the feature. Let's use the following example to understand how Cisco IOS controls and manages IP broadcasts.

```
ip forward-protocol spanning-tree
 bridge 1 protocol dec
access-list 201 deny 0x0000 0xFFFF
interface ethernet 0
 bridge-group 1
 bridge-group 1 input-type-list 201
interface ethernet 1
 bridge-group 1
 bridge-group 1 input-type-list 201
interface serial 0
 bridge-group 1
 bridge-group 1 input-type-list 201
interface serial 1
 bridge-group 1
 bridge-group 1 input-type-list 201
```

In this example, Ethernet 0 and Ethernet 1, along with the two serial interfaces, support the flooding of default protocols TFTP, DNS, Time, NetBIOS, and BOOTP. This example provides the capability to flood a network with the default protocols. The **ip forward-protocol spanning-tree** command enables transparent bridging, which is a requirement for broadcast flooding. The **access-list** filters all protocols from being bridged, with the exception of the default protocols. This access list is applied to each of the interfaces as an input filter, thereby protecting the propagation of all unwanted protocol broadcasts.

Packets must meet the following criteria to be considered for flooding:

- The packet must be a MAC-level broadcast.
- The packet must be an IP-level broadcast.
- The packet must be a TFTP, DNS, Time, NetBIOS, ND, or BOOTP packet, or a UDP protocol specified by the **ip forward-protocol udp** global configuration command.
- The packet's time-to-live (TTL) value must be at least two.

These are the same criteria used to consider packet forwarding using IP helper addresses.

To facilitate network broadcast requirements, such as workstations getting their network configuration parameters using Dynamic Host Configuration Protocol (DHCP), Cisco IOS redirects the broadcast to a specific IP address. Using the following example,

```
ip forward-protocol udp
!
interface ethernet 0
 ip address 10.1.1.1 255.255.255.0
 ip helper-address 10.4.2.7
interface ethernet 1
 ip address 10.1.2.1 255.255.255.0
 ip helper-address 10.4.2.7
```

the **ip forward-protocol udp** global command is entered to allow the following UDP application protocols to be forwarded:

- Trivial File Transfer Protocol (TFTP) (port 69)
- DNS (port 53)
- Time service (port 37)
- NetBIOS Name Server (port 137)
- NetBIOS Datagram Server (port 138)
- Boot Protocol (BOOTP) client and server datagrams (ports 67 and 68)
- TACACS service (port 49)

Other UDP applications' protocol broadcasts can be forwarded by supplying the appropriate UDP port number at the end of the **ip forward-protocol udp** command. In Figure 14-8, we see that the workstations on

Ethernet 0 and Ethernet 1 send a BOOTP (DHCP) broadcast to locate a DHCP server for acquiring network configuration parameters. The router forwards the request to the IP address provided by the ip helper-address defined for each interface. Multiple ip helper-address commands can be entered for each interface. Having multiple ip helper-address commands enables load distribution, redundant service, and multiple services supported for each interface.

Configure IP Services

Cisco IOS supports many different services specific to IP. Among the various services discussed here are ICMP, filtering with access lists, redundancy using HSRP, accounting, and performance tuning.

Disable ICMP Unreachable Messages

Cisco IOS automatically replies to an ICMP message for an unknown protocol by sending an ICMP Protocol Unreachable message back to the sending IP address. Likewise, if the ICMP message is undeliverable to the destination IP host address, it returns an ICMP Host Unreachable message to the sender.

Entering the following command for any interface under interface configuration mode disables the ICMP Unreachable messages:

no ip unreachables

Reenabling the ICMP Unreachable message for an interface is accomplished by entering the

Figure 14-8
Directing UDP DHCP broadcast using ip helper-address.

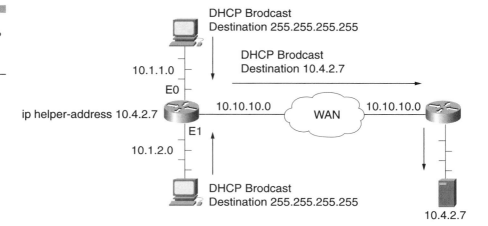

ip unreachable

interface configuration command. You may want to disable ICMP Unreachable messages on interfaces connecting to outside networks. Hackers sometimes use this information to obtain the reachability and available protocols that are allowed through the firewall.

Disable ICMP Redirect Messages

By default, the ICMP Redirect message is enabled for all interfaces supporting IP on the router. The ICMP Redirect message is sent to the originator of the packet, indicating the destination of the packet is either on the same subnet or there is a more direct path to the destination. In this case, the originating host places the IP address provided by the router that sent the ICMP Redirect message in the packet. The ICMP Redirect is disabled using the following interface configuration command:

no ip redirects

Again, hackers will use the ICMP Redirect message to break into a private network. To reenable the ICMP Redirect messages, enter the

ip redirects

interface configuration command for the interface on which ICMP redirects are desired.

Disable ICMP Mask Reply Messages

Another technique used by hackers is to request the IP address mask of an IP address by using the ICMP Mask Request message. The ICMP Mask Reply provides the final piece of the puzzle for hackers to gain access to your network. To disable the ICMP Mask Reply, enter the following command under interface configuration mode:

no ip mask-reply

Again, to reenable the command on a specific interface that has already disabled this function, enter the following command under interface configuration mode:

ip mask-reply

Support for Fragmenting Large IP Packets

The maximum transmission unit (MTU) size is applied to all defined Cisco router interfaces. The MTU size is the largest size packet supported on the defined interface. The MTU defaults are different for each interface type defined on the router. The largest possible size MTU on a route when using IP is determined by the IP Path MTU Discovery mechanism.

All Cisco routers employ the IP Path Discovery mechanism. As a router receives a packet on an interface, it determines the size of the packet, the MTU size allowed on the next hop interface, and whether the don't fragment (DF) bit is set by the origin IP host. Figure 14-9 illustrates an example in which the sending device sends a packet larger than that allowed on the destination LAN segment and the sending device has the DF bit set.

In this case, the destination router returns an ICMP Destination Unreachable message to the sending IP host with the code field indicating that fragmentation is needed to complete the delivery, but that the DF bit is set. The sending IP host must support the IP Path MTU Discovery mechanism in order to complete the delivery of the packet. If the sending IP host does not support the mechanism, the connection fails. The sending IP host

Figure 14-9
IP Path MTU
Discovery mechanism
with Cisco routers.

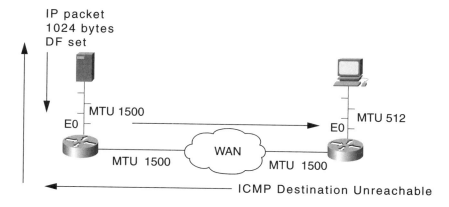

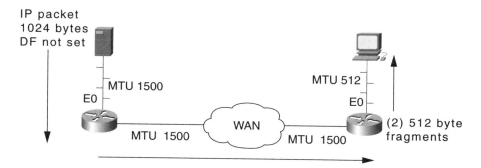

will require that its largest packet size be reduced to a size manageable by the majority of the connected networks. Most network designers end up avoiding this problem by making the MTU of an interface, and consequently the IP MTU size, 1500 bytes, which is typically the largest packet size allowed on an Ethernet LAN.

The MTU packet size is the largest size available for any protocol on the interface. This varies depending on the interface type. The following command can be used to modify just the IP protocol MTU size when specified under the interface configuration mode,

ip mtu *bytes*

where *bytes* is the size of the largest IP MTU allowed on the network supported by the interface being defined. The minimum is 128 and the maximum is dependent on the media connected to the interface. If the DF bit is not set, the Cisco router will automatically fragment the packet to the supported MTU size of the next hop interface.

Filter IP Packets Using Access Lists

The most widely used method for controlling access to a router, and subsequently networks attached to a router, is the access list feature of Cisco IOS. The access list is a filter that either permits the packet to pass through the router or denies the packet and returns an ICMP Destination Unreachable message to the source IP host of the denied packet. There are four types of access lists: standard, extended, dynamic, and reflexive.

An access list is a sequential comparison of the packet to the filters defined by the access-list global configuration command. The filters created can be applied to the following:

- Control packet transmissions on an interface
- Control access via virtual terminal lines
- For restricting the contents of routing updates

The packet IP address is tested against the conditions defined for each access list. The Cisco IOS software performs the test sequentially down the list. The first match found is the action taken on the packet and further conditional testing on the packet stops.

A list number or a name identifies access lists. IP access list numbers 1 to 99 are for use by standard access lists, while list numbers 100 to 199 are reserved for extended access lists. Standard IP access lists apply the condition to the source IP address field only. Extended access lists apply the condition test to protocols and possibly port numbers along with the source and destination IP addresses.

The dynamic filter is a feature of the extended IP access list that is used to grant access on a per-user basis by applying a conditional test to the source or destination IP host using a user authentication process, thereby allowing dynamic access without compromising security. The reflexive access list is nested within an extended named IP access list, basing the filter on session information. Using a name to identify an IP access list enables the router administrator to use more than 199 filters against IP packets.

NOTE: *Cisco IOS Release 11.1 and higher have modified IP access lists. The IP access lists created by releases prior to IOS 11.1 are automatically converted to the new IP access list format.*

Do not use an access list created with Cisco IOS 11.1 or higher on pre-11.1 IOS releases. Pre-11.1 releases are not compatible with the new access list format. This may result in security violations.

The IP access lists are applied to an interface on which a filter is required. The application of the filter is specific to packets inbound to the interface or outbound to the interface. An IP access list is applied to an interface under interface configuration mode using

ip access-group *access-list-number | access-list-name* [**in** | **out**]

The access list by default is applied to the outbound packets when neither the **in** or **out** keywords are specified on the **ip access-group** command. The access list itself is identified by either specifying the appropriate *access-list-number* or *access-list-name* of a previously defined access list. If a value is used that is not defined by an access list statement, all packets are permitted. Either a number or a name can be used when the access list is applied to a router interface. Only a number is allowed when applying an access list to a virtual terminal line.

NOTE: *Enabling outbound access lists automatically disables autonomous switching for the interface. Inbound access lists on a cbus or cxbus interface board disable autonomous switching for all the interfaces on the board, with the exception of those using SSE switching and simple access lists for outbound packets, and they still perform SSE switching. All other packets are sent using process switching.*

Create Standard Access Lists Using Numbers and Names

The format for creating a standard IP access list is

access-list *access-list-number* {**deny** | **permit**} **any** | *source* [*source-wildcard*] [**log**]

The *access-list-number* value is any available number in the range of 1 through 99, indicating a standard IP access list. More than one access-list command can be defined with the same access-list number. Be aware that all the conditions defined in the list group are applied to the packet being tested.

The **deny** | **permit** keywords indicate that if the condition being tested is true, the packet is dropped (deny) or forwarded (permit). The **any** keyword defines the use of the standard IP access list when the *source* is 0.0.0.0 and the *source-wildcard* is 255.255.255.255, essentially meaning all packets. The *source* variable is a four-part dotted decimal IP address and the *source-wildcard* is a dotted decimal value, indicating which bits of the *source* value are to be tested. The bits set to a one in the *source-wildcard* value are ignored.

The **log** keyword first appeared in IOS Release 11.3(3)T. Specifying this keyword causes the filtering process to write messages to the router message log. These messages include the *access-list-number*, whether the packet was permitted or denied, what the source address of the packet was, and the number of packets filtered. After the first successful match, a message is generated every five minutes with the number of packets permitted or denied within that interval.

NOTE: *An implicit deny filter for all packets can be found at the end of each access list.*

Suppose a resource with IP address 192.168.22.8, for example, requires access to the network, but all other hosts of the 192.168.0.0 network are restricted. The standard IP access list would be defined as

```
interface serial 0
 ip address 10.10.100.100 25.255.255.0
 ip access-group 1 in
access-list 1 permit 192.168.22.8 0.0.0.0
```

or

```
access-list 1 permit 192.168.22.8
```

The difference between the two statements is the exclusion of the *source-wildcard* value in the second access-list statement. Not coding the *source-wildcard* value assumes that the whole IP address entered as the *source* is tested. If a packet arrives with 192.168.22.10, it will fail the conditional testing, due to the implicit deny statement for the access list. All packets other than those with 192.168.22.8 will be discarded when applied against the defined access list.

In another example, suppose packets with 10.8.1.0 have restricted access with this router, but all other IP hosts in the 10.0.0.0 network are allowed. One other twist, address 10.8.1.23 needs access to the resources attached to this router. The standard access list is coded as

```
interface serial 0
 ip address 10.10.100.100 25.255.255.0
 ip access-group 1 in
access-list 1 permit 10.8.1.23
access-list 1 deny 10.8.1.0 0.0.0.255
access-list 1 permit 10.0.0.0 0.255.255.255
```

The statements' order of appearance in this access list is crucial for delivering the desired outcome. This example illustrates the best practice for defining access lists. Coding the most granular permits first, followed by the most granular denies, enables more global permits or denies to take place. Suppose a packet with IP address 10.8.2.200 is presented to the access list conditions. In this case, the packet is permitted because the IP address 10.8.2.200 falls into a different subnet than the deny statement.

NOTE: *Coding an explicit deny all statement causes the Cisco IOS to add new access list statements after the explicit deny all statement, causing the new access-list statements to be ignored. Because of this, the implicit **deny all** statement is recommended.*

Using a name as the access list identifier alleviates the IP access list restriction to 199 conditions. Only packet and route filters are currently supported using named access lists. The use of a name was first introduced in Cisco IOS Release 11.2 software. Thus, Cisco IOS releases previous to Release 11.2 will not be compatible with the use of names for access lists. The global configuration commands required to assign a name to an IP standard access list are as follows:

ip access-list standard *name*
deny {*source* [*source-wildcard*] | **any**}[**log**]
permit {*source* [*source-wildcard*] | **any**}[**log**]

The variables and keywords of the deny and permit statements shown have the same meaning as that discussed for creating access lists with number identifiers. The difference in using names is that the **deny** and **permit** statements are subcommands of the **ip access-list standard** command. The *name* variable of the **ip access-list standard** command is a unique name assigned to this named list of deny and permit subcommands.

NOTE: *As with numbered lists, additional deny or permit statements are added to the bottom of the list. The no deny or no permit command, however, can be entered against a named access list to remove the condition taking immediate effect.*

Applying names to the previous numbered access lists in our examples results in the following configuration:

```
interface serial 0
 ip address 10.10.100.100 255.255.255.0
 ip access-group customer in
 ip access-group sales out
!
ip access-list standard customer
permit 192.168.22.8 log
!
ip access-list standard sales
permit 10.8.1.23
deny 10.8.1.0 0.0.255.255
permit 10.0.0.0 0.255.255.255
```

The **log** keyword is added to the customer access list definition to log messages on the activity used by the permitted resource. The use of names is an added value since they now give an identity to the reason or group of users against which the filter is applied.

Extended Access Lists

The extended format of the IP access-list command is

access-list *access-list-number* {**deny | permit**} *protocol source source-wildcard destination destination-wildcard* [precedence *precedence*] [tos *tos*] [log]

The access-list-number is the extended access list identifier. The valid range for extended IP access lists is from decimal 100 to 199. The extended access list differs from a standard access list in its use of destination IP networks or IP host addresses, a precedence field, a Type of Service (TOS) field, and the keyword established. The variables are
protocol, source, source-wildcard, destination, and *destination-wildcard*

The *protocol* variable can be any of the following IP protocol names or a valid integer assigned to the protocol, such as

eigrp, gre, icmp, igmp, igrp, ip, ipinip, nos, ospf, tcp, or **udp.**

A value of **ip** denotes that all IP protocols listed will provide a match.

The *source* and *destination* variable values identify the IP network or IP host address to which the filter is applied. The *source-* and *destination-wildcard* variable values define the interesting bits of the IP network or IP host address to which the filter applies. These can be specified in the following ways:

- Using dotted-decimal format, such as 10.10.200.20 or 192.168.63.0.

- Using the any keyword when the filter applies to a value IP network or IP host address of 0.0.0.0 and the accompanying wildcard variable is 255.255.255.255.

- Using the host keyword when the wildcard value being applied is 0.0.0.0, indicating all bits are interesting.

The optional *precedence* variable is optional and is used to further define the type of packet being filtered by referencing the importance of the packet type. The possible values for *precedence* are listed below:

critical matches packets with critical precedence (5).

flash matches packets with flash precedence (3).

flash-override matches packets with flash override precedence (4).

immediate matches packets with immediate precedence (2).

internet matches packets with internetwork control precedence (6).

network matches packets with network control precedence (7).

priority matches packets with priority precedence (1).

routine matches packets with routine precedence (0).

The optional *tos* variable allows the extended filter to be placed against a specific type of service that meets the source and destination packet criteria. The *tos* variable values that can be used are listed below:

<0-15> is the type of service value.

max-reliability matches packets with max reliable TOS (2).

max-throughput matches packets with max throughput TOS (4).

min-delay matches packets with min delay TOS (8).

min-monetary-cost matches packets with min monetary cost TOS (1).

normal matches packets with normal TOS (0).

The specification of the optional **log** keyword indicates that any packets meeting the filter criteria will be written to the router's log file.

Further detailed filtering of ICMP, IGMP, TCP, and UDP protocols is possible using the extended access list. Specifying any of these protocols for the protocol variable modifies the format of the command to accept parameters with specific criteria within the protocol.

The complete format for specifying the ICMP as the protocol variable value is

access-list *access-list-number* {**deny** | **permit**}
icmp *source source-wildcard destination destination-wildcard*
[*icmp-type* [*icmp-code*] | *icmp-message*] [**precedence** *precedence*] [**tos** *tos*]
[**log**]

In the **icmp** format of the extended access list are three optional variables for further granular filtering. The *icmp-type*, along with the optional *icmp-code* parameter, allows criteria for an ICMP packet against the numerical values associated with the ICMP protocol. The numeric value is 0–255 for both the *icmp-type* and *icmp-code* variables. The *icmp-message* variable can be used, instead of the paired *icmp-type* and *icmp-code* variables. Using the *icmp-message* variable, ICMP packets are filtered based on a valid name provided by Cisco IOS software that describes the ICMP message type or ICMP message type and code within the message type. The following is the list of possible icmp-message values available:

administratively-prohibited: Administratively prohibited

alternate-address: Alternate address

conversion-error: Datagram conversion

dod-host-prohibited: Host prohibited

dod-net-prohibited: Net prohibited

echo: Echo (ping)

echo-reply: Echo reply

general-parameter-problem: Parameter problem

host-isolated: Host isolated

host-precedence-unreachable: Host unreachable for precedence

host-redirect: Host redirect

host-tos-redirect: Host redirect for TOS

host-tos-unreachable: Host unreachable for TOS

host-unknown: Host unknown

host-unreachable: Host unreachable

information-reply: Information replies

information-request: Information requests

mask-reply: Mask replies

mask-request: Mask requests

mobile-redirect: Mobile host redirect

net-redirect: Network redirect

net-tos-redirect: Net redirect for TOS

net-tos-unreachable: Network unreachable for TOS

net-unreachable: Net unreachable

network-unknown: Network unknown

no-room-for-option: Parameter required but no room

option-missing: Parameter required but not present

packet-too-big: Fragmentation needed and DF set

parameter-problem: All parameter problems

port-unreachable: Port unreachable

precedence-unreachable: Precedence cutoff

protocol-unreachable: Protocol unreachable

reassembly-timeout: Reassembly timeout

redirect: All redirects

router-advertisement: Router discovery advertisements

router-solicitation: Router discovery solicitations

source-quench: Source quenches

source-route-failed: Source route failed

time-exceeded: All time exceeded

timestamp-reply: Timestamp replies

timestamp-request: Timestamp requests

traceroute: Traceroute

ttl-exceeded: TTL exceeded

unreachable: All unreachables

In the following example, the serial 0 interface connects the router to the Internet. The access list 100 is applied to the outbound packets of the serial 0 interface, allowing the internal network to ping devices on the Internet. The access-list 101 is applied to inbound packets of the serial0 interface, thereby prohibiting Internet IP hosts from being able to ping internal IP hosts. The filters also allow echo-reply messages to flow.

```
interface serial 0
 ip address 209.196.9.34 255.255.255.0
 ip access-group 100 out
 ip access-group 101 in
access-list 100 permit icmp 10.0.0.0 0.255.255.255 any echo log
access-list 101 deny icmp any 10.0.0.0 0.255.255.255 echo log
```

When specifying the Internet Group Management Protocol (IGMP) on an extended access list, the format allows for the inclusion of specific IGMP message types. The format of the IGMP extended access list is

access-list *access-list-number* {**deny** | **permit**}
igmp *source source-wildcard destination destination-wildcard* [*igmp-type*]
[**precedence** *precedence*] [**tos** *tos*] [**log**]

The igmp-type variable can be a valid IGMP message type number ranging from 0 to 15, or it can be one of the IGMP message names found in the following list:

dvmrp: Distance Vector Multicast Routing Protocol

host-query: Host query

host-report: Host report

pim: Protocol Independent Multicast

trace: Multicast trace

In the following example, the serial0 interface connects the router to the Internet. The host-report IGMP message is prohibited from being transmitted between any internal hosts and any external hosts on the Internet.

```
interface serial 0
 ip address 209.196.9.34 255.255.255.0
 ip access-group 102 out
access-list 102 deny igmp any any host-report log
```

Specifying the TCP protocol on an extended access list enables the Cisco IOS software to apply filter criteria to packets that indicate a TCP connection is already traversing the router along with applying a comparison to specific TCP applications using the applications port number. The format of the extended access list when applying the filter to TCP is

access-list *access-list-number* {**deny** | **permit**}
tcp *source source-wildcard* [*operator port* [*port*]] *destination destination-wildcard* [*operator port* [*port*]] [**established**] [**precedence** *precedence*] [**tos** *tos*] [**log**]

The optional **established** keyword is used to match the filter and the packet only if the ACK or RST bits of the TCP header are set. This means that the filter is not applied to the packets during the initial TCP handshake used to form the connection.

The optional *operator* variable can be applied to the source and/or destination IP network or IP host address. The variable can be any of the following values:

eq matches only packets on a given port number.

gt matches only packets with a greater port number.

lt matches only packets with a lower port number.

neq matches only packets not on a given port number.

range matches only packets in the range of port numbers.

The *operator* value specified indicates the scope of the filter. Using the range value for the operator variable requires a second port number, thereby restricting the match within a sequential range of TCP port numbers.

The port variable is a TCP port number used by the packets of interest. The Cisco IOS software has the following list of port numbers that can also be assigned using the associated TCP port number name. These are

bgp: Border Gateway Protocol (179)

chargen: Character generator (19)

cmd: Remote commands (rcmd, 514)

daytime: Daytime (13)

discard: Discard (9)

domain: Domain Name Service (53)

echo: Echo (7)

exec: Exec (rsh, 512)

finger: Finger (79)

ftp: File Transfer Protocol (21)

ftp-data: FTP data connections (used infrequently, 20)

gopher: Gopher (70)

hostname: NIC hostname server (101)

ident: Ident Protocol (113)

irc: Internet Relay Chat (194)

klogin: Kerberos login (543)

kshell: Kerberos shell (544)

login: Login (rlogin, 513)

lpd: Printer service (515)

nntp: Network News Transport Protocol (119)

pop2: Post Office Protocol v2 (109)

pop3: Post Office Protocol v3 (110)

smtp: Simple Mail Transport Protocol (25)

sunrpc: Sun Remote Procedure Call (111)

syslog: Syslog (514)

tacacs: TAC Access Control System (49)

talk: Talk (517)

telnet: Telnet (23)

time: Time (37)

uucp: Unix-to-Unix Copy Program (540)

whois: Nicname (43)

www: World Wide Web (HTTP, 80)

The TCP port numbers listed represent well-known port numbers reserved for standardized TCP protocols.

NOTE: *If applying a filter to a user-defined TCP application, the port number must be specified since the user-defined TCP application name is unknown to the Cisco IOS.*

In the following example, the TCP protocol is being filtered on the inbound side of the serial 0 interface, which connects the router to the Internet. In this filter, a remote IP host with the address 192.168.39.8 is allowed to access an internal IP host at IP address 10.1.1.200 with only the Telnet protocol. Placing the filter on the inbound side of the serial interface ensures that the remote IP host cannot try to access any other host on the internal network.

```
interface serial 0
 ip address 10.200.20.1 255.255.255.0
 ip access-group 103 in
access-list 103 permit tcp host 192.168.39.8 eq telnet host
 10.1.1.200 eq telnet log
```

Applying an extended access list to UDP, like TCP, allows for comparison to UDP port numbers on the source and/or destination IP network or IP host address. The format of the extended access list for use with filtering UDP messages is

access-list *access-list-number* {**deny** | **permit**}
udp *source source-wildcard* [*operator port* [*port*]] *destination destination-wildcard* [*operator port* [*port*]] [**precedence** *precedence*]
[**tos** *tos*] [log]

The function of the operator and port variables is identical to the function and values of their use with TCP. However, UDP port numbers are unique to UDP applications. The UDP application names available for the port variable value, along with their associated port number, are as follows:

biff: Biff (mail notification, comsat, 512)

bootpc: Bootstrap Protocol (BOOTP) client (68)

bootps: Bootstrap Protocol (BOOTP) server (67)

discard: Discard (9)

dnsix: DNSIX security protocol auditing (195)

domain: Domain Name Service (DNS, 53)

echo: Echo (7)

mobile-ip: Mobile IP registration (434)

nameserver: IEN116 name service (obsolete, 42)

netbios-dgm: NetBios datagram service (138)

netbios-ns: NetBios name service (137)

ntp: Network Time Protocol (123)

rip: Routing Information Protocol (router, in.routed, 520)

snmp: Simple Network Management Protocol (161)

snmptrap: SNMP Traps (162)

sunrpc: Sun Remote Procedure Call (111)

syslog: System Logger (514)

tacacs: TAC Access Control System (49)

talk: Talk (517)

tftp Trivial File Transfer Protocol (69)

time: Time (37)

who: Who service (rwho, 513)

xdmcp: X Display Manager Control Protocol (177)

For both TCP and UDP, the valid range for the port value when using a number to identify the port is 0 through 65535.

In the following UDP example for extended access lists, the Ethernet interface 0 connects the router to the DMZ of the firewall for access to the Internet. To ensure that Internet RIP packets do not enter the router, an inbound filter denying RIP UDP packets is applied using access-list number 104.

```
interface ethernet 0
  ip address 10.200.10.1 255.255.255.0
  ip access-group 104 in
access-list 104 permit udp any any neq rip log
access-list 104 deny udp any any eq rip log
```

The extended access lists can also be defined using names. The format of the commands are as follows:

ip access-list extended *name*
{**deny** | **permit**} *protocol source source-wildcard destination destination-wildcard* [**precedence** *precedence*] [**tos** *tos*] [**established**] [**log**]
   or
{**deny** | **permit**} *protocol* **any any**
   or
{**deny** | **permit**} *protocol* **host** *source* **host** *destination*

For ICMP filtering using names on extended access lists, you would use the following format:

{**deny**|**permit**} **icmp** *source source-wildcard destination destination-wildcard* [*icmp-type* [*icmp-code*] | *icmp-message*] [**precedence** *precedence*] [**tos** *tos*] [log]

For IGMP filtering using names on extended access lists:

{**deny** | **permit**} **igmp** *source source-wildcard destination destination-wildcard* [*igmp-type*] [**precedence** *precedence*] [**tos** *tos*] [log]

For TCP filtering using names on extended access lists:

{**deny** | **permit**} **tcp** *source source-wildcard* [*operator port* [*port*]] *destination destination-wildcard* [*operator port* [*port*]] [**established**] [**precedence** *precedence*] [**tos** *tos*] [log]

For UDP filtering using names on extended access lists:

{**deny** | **permit**} **udp** *source source-wildcard* [*operator port* [*port*]] *destination destination-wildcard* [*operator port* [*port*]] [**precedence** *precedence*] [**tos** *tos*] [log]

The values and placements for extended access lists using names are the same for specifying the denial or permission of a packet. The **ip access-list extended** command followed by a unique *name* indicates to the Cisco IOS software that the following statements are grouped under the specified *name*.

We can apply the numbered extended access list examples using a name by specifying them using the descriptions listed below.

Using named extended access lists on ICMP echo messages to and from the Internet connection on serial 0 interface:

```
interface serial 0
 ip address 209.196.9.34 255.255.255.0
 ip access-group pingnet out
 ip access-group pingnet in
ip access-list extended pingnet
 permit icmp 10.0.0.0 0.255.255.255 any echo log
 deny icmp any 10.0.0.0 0.255.255.255 echo log
```

Prohibiting the host-report IGMP message from leaving the router on interface serial0 to the Internet:

```
interface serial 0
 ip address 209.196.9.34 255.255.255.0
 ip access-group igmpout out
ip access-list extended igmpout
 deny igmp any any host-report log
```

Permitting Telnet access only between an Internet IP host at 192.168.39.8 and an internal IP host at 10.1.1.200 through the serial 0 interface using named extended access lists:

```
interface serial 0
 ip address 209.196.9.34 255.255.255.0
 ip access-group port25 in
ip access-list extended port25
 permit tcp host 192.168.39.8 eq telnet host 10.1.1.200 eq telnet
 log
```

In the last example, an RIP protocol is filtered out on the inbound side of an Ethernet connection:

```
interface ethernet 0
  ip address 10.200.10.1 255.255.255.0
  ip access-group norip in
ip access-list extended norip
  deny udp any any eq rip log
```

Fault-Tolerant Routing of IP Packets

The Cisco IOS software can provide backup and recovery of the IP default gateway address using the Hot Standby Router Protocol (HSRP). Let's use Figure 14-10 as the first example on understanding how HSRP works with Cisco routers.

The virtual IP address of 10.1.1.1 is the default IP gateway address for ELAN1 on the Cisco Catalyst 5000 switch in Figure 14-10. The actual IP addresses HSRP assigns a virtual MAC address for the LAN interface associating the virtual IP address. The ATM-specific definitions are discussed in detail in Chapter 20, "Defining ATM (LANE, Classical IP, and MPOA)."

The following is the configuration for PRI-Router:
hostname PRI-Router

```
!
interface ethernet 0
 ip address 10.10.10.3 255.255.255.0
 standby 1 ip 10.10.10.1
 standby 1 preempt
 standby 1 priority 110
 standby 1 authentication group1
 standby 1 timers 5 15
```

The following is the configuration for SEC-Router:
hostname SEC-Router

```
!
interface ethernet 0
 ip address 10.10.10.2 255.255.255.0
 standby 1 ip 10.10.10.1
 standby 1 preempt
 standby 1 authentication group1
 standby 1 timers 5 15
```

Figure 14-10
HSRP in support of
providing IP gateway
address backup and
recovery.

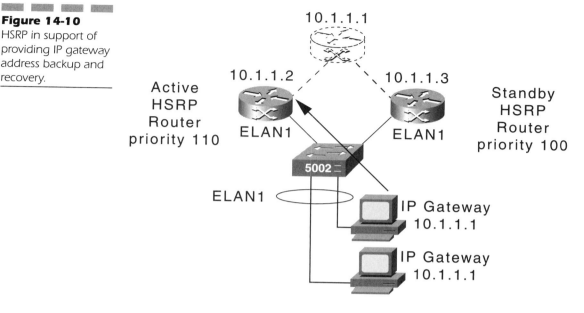

Figure 14-10
HSRP in support of
providing IP gateway
address backup and
recovery.

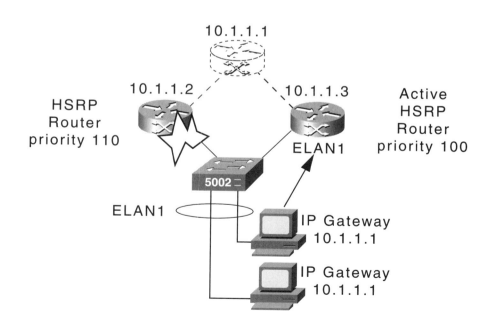

The HSRP feature is enabled by specifying the interface configuration command, **standby ip**. The format of this command is

standby [*group-number*] **ip** [*ip-address* [**secondary**]]

The *group-number* is an optional numeric identifier used to designate the routers that belong to the HSRP group. The default is 0 with a valid range of 0 to 255. The *ip-address* variable is the virtual IP address being assigned to the HSRP group. The secondary keyword is used when HSRP is being applied as a **secondary** IP address. In our example, the HSRP group is group 1 and the 10.10.10.1 is the virtual IP address.

NOTE: *Ethernet, ATM LANE, and FDDI support up to 255 Hot Standby groups. Token Ring LANs can support only three Hot Standby groups numbered 0, 1, and 2.*

The **standby priority** HSRP interface command is used on a router interface with HSRP to ensure the election of this router interface as the primary router. The format of this command is

standby [*group-number*] **priority** *priority* [**preempt** [**delay** *delay*]]

The *group-number* associates this command with an HSRP group. The *priority* value is a defined numeric value in the range of 1 to 255, defaulting to 100 and denoting the preference of this interface to act as the primary for the virtual IP address. The **preempt** keyword, if specified, directs the Cisco IOS to assume control as the active virtual IP address if the router has a higher priority than the current primary virtual interface. The *delay* variable determines the amount of time in seconds that the router will postpone its attempt to become the active primary interface for the virtual IP address. The *delay* variable defaults to 0 and can range from 0 to 3600 seconds.

In the example, PRI-Router has the *priority* set to 110, while SEC-Router defaults to a priority of 100. During the UDP hello exchanges that occur with HSRP, PRI-Router is elected as the primary interface for servicing the virtual IP address. Should PRI-Router's HSRP interface go inactive, the Ethernet interface on SEC-Router will become the active interface. Once PRI-Router's Ethernet interface becomes active again, it immediately attempts to become the active interface since the **preempt** keyword is coded and the delay value defaults to a 0. If the **preempt** keyword is not coded, the PRI-Router becomes the active router again when SEC-Router Ethernet is inactivated.

An authentication string can be used that ensures the proper learning of the virtual IP address and timer values interpreted for the appropriate HSRP group. The format of the command is

standby [*group-number*] **authentication** *string*

The *group-number* identifies which HSRP group the authentication *string* applies. All routers participating in the same HSRP group must use the same authentication string. The string value defaults to the string "cisco" and is one to eight characters in length. In our example, the authentication string of group1 is used to verify that the parameters are for use with the HSRP standby group number 1.

HSRP uses UDP hello messages to discover and convey other HSRP routers' participation. The standby timer's interface command allows the router administrator to fine-tune the interval between Hello messages and the delay in determining that an active or other standby router is no longer available. The format for the command is

standby [*group-number*] **timers** *hellotime holdtime*

The *group-number* value identifies which standby group to apply to the timer values. The *hellotime* variable is the number of seconds from 1 to 255 the router will wait between sending Hello messages. Its default is three seconds. The *holdtime* value ranges from 1 to 255 and defaults to 10 seconds. This value denotes the amount of time that must pass without receiving a Hello message from a previously known HSRP router interface before it is determined as unavailable. The timers configured on the active router override all timer settings. If coding the standby timers interface command, be sure to code it the same on all interfaces participating in the same standby group.

The *holdtime* is typically greater than or equal to three times the *hellotime* value. In our example, we follow this rule by having the Hello messages sent every five seconds and the receipt of a Hello message every 15 seconds the sending router interface has become unavailable.

Using the concept of HSRP groups, multiple groups can be created that can enable a single router to be the backup for multiple routers or even for creating load sharing. Figure 14-11 illustrates the capability of providing load sharing on Cisco routers with HSRP.

The following is the HSRP configuration portion of router R1:

```
hostname R1
!
interface ethernet 0
 ip address 10.1.1.1 255.255.255.0
 standby 1 ip 10.1.1.253
 standby 1 priority 110
 standby 1 preempt
```

```
standby 2 ip 10.1.1.254
standby 2 preempt
```

The following is the HSRP configuration portion of router R2:

```
hostname R2
!
interface ethernet 0
 ip address 10.1.1.2 255.255.255.0
 standby 1 ip 10.1.1.253
 standby 1 preempt
 standby 2 ip 10.1.1.254
 standby 2 priority 110
 standby 2 preempt
```

The above configurations demonstrate the use of two Cisco routers supporting fault-tolerance for two IP gateway addresses on the same subnet. IP address 10.1.1.253 is the virtual IP address supporting LAN devices requiring 10.1.1.253 as the default IP gateway. Router R1 is the active router for LAN devices using 10.1.1.253 as the default gateway due to the higher priority defined on standby group 1, which defines 10.1.1.253 as the virtual IP address. Router R2 assumes the active router responsibilities, should the Ethernet interface on router R1 become unavailable. If this happens, the physical interface on router R2 supports three IP addresses and responds to all three: the interface IP address and the group1 and group 2 standby IP addresses.

NOTE: *In order to minimize the potential for connection or session outages for all HSRP configurations during the election of a new active router, it is best to use a fast-converging routing protocol like EIGRP.*

Figure 14-11
Support for fault-tolerant load sharing between two Cisco routers.

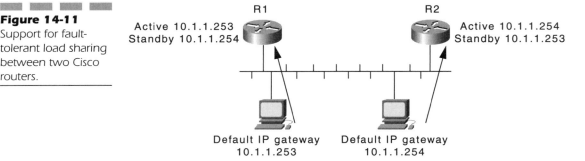

This same method can be used to plan load balancing over two routers that support the same multiple LANs. For instance, if both routers in Figure 14-11 support the same four Ethernet LAN segments, the configuration to load balance two segments on one router and two segments on the other router during a stable network would look like the following code.

The following section is the HSRP configuration portion of router R1:

```
hostname R1
!
interface ethernet 1/0
 ip address 10.1.1.1 255.255.255.0
 standby 1 ip 10.1.1.253
 standby 1 priority 110
 standby 1 preempt
 standby 2 ip 10.1.1.254
 standby 2 preempt
!
interface ethernet 1/1
 ip address 10.1.2.1 255.255.255.0
 standby 3 ip 10.1.2.253
 standby 3 priority 110
 standby 3 preempt
 standby 4 ip 10.1.2.254
 standby 4 preempt
!
interface ethernet 1/2
 ip address 10.1.3.1 255.255.255.0
 standby 5 ip 10.1.3.253
 standby 5 priority 110
 standby 5 preempt
 standby 6 ip 10.1.3.254
 standby 6 preempt
!
interface ethernet 1/3
 ip address 10.1.4.1 255.255.255.0
 standby 7 ip 10.1.4.253
 standby 7 priority 110
 standby 7 preempt
 standby 8 ip 10.1.4.253
 standby 8 preempt
```

The following is the HSRP configuration portion of router R2:

```
hostname R2
!
interface ethernet 0
 ip address 10.1.1.2 255.255.255.0
 standby 1 ip 10.1.1.253
 standby 1 preempt
 standby 2 ip 10.1.1.254
 standby 2 priority 110
 standby 2 preempt
```

IP Performance Tuning

The focus of IP performance-tuning in Cisco IOS is on TCP. The performance options available for tuning IP deal with the compression of TCP packet headers, MTU path discovery time, and selective acknowledgment to reduce retransmission of TCP packets, the TCP read size, the TCP window size, and outgoing queue size.

Compressing TCP Headers

Compressing TCP headers of TCP segments reduces the size of the IP datagram and therefore reduces the bandwidth requirement on the WAN connections. TCP header compression is supported by the following:

- HDLC serial lines
- Frame Relay serial lines
- PPP encapsulation on serial lines

TCP packet header compression is best suited for networks in which many small TCP packets traverse the WAN connection. This type of traffic is typical of interactive transaction processing from display terminals. The format of the interface configuration command is as follows:

ip tcp header-compression [passive]

Specifying the command on the serial interface with the optional **passive** keyword indicates that outgoing TCP packets are compressed only if the incoming TCP packets of the same interface are compressed. Not coding the passive keyword indicates that all incoming and outgoing TCP headers are compressed.

NOTE: *Fast switching is disabled when compression is enabled for a serial interface. Because of this, using TCP header compression on T1 serial interfaces and higher bandwidths may result in router overload.*

An associated command used with **ip tcp header-compression** is the **ip tcp compression-connections** interface configuration command. The format of this command is

ip tcp compression-connections *number*

The number variable is the total number of header compression connections supported by the router on the serial interface. The range is 3 through 256, and it defaults to 16 cache entries if the ip tcp compression-connections interface command is not defined with the ip tcp header-compression interface command. A sample configuration is

Router 1

```
host router1
!
interface serial 1/1
 ip 10.20.30.40 255.255.255.0
 ip tcp header-compression
 ip tcp compression-connections 20
```

Router 2

```
host router2
!
interface serial 2/1
 ip 10.20.30.50 255.255.255.0
 ip tcp header-compression
 ip tcp compression-connections 20
```

When using TCP header compression, both sides of the serial line must have ip tcp header-compression specified for proper connectivity.

Enable TCP Path MTU Discovery

The discovery of the largest MTU size over a path between the source and destination router is performed on the initial setup of the TCP connection. Using a dynamic TCP Path MTU Discovery mechanism enables the MTU size to be updated prior to any new TCP connection request. This is done using the interface command:

ip tcp path-mtu-discovery [**age-timer** {*minutes* | **infinite**}]

Applying this command on an interface definition enables the router to dynamically determine the largest MTU size between distinct subnets. This is useful to maximize bandwidth for connections that transmit bulk data between the two distinct subnets. The *minutes* variable is the number of minutes the discovery process will wait prior to discovering a new MTU size. The default is 10 minutes and the maximum is 30 minutes. Specifying the infinite value as the variable for the age-timer keyword turns off the age-timer and the MTU size discovery process uses the most current MTU size discovered, until modified by the router administrator.

Performance Enhancements Through Switching Features

Cisco IOS software and microcode together enable the router to move packets between interfaces based on the next-hop destination Layer 3 address. Fast switching is enabled on all interfaces by default. The types of switching supported with Cisco IOS software are

- Process
- Fast
- Optimum
- Silicon Switch Engine (SSE)
- Autonomous
- Distributed
- NetFlow

Access-control lists play a major role in the throughput of packets. Depending on the switching mechanism in use, along with the access filters being applied, packet performance is directly affected. Optimum switching is the most efficient with the highest throughput available on the routers when access filtering is not being used. NetFlow switching is the second-most efficient, even when applying access filters. Fast switching without access filters is the third-most efficient, followed by process switching.

NOTE: *Using optimum and fast switching is compromised to process switching when an access list is applied to an interface. NetFlow switching is the only mechanism that enables switching while access list processing is enabled.*

Enabling Process Switching

In process switching, each frame is sent to the route processor CPU and the CPU encapsulates or de-encapsulates the data. In addition, route selection and filtering is performed during process switching. Process switching is CPU-intensive and slows down packet throughput, using valuable CPU. If you use priority queuing, custom queuing, or filtering, frames become process-switched. Since fast switching is enabled by default, process switching is administratively enabled by issuing the following interface command:

no ip route-cache

Entering this command on an interface disables all switching and forces process switching.

Enabling Fast Switching

Fast switching is the default method used on Cisco routers when a Cisco cbus interface processor is installed. Fast switching enables the passing of a frame that is destined to a port on another cbus interface processor directly over the router cbus backplane at the interrupt level without copying the frame to the system memory first. This bypasses the involvement of the router processor CPU and therefore provides better performance. Enabling fast-switch processing if it has been disabled is accomplished by entering the interface command:

ip route-cache

NOTE: *A bus is the common electrical connection used by all the interface processors on a router. The Cisco cbus architecture is a high-speed backplane for connecting the router's interface processors.*

Enabling Fast Switching on the Same Interface

Fast switching on the same interface allows the switching of packets back out the interface without passing over the bus. This is useful for NBMA networks like Frame Relay and ATM. To enable the same interface ith fast switching, enter the following interface command:

ip route-cache same-interface

This command is only viable for non-broadcast multi-access (NBMA) networks where subinterfaces are defined to create multipoint connections.

Enabling Autonomous Switching

Autonomous switching occurs without an interrupt or the route processor CPU intervening. Autonomous switching performs better than fast-switch processing and is advantageous for traffic between cbus interfaces and functions for two-port or multiport bridging on the same router. Enabling autonomous switching is accomplished by entering the configuration interface command:

ip route-cache cbus

Entering the ip route-cache cbus interface command enables both autonomous and fast switching for the interface.

Enabling Silicon Switch Engine (SSE) Switching

The switching of packets using a software solution is now a viable alternative to the previous switching methods that utilized a hardware bus handler processor. The software solution speeds the switching of packets through the cbus since the SSE is a programmable cache. To enable SSE, the following configuration interface command must be entered:

ip route-cache sse

This interface command is specific to the Silicon Switch Processor (SSP) board of the Cisco 7000 series routers, which use a cxbus architecture.

Optimum Fast Switching

The highest switching throughput and most efficient mechanism for switching on the router is optimum switching. The feature is specified to the Cisco 7500 series routers where IP is enabled on Ethernet, FDDI, and serial interface. Optimum switching on serial interfaces is only supported when HDLC is the encapsulation method. To specify optimum switching, enter the following interface command:

ip route-cache optimum

NetFlow Switching

NetFlow switching is used on Cisco RSP7000/7000CI, 7200, and 7500 series routers. NetFlow switching is supported for IP and IP-encapsulated traffic on all interfaces. The exception to this is when more than one input access control list is applied to an ISL/VLAN, ATM, or Frame Relay interface. ATM

LANE interfaces also do not support the NetFlow switching feature at this time.

NetFlow switching creates a network flow cache based on the network layer source and destination IP address and the transport-layer port number. A flow is defined in the flow cache using the following fields found in IP datagram:

- Source/destination IP address
- Source/destination port number
- Protocol type
- Type of service
- Input/output interface
- Source/destination subnet mask
- BGP source/destination AS

NetFlow switching applies access list processing to the first packet of an identified flow. Subsequent packets are then handled on a connection-oriented basis, thereby bypassing the access-list processing of subsequent packets within a flow. This is in contrast to the standard access-list processing in which each packet is checked against the applied access list, thereby forcing process switching that causes degradation in the throughput.

Enabling NetFlow switching on an interface disables all other switching modes for the interface. The cache created is based on processing the first packet of flow through either fast or optimum switching processes. After the creation of the cached entry, the packet is flow switched based on the information found in the flow cache. NetFlow switching on a interface is enabled using the following interface command:

ip route-cache Flow

An advantage to using NetFlow switching is the capability to create call detail recording (CDR) records based on the flow entries found in the NetFlow cache. These data can be exported to the Cisco NetFlow Collector application residing on a workstation or server using the following global command:

ip flow-export destination {*hostname* | *ip-address*} *udp-port*

This command instructs the NetFlow feature to send the cached entry statistics of an expired entry to the NetFlow Collector application at *hostname* or *ip-address* using the *udp-port* number supported by the application. For example, if we entered

```
ip flow-export destination manager 125
```

the NetFlow process on the router sends the statistics to the workstation named manager using UDP port number 125. The data provided by the NetFlow entry can be used for network management and planning, enterprise accounting and departmental charge-backs, ISP billing, and data warehousing/mining for marketing purposes, as well as capacity planning.

Because NetFlow tracks the identified flows along with traffic counts, the process uses more memory and CPU resources than the other types of switching mechanisms. The default size of the NetFlow cache is 64K of memory. Each cache entry requires 64 bytes of storage; thus, a default memory requirement is 4 MB of DRAM. The NetFlow process has a memory management mechanism that attempts to age 30 flow entries using an accelerated timeout when approximately 10 remaining free flow entries are available in the cache. If the number of free flow entries is one, NetFlow automatically ages the oldest 30 flow entries. This mechanism is used each time a free flow entry in the cache is used for a new flow entry. The following global command can be used to change the NetFlow DRAM memory allocation:

ip flow-cache *entries*

The *entries* variable is the number of entries to be supported on the router. The range is 1024 to 524288 with the default number of entries being 65536. Cisco recommends that the default be used as much as possible since increasing the entries value may cause poor network performance and problems.

The record type exported to the NetFlow Collector on a workstation is defined by using the global command:

ip flow-export version {1 | 5 [**origin-as** | **peer-as**] }

If this command is not specified, the default record type is version 1. The version type is dependent on the version supported by the NetFlow Collector application on the workstation. If version 5 is supported, you may also specify either the origin (origin-as) or peer (peer-as) BGP autonomous-system number. Specifying version 5 defaults to neither origin nor peer AS numbers for the record and provides for better performance. The version 5 format also includes the source and destination AS addresses, source and destination prefix masks, and a sequence number to determine lost UDP packets.

The NetFlow collector application on a workstation can request NetFlow data and identify an IP address as the source of the NetFlow record through the use of the following global configuration command:

ip flow-export source *interface*

The interface variable provides the name of the interface that identifies the router IP address to use as the source of the NetFlow data and to allow the NetFlow Collector application to perform SNMP queries to the router using the IP address of the specified interface. In this instance, it is good practice to use the loopback interface IP address since it is not tied to a physical interface and is always considered active. An example of specifying the NetFlow source address is

```
interface loopback 0
 ip address 10.1.1.1 255.255.255.0
interface etherent 0/1
 ip address 10.2.2.1 255.255.255.0
 ip route-cache flow
 ip flow-export destination manager 125
 ip flow-export source loopback0
```

Using NetFlow switching provides a powerful tool for network-analysis gathering in order to determine traffic characteristics, which can then lead to network topology changes and performance tuning.

Distributed Switching

When using distributed switching, a cache entry is built and propagated to all switching caches of the VIPs that are enabled for distributed switching. Thus, switching caches are synchronized for all VIPs that are enabled for distributed switching. This allows VIP-to-VIP switching decisions to be made by the inbound VIP, even if the destination is to a different VIP card. The format of the interface command for implementing distributed switching is

```
ip route-cache distributed
```

Defining RIP Routing Protocol

Routing Information Protocol (RIP) is the first open standard used between router vendors and, as such, is a simple protocol. RIP comes in two versions. The initial introduction of RIP is based on IETF RFC 1058 and was developed to support small networks. It is now referred to as RIP version 1. The newest version of RIP, named RIP version 2 (RIP-2), like RIP version 1, is still based on classical distance-vector routing algorithms. RIP-2, however, incorporates some of the advanced features required in today's larger networks such as authentication, route summarization, classless inter-domain routing (CIDR), and variable-length subnet masks (VLSM). None of these advanced features are not supported by RIP version 1.

The Basics of RIP

RIP uses broadcast User Datagram Protocol (UDP) data packets for sending routing table entries to neighboring routers. Since RIP uses UDP as its delivery mechanism, the routing table updates sent to the neighboring routers are not guaranteed. The sending of the RIP table entries between routers defaults to 30 seconds after the initial startup of the router. This "advertising" of routes occurs also between two routers when a router becomes active on a connection to an already active router. Figure 15-1 illustrates this advertising of routing tables.

Routers using RIP expect an update from a neighboring router within 180 seconds. If a routing table update is not received from the neighboring router within this time, the routes to networks through the non-updating router are marked as unusable, forcing returned ICMP network-unreachable messages to originating requesters for resources connected through the non-updating router. Once the received update timer has reached 240 seconds, the non-updating router route entries are removed from the routing table. Packets now received by the router for networks connected through the non-updating router can now be directed to the default network path for this router. The "default route" is learned by RIP or a gateway of last resort is defined with a default RIP metric. Packets with destination networks not found in the routing table are directed out the interface on which the default route is defined.

In Figure 15-2, the Cisco IOS command, show ip route, is entered on a Cisco router. The displayed output identifies the default route for this router to be found at address 10.163.17.5 to network 0.0.0.0, the pseudo network used by Cisco IOS for implementing the default-routing feature. The result of this feature is that any destination IP addresses within the networks found in the routing table that are not found explicitly in the routing

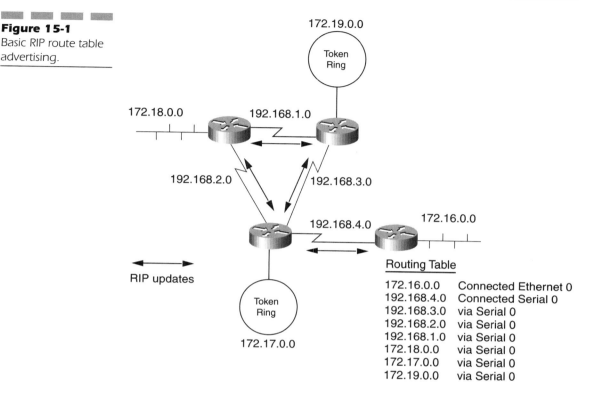

Figure 15-1

Basic RIP route table
advertising.

table are routed out of the interface defined by IP address 10.163.17.5. In
this case, the ATM interface on slot 3 subinterface 0.2 is used as the default
route to subnets within the known and unknown networks.

Why Use RIP as the Routing Protocol?

RIP is the most commonly found routing protocol and, as such, is available
on all IP-routing platforms. For example, as depicted in Figure 15-3, when
using RIP, a Cisco router can use another vendor's router, such as a Bay
Network router, for connecting network resources.

Also found in many networks is the use of Sun workstations as a router
supporting RIP as the routing protocol. Because RIP is the most common
denominator for connecting different vendor equipment, it is often used in
vendor equipment migrations and to grandfather entrenched, antiquated
network topologies, along with its ease of implementation.

Figure 15·2

The Cisco IOS show
ip route command
for identifying the
default route.

```
r1 >SH IP ROUTE
Codes: C - connected, S - static, I - IGRP, R - RIP, M - mobile, B - BGP
 D - EIGRP, EX - EIGRP external, O - OSPF, IA - OSPF inter area
 N1 - OSPF NSSA external type 1, N2 - OSPF NSSA external type 2
 E1 - OSPF external type 1, E2 - OSPF external type 2, E - EGP
 i - IS-IS, L1 - IS-IS level-1, L2 - IS-IS level-2, * - candidate default
 U - per-user static route, o – ODR

Gateway of last resort is 10.163.17.5 to network 0.0.0.0

R* 0.0.0.0/0 [120/1] via 10.163.17.5, 00:00:18, ATM3/0.2
 [120/1] via 10.163.17.2, 00:00:27, ATM3/0.2
 [120/1] via 10.163.17.4, 00:00:16, ATM3/0.2
```

Defining RIP as a Routing Protocol on the Router

Cisco routers enable routing protocols through the use of the following global configuration command:

router

The IOS enables the RIP-routing protocol by entering the following global configuration command:

router rip

After entering this command, the router is running the RIP process, but no RIP routing table is created. Creating the RIP-routing table is accomplished by following the **router rip** global configuration command with the network command. The format of the network command is

network *network-number*

The variable network number is the network number of a network directly connected to the router. For example, in Figure 15.4, three routers are connected to each other using the RIP routing protocol. Each router must specify the network addresses directly connected to it in order for RIP

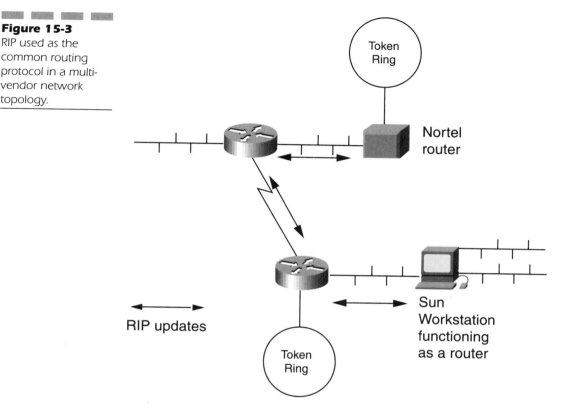

Figure 15-3
RIP used as the
common routing
protocol in a multi-
vendor network
topology.

to advertise the IP network to its neighbors. The network number is the
Class A, B, or C IP network assigned to the interfaces on the router. The use
of subnet masks for identifying the network is not needed on the network
command. In Figure 15-4, network 10.0.0.0 is defined to all the routers,
while network 192.168.5.0 is defined to only router 1, network 192.168.6.0
is defined to router 2, and network 192.168.4.0 is defined to router 3 only.

The RIP specific commands for each router are as follows:

Router 1:

```
router rip
 network 10.0.0.0
 network 192.168.5.0
```

Router 2:

```
router rip
 network 10.0.0.0
 network 192.168.6.0
```

Router 3:

```
router rip
 network 10.0.0.0
 network 192.168.4.0
```

RIP sends and receives routing updates only on the interfaces matching the networks defined by the network command. If a network is defined on an interface but not defined to the RIP process using a network statement, that network will not be advertised to the rest of the network and is essentially isolated from that part of the network.

Figure 15-4
RIP-routing protocol used between Cisco routers.

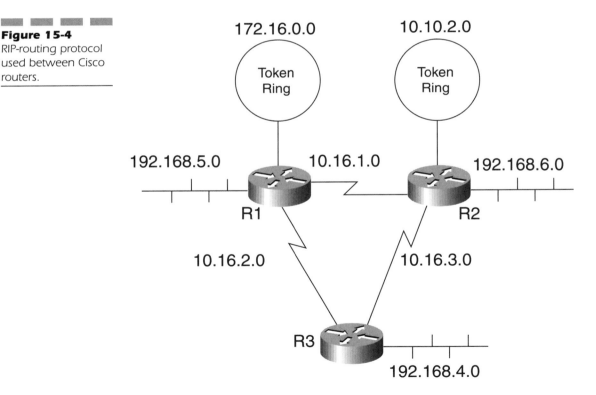

As shown in Figure 15-4, the serial interfaces connecting the routers along with the Ethernets on all the routers have their networks in the routing tables. The Token Ring network on router 1, however, is not included in the network statements under the router rip definition and therefore is not in the RIP-routing table. The devices on the Token Ring thus do not receive RIP updates from router 1. The Token Ring segment on router 2, however, is included in the RIP-routing tables because the interface has the IP address, 10.10.2.1, and a mask of 255.255.255.0, falling within network 10.0.0.0, which is defined by the network command on router 2.

Allow Point-to-Point (NBMA) Updates for RIP

X.25 and Frame Relay Non-Broadcast Multi-Access (NBMA) networks provide multiple connections over a single interface. Shown in Figure 15-5, the NBMA topology provides a single physical interface on the router to a public network. The public network provider then delivers the packets or frames to the destination NBMA address or identifier. The Cisco IOS software must be defined in such a scenario to specifically identify the RIP routers over the single interface by specifying the neighboring routers' IP addresses. For example, in Figure 15-5, router R1 must define the IP addresses of router R2 and R3 under the RIP-routing protocol definition to send RIP updates to the adjacent routers R2 and R3 through the single Frame Relay interface.

The router R1 specifies the IP address of the neighboring routers R2 and R3, connecting over the single frame relay interface using the global configuration command neighbor. The format of the command is

neighbor *ip-address*

The *ip-address* value is the IP address assigned to the routers on the far end of the public NBMA network connection. In Figure 15-5, the configuration in router R1 is specified as the following:

Router R1 Configuration:

```
interface serial 0
 encapsulation frame-relay
 ip address 10.163.7.1 255.255.255.0
!
interface ethernet 0
```

Figure 15-5
RIP-routing updates
over a single Frame
Relay interface using
the neighbor
command.

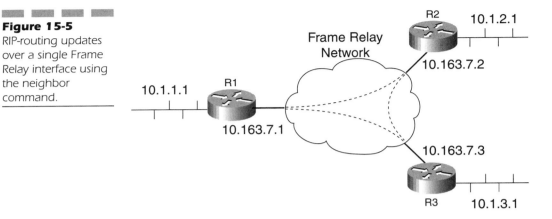

```
 ip address 10.1.1.1 255.255.255.0
!
router rip
 network 10.0.0.0
 neighbor 10.163.7.2
 neighbor 10.163.7.3
```

Router R1 sends RIP updates to the IP addresses 10.163.7.2 and
10.163.7.3 and has learned of the DLCI for each of these on the Frame
Relay multipoint connection using Frame Relay Inverse ARP. The Frame
Relay Inverse ARP builds a table, mapping the DLCI numbers to the IP
addresses dynamically. The configuration for router R2 and router R3 are
as follows:

Router R2 Configuration:

```
interface serial 0
 encapsulation frame-relay
 ip address 10.163.7.2 255.255.255.0
!
interface ethernet 0
 ip address 10.1.2.1 255.255.255.0
!
router rip
 network 10.0.0.0
 neighbor 10.163.7.1
 neighbor 10.163.7.3
```

Router R3 Configuration:

```
interface serial 0
 encapsulation frame-relay
 ip address 10.163.7.3 255.255.255.0
!
interface ethernet 0
 ip address 10.1.3.1 255.255.255.0
!
router rip
 network 10.0.0.0
 neighbor 10.163.7.1
 neighbor 10.163.7.2
```

NOTE: *It is recommended that dynamic routing be enabled to avoid configuration changes and to allow the network to change dynamically. This is done in frame relay networks by defining subinterfaces as point-to-point. See Chapter 4, "Frame Relay Network Design," for more information.*

Another use of the neighbor command is to selectively define which routers on a given interface will participate in routing updates along with the passive-interface command. In this sample configuration, the workstations connected to R1 LAN segment Ethernet 1 need only to communicate with the R2 router to connect to the WAN and the stations on segment Ethernet 1 router R2. The following configuration demonstrates this concept:

Router R1 Configuration:

```
interface Ethernet 0
 ip address 10.17.2.1 255.255.255.0
!
interface Ethernet 1
 ip address 10.1.2.1 255.255.255.0
!
router rip
 network 10.0.0.0
 neighbor 10.17.2.2
 passive-interface Ethernet 0
 passive-interface Ethernet 1
```

Router R2 Configuration:

```
!
interface Serial 0
 ip address 172.16.1.1 255.255.255.0

interface Ethernet 0
 ip address 10.17.2.2 255.255.255.0
!
```

```
interface Ethernet 1
 ip address 10.2.2.1 255.255.255.0
!
router rip
 network 10.0.0.0
 network 172.16.0.0
 passive-interface Ethernet 1
```

Router R3 Configuration:

```
interface Ethernet 0
 ip address 10.17.2.3 255.255.255.0
!
interface Ethernet 1
 ip address 10.3.2.1 255.255.255.0
!
router rip
 network 10.0.0.0
 neighbor 10.17.2.2
 passive-interface Ethernet 0
 passive-interface Ethernet 1
```

In this configuration example, router R3 does not receive updates from router R1 because the passive-interface command is specified for the Ethernet interface, connecting router R1 on IP subnet 10.17.2.0. The same holds true for R1 for receiving updates from R3. The passive-interface command indicates to the Cisco IOS that the interface specified on the command will not be used for sending routing updates, but the specified interface can receive updates. Router R2 receives and exchanges routing updates with R1 and R3 because the IP address of R2 is defined on the neighbor command of router R1 and R3. Figure 15-6 illustrates this network topology. Further RIP-update reduction is possible by implementing the passive-interface command for LAN segments connecting end-user stations only. This eliminates the unnecessary RIP-update traffic entering the network interface cards of the workstations.

The result of this configuration is that update packets are exchanged only between R1 and R2 and between R2 and R3. Using this method, the interface cards on routers not requiring RIP-routing table updates will not have to process unneeded packets. In another example, if the same three routers are attached through a switch, then the workstations attached to the same switch no longer receive unnecessary RIP-routing updates. This is especially true in switched networks employing ATM LANE topologies where unicast-directed RIP-routing updates are only forwarded to the destination MAC address within the packet, instead of an all-broadcast destination MAC address, as is normally found with RIP update packets.

Also required here is the no ip slit-horizon command on the interface E0 of R2. Figure 15-7 illustrates this configuration. Using this concept on switched connections saves switch processor resources and eliminates the RIP updates from being propagated to all the workstations also connected on the same switch.

Figure 15-6

Reducing RIP updates
on an Ethernet
backbone.

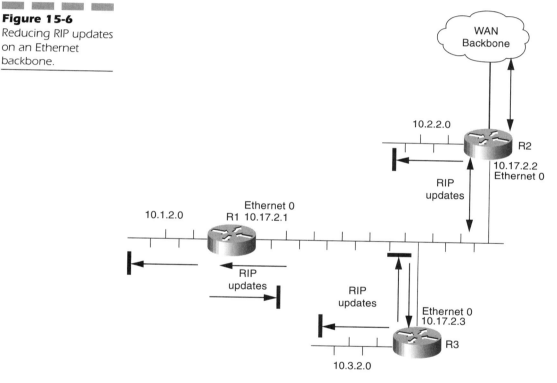

Figure 15-7
Reducing RIP updates
in an ATM LANE
network.

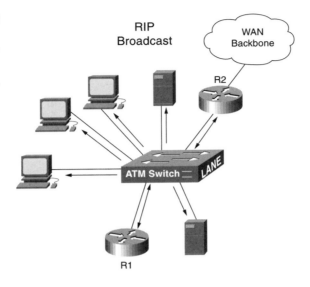

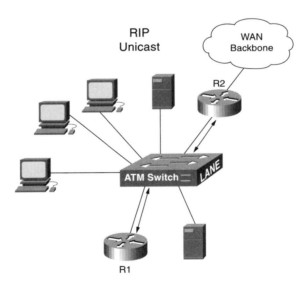

Specifying the Version of RIP

Two versions of RIP are available using Cisco IOS software. Specifying the
following command in the configuration

```
router rip
```

enables the Cisco IOS to receive RIP version 1 and version 2 packets. However, without specifically specifying the following commands

```
router rip
 version 2
```

only RIP version 1 is sent. Specifying the command version 2 as above indicates to the Cisco IOS that only RIP version 2 packets are sent and received. The Cisco router is instructed to send and receive RIP version 1 packets only by the following commands:

```
router rip
 version 1
```

Table 15-1 lists the various combinations of RIP packets being sent and received as the default behavior of RIP on a Cisco router.

Because there is the potential for two versions of RIP, the Cisco IOS software allows the router administrator to specify the version used on any specific interface to send and receive packets. This is useful in networks where legacy configurations are using UNIX workstations as routers. These older UNIX systems use RIP version 1 packet formats. For example, in Figure 15-8, a Sun workstation has multiple network interface cards and acts as a router to the various Ethernet segments. Subnet 10.1.1.0 on the Sun workstation is connected to the department backbone that connects the Cisco router.

The other two subnets on the Sun workstation, 10.1.2.0 and 10.1.3.0, require connectivity to the network 10.1.4.0, which is connected to the Cisco router R2. The RIP update between the routers is version 2. The Sun workstation acting as a router needs to learn of the 10.1.4.0 network through Cisco router R1.

The configuration on router R1 to accomplish RIP version 2 updates for router R2 and RIP version 1 updates for the Sun workstation is as follows:

Table 15-1	**Command Sequence**	**RIP Packet Support**
RIP Packet Default Support Based on RIP Definitions	router rip	Receives version 1 and version 2 / Sends version 1
	router rip version 1	Receives and sends version 1 packets only
	router rip version 2	Receives and sends version 2 packets only

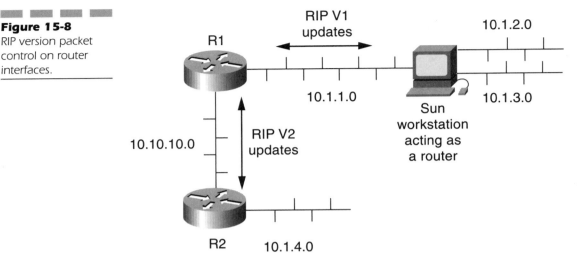

Figure 15-8
RIP version packet
control on router
interfaces.

Router R1 Configuration:

```
interface Ethernet 0
 description To Sun workstation
 ip address 10.1.1.2 255.255.255.0
 ip rip send version 1
 ip rip receive version 1
!
interface Ethernet 1
 description To router R2
 ip address 10.10.10.1 255.255.255.0
!
router rip
 version 2
 network 10.0.0.0
```

There is no need to specifically define the RIP version type on the interface Ethernet 1 since it defaults to the packet specified under the router rip command. In this case, interface Ethernet 1 sends and receives version 2 packets only. Table 15-2 lists the interface commands and their resulting functions.

If a Cisco router is placed on the departmental backbone, connecting router R1, and the Sun workstation acts as a router while RIP version 2 is used between the routers to support variable length subnet masks (VLSM) for networks connected to router R3, as shown in Figure 15.9, the configuration on router R1 is modified as follows:

Table 15-2	**RIP Version Interface Command**	**Resulting Function**
RIP Packet Version Interface Specific Commands	**ip rip send version 1**	Sends only RIP version 1 packets.
	ip rip receive version 1	Accepts only RIP version 1 packets.
	ip rip send version 2	Sends only RIP version 2 packets.
	ip rip receive version 2	Accepts only RIP version 2 packets.
	ip rip send version 1 2	Sends RIP version 1 and version 2 packets.
	ip rip receive version 1 2	Accepts both RIP version 1 or 2 packets.

Router R1 Configuration:

```
interface Ethernet 0
description To Sun workstation and router R3
ip address 10.1.1.2 255.255.255.0
ip rip send version 1 2
ip rip receive version 1 2
!
interface Ethernet 1
description To router R2
ip address 10.10.10.1 255.255.255.0
!
router rip
 version 2
 network 10.0.0.0
```

Router R1 requires the specification of both packet versions on interface Ethernet 0. This is because the packet version specified on the interface overrides the global default packet version defined under the router rip definition.

Enabling RIP Version 2 Authentication

RIP Version 2 supports router authentication as a means of providing security for routing table updates. RIP Version 1, however, does not support authentication. When using authentication, Cisco routers are protected from both advertising routes to and receiving routes from promiscuous

Figure 15-9
Use of RIP version 1
and 2 for sending
and receiving on the
same interface.

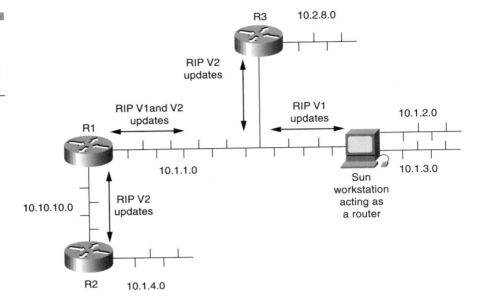

unauthorized routers. Authentication is defined on the interface level and hence provides for discreet selection of the interfaces that must use authentication.

Authentication is determined by the configuration of a key chain specific to the interface. The key chain is identified by using the following interface command:

ip rip authentication key-chain *name-of-chain*

The *name-of-chain* operand is the name given to the valid group of keys. Specifying the **ip rip authentication key-chain** command enables RIP version 2 authentication. If this command is not specified on an interface using RIP Version 2, then authentication is not performed.

Along with enabling authentication, the mode of authentication can be specified as well. The mode of authentication defaults to plain clear text, which becomes a security risk on connections that are deemed unsecured. Encrypted authentication must be specifically specified. The following interface command is used to define the type of mode used for authentication on an interface:

ip rip authentication mode {**text** | **md5**}

The **text** value is the default and should only be used on connections where security is not an issue. The **md5** value implements a keyed authentication based on the MD5 standard.

Authentication is enabled using the ip rip authentication key-chain interface command, but the authentication keys must be defined in order for authentication to occur. Authentication keys themselves are defined using the following global configuration commands:

key chain *name-of-chain*
key *number*
key-string *text*
accept-lifetime *start-time* {**infinite** | *end-time* | **duration** *seconds*}
send-lifetime *start-time* {**infinite** | *end-time* | **duration** *seconds*}

The value of the *name-of-chain* variable on the key-chain command must match a defined **ip rip authentication key-chain** command on an interface to exercise the authentication key chain. The *number* variable of the **key** command identifies the number of the key being defined. The *text* variable on the *key-string* command is the authentication text identified by the **key** *number* command used for authentication. Multiple keys can be configured. The key numbers supplied in the key chain definition are searched from lowest to highest, and the first valid key found is then authenticated. The router sends only one authentication packet despite multiple key definitions. The **key** *number* value in combination with the interface associated with the packet is used by the authentication algorithm and MD5 authentication to uniquely identify the authentication key.

The keys can be set to be active during specific times of a given day. This is done with the **accept-lifetime** and **send-lifetime** commands. The *start-time* variable of the accept-lifetime and send-lifetime commands defines the beginning time when the key will be in use. The *end-time* of the accept-lifetime and send-lifetime commands defines the end on a given day when the key will no longer be in use. The format of the *start-time* and *end-time* variable is

hh:mm:ss month day year

The *hh:mm:ss* variable is the two-digit 24-hour clock representation of the time of day. The month variable is the first three letters of the month. The day is the number of the day of the month, and the year variable is the four-digit number for the year. The *start-time* and *end-time* variables default to an infinite time period starting from January 1, 1993. The **infinite** keyword can be used as the end-time value, indicating that the key never times out after the value of the *start-time* variable has been reached. The **duration** keyword, followed by a valid value for the *seconds* variable, can also be used instead of the end-time variable value to define the usage length for the key. The following is an example of a configuration using RIP Version 2 and authentication between two Cisco routers.

Router R1 Configuration:

```
interface Ethernet 0
 ip address 10.163.8.1 255.255.255.0
 ip rip authentication key-chain colors
 ip rip authentication mode md5
!
router rip
 network 10.0.0.0
 version 2
!
key chain colors
 key 1
 key-string blue
 accept-lifetime 07:00:00 Feb 28 1999 duration 7200
 send-lifetime 08:00:00 Feb 28 1999 duration 3600
 key 2
 key-string green
 accept-lifetime 00:00:00 Mar 1 1999 infinite
 send-lifetime 00:30:00 Mar 1 1999 infinite

Router R2 Configuration:

interface ethernet 0
 ip address 10.163.8.2 255.255.255.0
 ip rip authentication key-chain colors
 ip rip authentication mode md5
!
router rip
 network 10.0.0.0
 version 2
!
key chain colors
 key 1
 key-string blue
 accept-lifetime 07:30:00 Feb 28 1999 duration 7200
 send-lifetime 06:30:00 Feb 28 1999 duration 3600
 key 2
 key-string green
 accept-lifetime 23:30:00 Feb 28 1999 infinite
 send-lifetime 00:00:00 Mar 1 1999 infinite
```

In these configurations, the two routers first use the keys identified by number 1 because the search order is from lowest to highest. The routers then use the number 2 key to authenticate routing updates between them.

The start time on router R1 is defined to ensure the acceptance and delivery of RIP version 2 packet updates to router R2, given a 30-minute cushion on the time differences between the routers. The second key (number 2) on each router takes effect once the clocks on each router have met the start-time criteria and last indefinitely.

NOTE: *Both routers must use RIP Version 2 and have authentication enabled, in addition to the accept and send lifetime value being coordinated. Both routers must also specify the same key-string that will then force the router to examine the accept and send lifetime values.*

Disable RIP Version 2 Route Summarization

Route summarization is enabled by default when using the RIP Version 2 routing protocol. The Cisco IOS software summarizes the RIP Version 2 routes across classful network boundaries. This is in contrast to RIP Version 1, which is also a classful routing protocol but does not communicate the subnets across different major networks.

Route summarization is the process of summarizing routes with long masks to routes with shorter masks that still meet the initial routing requirement. Classful routing protocols only use the full prefixes of each IP network classification if a subnetted network is directly connected to the router, meaning 8 bits for a Class A, 16 bits for a Class B, and 24 bits for a Class C address. Summarization is useful in RIP Version 2 due to its support of VLSM. In Figure 15.10, for example, router R1 connects to router R2 through serial interface 0 and router R3 through serial interface 1.

The networks connected to router R2 and router R3 are summarized in the RIP Version 2 update packets to router R1 from router R2 and R3. RIP Version 2 summarizes the following network addresses into two routing entries using RIP Version 2:

Using the router sh ip route command on router R1, the summarized routing entries will be displayed as

```
R 172.16.0.0/16 [120/1] via 172.30.1.1, 00:00:01, Serial0/0
R 172.20.0.0/16 [120/1] via 172.31.1.1, 00:00:01, Serial0/1
```

Figure 15-10

RIP Version 2
network
configuration used
for route
summarization.

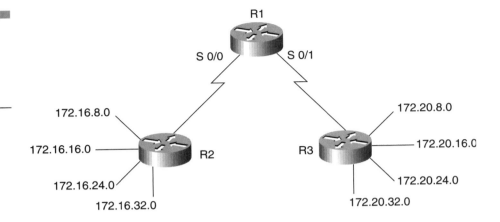

Table 15-3

Network addresses
to be summarized
in Figure 15-10.

IP Subnet	Subnet Mask
172.16.8.0	255.255.255.0
172.16.16.0	255.255.255.0
172.16.24.0	255.255.255.0
172.16.32.0	255.255.255.0
172.20.8.0	255.255.255.0
172.20.16.0	255.255.255.0
172.20.24.0	255.255.255.0
172.20.32.0	255.255.255.0

Using route summarization with RIP Version 2 reduces router overhead and bandwidth required to send routing updates.

Route summarization is the desired approach when using RIP Version 2. If a subnet is disconnected, however, the routers will not be able to correctly advertise the subnets. Figure 15-11 illustrates this issue. Router R2 has subnet 172.20.8.0 and router R3 has subnet 172.20.16.0, causing a disconnect of the subnets. Router R1, after receiving summarized entries from router R2 and R3, indicates two ways to the 172.20.0.0 network, which is not really the case.

The sh ip route command displays the following on router R1, based on router summarization updates from R2 and R3:

```
R 172.20.0.0/16 [120/1] via 172.31.1.1, 00:00:01, Serial0/0
R 172.20.0.0/16 [120/1] via 172.30.1.1, 00:00:01, Serial0/1
```

The resulting routing table will cause connectivity problems for two reasons. First, due to the fact that the hop count is the same, the router will load balance packets between serial interface 0/0 and serial interface 0/1. Secondly, this will cause only 50 percent of the packets to successfully reach their true destination. This type of topology can be corrected by disabling route summarization using the following router configuration mode command:

no auto-summary

Entering this in the configuration for routers R2 and R3 will disable summarization and cause the full subnet and host-routing information to be transmitted to router R1. The sh ip route command issued on router R1 will now display the following entries:

```
R 172.20.8.0/24 [120/1] via 172.30.1.1, 00:00:01, Serial0/0
R 172.20.16.0/24 [120/1] via 172.31.1.1, 00:00:01, Serial0/1
```

The no–auto-summary command on router R2 and R3 forces the RIP Version 2 updates to advertise the full mask for each of the subnets. Now packets through router R1 for resources on subnet 172.20.8.0 will only be directed out serial interface 0/0. Likewise, packets through router R1 for resources on subnet 172.20.16.0 will only be directed out serial interface 0/1.

Figure 15-11
Disconnected networks and RIP V2 route summarization.

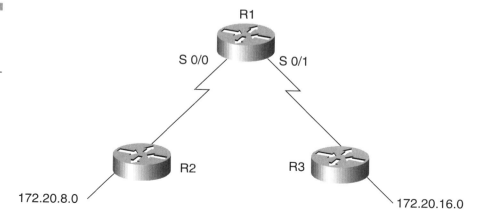

Disabling the Validation of Source IP Addresses

Many network configurations require multiple IP network definitions. RIP validates the source IP address of the routing update being received. If the source IP address of the routing update packet being received is on the same network as the IP address of the interface receiving the update, the routing update packet is processed. If the received routing update packet source IP address is not on the same network as the interface receiving the routing update packet, then the packet is discarded. A scenario where this is possible is the use of secondary IP addressing on interfaces. Figure 15-12 illustrates this configuration.

Router R1 in Figure 15-12 is connected to the same Ethernet segment as router R2 via a hub. Router R1 has its Ethernet interface defined as IP address 172.16.1.1, using 255.255.0.0 as the subnet mask. This same interface on router R1 also has a secondary IP address defined as 172.17.1.1, using 255.255.255.0 as the subnet mask. Router R2 connected to the same hub defines its Ethernet connection as 172.17.1.2, using 255.255.255.0 as the subnet mask. When the routers begin sending RIP-routing updates, the following message can be observed in the log of router R2, using the Debug IP Routing Information Protocol privileged command:

Ignored v1 update from bad source 172.16.1.1 on Ethernet0

This message indicates that the RIP update packets being received on Ethernet 0 of router R2 are not on a connected network. The source IP address of the routing packet received from router R1 is not a network connected to interface Ethernet 0 on router R2 and is hence discarded by router R2. To overcome this in the network configuration presented in Figure 15-12, the validation of the source IP address can be disabled using the following command:

no validate-update-source

Using this command, the validation process of incoming RIP update packets is disabled and the router, which in this case is router R2, receives the routing updates. The configuration of the two routers in Figure 15.12 that utilize this command is as follows:

Figure 15-12

The off-network routing configuration and the effect of disabling source IP address validation.

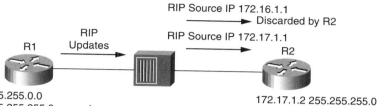

Validated Source IP Address

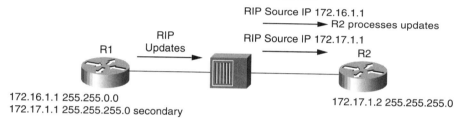

Non-validated Source IP Address

Configuration router R1:

```
interface Ethernet 0
 ip address 172.17.1.1 255.255.255.0 secondary
 ip address 172.16.1.1 255.255.0.0
 !
router rip
 network 172.16.0.0
 network 172.17.0.0
```

Configuration router R2:

```
interface Ethernet 0
 ip address 172.17.1.2 255.255.255.0
 !
router rip
 network 172.17.0.0
 no validate-update-source
```

This enables router R2 to place updates provided by router R1 source IP address 172.16.1.1 into its routing table. It is recommended that this command not be used because it can lead to confusion in the routing tables and possibly cause routing loops.

Reducing Routing Loops with Split-horizon

A router advertising routes out of an interface that the routing information was received on frequently causes routing loops. The split-horizon feature employed for distance-vector routing protocols like RIP reduces the possibility of routing loops by blocking routing updates to connected routers from which the routing update was originally received. Figure 15-13 diagrams this scenario.

This type of scenario is most prevalent on broadcast type IP networks such as LANs. As shown in Figure 15-13, the routing advertisements received by router R1 for networks connected to router R2 are not sent to router R2 from router R1 in its routing update packets. Likewise, router R2 does not send routing advertisements to router R1 for networks attached to router R1.

Non-broadcast networks like Frame Relay, however, require split-horizon to be disabled. The Cisco IOS automatically disables split-horizon for Frame Relay, ATM, and SMDS networks when subinterfaces are defined on the physical interface, but split-horizon is enabled for all other network connections. If split-horizon is disabled on an interface connecting a packet-switched network like X.25, it must be disabled on all other routers connecting to the same packet-switched network.

Spilt-horizon is disabled using the following interface configuration command:

no ip split-horizon

Enabling split-horizon for a specific interface is accomplished by entering the following interface command:

ip split-horizon

Tuning RIP Update Packet Delays

In many situations, the network topology consists of a high-end Cisco router acting as a hub router that connects multiple remote routers. The remote routers are usually lower-end routers servicing small remote offices. The high-end Cisco router at the hub is a higher-performance router and hence can cause the lower-end remote office router CPU to become overutilized

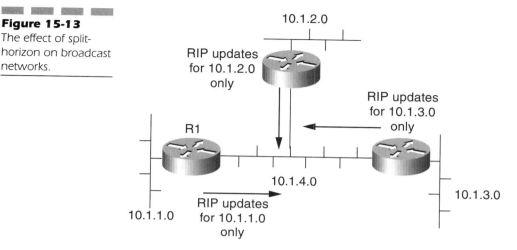

Figure 15-13
The effect of split-
horizon on broadcast
networks.

when processing RIP updates. The Cisco IOS allows for the router administrator to delay the packets for delivery through the use of the following
router configuration command:

output-delay *delay*

The router will delay the sending of RIP update packets to all RIP interfaces by the value defined for the delay variable in the output-delay router
command. The delay variable can be specified in the range of 8 to 50
expressed in milliseconds.

RIP Updates and the Effect on Bandwidth

RIP-routing updates are sent every 30 seconds to all RIP routers on interfaces supporting the RIP-routing protocol. Remember that the RIP process
on the router can determine which interface to send RIP updates on by
using the networks specified under the router-rip configuration. Because
RIP automatically sends updates every 30 seconds, there can be a sudden
increase in temporary bandwidth required.

An RIP update packet can have up to 25 route entries. The RIP update header is 36 bytes and each route entry is 20 bytes. A single routing update packet can then be as large as 536 bytes.

To determine the amount of bandwidth used by RIP in your network, use the following formula:

\# of advertised routes / 25 entries = # of packets
\# of packets x 36 bytes of header = # of bytes for headers
\# of advertised routes x 20 bytes for each entry = # of bytes for entries
\# of bytes for headers + # of bytes for entries = # of bytes (every 30 seconds)
\# of bytes / 30 second updates x 8 bits per second = bandwidth required for sending RIP updates

Suppose the RIP network has 200 advertised routes, for example. Using the formula, the bandwidth used every 20 seconds on RIP interfaces is as follows:

200/25 = 8 packets
8 x 36 = 288 bytes for headers
200 x 20 = 4,000 bytes for entries
288 + 4000 = 4,288 bytes
(4288/30) x 8 = 1,143 bps or 1.1 Kbps

This does not seem like much for many serial-line connections. But suppose the serial line is connecting to a Frame Relay network with 50 DLCIs connecting to the interface. The bandwidth requirement is now 50 x 1.1 Kbps, or 50.5 Kbps on the serial interface. This can lead to severe bandwidth constraints on the Frame Relay connection for remote locations where 56 Kbps is often used as the Frame Relay bandwidth.

Connecting 50 remote locations over the 56-Kbps Frame Relay connection in this scenario will require a full-committed information rate (CIR) of 56 Kbps to guarantee that the RIP update packets will be sent through the network. If the CIR is low, then there is the potential that the RIP updates will be dropped by the public Frame Relay network switches and hence the routers will not be updated appropriately.

CHAPTER 16

Configuring
IGRP Routing
Protocol

Interior Gateway Routing Protocol (IGRP) is a Cisco proprietary distance-vector-based routing protocol. IGRP uses metrics (termed vectors) to determine the best route to a network. IGRP uses delay, bandwidth, reliability, and load for determining the calculated optimal route. Cisco IOS allows router administrators to set weights to these metrics in order to influence the metric calculation.

Cisco IGRP enhances routing through the use of multiple paths between two networks. IGRP can use these equal-cost paths to perform load balancing on a packet-by-packet or destination-by-destination round-robin fashion. If a connection becomes inoperative in a dual equal-bandwidth configuration, IGRP can perform an automatic switchover to the remaining connection. In addition, IGRP provides the mechanism with multiple paths of unequal cost between routers in order to improve performance. In such a situation, the lower-cost path will be used more often than the higher-cost one.

IGRP has three flavors of route entries in its routing table: interior, system, and exterior routes. As shown in Figure 16-1, interior routes are advertisements describing paths between subnetworks attached to a router interface. Interior route entries include the subnet mask for the interface. If the network defined to a router interface is not subnetted, IGRP does not advertise this route as an interior route. Instead, non-subnetted interfaces are advertised using system routes.

Figure 16-1
IGRP route types within a network topology.

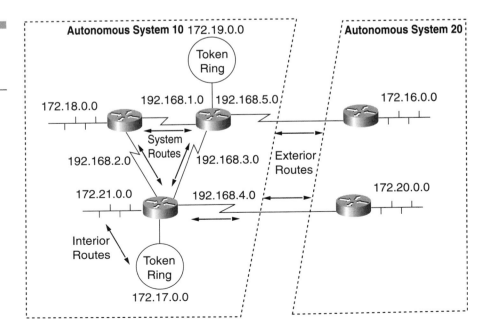

System route advertisements describe routes between networks within the same autonomous system. IGRP uses the concept of autonomous systems (AS) to isolate routing domains. The system routes are determined by the network definition of an interface and system route information gathered from the receipt of other IGRP routers within the autonomous system. The system routes describe the path on the network boundary and do not include subnet mask information.

The final route advertisement describes paths to exterior routes. Exterior routes describe to other autonomous systems the path that is used by the routing in determining the gateway of last resort. The gateway of last resort is chosen from the exterior routes and is chosen for packets that are destined for networks that are not known within the autonomous system routing tables. In networks with multiple routers, connecting the same two autonomous systems can have different gateway-of-last-resort routes.

Managing IGRP Updates and Route Advertisements

IGRP, like RIP, has a set period for delivering the routing table entries between adjacent routers. IGRP defaults the period to 90 seconds. This is a modifiable time period, but most networks operate smoothly using this default value.

The IGRP process must first recognize that an interface has become active and the IP network address assigned to the interface is defined for IGRP routing. After this recognition, the router broadcasts the IGRP routing table out of the interface. At this point, the IGRP process begins the 90-second timer.

Like RIP, IGRP uses UDP to send the route entries and hence the router has no knowledge as to whether the updates were successfully delivered to an adjacent router. Because of this, IGRP will declare a route as inaccessible if an update is not received from a router on the interface defined as the outbound port within three routing updates. That is, 270 seconds must pass by for the route to be labeled as inaccessible. If seven route-update periods have elapsed (630 seconds), the IGRP process removes the route from the routing table.

One of the advantages of using IGRP over RIP version 1 is the reduced time for route convergence. IGRP implements three different algorithms to minimize convergence time: holddowns, split-horizons, and poison-reverse updates.

The Holddown Algorithm for IGRP

The holddown algorithm instructs the IGRP process in updating and then propagating a new calculated route due to a connection that has become inoperable for a period of time. The time period calculated by IGRP is just a little longer than the time period calculated to update all the routers within the network of the new calculated route(s). Using this holddown algorithm, a Cisco router using IGRP avoids erroneous routing updates.

For example, in Figure 16-2, a router (R1) looses its connection to router R2, which detects the outage due to the lack of routing updates. Router R2 recalculates new routes for networks once reachable through router R1 and sends the update routes to its neighbors. This causes router R3 in Figure 16-2 to then recalculate its routes to the networks connected to router R1 based on information from router R2. This triggered update mechanism is propagated throughout the network.

Herein lies the problem. Some routers in the network, not yet being updated with the outage, will send the previously known viable calculated route, as is the case with router R4. Router R4 sends its update prior to recognizing the outage of router R1, as if it is still available. Router R3 now contains an update that router R4 can get to the networks on router R1. This update is sent to router R2, which then calculates a new route for networks off of router R1 based on the originating update from router R4. Router R1 now believes that it can route packets destined for networks connected to router R1 through router R3, which then in turn will route the packets to router R4.

Now router R4 has recognized that connectivity to router R1 is down and sends an update to R3, which then forwards an update to R2. The holddown mechanism prevents router R2 from updating its routing table with the outage and then sends an updated routing table after the above scenario has taken place, thus avoiding an erroneous routing table information and long convergence time.

The Split-horizon Algorithm for IGRP

Split-horizons work for IGRP, just as with RIP. Route information received on an interface is never sent back out the same interface. Without split-horizon in effect, a routing loop, as shown in Figure 16-3, is possible.

In Figure 16-3, a routing loop is created when the Ethernet to network 192.168.7.0 becomes inactive if split-horizon is not implemented. Router R2, having learned of the existence of network 192.168.7.0 from router R1,

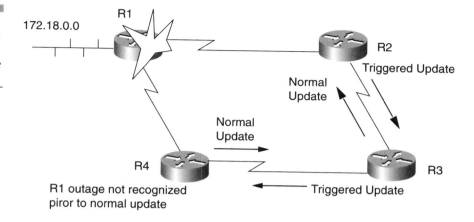

Figure 16-2
IGRP-routing updates
of a lost connection
with and without the
use of holddown.

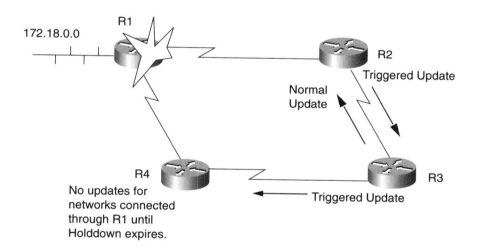

sends an update to router R1 that network 192.168.7.0 can be reached in two hops. Router R1 now sends an update back to router R2, increasing the hop count and updates the routing table in R2. Now router R2 does it again. This iteration continues until delay has reached 167 seconds and the network connection is marked as unreachable. Split-horizon prevents such a loop from happening. Holddowns, in concert with split-horizon for IGRP-based routing environments, add a greater degree of stability to the network than with RIP V1.

Figure 16-3
A routing loop
created from split-
horizon being
disabled.

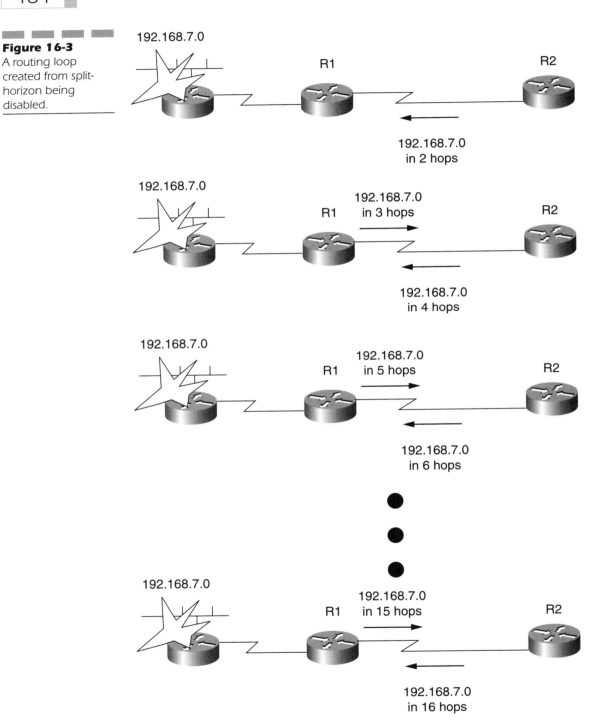

The Poison-reverse Updates Algorithm for IGRP

As a router receives an update from a neighbor with an increased metric, it marks the route as unusable. The router will update the path as usable after it has received a follow-up update confirming the metric change. The confirmation happens within the periodic routing-table update time of 90 seconds. This enables IGRP routers to defeat larger routing loops that may occur within the network.

As the increased metric indicates a loop, it does not necessarily mean that there is a loop. IGRP sends a poison-reverse update to adjacent routers that instructs the IGRP process to place the route in question in holddown. Cisco's IGRP sends poison-reverse updates when a metric has increased by a factor of 1.1 or greater.

Defining IGRP as a Routing Process

The following global configuration command is used to identify to the Cisco IOS that a routing protocol is being defined:

router

Cisco IOS starts the IGRP routing protocol process by entering the following global configuration command:

router igrp *autonomous-system*

The *autonomous-system* variable is either a registered or an internal-use-only autonomous-system number that identifies the routes of the IGRP network. This value is also used to identify the IGRP process executing in the router. It can also be referred to as the process-id for the IGRP route process being defined. Each router using IGRP must specify the same autonomous-system number in order for the routers to exchange and update IGRP routing tables.

The routing tables are defined by entering the network command under the router igrp command. The format of the network command is

network *network-number*

The variable *network-number* is the network number of a network directly connected to the router. For example, in Figure 16-4, the three routers are connected using IGRP as the routing protocol. Each router specifies the network address of a directly connected network under the router IGRP definition. This enables each router to advertise the IP network to its neighboring IGRP routers. The *network-number* is the Class A, B, or C IP network assigned to the interfaces on the router. The use of subnet masks for identifying the network is not used on the network command.

Also in the figure, network 10.0.0.0 is defined to all the routers, while network 192.168.15.0 is defined to only router 1, network 192.168.16.0 is defined to router 2, and network 192.168.14.0 is defined to router 3 only.

The IGRP configuration commands for each router are as follows:

Router 1:

```
interface serial 0
 ip address 10.16.1.1 255.255.255.0
!
interface serial 1
 ip address 10.16.2.1 255.255.255.0
!
interface Ethernet 0
 ip address 192.168.15.1 255.255.255.0
!
router igrp 100
 network 10.0.0.0
 network 192.168.15.0
```

Router 2:

```
interface serial 0
 ip address 10.16.1.2 255.255.255.0
!
interface serial 1
 ip address 10.16.3.2 255.255.255.0
!
interface Ethernet 0
 ip address 192.168.16.1 255.255.255.0
!
router igrp 100
 network 10.0.0.0
 network 192.168.16.0
```

Router 3:

```
interface serial 0
 ip address 10.16.2.3 255.255.255.0
!
interface serial 1
 ip address 10.16.3.3 255.255.255.0
!
```

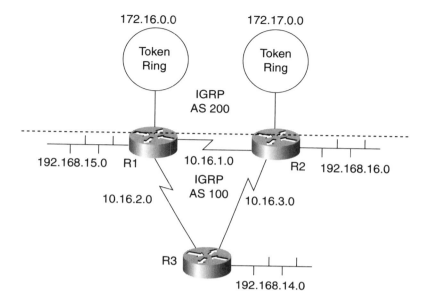

Figure 16-4

IGRP-routing protocol
used between Cisco
routers.

```
interface Ethernet 0
 ip address 192.168.14.1 255.255.255.0
!
router igrp 100
 network 10.0.0.0
 network 192.168.14.0
```

IGRP sends and receives updates for networks only on interfaces where the network is connected and only to the IGRP autonomous system neighbors being advertised with autonomous system number 100. If a second IGRP process were defined with different networks, they would not communicate with the networks of the other autonomous system.

As seen in Figure 16-4, the serial interfaces connecting the routers, along with the Ethernets on all the routers that have their networks in the routing tables, are in IGRP 100. The Token Ring networks on the routers, as well as the serial links, are defined in IGRP network 200. The devices on the Token Ring cannot communicate with the devices on the Ethernet in this configuration. This is because the IGRP autonomous systems are viewed as two independent networks. Routers R1 and R2 have two separate routing tables, one for each AS defined. The following configuration illustrates the new definitions to support the two IGRP autonomous system networks:

Router 1:

```
interface serial 0
 ip address 10.16.1.1 255.255.255.0
!
interface serial 1
 ip address 10.16.2.1 255.255.255.0
!
interface Ethernet 0
 ip address 192.168.15.1 255.255.255.0

interface Tokenring 0
 ip address 172.16.1.1 255.255.255.0
!
router igrp 100
 network 10.0.0.0
 network 192.168.15.0
!
router igrp 200
 network 10.0.0.0
 network 172.16.0.0
```

Router 2:

```
interface serial 0
 ip address 10.16.1.2 255.255.255.0
!
interface serial 1
 ip address 10.16.2.2 255.255.255.0
!
interface Ethernet 0
 ip address 192.168.16.1 255.255.255.0

interface Tokenring 0
 ip address 172.17.1.1 255.255.255.0

router igrp 100
 network 10.0.0.0
 network 192.168.16.0
!
router igrp 200
 network 10.0.0.0
 network 172.17.0.0
```

Router 3:

```
interface serial 0
 ip address 10.16.2.3 255.255.255.0
!
interface serial 1
 ip address 10.16.3.3 255.255.255.0
!
interface Ethernet 0
 ip address 192.168.14.1 255.255.255.0
!
router igrp 100
 network 10.0.0.0
 network 192.168.14.0
```

In order for devices on these two IGRP networks to communicate, the router must redistribute the routes between the two IGRP networks. Router redistribution among routing protocols is discussed in Chapter 19, "Route Redistribution."

Using Unicast IGRP Routing Updates

Non-Broadcast Multi-Access (NBMA) networks, like X.25 and Frame Relay, provide multiple connections over a single interface. As in Figure 16-5, the NBMA topology provides for a single physical interface on the router to a public network. The public network provider delivers the packets or frames to the destination NBMA address or identifier.

The Cisco IOS software must be defined in such a scenario to specifically identify the IGRP routers over the single interface by specifying the neighboring routers' IP addresses. For example, in Figure 16-5, router R1 must define the IP addresses of router R2 and R3 under the IGRP-routing protocol definition to send IGRP updates to the adjacent routers R2 and R3 through the single Frame Relay interface.

Router R1 specifies the IP addresses of the neighboring routers R2 and R3 connecting over the single Frame Relay interface by using the global configuration command neighbor. The format of the command is

neighbor *ip-address*

The *ip-address* value is the IP address assigned to the routers on the far end of the public NBMA network connection. In Figure 16-5, the configuration in router R1 is specified as the following:

Router R1 Configuration:

```
interface serial 0
 encapsulation frame-relay
 ip address 10.16.17.1 255.255.255.0
!
interface ethernet 0
 ip address 10.1.10.1 255.255.255.0
!
router igrp 100
 network 10.0.0.0
 neighbor 10.16.17.2
 neighbor 10.16.17.3
```

Figure 16-5
IGRP unicast updates
using the neighbor
command.

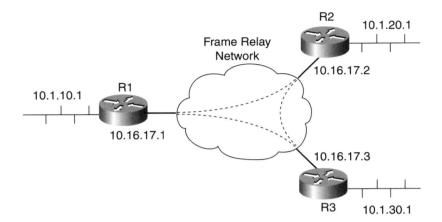

Router R1 sends IGRP updates to the IP addresses 10.16.17.2 and 10.16.17.3 and has learned of the DLCI for each of these on the Frame Relay multipoint connection using Frame Relay Inverse ARP. The Frame Relay Inverse ARP builds a table mapping the DLCI numbers to the IP addresses dynamically. The configuration for router R2 and router R3 are as follows:

Router R2 Configuration:

```
interface serial 0
 encapsulation frame-relay
 ip address 10.16.17.2 255.255.255.0
!
interface ethernet 0
 ip address 10.1.20.1 255.255.255.0
!
router igrp 100
 network 10.0.0.0
 neighbor 10.16.17.1
 neighbor 10.16.17.3
```

Router R3 Configuration:

```
interface serial 0
 encapsulation frame-relay
 ip address 10.16.17.3 255.255.255.0
!
interface ethernet 0
 ip address 10.1.30.1 255.255.255.0
!
router igrp 100
 network 10.0.0.0
 neighbor 10.16.17.1
 neighbor 10.16.17.2
```

NOTE: *It is highly recommended to use subinterfaces to enable broadcast-routing updates. See Chapter 22, "Defining Frame Relay" for more information.*

As was discussed with RIP unicast topologies, the neighbor command can be used to selectively define which routers on a given interface will participate in routing updates along with the passive-interface command. In this sample configuration, the workstations connected to R1 LAN segment Ethernet 1 need only communicate with the R2 router to connect to the WAN and the stations on segment Ethernet 1 router R2. The network topology is diagrammed in Figure 16-6 and the following IGRP configuration demonstrates this concept:

Router R1 Configuration:

```
interface Ethernet 0
 ip address 10.17.2.1 255.255.255.0
!
interface Ethernet 1
 ip address 10.12.2.1 255.255.255.0
!
router igrp 100
 network 10.0.0.0
 neighbor 10.17.2.2
 passive-interface Ethernet 0
 passive-interface Ethernet 1
```

Router R2 Configuration:

```
!
interface Serial 0
 ip address 172.16.10.1 255.255.255.0

interface Ethernet 0
 ip address 10.17.20.2 255.255.255.0
!
interface Ethernet 1
 ip address 10.22.2.1 255.255.255.0
!
router igrp 100
 network 10.0.0.0
 network 172.16.0.0
 passive-interface Ethernet 1
```

Router R3 Configuration:

```
interface Ethernet 0
 ip address 10.17.2.3 255.255.255.0
!
 interface Ethernet 1
```

```
    ip address 10.32.2.1 255.255.255.0
    !
router igrp 100
    network 10.0.0.0
    neighbor 10.17.2.2
    passive-interface Ethernet 0
    passive-interface Ethernet 1
```

In this configuration example, router R3 does not receive updates from router R1 because the passive-interface command is specified for the Ethernet interface connecting router R1 on IP subnet 10.17.2.0. The same holds true for R1 for receiving updates from R3. The passive-interface command indicates to the Cisco IOS that the interface specified on the command will not be used for sending routing updates, but the specified interface can receive updates. Router R2 receives and exchanges routing updates with R1 and R3 because the IP address of R2 is defined on the neighbor command of router R1 and R3. Figure 16-6 illustrates this network topology.

Further IGRP update reduction is possible by implementing the passive-interface command for LAN segments connecting end-user stations only.

Figure 16-6
Reducing IGRP-update reduction on an Ethernet backbone using unicast.

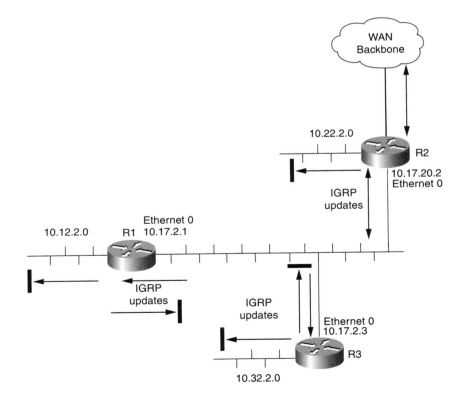

This eliminates the unnecessary IGRP update traffic entering the network interface cards of the workstations.

The result of this configuration is that update packets are exchanged only between R1 and R2 and between R2 and R3. Using this method, the interface cards on routers not requiring IGRP routing table updates will not have to process unneeded packets. In another example, if the same three routers are attached through a switch, then the workstations attached to the same switch no longer receive unnecessary IGRP-routing updates. This is especially useful in switched networks employing ATM LANE topologies where unicast-directed IGRP-routing updates are only forwarded to the destination MAC address within the packet, instead of an all-broadcast destination MAC address, as is normally found with IGRP update packets. Figure 16.7 illustrates this configuration.

Using this concept on switched connections saves switch processor resources and eliminates the IGRP updates from being propagated to all the workstations also connected on the same switch.

Increasing Throughput and Reliability Using Unequal-cost Paths

Both RIP and IGRP distribute IP packets over equal cost paths on a packet-by-packet basis or on a destination-by-destination basis. IGRP, however, can provide for load balancing over unequal cost paths, enabling greater throughput and reliability with minimal convergence. The unequal-cost load balancing is provided over a maximum of four paths to a given destination network. The paths considered by IGRP must be calculated as feasible paths. A feasible path is determined by the route update from an adjacent router. If the adjacent router's routing update for a destination network has a lower value than the calculated metric of this router and the final calculated metric for the alternate route is equal to or greater than the best metric for the destination network on this router.

The following configuration illustrates the use of the variance definition for determining the feasibility of alternate routes for use in unequal-cost load balancing.

Router R1 in Figure 16-8:

```
router igrp 100
  variance 10
```

Figure 16-7
IGRP updates
reduction in an ATM
LANE network using
unicast.

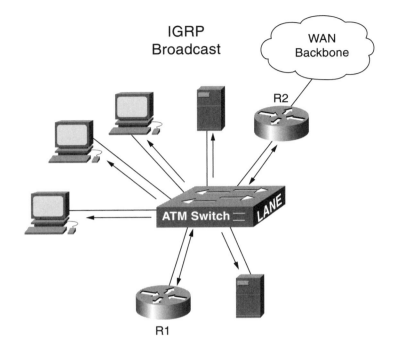

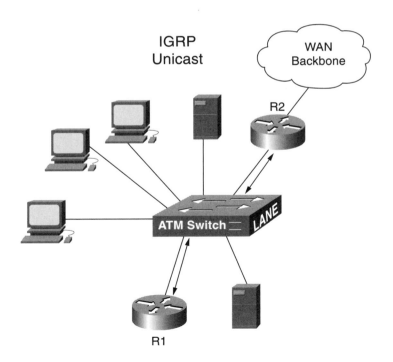

The variance command value of 10 in the example is the multiplier used for determining the feasibility of the alternate routes. It represents the metric multiplier. If you multiply the metric of the route with the best (lowest) metric by the variance value, all routes with a metric less than or equal to that result will be considered equal cost paths, provided that the loop prevention conditions (metric through the next router) are met. Metrics with resulting values equal to or greater than that will be considered unequal-cost paths. The metric value for the variance command can range from 0 to 128. The default multiplier is 1 for the variance command.

Figure 16-8 illustrates the unequal-cost path feasibility calculation. Router R1 connects to network 172.16.0.0 and has a metric of 50. Router R2 updates router R1 for network 172.16.0.0 with a metric of 40. Using the variance value of 10 for the IGRP autonomous system router R1 will add and use the route through router R2 for connection to network 172.16.0.0. This occurs because:

1. The metric for network 172.16.0.0 is greater than the received metric from router R2.

2. The resulting product of router R1's metric (50) multiplied by the variance value (10) is greater than or equal to the calculated metric of router R1 using router R2 to route traffic to the 172.16.0.0 network.

In concert with the variance command, the traffic-share command can be specified to manage just how packets are balanced across unequal-cost paths. The command format is

traffic-share {balanced | min}

The **traffic-share balanced** command shares the traffic proportionately to the ratio of metrics for the routes. The **traffic-share min** command uses the route with the minimum cost. The **variance** command allows you to specify the multiplier for the load balancing to skew the load. Both commands are for IGRP and EIGRP only.

Altering IGRP Routing and Metric Computations

IGRP router metrics are altered using five constants and the type of service for the route. A router administrator can alter these metric values

Figure 16-8
IGRP unequal-cost
path feasibility
topology.

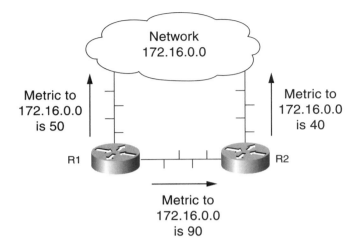

using the metric weights router configuration command. The format of the command is

metric weights *tos k1 k2 k3 k4 k5*

The *tos* variable currently defaults to the value of 0 and must always be specified as 0. The *k1* through *k5* values default to the following:

k1: 1

k2: 0

k3: 1

k4: 0

k5: 0

The values placed in the positional parameters of the metric weights command provide the values used as IGRP metric coefficients when determining the calculated metric for an IGRP route. Changing the defaults for these values changes the default behavior for all IGRP routing and metric calculations. Thus, changing the metrics can greatly affect network performance. The valid range for the numeric value of *k1-k5* is 0 to 4,294,967,295. Using 4,294,967,295 as a value for any of the coefficients results in the route being marked as unusable. The k1-k5 values are used in the IGRP metric calculation against the four major metric components of IGRP route calculation. These components are bandwidth, load, delay, and reliability.

NOTE: *Great care should be taken when modifying the default metric values for IGRP. It is strongly advised that the metric weight values should not be modified unless consulting with the Cisco TAC prior to and during the modification.*

The IGRP process calculates the metric by adding weighted values of different characteristics of the route entry. The standard formula for determining the metric is as follows:

metric = k1 x bandwidth + (k2 x bandwidth / (256 - load) + k3 x delay

The default metric values for k1-k5 affect this overall calculation by realizing that the k1 and k3 values both are 1 and the k2, k4, and k5 values equal 0. Applying the default values for the **metric weights** router command results in the following calculation:

metric = bandwidth + delay

Understanding this results in the need to understand the interface command **bandwidth**. The interface configuration command bandwidth allows for a router administrator to modify the bandwidth of the physical medium. For example, entering the following command

```
interface etherent 0
  bandwidth 5000
```

will end up causing interface Ethernet 0 on this router to have a less favorable metric than a router that uses the default bandwidth for a 10-Mbps Ethernet, which is 10,000 Kbps. The bandwidth command is expressed as

bandwidth *kilobits*

The *kilobits* value is in the valid range of 1 to 10,000,000, expressed in Kbps. This allows the router administrator to place a value as high as 10 terabits per second (Tbps) on an interface. With 1 Tbps technology proven and the capability to continually increase the bandwidth on fiber optic networks, this value may have a shorter life span than anticipated. The metric bandwidth value used by Cisco IOS running the IGRP process for serial interfaces defaults to 1.544 Mbps (T1 speed). This warrants that if the serial lines connecting to the router are less than a T1, then the bandwidth interface command must be specified to allow IGRP to calculate the true metric. For example, a 56-Kbps serial connection should be defined as

```
interface serial 0
  bandwidth 56
```

Since bandwidth is such a major factor in determining the metric for a route, great care must be used when using the bandwidth interface command.

Suppose the metric weights command were entered where the k2 value was changed from 0 to a value of 1. The command sequence is as follows:

```
router igrp 100
  metric weights 0 1 1 1 0 0
```

In this instance, the load metric becomes the deciding variable. The load value for an interface is calculated every five seconds, based on a five-minute weighted average. The load is presented as a fraction of 255, where 255 is a saturated link experiencing 100 percent utilization.

Setting the k2 coefficient to 1 can result in a route going into holddown when there is an increase in load, due to a large FTP or some other type of action that can consume bandwidth over a period of time. The net effect is that the metric ends up doubling the bandwidth, which can possibly make a slow link artificially inflated with bandwidth. In such a scenario, not only can a load rise fast enough to make a route unstable, it can also fall just as fast. A falling load will change the metric to become favorable and cause the Cisco router to use the Cisco IOS feature called flash update.

Flash update is a mechanism whereby the routing table is broadcast to the router's neighbors, prior to the update timer being expired. In the scenario described, multiple flash updates may occur due to the variant load, thus causing not only an unstable route for the specific path but causing the network to continuously perform convergence, which ends up in a convergence storm and an unstable network. It is because of the undeterministic characteristics found with IP networks that the metric defaults remain unaltered.

In addition to the formula noted above involving k values k1 through k3, k5 and k4 come into play if the k5 value specified on the metric weights IGRP router command is not zero. When this occurs, the following formula is also calculated to create the final metric for the route:

metric = metric x [k5 / (reliability + k4)]

A long-hand method for determining the metric can be performed for a specific router by performing the following:

1. Determine the smallest of all the bandwidths from outgoing interfaces and divide 10,000,000 by that number. (The bandwidth is scaled by 10,000,000 in kilobits per second.)

2. Add all the delays from the outgoing interfaces and divide this number by 10. (The delay is in 10s of microsecs.)

The path with the smallest metric is the best path. The router configuration for determining metric values is shown in Figure 16-9 and the default delay and bandwidth values used by IGRP for specific media types are shown in Table 16-1. These values can be found by issuing the router operation command show interfaces. An example for this is as follows:

```
R1#sh int e 0
Ethernet 0 is up, line protocol is up
Internet address is 192.168.9.22, subnet mask is 255.255.255.0
MTU 1500 bytes, BW 10000 Kbit, DLY 1000 usec, rely 255/255, load 1/255
Serial 0 is up, line protocol is up
Internet address is 192.168.19.9, subnet mask is 255.255.255.224
MTU 1500 bytes, BW 784 Kbit, DLY 20000 usec, rely 255/255, load 20/255

R2#sh int s 0
Serial 0 is up, line protocol is up
Internet address is 192.168.42.1, subnet mask is 255.255.255.224
MTU 1500 bytes, BW 448 Kbit, DLY 20000 usec, rely 255/255, load 1/255
Serial 1 is up, line protocol is up
Internet address is 192.168.19.8, subnet mask is 255.255.255.224
MTU 1500 bytes, BW 224 Kbit, DLY 20000 usec, rely 255/255, load 3/255

R1# sh ip route R2-s0
Total delay is 40000 microseconds, minimum bandwidth is 448 Kbit
   Known via "igrp 2022", distance 100, metric 26321
```

The calculation:

$$\text{Metric} = \text{bandwidth} + \text{delay}$$
$$= 10{,}000{,}000/448 + (20{,}000+20{,}000)/10$$
$$= 26321$$

```
R2# sh ip route R1-e0
Total delay is 21000 microseconds, minimum bandwidth is 224
Kbit Known via "igrp 2022", distance 100, metric 46742
```

$$\text{Metric} = \text{bandwidth} + \text{delay}$$
$$= 10{,}000{,}000/224 + (20.000 + 1000)/10$$
$$= 46742$$

Decreasing IGRP Route Convergence

The holddown mechanism is used by IGRP to assist in avoiding routing loops due to changes in route metrics. The Cisco IOS software places a route in a holddown state after receiving an update from a neighboring router

Figure 16-9
The router
configuration for
determining metric
values.

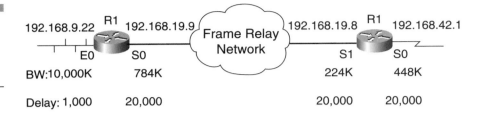

Table 16-1

Default Delay and
Bandwidth Values
Used by IGRP for
Specific Media
Types

Media Type	Delay	Bandwidth
Satellite	5120 (2 seconds)	5120 (500 Mbits)
Ethernet	25600 (1 ms)	256000 (10 Mbits)
1.544 Mbps	512000 (20,000 ms)	1,657,856 bits
64 kbps	512000 (20,000 ms)	40,000,000 bits
56 kbps	512000 (20,000 ms)	45,714,176 bits
10 kbps	512000 (20,000 ms)	256,000,000 bits
1 kbps	512000 (20,000 ms)	2,560,000,000 bits

that the network found on the route in question is now a greater distance
from the router or the network is no longer available. During the holddown
period, the known route metrics for the network in question is still advertised to the neighboring routers. Advertisements received from other
routers concerning the network in question are ignored. The ignoring of
updates to the network in question after receiving a metric update change
helps avoid the route loop. The time it takes for the routers to determine the
correct route and metric, however, can them increase the convergence time
for IGRP. In some instances, it is favorable to eliminate the holddown
mechanism, which reduces the time for convergence. Disabling the holddown mechanism is accomplished by entering the following configuration
IGRP router command:

```
no metric holddown
```

Entering this command disables the holddown mechanism. This configuration, however, must be the same for all routers in the IGRP autonomous system. Not disabling the holddown metric on all the IGRP autonomous system routers may result in routing loops.

To reenable the holddown mechanism after it has been disabled, the following IGRP router command must be entered on all the IGRP autonomous system routers:

```
metric holddown
```

Tuning IGRP Route Convergence

IGRP uses five timers for determining how routing tables are managed. These timers include an update timer, an invalid timer, a holddown timer, a flush timer, and a sleeptime timer.

- The `update timer` determines the amount of time measured in seconds for sending routing updates. The default value is 90 seconds.

- The `invalid timer` determines the amount of time measured in seconds that must expire without the router receiving route updates from neighboring routers for a known route. The default value is 270 seconds. If the invalid timer stops, the route is marked inaccessible and the route is advertised by the router to neighboring routers as unreachable. The route at this point has entered holddown state. Packets destined for the network in question, however, are still forwarded on the route.

- The `holddown timer` is measured in seconds and defaults to 280 seconds. This is the amount of time that updates for the route in holddown state are ignored. After the holddown period, updates for the route are now applied and the route is now reachable.

- The `flush timer` is the number of seconds that must pass prior to a route being removed from the routing table. This timer must be at minimum the sum of the interval and holddown timer values. The default is 630 seconds. Specifying a value that is less than the sum of the interval and holddown timer values results in the holddown timer never expiring. This allows an improper route to be added to the routing table on the update received.

The `sleeptime timer` is measured in milliseconds and delays routing updates due to a flash update. The sleeptime timer value should be less than the update timer to avoid unsynchronized routing tables. The default for this timer is 0 milliseconds.

The timers start after the routing table has been calculated. Modifying the timer values is accomplished using the IGRP router command:

timers basic *update invalid holddown flush* [*sleeptime*]

The *update* and *holddown* variables' range is from 0 to 429,496,729. The *invalid, flush,* and *sleeptime* variables' range from 1 to 4294967295.

In the following example, the IGRP process sends routing updates every 20 seconds.

```
router igrp 100
  timers basic 20 60 70 130
```

In 60 seconds, a route to a neighboring router is determined to be inaccessible if an update has not been received from the neighbor. The route then enters holddown. The holddown time of 70 seconds indicates that the updating of the route is ignored for an additional 70 seconds. At the end of the holddown period, the route is flushed from the routing table. The router then adds a new route based on the next received routing update for the original network in question. Making the timers to small may result in increased router utilization in large networks.

Controlling the Logical Size of an IGRP Network

IGRP being a distance-vector routing protocol measures distance between routers based on the hop count. Although RIP reaches its maximum at 16 (meaning infinity), IGRP can reach as high as 255 hop counts before declaring a route unreachable. Using the following command with IGRP, an autonomous system can be protected from a potential count-to-infinity problem. The format of this command is

metric maximum-hops *hops*

The *hops* value is a decimal value ranging from 1 to 255. The default is 100. For large networks, it may be necessary to increase the default value to enable routes over a complex routed WAN environment. The default of 100 indicates that any route with a hop count greater than 100 is advertised to its neighbors as unreachable.

Validate Source IP Addresses

Many network configurations require multiple IP network definitions. IGRP validates the source IP address of the routing update being received. If the source IP address of the routing update packet being received is on the same network as the IP address of the interface receiving the update, the routing update packet is processed. If the received routing update packet source IP address is not on the same network as the interface receiving the routing update packet, the packet is discarded. A scenario where this is possible is the use of secondary IP addressing on interfaces. Figure 16-10 illustrates this configuration.

Router R1 in Figure 16-10 is connected to the same Ethernet segment as router R2 via a hub. Router R1 has its Ethernet interface defined as IP address 192.168.16.1, using 255.255.0.0 as the subnet mask. This same interface on router R1 also has a secondary IP address defined as 192.168.17.1, using 255.255.255.0 as the subnet mask. Router R2 connected to the same hub defines its Ethernet connection as 192.168.17.2, using 255.255.255.0 as the subnet mask. When the routers begin sending RIP routing updates, the following message can be observed in the log of router R2, using the Debug IP Routing Information Protocol privileged command:

```
Ignored v1 update from bad source 192.168.16.1 on Ethernet0
```

This message is an indicator that the IGRP update packets being received on Ethernet 0 of router R2 are not on a connected network. The source IP address of the routing packet received from router R1 is not a network connected to interface Ethernet 0 on router R2 and is hence discarded by router R2. To overcome this in the network configuration presented in Figure 16-10, the validation of the source IP address can be disabled using the following command:

```
no validate-update-source
```

Using this command, the validation process of incoming IGRP update packets is disabled and the router, in this case router R2, receives the routing updates. The configuration of the two routers in Figure 16-10 using this command is as follows:

Configuration router R1:

```
interface Ethernet 0
 ip address 192.168.17.1 255.255.255.0 secondary
 ip address 192.168.16.1 255.255.0.0
 !
router igrp 100
 network 192.168.16.0
 network 192.168.17.0
```

Figure 16-10
The off-network
routing configuration
and the effect of
disabling the source
IP address validation.

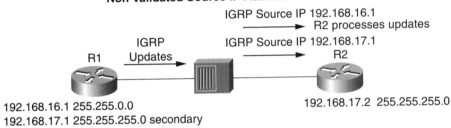

Validated Source IP Address

IGRP Source IP 192.168.16.1
→ Discarded by R2

IGRP
Updates
R1
IGRP Source IP 192.168.17.1
→ R2

192.168.16.1 255.255.0.0
192.168.17.1 255.255.255.0 secondary

192.168.17.2 255.255.255.0

Figure 16-10
The off-network
routing configuration
and the effect of
disabling the source
IP address validation.

Non-validated Source IP Address

IGRP Source IP 192.168.16.1
→ R2 processes updates

IGRP
Updates
R1
IGRP Source IP 192.168.17.1
→ R2

192.168.16.1 255.255.0.0
192.168.17.1 255.255.255.0 secondary

192.168.17.2 255.255.255.0

```
Configuration router R2:

interface Ethernet 0
 ip address 192.168.17.2 255.255.255.0
 !
router igrp100
 network 192.168.17.0
 no validate-update-source
```

This enables router R2 to place updates provided by router R1 source IP address 192.168.16.1 into its routing table. It is recommended that this command not be used, however, since it can lead to confusion in the routing tables and potentially cause routing loops.

IGRP Updates and the Effect on Bandwidth

Generally, IGRP updates flow every 90 seconds. Each IGRP packet can contain 104 route entries, for a total of 1,492 bytes, 38 of which are header information, and each route entry is 14 bytes. Advertising 1,000 routes over a Frame Relay link configured with 50 DLCIs, the request is approximately 720 KB of routing update data every 90 seconds, or 64 Kbps of bandwidth consumed. On a T1 link, this bandwidth would represent 4.2 percent of the bandwidth, with each update duration being 3.7 seconds. This overhead is an acceptable amount:

$$1000 / 104 = 9 \text{ packets X } 38 = 342 \text{ header bytes}$$

$$1000 \text{ X } 14 = 14{,}000 \text{ bytes of route entries}$$

$$\text{Total} = 14{,}342 \text{ bytes X } 50 \text{ DLCIs}$$
$$= 717 \text{ KB of IGRP updates every } 90 \text{ seconds}$$

$$717{,}000 \text{ bytes } / 90 \text{ X } 8 \text{ bits} = 63.7 \text{ kbps}$$

Configuring Enhanced IGRP Routing Protocol

Enhanced IGRP (EIGRP) is the Cisco proprietary routing protocol that fuses the best attributes of distance-vector routing protocols with those of link-state routing protocols. EIGRP is configured just like IGRP and uses the same metrics as IGRP. The enhancement is provided by the inclusion of using the Diffusing Update Algorithm (DUAL). DUAL was developed by SRI International under the direction of J.J. Garcia to achieve a rapid convergence routing protocol that virtually guarantees a loop-free network. The marriage of distance-vector, link-state, and DUAL results in the following characteristics of EIGRP:

- Rapid convergence
- Reduced bandwidth
- Increased network size
- Reduced router CPU utilization

Rapid convergence is due to the use of DUAL. This rapid convergence is achieved by a router using EIGRP to keep backup routes within the routing table. In other words, the least-cost (successor) and second-to-least-cost (feasible successors) routes for a destination network are kept within the routing table. This enables a router to quickly adapt to link outages without causing major network disruption within the network. The favored and backup routes are recalculated based on updates from neighboring routers. EIGRP updates neighboring routers after the initial convergence only when there is a change in a route and only for the changed route.

Because EIGRP sends updates on routes to neighbor EIGRP routes only when the state of a route to a destination network changes or when the metric for a route changes, these partial updates require considerably less bandwidth. In addition, the route update is sent only to the neighboring routes that require knowledge of the state change. Due to the incremental updates, EIGRP uses less CPU than IGRP.

Large networks have difficulty using RIP as the IP routing protocol due to the 15 hop limit. EIGRP enables much larger networks to be architected, increasing the hop limit to 255. This means that the EIGRP-calculated metric supports hop counts in the thousands, enabling very large network configurations. Using EIGRP also moves the network size restrictions up the protocol stack to the transport layer. EIGRP facilitates the transport layer deficiency of 15 hops by incrementing the transport control field by one after the packet has passed through 15 EIGRP routers and the next hop is an EIGRP router. If non-EIGRP routers on the packets utilize next hop, the transport control field is incremented.

Because EIGRP is a Cisco proprietary routing protocol, it has an additional benefit not found with open-standard routing protocols. EIGRP can also be used for delivering the routing and services information of Novell IPX RIP/SAP updates and AppleTalk Routing Table Maintenance Protocol (RTMP). The greater advantage in using EIGRP on these other routing protocols is that with Novell IPX networks, EIGRP sends incremental RIP/SAP updates between EIGRP routers. These updates are sent only when there is a change in the IPX entry. Furthermore, when using EIGRP for Novell networks, the hop count is now 255 versus the IPX RIP hop count of 15. EIGRP used for Novell IPX selects the best route to a destination based on the EIGRP metrics of bandwidth and delay, instead of the IPX metrics of tick and hop counts.

EIGRP uses three types of tables to determine routes. All these tables are used for the three networking protocols supported by EIGRP. These tables are named Neighbor, Topology and Routing. Each EIGRP router lists the address of the next hop router (the neighbor network layer address) and the interface on the router to which the neighbor is connected. The EIGRP process to verifies bidirectional communication using this table. The topology table contains the destination networks and up to six learned routes to each destination. These include the successor (best route) and feasible successors (backup routes). The routing table is the list of the best route (successor) to a destination network. The routing table is populated from the best route entries in the routing table for each destination network.

EIGRP maintains a set of tables for all enabled, supported network layer protocols. The IP network layer protocol is further supported by EIGRP using Variable Length subnet mask (VLSM) IP addressing and route summarization.

NOTE: *This chapter concerns the configuration of IP network layer protocol with EIGRP. Configuring EIGRP for Novell networks is discussed later in the book.*

Enable EIGRP as a Routing Protocol

Cisco IOS starts the EIGRP routing protocol process by entering the following global configuration command:

router eigrp *autonomous-system*

The *autonomous-system* variable is either a registered or an internal-use-only autonomous system number that identifies the routes of the EIGRP network. This value ranges from 1 to 65535 and is also used to identify the EIGRP process executing in the router. It can also be referred to as the process-id for the EIGRP route process being defined. Each router using EIGRP must specify the same autonomous system number in order for the routers to exchange and update EIGRP routing tables.

The topology tables are defined by entering the network command under the router eigrp command. The format of the network command is

network *network-number*

The variable *network-number* is the classful network number of a network directly connected to the router. For example, in Figure 17-1, the three routers are connected using EGRP as the routing protocol. Each router specifies the network address of a directly connected network under the router EIGRP definition. This enables each router to advertise the IP network to its neighboring IGRP routers. The network number is the Class A, B, or C IP network assigned to the interfaces on the router. The use of subnet masks for identifying the network is not used on the network command. In Figure 17-1, network 10.0.0.0 is defined to all the routers, while network 172.16.0.0 is defined to only router 1, network 172.17.0.0 is defined to router 2, and network 172.16.0.0 is defined to router 3 only.

The EIGRP configuration commands for each router are as follows:

Router 1:
```
interface serial 0
 ip address 10.16.1.1 255.255.255.0
!
interface serial 1
 ip address 10.16.2.1 255.255.255.0
!
router eigrp 200
 network 10.0.0.0
 network 172.16.0.0
```

Router 2:
```
interface serial 0
 ip address 10.16.1.2 255.255.255.0
!
interface serial 1
 ip address 10.16.3.2 255.255.255.0
!
router eigrp 200
 network 10.0.0.0
 network 172.17.0.0
```

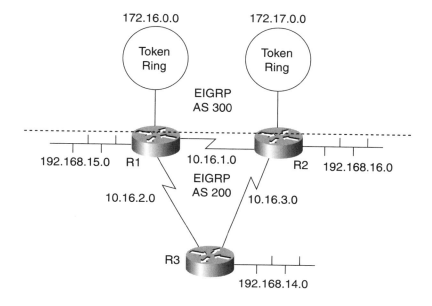

Figure 17-1
EIGRP routing
protocol used
between Cisco
routers.

Router 3:

```
interface serial 0
 ip address 10.16.2.3 255.255.255.0
!
interface serial 1
 ip address 10.16.3.3 255.255.255.0
!
router eigrp 200
 network 10.0.0.0
 network 172.18.0.0
```

EIGRP sends and receives updates for networks only on interfaces where the network is connected and sends updates only to the EIGRP autonomous system neighbors being advertised with autonomous system number 200. If a second EIGRP process is defined with different networks, they would not communicate with the networks of the other autonomous system. As seen in Figure 17-1, the serial interfaces connecting the routers, along with the Ethernets on all the routers that have their networks in the routing tables, are in EIGRP 200. The Token Ring networks on the routers as well as the serial links are defined in EIGRP network 300. The devices on the Token Ring cannot communicate with the devices on the Ethernet in this configuration. This is because the EIGRP autonomous systems are viewed as two independent networks. Each router will have two separate routing tables. The following configuration illustrates the new definitions to support the two EIGRP autonomous system networks. Expand these configurations using the serial, Ethernet, and Token Ring definitions.

Router 1:

```
interface serial 0
 ip address 10.16.1.1 255.255.255.0
!
interface serial 1
 ip address 10.16.2.1 255.255.255.0
!
router eigrp 200
 network 10.0.0.0
 network 172.16.0.0
!
router eigrp 300
 network 10.0.0.0
 network 192.168.100.0
```

Router 2:

```
interface serial 0
 ip address 10.16.1.2 255.255.255.0
!
interface serial 1
 ip address 10.16.2.2 255.255.255.0
!
interface Ethernet 0
 ip address 192.168.16.1 255.255.255.0

interface Tokenring 0
 ip address 172.17.1.1 255.255.255.0
!
router eigrp 200
 network 10.0.0.0
 network 172.17.0.0
!
router eigrp 300
 network 10.0.0.0
 network 192.168.200.0
```

Router 3:

```
interface serial 0
 ip address 10.16.2.3 255.255.255.0
!
interface serial 1
 ip address 10.16.3.3 255.255.255.0
!
interface Ethernet 0
 ip address 192.168.14.1 255.255.255.0
!
router eigrp 200
 network 10.0.0.0
 network 192.168.14.0
```

In order for devices on these two EIGRP networks to communicate, the router must redistribute the routes between the two EIGRP networks. Router redistribution among routing protocols is discussed in a later chapter.

Migrating to EIGRP from IGRP

Because EIGRP has its foundation in IGRP and both these protocols are proprietary to Cisco IOS, the migration from IGRP to EIGRP is extremely simple. The topology in Figure 17-2 illustrates the use of having IGRP and EIGRP in the same network. When both IGRP and EIGRP are configured using the same autonomous system number, the routes learned by both protocols are redistributed automatically. This makes for an ease of migration between IGRP and EIGRP.

In Figure 17-3, router R2 acts as the autonomous system boundary router (ASBR) between the IGRP network and the EIGRP network. Selecting an ASBR is paramount to the success of the migration effort. The configuration for the routers is listed below. Expand these configurations using the serial and Ethernet and Token Ring definitions.

Router 1:

```
interface serial 1
 ip address 10.1.2.1 255.255.255.0
!
interface Ethernet 0
 ip address 172.16.1.1 255.255.255.0
!
router igrp 100
 network 10.0.0.0
 network 172.16.0.0
```

Router 2:

```
interface serial 0
 ip address 10.2.3.2 255.255.255.0
!
interface serial 1
 ip address 10.1.2.2 255.255.255.0
!
router eigrp 100
 network 10.0.0.0
 passive-interface serial 1
!
router igrp 100
 network 10.0.0.0
 passive-interface serial 0
```

Figure 17-2
Migrating from IGRP
to EIGRP.

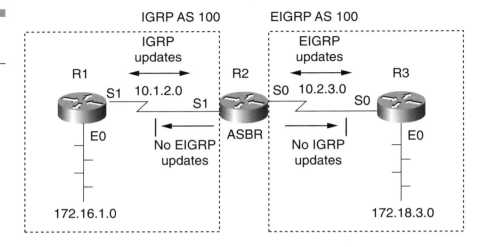

Router 3:

```
interface serial 0
 ip address 10.2.3.3 255.255.255.0
!
interface Ethernet 0
 ip address 172.18.3.3 255.255.255.0
!
router eigrp 100
 network 10.0.0.0
 network 172.18.0.0
```

The routes in router R2 are automatically redistributed between the EIGRP and IGRP processes, enabling router R1 and its attached network to use IGRP as its routing protocol while learning the routes to networks connected to router R3. Likewise, router R3 EIGRP routing tables are populated with routes for networks attached to router R1 while using EIGRP as the routing protocol. If the autonomous system numbers used by IGRP and EIGRP are different, then router R2 would have to redistribute the IGRP-learned routes into EIGRP routes and EIGRP-learned routes into IGRP routes. Using the same AS number removes the necessity of route redistribution, which reduces CPU utilization.

In the configuration example, the passive-interface command is used on router R2 to eliminate unnecessary routing update traffic not used by the adjacent router. The command passive-interface serial 2 under the router eigrp 100 command blocks EIGRP routing updates and hello packets from being sent to the adjacent IGRP router that would just discard these packets anyway. Likewise, the passive-interface serial 3 statement under the router igrp 100 command blocks IGRP routing protocol packets from being sent to the adjacent EIGRP-only router. Running EIGRP with RIP and OSPF is discussed in a later chapter.

Monitoring Neighbor Adjacency Changes

The establishment of EIGRP neighbors and the building of neighbor tables is a key element in the rapid convergence of EIGRP. Figure 17-3 provides a sample output of an EIGRP neighbor table for IP network layer protocol. EIGRP maintains a similar table for both IPX and AppleTalk.

The neighbor table is built on hello packet responses from adjacent EIGRP routers, and the hello packets are multicast packets. EIGRP uses the IP multicast group address 224.0.0.10 for the hello packets, which are sent by default every five seconds on a multi-access or point-to-point network. On NBMA networks like frame relay or X.25, the sending of hello packets defaults to 60 seconds. The hello packets are not acknowledged, while the update packets are unicast to neighbors, guaranteed delivery, and are acknowledged.

The neighbor table display resulting from the IOS EXEC command show ip eigrp neighbors lists the contents of the neighbor table. The Address column identifies the IP address of an adjacent neighbor. The Interface column identifies the interface on which the adjacent neighbor is attached. The Hold column specifies the number of seconds the router will wait without receiving any packets from the neighbor before marking the connection unavailable.

Figure 17-3

Router output of EIGRP neighbor table.

```
r1-njdc#SH IP EIGRP NEI
IP-EIGRP neighbors for process 10
H    Address        Interface    Hold Uptime   SRTT   RTO   Q     Seq
                                 (sec)         (ms)         Cnt   Num
6    10.16.1.4      AT3/0.2      13   2d19h    132    792   0     185923
11   10.16.1.6      AT3/0.2      12   2d20h    30     200   0     15956409
5    10.16.1.25     AT3/0.2      12   2d20h    32     200   0     2024
8    10.16.1.3      AT3/0.2      11   2d20h    9      200   0     8657
4    10.16.1.2      AT3/0.2      12   2d21h    26     200   0     7307774
0    10.16.1.5      AT3/0.2      14   2d21h    40     240   0     143003
9    10.16.1.7      AT3/0.2      12   2d21h    36     216   0     16160182
7    10.16.1.8      AT3/0.2      14   2d21h    44     264   0     312020
3    10.16.1.10     AT3/0.2      12   2d21h    28     200   0     7045242
2    10.16.1.1      AT3/0.2      11   2d21h    20     200   0     8660
1    10.16.1.9      AT3/0.2      10   2d21h    37     222   0     7080567
```

In the early releases of EIGRP, only the receipt of hello packets was measured. The current releases now measure the hold time for any EIGRP packet received after the first hello packet is received from the neighbor. The Uptime column indicates the amount of time this neighbor has been connected. The SRTT column represents the Smooth Round Trip Time (SRTT), which is a measurement in milliseconds of the average round-trip time for packets to travel between the routers. This time is used to determine the retransmit interval (RTO) values. The Q CNT (Queue Count) column is the number of packets waiting in the send queue. A value that is consistently higher than zero indicates link congestion.

The status of neighbor routers can assist in determining routing problems within the network. Changes to adjacent neighbors are normally not logged by Cisco IOS software. Logging is enabled using the following router eigrp configuration command:

eigrp log-neighbor-changes

Figure 17-4 provides a listing of a sample output from the Cisco IOS log when neighbor logging is enabled.

The %DUAL-5-NBRCHANGE message identifier indicates that EIGRP process ID 10 for IP routing has recognized a change in neighbor status. Neighbor 10.16.3.3, upon connecting to the network, has contacted this router and exchanged identification to form an adjacency. The neighbor connected using IP address 10.16.1.2 has not responded to EIGRP messages past the hold time and, as such, the router has determined that the neighbor is down. Once this neighbor rejoins the network, the logging process records it. Note that if a connection on this router to a neighbor goes down administratively, as shown in Figure 17-4, the logging process for ELAN test1 does not indicate a neighbor being disconnected. However, once the interface is brought back to an active state, the logging process indicates connection to the neighbor and forms an adjacency.

Figure 17-4

EIGRP neighbor changes logging output.

```
Feb 8 16:23:09: %DUAL-5-NBRCHANGE: IP-EIGRP 10: Neighbor 10.16.3.3
    (ATM3/0.9) is up: new adjacency
Feb 8 16:24:48: %DUAL-5-NBRCHANGE: IP-EIGRP 10: Neighbor 10.16.1.2
    (ATM3/0.2) is down: holding time expired
Feb 8 16:25:47: %DUAL-5-NBRCHANGE: IP-EIGRP 10: Neighbor 10.16.1.2
    (ATM3/0.2) is up: new adjacency
Feb 8 16:26:38: %LANE-5-UPDOWN: ATM3/0.9 elan test1: LE Client changed
    state to down
Feb 8 16:27:12: %LANE-5-UPDOWN: ATM3/0.9 elan test1: LE Client changed
    state to up
Feb 8 16:27:16: %DUAL-5-NBRCHANGE: IP-EIGRP 10: Neighbor 10.16.3.3
    (ATM3/0.9) is up: new adjacency
```

Managing EIGRP Bandwidth Utilization

Another advantage EIGRP has over other routing protocols is its inherent limit on the amount of bandwidth that routing updates will consume. Other routing protocols can quickly consume bandwidth during initial router connectivity and during normal periodic routing updates for distance-vector protocols and convergence in unstable networks. EIGRP guards against overutilizing the link for its own requirements by having an inherent limit of 50 percent link utilization imposed. The link utilization is based on the media default or value specified on the bandwidth interface command. Modifying the EIGRP utilization on a link is performed by entering the following interface command under the interface of the affected link:

ip bandwidth-percent eigrp *as-number percent*

The *as-number* value identifies the EIGRP process defined on this router that is being modified for link utilization. The percent value is the maximum amount of link utilization that EIGRP can consume on the link connected to the interface in question. The value 1 through 999,999 is valid for the percent variable.

Because the bandwidth interface command is used in some instances to influence the metric calculation for routes, EIGRP link utilization may end up becoming a factor that inadvertently causes performance problems. Or, for that matter, may require a link utilization that is greater than 100 percent due to bandwidth values that are specified as being much lower than the actual bandwidth of the connected link.

In Figure 17-5, we see a typical configuration where EIGRP would select the route R1-S1-R2-S0-R3-S0-R4-E0 to get from network 172.16.0.0 on router R1 to 172.24.0.0 on router R4. This route is simply based on the higher bandwidth and minimal delay. R1-S0 connects to R4-S0, however, using a direct 56-Kbps connection.

Because 56 Kbps is perceived by EIGRP to be a less favorable route, it is not the preferred path. The router administrator knows, however, that the connection between R1 and R4 over the 56-Kbps link have been traditionally more stable than the link between R2 and R3. Because of this, the bandwidth value for the serial interfaces connecting router R1 and router R4 are artificially increased to that of an T1 (1.544 Mbps) to establish this as the preferred route.

EIGRP, however, will now use this new value to determine its link utilization. At a default of 50 percent link utilization, the link would require

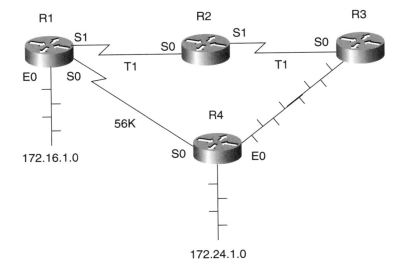

722 Kbps of bandwidth to support the EIGRP link utilization default. Obviously, this will saturate a 56-Kbps line. To protect the line from EIGRP overutilization, the following configuration for the serial interfaces on router R1 and router R4 is defined:

Router R1:

```
interface serial 0
 description Actual link bandwidth is 56Kbps
 bandwidth 1544
 ip bandwidth-percent eigrp 200 2
```

Router R4:

```
interface serial 0
 description Actual link bandwidth is 56Kbps
 bandwidth 1544
 ip bandwidth-percent eigrp 200 2
```

Utilizing the value of two percent on the artificially raised bandwidth, EIGRP uses a maximum of 30 Kbps, which is similar to the normal default of 28 Kbps for a 56-Kbps link.

In Figure 17-6, we see a configuration in which the serial link between R1 and R4 is actually a T1, but the router administrator wants to force EIGRP to use a public Frame Relay network. The frame relay multipoint connection has a total CIR of 768 Kbps. The router administrator modifying the bandwidth values for router R1 and router R4 on the T1 connection

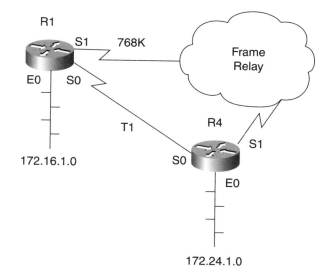

Figure 17-6
*EIGRP link utilization
configuration for
specifying more than
100 percent of a link.*

accomplishes this. The frame relay connection link between R1 and R4 is now favored.

Router R1:

```
interface serial 0
 description Actual link bandwidth is T1
 bandwidth 56
 ip bandwidth-percent eigrp 200 1000

interface serial 1
 description Frame Relay CIR bandwidth is 768K
 bandwidth 768
```

Router R4:

```
interface serial 0
 description Actual link bandwidth is T1
 bandwidth 56
 ip bandwidth-percent eigrp 200 1000

interface serial 1
 description Frame Relay CIR bandwidth is 768K
 bandwidth 768
```

The router R1 has its T1 serial interface bandwidth command specified as 56 Kbps. Likewise, router R4 has the T1 serial bandwidth specified as 56 Kbps. The requirement is met here, yet EIGRP router convergence will be affected, due to the default of 50 percent link utilization based on the bandwidth value. In order to compensate for this, the percent variable on the ip bandwidth-percent eigrp interface command is set above 100 percent to 1000 percent, allowing EIGRP to use the actual available bandwidth on the link. The Frame Relay links must have the bandwidth interface command specified, since EIGRP will default the route calculation for the serial interface to that of a T1 (1.544 Mbps).

Modifying EIGRP Metric Weights

EIGRP router metrics are altered using five constants and the type of service for the route. A router administrator may alter these metric values using the metric weights router configuration command. The format of the command is

metric weights tos k1 k2 k3 k4 k5

The *tos* variable currently defaults to the value of 0 and must always be specified as 0. The *k1* through *k5* values default to the following:

k1: 1

k2: 0

k3: 1

k4: 0

k5: 0

The values placed in the positional parameters of the metric weights command provide the values used as EIGRP metric coefficients when determining the calculated metric for an EIGRP route. Changing the defaults for these values thus changes the default behavior for all EIGRP routing and metric calculations. Therefore, changing the metrics can greatly affect network performance. The valid range for the numeric value of *k1-k5* is 0 through 4294967295. Using 4294967295 as a value for any of the coefficients results in the route being marked unusable. The k1-k5 values are used in the EIGRP metric calculation against the four major metric components of IGRP route calculation. These components are bandwidth, load, delay, and reliability.

NOTE: *It is strongly advisable to not modify the metric weight values unless consulting with the Cisco TAC prior to and during the modification.*

The EIGRP process calculates the metric by adding together weighted values of different characteristics of the route entry. The standard formula for determining the metric is as follows:

metric = k1 x bandwidth + (k2 x bandwidth / (256 - load) + k3 x delay

The default metric values for k1-k5 affect this overall calculation by realizing that the k1 and k3 values both are 1 and the k2, k4, and k5 values equal 0. Applying the default values for the **metric weights** router command results in the following calculation:

metric = bandwidth + delay

Understanding this results in the need to understand the interface command **bandwidth.** It allows for a router administrator to modify the bandwidth of the physical medium. For example, entering the following command:

```
interface ethernet 0
 bandwidth 5000
```

will end up causing interface Ethernet 0 on this router to have a less favorable metric than a router that uses the default bandwidth for a 10-Mbps Ethernet, which is 10,000 Kbps. The bandwidth command is expressed as

bandwidth *kilobits*

The *kilobits* value is in the valid range of 1 to 10,000,000, expressed in Kbps. This allows the router administrator to place a value as high as 10 terabits per second (Tbps) on an interface. With one-Tbps technology proven and the capability to continually increase the bandwidth on fiber optic networks, this value may have a shorter life span than anticipated. The metric bandwidth value used by Cisco IOS running the EIGRP process for serial interfaces defaults to 1.544 Mbps (T1 speed). This warrants that if the serial lines connecting to the router are less than a T1, then the bandwidth interface command can be specified to allow EIGRP to calculate the true metric. For example, a 56-Kbps serial connection should be defined as

```
interface serial 0
 bandwidth 56
```

Since bandwidth is such a major factor in determining the metric for a route, great care must be used when using the bandwidth interface command.

Suppose the metric weights command was entered where the k2 value was changed from 0 to a value of 1. The command sequence is as follows:

```
router eigrp 200
 metric weights 0 1 1 1 0 0
```

In this instance, the load metric becomes the deciding variable. The load value for an interface is calculated every five seconds based on a five-minute weighted average. The load is presented as a fraction of 255, where 255 is a saturated link experiencing 100 percent utilization. Setting the k2 coefficient to a 1 can result in a route going into holddown when there is an increase in load due to a large FTP or some other type of action that can consume bandwidth over a period of time. The net effect is that the metric ends up doubling the bandwidth, which can possibly make a slow link artificially inflated with bandwidth. In such a scenario, not only can a load rise fast enough to make a route unstable, it can also fall just as fast. A falling load can change the metric to become favorable and cause the Cisco router send link state updates.

In addition to the formula noted above involving k values k1-k3, k5 and k4 come into play if the k5 value specified on the metric weights EIGRP router command is not zero. When this occurs, the following formula is also calculated to create the final metric for the route:

metric = metric x [k5 / (reliability + k4)]

A long-hand method for determining the metric can be performed for a specific router by performing the following:

1. Determine the smallest of all the bandwidths on the route from outgoing interfaces and divide 10,000,000 by that number. (The bandwidth is scaled by 10,000,000 in kilobits per second.)

2. Add all the delays on the route from the outgoing interfaces and divide this number by 10. (The delay is in 10s of microsecs.)

The path with the smallest metric is the best path. These values can be found by issuing the router operation command show interfaces. An example for this is as follows:

```
R1#sh int e 0
 Ethernet 0 is up, line protocol is up
 Internet address is 172.16.9.22, subnet mask is 255.255.255.0
 MTU 1500 bytes, BW 10000 Kbit, DLY 1000 usec, rely 255/255, load
   1/255
Serial 0 is up, line protocol is up
 Internet address is 172.18.19.9, subnet mask is 255.255.255.224
 MTU 1500 bytes, BW 784 Kbit, DLY 20000 usec, rely 255/255, load
   20/255

R2#sh int s 0
 Serial 0 is up, line protocol is up
 Internet address is 172.19.42.1, subnet mask is 255.255.255.224
 MTU 1500 bytes, BW 448 Kbit, DLY 20000 usec, rely 255/255, load
   1/255
Serial 1 is up, line protocol is up
 Internet address is 172.18.19.8, subnet mask is 255.255.255.224
```

```
      MTU 1500 bytes, BW 224 Kbit, DLY 20000 usec, rely 255/255, load
        3/255
     R1# sh ip route R2-s0
      Total delay is 40,000 microseconds, minimum bandwidth is 448 Kbit
      Known via "eigrp 2022", distance 100, metric 26321
```

The calculation:

$$\text{Metric} = \text{bandwidth} + \text{delay}$$

$$= 10,000,000/448 + (20,000 + 20,000)/10$$

$$= 26321$$

```
     R2# sh ip route R1-e0
     Total delay is 21,000 microseconds, minimum bandwidth is 224 Kbit
     Known via "eigrp 2022", distance 100, metric 46742
```

$$\text{Metric} = \text{bandwidth} + \text{delay}$$

$$= 10,000,000/224 + (20.000 + 1000)/10$$

$$= 46742$$

Figure 17-7

Router configuration for determining metric values.

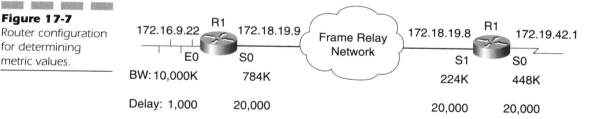

172.16.9.22 — R1 — 172.18.19.9 — Frame Relay Network — 172.18.19.8 — R1 — 172.19.42.1

	E0	S0			S1	S0
BW:	10,000K	784K			224K	448K
Delay:	1,000	20,000			20,000	20,000

Table 17-1

Default Delay and Bandwidth Values Used by EIGRP for Specific Media Types

Media Type	Delay	Bandwidth
Satellite	5,120 (2 seconds)	5,120 (500 Mbits)
Ethernet	25,600 (1 ms)	256,000 (10 Mbits)
1.544 Mbps	512,000 (20,000 ms)	1,657,856 bits
64 kbps	512,000 (20,000 ms)	40,000,000 bits
56 kbps	512,000 (20,000 ms)	45,714,176 bits
10 kbps	512,000 (20,000 ms)	256,000,000 bits
1 kbps	512,000 (20,000 ms)	2,560,000,000 bits

Routing Between Disconnected Networks with EIGRP

Route summarization is enabled by default when using both IGRP and EIGRP routing protocols. The Cisco IOS software will summarize the IGRP or EIGRP routes to the classful network boundary across classful network boundaries. Route summarization is the process of summarizing routes with long masks to routes with shorter masks that still meet the initial routing requirement. Summarization only uses the full prefixes of each IP network classification, meaning 8 bits for a Class A, 16 bits for a Class B, and 24 bits for a Class C address.

Summarization is useful in EIGRP due to its support of VLSM. For example, in Figure 17-8, router R1 connects to router R2 through serial interface 0 and router R3 through serial interface 1.

The networks connected to router R2 and router R3 are summarized in the EIGRP update packets to router R1 from router R2 and R3. EIGRP will summarize the following network addresses:

IP Subnet	Subnet Mask
172.16.8.0	255.255.255.0
172.16.16.0	255.255.255.0
172.16.24.0	255.255.255.0
172.16.32.0	255.255.255.0
172.20.8.0	255.255.255.0
172.20.16.0	255.255.255.0
172.20.24.0	255.255.255.0
172.20.32.0	255.255.255.0

into two routing entries using EIGRP. Using the router sh ip route command on router R1, the summarized routing entries will be displayed as

```
D 172.16.0.0/16 [120/1] via 172.30.1.1, 00:00:01, Serial0/0
D 172.20.0.0/16 [120/1] via 172.31.1.1, 00:00:01, Serial0/1
```

Using route summarization with EIGRP reduces router overhead and bandwidth required to send routing updates.

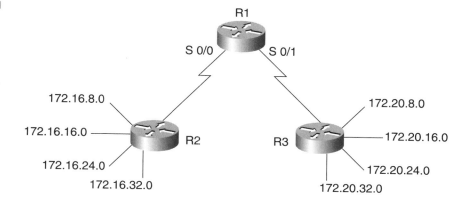

Figure 17-8
EIGRP network configuration used for route summarization.

Route summarization is the desired approach when using EIGRP. If a subnet is disconnected, however, the routers will not be able to correctly advertise the subnets. Figure 17-10 illustrates this issue. Router R2 in the figure has subnet 172.20.8.0 and router R3 has subnet 172.20.16.0, causing a disconnect of the subnets. Router R1 receives summarized entries from router R2 and R3 will indicate two paths to the 172.20.0.0 network, which is not really the case.

The sh ip route command displays the following on router R1 based on router summarization updates from R2 and R3:

```
D 172.20.0.0/16 [120/1] via 172.31.1.1, 00:00:01, Serial0/0
D 172.20.0.0/16 [120/1] via 172.30.1.1, 00:00:01, Serial0/1
```

The resulting routing table will cause connectivity problems for two reasons. First, due to the fact that the hop count is the same, the router will load balance packets between serial interface 0/0 and serial interface 0/1. Secondly, this will cause only 50 percent of the packets to successfully reach their true destination. This type of topology is corrected by disabling route summarization using the following router configuration mode command:

no auto-summary

Entering this in the configuration for routers R2 and R3 will disable summarization and cause the full subnet and host routing information to be transmitted to router R1. The sh ip route command issued on router R1 will now display the following entries:

```
D 172.20.8.0/24  [120/1] via 172.30.1.1, 00:00:01, Serial0/0
D 172.20.16.0/24 [120/1] via 172.31.1.1, 00:00:01, Serial0/1
```

Figure 17-9
Disconnected
networks and EIGRP
route summarization.

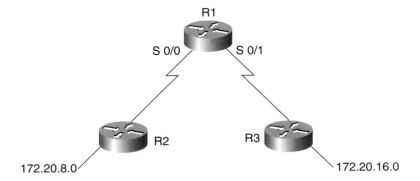

The no auto-summary command on router R2 and R3 forces the EIGRP updates to advertise the full mask for each of the subnets. Now packets through router R1 for resources on subnet 172.20.8.0 will only be directed out serial interface 0/0. Likewise, packets through router R1 for resources on subnet 172.20.16.0 will only be directed out serial interface 0/1.

Summarizing Routes for Advertisements out Specific Interfaces

Further summarization of routes is possible through the use of the following interface configuration command:

ip summary-address eigrp *autonomous-system-number address mask*

The *autonomous-system-number* variable specifies a valid EIGRP AS number in use by this router. The *address* variable is the IP address being summarized. The *mask* variable is the subnet mask that is applied to the value of the *address* variable. Applying this interface command to any interface definition causes the EIGRP process to summarize routes out of this interface that may not be normally summarized. This command is normally not used since EIGRP defaults to route summarization. In instances such as disconnected networks where auto-summarization is disabled, however, the ip summary-address interface command is useful to summarize routes to portions of the network not involved with the disconnected networks.

Figure 17-10 diagrams such a situation. In this figure, network 172.16.0.0 is subnetted using 255.255.252.0 as the subnet mask. In default mode, EIGRP would summarize the route update to router R2 and R3 from router R1. Because auto-summarization is disabled to handle the disconnected network 172.20.0.0, however, each subnet associated with the 172.16.0.0 network would be sent to the neighboring routers. Using the ip summary-address eigrp interface command, the 172.16.0.0 network can be summarized to router R2 and R3, thus reducing routing table overhead and creating a more efficient path for router R2 and R3 to route packets to the 172.16.0.0 network.

The router configuration for aggregating the 172.16.0.0 routes follows:

Router R1 Configuration:

```
interface serial 0/0
 ip address 172.30.1.1 255.255.255.0
 ip summary-address eigrp 200 172.16.0.0 255.255.0.0
!
interface serial 0/1
 ip address 172.31.1.1 255.255.255.0
 ip summary-address eigrp 200 172.16.0.0 255.255.0.0
!
interface Ethernet 0
 ip address 172.16.4.1 255.255.252.0
!
interface Ethernet 1
 ip address 172.16.8.1 255.255.252.0
!
interface Ethernet 2
 ip address 172.16.12.1 255.255.252.0

router eigrp 200
 network 172.16.0.0
 network 172.30.0.0
 network 172.31.0.0
 no auto-summary
```

Tuning Hello Packet and the Hold Time intervals

Hello packets are sent periodically over interface connections between routing devices to enable the discovery of neighbor EIGRP routers. The hello packets are sent only over interface connections whose IP address network is specified under the router eigrp command using the router configuration network command. These hello packets are also used to determine if a neighbor has become unreachable or inoperative.

Figure 17-10
Aggregating route
summarization for a
specific network.

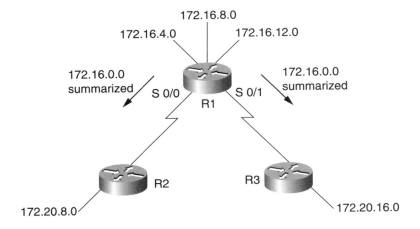

172.16.8.0
172.16.4.0   172.16.12.0
172.16.0.0   172.16.0.0
summarized   S 0/0   S 0/1   summarized
R1

R2   R3
172.20.8.0   172.20.16.0

Every five seconds the EIGRP process sends a hello packet out EIGRP interfaces by default for multi-access networks and high-speed point-to-point interfaces. For low-speed serial interfaces and NBMA networks, the hello packet is sent every 60 seconds by default. In high-speed NBMA networks, the default is also five seconds.

NOTE: *Frame Relay and SMDS networks are considered NBMA networks only when the interface is not configured to use physical multicasting.*

Because EIGRP uses the bandwidth value assigned to an interface to determine the speed of a link, it can also alter the number of hello packets sent over the connection.

To help avoid sending too many hello packets over slow links due to inflated bandwidth or too few over-artificially low bandwidth values, use the following interface command:

ip hello-interval eigrp *autonomous-system-number seconds*

The *autonomous-system-number* variable specifies a valid EIGRP AS number in use by this router. The variable is the interval in seconds for sending hello packets out the specified interface.

The hold time is the amount of time advertised to the neighbor that the sender on this link is operational, even if hello packets have not been received. The hold time value defaults to 180 seconds for slow serial links and slow NBMA networks. For high-speed NBMA and multiaccess networks, the default hold time is three times the hello-packet interval. These defaults may not be a long enough interval in congested and very large networks, but because the hold time is affected by the value of the bandwidth interface command and its direct affect on route convergence within the network, great care and planning is advised be entered:

ip hold-time eigrp *autonomous-system-number seconds*

The *autonomous-system-number* variable specifies a valid EIGRP AS number in use by this router. The variable is the interval in seconds allowed without receiving hello-packets prior to determining that the neighbor router and routes pointing to it are unavailable.

Split-Horizon and EIGRP

A router advertising routes out of an interface that the routing information was received on frequently causes routing loops. The split-horizon feature employed for distance-vector routing protocols like RIP reduces the possibility of routing loops by blocking routing updates to connected routers from which the routing update was originally received.

As an added insurance, EIGRP also uses the split-horizon algorithm. Figure 17-11 diagrams this scenario. This type of scenario is most prevalent on broadcast type IP networks such as LANs. As shown in the figure, the routing advertisements received by router R1 for networks connected to router R2 are not sent to router R2 from router R1 in its routing update packets. Likewise, router R2 does not send routing advertisements to router R1 for networks attached to router R1.

Spilt-horizon is disabled using the following interface configuration command:

no ip split-horizon eigrp *autonomous-system-number*

Enabling split-horizon for a specific interface is accomplished by entering the following interface command:

ip split-horizon eigrp *autonomous-system-number*

Non-broadcast networks like Frame Relay, however, require split-horizon to be disabled. The Cisco IOS automatically disables split-horizon for Frame Relay and SMDS networks when EIGRP is used as the routing pro-

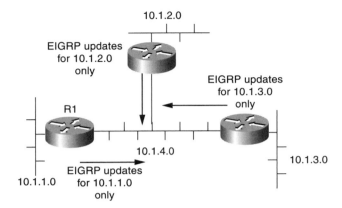

Figure 17-11
The effect of split-horizon on broadcast networks with EIGRP.

tocol for those connections. Split-horizon is enabled for all other network connections. If split-horizon is disabled on an interface connecting a packet-switched network like X.25, it must be disabled on all other routers connecting to the same packet-switched network.

MD5 Authentication with EIGRP

EIGRP supports router authentication as a means of providing security for routing table updates. Using MD5 authentication, Cisco routers are protected from advertising routes to and receiving routes from promiscuous unauthorized routers. Authentication is defined on the interface level and hence provides for discreet selection of which interfaces must use authentication.

Authentication is determined by the configuration of a key chain specific to the interface. The key chain is identified by using the following interface command:

ip authentication key-chain eigrp *autonomous-system key-chain*

The *key-chain* operand is the name given to the valid group of keys. Specifying the **ip authentication key-chain eigrp** command enables EIGRP authentication. If this command is not specified on an interface using EIGRP, then authentication is not performed.

Along with enabling authentication, the mode of authentication can be specified. The mode of authentication defaults to plain, clear text that becomes a security risk on connections and can be deemed unsecured.

Encrypted authentication must be specifically specified. The following interface command is used to define the type of mode used for authentication on an interface:

ip authentication mode eigrp *autonomous-system* **md5**

The *autonomous-system* value is the AS number of an EIGRP process. The **md5** authentication technique is the only valid keyed authentication algorithm used with EIGRP.

Authentication is enabled using the **ip authentication key-chain eigrp** interface command, but the authentication keys must be defined in order for authentication to occur. Authentication keys themselves are defined using the following global configuration commands:

```
key chain name-of-chain

key number

key-string text

accept-lifetime start-time {infinite | end-time | duration seconds}

send-lifetime start-time {infinite | end-time | duration seconds}
```

The value of the *key-chain* variable on the key-chain command must match a defined **ip authentication key-chain eigrp** command on an interface to exercise the authentication key chain. The *number* variable of the key command identifies the number of the key being defined. The *text* variable on the key-string command is the authentication text identified by the key number used for authentication. Multiple keys can be configured as well.

The key numbers supplied in the key chain definition are searched from lowest to highest, and the first valid key found is then authenticated. The router sends only one authentication path despite multiple key definitions. The key number value, in combination with the interface associated with the packet, is used by the authentication algorithm and MD5 authentication to uniquely identify the authentication key.

The keys can be programmed to be active during specific times of a given day. This is done with the **accept-lifetime** and **send-lifetime** commands. The *start-time* variable of the accept-lifetime and send-lifetime commands defines when the key will be activated. The *end-time* of the accept-lifetime and send-lifetime commands defines the end on a given day when the key will no longer be in use. The format of the *start-time* and *end-time* variable is

hh:mm:ss month day year

The *hh:mm:ss* variable is the two-digit 24-hour clock representation of the time of day. The month variable is the first three letters of the month, the day is the number of the day of the month, and the year variable is the four-digit number for the year. The *start-time* and *end-time* variables default to an infinite time period starting from January 1, 1993. The **infinite** keyword can be used as the end time value, indicating that the key never expires after the value of the *start-time* variable has been reached. The **duration** keyword, followed by a valid value for the *seconds* variable, can also be used instead of the end-time variable value to define the usage length for the key. The following is an example of a configuration using RIP Version 2 and authentication between two Cisco routers.

Router R1 Configuration:

```
interface Ethernet 0
 ip address 10.16.8.1 255.255.255.0
 ip authentication mode eigrp 200 md5
 ip authentication key-chain eigrp 200 colors
!
router eigrp 200
 network 10.0.0.0
!
key chain colors
 key 1
 key-string blue
 accept-lifetime 07:00:00 Feb 28 1999 duration 7200
 send-lifetime 08:00:00 Feb 28 1999 duration 3600
 key 2
 key-string green
 accept-lifetime 00:00:00 Mar 1 1999 infinite
 send-lifetime 00:30:00 Mar 1 1999 infinite
```

Router R2 Configuration:

```
interface ethernet 0
 ip address 10.16.8.2 255.255.255.0
 ip authentication mode eigrp 200 md5
 ip authentication key-chain eigrp 200 colors
!
router eigrp 200
 network 10.0.0.0
 version 2
!
key chain colors
 key 1
 key-string blue
 accept-lifetime 07:30:00 Feb 28 1999 duration 7200
 send-lifetime 06:30:00 Feb 28 1999 duration 3600
 key 2
 key-string green
 accept-lifetime 23:30:00 Feb 28 1999 infinite
 send-lifetime 00:00:00 Mar 1 1999 infinite
```

In these configurations, the two routers first use the keys identified by number 1 because the search order is from lowest to highest. The routers then use the number 2 key to authenticate routing updates between them. The start time on router R1 is defined to ensure the acceptance and delivery of EIGRP updates to router R2, given a 30-minute cushion on the time differences between the routers. The second key (number 2) on each router takes effect once the clocks on each router have met the start-time criteria and last indefinitely.

NOTE: *Both routers must be using EIGRP and have authentication enabled, in addition to the accept and send lifetime values being coordinated. Both routers must also specify the same key-string that will then force the router to examine the accept and send lifetime values.*

CHAPTER 18

Configuring OSPF Routing Protocol

Open Shortest Path First (OSPF) is a link-state IP routing protocol. Developed in 1988 by the Internet Engineering Task Force (IETF) and recently updated in RFC 2178, OSPF addresses the scalability concerns of large global IP networks that are not addressable by distance-vector-based IP routing protocols such as RIP and IGRP. OSPF meets the scalability concerns of distance-vector routing protocols by addressing the following:

- *Convergence:* OSPF route convergence uses a flooding mechanism to update neighboring OSPF routers within an area of new routes. Only the affected routes are updated and, due to route summarization, if the route is part of a summarized route to another area, the update remains only within the area affected.

- *Variable Length Subnet Mask (VLSM) support:* RIP1 and IGRP do not support VLSM, which makes OSPF a viable alternative for managing large IP networks within a restrictive address range.

- *Network Diameter:* In RIP, IGRP, and EIGRP networks the diameter (hops) between networks has a limit. The concept of areas and building hierarchical networks based on the areas enables OPSF to have a virtually limitless diameter.

- *Efficient bandwidth use:* Because OSPF is a link-state routing protocol, only updates of affected routes are sent to neighboring routers, instead of the entire routing table. OSPF uses a multicast link-state update (LSU) packet to accomplish the routing updates and only sends the LSU when a network change has occurred.

- *Advanced route selection:* OSPF uses bandwidth as a deciding factor in determining the optimal path between two networks. RIP1 and RIP2 rely on hop counts.

OSPF routers establish adjacencies upon the activation of the connections defined to the OSPF routing protocol process. The adjacencies are established using the Hello protocol. There are nine variables used in the Hello protocol that enable an OSPF router to form bidirectional communication with adjacent OSPF routers. Table 18-1 lists a table identifying these nine variables.

OSPF routers have a unique identifier for the router, called the router ID. Each router selects the highest dotted-decimal IP address on any active interface as the router ID. The exception to this rule is when the loopback interface is specified on the router. When loopback interfaces are defined, the highest IP address assigned to any of the loopback interfaces is chosen as the router ID. The router ID is important in the selection of the designated and backup routers for the OSPF network. If the interface goes down,

Table 18-1

OSPF Adjacency
Variables Found in
the Hello Packet

OSPF Adjacency Variable	Variables that Must Match Between Adjacencies
Router-ID	
Hello/Dead intervals	■
Neighbors	
Area-ID	■
Router priority	
Designated router (DR) IP address	
Backup DR (BDR) IP address	
Authentication password	■
Stub area flag	■

the router is unreachable. To avoid this situation, it is prudent to define a loopback interface as the forced OSPF router ID.

The hello/dead intervals are the predetermined timers used by all adjacent routers for specifying the frequency in seconds that a router will send hello packets or determine that an adjacent neighbor router is declared down. Neighboring routers must be using the same timing values for these intervals. If the values do not agree, the neighbors may believe that a router has gone down but is, in fact, still active on the network. The default of hello messages is 10 seconds and for dead intervals it is 40 seconds on non-NBMA interfaces.

The value for neighbors in the Hello packet is the list of adjacencies created by the router sending the hello packet. In initial contacts, this field is empty.

The area-ID is a definition that creates a segmented OSPF network. Using the same area-ID in all OSPF routers denotes a single commonly shared network, including the IP address subnet and mask. Each router on the shared segment with the same area-ID will have the same link-state database.

The router priority field of the hello packet indicates to the neighboring router(s) whether this router is eligible to become a designated or backup router. The router with the highest priority is the selected designated router (DR) and the router with the second highest priority is the backup designated router (BDR). If the highest priority values are equal, the router with the highest router-ID becomes the DR and the router with the second highest router id becomes the BDR. A router specified with a priority of 0 can never be eligible as a DR or BDR, and Cisco IOS defaults the priority value to 1. The DR and BDR fields in the hello packet are the IP addresses of the current DR and BDR.

The authentication password field is filled in only when authentication is enabled on the router. The password provided by the Cisco IOS for authentication must be the same on the routers exchanging the hello packets. If authentication is set for one router and not another, an adjacency is not established. To ensure adjacencies with authentication, all peer routers participating on the OSPF network should use the same authentication password.

The last field used in the hello packet is the stub area flag. This field indicates to the peer router that the router sending the hello packet is in a stub area. A stub area is generally defined as a network with a single router having a single exit point from a router into the OSPF network. It is the exchange of the information in the hello packets that enables an OSPF network to function appropriately.

OSPF with Cisco IOS

Cisco IOS fully supports the OSPF RFC 2178, Not-So-Stubby-Area (NSSA) RFC 1587, and OSPF over-demand circuit RFC 1793. Cisco IOS at this point in time does not support Multicast-OSPF (MOSPF) Link State Advertisement (LSA) Type 6 packets. The enhancements to OSPF, specific to Cisco IOS features, include the following:

Totally Stubby Areas: This Cisco IOS-specific feature works only when Cisco routers are involved between a stub area and an OSPF area. The feature reduces OSPF routing information from the network link between the OSPF Area Border Router (ABR) that connects to the stub area. The Cisco ABR forwards the default summary link 0.0.0.0 into the stub area. In this way, as shown in Figure 18-1, bandwidth on the link to the totally stubby area router is saved for data traffic. The totally stubby area feature blocks external type5 LSAs and summary type 3 and 4 intra-area LSAs from being sent into the stub area.

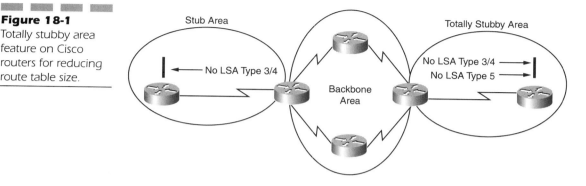

Figure 18-1
Totally stubby area feature on Cisco routers for reducing route table size.

NOTE: *Use Totally Stubby Areas only* with Cisco routers. In a mixed Cisco *and non-Cisco environment, specify the area configuration as a stub network.*

Cisco further increases OSPF network stability and scalability by employing an interface output cost, retransmission timer, and interface transmit delay timers.

Link output cost: Cisco IOS allows the router administrator to apply a cost to a specific link. This is useful in forcing OSPF route selection over preferred physical connections to destination networks from the router.

LSA retransmit interval: Using this feature, the router administrator can increase or decrease the default retransmission of LSAs to the neighbor router. The retransmit is used if the neighbor route has not responded to the LSA previously sent.

LSA transmit delay: The value specified here is used in conjunction with the retransmit interval in determining an unsuccessful delivery of an LSA over a link.

Specifying OSPF on Cisco Routers

Taking the defaults for all router configurations within an OSPF area's internal routers, area border routers, and autonomous system boundary routers (ASBR) will most certainly provide an operational network. Much of the decision making is up to the OSPF neighbor adjacency negotiations for determining the DR and BDR, however, with no authentication of peer routers joining the network, and no default values that protect valuable bandwidth and processor utilization. Defining network-specific values for the OSPF area will enable the network engineer to create a deterministic OSPF configuration versus an undetermined topology.

Creating the OSPF Routing Process

The Cisco IOS software initializes an OSPF routing protocol process by the router administrator entering the global configuration command:

router ospf *process-id*

Defining **router ospf**, followed by a *process-id* number, spawns an OSPF routing process with the assigned process-id. Unlike IGRP and EIGRP, the value here is specific to the router and is not used to identify different OSPF autonomous systems. Multiple OSPF processes can be executed on any given router using unique process-ids for each. It is more common practice, however, to have one OSPF process running on any given router. The value for the process-id parameter ranges from 1 to 65535.

The OSPF process defined must be associated with an active IP interface on the router in order for OSPF to begin building neighbor adjacencies and routing tables. The process becomes aware of which interfaces are using OSPF by defining the network area command in the following format under the router ospf global command:

network *address wildcard-mask* **area** *area-id*

The *address* parameter can be either the IP address of the interface, the subnet, or network address of the interface to which OSPF routing is to be applied.

Paired with the *address* parameter is the *wildcard-mask* parameter. The value specified for the *wildcard-mask* parameter identifies which bit of the *address* parameter value is used for interpreting the address parameter value. The *wildcard-mask* is expressed in dotted-decimal format. Using the following example,

```
network 172.16.0.0 0.0.255.255 area 0
```

the network address value, 172.16.0.0, is used with an applied mask of 0.0.255.255. All interfaces on the router using the Class B network address of 172.16.x.x will have LSA sent and received, as well as Hello protocol packets being sent for neighbor adjacency establishment and DR/BDR determination. If the example

```
network 172.16.8.0 0.0.0.255 area 0
```

were used, the wildcard-mask implies that only interfaces using the 172.16.8.0 subnet would use OSPF as the routing protocol. The mask applied to the address is an entity unto itself and it does not have to match the mask used for the IP address defined on the interface. For example, if the router were configured as follows,

```
interface serial 0
 ip address 172.16.8.16 255.255.255.248
!
interface serial 1
 ip address 172.16.8.24 255.255.255.248
!
router ospf 1
 network 172.16.8.0 0.0.0.255 area 0
```

the OSPF process would use both interfaces for OSPF routing since the first three bytes of the address parameter value are met by the wildcard-mask. If the following configuration were in use,

```
interface serial 0
 ip address 172.16.8.1 255.255.255.0
!
interface serial 1
 ip address 172.16.9.1 255.255.255.0
!
router eigrp 100
 network 172.16.0.0
!
router ospf 1
 network 172.16.9.1 0.0.0.0 area 0
```

then interface serial 0 would use only EIGRP routing protocol, while interface serial 1 would use both EIGRP and OSPF as routing protocols. When defining a specific interface to use the OSPF routing protocol, the full IP address assigned to the interface can be specified. In such a case as this example illustrates, the *wildcard-mask* must specify all 0s, indicating an exact match is required.

The *area-id* parameter value identifies to which OSPF area the specified network is associated. The *area-id* can be a decimal number in the range of 0 to 4294967295, or it can be written in the dotted-decimal format of an IP address. Using an IP network or subnet dotted-decimal format to represent the area is often used to assist in identifying the attached area with a true network meaning. In the following example, the IOS configuration

```
router ospf 1
 network 10.0.0.0 0.255.255.255 area 10.1.0.0
```

is particularly useful because the area-id value specified identifies the IP subnet of the attached network. For the most part, installations use decimal values. If the OSPF network being defined has a single area, the area-id value must equal 0. This is because OSPF treats area 0 as the backbone area that connects all other OSPF areas.

The address parameter value must specify the primary IP address, subnet, or network of an active interface to enable OSPF for the interface. Specifying the IP address, subnet, or network of a secondary IP address for an active interface will not enable OSPF for the interface. Here's an example:

```
interface Ethernet 0
 ip address 172.16.1.1 255.255.255.0 secondary
 ip address 10.1.1.1 255.255.255.0
 !
router ospf 1
 network 172.16.0.0 0.0.255.255 area 0
```

The Ethernet connected to interface Ethernet 0 will not be accessible from networks connecting to this router from other routers because the primary IP network 10.0.0.0, the subnet 10.1.1.0, and the exact IP address 10.1.1.1 are not specified on the network area command.

The Cisco IOS performs an OR operation when determining whether an interface is to have OSPF enabled. The process is as follows:

1. The *wildcard-mask* value is logically ORed with the IP address of each active interface.
2. The *wildcard-mask* value is then logically ORed against the address parameter value of the network area command.
3. The resulting ORed values are compared.
4. If the resulting values match, then the Cisco IOS enables OSPF for the interface and attaches the interface to the OSPF area specified by the area-id parameter value.

For example, if the IP address of an interface is 8.2.2.1 and the *wildcard-mask* is 0.0.255.255, the ORed value is

```
00001000.00000010.00000010.00000001
00000000.00000000.11111111.11111111
00001000.00000010.11111111.11111111
```

If the **network area** command *address* parameter specifies 8.2.0.0 with a *wildcard-mask* of 0.0.255.255, the ORed value is

```
00001000.00000010.00000000.00000000
00000000.00000000.11111111.11111111
00001000.00000010.11111111.11111111
```

Comparing the resulting values, we find that the results match and hence any interface using 8.2.x.x in the first two octets of the IP address field will have OSPF enabled. Now suppose the IP address of the interface is 8.3.1.1 and the *wildcard-mask* is 0.0.255.255:

```
00001000.00000011.00000001.00000001
00000000.00000000.11111111.11111111
00001000.00000011.11111111.11111111
```

Now we compare this interface logically ORed result with the network area result found earlier:

```
00001000.00000011.11111111.11111111 IP address 8.3.1.1 logically ORed result
00001000.00000010.11111111.11111111 network area 8.2.0.0 logically ORed result
```

The resulting values do not match; hence, the interface using the 8.3.1.1 IP address will not have OSPF enabled.

In Figure 18-2, a single OSPF area topology is shown. The three routers within the figure are all connected using serial attached lines. Since serial point-to-point links are connecting only two routers, there is no use for a DR or BDR.

Figure 18-2

A simple point-to-point OSPF single area network.

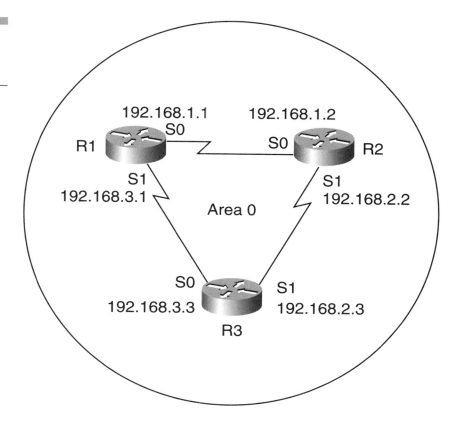

The following are the configurations used to enable OSPF in Figure 17-2.

Router R1 Configuration:

```
interface serial 0
 ip address 192.168.1.1 255.255.255.0
!
interface serial 1
 ip address 192.168.3.1 255.255.255.0
!
router ospf 1
 network 192.168.0.0 0.0.255.255 area 0
```

Router R2 Configuration:
```
interface serial 0
 ip address 192.168.1.2 255.255.255.0
!
interface serial 1
 ip address 192.168.2.2 255.255.255.0
!
router ospf 1
 network 192.168.0.0 0.0.255.255 area 0
```

Router R3 Configuration:

```
interface serial 0
 ip address 192.168.3.3 255.255.255.0
!
interface serial 1
 ip address 192.168.2.3 255.255.255.0
!
router ospf 1
 network 192.168.0.0 0.0.255.255 area 0
```

In these configurations, the OSPF process in each router is specified as 1. This is done simply to ease configuration effort. The OSPF process-id in each router could have been defined using different values in each router, which must specify the same area-id value. If the area-id values are not in agreement, the exchange of hello packets would not result in the formation of neighbor adjacencies and hence each router would not be able to reach the networks attached to the adjacent routers. Since this is a single OSPF area network, the area-id must have a 0 specified in order for OSPF to create a routing table.

DR and BDR Election Using a Loopback Interface

Suppose the network were a data center backbone configuration, as shown in Figure 18-3, where each router on the Ethernet backbone is participating in the OSPF area. In this configuration, the routers would be sitting on a broadcast network and would therefore go through a DR and BDR election process.

Figure 18-3
A single area OSPF network over Ethernet using DR and BDR.

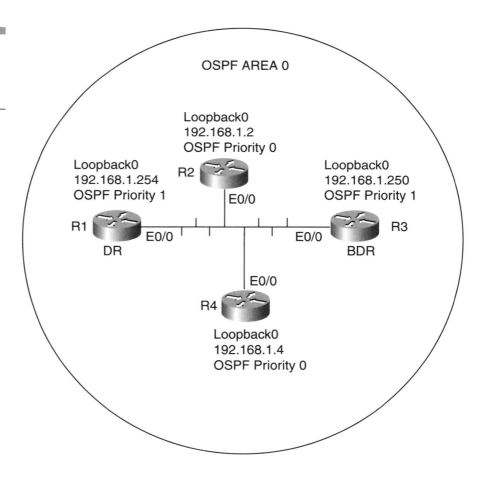

The following router configurations detail the OSPF parameters:

Router 1 Configuration:

```
interface Ethernet 0/0
 ip address 172.16.1.1 255.255.255.0
!
interface loopback 0
 ip address 192.168.1.254 255.255.255.252
!
router ospf 1
 network 172.16.0.0 0.0.255.255 area 0
 network 192.168.1.254 0.0.0.0 area 0
```

Router 2 Configuration:

```
interface Ethernet 0/0
 ip address 172.16.1.2 255.255.255.0
 ip ospf priority 0
!
interface loopback 0
 ip address 192.168.1.2 255.255.255.252

router ospf 1
 network 172.16.0.0 0.0.255.255 area 0
 network 192.168.1.4 0.0.0.0 area 0
```

Router 3 Configuration:

```
interface Ethernet 0/0
 ip address 172.16.1.3 255.255.255.0
!
interface loopback 0
 ip address 192.168.1.250 255.255.255.252

router ospf 1
 network 172.16.0.0 0.0.255.255 area 0
 network 192.168.1.250 0.0.0.0 area 0
```

Router 4 Configuration:

```
interface Ethernet 0/0
 ip address 172.16.1.4 255.255.255.0
ip ospf priority 0
!
interface loopback 0
 ip address 192.168.1.4 255.255.255.252

router ospf 1
 network 172.16.0.0 0.0.255.255 area 0
 network 192.168.1.4 0.0.0.0 area 0
```

In this configuration example, the use of the loopback interface, along with optional OSPF interface commands, is shown in determining the DR and BDR for the OSPF area. The DR election process is determined by first discovering which router on the OSPF broadcast network has the highest router priority. The second-highest router priority value presented by a router in the OSPF broadcast network becomes the BDR.

The OSPF process in Cisco IOS defaults the router priority value to 1. Since this automatically generates a tie with any other participating OSPF router, the tie is broken by determining the highest router ID. The router ID within a router is determined by the OSPF process of selecting the highest IP address assigned to any enabled OSPF interface, which is only superseded by the configuration of a loopback interface.

Allowing the OSPF election process to decide on the DR and BDR can become critical in busy backbone areas and creates an unknown topology. A Cisco router administrator can modify the OSPF DR/BDR election process by using the interface command ip ospf priority. The format of the command is as follows:

ip ospf priority *number*

The *number* parameter value can range from 0 to 255, where 0 is the default value. The value 255 is the highest value allowed. As shown in the configurations above that detail the topology diagrammed in Figure 18-3, we can see how using the ip ospf priority interface command, along with the IP address assignment of a loopback interface, can predetermine the DR and BDR on a broadcast network.

The OSPF process for Cisco automatically selects a loopback interface IP address as the preferred router ID over other interfaces. This is because the loopback interface is always active. If multiple loopback interfaces are defined, the OSPF process selects the highest IP address of all the defined loopback interfaces as the router ID.

Combining this knowledge with the ip ospf priority command, router R1 becomes the DR, and router R3 becomes the BDR for the sample network configuration. The election of router R1 as the DR is due to the fact that the ip ospf priority value defaults to 1, and the router ID presented in the Hello packet is the IP address 192.168.1.254 on the loopback 0 interface of router R1. Router R3 defaults the ip ospf priority value to a 1, making it DR-eligible. Because the router ID presented by router R3 is the IP address 192.168.1.250, however, which is found on the loopback 0 interface of router R3, it is elected as BDR since its IP address is lower than that presented by router R1.

Routers R2 and R4 each have loopback 0 interface definitions, yet the ip ospf priority value of 0 defined on the Ethernet interface connecting the router to OSPF area 0 indicates that these routers are not DR-eligible and therefore will not participate in the election process.

Predetermining the DR and BDR on a broadcast network, as described above, enables reduced link-state updates because LSAs are only delivered to the assigned DR and BDR routers. This allows for added design enhancements so that these routers only take care of the OSPF routing tables and are not part of delivering the data traffic to end user networks. Secondly, if all the routers are DR-eligible, an election storm process could occur on large router backbone networks. If the DR were to become inoperative, the BDR becomes the DR. In the above example, there is no BDR once this happens. However, once the router R1 connects to the network again, it becomes the new BDR until router R3 disconnects from the network.

Multi-Area OSPF Networks

The concept of areas within an OSPF network enables extremely large scalable network topologies. Using OSPF hierarchical area topologies addresses the scalable issues found in a single large OSPF area network. The advantages to a hierarchical topology are as follows:

- CPU overhead is reduced, due to frequent Shortest Path First (SPF) calculations.
- Routing table size is kept to a minimum.
- Route summarization minimizes the LSU overhead, protecting bandwidth.

Figure 18-4 illustrates a simple OSPF hierarchical topology, which is also referred to as hierarchical routing. A hierarchical routed network is a single autonomous system broken into smaller, more manageable networks termed areas. Routing between the areas is called inter-area routing, and routing within an area is termed intra-area routing. Because OSPF views each area as a network unto itself, SPF calculations for changes within an area are performed only by the routers within the area. In designing an OSPF hierarchical routing network, architecting a well-thought out IP addressing scheme can further reduce routing table updates between areas by using route summarization. Because of this summarization, fewer LSUs are required to update the entire OSPF network.

OSPF Route Summarization

Summarizing routes between OSPF areas is the key to achieving a scalable hierarchical routing topology. OSPF summarizes two types of routes: intra-area (IA) routes and external routes. The IA routes are summarized by Area Border Routers (ABR) and external routes are summarized by Autonomous System Border Routers (ASBR). A router can perform both the ABR and ASBR functions simultaneously. Proper route summarization requires a contiguous IP address space for each OSPF area. Using discontiguous IP addressing between areas can cause an OSPF router to forward packets erroneously.

Figure 18-4
OSPF hierarchical
routing topology.

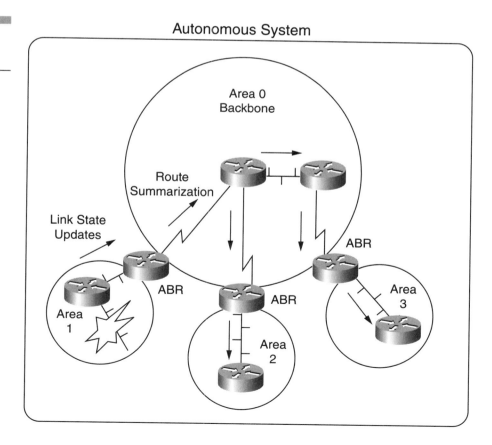

Figure 18-5 illustrates the use of route summarization between OSPF areas. Both router R1 and R2 are ABR routers connecting OSPF area 0 to OSPF area 1 and area 2. Router R1 connects both area 0 and area 1, while router R2 connects area 0 to area 2. Summarizing routes between these areas enables summarization in both directions. Area 0 has reserved the address range 172.20.96–127.0, using 255.255.255.0 as the mask. Area 1 has reserved the address range 172.20.32–63.0, using 255.255.255.0 as the mask. Area 2 has reserved the address range 172.20.64–95.0, using 255.255.255.0 as the address range.

The following configuration example highlights the commands for the topology in Figure 18-5:

Router 1 Configuration:

```
interface Ethernet 0
 ip address 172.20.96.1 255.255.255.0
!
interface serial 0
 ip address 172.20.32.1 255.255.255.0
!
router ospf 1
 network 172.20.96.1 0.0.0.0 area 0
 network 172.20.32.1 0.0.0.0 area 1
 area 0 range 172.20.96.0 255.255.224.0
 area 1 range 172.20.32.0 255.255.224.0
```

Figure 18-5
OSPF router summarization between areas.

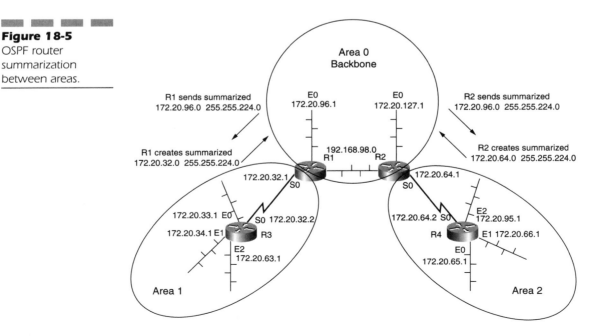

Router 3 Configuration:

```
interface Ethernet 0
 ip address 172.20.33.1 255.255.255.0
!
interface Ethernet 1
 ip address 172.20.34.1 255.255.255.0
!
interface Ethernet 2
 ip address 172.20.63.1 255.255.255.0

interface serial 0
 ip address 172.20.32.2 255.255.255.0
!
router ospf 1
network 172.20.0.0 0.0.255.255 area 1
```

Router R2 Configuration:

```
interface Ethernet 0
 ip address 172.20.127.1 255.255.255.0
!
interface serial 0
 ip address 172.20.64.1 255.255.255.0
!
router ospf 1
 network 172.20.127.1 0.0.0.0 area 0
 network 172.20.64.1 0.0.0.0 area 2
 area 0 range 172.20.127.0 255.255.224.0
 area 2 range 172.20.64.0 255.255.224.0
```

Router R4 Configuration:

```
interface Ethernet 0
 ip address 172.20.65.1 255.255.255.0
!
interface Ethernet 1
 ip address 172.20.66.1 255.255.255.0
!
interface Ethernet 2
 ip address 172.20.95.1 255.255.255.0
!
interface serial 0
 ip address 172.20.64.2 255.255.255.0
!
router ospf 1
 network 172.20.0.0 0.0.255.255 area 2
```

The summarization of the routes between the areas is accomplished by specifying the **area range** router command. The format of the command is as follows:

area *area-id* range *address mask*

The *area-id* parameter value denotes the OSPF area to which the summarization is being applied. The *address* parameter value is the IP address value used to define the range of addresses being summarized. The *mask* parameter value is the bit mask applied to the IP address specified by the address parameter.

In the above example configuration, the router R1 and R2 are ABR routers. Route summarization is performed only on ABR routers. The command area 0 range 172.20.96.0 255.255.224.0 on both router R1 and R2 denotes a summarized route. The applied summarization mask is a full 19-bit mask, which applies to the range of addresses for the subnets assigned to the three areas.

Suppose the subnet range in area 1 began at 8 with a mask of 255.255.252.0 applied to the IP addresses. In this case, multiple area range commands would be necessary to summarize the routes. For example, the IP networks coming from area 1 would consist of the following:

IP subnet address	Binary	Summarized mask
172.20.8.0	00001000	255.255.248.0
172.20.12.0	00001100	255.255.248.0
172.20.16.0	00010000	255.255.240.0
172.20.20.0	00010100	255.255.240.0
172.20.24.0	00011000	255.255.240.0
172.20.28.0	00011100	255.255.240.0
172.20.32.0	00100000	255.255.224.0
172.20.36.0	00100000	255.255.224.0
172.20.60.0	00100000	255.255.224.0

The resulting area range commands used in router R1 to summarize these new routes are

```
area 1 range 172.20.8.0 255.255.248.0
area 1 range 172.20.16.0 225.255.240.0
area 1 range 172.20.32.0 255.255.224.0
```

All 14 subnets are summarized into these three summary statements. It must be restated here that the IP addressing scheme deployed is paramount in using effective route summarization. If overlapping subnet masks are used, then summarization would be impossible and would cause undue SPF calculations and LSUs to traverse the links.

It is not prudent to summarize routes between OSPF areas when more than one ABR connects the two areas. Sending summarized routes between areas in such a topology reduces routing table size, but can also lead to the selection of a suboptimal path. This is especially important to note for ABR connectivity to OSPF area 0.

NOTE: *In an OSPF hierarchical routing topology, the* **router ospf** *process-id parameter is used to identify the autonomous system number of the OSPF network. Every OSPF router participating in an OSPF routing protocol must be using the same autonomous system number in order to exchange link state databases.*

In very large OSPF networks, it may be advantageous to divide the single OSPF autonomous system into smaller hierarchical networks with multiple autonomous systems defined. For example, in Figure 18-6, a large corporation has multiple areas within a large geographical area. The OSPF routing tables, due to expansion, have grown excessively large. Dividing the network into multiple autonomous systems would allow summarization between autonomous systems.

The ASBR routers R4 and R5 summarize the entire AS 1 routing table and forward the summarized route to router R2 and R6, which are part of AS 2. Likewise, R4 and R5 summarize the entire AS 2 routing table and forward the summarized route to router R1 and R3 in AS 1. Routers R4 and R5 are configured as follows:

Router R4 Configuration:

```
interface Ethernet 0
 ip address 10.1.1.1 255.255.255.0
!
interface Ethernet 1
 ip address 20.1.1.1 255.255.255.0
!
router ospf 1
 network 10.1.1.1 0.0.0.0 area 0
 summary-address 20.0.0.0 255.0.0.0
!
router ospf 2
 network 20.1.1.1 0.0.0.0 area 0
 summary-address 10.0.0.0 255.0.0.0
```

Figure 18-6
ASBR route
summarization.

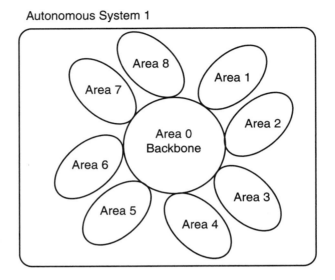

Autonomous System 1

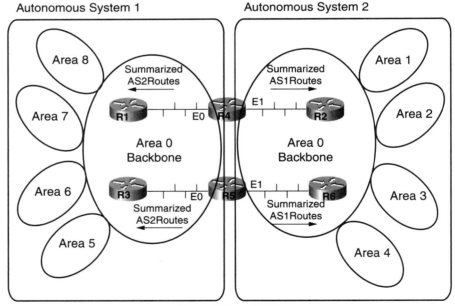

R4 and R5 are ASBRs

Router R5 Configuration:

```
interface Ethernet 0
 ip address 10.1.1.5 255.255.255.0
 !
interface Ethernet 1
 ip address 20.1.1.5 255.255.255.0
 !
router ospf 1
 network 10.1.1.5 0.0.0.0 area 0
 summary-address 20.0.0.0 255.0.0.0
 !
router ospf 2
 network 20.1.1.5 0.0.0.0 area 0
 summary-address 10.0.0.0 255.0.0.0
```

The summary-address router command is used to summarize the OSPF routes from AS1 and AS2. The format of the command is

summary-address *address mask*

The *address* parameter value is the IP network address on which the mask will be applied. The *mask* parameter consists of the relative bits for performing the external route summarization.

Stub, Totally Stubby, and Not-So-Stubby-Area (NSSA) OSPF Areas

OSPF link-state advertisement (LSA) type-5 defining routes to external networks are not flooded into the stub area. Instead, the ABR connecting to the stub area sends a default route (0.0.0.0) for external networks into the stub area. This allows a router within the stub area to forward a packet destined for a network that is not found in the stub area router routing table. The stub area router will forward packets for networks not found in its own table to the ABR router that sent the 0.0.0.0 LSA. Figure 18-7 illustrates the topology of a stub area in OSPF.

Cisco IOS further reduces the size of a routing table within a stub area router by using the totally stubby area feature. A totally stubby area blocks OSPF LSA type-5, as does a stub area, but also blocks OSPF type 3 and 4 summary LSA for intra-area routes from being introduced into the stub area. Using this Cisco-specific feature, only intra-area stub routes and the default 0.0.0.0 routes are known in the stub area routers. An ABR forwards a summary LSA type 3 and 4 into the totally stubby area, which enables the stub area route to select the closest ABR gateway to all networks outside of the totally stubby area.

Stub and totally stubby areas are typically found in a hub and spoke topology. The stub or totally stubby area is the spoke. This is very common when using Frame Relay on the WAN. Further discussion on using Frame Relay with OSPF is found in Chapter 21, "Defining Frame Relay."

The OSPF Not-So-Stubby-Area (NSSA) option is defined in RFC 1587 and became a requirement under OSPF to enable a stub area router to use a non-OSPF routing protocol. This hybrid situation allows LSA type-7 (autonomous system external routes) to be forward to the OSPF network. Figure 18-8 illustrates the topology.

As shown in Figure 18-8, the NSSA connecting router R1 to router R2 must forward the routes from router R2 that are not OSPF routes. In this case, these routes are created from the RIP process on router R2, which is defined as an ASBR router. Router R2 is configured to perform RIP and OSPF routing. When router R2 receives an RIP update for networks 10.100.0.0/16, 10.110.0.0/16, and 20.20.0.0/8, it imports them into type-7 LSAs and forwards these LSAs to router R1. Router R1 is configured as an ABR, connecting to the OSPF backbone area 0 network. After router R1 performs SPF calculation, the type-7 LSAs are translated into type-5 LSAs and are flooded to area 0. Router R1 can also perform route summarization on these external routes received from the NSSA or it can filter these routes from the backbone area 0.

Figure 18-7
Stub and totally
stubby network
topology.

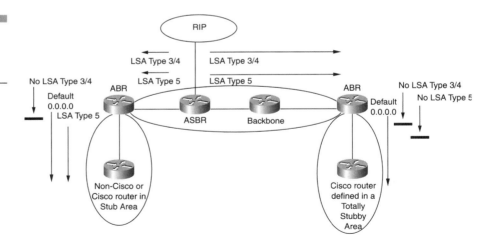

Figure 18-8
NSSA OSPF network
topology.

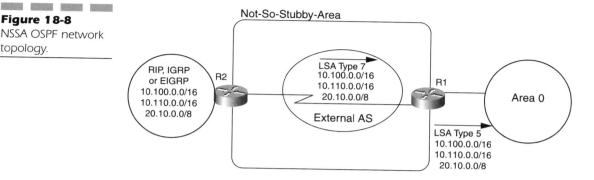

Configuring a Stub and Totally Stubby Areas

A stub area is identified by specifying the area stub command on all routers participating in the OSPF stub area. The area stub command has the following format:

area *area-id* **stub [no-summary]**

The *area-id* parameter is the identifier associated with the stub or totally stubby area. It can be either a decimal value ranging from 0 to 4,294,967,295 or in a dotted-decimal format akin to an IP address. The optional no-summary keyword is used to define the stub area as a totally stubby area, eliminating the type 3 and 4 LSAs, along with LSA type 5, from entering the area.

In Figure 18-9, a typical topology for using a stub or totally stubby area is illustrated. The following configuration details the configuration for routers R1, R2, and R3 in forming the stub area.

Router R1 Configuration:

```
interface Ethernet 0
 ip address 10.10.10.1 255.255.255.0
!
interface serial 0
 ip address 10.20.20.1 255.255.255.0
!
interface serial 1
 ip address 10.30.30.1 255.255.255.0
!
router ospf 1
 network 10.10.10.1 0.0.0.0 area 0
 network 10.20.20.1 0.0.0.0 area 1
 network 10.30.30.1 0.0.0.0 area 2
 area 1 stub
 area 2 stub
```

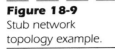

Figure 18-9
Stub network
topology example.

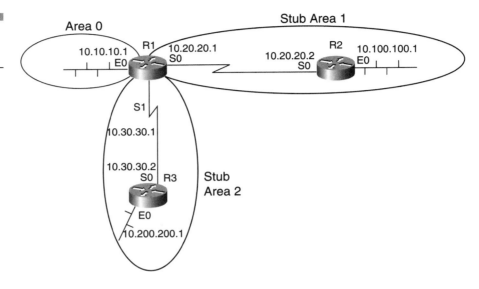

Router R2 Configuration:

```
interface Ethernet 0
 ip address 10.100.100.1 255.255.255.0
!
interface serial 0
 ip address 10.20.20.2 255.255.255.0
!
router ospf 1
 network 10.0.0.0 0.0.0.0 area 1
 area 1 stub
```

Router R3 Configuration:

```
interface Ethernet 0
 ip address 10.200.200.1 255.255.255.0
!
interface serial 0
 ip address 10.30.30.3 255.255.255.0
!
router ospf 1
 network 10.0.0.0 0.0.0.0 area 2
 area 2 stub
```

The stub area 1 in the example configuration is changed to a totally stubby area by changing the router R1 configuration to include the no-summary keyword on the area stub command. This causes router R1 to forward a default route of 0.0.0.0 for all external routes out of the stub area. The resulting IOS configuration for router R1 is as follows:

Router R1 configuration for totally stubby areas:

```
interface Ethernet 0
 ip address 10.10.10.1 255.255.255.0
!
interface serial 0
 ip address 10.20.20.1 255.255.255.0
!
interface serial 1
 ip address 10.30.30.1 255.255.255.0
!
router ospf 1
 network 10.10.10.1 0.0.0.0 area 0
 network 10.20.20.1 0.0.0.0 area 1
 network 10.30.30.1 0.0.0.0 area 2
 area 1 stub no-summary
 area 2 stub
```

Defining the area stub with the no-summary command enables the totally stubby Cisco-specific feature. This command is needed only on the ABR router that connects the OSPF standard area with the stub area.

Configuring a NSSA

NSSA configurations are most useful in situations where the OSPF hierarchical routing network must connect to a non-OSPF network. This is typically used in Internet Service Provider (ISP) connections and in merged corporate networks due to corporate acquisitions or during migration from non-OSPF to OSPF hierarchical routing.

Shown in Figure 18-10 is an example NSSA network configuration with router R1 and R2 forming the NSSA OSPF area. Router R1 performs the non-OSPF-to-OSPF translation of non-OSPF routing updates to OSPF external link-state advertisement type-7. Router R2 translates these received type-7 LSAs to type-5 LSAs and can further summarize or filter routes to the NSSA area. Prior to using NSSA, this type of configuration required the non-OSPF and OSPF routing protocols to be executing on the standard OSPF area, which in this case is router R2.

The following is the configuration for router R1 and R2 referencing Figure 18-10:

Router R1 Configuration for NSSA:

```
interface serial 0
 ip address 192.168.1.1 255.255.255.252
!
```

Figure 18-10
NSSA topology
connecting a RIP
network to an OSPF
hierarchical network.

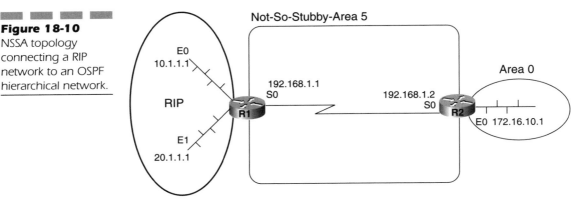

```
interface Ethernet 0
 ip address 10.1.1.1 255.255.255.0
!
interface Ethernet 1
 ip address 20.1.1.1 255.255.0.0
!
router rip
 network 10.0.0.0
 network 20.0.0.0
router ospf 1
 redistribute rip subnets
 network 192.168.1.1 0.0.0.0 area 5
 area 5 nssa
```

Router R2 Configuration for NSSA:

```
interface serial 0
 ip address 192.168.1.2 255.255.255.252
!
interface Ethernet 0
 ip address 172.16.10.1 255.255.255.0
!
router ospf 1
 summary-address 10.0.0.0 255.0.0.0 tag 16
 summary-address 20.0.0.0 255.0.0.0 tag 8
 network 192.168.1.2 0.0.0.0 area 5
 network 172.16.10.1 0.0.0.0 area 0
 area 5 nssa
```

The router R1 configuration indicates that the Ethernet interfaces 0 and 1 are using RIP as the routing protocol to the external network. This is determined by the network commands following the router rip command. The serial interface 0 on router R1 uses OSPF as the routing protocol and OSPF knows to use serial 0 interface because of the network area command found under the router ospf command. The redistribute rip subnets command under the router ospf command in router R1 directs the OSPF process on router R1 to translate the RIP updates into OSPF external link-state advertisement type-7 LSAs. The translation is to type-7 LSAs based on the area nssa command. In the router R1 configuration example, the NSSA area-id is defined as the decimal number 5. The format of the area nssa command is

area *area-id* nssa [no-redistribution]
[default-information-originate]

The *area-id* parameter can be either a decimal number ranging from 1 to 4294967295 or a dotted-decimal format in the form of an IP address. The optional **no-redistribution** keyword is used only on the NSSA ABR router, in our example router R2, and directs the OSPF process to import routes only into the standard OSPF areas and not the NSSA areas. The **default-information-originate** optional keyword may be used to tell the NSSA ABR to send a default type-7 LSA into the NSSA area.

An optional command under the router ospf command in the router R2 configuration is included to discuss route aggregation. The command is summary-address and the format is as follows:

summary-address *address mask* [*prefix mask*] [not-advertise]
[tag *tag*]

The *address* parameter value is the IP address used to identify the range of addresses. The first *mask* parameter value is the bit mask applied to the address value to identify the summarized route. The optional parameter *prefix* is the IP address of a destination network that can be summarized. The following optional *mask* parameter value is the mask applied to the *prefix* value. The optional keyword **not-advertised** is used to suppress the routes that match the prefix/mask pairing so the routes are not advertised at all. The optional **tag** keyword and parameter *tag* are used to determine a match value in redistributing routes using route maps. The value used for *tag* ranges from 0 to 4294967295.

Using OSPF Virtual Links

OSPF hierarchical routing is based on the premise that all areas connect to the backbone area 0 network. There may be times in the course of network implementation when operational cost requires the connectivity of a new OSPF area to the backbone area 0 network through another standard area. OSPF virtual links perform this task, connecting a disconnected area to the OSPF backbone area 0 network.

OSPF virtual links provide a logical path from the disconnected area to the backbone area. Virtual links have multiple purposes. The first is to connect a remote area with no physical connectivity to the backbone area. The second is to add a connection to a discontinuous backbone area. A third use is to provide redundancy when a router failure could cause a divided backbone area. The logical path connecting the disconnected areas is that the virtual link must be defined on the two routers that can share the common area and one of these routers must be connected to the backbone. The common area used for making the logical connection cannot be a stub area. The common area used for establishing the virtual link to the backbone is termed the transit area.

Configuring Virtual Links

In Figure 18-11, a virtual link topology connecting a remote location to the OSPF backbone area over serially connected routers is illustrated. Router R1 connects to the backbone area 0 network as well as to area 1 over a serial line to router R2. Router R2 connects over a serial line to router R3, which has been defined with area 2 attached to it. This type of topology is very plausible when the cost of establishing a physical link from router R3 to the backbone ABR is excessive over the connection to router R2.

In this figure, router R3 connects area 1 and area 2. It is then an ABR router and meets the virtual link requirement. Secondly, router R1 is connected to the backbone area and it is also an ABR router. Router R2, being in area 1, participates in the virtual link as a pass-through node, delivering the LSUs between router R1 and router R3. Area 1 becomes the transit area for the virtual link.

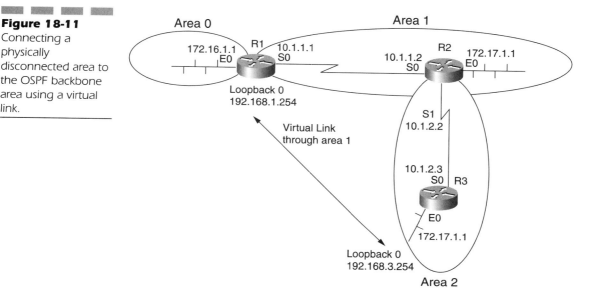

Figure 18-11
Connecting a physically disconnected area to the OSPF backbone area using a virtual link.

The following example configurations detail the virtual link connection for Figure 18-11:

Router R1 Configuration for Virtual link to router R3:

```
interface serial 0
 ip address 10.1.1.1 255.255.255.0
!
interface loopback 0
 ip address 192.168.1.254 255.255.255.252
!
interface Ethernet 0
 ip address 172.16.1.1 255.255.255.0
!
router ospf 1
 network 10.1.1.1 0.0.0.0 area 1
 network 172.16.0.0 0.0.255.255 area 0
 area 1 virtual-link 192.168.3.254
```

Router R2 Configuration for Virtual link to router R3:

```
interface serial 0
 ip address 10.1.1.2 255.255.255.0
!
interface serial 1
 ip address 10.1.2.2 255.255.255.0
!
```

```
interface loopback 0
 ip address 192.168.2.254 255.255.255.252
!
interface Ethernet 0
 ip address 172.17.1.1 255.255.255.0
!
router ospf 1
 network 10.1.0.0 0.0.255.255 area 2
 network 172.17.0.0 0.0.255.255 area 1
```

Router R3 Configuration for Virtual link to router R1:

```
interface serial 0
 ip address 10.1.2.3 255.255.255.0
!
interface loopback 0
 ip address 192.168.3.254 255.255.255.252
!
interface Ethernet 0
 ip address 172.18.1.1 255.255.255.0
!
router ospf 1
 network 10.1.2.0 0.0.0.255 area 1
 network 172.18.0.0 0.0.255.255 area 2
 area 1 virtual-link 192.168.1.254
```

In the example configurations, the router ID of router R3 is defined in the configuration for router R1 as the end point of the virtual link, connecting through transit area 1. In router R3, the router ID of router R1 is defined as the end point of the virtual link through transit area 1. The router IDs for the example use the IP address of the loopback interface of each router. The configuration in router R1 does not have any special definitions to allow the virtual connection. Although it may appear as a stub area, it is not defined as such and can therefore be used for establishing the virtual link.

The format of the area virtual-link command is as follows:

area *area-id* **virtual-link** *router-id* [**hello-interval** *seconds*] [**retransmit-interval** *seconds*] [**transmit-delay** *seconds*] [**dead-interval** *seconds*] [[**authentication-key** *key*] | [**message-digest-key** *keyid* **md5** *key*]]

The *area-id* parameter is the decimal or IP address dotted-decimal format identifier for the area being used as the transit area for the virtual link. The *router-id* parameter is the router-ID of the end point to which the router is defining the virtual link. The optional keyword **hello-interval** parameter *seconds* defaults to a value of 10 seconds and can range from 1 to 8192, measured in seconds. The value specified here must be defined on all participating routes on the common network. The value specifies the number of seconds the router will wait between sending hello-packets on the virtual link.

The optional **retransmit-interval** keyword parameter *seconds* defaults to five seconds with a range of 1 to 8192. This value specifies the time in seconds for retransmitting LSAs to adjacency routers. The value must be greater than the expected round-trip delay between the routes on the virtual link. The optional **transmit-delay** keyword parameter *seconds* defaults to one second and can range from 1 to 8192. The value specified increments the age count on the LSU packet before transmitting on the virtual link.

The optional keyword **dead-interval** parameter *seconds* defaults to four times the hello interval and also ranges from 1 to 8192. The value specified here must be the same on all routers attached to the same common network. This interval is the time in seconds that must expire without the router receiving hello packets from the far end of the virtual link in order to declare the far-end router down. The optional authentication-key parameter key value is the password used on hello packets to the far end of the virtual link to authenticate the far-end router. The value is a continuous string of up to eight characters long. The far end must use the same password so that the routers establish a full state between them.

The configuration global command service password-encryption affects the key value, making the value from the **sh config**, **sh run**, **sh start**, and **wr terminal** display output encrypted for the key value. The optional **message-digest-key md5** parameter *keyid* is a decimal value ranging from 1 to 255, and the *key* parameter is an alphanumeric string up to 16 characters long. These values are used by the far-end router on the virtual point connection when MD5 authentication is in use. Again, all routes on the common network must use the same *keyid* and *key* values for OSPF to operate properly.

Non-Broadcast and Broadcast Network Configurations

OSPF, as of Cisco IOS Release 12.0, can configure NBMA networks as broadcast networks and broadcast networks as NBMA networks. This capability allows you to override the default media type for an interface. This capability is especially useful in point-multipoint networks like Frame Relay. However, the point-multipoint feature available with Cisco IOS can also be applied to an Ethernet, Token Ring, or FDDI network as well. If a network is to be viewed as an NBMA-type network, a neighbor must be specified for each router connection that requires OSPF routing information. Defining a link as an OSPF point-to-multipoint connection enables broadcasting on NBMA networks. The point-multipoint feature has the following advantages:

- Explicit configuration of neighbor routers is not required.
- Only one IP subnet is used for the entire point-to-multipoint connection.
- Routing between the end points is accomplished through the common point connecting them.
- No DR election is required.
- It does not require a fully meshed network topology.

In some broadcast topologies there will be routers that do not support multicasting. In these networks, even if they are broadcast-based (such as Ethernet), a Cisco router can view the network as a non –broadcast network and therefore require neighbor routers be defined.

Configuring OSPF Point-to-Multipoint

Three OSPF commands are specific to the point-multipoint feature. The first of these is the ip ospf network command. The format of the command is as follows:

ip ospf network {broadcast | non-broadcast | {point-to-multipoint [non-broadcast]}}

This command is entered under the interface on which the default media type is being overridden for OSPF. The broadcast keyword uses an NBMA or point-to-point connection as if it were actually a broadcast network. The non-broadcast keyword modifies the use of a broadcast network to that of a NBMA network, requiring the router administrator to define the router neighbors connected to the network. The point-to-multipoint keyword enables an NBMA network connection to be used by OSPF as if it were a broadcast network. The optional non-broadcast keyword of the point-multipoint keyword forces OSPF to use the point-to-multipoint connection it is defined on as a non-broadcast connection, requiring the definitions of the routing neighbor at the far end of the connection.

The neighboring routers on non-broadcast configurations are defined using the neighbor command under the router ospf command. The format of the neighbor command is as follows:

neighbor *ip-address* **[priority** *number*] **[poll-interval** *seconds*] **[cost** *number*]

The ip-address parameter of the neighbor command is the interface IP address assigned to the router at the other end of the connection. The optional priority keyword and parameter number are used in assigning the eligibility of this neighbor as a DR or BDR router. The default is 0 and can range from 1 to 255. This keyword does not apply when the ip ospf network point-to-multipoint command is specified for the neighbors interface on this router. The optional poll-interval keyword and its parameter seconds indicates the number of seconds between hello packets being sent to the neighbor after the dead-interval has expired and the neighboring router is declared down. The optional cost keyword and parameter number allows the router administrator to apply an OSPF cost to the link connecting to the neighbor. This keyword is ignored when used for an interface that is defined as an NBMA connection.

Figure 18-12 illustrates the use of a point-to-multipoint connection over a Frame Relay network. Router R1 in Figure 18-12 uses a single Frame Relay serial link connection to router R2 and router R3. All three routers define the Frame Relay connection as point-to-multipoint and specify the broadcast keyword on the Frame Relay map ip command defined for the interface. The Frame Relay-specific commands are discussed in Chapter 22, "Defining Frame Relay."

The following is the example router configuration for Figure 18-12:

Router 1 Configuration:

```
interface serial 0
 ip address 172.16.10.1 255.255.255.0
 ip ospf network point-to-multipoint
 encapsulation frame-relay
 frame-relay map ip 172.16.10.2 30 broadcast
 frame-relay map ip 172.16.10.3 31 broadcast
!
router ospf 1
 network 172.16.10.1 0.0.0.255 area 0
```

Figure 18-12
An OSPF point-to-
multipoint Frame
Relay connection as a
broadcast network.

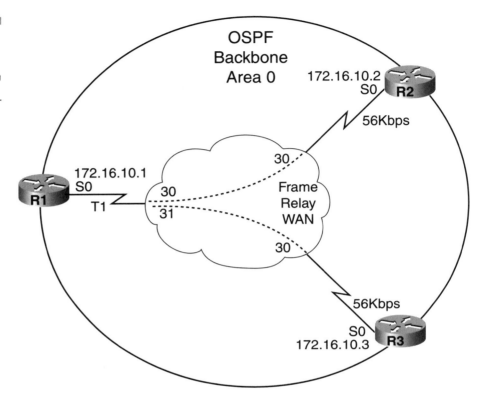

Router 2 Configuration:

```
interface serial 0
 ip address 172.16.10.2 255.255.255.0
 ip ospf network point-to-multipoint
 encapsulation frame-relay
 clockrate 56
 frame-relay map ip 172.16.10.1 30 broadcast
!
router ospf 1
 network 172.16.10.2 0.0.0.0 area 0
```

Router 3 Configuration:

```
interface serial 0
 ip address 172.16.10.3 255.255.255.0
 ip ospf network point-to-multipoint
```

```
 encapsulation frame-relay
 clock rate 56
 frame-relay map ip 172.16.10.1 30 broadcast
!
router ospf 1
 network 172.16.10.3 0.0.0.0 area 0
```

The above configuration listed for Figure 18-12 illustrates the use of the point-to-multipoint configuration for OSPF over Frame Relay as an NBMA network. In the next example, the same network topology is used, but the network is defined as a non-broadcast point-to-multipoint configuration. In this instance, the neighbor command is required to identify the router peer at the far end of the Frame Relay connection.

Router 1 configuration using point-to-multipoint non-broadcast:

```
interface serial 0
 ip address 172.16.10.1 255.255.255.0
 ip ospf network point-to-multipoint non-broadcast
 encapsulation frame-relay
 frame-relay local-dlci 200
 frame-relay map ip 172.16.10.2 30
 frame-relay map ip 172.16.10.3 31
!
router ospf 1
 network 172.16.10.1 0.0.0.0 area 0
 neighbor 172.16.10.2 cost 15
 neighbor 172.16.10.3 cost 20
```

Router 2 configuration using point-to-multipoint non-broadcast:

```
interface serial 0
 ip address 172.16.10.2 255.255.255.0
 encapsulation frame-relay
 ip ospf network point-to-multipoint non-broadcast
 frame-relay local-dlci 30
 frame-relay map ip 172.16.10.1 30
!
 router ospf 1
 network 172.16.10.2 0.0.0.0 area 0
```

Router 3 configuration using point-to-multipoint non-broadcast:

```
interface serial 0
 ip address 172.16.10.3 255.255.255.0
 encapsulation frame-relay
 ip ospf network point-to-multipoint non-broadcast
 frame-relay local-dlci 31
```

```
frame-relay map ip 172.16.10.1 31
!
router ospf 1
 network 172.16.10.3 0.0.0.0 area 0
```

In the non-broadcast configuration, the neighbor command is used only on the hub router, which in this scenario is router R1. A cost is applied to each individual neighbor on the physical serial interface of router R1, enabling OSPF to calculate a different cost for routes to each neighboring router. Prior to IOS Release 12.0, the ip ospf cost interface command had to be used to apply a cost to the connection, but now the ip ospf cost value is applied to all the virtual circuits connecting to the physical Frame Relay connection. Using the neighbor command allows unique costs to be applied to each DLCI of a Frame Relay connection. Frame Relay DLCI connections, defined using subinterfaces, can safely use the ip ospf cost command as a means of applying a cost to the DLCI connection without defining neighbors. The format of the ip ospf cost command is

ip ospf cost *cost*

The cost parameter is an unsigned decimal value ranging from 1 to 65535. Applying this command to an interface overrides the default OSPF cost for the media type. The default cost of an OSPF link is determined by using the following formula:

10^8 / bandwidth value

The bandwidth-value is the default bandwidth of the connected interface. The default OSPF path cost for the following links are listed here:

- 56-kbps serial link: 1785
- 64-kbps serial link: 1562
- T1 (1.544-Mbps serial link): 65
- E1 (2.048-Mbps serial link): 48
- 4-Mbps Token Ring: 25
- Ethernet: 10
- 16-Mbps Token Ring: 6
- FDDI and ATM (OC-3 and higher): 1

The ip ospf cost interface command can be used for any OSPF network connection and is not specific to NBMA or broadcast topologies.

NOTE: *The interface command bandwidth changes the OSPF calculated cost of a link when the ip ospf cost command is not specified for the interface.*

CHAPTER 19

Configuring BGP Routing Protocol

The Border Gateway Protocol (BGP) is an IETF standard defined in RFCs 1163, 1267, 1654, 1655, and 1771, with the latest standard being termed BGP4 for version 4. Cisco IOS supports versions 2, 3, and 4. BGP provides a loop-free routing environment for autonomous systems (AS). Under BGP, an autonomous system is a unique IP network of routers under control of a specific entity. Each AS can potentially use multiple interior gateway protocols (IGPs) for the exchange of routing tables within the AS, which uses an exterior gateway protocol (EGP) to send packets outside of the AS.

BGP is not always a requirement for connecting between autonomous systems. In most cases, the driving force for implementing BGP is the routing policies enacted between the connecting AS networks. If the routing policy of the one AS is the same as the connecting AS network, BGP is not even necessary. For example, a static route and default networks can be defined within the corporate network to provide connectivity to the connecting AS, which uses BGP to connect to other networks. This is often used when connecting a corporate network to an ISP provider that uses BGP to connect to the Internet. Many corporations use two ISPs or connections to the Internet to facilitate redundancy, load sharing, and cost-reduction through connection options that enable lower tariffs for off-hours use. In the redundancy case, using backup link static and default network routes may be suitable, instead of implementing BGP. Configuring the ISP connections for load sharing will most likely require BGP.

A typical BGP network topology is illustrated in Figure 19-1. The corporate network has two ISP connections that enable the company to have redundancy, availability, and load sharing. In Figure 19-1, ISP1 connects to the corporate network in San Diego, while ISP2 connects to the corporate network in Atlanta. The policy of the corporate network in agreement with the ISP vendors is to have the majority of Internet traffic traversing the connection in Atlanta during the off-peak hours for the West Coast and the San Diego connection used during off-peak hours for the East Coast. This provides the lowest tariff rates for the corporation while maintaining redundancy, availability, and load sharing.

Routing policy plays an important role in determining the use of BGP. In Figure 19-2, a new AS (AS 60) is connected to the existing network. Router R1 is attached to AS 10 and uses BGP to communicate to AS 20 and AS 30. Router R6 initially connects to router R3 using a static route definition in the routing tables. The routes to networks in AS 60 will be viewed from router R1 as having the same policy as the networks existing in AS 20. This is because the AS 60 is not differentiated using BGP. AS 60 is also seen as an extension of AS 20. Therefore, router R1 cannot use a unique routing policy to networks from AS 10. By enabling BGP between router R6 and

Figure 19-1
High availability
using BGP on two ISP
networks connecting
to the Internet.

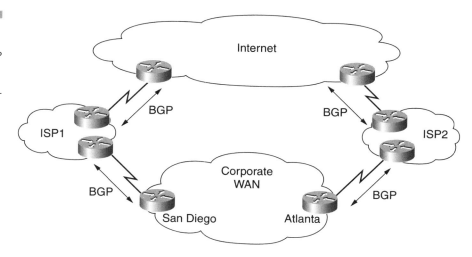

Router R3, AS 60 is announced into the AS 20 network as a unique AS connection. This is propagated to AS 10 and AS 30, thereby enabling a clarified routing policy to networks residing in AS 60.

Traffic on BGP is carried using a reliable transport. The Transmission Control Protocol (TCP) carries the BGP traffic over an established TCP connection that is formed over TCP port 179. BGP routers that form a connection are referred to as peer routers or neighbors. The connection enables the exchange of connection parameters and full BGP routing tables. The entire BGP routing table is exchanged at the onset of a TCP connection. After the full exchange, only incremental updates are sent between neighbors. The BGP table has a version number assigned to it that is used by all of the BGP peers. The version number increments after a BGP update occurs. The neighbors keep their connection alive by sending keepalive packets between the peers. If errors occur in the transmission of packets or a special condition occurs on a peer notification, the packets are still sent.

Exterior and Interior BGP Sessions

More than one BGP connection can occur in a single AS. In such a scenario, the AS with multiple BGP connections can be used as a transit AS. Two types of BGP sessions can exist when implementing BGP: Exterior BGP (EBGP) and Interior BGP (IBGP) sessions. Figure 19-3 highlights the EBGP and IBGP topology.

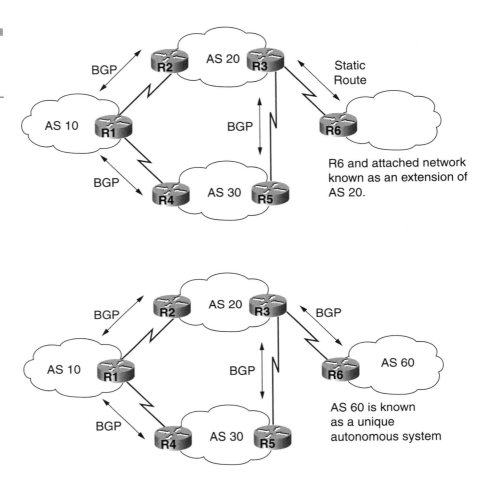

Figure 19-2
Using BGP for
creating a routing
policy.

The EBGP sessions are established between two unique AS networks. In Figure 19-3, AS 10 and AS 30 establish an EBGP session with AS 20. Adjacent routes sharing the same media and subnet connect EBGP sessions. The network in AS 20 also implements BGP, yet since the connection is between multiple routers within its network, it uses IBGP for communicating BGP routing tables. An IBGP session occurs between two routers of the same AS. This allows the IBGP routers to coordinate and synchronize routing policies for the AS. The IBGP peer connections do not have to be adjacent to each other. The peer connections for IBGP can be several hops away but must remain within the AS.

Figure 19-3
EBGP and IBGP
sessions and transit
AS topology.

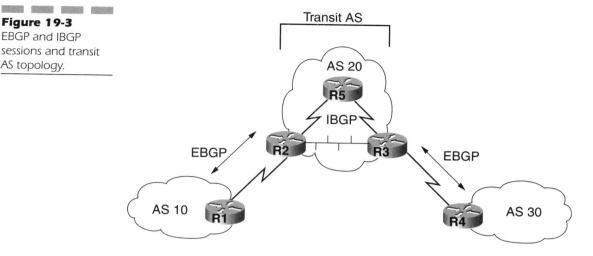

Path Selection Under BGP

BGP has two mechanisms for selecting a path. The first mechanism is used for choosing a single path. BGP defaults to a single path in the IP routing table. In a single path selection scenario, the following process is implemented:

- Inaccessible next-hop routes are not considered.
- The routers with the highest BGP administrative weights are considered first.
- The routers with a high local preference in a tie for the highest BGP administrative weight are preferred.
- When the local preference is equal, the route originated by the local router is preferred.
- If the local router did not originate the route, the shortest autonomous system path is selected.
- Paths having the same autonomous system path length are then arranged by the lowest origin code first. IGP routes have a lower origin code than EGP routes, which are lower than incomplete routes.
- If all the paths are from the same autonomous system and the origin code list results in equal origin codes, then the tiebreaker is the path with the lowest Multi Exit Discriminator (MED) metric value. If the path has a missing metric value, it is assumed to be equal to 0.

- In the case where the MED values are equal, external paths are selected over internal paths.

- If only internal paths are remaining in the selection list and IGP synchronization is disabled, the BGP selects the closest neighbor as the best path.

- If, at this point, there is a tie as to which neighbor is closest, BGP selects the neighbor with the lowest BGP router ID value.

In situations when multiple paths are designed into the topology for EBGP connections to a neighboring AS, the path that the lowest BGP router-id is presented on is the preferred single path. Enabling multipath BGP support for EBGP paths determined from the same neighboring autonomous system allows for up to six paths installed in the routing table. BGP will then either load balance over the multiple paths on a per-packet or per-destination basis.

Defining the BGP Process

Four basic commands are required to initialize the BGP process on Cisco routers. These commands define the BGP process, what networks originate in this router, what BGP neighbors establish a connection to this router, and a means of reinitializing the BGP connections and routing table after configuration changes.

Enabling the BGP Process

The Cisco IOS begins a BGP process when the router administrator enters the router bgp global configuration command. The format of the command is

router bgp *autonomous-system*

The AS parameter value ranges from 1 to 65,535. The value specified must be the same for all routers participating in the IBGP network connections in order for the routers to exchange BGP routing updates within the same AS. The AS value code is also used as a tag for the information exchanged between the BGP peers. For example, in the two configurations below, the BGP specific parameters are shown:

Router R1 BGP Configuration:

```
router bgp 10
```

Router R2 BGP Configuration:

```
router bgp 20
```

These configurations identify two unique AS networks. Router R1 is defined as a router belonging to AS 10 and Router R2 is defined as a router belonging to AS 20.

Establishing BGP Peer Connections

The BGP process is made aware of which BGP routers will be peers with the local router through the definition of neighbors. Once defining the neighbors, the BGP process attempts to establish a BGP peer connection with the defined neighbor. BGP routing table updates will only be sent after a successful TCP peer connection has been established.

Upon establishing the peer connection, the peers send "open messages" to each other that identify the AS number, BGP version number, BGP route ID, and keepalive hold-time values, among others. The neighbor connection must be in an established state for the exchange of routing updates. If the neighbor connection state is not shown as established, the BGP update exchange has not occurred and BGP routing over these routers will not take place.

Identifying the neighbors is accomplished using the router bgp command neighbor remote-as. The format of the command is

neighbor {*ip-address* | *peer-group-name*} **remote-as** *number*

The *ip-address* parameter is the value of the IP address used to locate a BGP neighbor. The value must be in the dotted-decimal IP address format. The parameter *peer-group-name* value is a label given to a group of BGP peers that are recognized collectively as a group. The *ip-address* and *peer-group-name* parameter values are mutually exclusive. The *number* parameter following the remote-as keyword is the AS number to which the neighbor being defined belongs. BGP peer groups are discussed later in this chapter.

If the remote-as *number* value assigned to the neighbor is the same as the AS number assigned on the router bgp command, then the BGP process will be performing IBGP to the neighbor. If the remote-as number value is different form the local router's AS number assigned on the router bgp command, then the BGP process will perform EBGP to the neighbor.

NOTE: *To verify IP connectivity between two neighbors prior to definition, use the Cisco IOS extended PING command, placing the IP address of the neighbor as the source address in the command.*

BGP implementation with Cisco IOS defaults to using BGP Version 4 protocol and then negotiates sequentially downward to determine the appropriate version on the neighbor. However, Cisco IOS enables the router administrator to define the BGP version being used by the neighbor using the neighbor version command. The format of the command is

neighbor {*ip-address* | *peer-group-name*} **version** *value*

The *ip-address* parameter is the IP address value of a defined BGP neighbor. The value must be in the dotted-decimal IP address format. The parameter *peer-group-name* value is a label given to a group of BGP peers that are recognized collectively as a group. The *ip-address* and *peer-group-name* parameter values are mutually exclusive. The *value* parameter following the version keyword defines the BGP version number to use for the TCP connection with the identified neighbor. The *value* parameter can be either 2, 3, or 4, with 4 being the default.

In Figure 19-4, the following configuration is applied:

Router R1:

```
router bgp 10
 neighbor 172.21.1.1 remote-as 20
```

Router R2:

```
router bgp 20
 neighbor 172.21.1.2 remote-as 10
 neighbor 192.168.1.2 remote-as 20
```

Router R3:

```
router bgp 20
 neighbor 192.168.3.1 remote-as 20
 neighbor 192.168.4.1 remote-as 30
```

Router R4:

```
router bgp 30
 neighbor 192.168.4.3 remote-as 20
```

All the routers in this configuration are assumed to be using BGP Version 4, since the neighbor version command was not explicitly entered. Since the AS number defined on the router bgp command for router R1 is different than the AS number defined on the neighbor command in the router R1 configuration, EBGP will be used from router R1 to the neighbor at 172.21.1.1. Router R2 uses IBGP to communicate with router R3. Recall that BGP uses TCP connections to deliver BGP routing updates. As such, the topology in Figure 19-4 illustrates that the BGP peers do not necessarily need to be directly connected for IBGP. Router R5 in the figure is used as the routing node for establishing the BGP TCP connection between router R2 and router R3. The BGP TCP connection between router R3 and router R4 completes the illustration and uses EBGP since this connection is established using different AS numbers.

When making BGP configuration changes, it is good practice to always reinitialize the BGP routing table and BGP TCP connections with the defined neighbors to ensure that the change has taken place. This is done by entering the following command:

clear ip bgp {* | *address* | *peer-group name*} [soft [in | out]]

The * value used in the command causes the current BGP peer connections to reset and a new routing table is built. The address parameter value is used when a specific neighbor connection needs to be reset and the routes

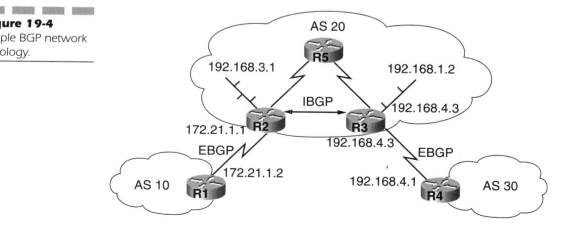

Figure 19-4
Simple BGP network topology.

received from that neighbor are updated. Using the peer-group-name value will reset all the connections from the local router to all members of the peer group. The *peer-group-name* must be the name assigned to a previously defined peer group in the local router.

The optional **soft** keyword indicates that the current BGP sessions are not reset, but the router will send routing updates. When using the **soft** keyword, the entire table is only updated if the **neighbor soft-reconfiguration** command is entered. Performing this function is memory-intensive and may cause long packet delays for connections traversing through the local router. The **in** variable of the optional **soft** keyword triggers only inbound reconfiguration, while the **out** variable of the soft keyword generates only outbound soft reconfiguration. Not specifying either variable triggers both inbound and outbound soft reconfiguration.

The clear ip bgp command should be used when the BGP configuration is changed in accordance with the following:

- BGP access list adds, changes, or deletions

- BGP weights have been altered

- BGP distribution-list adds, changes, or deletions

- BGP-specific timers

- Altering BGP administrative distance

- Using the route map command for BGP

  By issuing the following command

```
clear ip bgp *
```

all the BGP peer connections are reset and the BGP peers will reestablish their connections and then exchange routing updates.

Forcing a Loopback Interface as the BGP Neighbor

BGP uses the best local address to a neighbor as the source for sending updates. This is usually the IP address of the interface with the best path to the neighbor. In cases where multiple links are available to connect to a neighbor, usually found in IBGP topologies, greater availability is possible by using a loopback interface as the BGP neighbor of the local router. To identify the use of a loopback interface as the BGP peer on the local router, the following router bgp command is used:

neighbor {*ip-address* | *peer-group-name*} **update-source** *interface*

The *ip-address* parameter is the value of the IP address of a defined BGP neighbor. The value must be in the dotted-decimal IP address format. The parameter *peer-group-name* value is a label given to a group of BGP peers that is recognized collectively as a group. The *ip-address* and *peer-group-name* parameter values are mutually exclusive.

The *interface* parameter of the **update-source** keyword identifies the loopback interface used as the neighbor. The IP address defined under the specified loopback interface becomes the IP address used in the neighbor remote-as command in the BGP peer router configuration. For example, in Figure 19-5, router R1 uses a loopback interface IP address as its neighbor address. Router R2 and Router R3 both use the loopback interface IP address defined on router R1 as the neighbor ip-address on their respective neighbor remote-as commands.

The following configuration examples illustrate the requirement of router R2 and router R3 defining the IP address of the loopback interface for router R1 as the neighbor IP address with which TCP connections are established.

Router R1 Configuration for illustrating the use of loopback interface on a single BGP router:

```
ip subnet-zero
!
interface serial 0
 ip address 192.168.1.1 255.255.255.252
!
interface serial 1
 ip address 192.168.1.5 255.255.255.252
!
interface loopback 0
 ip address 192.168.1.254 255.255.255.252
!
router eigrp 10
 network 192.168.1.0
!
router bgp 10
 network 192.168.1.0 mask 255.255.255.252
 neighbor 192.168.1.2 remote-as 10
 neighbor 192.168.1.6 remote-as 10
 neighbor 192.168.1.2 update-source loopback 0
 neighbor 192.168.1.6 update-source loopback 0
```

Router R2 configuration for Figure 19-5:

```
ip subnet-zero
!
interface serial 0
```

Figure 19-5
BGP topology for
using a loopback
interface as the BGP
neighbor.

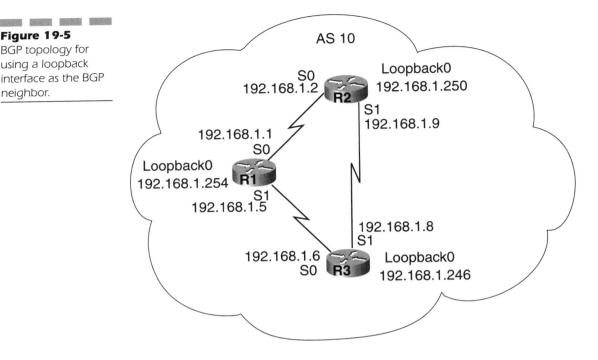

```
 ip address 192.168.1.2 255.255.255.252
!
interface serial 1
 ip address 192.168.1.9 255.255.255.252
!
router eigrp 10
 network 192.168.1.0
!
router bgp 10
 network 192.168.1.0 mask 255.255.255.252
 neighbor 192.168.1.254 remote-as 10
 neighbor 192.168.1.8 remote-as 10
```

Router R3 configuration for Figure 19-5:

```
ip subnet-zero
!
interface serial 0
 ip address 192.168.1.6 mask 255.255.255.252
!
interface serial 1
 ip address 192.168.1.8 255.255.255.252
!
router eigrp 10
 network 192.168.1.0
!
```

```
router bgp 10
 network 192.168.1.0 mask 255.255.255.252
 neighbor 192.168.1.254 remote-as 10
 neighbor 192.168.1.9 remote-as 10
```

As shown above, the neighbor update-source is only used for router R1 since it uses a loopback interface as the BGP peer IP address when communicating to both router R2 and router R3. The configuration for router R2 and router R3 uses the loopback IP address 192.168.1.254, defined on router R1 as the neighbor IP address on the respective neighbor remote-as commands for identifying router R1 as a neighbor. When using this configuration, should the link between R1 and R3 go down, R1 will not be able to establish a BGP TCP connection to R3, even if the link between R2 and R3 is active. This is because the IP address used as the BGP neighbor for R3 from R1 is the IP address associated with the link between R1 and R3.

A failsafe configuration is shown below, whereby if any physical interface goes down the BGP TCP connections can reroute their session through the other surviving connection because the loopback interface on all three routers is being used.

Router R1 Configuration for Figure 19-5:

```
ip subnet-zero
!
interface serial 0
 ip address 192.168.1.1 255.255.255.252
!
interface serial 1
 ip address 192.168.1.5 255.255.255.252
!
interface loopback 0
 ip address 192.168.1.254 255.255.255.252
!
router eigrp 10
 network 192.168.1.0
!
router bgp 10
 network 192.168.1.0 mask 255.255.255.252
 neighbor 192.168.1.250 remote-as 10
 neighbor 192.168.1.246 remote-as 10
 neighbor 192.168.1.250 update-source loopback 0
 neighbor 192.168.1.246 update-source loopback 0
```

Router R2 configuration for Figure 19-5:

```
ip subnet-zero
!
interface serial 0
 ip address 192.168.1.2 255.255.255.252
!
interface serial 1
```

```
  ip address 192.168.1.9 255.255.255.252
 !
 interface loopback 0
  ip address 192.168.1.250 255.255.255.252
 !
 router eigrp 10
  network 192.168.1.0
 !
 router bgp 10
  network 192.168.1.0 mask 255.255.255.252
  neighbor 192.168.1.254 remote-as 10
  neighbor 192.168.1.246 remote-as 10
  neighbor 192.168.1.254 update-source loopback 0
  neighbor 192.168.1.246 update-source loopback 0
```

Router R3 configuration for Figure 19-5:

```
 ip subnet-zero
 !
 interface serial 0
  ip address 192.168.1.6 255.255.255.252
 !
 interface serial 1
  ip address 192.168.1.8 255.255.255.252
 !
 interface loopback 0
  ip address 192.168.1.246 255.255.255.252
 !
 router eigrp 10
  network 192.168.1.0
 !
 router bgp 10
  network 192.168.1.0 mask 255.255.255.252
  neighbor 192.168.1.254 remote-as 10
  neighbor 192.168.1.250 remote-as 10
  neighbor 192.168.1.254 update-source loopback 0
  neighbor 192.168.1.250 update-source loopback 0
```

The network mask command is used under the router bgp command to identify the networks of this AS that we want BGP to distribute to peers. This command is used to quantify which networks the BGP process will advertise. The format of the command is

network *network-number* [**mask** *network-mask*]

The *network-number* is the full class network to be advertised by BGP. Using the optional *network-mask* parameter enables BGP to advertise specific subnets or supernets, instead of just the full class network address. A maximum of 200 network commands is allowed for each BGP process executing in a router. The networks included on the command do not have to be directly connected networks associated with the local router. These networks can be directly connected, dynamically learned, or from static route definitions.

For instance, if router R1 has a network, 192.168.20.0, directly connected to it and this network is advertised using an IGP to a BGP router, the BGP router can include the learned network in its advertisements using the network command. In the example above, since we are using the 192.168.1.0 Class C network with a 255.255.255.252 subnet mask on the loopback interface, we would want the BGP process to advertise the network to its peers to enable connectivity.

Multihop EBGP Connections

Some instances occur when the EBGP TCP connection is not the directly connected IP address. This may happen when the external BGP AS uses a single router for connectivity to the internal BGP AS, or when the external BGP is using a loopback interface as the neighbor IP address for the TCP connection to the EBGP router.

Figure 19-6 illustrates a scenario in which the connection between AS 10 and AS 20 is accomplished using a router acting as the conduit to the internal network of AS 20. In such a scenario, the router administrator of the BGP router R2 in AS 20 has decided that the critical point is the Ethernet connection to their internal network on router R2. If the Ethernet 0 interface on router R2 goes down, then there is no reason for BGP TCP connections to AS 10. This type of situation is termed a multihop configuration.

The following configuration example applies to the topology illustrated in Figure 19-6:

Router R1 Configuration:

```
interface serial 0
 ip address 192.168.1.1 255.255.255.0
!
router bgp 10
 network 192.168.1.0
 neighbor 172.16.1.1 remote-as 20
 neighbor 172.16.1.1 ebgp-multihop
```

Router R2 Configuration:

```
interface serial 0
 ip address 192.168.1.2 255.255.255.0
!
interface Ethernet 0
 ip address 172.16.1.1 255.255.255.0
!
router eigrp
 network 172.16.0.0
 network 192.168.1.0
```

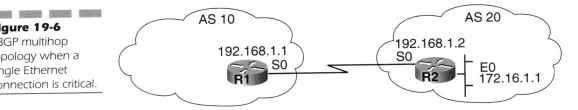

Figure 19-6
EBGP multihop
topology when a
single Ethernet
connection is critical.

```
!
router bgp 20
 network 172.16.0.0
 neighbor 192.168.1.1 remote-as 10
```

The neighbor defined on router R1 references the Ethernet 0 address of router R2. The EBGP peer connection is established by the inclusion of the neighbor ebgp-multihop command in router R1. The format of the neighbor ebgp-multihop command is

neighbor {*ip-address* | *peer-group-name*} **ebgp-multihop** [*ttl*]

The *ip-address* parameter is the IP address value of a defined BGP neighbor. The value must be in the dotted-decimal IP address format. The parameter *peer-group-name* value is a label given to a group of BGP peers that is recognized collectively as a group. The *ip-address* and *peer-group-name* parameter values are mutually exclusive. The optional *ttl* variable following the **ebgp-multihop** keyword provides the mechanism for determining the timeout of the TCP connection created for the neighbor IP address defined. The range for the optional *ttl* variable value is 1 to 255.

NOTE: *Cisco IOS does not establish the multihop peer connection if the only available route to the defined neighbor is the default 0.0.0.0 route.*

Load balancing over parallel links between two routers of different autonomous systems is made possible by using the loopback interface as the neighbor IP address. Because the loopback interface is not a directly connected EBGP, multihop is required. Figure 19-7 illustrates this scenario. In the standard EBGP connection, BGP will select one of the links for sending packets. However, by using EBGP multihop and loopback interfaces, the

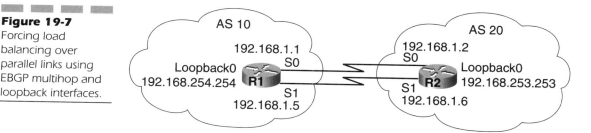

Figure 19-7
Forcing load
balancing over
parallel links using
EBGP multihop and
loopback interfaces.

BGP process is manipulated into using both physical connections and thereby performs load balancing.

The following configuration example details Figure 19-7:

Router R1 configuration:

```
ip subnet-zero
!
interface serial 0
 ip address 192.168.1.1 255.255.255.252
!
interface serial 1
 ip address 192.168.1.5 255.255.255.252
!
interface loopback 0
 ip address 192.168.254.254 255.255.255.252
!
router bgp 10
 network 192.168.254.0
 neighbor 192.168.253.253 remote-as 20
 neighbor 192.168.253.253 ebgp-multihop
 neighbor 192.168.253.253 update-source loopback 0
!
ip route 192.168.253.0 255.255.255.0 192.168.1.2
ip route 192.168.253.0 255.255.255.0 192.168.1.6
```

Router R2 configuration:

```
ip subnet-zero
!
interface serial 0
 ip address 192.168.1.2 255.255.255.252
!
interface serial 1
 ip address 192.168.1.6 255.255.255.252
!
interface loopback 0
 ip address 192.168.253.253 255.255.255.252
!
router bgp 20
 network 192.168.253.0
 neighbor 192.168.254.254 remote-as 10
```

```
neighbor 192.168.254.254 ebgp-multihop
neighbor 192.168.254.254 update-source loopback 0
!
ip route 192.168.254.0 255.255.255.0 192.168.1.1
ip route 192.168.254.0 255.255.255.0 192.168.1.5
```

Static routes are introduced into the configuration using the ip route command in each router. This allows each router to create two equal cost paths to reach the BGP neighbor addresses. An IGP can also be used to establish the equal cost path.

Controlling Routing Information Using Route Maps

The **route-map** configuration command is used in the context of BGP to define conditions for redistributing routing information to other routing protocols or for controlling routing information inbound or outbound from the BGP autonomous systems. The format of the command is

route-map *map-tag* [[**permit** | **deny**] | [*sequence-number*]]

The *map-tag* variable value is a name that is associated with the route map. More than one instance of the same *map-tag* value can be defined in the router. The *sequence-number* variable value defines the position of the route-map entry in the list of route maps configured with the same *map-tag* value.

As an example, the following configuration identifies a single route-map named MAP1 with two instances. The first instance is defined using sequence-number 10 and the second is defined using sequence number 20:

route-map MAP1 permit 10

▪

▪

▪

route-map MAP1 permit 20

▪

▪

▪

The statements following the **route-map** command describe the set of conditions applied to the *sequence- number* of the *map-tag*. In this example, if the conditions following the MAP1 instance 10 are not met, the IOS proceeds to the next higher instance of the same *map-tag* value. In this case, MAP1 instance 20 and its associated conditions are applied. The **permit** and **deny** keywords of the **route-map** command indicate the action taken on the on the routing information.

The conditions that follow a **route-map** command are defined using match and set configuration commands. The **match** command defines the criteria used to determine if the routing information is of interest, and the **set** command specifies the action to take against the routing information. For example, if the route-map conditions are

```
match ip address 10.1.20.100
set metric 10
```

and the **permit** keyword is specified on the **route-map** command, the routes are redistributed or controlled in accordance with the set command following the **match** command. In this case, the routing information will have its distance metric set to 10. If the **route-map** command has the **deny** keyword applied, the route is not redistributed or controlled and the IOS breaks out of the list. On the other hand, if the match is not met at all and either **permit** or **deny** is specified on the **route-map** command, the next instance of the **route-map** is checked. This checking continues until a match is made to the list. Perchance that a match is not found in the list, the route will not be accepted, nor will it be forwarded.

NOTE: *route-map, when used for filtering BGP updates instead of redistributing between protocols, is not capable on filtering inbound when using a match on the ip address. Only outbound filtering when using a match on ip address is allowed. Route-map functions are available to all other routing protocols.*

Table 19-1 lists all the match and set conditions available using the route-map configuration command for BGP redistribution and routing information control.

In the following router configuration example, a typical configuration exists in which one AS is running RIP and the connection to another AS is done using BGP. Shown in Figure 19-8, router R1 and router R2 are using RIP within their AS. Router R2 of AS 100 and router R3 of AS 200 utilize BGP for routing information updates. Router R2 redistributes the BGP updates received from router R3 to RIP for distribution to router R1. If the routes to 172.16.0.0 are to be favored through router R2 versus some other

Table 19-1

"match" and "set"
Commands for the
route-map Configu-
ration Command

"match" on	"set" Variable
match as-path	set as-path
match community	set clns
match clns	set automatic-tag
match interface	set community
match ip address	set interface
match ip next-hop	set default interface
match ip route-source	set ip default next-hop
match metric	set level
match route-type	set local-preference
match tag	set metric
	set metric-type
	set next-hop
	set origin
	set tag
	set weight

connection, we can set the metric to a value of 2 and all other routers with a metric of 10.

The following router configurations can be used to accomplish the setting of the metrics discussed above. The configurations only display the pertinent route configuration commands:

Configuration for router R2 in Figure 19-8:

```
R2#
router rip
 network 172.16.0.0
 network 172.18.0.0
 network 172.20.0.0
 passive-interface Serial0
 redistribute bgp 100 route-map METRIC2
router bgp 100
 neighbor 172.18.2.3 remote-as 200
 network 172.20.0.0
 route-map METRIC2 permit 10
```

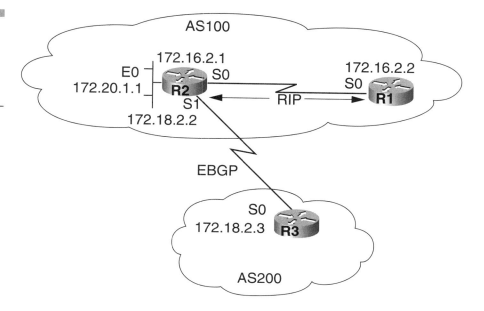

Figure 19-8
Using route-map conditions to set metrics for redistributed RIP routes.

```
match ip-address 1
set metric 2
route-map METRIC2 permit 20
set metric 10
access-list 1 permit 172.17.0.0 0.0.255.255
```

In this example, the first instance of METRIC2 uses the access-list 1 for IP access-list conditions to set the metric to 2. If the route matches the IP address 172.17.0.0, it will have a metric of 2 applied to the route and the IOS will break out of the list. If the route does not match, however, the next sequential instance is compared.

In this case, instance 20 is compared. Instance 20 of METRIC2 does not even provide a match command and therefore provides a default metric value of 10 for all other routes that do not provide routing information for the 172.17.0.0 network. This example also demonstrates the requirement to ask what will happen to route information that does not match any of the conditional criteria. If a second instance for all other routes was not included, the route would be dropped and not forwarded to any other routers.

Since the matching on IP addresses for inbound updates is not possible, outbound route maps must be applied. In the above example, route updates for 172.17.0.0 can be filtered from AS 100 by applying an outbound route map to router R3. Using the same topology as in Figure 19-8, router R3 can filter updates about 172.17.0.0 to router R2 and AS 100 using the following router configuration:

Router R3 configuration for filtering 172.16.0.0 updates to AS 100:

```
router bgp 200
 network 172.17.0.0
 neighbor 172.18.2.2 remote-as 100
 neighbor 172.18.2.2 route-map NO17217 out
route-map NO17217 permit 10
 match ip-address 1
access-list 1 deny 172.17.0.0 0.0.255.255
access-list 1 permit 0.0.0.0 255.255.255.255
```

In this configuration example, the IP access-list number 1 applies a deny to the IP network 172.17.0.0 and permits any other network. The neighbor route-map command under the router bgp command applies the route-map tag named NO17217 to outbound routing updates. The route-map command map-tag named NO17217 indicates that the IOS will permit routing updates that pass through the access-list number 1 successfully. For example, if the 10.0.0.0 network is in AS 200 and a route for this network is being sent to router R2 in AS 100, the access-list number 1 in router R3 would allow the route, and the route-map command would then permit the route to be sent to the neighbor BGP router at address 172.18.2.2 in AS 100.

Redistributing IGP Routes into BGP

Interior Gateway Protocols (IGPs) such as IGRP, RIP, OSPF, and EIGRP can be advertised using BGP through route redistribution. This means that the internal routes of your AS will be advertised as BGP routes. In some cases, this may cause duplication of routes since BGP may have already learned of these IGP routes. In this case, using filters will help avoid the duplication of routes to the Internet and also enable the advertising of only those routes required. A further discussion of route redistribution is found in Chapter 19, "Route Redistribution."

In Figure 19-9, we see three AS's in which router R1 in AS 100 is advertising 192.168.1.0 and router R3 is advertising network 172.22.0.0. Using router R3 as an example, the router is using EIGRP as the IGP and redistributing EIGRP routes into BGP AS 200.

The router R3 configuration using only the network command AS:

```
router eigrp 10
 network 172.22.0.0
 redistribute bgp 200
```

Figure 19-9
Using route
redistribution
between EIGRP and
BGP.

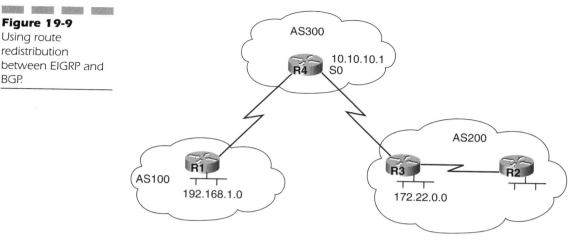

```
default-metric 1000 100 250 100 1500
router bgp 200
 neighbor 10.10.10.1 remote-as 300
 network 172.22.0.0 mask 255.255.0.0
```

Using only the network command under the router bgp definition limits the networks originated by AS 200 to 172.22.0.0. However, applying the redistribute command under the router bgp definition, as follows

```
router eigrp 10
 network 172.22.0.0
redistribute bgp 200
 default-metric 1000 100 250 100 1500
router bgp 200
 neighbor 10.10.10.1 remote-as 300
 redistribute eigrp 10
```

causes 192.168.1.0, known by EIGRP, to be injected into BGP. Since AS 200 is not the source of the address, filters are needed to stop the 192.168.1.0 network from being sourced by AS 200. This is accomplished using access-lists. The following configuration for router R3 in Figure 19-9 illustrates the uses of the filter to achieve the route redistribution without sourcing 192.168.1.0 from AS 200.

Router R3 configuration using access-list filters for route redistribution:

```
router eigrp 10
 network 172.22.0.0
 redistribute bgp 200
 default-metric 1000 100 250 100 1500
```

```
router bgp 200
 neighbor 10.10.10.1 remote-as 300
 neighbor 10.10.10.1 distribute-list 1 out
 redistribute eigrp 10
access-list 1 permit 172.22.0.0 0.0.255.255
```

Using this configuration, the neighbor distribute-list command under router bgp 200 applies an outbound filter that points to access-list 1, which permits only 172.22.0.0 routes to be advertised. All other routes are denied due to the implicit deny of an access list.

Static routes can also be used to identify originating networks or subnets within a router. BGP, however, considers static routes as having an unknown origin. This is also termed as incomplete origin. Using static routes to accomplish the routing in the previous example, router R3 could have been configured as

```
router eigrp 10
 network 172.22.0.0
 redistribute bgp 200
 default-metric 1000 100 250 100 1500
router bgp 200
 neighbor 10.10.10.1 remote-as 300
 redistribute static
ip route 172.22.0.0 255.255.255.0 null0
```

The static route defined using the ip route command forces the route into the routing table; however, the actual packets are discarded due to the route pointing to the null0 interface. Using this type of method, a supernet can be safely advertised. Remember that the routes generated from the above methods are in addition to BGP routes learned from BGP neighbors either internal or external. Using redistribution, static, or the network command generates routes as originating from the AS of the router.

Nexthop Attribute and Multiaccess/NBMA Networks

In Figure 19-10, two autonomous systems are connected using router R1 and R3. The next-hop address is always the IP address specified on the neighbor command for EBGP connections. In the figure, router R3 uses 172.16.2.2 as the next-hop address when advertising route 172.16.0.0 to router R1. Router R1 will use the next-hop address 172.16.2.1 when advertising the network 172.31.0.0 to router R3. The IBGP protocol requires that the next-hop advertised by EBGP be carried into IBGP. This forces router R1 to advertise 172.16.0.0 to router R2, its IBGP peer with a next-hop of

172.16.2.2. Because of this, router R2 uses the next-hop address of 172.16.2.2 and not 172.31.2.1 to reach the 172.16.0.0 network.

A key to this configuration is that router R2 must be able to reach the next-hop address of 172.16.2.2 using the IGP of the AS. One way to accomplish this is to run the IGP on router R1 network 172.16.0.0 and make the IGP link passive to router R3 so only BGP information is exchanged. The following configuration demonstrates this technique as applied against Figure 19-10:

Router R1 configuration for Figure 19-10:

```
router bgp 100
 neighbor 172.16.2.2 remote-as 300
 neighbor 172.31.5.1 remote-as 100
 network 172.31.0.0
```

Router R2 configuration applied to Figure 19.10:

```
router bgp 100
 neighbor 172.31.3.1 remote-as 100
```

Router R3 configuration as applied to Figure 19-10:

```
router bgp 300
 neighbor 172.16.2.1 remote-as 100
 network 172.16.0.0
```

The result of these configurations is the advertisement of 172.16.0.0 from router R3 to router R1 will use 172.16.2.2 as the next-hop address. Router R1 will use 172.16.2.2 as the next-hop address when router R1 advertises 172.16.0.0 to router R2.

On multiaccess networks, as illustrated in Figure 19-11, the EBGP router advertises the actual address of the router originating the advertised network, instead of its own, since the EBGP routers and the target IBGP router are on the same multiaccess network. As shown in Figure 19-11, router R1 in AS 100 connects to AS 200 using a common Ethernet segment on which router R3 and R4 are attached. Router R3 is the EBGP peer-to-router R1.

The router R3 sends a BGP update to router R1 using the next-hop address of 172.16.2.3 for network 172.30.0.0, instead of its own IP address 172.16.2.2 for the common Ethernet. This is done to avoid an unnecessary hop to access the networks originating on router R4.

In NBMA networks where connections between BGP AS's are not provided, using a full-mesh routing fails because the next-hop IP address advertised is not reachable by some of the routers connected to the NBMA network. This is diagrammed using Figure 19-12. Router R3 advertises a next-hop address of 172.16.2.3 to router R1 for the network 172.31.0.0, which is connected to router R4. Router R3 knows of this next-hop address because it has a Frame Relay PVC connecting to router R4. However, router R1 does not have a PVC to router R4 and will not be able to route packets to the next-hop address specified by router R3 in its advertisement of the 172.31.0.0 network. The Cisco IOS solves this dilemma by incorporating a command feature called nexthopself.

Figure 19-10
Next-hop attribute assignment BGP router configuration.

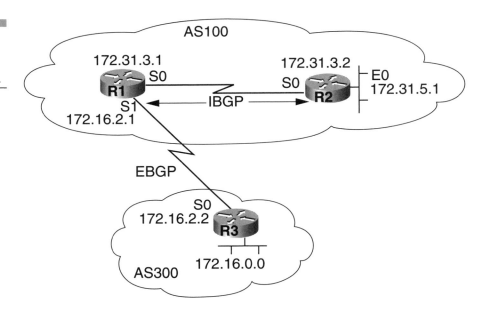

Figure 19-11
Next-hop addressing on multiaccess networks.

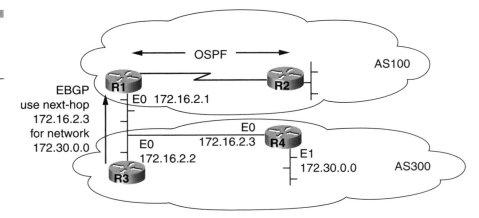

The nexthopself feature is applied to the neighbor command as follows:

neighbor {*ip-address* | *peer-group-name*} **next-hop-self**

The *ip-address* variable value is the IP address of the neighbor. A *peer-group-name* can be used instead of an IP address to identify a group of BGP peers to which this command applies. The command is most useful on NBMA networks where the BGP neighbors do not have direct access to each other even though they are on the same IP network or subnet. Using this command causes the router to override the true default next-hop IP address and places instead in the advertisement its own IP address for the interface connecting to the neighbor identified by the *ip-address* or *peer-group-name* values.

In the configuration laid out in Figure 19-12, the following is entered on router R3 to identify itself as the next-hop address, instead of 172.16.2.3 as the next-hop address for network 172.31.0.0:

Router R3 configuration as applied to Figure 19-12:

```
router bgp 300
 neighbor 172.16.2.1 remote-as 100
 neighbor 172.16.2.1 next-hop-self
```

Figure 19-12
Next-hop addressing configuration for NBMA networking example.

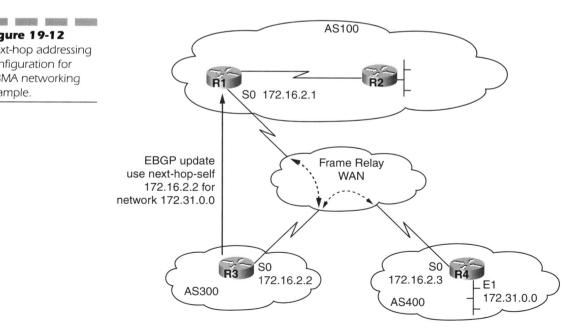

Using this configuration, router R3 sends a EBGP update to router R1, specifying its own IP address of 172.16.2.2 as the next-hop address for network 172.31.0.0 and enabling connectivity for AS100 to AS 400.

Forcing BGP to Prefer a IGP Route Using the Backdoor Command

In some cases, AS connectivity may be a combination of EBGP and IGP. In Figure 19-13, Router R1 in AS 100 connects to router R2 in AS 200 and uses an IGP (IGRP, EIGRP, OSPF, RIP) to build routing tables between the two networks. Router R1 and Router R2 both use EBGP to communicate routing information with router R3 of AS 300. In the figure, router R1 will receive two routing updates for network 172.16.0.0 (160.10.0.0), which is connected to router R2 in AS 200.

You can indicate which networks are reachable by using a *backdoor* route that the border router should use. A backdoor network is treated as a local network, except that it is not advertised. To configure backdoor routes, use the following command in router configuration mode:

network *address* **backdoor**

The *address* variable value for the network backdoor configuration command is the IP network reachable using the IGP. Using Figure 19-13, a backdoor command can be added to the configuration for router R1, enabling a route to be used for the more direct path to network 172.16.0.0 as follows:

Configuration for router R1 using the network backdoor command
applied to Figure 19-13:

```
router eigrp 10
 network 172.16.0.0
router bgp 100
 neighbor 10.20.20.1 remote-as 300
 network 172.16.0.0 backdoor
```

Router R1 learns of network 172.16.0.0 from router R2 using EIGRP with a default distance of 90. R1 also receives a routing update from router R3 via EBGP with a default distance of 20. The EBGP route, because of the lower distance value, is normally the preferred route, but because the network backdoor command is used in the configuration, the EIGRP route becomes the preferred route.

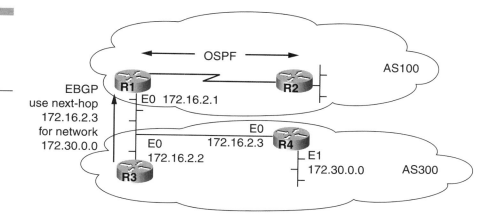

Figure 19-13
EBGP and IGP
network
configuration and
backdoor routing.

Synchronization of Routes

BGP does not advertise a route until all routes within the AS have learned of the route through the IGP. Once the IGP has propagated the route to all other routers within the AS, BGP then advertises it to the external peers. This mostly happens when traffic is passing from one AS to another AS using the local AS. Figure 19-14 illustrates this concept.

The synchronization between BGP to IGP routes is demonstrated using Figure 19-14. In the figure, router R3 in AS300 sends routing updates about its connected network, 172.16.0.0. Router R1 and R2 use IBGP, enabling R2 to receive updates for network 172.16.0.0 by using 10.20.20.1 as the next hop, and are not redistributing routes into IGP. For R2 to reach the next-hop address 10.20.20.1, it sends traffic to router R5. This creates a problem because router R5 is not aware of the 172.16.0.0 network. Router R2 using BGP synchronization will not advertise the 172.16.0.0 route until it is learned using the IGP. Once learning of the route, router R2 updates router R4. To facilitate the process, a static route in router R2 can be added, forcing router R2 to add the 172.16.0.0 network into the IGP routing table.

This synchronization process is enabled under BGP by default, but in some scenarios synchronization is not warranted. An example would be when the AS is not acting as a transient AS for traffic between two other autonomous systems, or when all routes within the AS are running BGP. In these cases, synchronization can be disabled, which reduces the routes in the IGP routing table while providing quicker convergence for BGP. Disabling BGP synchronization is accomplished using the following BGP router configuration command:

▬ ▬ ▬ ▬

Figure 19-14
Network
configuration
illustrating route
synchronization.

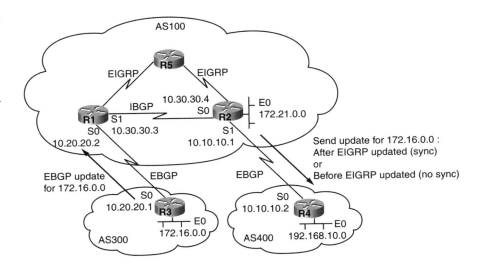

no synchronization

Employing this command under the router bgp configuration command enables BGP to advertise routes to peers without synchronizing the route to the IGP. Using the Figure 19-14 for the following sample configuration, the no synchronization command can be added to router R2, which enables R2 to place the 172.16.0.0 network in the IP routing table and advertises to router R4 without the route being included in the IGP routing table.

Configuration for Router R2 in Figure 19-14 to disable synchronization:

```
router bgp 100
 network 172.21.0.0
 neighbor 10.10.10.2 remote-as 400
 neighbor 10.30.30.3 remote-as 100
 no synchronization
```

Router R1 configuration for Figure 19-14:

```
router bgp 100
 network 172.21.0.0
 neighbor 10.30.30.4 remote-as 100
```

Router R4 configuration for Figure 19.14

```
router bgp 400
 neighbor 10.10.10.1 remote-as 100
 network 192.168.10.0
```

In order for the no synchronization command to take effect, the following command must be entered in EXEC operator mode to reset the BGP peer connections:

clear ip bgp *address*

The address variable value is the IP address of the neighbor for which the BGP routes are cleared. In the example, the following commands entered sequentially will clear the neighbor routes and reset the BGP peer connection for the R1 and R4 routers in Figure 19-14:

```
clear ip bgp 10.30.30.3
clear ip bgp 10.10.10.2
```

Best Path Selection Using the Weight Attribute

Cisco IOS Release 10.0 introduced a Cisco-specific BGP attribute to identify preferred paths when multiple paths for a network exist. The router bgp configuration command neighbor weight command is as follows:

neighbor {*ip-address* | *peer-group-name*} **weight** *weight*

The *ip-address* variable is the IP address of the neighbor to which the *weight* is applied. The *peer-group-name* can be used instead of the *ip-address* variable and identifies a BGP peer group to which the *weight* will be applied to all the neighbors in the group. The *weight* variable of the **weight** keyword can range from 0 to 65,535. The preferred path is the weight with the higher value.

Normally, without coding the neighbor weight command routes learned from other BGP peers have a default weight of 0. Routes originating within the local router use 32,768 as the default weight.

Using Figure 19-15, router R1 knows of the 172.21.0.0 network from AS400. Router R1 provides router R3 with this information through routing updates. Router R2 also knows of the 172.21.0.0 network via AS400 and sends routing updates to router R3. Router R3 now has in its routing tables two viable paths to reach the 172.21.0.0 network. By setting the weight attribute higher on router R3 for updates from router R1 over updates from router R2, the preferred path to the 172.21.0.0 network for router R3 is through the router R1 BGP peer connection with a next hop of 172.21.0.0. The following configuration illustrates the commands used in router R3 to achieve the preferred path through router R1:

Router R3 configuration to prefer R1 in Figure 19-15:

```
router bgp 300
 neighbor 10.10.10.1 remote-as 100
 neighbor 10.10.10.1 weight 200
 neighbor 10.20.20.2 remote-as 200
 neighbor 10.20.20.2 weight 100
```

The result of the configuration causes the connection from router R3 to router R1 to be the selected route since its defined weight is higher (200) than that of the weight assigned to the peer connection between router R3 and router R2.

Forcing a Preferred AS Exit Path

In many network topologies, multiple paths can be selected from among the AS's. A preferred path out of an AS can be identified as a preferred path by modifying the local preference attribute of BGP. The local preference attribute is set using the Cisco IOS command:

bgp default local-preference *value*

The value variable is a valid decimal integer ranging from 0 to 4294967295. The higher the number, the greater preference is given to the route being advertised to reach the AS. If the local preference attribute is not set through IOS commands, it defaults to 100. In Figure 19-16, a typical configuration is illustrated, showing the local preferences for the various BGP routers within the network.

In Figure 19-16, AS200 receives routing information for the 172.16.0.0 network from router R1 of AS100 and router R2 of AS300. The local preference attribute set in the routes enables the BGP process to determine the best path to exit AS200 when reaching the 172.16.0.0 network. The following configuration examples sets router R4 as the preferred exit from AS 200.

Configuration for router R3 in Figure 19-16:

```
router bgp 200
 neighbor 10.10.10.1 remote-as 100
 neighbor 192.168.11.2 remote-as 200
 bgp default local-preference 1500
```

Configuration for Router R4 in Figure 19-16:

```
router bgp 200
 neighbor 10.30.30.4 remote-as 300
 neighbor 192.168.11.1 remote-as 200
 bgp default local-preference 2000
```

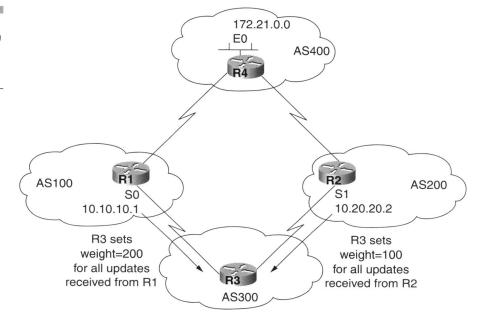

Figure 19-16
The effect of the local
preference attribute
for selecting the
preferred AS exit
path.

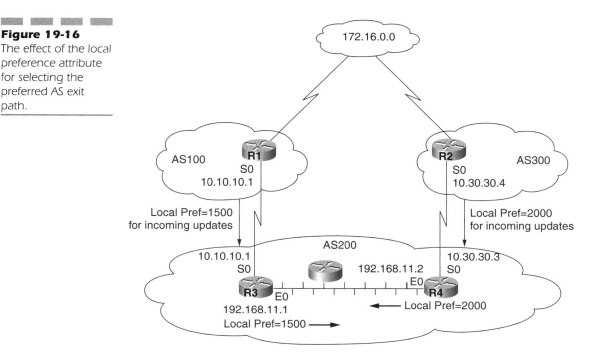

Because the BGP local preference attribute value is exchanged between BGP peers within an AS, router R3 and R4 of AS200 determine that the 172.16.0.0 network is given a higher local preference when connectivity is made from AS300 over AS100. All traffic destined for the 172.16.0.0 network, including traffic originating at networks on router R3, will traverse the path from router R4 to router R2.

Influencing the Preferred Path into an AS

Many configurations use multiple paths between the autonomous systems for redundancy and availability. Modifying the metric attribute allows an AS to influence the preferred path dynamically between the autonomous system connections when multiple entry points exist. If BGP4 is being used, the metric attribute is known as the Multi-exit discriminator (MED) attribute. In BGP3, the metric attribute is called the Inter-As attribute. Unlike the local preference, which is specific to the BGP routing process within a Cisco router, the metric attribute is exchanged with the external BGP neighbors. However, the metric received is not sent to another AS. BGP defaults the metric attribute value to 0 and prefers the lowest metric attribute presented in the compared routing information updates received for a given network. Figure 19-17 illustrates the use of the metric attribute.

Routers R2, R3, and R4 are sending routing information to AS 100 for the 192.168.180.0 (180.10.0.0) network. R2 is in AS 400, and R3 and R4 are in AS 300. Each router influences the preferred path into AS 100 by setting the metric attribute using the following configurations:

Router R2 configuration for Figure 19-17:

```
router bgp 400
 neighbor 10.40.40.4 remote-as 100
 neighbor 10.40.40.4 route-map setmetricout out
route-map setmetricout permit 10
 set metric 50
```

Router R3 configuration for Figure 19-17:

```
router bgp 300
 neighbor 10.20.20.2 remote-as 100
 neighbor 10.20.20.2 route-map setmetricout out
 neighbor 10.10.10.2 remote-as 300
route-map setmetricout permit 10
 set metric 120
```

Figure 19-17
Influencing the preferred path into an AS using the metric attribute.

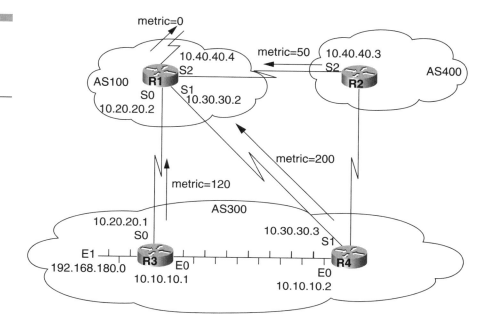

Router R4 configuration for Figure 19-17:

```
router bgp 300
 neighbor 10.30.30.2 remote-as 100
 neighbor 10.30.30.2 route-map setmetricout out
 neighbor 10.10.10.1 remote-as 300
route-map setmetricout permit 10
 set metric 200
```

Routers R2, R3, and R4 each set the metric attribute using the **route-map setmetricout** and **set metric** commands. Router R2 sets the metric attribute for routes coming from R2 to 50. Routes coming from router R3 are set to 120 and the ones from router R4 are set to 200.

By default, routers compare only the metrics from neighbors of the same AS. In the example, the routing information provided by routers R3 and R4 are compared by router R1. The routing information from router R2 is not compared because router R2 is in a different AS than router R3 and R4. Router R1 also receives a routing update for the 192.168.180.0 network from router R2. This metric attribute shows a lower value of 50, but router R1 cannot compare the routing information received from routers R3 and R4 with that of R2 because R2 is in a different AS than routers R3 and R4.

Router R1 then chooses the preferred route to 192.168.180.0 based on other BGP attributes. R1 can be configured, however, to compare routing information received from all connected autonomous systems in an effort to compare the metric attribute of a network to all external BGP neighbors by specifying the following command under the router bgp command:

bgp always-compare-med

Using this command in the configuration for router R1 causes the BGP process to compare the metric attribute of all alternate paths to a destined network. In Figure 19-17, router R1 is configured to take advantage of this enhancement as follows:

Router R1 configuration for Figure 19-17:

```
router bgp 100
 neighbor 10.20.20.1 remote-as 300
 neighbor 10.30.30.3 remote-as 300
 neighbor 10.40.40.3 remote-as 400
 bgp always-compare-med
```

By including the **bgp always-compare-med** command in router R1, the preferred path to 192.168.180.0 network is router R2. Without the inclusion of the **bgp always-compare-med** command in router R1, the preferred path to the 192.168.180.0 network is to router R3. In this example, the extra hop through router R2 is warranted because of the low line speeds connecting router R3 and R4 to R1. The R1-R2 and R2-R4 connections use T1 line speeds and hence will have a greater probability of throughput.

Grouping Destinations That Share a Common Attribute

There are many network configuration instances in which multiple destinations can be grouped by shared common attributes. By grouping these destinations into a community, routing decisions and other BGP attributes can be applied to all the destination networks belonging to the community. The communities attribute is optional and is not sent to a neighbor, but if the set community command is used in conjunction with a route-map and match command, a destination is assigned all the attributes belonging to the community as a whole. The format of the **set community** command is

set community {*community-number* [**additive**]} | **none**

The *community-number* variable value can be in the range of 1 to 4294967200, or the keyword **no-export** or **no-advertise**. The default *community-number* value is the well-know community name **internet**. Every

BGP router belongs to the **internet** community. When using the **no-export** value for *community-number*, the route is not advertised to EBGP peers. The **no-advertise** keyword value for the *community-number* variable indicates to the BGP process that the route in question is not advertised to either an internal or external BGP peer.

The **additive** keyword following the *community-number* value indicates that the network route being interpreted will have the specified community added to its routing information. Without the **additive** keyword, the specified community will replace all previously defined communities for the destination network in any further route information updates. The final keyword **none** directs the BGP process to strip away the communities attribute from the prefix of any route that passes the route-map criteria.

In order for BGP neighbors to learn of the different communities for destination networks, the neighbor send-community command must be entered into the router configuration. The format of the command is

neighbor {*ip-address* | *peer-group-name*} **send-community**

The *ip-address* variable is the IP address of the BGP neighbor to which the communities attribute is sent. The *peer-group-name* variable can be used in place of the *ip-address* variable, resulting in the same action.

The following router configuration provides an example for using the communities attribute.

```
router bgp 100
 neighbor 192.168.171.50 remote-as 200
 neighbor 192.168.171.50 send-community
 neighbor 192.168.171.50 route-map set-community out
 !
route-map community 10 permit
 match address 1
 set community no-export
 !
route-map community 20 permit
 match address 2
```

In this example, the route map named **community** is applied to the outbound routing updates of the neighbor using the 192.168.171.50 IP address. The actions are applied to the outbound updates based on the out keyword specified on the **neighbor route-map** command. As the BGP routes are processed, they pass through access list 1 and 2. The routes passing access list 1 are set to the well-known community name of no-export. Any routes that fail the criteria for instance 10 are processed by instance 20 of the community route-map where they are advertised as normal since no community attribute is applied to their routing information. Routes meeting the criteria for instance 10 of the community route-map will not be advertised to EBGP peers.

Suppose in Figure 19-18, the BGP routes advertised from router R2 to R3 are not to be sent by router R3 to any other external peers. The following configuration is used:

Router R2 configuration for Figure 19-18:

```
router bgp 200
 network 172.16.0.0
 neighbor 10.30.30.1 remote-as 300
 neighbor 10.30.30.1 send-community
 neighbor 10.30.30.1 route-map setnoexport out
route-map setnoexport
 match ip address 1
 set community no-export
access-list 1 permit 0.0.0.0 255.255.255.255
```

Router R2 sets all outbound routing updates to router R3 with the no-export communities attribute forcing router R3 to not forward the routes received from router R2 to router R1. Again, this is indicated by using the neighbor send-community command in concert with the neighbor route-map out command.

The communities attribute can also be used to set other attributes like weight and metric. In the following configuration examples applied to Figure 19-18, router R2 now sets the communities attribute to include the 300 and 400 communities with any other communities attribute found on the route. We can also have router R3 set the weight for these routes.

Router R2 configuration using the additive keyword applied to Figure 19-18:

```
router bgp 200
 network 172.16.0.0
 neighbor 10.30.30.1 remote-as 300
 neighbor 10.30.30.1 send-community
 neighbor 10.30.30.1 route-map set-community out
route-map set-community
 match ip address 2
 set community 300 400 additive
access-list 2 permit 0.0.0.0 255.255.255.255
```

Router R3 configuration applied to Figure 19-18:

```
router bgp 300
 neighbor 10.30.30.3 remote-as 200
 neighbor 10.30.30.3 route-map community-check in
route-map community-check permit 10
 match community 1
 set weight 20
route-map community-check permit 20
```

Figure 19-18
Using the community
attribute for route
filtering.

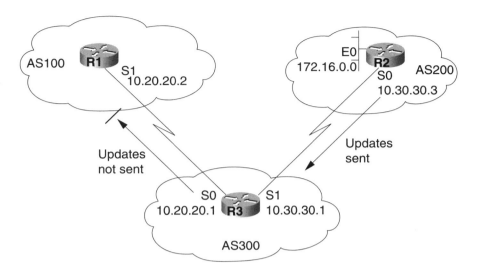

```
 match community 2 exact
 set weight 10
route-map community-check permit 30
 match community 3
ip community-list 1 permit 300
ip community-list 2 permit 400
ip community-list 3 permit internet
```

The result of these configurations matches any route with 300 in the communities attribute by match list 1. The action taken in match list 1 sets the weight of the route to 20. Match list 2 applies to any route that only has the 400 community name in the communities attribute because of the exact keyword used on the match community statement. If only the 400 community is assigned to the communities attribute, it will be set to a weight of 20. The last instance of the community-check route map catches any other type of route and assigns the well-known community name of internet to the communities attribute.

This filtering is made possible by the use of the ip community-list command. This command groups communities together for use in a match clause statement of a route-map command. The format of the ip community-list command is

ip community-list *community-list-number* {**permit** | **deny**}
    community-number

The *community-list-number* variable value ranges from 1 to 99 and identifies one or more permit or deny community groups. The **permit** keyword grants access for the matching condition specified, while the **deny** keyword prohibits access when a matching condition is found. The *community-number* variable value is a valid *community-number* defined on a previous **set community** command.

It is important to remember that an implicit deny will follow the first permit community list. It is therefore always necessary to permit any routes that do not meet any of the previous match criteria. This is shown in the sample configuration above for router R3.

Route and Path Information Filtering

As in all other routing protocols, managing and controlling the number of routing updates is an important practice for conserving network resources. Three basic filtering techniques are used for controlling BGP routing updates. These filtering methods are based on route information, path information, and communities. In the previous section, we discussed filtering on communities. This section concentrates on filtering using route and path information.

Routing information updates can be managed by using access-lists that are defined and applied to the BGP routing updates both received and sent. Cisco IOS achieves this filtering by using the neighbor distribute-list command under the router bgp command. The format of the neighbor distribute-list command is

neighbor {*ip-address* | *peer-group-name*}
   distribute-list {*access-list-number* | *name*} {**in** | **out**}

The *ip-address* variable value is the IP address of a BGP neighbor. The *peer-group-name* variable can be used instead of the *ip-address* variable. The *access-list-number* variable is a valid integer from 1 to 199, identifying a standard or extended access list that is applied to the routing updates to or from the identified neighbor. The *access-list-name* can be used instead of the *access-list-number*. The **in** keyword applies the identified access list to the incoming routing updates and the **out** keyword applies the identified access list to the outgoing routing updates.

Suppose in Figure 19-19 updates for network 172.16.0.0 originating from router R2 and received by router R3 are filtered to stop these updates from being propagated into AS100. Using the neighbor distribute-list command, router R3 can filter these updates by applying the filter for routing information to router R1.

Figure 19-19

Using an access list to control updates to/from BGP neighbors.

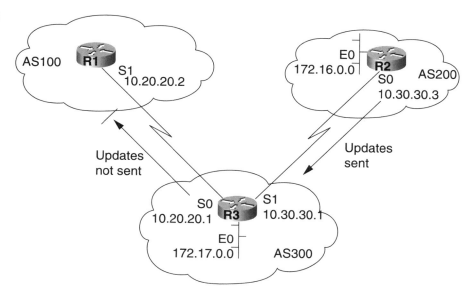

Router R3 configuration applied for Figure 19-19:

```
router bgp 300
 network 172.17.0.0
 neighbor 10.30.30.3 remote-as 200
 neighbor 10.20.20.2 remote-as 100
 neighbor 10.20.20.2 distribute-list 1 out
access-list 1 deny 172.16.0.0 0.0.255.255
access-list 1 permit 0.0.0.0 255.255.255.255
```

The router R3 configuration filters outbound routing updates to the neighbor identified by IP address 10.20.20.2 using access-list number 1. This is denoted on the neighbor 10.20.20.2 distribute-list 1 out command. The access-list 1 defined in router R3 first denies all routes specific to the 172.16.0.0 network. Any network IP address that does not meet this criterion is then permitted by using the access-list 1 permit 0.0.0.0 255.255.255.255 command.

In many BGP network configurations, supernets (CIDR) addressing is used. Taking the above example, suppose router R2 has many different 172.16.0.0 subnets and that the network 172.16.0.0 is a CIDR network with a mask of 255.240.0.0, creating a supernet. To meet the original objective, the filter must be applied to an 8-bit mask or 172.0.0.0 network with a 255.0.0.0 subnet mask. The first impulse is to apply an access-list permit command to the 172.0.0.0 network with a 0.255.255.255 mask applied, but this permits all the network addresses beginning with 172.0.0.0. Further filtering must be applied to identify the specific network address when using supernets. This is done using the extended access list. In applying the extended access-list permit, only the 172.0.0.0 8-bit subnet mask network must be applied:

```
access-list 101 172.0.0.0 0.255.255.255 255.0.0.0 0.0.0.0
```

Using this access list and specifying the neighbor distribute list command that identifies the 101 access list, only the network routing updates for 172.0.0.0 255.0.0.0 are permitted. All other networks are denied. For more information on extended access lists, consult Chapter 13, "IP Configuration."

The route filtering controls routing updates to specific neighbors based on network numbers. Path filtering applies filters for both inbound and outbound routing updates based on autonomous system paths in a BGP network configuration. Path filtering is applied using the Cisco IOS feature called regular expressions.

Regular expressions are a means of defining a pattern or a string that must match the given input. For BGP, the string consists of the path information. Table 19-2 lists the variable uses in a regular expression.

Using regular expressions path filtering can be applied to the whole AS. For example, in Figure 19-20, a network topology illustrates four autonomous systems serially connected. Suppose, as shown the figure, that AS100 does not require updates about the 172.16.0.0 (160.10.0.0) network. Using access lists again in the router R3 configuration, we can stop routing updates with AS200 as the origin from entering AS100. This path filtering is accomplished using two configuration commands. The first of these is the ip as-path access-list global command. The format of this command is

ip as-path access-list *access-list-number* {**permit** | **deny**}
as-regular-expression

The *access-list-number* variable value points to a regular expression access list number that defines the filtering. The **permit** keyword grants access on the matching condition, while the **deny** keyword stops access on the matching condition. The *as-regular-expression* variable is the matching criteria used in the access list of the autonomous system. The **access-list** filter can be applied to both inbound and outbound flows. The Cisco IOS process examines the regular expression specified on the **ip as-path access-list** command against the autonomous system path of the route as an ASCII string. If there is a match, the defined condition is applied. An autonomous system path will not have the AS of the local router.

The second router configuration command required to use path filtering is the **neighbor filter-list** command. This command follows the **router bgp** command to which the filter is to be applied. The format of the command is

Table 19-2

Regular Expressions

Ranges	Ranges are written as a sequence of characters that are contained within left and right square brackets, such as [10ABC].
Atoms	An atom is a single character being matched in the following manner:
	. — The character in this position matches any single character
	^ — The characters match the beginning of the input string
	$ — The characters match the end of the input string
	\ — An exact match to the character
	_ — The character matches a comma (,), left brace ({), right brace (}), the beginning of the input string, the end of the input string, or a space
	e.g.: _400_ routes via AS400
	^400$ routes with AS400 as the origin
	^400.* routes coming from AS400
	^$ routes originating from this autonomous system
Pieces	A piece is an atom followed by either a
	* — matching 0 or more sequences of the atom, such as a*, in which there is the letter a or a followed by anything else
	+ — matches 1 or more sequences of the atom, such as a+, in which one occurrence of a or more should be found
	? — matches the entire atom or the null string, such as ab?a, which matches abaa or aba
Branch	A branch is a concatenation of pieces.

neighbor {*ip-address* | *peer-group-name*}
filter-list *access-list-number* {**in** | **out** | **weight** *weight*}

The *ip-address* variable is the IP address of the neighbor to which the filter is to be applied. The *peer-group-name* variable can be used instead of the *ip-address* variable. If the *peer-group-name* variable is used, then the filter is applied to all the neighbors associated with the peer-group. The *access-list-number* variable is the access-list number defined on the **ip as-path access-list** command. The **in** keyword applies the filter to the incoming routes and the **out** keyword applies the filter to the outbound routes. The **weight** keyword and its associated *weight* variable allow the router administrator to assign a value from 0 to 65,535 to incoming routes matching the AS paths. This value provides a relative importance to the matching incoming AS path.

NOTE: *The weight values specified on the* **neighbor weight** *and* **neighbor filter-list** *commands are overridden by the weight values specified on the* **match as-path** *and* **set weight** *route-map commands.*

Following through on the supposition, router R3 in Figure 19-20 is configured as follows to prevent R3 from sending updates on the 172.16.0.0 network to router R1.

Configuration for router R3 in Figure 19-20:

```
router bgp 300
 neighbor 10.30.30.3 remote-as 200
 neighbor 10.20.20.2 remote-as 100
 neighbor 10.20.20.2 filter-list 1 out
ip as-path access-list 1 deny ^200$
ip as-path access-list 1 permit .*
```

The access-list number referred in the neighbor filter-list command identifies the ip as-path access list to be applied to the routing updates to or from the identified neighbor. The configuration denies any updates that have AS path information that starts with 200 (^200) and ends with 200 (200$). Updates for the 172.16.0.0 network sent from router R2 having path information beginning and ending with 200 match the filter and are then denied.

The ip as-path permit command in router R3 configuration uses the ".*" regular expression. The use of the dot (.) indicates that any character will be a match. The "*" represents the repetition of the character found in the dot position. These characters together indicate that any path information is allowed. This statement is needed to override the implicit deny found for all access lists.

Verifying the paths that have matched a regular expression for BGP is possible using the command, **sh ip bgp regexp** *regular-expression*. The *regular-expression* value is the expression used on the ip as-path access-list command. In the above example, to verify that the AS paths beginning and ending with 200 are being filtered, the command would be entered as **sh ip bgp regexp ^200$**.

The **ip as-path access-list** command can also be used in conjunction with the **neighbor route-map** command when matching routing information using the **match as-path** statement. The topology shown in Figure 19-21 illustrates this combination.

Suppose in Figure 19-21 router R3 is to learn only of local networks of AS200. In addition, the weight of the permitted routes are set to 20. The

■■■ ■■■ ■■■ ■■
Figure 19-20
A path-filtering
topology example for
controlling updates
to/from BGP
neighbors.

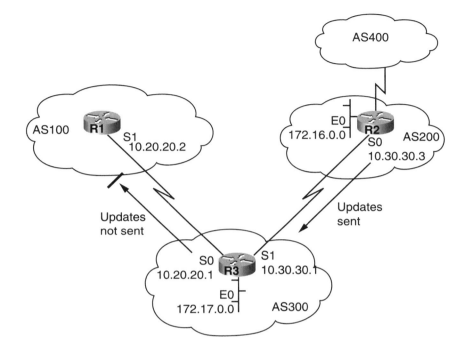

■■■ ■■■ ■■■ ■■
Figure 19-21
Network topology for
using neighbor
route-map and ip as-
path access-list
commands to control
BGP routing updates.

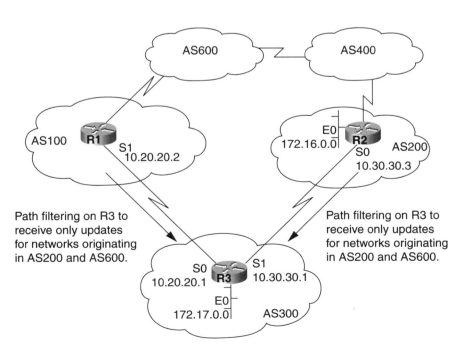

filter to perform this task is applied to router R3 and has the following configuration:

Configuration for router R3 of Figure 19-21:

```
router bgp 300
 network 172.17.0.0
 neighbor 10.30.30.3 remote-as 200
 neighbor 10.30.30.3 route-map only200 in
route-map only200
 match as-path 1
 set weight 20
ip as-path access-list 1 permit ^200$
```

Updates that originate from AS200 will have the AS path information starting and ending with 200. Applying the ip as-path access-list filter with ^200$ as the regular expression ensures that only this path is permitted. All other updates are dropped. The ip as-path access-list is identified under the route-map named only200 by the match as-path statement. The only200 route-map is identified by the **neighbor route-map** command under router bgp. The routes accepted will be given a weight of 20.

To complicate the scenario, all routes other than paths originating in AS200 will be given a weight of 10 and updates originating from AS400 are to be dropped. Again the filter is applied to router R3 in the following manner:

Configuration for router R3 in Figure 19-21 dropping AS400 and applying a weight of 10 to all other paths:

```
router bgp 300
 network 172.17.0.0
 neighbor 10.30.30.3 remote-as 200
 neighbor 10.30.30.3 route-map drop400 in
route-map drop400 permit 10
 match as-path 1
 set weight 20
route-map drop400 permit 20
 match as-path 2
 set weight 10
ip as-path access-list 1 permit ^200$
ip as-path access-list 2 permit ^200 600 .*
```

In this expanded example, paths originating from AS200 are still set to a weight of 20, but all other permitted paths are set to a weight of 10. Setting the other permitted paths to a weight of 10 is accomplished by the second instance of the drop400 route-map specification. The second instance of the drop400 route-map applies ip as-path access-list number 2 to the AS path information. This filter permits only paths that begin with 200 followed by 600, thereby causing router R3 to accept paths for updates behind AS400 while dropping AS400 paths.

Manipulating the Path Information Order

The BGP decision process can be influenced through changing the order of the AS path information in an update. This is a common practice to influence path load balancing. The path information of a BGP update can be manipulated using the set as-path prepend command following a route-map statement. The format of the set as-path prepend command is

set as-path {tag | prepend *as-path-string***}**

The **tag** keyword directs the IOS to convert the tag associated with a route into an AS path. The **tag** keyword can only be used for redistributing routes into BGP. The **prepend** keyword and its associated variable named *as-path-string* appends the value of *as-path-string* to the AS path information of the route matched by the route-map definitions. The changing of the AS path in this manner applies to both inbound and outbound BGP route maps. The **set as-path** command artificially increases the length of the AS path information.

In Figure 19-22, AS300 is getting all its traffic from AS100 because the AS path length received from AS100 is shorter (100, 300) than the AS path length received from AS400 (400, 200, 300). This is verified by interrogating router R3 in Figure 19-22. Router R3 advertises its local network 172.17.0.0 to both AS100 and AS200. AS600 receives this information and determines reachability about 172.25.0.0 via two routes. The first is from AS100 and the second from AS400. If all the other attributes are the same, AS600 will use the shortest path to router R3, in this case the route through AS100. Although this makes sense from a BGP-routing perspective, it may not be preferred based on bandwidth availability and router performance.

Suppose in Figure 19-22 the bandwidth connecting AS100 to AS300 is 56 Kbps and the router R1 is a Cisco 4500 series router. The physical connection from AS100 to AS600 is also a 56-Kbps line, but router R6 is a Cisco 7500 series router using an RSP4 and VIP-2 processors. The connection from AS600 through AS400 to AS200 through to router R3 in AS300 is T3 (45 Mbps) with low utilization. In such a case, it is prudent to manipulate the AS path in such a way as to increase the AS length of the path received from AS100 to a length greater than that received from AS200. The configuration used in router R3 to produce this desired effect is as follows:

```
router bgp 300
 network 172.17.0.0
 neighbor 10.20.20.2 remote-as 100
 neighbor 10.20.20.2 route-map prefer-AS400 out
route-map prefer-AS400
 set as-path prepend 300 300
```

Figure 19-22
Network topology for
using the set as-path
prepend command
to increase the AS
path length.

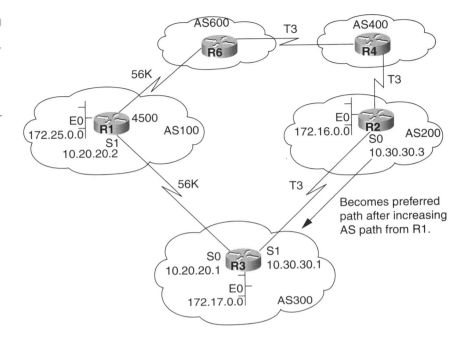

A common way of increasing the AS path is to replicate the local AS number in the path information. This is done in the above example using the **set as-path prepend 300 300** command. By implementing this statement, AS600 receives updates on network 172.17.0.0 from AS100 with path information such as 100, 300, 300, 300. This now creates a path length longer than the natural path length generated from AS400 (400, 200, 300).

Using BGP Peer Groups

In many of the previous discussions, the peer-group-name variable is discussed on many of the commands affecting BGP. A BGP peer group is a list of BGP neighbors having the same update policy requirements. Peer groups enable the router administrator to assign the same update policies, such as route maps, distribute-lists, and filter-lists, to the group, rather than defining the same policies to the individual neighbors. The peer group is created using the neighbor peer-group routing configuration command. The format of the command is

neighbor *peer-group-name* **peer-group**

The *peer-group-name* variable is the name assigned to the peer group. Neighbors are assigned to a peer group using the following router configuration command:

neighbor *ip-address* **peer-group** *peer-group-name*

The *ip-address* variable is the value of the IP address for a BGP neighbor belonging to the peer group. The *peer-group-name* variable following the **peer-group** keyword is the BGP peer group to which the neighbor is a member.

Each member of the peer group inherits the following configuration options:

```
remote-as (only if the peer-group-name is used on a neighbor
remote-as command)
version
update-source
out-route-map
out-filter-list
out-dist-list
minimum-advertisement-interval
next-hop-self
```

Using Figure 19-23, peer groups can be applied for internal and external BGP neighbors. When defining internal BGP peer groups, the neighbor peer-group-name remote-as command format is useful since the configuration options are affecting only the routers within the internal BGP network. For example, router R3 in Figure 19-23 can be configured using a BGP peer group and applies filter-lists to inbound and outbound updates. The filters being applied are not pertinent to the example so they are not coded. However, they are included to illustrate that the lists affect the entire peer group.

Configuration for router R3 for internal BGP neighbors in Figure 19-23:

```
router bgp 300
 neighbor IBGPmap peer-group
 neighbor IBGPmap remote-as 300
 neighbor IBGPmap route-map SETMETRIC out
 neighbor IBGPmap filter-list 1 out
 neighbor IBGPmap filter-list 2 in
 neighbor 10.50.50.2 peer-group IBGPmap
 neighbor 10.60.60.2 peer-group IBGPmap
 neighbor 10.30.30.2 peer-group IBGPmap
 neighbor 10.30.30.2 filter-list 3 in
```

In the sample configuration for router R3, the peer group named IBGPmap has enlisted routers R5, R6, and R7 as members of the peer group. A neighbor peer-group command is used to associate each internal BGP neighbor with the IBGPmap peer group. A separate filter list is defined for neighbor 10.30.30.2 (router R5) that will override the filter-list 2 applied to the entire peer group. When using peer groups, options can only be overridden that affect inbound updates.

External BGP peer groups can also be defined to further control the effects of options to multiple neighbors. In the following router configuration example, router R3 has defined external BGP neighbors into a peer group named EBGPmap. The **neighbor** *peer-group-name* **remote-as** command format is not used in defining external BGP peer groups because multiple autonomous system numbers must be defined.

Configuration for router R3 using external BGP peer group definition applied to Figure 19-23:

```
router bgp 300
 neighbor EBGPmap peer-group
 neighbor EBGPmap route-map SETMETRIC
 neighbor EBGPmap filter-list 1 out
 neighbor EBGPmap filter-list 2 in
 neighbor 10.20.20.2 remote-as 100
 neighbor 10.20.20.2 peer-group EBGPmap
 neighbor 10.40.40.2 remote-as 600
 neighbor 10.40.40.2 peer-group EBGPmap
 neighbor 10.10.10.2 remote-as 200
 neighbor 10.10.10.2 peer-group EBGPmap
 neighbor 10.10.10.2 filter-list 3 in
```

For each external BGP neighbor, a **neighbor remote-as** and **neighbor peer-group** command pair is specified.

Aggregate Addresses

BGP4 is the only version of BGP that supports Classless Interdomain Routing (CIDR). CIDR removes the notion of IP class type addressing by allowing what is termed supernets. Supernets are mostly used on Class B and Class C address format. For example, the class C address of 192.168.200.0 with a 255.255.255.0 subnet mask can become a supernet using just 192.168.0.0 with a 255.255.0.0 subnet. Using CIDR supernets is very useful in reducing the size of the routing updates, and hence the routing tables.

BGP allows for network address aggregation by propagating the most common bits of an IP network address together so that a single route is advertised for building routing tables to the supernet. Using Figure 19-24, the networks originating from AS200 router R2 are 172.16.0.0, 172.17.0.0, and 172.30.0.0. Aggregate addressing and the notion of supernets allows

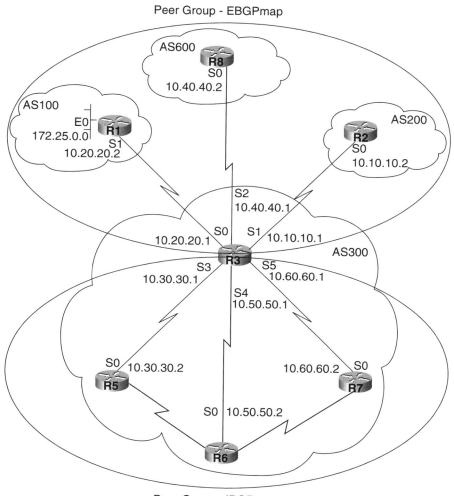

Figure 19-23

Network topology for
defining a BGP peer
group example.

Peer Group - EBGPmap

AS600
R8
S0
10.40.40.2

AS100
E0 R1
172.25.0.0
S1
10.20.20.2

AS200
R2
S0
10.10.10.2

S2
10.40.40.1

S0   S1 10.10.10.1
10.20.20.1

AS300

R3
S3   S5
10.30.30.1   10.60.60.1

S4
10.50.50.1

S0 10.30.30.2   10.60.60.2 S0
R5   R7

S0 10.50.50.2

R6

Peer Group - IBGPmap

the router administrator to reduce the three route advertisements into the
172.0.0.0 supernet.

In Figure 19-24, router R2 sends routing updates for the 172.16.0.0,
172.17.0.0, and 172.30.0.0 networks. Router R3 can be configured as follows
to forward a supernet route advertisement of the 172.0.0.0 network to
router R1. The following configuration demonstrates the specification of
simple aggregate addressing:

Figure 19-24
A simple topology for
BGP route
aggregation.

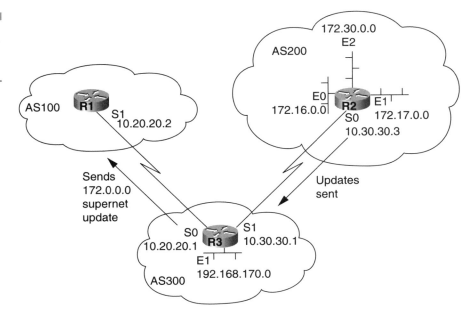

Router R2 configuration applied to Figure 19-24:

```
router bgp 200
 neighbor 10.30.30.1 remote-as 300
 network 172.16.0.0
 network 172.17.0.0
 network 172.30.0.0
```

Router R3 Configuration applied to Figure 19-24:

```
router bgp 300
 neighbor 10.30.30.3 remote-as 200
 neighbor 10.20.20.2 remote-as 100
 network 192.168.170.0
 aggregate-address 172.0.0.0 255.0.0.0
```

The above sample configuration uses the simplest form of the aggregate-address command. The full format of the command is as follows:

aggregate-address *address mask* **[as-set] [summary-only] [suppress-map** *map-name*] **[advertise-map** *map-name*] **[attribute-map** *map-name*]

The *address* variable is the aggregate or supernet address being used to summarize the routes. The *mask* variable is the bit mask applied to the *address* variable to determine the supernet. Specifying only the *address* and *mask* variables on the command causes BGP to advertise the supernet, also called the prefix route in addition to the more specific routes.

In the previous example, not only will the 172.0.0.0 network be advertised but also the more specific 172.16.0.0, 172.17.0.0 and 172.30.0.0 networks are advertised to router R1. Aggregate addressing is only possible if a more specific route is found in the BGP routing table. For example, router R2 cannot aggregate the 172.x.x.x networks if it does not have a more specific entry for the network in its own BGP routing table. Specific entries can be included in the BGP routing table from either incoming routing updates received from other autonomous systems, the redistribution of IGP static routes into BGP, or using the network command.

Based on this discussion, the above configuration example did not reduce routing updates or the routing table but actually increased it by one route. To accomplish the actual reduction of routing updates and minimizing the size of the BGP routing table, the **summary-only** keyword is applied to the **aggregate-address** *address mask* command. Specifying the **aggregate-address** command with the **summary-only** keyword is formatted as

aggregate-address *address mask* **summary-only**

where the *address* variable is the IP address of the network to aggregate and the *mask* is the bit mask applied to the *address* variable. The **summary-only** keyword causes BGP to advertise only the prefix address and not the more specific addresses. Attention, however, must be given to how the networks are included in BGP. Defining networks on the **network** statement causes the network address to be included in BGP updates even when the **summary-only** keyword is specified.

Including the optional **as-set** keyword causes the BGP process to create AS set path information for both the prefix address advertisement and the more specific routes. The format for using the **as-set** keyword is

aggregate-address *address mask* **as-set**

again where *address* is the IP address of the supernet and the *mask* is the bit mask applied to the *address* variable.

The **as-set** keyword of the aggregate-address command is used primarily on aggregate route information where the path attribute has lost information due to the function of the AS-SETS process when using aggregation. The AS-SETS process reduces the path information length by including an AS number only once, even though it may be in multiple paths used to build the aggregate.

In Figure 19-25, router R3 is to aggregate using network 172.0.0.0 255.0.0.0 and send the path to router R4. Router R4 will not be aware of the origin of this route if router R3 does not use the `as-set` keyword on the aggregate address command to generate path information as a set. The set includes all the path information regardless of which path was received first.

The router configuration used to accomplish the desired outcome is as follows:

Router R1 configuration applied to Figure 19-25:

```
router bgp 100
 network 172.20.0.0
 neighbor 10.20.20.1 remote-as 300
```

Router R2 configuration applied to Figure 19-25:

```
router bgp 200
 network 172.16.0.0
 neighbor 10.30.30.1 remote-as 300
```

Router R3 configuration applied to Figure 19-25:

```
router bgp 300
 neighbor 10.30.30.3 remote-as 200
 neighbor 10.20.20.2 remote-as 100
 neighbor 10.40.40.4 remote-as 400
 aggregate-address 172.0.0.0 255.0.0.0 summary-only
 aggregate-address 172.0.0.0 255.0.0.0 as-set
```

Applying the above configurations, router R3 sends updates on the supernet 172.0.0.0 255.0.0.0 to router R4 with the AS-SET of ({100 200}) included in the path information. Without configuring the aggregate-address as-set command in router R3, router R4 would not be aware that the 172.0.0.0 supernet is actually originating from two different autonomous systems. Using the **as-set** keyword on a supplementary **aggregate-address** command protects router R4 from creating a loop to AS100 through an unknown backdoor connection.

The **suppress-map** keyword followed by its *map-name* variable enables the suppression of more specific routes when performing aggregate address summarization using a route map that is applied to the aggregate entry. For example, in Figure 19-25, when using **suppress-map** on the aggregate-address with associated route-map and access-list statements, the supernet 172.0.0.0 and 172.16.0.0 networks can be advertised while the specific routes for 172.20.0.0 can be suppressed. The following configuration demonstrates this for router R3:

Router R3 configuration suppressing the 172.20.0.0 network:

```
router bgp 300
 neighbor 10.30.30.3 remote-as 200
```

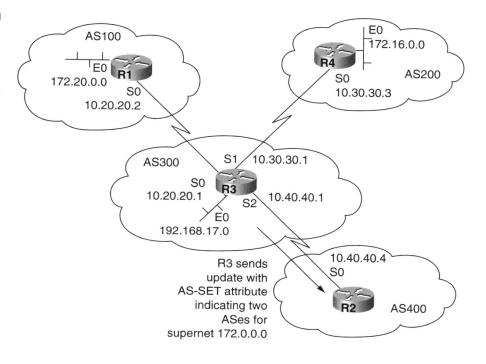

Figure 19-25
Network topology used for **as-set** aggregate command.

```
neighbor 10.20.20.2 remote-as 100
network 192.168.17.0
aggregate-address 172.0.0.0 255.0.0.0 suppress-map NO172-20

route-map NO172-20 permit 10
 match ip address 1
access-list 1 deny 172.20.0.0 0.0.255.255
access-list 1 permit 0.0.0.0 255.255.255.255
```

The **advertise-map** keyword and its associated *map-name* identify the route map used for selecting routes when creating AS-SET origin communities. The **attribute-map** keyword followed by its *map-name* variable value identifies the route map used for setting the various attributes of the advertised aggregate route.

Grouping Multiple Autonomous Systems into a BGP Confederation

Many Internet Service Provider (ISP) networks have large IBGP mesh configurations within their AS. Using the concept of a confederation, a large AS can be divided into smaller autonomous systems, grouped together as a single confederation that is assigned its own AS. Each of the new autonomous systems has an IBGP mesh with connections to the other new autonomous systems in the confederation.

Because they belong to a confederation, the EBGP peering between the new autonomous systems exchanges their routing updates as if they are connected using IBGP. This means that next-hop, metric, and local preference information is passed between the EBGP peers of the confederation, even though normally EBGP connections do not propagate this information. Connections from networks to the confederation use the confederation AS number despite the physical connection. Figure 19-26 illustrates a BGP confederation topology.

A BGP confederation is built using two bgp commands. The first of these defines the AS number associated with the confederation. The format for this command is

bgp confederation identifier *autonomous-system*

The value specified for the *autonomous-system* variable of the **bgp confederation identifier** command is the AS number associated with the BGP confederation. The value can range from 1 to 65535 and must be unique within the network.

The second required definition for using BGP confederation is the bgp confederation peers command. BGP peers become members of the confederation by their specification of the bgp confederation peer command in their router configuration. The format of the command is

bgp confederation peers *autonomous-system* [*autonomous-system*]

The *autonomous-system* variable(s) identifies the BGP AS numbers of routers belonging to the confederation defined under the router bgp command.

In Figure 19-26, the AS500 consists of nine BGP routers with EBGP connections to other AS's. Creating a full mesh within AS500 requires nine peer connections for each router broken down into eight IBGP peers and one EBGP peer to an external AS. Using a confederation, the AS500 can safely be divided into three AS's, each having a full IBGP mesh. The following illustrates the BGP confederation configuration for routers R1, R3, and R4 in Figure 19-26:

Router R1 configuration for defining BGP confederations in Figure 19-26:

Figure 19-26
A BGP confederation
topology.

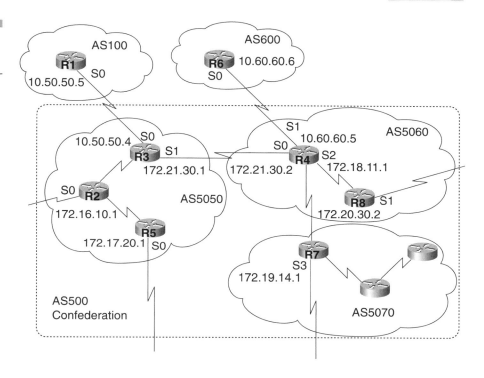

```
router bgp 100
 neighbor 10.50.50.4 remote-as 500
```

Router R3 configuration for defining BGP confederations in Figure
  19-26:

```
router bgp 5050
 bgp confederation identifier 500
 bgp confederation peers 5060 5070
 neighbor 172.16.10.1 remote-as 5050
 neighbor 172.17.20.1 remote-as 5050
 neighbor 172.18.11.1 remote-as 5060
 neighbor 172.19.14.1 remote-as 5070
 neighbor 10.50.50.5 remote-as 100
```

Router R4 configuration for defining BGP confederations in Figure
  19-26:

```
router bgp 5060
 bgp confederation identifier 500
 bgp confederation peers 5050 5070
 neighbor 172.20.30.2 remote-as 5060
 neighbor 172.21.30.1 remote-as 5050
 neighbor 172.19.14.1 remote-as 5070
 neighbor 10.60.60.6 remote-as 600
```

Router R1 does not know of the new AS's 5050, 5060, and 5070, which were created for the confederation. Router R1 contacts peers using the 500 AS number. The 500 is the BGP confederation identifier defined in router R3 and R4. The bgp confederation peers command for router R3 identifies AS 5060 and 5070 as being a part of the confederation using identifier 500. Router R4 defines AS 5050 and 5070 as members of the confederation using the same identifier 500.

Reducing IBGP Peering Using Route Reflectors (RR)

Internal BGP peering does not have IBGP peers forward advertised routes learned by other IBGP peers to a third IBGP peer. IBGP peers providing learned routes to other IBGP routers within the AS are called route reflecting. An IBGP router acting as a route reflector (RR) performs a function akin to a hub and spoke configuration. The router using the RR feature has peer connections with all the routers in the AS and updates their tables. The non-RR routers have peer connections only with the RR router, as illustrated in Figure 19-27.

In this simple configuration, the normal full IBGP mesh for connecting router R1, R2, and R3 in AS100 is not needed because router R3 is performing the RR function. Router R1 and R2 do not peer with each other. Instead, they learn of the routes from only router R3. Router R3 "reflects" routing updates received from R1 to R2 and updates from R2 to R1. The router acting as the RR refers to the neighbors receiving updates from it as clients. The combination of the RR and its clients is called a cluster.

In Figure 19-27, router R1, R2, and R3 form the cluster with only router R3 as the single RR in the AS. IBGP peers of the RR that are not defined as clients are called non-clients. A router becomes an RR by including in its router bgp configuration the **neighbor route-reflector-client** command. The format of this command is

neighbor *ip-address* **route-reflector-client**

The *ip-address* variable value is the IP address of a BGP neighbor being established as a client of the router. Specifying this command causes the router to act as a route reflector.

More than one RR can exist in an AS, and if more than one RR is present then there can be multiple clusters. A RR communicates with other RRs as if they were IBGP peers. The multiple RRs can be defined in the same cluster

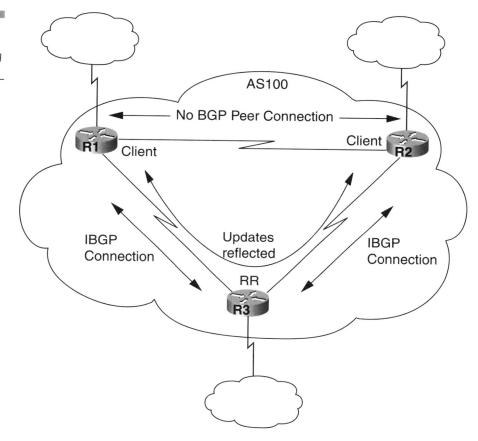

Figure 19-27
Simple network
topology for defining
RR.

or to other clusters. For example, in Figure 19-28, router R1, R2, and R3 are defined as a single cluster and R3 is the RR for the cluster. A second cluster is defined by the RR definition in router R4 whose clients are R5 and R6. Router R7 is an RR unto itself, forming a third cluster within the AS. The three RRs are fully meshed. The clients of each cluster, however, do not peer with the clients of other clusters.

When a RR receives a route from a non–client peer, it reflects the route to all the clients of its cluster. If the RR receives a route from a client peer, the route is reflected to all the non-client peers as well as the client peers. Finally, if the route received by a RR is from an external BGP peer, the RR sends the update to all client and non-client peers.

The following router configurations highlight the definitions for the BGP routers R2, R3, and R4 of Figure 19-28.

Figure 19-28
Multiple RR network
topology.

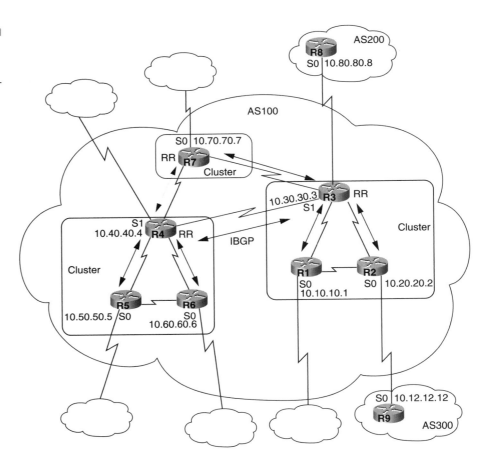

Router R2 configuration applied to Figure 19-28:

```
router bgp 100
neighbor 10.30.30.3remote-as 100
neighbor 10.12.12.12 remote-as 300
```

Router R3 configuration applied to Figure 19-28:

```
router bgp 100
neighbor 10.20.20.2 remote-as 100
neighbor 10.20.20.2 route-reflector-client
neighbor 10.10.10.1 remote-as 100
neighbor 10.10.10.1 route-reflector-client
neighbor 10.70.70.7 remote-as 100
neighbor 10.40.40.4 remote-as 100
neighbor 10.80.80.8 remote-as 200
```

Router R4 configuration applied to Figure 19-28:

```
router bgp 100
 neighbor 10.60.60.6 remote-as 100
 neighbor 10.60.60.6 route-reflector-client
 neighbor 10.50.50.5 remote-as 100
 neighbor 10.50.50.5 route-reflector-client
 neighbor 10.70.70.7 remote-as 100
 neighbor 10.30.30.3 remote-as 100
```

Because routes are reflected, it is possible the learned internal BGP routes will end up causing a routing information loop. The schema used for route reflecting, however, employs two methods to avert a routing information loop. The first method uses the originator-id optional attribute that is four bytes in length and is created by the RR. The attribute value is actually the route-id of the route originator in the local AS. This enables the route originator to determine if the route has come back to itself, thereby enabling the originator of the route to ignore the routing update.

The second method of route reflecting is the use of cluster lists. The cluster list is also a non-transitive BGP optional attribute as well as a sequence of cluster-ids that a route has passed through. A RR will append its local cluster ID to the cluster list when reflecting a route from a client to non-client peers.

Using a cluster list, a RR can determine if a loop exists by discovering its own cluster ID in the cluster list of the router advertisement. If the RR finds its own cluster ID in the cluster list, the advertisement is ignored. If the cluster list is empty, the RR creates begins a new cluster list. Cluster IDs are defined using the bgp cluster-id command. The format of the command is

bgp cluster-id *cluster-id*

where the cluster-id variable value is the ID assigned to the cluster by the RR. The value can be up to four bytes.

The cluster-id is important in configurations employing redundancy to avoid a single point of failure for the RR of a cluster. Pictured in Figure 19-29 is such a network topology. Multiple RRs are defined within a cluster to provide redundancy. Each RR of a cluster must use the same cluster-id in order to utilize the cluster-list method of avoiding loops.

Routers R4, R5, R6, and R8 in Figure 19-29 are part of a single cluster in which R4 and R8 provide the services of a RR for the cluster. Each RR in the cluster must use the same cluster-id in order to determine if a route advertisement is causing a loop. In the following router configuration examples, router R4 and R8 define a cluster-id of 1111. Router R3 does not have a cluster ID defined since it is the only RR within its cluster.

Figure 19-29
Multiple RRs in a
cluster to avoid a
single point of failure.

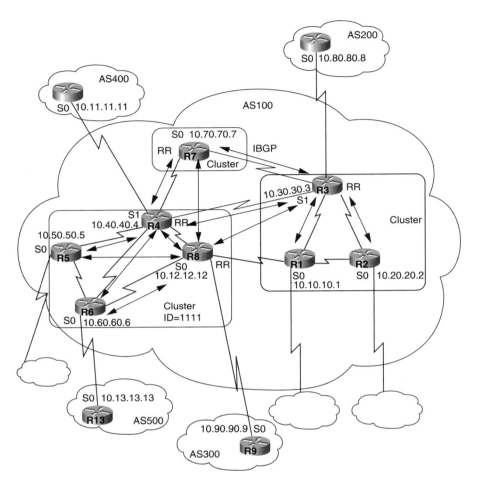

Router R3 configuration applied to Figure 19-29:

```
router bgp 100
 neighbor 10.10.10.1 remote-as 100
 neighbor 10.10.10.1 route-reflector-client
 neighbor 10.20.20.2 remote-as 100
 neighbor 10.20.20.2 route-reflector-client
 neighbor 10.40.40.4 remote-as 100
 neighbor 10.70.70.7 remote-as 100
 neighbor 10.12.12.12 remote-as 100
 neighbor 10.80.80.8 remote-as 200
```

Router R4 configuration applied to Figure 19-29:

```
router bgp 100
 neighbor 10.12.12.12 remote-as 100
```

```
neighbor 10.50.50.5 remote-as 100
neighbor 10.50.50.5 route-reflector-client
neighbor 10.60.60.6 remote-as 100
neighbor 10.60.60.6 route-reflector-client
neighbor 10.70.70.7 remote-as 100
neighbor 10.30.30.3 remote-as 100
neighbor 10.11.11.11 remote-as 400
bgp route-reflector 1111
```

Router R6 configuration applied to Figure 19-29:

```
router bgp 100
  neighbor 10.12.12.12 remote-as 100
  neighbor 10.40.40.4 remote-as 100
  neighbor 10.13.13.13 remote-as 500
```

Router R8 configuration applied to Figure 19-29:

```
router bgp 100
  neighbor 10.40.40.4 remote-as 100
  neighbor 10.50.50.5 remote-as 100
  neighbor 10.50.50.5 route-reflector-client
  neighbor 10.60.60.6 remote-as 100
  neighbor 10.60.60.6 route-reflector-client
  neighbor 10.70.70.7 remote-as 100
  neighbor 10.30.30.3 remote-as 100
  neighbor 10.90.90.9 remote-as 300
bgp route-reflector 1111
```

If clients of a cluster are meshed, route reflection is not required. By default, an RR has client-to-client reflection enabled. To disable this, enter the no bgp client-to-client reflection command. It is important to note that peer groups cannot be used if client-to-client reflection is enabled. Any clients of a route reflector cannot therefore be members of a BGP peer group. Having the clients as part of a peer group could cause invalid routes reflected to clients that are not part of the peer group.

In Figure 19-30, a topology is in in which where router R4, R5, and R6 understand router reflection, while routers R1, R2, and R3 are not configurable as RRs. Routers R1, R2, and R3 can be configured in a full IBGP mesh along with R4. When any of the routers R1, R2, or R3 are upgraded to support RR, the other two remaining traditional routers can become clients of the RR. In our example, R3 becomes the RR, and R1 and R2 become the clients of the R3 cluster. Once R3 is made an RR with R1 and R2 as clients, the full IBGP mesh that exists between the three can be removed.

The following router configurations coincide with routers R4 and R3 in Figure 19-30:

Router R3 configuration applied to Figure 19-30:

```
router bgp 100
  neighbor 10.40.40.4 remote-as 100
```

Figure 19-30
RR migration strategy
topology.

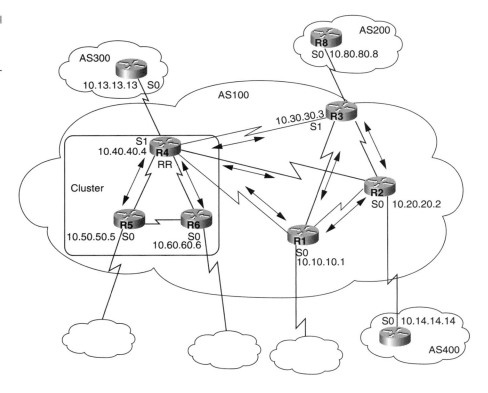

```
neighbor 10.20.20.2 remote-as 100
neighbor 10.10.10.1 remote-as 100
neighbor 10.14.14.14 remote-as 400
```

Router R4 configuration applied to Figure 19-30:

```
router bgp 100
  neighbor 10.60.60.6 remote-as 100
  neighbor 10.60.60.6 route-reflector-client
  neighbor 10.50.50.5 remote-as 100
  neighbor 10.50.50.5 route-reflector-client
  neighbor 10.30.30.3 remote-as 100
  neighbor 10.20.20.2 remote-as 100
  neighbor 10.10.10.1 remote-as 100
  neighbor 10.13.13.13 remote-as 300
```

Two features must be watched when employing RRs and avoiding routing loops. The first is the set clause command. When specified for outbound route-maps, it does not affect routes that are reflected to IBGP peers by a RR. The second item is the nexthop-self feature for RRs. Using the nexthop-self on a RR router only affects the nexthop of learned EBGP routes because the nexthop of a RR does not change.

Managing Unstable Routes

Unstable routes can greatly affect network performance. Each time a connection somewhere in the route fails or has an adverse performance, routes can be recalculated and then propagated throughout the network. As of Cisco IOS version 11.0, a feature was introduced to protect BGP from unstable routes known as route dampening.

A route that flip-flops between being available and not available is considered to be a flapping route. When a route flaps for the first time, the IOS BGP process places the route into a history state. When a route is placed in a history state, the route is not perceived to be the best route to the destination. Consecutive route flaps cause the IOS BGP process to place a penalty on the route. A penalty is valued at 1000 and is cumulative. The value of penalty is stored in the BGP, routing travel around the route in question until the penalty. The penalty is halved after a half-life period. This is performed and adjusted every five seconds in an effort to allow the route to establish itself as a stable route once again.

Over the course of time, the cumulative penalty placed on the route may become greater than a specified suppress limit. The suppress limit is the cumulative total of penalties weighed against a route. Once the suppress limit is exceeded, the state of the route changes from history to damp.

A route can only be considered suppressed for a maximum amount of time. This time defaults to four times the half-life value. In the damp state, the route is no longer advertised to the BGP neighbors. The router IOS places a route back into the BGP table and forwards the route to neighbors once the penalty value has dropped below a reuse-limit level. The process to determine if a route has fallen below the reuse-limit level occurs every 10 seconds. If a route is found to have its penalty below the reuse-limit level, the BGP process advertises the route to all of its neighbors.

This capability to dampen routes is disabled by default. The format for enabling route dampening is

bgp dampening [*half-life reuse suppress max-suppress-time*] [**route-map** *map*]

Specifying only **bgp dampening** enables route dampening using default values. The *half-life* optional variable defaults to 15 minutes. The *half-life* period default is specified when this positional variable is specified. The value for *half-life* ranges from one to 45 minutes.

The optional *reuse* variable defines the reuse-limit value for determining the penalty value under which the route can be unsuppressed. The *reuse* value can range from 1 to 20000 and defaults to 750.

The *suppress* variable is the value at which the cumulative penalty must exceed to change the state of the route from history to damp. The range for the *suppress* variable is 1 to 20000 and defaults to 2000. The *max-suppress-time* variable value is defined in minutes and defaults to the half-life value multiplied by four. The *max-suppress-time* value can range from 1 to 20000.

The **route-map** keyword followed by the *map* variable identifies the route map enabling route dampening. If any of the default values for the positional variables *half-life*, *reuse*, *suppress,* and *max-suppress-time* are altered to meet the network requirements, they must all be specified since they are positional variables.

Suppose, as shown in Figure 19-31, router R2 is taking the default values of the bgp dampening command. The two routers, R2 and R4, are defined as follows:

Router R2 configuration applied to Figure 19-31:

```
interface Serial0
  ip address 10.203.250.2 255.255.255.252
interface Serial1
  ip address 10.192.208.6 255.255.255.252
router bgp 100
  bgp dampening
  network 10.203.250.0
  neighbor 10.192.208.5 remote-as 300
```

Router R4 configuration applied to Figure 19-31:

```
interface Loopback0
  ip address 10.192.208.174 255.255.255.192
interface Serial0/0
  ip address 10.192.208.5 255.255.255.252
router bgp 300
 network 10.192.208.0
 neighbor 10.192.208.6 remote-as 100
```

Figure 19-31
Route flapping
network topology
example.

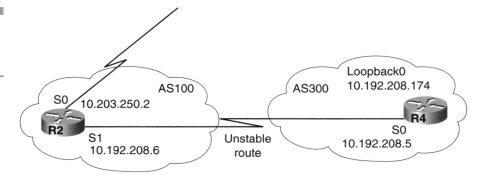

If the EBGP link to router R4 from router R2 becomes unstable, router R2 places the BGP entry for 10.192.208.0 into a history state. After several more flaps over a given time period, the route becomes dampened. Only after the penalty backs down below the reuse limit will the route again be advertised.

Route
Redistribution

A single IP routing protocol is the preferred method for managing IP routes within the network. Circumstances will arise, however, when more than one routing protocol is required. In previous chapters, we have alluded to some of these circumstances. More than likely, multiple routing protocols will be necessary during a migration from one interior gateway protocol (IGP) to another, such as migrating from RIP to EIGRP or RIP to OSPF. Another example is a historical network design where a Sun workstation is acting as a RIP router for a LAN but requires connectivity to the WAN that is using Cisco EIGRP or OSPF.

Another potential requirement for running multiple routing protocols is the mix of vendor router hardware and software. An example would be the merger of two companies. One company using non-Cisco router platforms running RIP and the other company running Cisco router platforms running EIGRP require both routing tables to be merged. Cisco IOS enables the simultaneous use of multiple routing protocols by using the route redistribution feature.

Understanding Route Redistribution

Cisco IOS enables the execution of multiple IP routing protocols. Each routing protocol and the networks serviced by the routing protocol are referred to as an autonomous system. Cisco IOS using the route redistribution feature enables the exchange of routing information built by one protocol with another. In a matter of speaking, Cisco IOS translates the routing information of one routing protocol into another.

For example, Figure 20-1 displays two AS's. The AS100 uses the Cisco IGRP routing protocol and the AS200 is using the Cisco EIGRP routing protocol. At least one router within the network must be using both routing protocols for each AS to learn of the routes between the AS's. A router using multiple routing protocols and redistributing the routes between the routing protocols is termed an Autonomous System Boundary Router (ASBR). The ASBR interconnects the two unique AS's so that the routes of both are advertised to each AS.

The Class C network 192.168.140.0 address used in AS200 with EIGRP is advertised to router R1 by the ASBR, router R2. The resulting IGRP routing table in router R1 includes the route to 192.168.140.0 with a 255.255.255.0 mask. The router R1 IGRP table will direct any 192.168.140.x routing request to serial interface S1 of router R1. Router R2 will receive the request and forward this request over serial interface S0 of router R2 to reach the 192.168.140.0 network. Router R3, in its EIGRP routing table, will then interpret the destination address of the request and match it against its routing table. The route for destination IP address 192.168.140.10 falls into the network address of 192.168.8.0 with a 255.255.248.0 mask. The EIGRP routing table in AS200 for router R3 forwards the packet to the Ethernet 0 interface on router R3, as indicated by the routing table.

The sending host in Figure 20-1 is IP address 172.16.1.2 with a 255.255.255.0 mask on Ethernet interface 1 of router R1 in AS200. Router R3 has included in its routing table a route for the 172.16.0.0 network that it has learned from the ASBR router R2 advertisement. The reply back in this simple configuration uses the reverse path. Both router R1 and R3 receive a summarized route advertisement from router R2.

The Redistribution Router Configuration Command

The router configuration command redistribution enables the Cisco IOS to translate the routes learned from one routing protocol into another routing protocol. The command format is as follows:

redistribute *protocol* [*process-id*] {**level-1** | **level-1-2** | **level-2**}
    [**metric** *metric-value*]

[**metric-type** *type-value*] [**match** {**internal** | **external 1** | **external 2**}]

[tag *tag-value*] [**route-map** *map-tag*] [**weight** *weight*] [**subnets**]

The *protocol* variable identifies the source-routing protocol. The routes derived from this routing protocol are the routes translated into the routing protocol under which this **redistribute** command is specified. The values available for the *protocol* variable are

Figure 20-1
A simple route redistribution configuration.

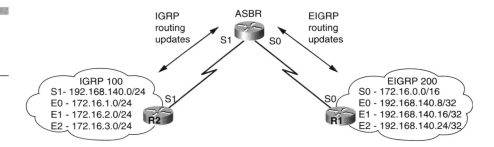

- **bgp**
- **eigrp**
- **igrp**
- **isis**
- **ospf**
- **static [ip]**
- **connected**
- **rip**

Specifying the **static [ip]** keywords together as the value for *protocol* is used to redistribute IP static routes into intersystem-to-intersystem (IS-IS). Specifying the **connected** keyword as the value for *protocol* is used when interfaces are enabled for IP but are not specified under a router configuration command using the **network** command. This situation is often seen when there is no reason to have the router send hello messages or routing update broadcasts onto LANs that do not have another router on the LAN.

If **connected** is used, OSPF and IS-IS redistribute these routes as external routes to the AS. The *process-id* variable is optional and is used to identify the bgp, eigrp, or igrp AS number of the BGP, EIGRP, or IGRP process, having its routes redistributed or the OSPF process number assigned to one of potentially multiple OSPF processes within the router. RIP does not require a *process-id* value. The **level-1, level-1-2,** and **level-2** keywords are used only for IS-IS.

The optional **metric** keyword, followed by its variable named *metric-value,* is a value ranging from 0 to any positive integer. The value used on the **redistribute** command for the **metric** *metric-value* variable overrides the *metric* value used on a **default-metric** command. The *metric-value* used is assigned as the seed metric for the redistributed route. (The seed metric will be covered later in Table 20-2.)

Redistributing routes in OSPF without specifying the *metric-value* variable on the **metric** keyword causes OSPF to use a default cost of 20 for the imported route for all redistributed routes, except those derived from BGP. In the case of redistributing BGP into OSPF with the **metric** keyword specified without a **metric-value**, BGP redistributed routes receive a cost metric of one. Redistribution of OSPF routes from one OSPF AS to another OSPF AS without the *metric–value* coded after the specification of the **metric** keyword causes the importing OSPF process to use the derived OSPF route cost metric.

The **metric-type** optional keyword followed by its *type-value* variable, when used for OSPF, defaults to a type 2 external route as the default route being advertised into the OSPF AS. Using a value of **1** indicates that the default route is a Type 1 external route. A value of **2** for the **metric-type** *type-value* variable specifies a default route advertisement of Type 2 external routes into the OSPF AS.

The optional keyword **match** and its arguments **internal, external1,** or **external2** are specifically for OSPF routes being redistributed into other routing protocols. Specifying the **internal** argument of the optional **match** keyword indicates that the routes are internal routes of the AS. Using the **external1** argument indicates that the routes are external to the AS but were calculated by OSPF as type 1 external routes. The **external2** argument indicates that the routes are external to the AS and that OSPF had created them as type 2 external routes.

The optional **tag** keyword and its associated *tag-value* variable assign a 32-bit decimal value to external routes. The *tag-value* specified is not used by the OSPF routing protocol but can be used by the ASBR. If a tag is not defined, the default tag used when redistributing BGP routes is the remote AS number of routes coming from BGP. The other routing protocols default the tag to 0.

The optional **route-map** keyword and its following *map-tag* variable identify the filter to apply to routes imported from the source routing protocol. Not specifying a **route-map** allows all routes to be redistributed, while not specifying a *map-tag* value is a means of filtering all the routes being redistributed. The **weight** keyword and its variable *weight* assigns an integer from 0 to 65535 to routes being redistributed into BGP. BGP then uses the *weight* value to determine the best path to the destination if multiple paths exist. The final optional keyword is the **subnets** keyword. This keyword is used for redistributing routes into OSPF, enabling granular redistribution versus summarized redistribution.

The following configuration code is an example of the redistribution command between RIP and OSPF:

```
router rip
 redistribute ospf 109 metric 10
router ospf 109
 redistribute rip metric 200 subnets
```

In this example, the OSPF-derived routes are redistributed into RIP routes having a hop count of 10. The RIP-derived routes being redistributed into OSPF routes as type 2 external routes are given an OSPF cost of 200.

Selecting the Best Path Based on a Routing Protocol

Each of the routing protocols discussed has a variance on the way common metrics between them can be used due to the metric structure and/or the algorithm used to derive the metric value. This makes redistribution difficult to implement. Cisco IOS utilizes a methodology for determining the best path to a destination when two or more routing protocols are used, resulting in two or more different routes to the destination. The methodology is based on an administrative distance and a default metric.

Altering Trusted or Believable Routes Using the Distance Command

The administrative distance is a metric value that determines the validity or believability of a routing protocol. The various routing protocols available in Cisco IOS are prioritized in the order of most to least believable. This is the first criterion used by the Cisco IOS in determining which of the multiple routes is the best to reach the destination. The default administrative distance values applied to the various routing protocols are listed in believability order in Table 20-1.

Judging from the table, if a router running RIP and EIGRP received a route advertisement for the 172.16.0.0 network from both of the routing protocols, the EIGRP route would be the most believable. Therefore, it is this route that is placed in the routing table.

Although the table displays the default values used by Cisco IOS for administrative distances, occasions will occur when the distance may need to be altered. For example, when migrating from RIP to EIGRP, the EIGRP routes can be given a higher administrative value than the default RIP, or RIP can be given a lower administrative distance value than the default EIGRP. This enables both routing protocols to build their own tables but provide a preference as to which routing protocol provides the best path. Once the EIGRP routing tables are built, the default distances can be reinstated and the EIGRP routing information for the connected networks will be used as the best path to the destination networks.

The administrative distance of a routing protocol can be altered by using the **distance** router configuration command. The format of the **distance** command is as follows:

distance *weight* [*address mask* [*access-list-number* | *name*]] [ip]

Table 20-1

The Default Admin-istrative Distances Used by Cisco IOS

Route Source	Default Distance
Connected interface	0
Static route	1
Enhanced IGRP summary route	5
External BGP	20
Internal Enhanced IGRP	90
IGRP	100
OSPF	110
IS-IS	115
RIP	120
EGP	140
External EIGRP	170
Internal BGP	200
Unknown	255

The *weight* variable is the actual administrative distance that is assigned to the routes built by the routing protocol to which the **distance** command is specified. The value of the *weight* variable can be a number ranging from 10 to 255. The administrative value is the default metric used by Cisco IOS when there is no other metric available for the route. A value of 255 specified for the *weight* variable instructs the Cisco IOS to not build an entry in the routing table for the routing protocol to which this **distance** command is applied. Assigning a value to the *weight* variable is purely a subjective versus quantitative approach. The *weight* value selected should be chosen to meet the objective for using the **distance** command.

The optional *address* variable is the network address to which the *weight* value is to be applied. The following *mask* variable, written in four-part dot-ted-decimal form, is the bit mask applied to the *address* variable value. Using these variables, only routes that match the *address/mask* variable value pair are given the administrative distance value specified by this command. The optional *access-list-number* or *name* variable value specifies the access-list number or name of a standard IP access list that is applied to the incoming routing update. The optional **ip** keyword is for IS-IS routing protocols, enabling the routing tables to build IP derived routes for IS-IS.

NOTE: *When applying the distance command to BGP, the value sets the administrative distance for the external BGP routing entries and not the internal BGP routing entries.*

The use of the access-list arguments applies to the insertion of a route into the routing table. Using this argument on the **distance** command enables the router administrator to filter networks based on the sending IP address supplying the routing update.

Multiple instances of the **distance** command can be used under the router configuration mode. As an example

```
router igrp 10
 network 192.168.31.0
 network 172.28.0.0
 distance 255
 distance 90 192.168.31.0 0.0.0.255
 distance 120 172.28.1.1 0.0.0.0
```

the router AS for this IGRP definition is 10. The IGRP router configuration includes the 192.168.31.0 and 172.28.0.0 networks. The first **distance** command applied to the routes received indicates that all the routes are ignored when the routing update does not have an explicit distance set. The second **distance** command applies an administrative distance of 90 to all routing updates from routers advertising the 192.168.31.0 network. The final **distance** command sets the administrative distance to 120 for all routing updates received from the router with the source address of 172.28.1.1.

Modifying the Seed Metric Using the default-metric Command

An ASBR uses the administrative distance value to determine which routing protocol to use for selecting the best route. The next step of the ASBR is to translate the metric(s) of the received routing update into a routing update appropriate for the other routing protocol. As an example, RIP uses a hop count as its metric. Redistributing RIP into OSPF requires that the hop count be assigned an OSPF cost value. Recall that cost is the determinant metric of OSPF. The determinant metric of each routing protocol is termed as the seed or default metric.

The seed metric, once established, increments normally within the AS. A router administrator can influence the route selection process by specifying the default metric value. The default metric value is modifiable using the router configuration mode command **default-metric**. There are two formats for the command. The first format, shown below, is used for settling the default metric value during route redistribution with the BGP, OSPF, and RIP-routing protocols. The format of the command when used for these routing protocols is

default-metric *number*

The value used for *number* variable ranges from 0 to any positive integer that reflects the values used by the seed metric of the routing protocol importing the redistributed route. The seed metric is listed in Table 20.2. The value of the *number* variable in the **default-metric** command is used as the metric value for the seed metrics of each respective routing protocol.

As an example, if the following were defined in a router running both RIP and OSPF, the OSPF-derived routes would be translated into RIP routes using 4 as the hop-count metric for the RIP routing information on all redistributed OSPF routes. The RIP routes translated into OSPF are assigned a cost value of 10 based on the **default-metric** command found under the router ospf configuration command:

```
router rip
 default-metric 4
 redistribute ospf 100
router ospf 100
 default-metric 10
 redistribute rip
```

Table 20-2

Seed Metrics for RIP, OSPF, and BGP

Routing Protocol	Seed Metric
RIP	Hop count
OSPF	Cost
BGP4	Multi-exit discriminator (MED) metric
BGP2 and BGP3	INTER_AS

NOTE: *Redistribution of OSPF routes between OSPF processes does not cause the OSPF processes to maintain route metrics. A default-metric statement is needed to ensure the proper metric assignment.*

When defining the default metric for route redistribution involving IGRP or EIGRP, the command format is different. This is because these routing protocols have five metrics. The format of the command is as follows when used with IGRP or EIGRP:

default-metric *bandwidth delay reliability loading mtu*

The variables of the **default-metric** command used for IGRP and EIGRP are positional and must all be specified when changing only one of the variables. The *bandwidth* variable is the minimum bandwidth in kilobits per second of the **default-metric** command. The *bandwidth* variable value can be set to 0 or any positive integer.

The *delay* variable value is measured in tens of microseconds. The *delay* variable can be set to 0 or any positive number. The actual value is the result of multiplying the *delay* variable value by 39.1 nanoseconds.

The *reliability* metric variable value indicates the capability of the route to successfully transmit packets. The number value for the *reliability* metric variable ranges from 0 to 255. The higher the value, the more reliable the route. A value of 255 indicates that the transmission of packets is considered to have a 100-percent success rate. A value of 0 for the reliability variable means the route is completely unreliable for transmitting packets.

The *loading* variable indicates the effective bandwidth, or percentage, on the route. The value for *loading* is a number ranging from 0 to 255, with 255 indicating that the bandwidth on the route is saturated or 100 percent utilized.

The final variable is the *mtu* (maximum transmission unit) size allowed on the route in bytes. The value for *mtu* can be set to 0 or be any positive integer.

NOTE: *When redistributing routes from BGP, OSPF, or RIP to EIGRP and IGRP, a default metric statement is needed. Only connected and static routes can be redistributed without a default metric. Redistributing routes between IGRP and EIGRP does not require a default metric command.*

As an example, the following router configuration redistributes RIP-sourced routes into EIGRP routes, using a bandwidth metric of 1,000, a delay of 50, a reliability of 255, a loading of 50, and a standard MTU size (mtu) of 1,500 bytes:

```
router rip
 network 131.110.0.0
router eigrp 100
 network 131.111.0.0
 redistribute rip
 default-metric 1000 50 255 50 1500
```

This example demonstrates a one-way redistribution. RIP-derived routes are being redistributed into EIGRP routes using the default-metric command. A two-way redistribution would involve the EIGRP-derived routes being redistributed into RIP.

Filtering Redistributed Routes Using the distribute-list Command

The filtering of the redistributed routes provides added control on which routes are allowed to be redistributed once received as routing updates and on being advertised into the AS. The filtering is accomplished using the **distribute-list** command. Two formats support the control functions. The first format controls which of the received routing updates are to be translated into the routing protocol process:

distribute-list {*access-list-number* | *name*} in [*type number*]

The **distribute-list in** command enables filtering of received updates prior to translation. The **distribute-list in** command is applicable to all routing protocols except IS-IS and OSPF. The use of the **distribute-list in** command is effective in preventing routing loops from being propagated.

Specifying the *access-list-number* or *name* variable identifies a Cisco IOS access list filter that is applied to the received routing update. The values specified must point to a standard IP access list number or name. The list specifies which networks can be received or which can be suppressed prior to redistribution.

The optional *type number* variable pair identifies which router interface the distribute-list applies. Not using this optional pair enables the **distribute-list in** to all interfaces on which the routing protocol executes. In the following example configuration, the EIGRP routing protocol permits only the default network of 0.0.0.0 and the network 172.16.0.0. Any network on incoming routing updates not matching these criteria are suppressed:

```
router eigrp 10
 network 172.16.0.0
 distribute-list 1 in
!
access-list 1 permit 0.0.0.0
access-list 1 permit 172.16.0.0
access-list 1 deny 0.0.0.0 255.255.255.255
```

The filtering mechanism required that controls routing updates during redistribution for OSPF and all other routing protocols is accomplished by using the distribute-list out router configuration command. The format of the command is

distribute-list {*access-list-number* | *name*} out
[*interface-name* | *routing-process* | *autonomous-system-number*]

Using the **distribute-list out** command, network advertisements can be suppressed during the sending of routing updates. Specifying the *access-list-number* or *name* variable identifies a Cisco IOS access list filter that is applied prior to sending routing updates. The values specified must point to a standard IP access list number or name. The list will specify which networks can be sent or which can be suppressed prior to sending the route updates. The out keyword is necessary to apply the **distribute-list** command to outbound routing updates.

The *interface-name* optional variable is used to identify a specific router interface on which the filter is applied for outgoing routing updates. The *routing-process* optional variable can be any of the following keywords:

- **bgp**
- **eigrp**
- **igrp**
- **isis**
- **ospf**
- **static**
- **connected**
- **rip**

The *autonomous-system-number* optional variable identifies the AS number of the routing process if an AS number is applicable. When using the optional *routing-process* optional variable, the filter is applied to only the routes derived from the *routing-process* value specified. It is only after the *routing-process*-derived routes are applied to the access-list filter that any other access list is applied to the *routing-process*-derived routes that are not suppressed by the **distribute-list out** access list.

In the following example, a **distribute-list out** command is used to allow only the 192.168.31.0 network of EIGRP AS 110 to be redistributed into EIGRP AS number 10:

```
router eigrp 10
 network 10.0.0.0
 redistribute eigrp 110
 distribute-list 1 out eigrp 110
 !
router eigrp 110
 network 192.168.31.0
 network 192.168.32.0
 !
access-list 1 permit 192.168.31.0
```

The **distribute-list 1 out eigrp 110** command under the router configuration for EIGRP AS 10 directs the routing update send process to use access-list 1. The access-list 1 permits only the 192.168.31.0 network to be sent from derived routes of EIGRP AS110 into the EIGRP AS 10 network.

Redistribution Considerations

Because route redistribution is such a powerful means for affecting routing within the network, it is important to understand its impact. When implementing redistribution, it is best to have a distinct boundary between the routing protocols in question. This enables a point of reference for determining routing problems, should they occur.

Using one-way route redistribution avoids routing loops and minimizes convergence time between the routing protocols. In a one-way route redistribution topology, it is suggested that in the reverse direction a default route be implemented, enabling reverse routing. Although two-way route redistribution provides a complete translation of routes between the routing protocols, it may require the use of default routes, route filters, or the specification of default metrics. Using one or many of these techniques will reduce the chances of creating routing loops between the AS's.

EIGRP and redistribution is a special case because EIGRP supports not only IP but Novell IPX and AppleTalk RTMP-routing protocols. Focusing in on IP-routing protocols, EIGRP can have its routes redistributed automatically with IGRP if both have the same AS number. If the EIGRP and IGRP AS numbers are different, however, the redistribution of routes with EIGRP by IGRP is treated just like the redistribution of the other IP-routing protocols. A distinct redistribute command must be entered, identifying the AS number of the routing protocol for routes to be redistributed. For example,

```
router igrp 10
 network 172.16.0.0
 router eigrp 10
 network 10.0.0.0
```

will have their routes redistributed automatically because they share the same AS number. In this case, the AS number is 10. However, if the two routing protocols were defined as

```
router igrp 10
 network 172.16.0.0
router eigrp 200
 network 10.0.0.0
```

then no route redistribution occurs automatically. In this case, the redistribute command is required. An example would be to code the following for two-way route redistribution:

```
router igrp 10
 network 172.16.0.0
 redistribution eigrp 200
router eigrp 200
 network 10.0.0.0
 redistribution igrp 10
```

Redistribution Examples

Route redistribution, as discussed earlier, may be required in many different scenarios. The most common are redistribution scenarios of RIP-to-OSPF, IGRP-to-EIGRP, and RIP-to-EIGRP. The following sections discuss these redistribution configurations.

RIP V1-to-OSPF Redistribution

Quite often, RIP V1-to-OSPF migrations are encountered to take advantage of the open-standard (such as interoperability between router vendors) and to utilize the minimized convergence time, VLSM support, and route summarization capabilities of OSPF over RIP Version 1. Shown in Figure 20-2 is a RIP V1 network using a Class B network addressing scheme with a full 24-bit network mask (8-bit subnet mask).

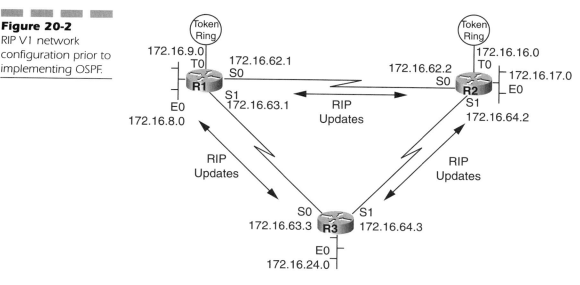

Figure 20-2
RIP V1 network
configuration prior to
implementing OSPF.

The network address assignments attaching to routers R1, R2, and R3 provide a range for use by each of the routers. For example, subnet 172.16.8-15.0 is for use on router R1 non-backbone connections. Router R2 has reserved subnets 172.16.16-23.0 for its non-backbone network connections. Router R3 is assigned subnets 172.16.24-31.0 for its non-backbone connections. The backbone connections (serial links) in Figure 20-2 are assigned subnet addresses of 172.16.62-64.0. For each of the routers in Figure 20-2, the following router configurations are in use prior to implementing OSPF:

Router R1 configuration for Figure 20-2 prior to implementing OSPF:

```
interface serial 0
 ip address 172.16.62.1 255.255.255.0
interface serial 1
 ip address 172.16.63.1 255.255.255.0
interface ethernet 0
 ip address 172.16.8.1 255.255.255.0
interface tokenring 0
 ip address 172.16.9.1 255.255.255.0
router rip
 network 172.16.0.0
```

Router R2 configuration for Figure 20-2 prior to implementing OSPF:

```
interface serial 0
 ip address 172.16.62.2 255.255.255.0
interface serial 1
 ip address 172.16.64.2 255.255.255.0
```

```
interface ethernet 0
 ip address 172.16.17.2 255.255.255.0
interface tokenring 0
 ip address 172.16.16.2 255.255.255.0
router rip
 network 172.16.0.0
```

Router R3 configuration for Figure 20-2 prior to implementing OSPF:

```
interface serial 0
 ip address 172.16.63.3 255.255.255.0
interface serial 1
 ip address 172.16.64.3 255.255.255.0
interface ethernet 0
 ip address 172.16.24.3 255.255.255.0
router rip
 network 172.16.0.0
```

Since the network address of all the interfaces on the routers are 172.16.0.0, only this network is required under the router rip configuration command of each router.

Typically, in a network, such as that shown in Figure 20-2, OSPF is first added to the backbone connections and given the assignment as OSPF area 0. Figure 20-3 illustrates the new network configuration utilizing OSPF Area 0 to connect the backbone routers R1, R2, and R3 as ASBRs.

The following router configurations apply to Figure 20-3 in support of using OSPF as the backbone-routing protocol and RIP as the edge-routing protocol. The configurations employ the use of the passive-interface, default-metric, and distribute-list out commands:

Router R1 configuration for Figure 20-3 with OSPF Area 0 on the backbone:

```
interface serial 0
 ip address 172.16.62.1 255.255.255.0
interface serial 1
 ip address 172.16.63.1 255.255.255.0
interface ethernet 0
 ip address 172.16.8.1 255.255.255.0
interface tokenring 0
 ip address 172.16.9.1 255.255.255.0
!
router rip
 default-metric 10
 network 172.16.0.0
 passive-interface serial 0
 passive-interface serial 1
 redistribute ospf 100 match internal external 1 external 2
 distribute-list 2 out ospf 100
```

Figure 20-3

RIP V1 network
configuration with
OSPF Area 0 assigned
to the backbone
connections.

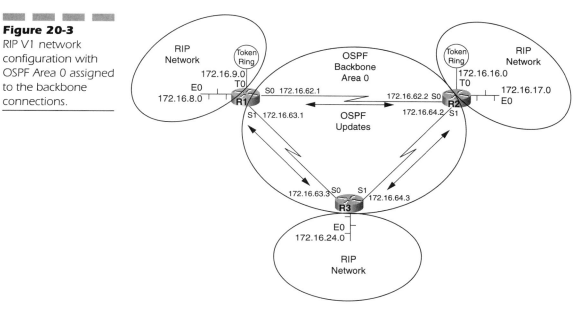

```
!
router ospf 100
 default-metric 20
 network 172.16.62.0 0.0.0.255 area 0
 network 172.16.63.0 0.0.0.255 area 0
 redistribute rip subnets
 distribute-list 1 out rip
!
access-list 1 permit 172.16.8.0 0.0.7.255
access-list 1 deny 0.0.0.0 255.255.255.255
access-list 2 deny 172.16.8.0 0.0.7.255
access-list 2 permit 0.0.0.0 255.255.255.255
```

Router R2 configuration for Figure 20-3 with OSPF Area 0 on the backbone:

```
interface serial 0
 ip address 172.16.62.2 255.255.255.0
interface serial 1
 ip address 172.16.64.2 255.255.255.0
interface ethernet 0
 ip address 172.16.17.2 255.255.255.0
interface tokenring 0
 ip address 172.16.16.2 255.255.255.0
!
```

```
router rip
 default-metric 10
 network 172.16.0.0
 passive-interface serial 0
 passive-interface serial 1
 redistribute ospf 100 match internal external 1 external 2
 distribute-list 2 out ospf 100
!
router ospf 100
 default-metric 20
 network 172.16.62.0 0.0.0.255 area 0
 network 172.16.64.0 0.0.0.255 area 0
 redistribute rip subnets
 distribute-list 1 out rip
access-list 1 permit 172.16.16.0 0.0.7.255
access-list 1 deny 0.0.0.0 255.255.255.255
access-list 2 deny 172.16.16.0 0.0.7.255
access-list 2 permit 0.0.0.0 255.255.255.255
```

Router R3 configuration for Figure 20-3 with OSPF Area 0 on the backbone:

```
interface serial 0
 ip address 172.16.63.3 255.255.255.0
interface serial 1
 ip address 172.16.64.3 255.255.255.0
interface ethernet 0
 ip address 172.16.24.3 255.255.255.0
!
router rip
 default-metric 10
 network 172.16.0.0
 passive-interface serial 0
 passive-interface serial 1
 redistribute ospf 100 match internal external1 external2
 distribute-list 2 out ospf 100
!
!
router ospf 100
 default-metric 20
 network 172.16.63.0 0.0.0.255 area 0
 network 172.16.64.0 0.0.0.255 area 0
 redistribute rip subnets
 distribute-list 1 out rip
access-list 1 permit 172.16.24.0 0.0.7.255
access-list 1 deny 0.0.0.0 255.255.255.255
access-list 2 deny 172.16.24.0 0.0.7.255
access-list 2 permit 0.0.0.0 255.255.255.255
```

Because OSPF is being used as a routing protocol on the backbone routers, the transmission of RIP-routing updates between routers R1, R2, and R3 is not needed. The RIP-routing updates are suppressed using the passive-interface command, specifying the applicable serial interface on each of the routers. Each of the three routers redistributes the RIP subnet routing updates into OSPF routes by the inclusion of the subnets keyword on the redistribute command under the router ospf configuration command. Without the subnets keyword only the 172.16.0.0 network is redistributed.

The RIP-routing process on each router is updated with the routes learned by OSPF through the redistribution of the RIP routes. Router R1's RIP process learns of routes from router R2 RIP process from the redistribution of RIP routes in router R2. The same process is used for router R1 and R3.

The **ospf** keyword on the redistribute command under the router rip configuration command indicates that all routes originating in the AS, routes derived as intra-area OSPF routes (external1), and routes derived as inter-area routes (external2) are to be redistributed into RIP routes. The default-metric command on each of the routers applies a default hop count of 10 for the OSPF routes translated into RIP.

As mentioned earlier, it is always good practice to provide the capability of blocking a potential routing loop, even if there is not a known configuration that may cause a loop. In the above router configuration examples, the potential for routing loops is addressed using the distribute-list out command under the router ospf configuration command for each router. The **distribute-list out** command identifies that the access-list number 1 will be applied to outgoing RIP updates only by the use of the **rip** keyword on the command. The access-list 1 permits only the subnet address range assigned to each of the routers for their end user interfaces. Any other RIP routing updates not meeting this criteria are suppressed by the deny statement following the permit statement of the access list.

The result of the distribute-list out command stops each router from advertising the networks derived by the other RIP-routing processes back into the OSPF backbone, which protects the backbone from creating a loop. To complete the loop-free environment configuration, the RIP process of each router should employ a distribute-list out command applied to the OSPF routes being redistributed in the same manner as the one that was applied to the OSPF process. By filtering on OSPF routes that are derived by OSPF from being redistributed into RIP, the duplication of routes is avoided and a loop-free configuration is achieved.

IGRP-to-EIGRP Redistribution

IGRP-to-EIGRP redistribution in its simplistic form is accomplished using the same AS numbers for the two routing protocols. For example, in Figure 20-4, router R5 connects an EIGRP network that requires connectivity to resources in an IGRP network. Router R5 becomes the ASBR for the redistribution and is configured to use both IGRP and EIGRP. Recall that IGRP and EIGRP use the same routing metrics in determining the best route to a destination network. Because of this commonality, when IGRP and EIGRP use the same AS number the routes are automatically redistributed and hence no redistribution command is necessary.

In Figure 20-4, router R6 uses EIGRP as the only routing process. Because the EIGRP AS is supporting only EIGRP routers, the router configuration for router R5 uses the passive-interface command on the connection to the EIGRP network for the IGRP route process, disabling the IGRP-routing update broadcasts to the EIGRP network. The following router configurations apply to the IGRP-to-EIGRP redistribution configuration diagrammed in Figure 20-4:

Router R5 configuration applied to Figure 20-4 supporting a single EIGRP AS connection to an IGRP AS:

```
interface ethernet 0
 ip address 192.168.42.121 255.255.255.248
interface ethernet 1
 ip address 192.168.42.9 255.255.255.248
!
router igrp 42
 network 192.168.42.0
router eigrp 42
 network 192.168.42.0
```

Router R6 configuration applied to Figure 20-4 supporting a single EIGRP AS connection to an IGRP AS:

```
interface ethernet 0
 ip address 192.168.42.17 255.255.255.248
interface ethernet 1
 ip address 192.168.42.10 255.255.255.248
!
router igrp 42
 network 192.168.42.0
router eigrp 42
 network 192.168.42.0
```

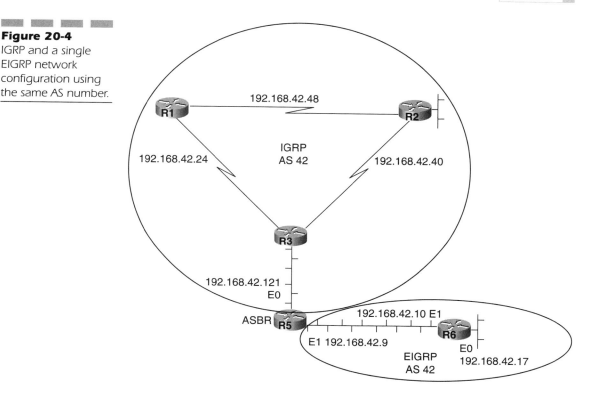

Figure 20-4
IGRP and a single
EIGRP network
configuration using
the same AS number.

The subnet 192.168.42.120 is viewed as an internal route for router R6 because router R5 is also running EIGRP along with IGRP. The other routes by router R6 are considered external routes because they are derived from the IGRP redistribution occurring on router R5.

The network configuration shown in Figure 20-5 illustrates the implementation of redistributing EIGRP networks into IGRP networks. Routers R1, R2, and R3 all use IGRP AS 60. Router R1 also uses static routes to the network 192.168.9.0 .

The following router configurations apply to Figure 20-5 prior to implementing EIGRP:

Router R1 configuration for Figure 20-5 prior to implementing EIGRP:

```
interface serial 0
 ip address 172.16.1.1 255.255.255.0
interface serial 1
 ip address 172.16.2.1 255.255.255.0
interface ethernet 0
 ip address 10.1.1.1 255.255.255.0
```

```
interface ethernet 1
 ip address 10.1.2.1 255.255.255.0
router igrp 60
 network 172.16.0.0
 network 10.0.0.0
 default-metric 1000 100 1 1 1500
 redistribute static
ip route 192.168.9.0 255.255.255.0 e0
```

Router R2 configuration for Figure 20-5 prior to implementing EIGRP:

```
interface serial 0
 ip address 172.16.1.2 255.255.255.0
interface serial 1
 ip address 172.16.3.1 255.255.255.0
router igrp 60
 network 172.16.0.0
```

Router R3 configuration for Figure 20-5 prior to implementing EIGRP:

```
interface serial 0
 ip address 172.16.2.2 255.255.255.0
interface serial 1
 ip address 172.16.3.2 255.255.255.0
interface ethernet 0
 ip address 172.16.11.4 255.255.255.0
interface ethernet 1
 ip address 172.17.12.1 255.255.255.0
router igrp 60
 network 172.16.0.0
 network 172.17.0.0
```

Figure 20-5
Implementing EIGRP
into an IGRP network
configuration.

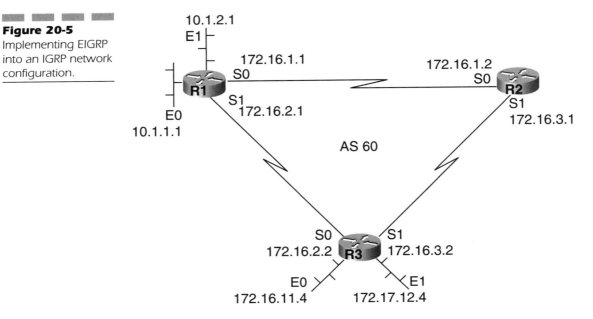

The default-metric command used in router R1 assigns the metrics to the static routes as they are translated into IGRP-routing entries. By adding the router eigrp 60 command to router R1, IGRP routes are automatically included in the EIGRP routing table. The following configuration is now applied to router R1 in Figure 20-5:

Router R1 configuration for Figure 20-5 implementing EIGRP:

```
interface serial 0
 ip address 172.16.1.1 255.255.255.0
interface serial 1
 ip address 172.16.2.1 255.255.255.0
interface ethernet 0
 ip address 10.1.1.1 255.255.255.0
interface ethernet 1
 ip address 10.1.2.1 255.255.255.0
router igrp 60
 network 172.16.0.0
 network 10.0.0.0
 default-metric 1000 100 1 1 1500
 redistribute static
!
router eigrp 60
 network 172.16.0.0
 network 10.0.0.0
 default-metric 1000 100 1 1 1500
 redistribute static
!
ip route 192.168.9.0 255.255.255.0 e0
```

Router R3 is now updated to include the IGPR-routing process. After this process is defined to router R3, EIGRP routing updates are exchanged between router R1 and R3. Routes for network 10.0.0.0 and 172.16.0.0 are automatically summarized in the EIGRP updates. Because EIGRP distance values are less than those derived by IGRP, the EIGRP routes learned now displace the IGPR routes in router R1 and R3 routing tables. Adding EIGRP routing to router R2 completes the inclusion of EIGRP into the network.

The following configurations show both IGRP and EIGRP routing in all three routers. At this point, the IGRP process can be removed from each router by entering no router igrp 60 in configuration mode. Connectivity is not disrupted because the EIGRP tables are being updated by the neighboring EIGPR routers. The following route configurations show the IGRP and EIGRP definitions as applied to Figure 20-5:

Router R2 configuration for Figure 20-5 with EIGRP:

```
interface serial 0
 ip address 172.16.1.2 255.255.255.0
interface serial 1
 ip address 172.16.3.1 255.255.255.0
!
router igrp 60
 network 172.16.0.0
!
router eigrp 60
 network 172.16.0.0
```

Router R3 configuration for Figure 20-5 with EIGRP:

```
interface serial 0
 ip address 172.16.2.2 255.255.255.0
interface serial 1
 ip address 172.16.3.2 255.255.255.0
interface ethernet 0
 ip address 172.16.11.4 255.255.255.0
interface ethernet 1
 ip address 172.17.12.1 255.255.255.0
router igrp 60
 network 172.16.0.0
 network 172.17.0.0
!
router eigrp 60
 network 172.16.0.0
 network 172.17.0.0
```

RIP-to-EIGRP Redistribution

RIP-to-EIGRP redistribution requires the mapping of unlike routing metrics. For example, in Figure 20-6, a RIP network and an EIGRP network require connectivity to support the merger of two companies. The ASBR in this case is router R1, which must support two-way redistribution between RIP and EIGRP. The configuration must also protect the network routing tables from having EGIRP sending routes learned via RIP back into the RIP network. It must also prevent the RIP process from sending routes learned via EIGRP back into the EIGRP network. This "route feedback" is what typically causes unstable routing tables and results in erroneous routing information with a high potential for routing loops to occur.

Router R1, acting as the ASBR, implements the stated requirements above. The router configuration for router R1 follows:

Router R1 configuration applied to Figure 20-6:

```
interface Ethernet 0
 ip address 172.16.1.1 255.255.255.0
interface Ethernet 1
 ip address 172.16.2.1 255.255.255.0
interface serial0
 ip address 172.16.10.1 255.255.255.0
!
router rip
 network 172.16.0.0
 redistribute eigrp 10
 default-metric 2
 passive-interface serial 0
!
router eigrp 10
 network 172.16.0.0
 redistribute rip
 default-metric 1544 100 255 1 1500
 distribute-list 1 in
 passive-interface ethernet 0
 passive-interface Ethernet 1
access-list 1 permit ip 172.16.1.0 255.255.255.0
access-list 1 permit ip 172.16.10.0 255.255.255.0
access-list 1 deny ip
```

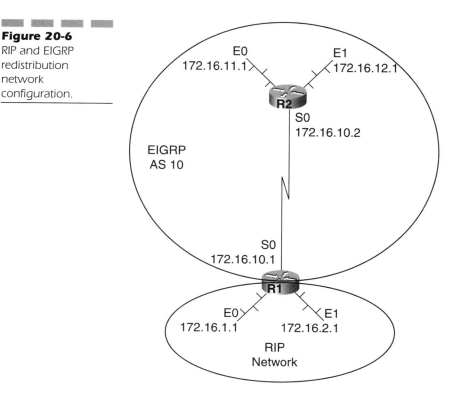

Figure 20-6

RIP and EIGRP redistribution network configuration.

In the above router configuration, router R1 stops routing updates on serial 0 for the RIP-routing protocol and on Ethernet 0 for the EIGRP-routing protocol by using the passive-interface command. The distribute-list in command is used under the router eigrp process to identify the routes that are filtered prior to being translated from RIP into EIGRP. In the example given, the 172.16.1.0 and 172.16.10.0 networks are redistributed, but the 172.16.2.0 network on ethernet 1 is suppressed from being redistributed because it does not pass through the filter applied by access-list 1.

The derived RIP routes are assigned EIGRP metric values by the default-metric router configuration command. The first value represents the minimum bandwidth assigned to the route. In this case, it describes the bandwidth as 1.544 Kbps. The second value of 100 specifies a route delay in tens of microseconds. The third value indicates that there is a 100 percent reliability of the link based on the 255 value being specified. The fourth value indicates that the effective bandwidth of the route is a 1 and the final value defines the MTU size available on the route.

Defining ATM (LANE, Classical IP, and MPOA)

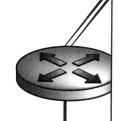

As discussed in Chapter 6, "ATM Internetworking Design," ATM was developed with the idea of supporting multiple services. The ATM transmission protocol could be a network solution due to its versatility or because it made more sense before Synchronous Optical Network (SONET) was offered for wide area connectivity.

Regardless of the reason for using ATM, Cisco provides solutions for implementation. The implementation could be on the Lightstream series ATM switch products, an ATM-capable router (see Chapter 6 for routers that are ATM-capable), or the Catalyst series switches. In this section on configuration for LANE services, Classical IP and MPOA (multiprotocol over ATM) will be discussed.

Configuring LANE

All components of LANE services can be configured on an ATM-capable router. A router can be a LAN emulation client (LEC), a LAN emulation server/broadcast unknown server (LES/BUS) pair, or a LAN emulation configuration server (LECS). A LEC participates in LANE by joining an ELAN, which involves the contacting of the LECS for ELAN definitions. Each ELAN definition includes a LES server and a BUS server that provide address resolution and broadcast capability within an ELAN. The LECS contains the address locations of the LES/BUS servers. From the LECS, a LEC can find its designated LES server to become a member of a particular ELAN. The configuration of these different components will be addressed in the following sections.

Initial Configuration for LANE

Before any of the components are configured on the router, a few parameters must be set first. There must be some ATM switch cloud to connect to first. The ATM prefix address for this switch cloud must be determined and set. This is not too important in the case of a private network where the preconfigured addresses of the devices can be used, but if a Private Network-Network Interface (PNNI) hierarchy is going to be used or if the network is going to link to a public ATM network, then a unique ATM prefix should be obtained.

After a proper ATM prefix is configured in the ATM switch cloud, two permanent virtual circuits (PVC) need to be set up for interim local management interface (ILMI) and switched virtual circuit management. ILMI is the network management system that provides configuration, perform-ance, and fault management within the user-to-network interface (UNI). The UNI is the connection between a LEC device and a PNNI device.

The two PVCs that are needed are virtual path indicator (VPI)/virtual circuit indicator (VCI) 0/5 and 0/16. VPI/VCI 0/5 is for signaling control to set up and tear down switch virtual circuits. VPI/VCI 0/16, the ATM forum circuit, is to communicate with ILMI. These PVCs are configured on the main ATM interface of the router.

The format for the configuration of the PVCs on the main ATM interface is as follows:

interface atm (*slot/0* | *slot/port-adapter/0* | *number*)

The **interface** keyword specifies that this will be an interface command and the interface is of type **ATM**. The slot number indicates where in the router the ATM module is located. Since the interface is the main interface, the number 0 or just the number of the interface is listed. If the interface is a subinterface, the syntax of the command would be 0.subinterface-number. The command for configuring a PVC on an ATM interface is

atm pvc *vcd vpi vci* **qsaal**

The **atm pvc** keywords are used to indicate that the router will set up a PVC. The *vcd* is the circuit identifier, which has the characteristics of being represented by virtual path identifier (*vpi*) and virtual channel identifier (*vci*). For each physical port on an ATM device, there can be 256 virtual paths. Each path contains 4,096 virtual channels. Each link between two ATM devices is a virtual circuit that is mapped to a virtual path. The **qsaal** indicates the type of ATM signaling. The command to configure the LANE setup PVC is

atm pvc *vcd vpi vci* **ilmi**

The other PVC definition is for ILMI, which is used for this initialization of LANE. Again, a vcd is used to indicate the circuit number. vpi is used to give the circuit a virtual path number and vci tells which virtual circuit in the virtual path to use. The ilmi informs router that the circuit is being used for interim local management interface traffic to configure and monitor LANE.

The example configuration for this is

```
interface ATM8/0
 atm pvc 1 0 5 qsaal
 atm pvc 2 0 16 ilmi
```

This example shows the configuration of the PVCs for LANE operation on a router with an AIP in the eighth slot. The configuration for the PVC has to be on the main interface, so a 0 is used for the interface number. The qsaal pvc of vpi 0 and vci 5 is the ATM Forum standard pvc for ATM signaling, which is used for building circuits as well as tearing them down. The ilmi pvc of vpi 0 and vci 16 is also an ATM forum standard for ILMI signaling, which includes communication between LANE components. Once the PVC is set up on the router and the router has a connection to an ATM switch, LANE components can be configured on the ATM interface of the router.

Configuring a LAN Emulation Client (LEC)

A router can be configured to be a LEC in the instance of performing routing for a specific emulated LAN (ELAN). This includes the routing for Ethernet-emulated LANs and Token Ring-emulated LANs. Some of the protocols specific to Ethernet are IP, IPX, AppleTalk, DECnet, Banyan VINES, and XNS-routed protocols, along with bridging between emulated LANs. Some of the protocols specific to Token Ring are IP from Token Ring to Ethernet, IPX from Token Ring to Ethernet, two-port and multiport source route bridging between Ethernet and Token Ring, IP and IPX multiring, SRB, SR/TLB, SRT, AppleTalk DECnet, Banyan VINES, and XNS protocols. Since this is a handbook dedicated to the entire router, the configuration examples for LANE will not cover every protocol but will include the most widely used implementations.

For a router to become a LEC, there must be a LAN Emulation Configuration Server (LECS) and LAN Emulation Server (LES) configured first. These components can be configured on a Catalyst switch, a Lightstream switch, or a router. Refer to documentation for configuration of the Catalyst or Lightstream switches.

The configuration for each of these LANE services on a router will be given in following sections. A LEC becomes operational after it contacts the LECS and finds the location of the LES of the ELAN the LEC is trying to become part of. All these components are interdependent of each other, so a sound design, along with fault tolerance, should be considered.

The first example will be a router participating in an Ethernet ELAN as a LEC. This gives the router the capability to route between its own emulated LAN and other emulated LANs that it is joined to or other legacy LANs that are defined on the router's other interfaces. For instance, if an ATM switch such as a Lightstream 1010 is at the core of the network providing the LANE services, the router could be used strictly for routing, as shown in Figure 21-1. As shown in the figure, the ATM switch has an LEC definition for two ELANs and the router can join both ELANs and route between them.

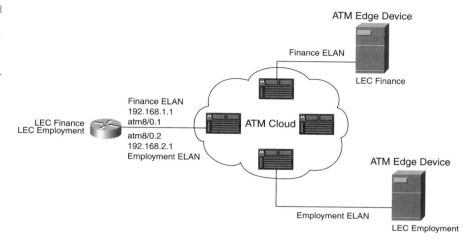

Figure 21-1

Cisco router acting as a LEC on an Ethernet ELAN.

Usually the configuration for a LEC is done as a subinterface on the router's ATM interface. Before the router can become part of the ELAN, a few important notes must be made clear before continuing. The name of the ELAN (case-specific) has to be known as well as the correct medium access sublayer (Ethernet or Token Ring). If the ELAN will eventually participate in MPOA, then the ELAN id should also be known. Once these parameters are determined, the configuration is

interface atm (*slot*/**0**.*subinterface-number* |
slot/*port adapter*/**0**.*subinterface-number* | *number.subinterface-number*)

The definition for a LEC is usually defined on the subinterface of an ATM interface. To define the subinterface, the slot where the ATM interface is located in the router is specified. The subinterface where the definition is going to reside is given by following the main interface number 0 by a period and then the subinterface number. As is shown, it is different with a port adapter or an interface number on the 4000 series routers. Once the subinterface is created, a LANE client can be bound to the subinterface with the following command:

lane client (**ethernet** | **tokenring**) *elan-name* [**elan-id** *id*]

To define the LANE client, the keyword **lane** is used and **client** tells which component of LANE is being configured. The media type used for the ELAN follows the client keyword. Either the **ethernet** or **tokenring** keyword is used to define the media type being emulated. The *elan-name* variable should be the name of the ELAN indicated in the LECS that the router is going to join. The **elan-id** *id* variable is used for configuring MPOA.

On the same subinterface of the ATM interface, the protocol should be added. If IP, IPX, or other protocols are needed, then they are added as if the interface was an Ethernet or Token Ring interface.

The example configuration relative to Figure 21-1 is

```
interface atm8/0.1 multipoint
 lane client ethernet finance elan-id 1
 ip address 192.168.1.1 255.255.255.0
!
interface atm8/0.2 multipoint
 lane client ethernet employment elan-id 2
 ip address 192.168.2.1 255.255.255.0
```

In the command sequence, subinterface number one of an ATM interface in the eighth slot is being configured. Subinterface number one is going to be a LANE client of the finance ELAN. The finance elan has an elan identifier of 1. The IP protocol will run on subinterface one, which has an IP address of 192.168.1.1 and a mask of 255.255.255.0. The command sequence also has another subinterface that is number two. Subinterface number two will be a LANE client of the employment ELAN. The IP protocol will run on subinterface number two. The IP address of the subinterface is 192.168.2.1 and the mask is 255.255.255.0. The router will have the capability to route IP packets between the two subinterfaces.

Once the interface is enabled, the following sequence takes place. The LEC establishes a direct virtual channel connection (VCC) usually though the ATM Forum's well-known address to the LECS. The LEC attempts to find the ATM address of the LES. If the address is found, then the LEC creates a direct VCC with the LES and attempts to join. If the join is successful, then the LEC does a LE_ARP_REQUEST to the LES to establish a multicast send VCC with the BUS. Now the LEC has address resolution and multicast capabilities as part of the ELAN.

LANE may not look attractive at first because it appears to lack redundancy. This is not the case since Cisco's HSRP can be implemented within LANE. LANE emulates layer 2 of the OSI Reference Model, so the configuration is the same as if two routers were Ethernet-attached. An example of HSRP within LANE is shown in Figure 21-2.

The configuration for the HSRP example of Figure 21-2 is as follows:

Router R1 configuration applied to Figure 21-2:

```
interface atm8/0.1 multipoint
 lane client ethernet finance elan-id 1
 ip address 192.168.1.2 255.255.255.0
 standby 1 ip 192.168.1.1
 standby 1 preempt
```

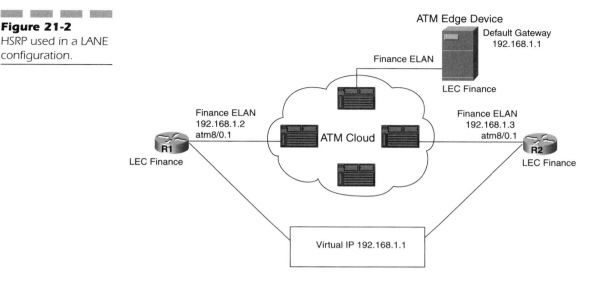

Figure 21-2
HSRP used in a LANE configuration.

```
standby 1 priority 150
standby 1 authentication corporate
```

Router R2 configuration applied to Figure 21-2:

```
interface atm8/0.1 multipoint
 lane client ethernet finance elan-id 1
 ip address 192.168.1.3 255.255.255.0
 standby 1 ip 192.168.1.1
 standby 1 preempt
 standby 1 authentication corporate
```

The configuration above is similar to that of HSRP between two Ethernet interfaces. LANE emulates what Ethernet does on layer two; as long as the two routers are part of the same ELAN, packets can flow between them as if they were physically connected. The connection now becomes more logical than physical. The HSRP hello packets can flow back and forth between the routers across the ATM cloud. The difference in the definition lies on both ATM subinterfaces. Each router becomes a LANE client of the same ELAN. Both interfaces have an IP assigned to them, as any Ethernet interface would, and the standby group definitions specified for HSRP are the same as those used for Ethernet interfaces.

Of course, the router does more than just route between two Ethernet ELANs. The following examples show the configuration of a LEC on a Token Ring ELAN and routing between ELANs and legacy networks.

A Token Ring LEC is needed for routing between Token Ring interfaces. This would be done in the case of having multiple physical rings on separate routers that become part of the same logical ring. An example of this is in Figure 21-3. If a router has more than one physical Token Ring interface, then a virtual ring is used. This way the traffic can flow within its ring and bridge to the virtual ring. The logical definition of the LANE Token Ring interface is applied to an ATM subinterface.

The configuration for a token ring ELAN is as follows:

interface atm (*slot* / **0**.*subinterface-number* |
slot / *port adapter* / **0**.*subinterface-number* | *number.subinterface-number*)

The definition of a Token Ring ELAN is also defined on the subinterface of an ATM interface. The subinterface is defined the same as an Ethernet ELAN is defined on a subinterface. The **interface** keyword indicates that the configuration is applied to an interface. The **atm** keyword signifies that the interface is an ATM interface. *Slot* is a number that tells which slot the ATM module is in, or *number* tells what interface number. The **0** is the indication of the main interface. The period followed by *subinterface* describes what logical subinterface the definition will be on. The command for configuring a Token Ring client is as follows:

lane client tokenring el*an-name* **elan-id** *id*

The Token Ring ELAN definition differs from Ethernet by indicating the ELAN type from the keyword **tokenring**. The *elan-name* is defined being case-sensitive and identifies the ELAN being joined. The **elan-id** *id* is used for future configurations of MPOA.

The same protocols that can be configured on a physical Token Ring interface can also be configured to operate on the LANE definition of Token Ring. IP, IPX, or other protocols can be defined.

Figure 21-3
Cisco routers
participating in a
Token Ring ELAN
configuration.

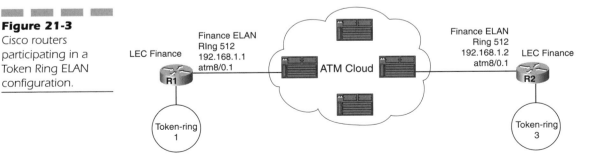

The example configuration relative to Figure 21-3 is as follows:

Router R1 configuration applied to Figure 21-3:

```
interface atm 8/0.1 multipoint
 lane client tokenring finance elan-id 1
 ip address 192.168.1.1 255.255.255.0
 source-bridge 512 1 1
 source-bridge spanning
!
interface tokenring 9/0
 ring-speed 16
 source-bridge 1 1 512
 source-bridge spanning
```

Router R2 configuration applied to Figure 21-3:

```
interface atm 8/0.1 multipoint
 lane client tokenring finance elan-id 1
 ip address 192.168.1.1 255.255.255.0
 source-bridge 512 3 3
 source-bridge spanning
interface tokenring 9/0
 ring-speed 16
 source-bridge 3 3 512
 source-bridge spanning
```

In Figure 21-3, the two separate routers each have a physical Token Ring interface. The separate Token Ring can be bridged into one logical ring between the routers. As can be seen, both Router R1 and Router R2 join the same Token Ring ELAN called finance. Each router Token Ring physical interface is bridged with the Virtual Ring defined on the ATM subinterface. This is done by using the source-bridge command. The command specifies that the first number indicate the local ring, which is unique to the interface. The second number indicates what bridge is going to be used. The third number indicates the target ring for the traffic.

On Router R1, the local Ring 512 on the ATM interface sends traffic through bridge 1 to the target ring 1. Traffic flows to the physical Token Ring interface by being the local ring, which is the target of the Token Ring ELAN. The traffic comes through bridge 1. The traffic also flows in the other direction from local ring 1 through bridge 1 to the target ring 512. The traffic can then flow on layer 2 between the routers by the Token Ring ELAN. Because all the traffic flows between the routers, one interface can be given an IP address to route IP packets in the logical ring.

If one of the routers has two physical Token Ring interfaces, then a virtual ring could be created to do source-route bridging between the two interfaces. This is shown in Figure 21-4 and the configuration is as follows:

Router R1 configuration applied to Figure 21-4:

```
source-bridge ring-group 4
!
interface atm8/0.1 multipoint
 lane client tokenring finance
 ip address 192.168.2.1 255.255.255.0
 source-bridge 1024 1 4
 source-bridge spanning
interface tokenring 9/0
 ring-speed 16
 source-bridge 1 1 4
 source-bridge spanning
interface tokenring 9/1
 ring speed 16
 source-bridge 3 3 4
 source-bridge spanning
```

The configuration above is useful when the router is connected logically to other devices that have Token Ring running on them. A Catalyst or another router may have an uplink to an ATM cloud. The ATM subinterface provides the versatility to configure the upper-layer protocols such as AppleTalk or IP as well the capability to make a network more organized on layer two. As was shown, this all can be done through LEC definitions on the router.

Figure 21-4

Bridging two Token Ring interfaces and a Token Ring ELAN using a virtual ring group.

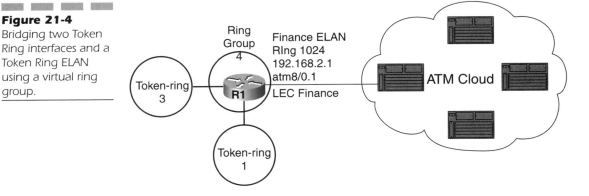

Configuring a LAN Emulation Configuration Server (LECS)

As previously described, a LEC joins an ELAN after finding the LES. The LEC does this by setting up a direct VCC to a LECS through ILMI. The LECS gives the LEC the ATM address of the LES server it is looking for. Without the LECS there would be a need for the broadcast mechanism to get address resolution for the LES. Since ATM is connection-oriented, this is not part of the protocol for initial LANE setup. It is easier for the LECS to be the central control point for LEC devices to find their designated LES.

The LECS is actually a database of ATM addresses of the LES that can be indexed by LEC devices. The database contains the address of the LES associated with ELAN names. This gives a LEC the capability to join an ELAN by name. Recall that the configuration of a client is

```
lane client ethernet finance
```

with finance being the name of the ELAN.

The LEC, which is the router, has to find the address for the LES of finance. The way the LEC finds this address is by connecting to the LECS through ILMI. Then from the address associated with finance in the LECS the LEC establishes a VCC to the LES to attempt to join the ELAN.

A router, a Catalyst switch, and a Lightstream switch can all be configured to run the LECS. Of course, the example here will use the router. The first thing to do is define the database, and then bind it to an interface. Once the LECS database is bound to an interface, an ATM address needs to be associated with the LECS. Cisco provides the capability to automatically compute the address of the LECS or define an explicit address. This is not important unless you are looking for redundancy, which will be explained a little later. The address assigned to the LECS has to be registered in the ATM switch cloud so the switches know the location of the LECS.

The format of a single LECS with a few ELAN definitions will be given just as a setup to build on later. Redundancy with multiple LECS and LES will be described later in the section. Initially, the database will need a name and then, upon naming the database, the ELAN definitions will be defined. The naming of the database is as follows:

lane database *database-name*

This command is done in global configuration mode. The **lane** keyword specifies that it is a LANE configuration command. The **database** keyword indicates that the definition is a LECS database with a specific name assigned by the *database-name* variable value. To add entries to the new database, the following commands are needed:

name *elan-name* **server-atm-address** *atm-address* **restricted** [**index** *number*]

name *elan-name* **local-seg-id** *segment-number*

ELAN definitions are the records in this database. The *elan-name* variable value defines the name of an ELAN. The address of the LES/BUS services for that ELAN is specified using the *atm-address* variable value. If the ELAN is going to be limited to just a few specified clients, then the keyword **restricted** is used. The index *number* optional operand is used to define which LES/BUS will be the primary for the ELAN in the case of Simple Server Redundancy Protocol (SSRP). If the ELAN is a Token Ring, then a *segment-number* is used.

To define a database with a LES/BUS for an Ethernet ELAN called finance and a LES/BUS for a Token Ring ELAN called employment, the sequence is

```
lane database Mycompany
 name finance server-atm-address 11111111111111111111111111111111111111111
 name employment server-atm-address 22222222222222222222222222222222222222222
 name employment local-seg-id 1250
```

This defines the database, but it will need to be bound to an interface for use. To bind the database to an interface, the following command is used:

interface atm (*slot*/**0** | *slot*/*port adapter*/**0** | *number*)

A LANE database must be defined on the main interface of the ATM module. The previous commands display the syntax for reaching the main ATM interface. This differs from a subinterface in that a subinterface number is not specified. Once the ATM main interface is located, the binding of the LANE database to that interface can be done by the following interface configuration command:

lane config database *database-name*

This command directs the IOS to build a LECS database with the name of the *database-name* variable value. The *database-name* should match the name of the database that was defined in the global command. After the database is bound to the interface, it now needs an ATM address. The ATM address should be the same addresses that the ATM switches in the ATM cloud point to for the LECS. The following commands define the ATM address:

lane config auto-config-atm-address | lane config fixed-config-atm-address | lane config config-atm-address *atm-address*

Specifying **lane config auto-config-atm-address** indicates that the LECS will run in SSRP and the ATM address of the LECS will be automatically given by the switch.

Entering the **lane config fixed-config-atm-address** command causes the LECS to run in SSRP and the ATM address of the LECS will be automatically given by the device or it will not run in SSRP and only the well-known address is used.

Configuring the **lane config config-atm-address** atm-address directs the LECS to run in SSRP and the address of the LECS to be designated by a 20-byte ATM address.

To finish up the example started above, the definitions are as follows:

```
interface atm 8/0
 lane config database Mycompany
 lane config auto-config-atm-address
```

Using the above configuration example, the device will determine the ATM address.

The above example is given in Figure 21-5 and explains a simple definition of setting up the LECS. Cisco provides redundancy with the LECS and the LES. The redundancy that Cisco provides is called Simple Server Redundancy Protocol (SSRP). The nice feature of SSRP in implementing the LECS is that you can have multiple LECS defined so if one fails, there is a backup LECS.

Cisco's implementation is that of having one master LECS based on a priority. If the master goes down, other LECS are there to backup the master. The definition of the LECS addresses is located on the ATM switches. When a LEC requests the LECS from the ATM switch, it gives the list of LECS addresses and the device should use the LECS with the highest priority. The priority is given by the definition of the LECS address on the ATM switch. This is determined by an index number associated with a LECS address. No matter what address scheme is being used to have the necessary redundancy, each LECS defined should have identical databases.

If the well-known address is the choice for LECS to run, then a few rules should be followed first. There should never be more than one LECS configured on the same switch. This will confuse the ATM switches that LECS refer to because they have the same ATM address. Use the lane config fixed-config-atm-address command for the LECS to listen to the well-known address.

It may be a good idea to use the well-known address scheme so that other third-party products will work with the configuration. The example of using SSRP for LECS redundancy is given in Figure 21-5 and the configuration for this is as follows:

Router R1 configuration applied to Figure 21-5:

```
lane database Mycompany
name finance atm-server-address 1111111111111111111111111111111111111111
name employment server-atm-address 2222222222222222222222222222222222222222
name employment local-seg-id 1250
!
interface atm 8/0
 lane config database Mycompany
 lane config fixed-config-atm-address
```

Router R2 configuration applied to Figure 21-5:

```
lane database Mycompany
name finance atm-server-address 1111111111111111111111111111111111111111
name employment server-atm-address 2222222222222222222222222222222222222222
name employment local-seg-id 1250
!
interface atm 8/0
 lane config database Mycompany
 lane config fixed-config-atm-address
```

The example shows two separate routers acting as the LECS with an ATM address being the well-known address. Both databases on both routers have the same database definition. The priority of which router will be the primary LECS is defined on the ATM switches.

This shows redundancy for the LECS but SSRP also provides for redundancy amongst the LES/BUS servers. The redundancy for the LES/BUS is done through the configuration on the LECS. To implement SSRP for the LES/BUS servers, multiple devices are running the LES/BUS service and are defined in the LECS. In the ELAN definition, each device running a LES/BUS for that ELAN is given by its address. An example of this is shown in Figure 21-6.

Figure 21-5
Using SSRP for LECS
redundancy.

Uses ATM Well-Known
Address for LECS
  ELAN employment
  ELAN finance
  LANE Database: Mycompany

Index of 1 **R1** Uses ATM Well-Known
                  Address for LECS

atm8/0
finance ELAN
employment ELAN
LANE database Mycompany

Definition of LECS
Address on ATM switch
along with priority

finance ELAN
employment ELAN
LANE database Mycompany
atm8/0

Uses ATM Well-Known
Address for LECS   **R2** Index of 2

LANE Database: Mycompany
ELAN finance
ELAN employment

The router configurations for Figure 21-6 follow:

Router R1 configuration applied to Figure 21-6:

```
lane database Mycompany
name finance atm-server-address 3333333333333333333333333333333333333333 index 1
name finance atm-server-address 4444444444444444444444444444444444444444 index 2
!
interface atm8/0
 lane config database Mycompany
 lane config fixed-config-atm-address
```

The index value specified identifies the LES/BUS server priority. The higher priority identifies which LES/BUS server is the master server.

Figure 21-6 contains separate devices denoted by the different ATM addresses. The different devices have LES/BUS definitions for the same ELAN named finance. When a LEC queries this LECS, the LECS responds with the first devices defined with an index of 1. If that device is not available, the LEC is directed to the other device with an index of 2.

There is no restriction to the number of LECS or LES/BUS that can be run. Cisco recommends two, or three at most, for the LECS. The network topology assists in determining the correct number of LECS and LES/BUS that are needed.

The last feature that can be determined in a LECS is restricting which device can join a certain ELAN. If there is a need for only certain devices to join a particular ELAN, that can be specified in the LECS. The configuration is as follows:

lane database *database-name*

name *elan-name* **server-atm-address** *atm-address* **restricted** [**index** *index-number*]

Figure 21-6

LES/BUS services on a Cisco router in support of LANE.

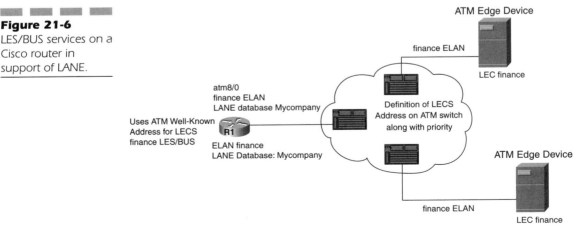

The previous two statements are the same as when defining any LECS database. The only thing that is added is the keyword **restricted** to indicate that an ELAN will be restricted to list LEC devices. To list the LEC devices that will only be able to participate in the ELAN, the following command is used:

client-atm-address *atm-address* **name** *elan-name*

This command defines the clients that can join by ATM address. The keywords **client-atm-address** are given, followed by the actual ATM address of the LEC device and the ELAN that the LEC is trying to join. The *elan-name* should be the same as the *elan-name* used in the LES/BUS definition. Here is an example of this:

```
lane database Mycompany
name finance atm-server-address 5555555555555555555555555555555555555555 restrict
client-atm-address 47.000000000ffe21085643223400.0800.0234.2345.01 name finance
```

This example restricts any other client from joining this ELAN named finance, except the device assigned to that ELAN. This may be useful in some situations, but the management of restricted ELANs could become cumbersome. Now that a way to join an ELAN has been defined, along with the facilities to join an ELAN, there is a need to know how to define the services on which an ELAN operates. The next section will discuss the definition of a LES server.

Configuring a LAN Emulation Server (LES)

In the previous sections, we saw how to configure a LEC for a router to participate in an ELAN. From the configuration, we saw that a LEC has to know the LES/BUS definition associated to the ELAN name. The LECS, which can be configured on a router, provides the definition of the location of the services for an ELAN.

The services of the ELAN are the LES and BUS servers. The LES provides address resolution within the ELAN. The BUS provides the broadcast facility, along with the unknown address resolution. Although the LES and BUS services are different entities, the definition on the router is a single definition for both servers. Like the LEC, the LES is done on an ATM subinterface. The configuration is as follows:

interface atm (*slot*/**0**.*subinterface-number* |
slot/*port-adapter*/**0**.*subinterface-number* | *number.subinterface-number*)

This is the same command given above to get to the subinterface of an ATM interface. This is indicated by providing the slot number of the ATM module followed by the subinterface number that is being created. Once the subinterface is created, the LES/BUS definition can be put in place by using the following interface command:

lane server-bus (**ethernet** | **tokenring**) *elan-name*

This statement defines the LES/BUS server on the router. It distinguishes whether the ELAN will emulate ethernet or tokenring. It also defines the ELAN by name. The name is what is used to configure the LEC devices that will attempt to become part of the ELAN.

An example configuration is

```
interface atm 8/0.1 multipoint
 lane server-bus ethernet finance
```

This is an example of the router acting as the LES/BUS for the ELAN named finance. Using this router configuration, the router R1 in Figure 21-6 can act as both a LEC and a LES/BUS for the finance ELAN.

The design in Figure 21-6 is a feasible configuration of an ELAN, but the single router now becomes the single point of failure. A better implementation would be to use SSRP and HSRP for redundancy. For each LES/BUS definition on a separate router, the LECS has to be updated to show the additional server as well as which server has the highest priority. The redundant design is shown in Figure 21-7.

The router configurations for Figure 21-7 are as follows:

Router R1 configuration applied to Figure 21-7:

```
lane database Mycompany
name finance atm-server-address 111111111111111111111111111111111111111 index 1
name finance atm-server-address 222222222222222222222222222222222222222 index 2
!
interface atm 8/0
 lane config database Mycompany
 lane config fixed-config-atm-address
!
interface atm8/0.1 multipoint
 lane server-bus ethernet finance
 lane client ethernet finance
 ip address 192.168.1.2 255.255.255.0
 standby 1 ip 192.168.1.1
 standby 1 preempt
 standby 1 priority 125
 standby 1 authentication corporate
```

Figure 21-7
Redundancy using
SSRP and HSRP.

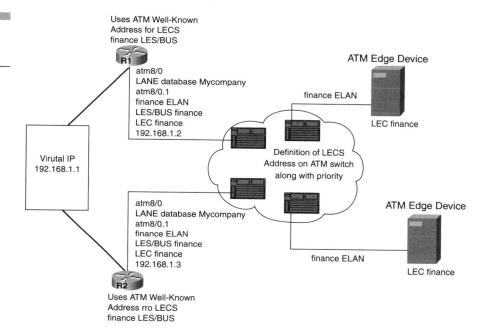

Router R2 configuration applied to Figure 21-7:

```
lane database Mycompany
name finance atm-server-address 1111111111111111111111111111111111111111 index 1
name finance atm-server-address 2222222222222222222222222222222222222222 index 2
!
interface atm 8/0
lane config database Mycompany
lane config fixed-config-atm-address
!
int atm8/0.1 multipoint
 lane server-bus ethernet finance
 lane client ethernet finance
 ip address 192.168.1.3 255.255.255.0
 standby 1 ip 192.168.1.1
 standby 1 preempt
 standby 1 authentication corporate
```

The router configuration examples for Figure 21-7 illustrate not only the use of SSRP for the LES/BUS but also the use of SSRP for the LECS. As can be seen, both databases are identical on both routers. From the example, the priority LECS could not be determined without seeing which router is defined as the priority LECS in the ATM switches. Both routers also provide SSRP for the LES/BUS. Each router has a LANE server definition for finance ELAN. This is indicated in the LECS database by router R1 having an ATM address of 1111111111111111111111111111.111111111111 and router R2 with 2222222222222222222222222222.222222222222, as the ATM address.

If a LEC is joined to the LES/BUS on R1 and R1 loses connectivity to the ATM cloud, the LEC will join the LES/BUS on R2.

The configurations also employ the use of HSRP for establishing routing redundancy between R1 and R2. If R1 loses connectivity, R2 becomes the primary routing interface for the ELAN. The LEC devices in the ELAN will be able to communicate outside of the ELAN through the router.

LANE gives the capability to utilize existing routing infrastructure to upgrade existing LAN technologies. In this section, we see how an existing router with ATM modules can do all the services that would be needed in a multiprotocol environment. Due to its dynamic nature, ATM may be a solution for backbone upgrade or wide-area connectivity. We will see other ATM protocols in the next sections that may or may not provide the services that LANE does.

Configure ATM over a Serial Interface

In an environment where the majority of the network is ATM, a remote site may be connected to the ATM network using a serial or high-speed serial interface connected to an ATM service data unit (ADSU). The connection is configured for communication through ATM-Data Exchange Interface (ATM-DXI) encapsulation. ATM-DXI gives the capability to transfer multiprotocols through a serial interface using encapsulation. This section will explain the configuration for setting up ATM-DXI encapsulation.

For multiprotocol traffic to flow from a serial interface through an ADSU, ATM-DXI encapsulation must be enabled and a permanent virtual circuit (PVC) must be set up. Once these parameters are in place, each of the protocols that are going to be transmitted out the serial interface have to be mapped to the PVC. When the PVC is initially configured, there are three types of encapsulation to distinguish from:

- snap, the encapsulation of multiprotocol LLC/SNAP compatible with RFC 1483

- nlpid, the network layer protocol identification multiprotocol encapsulation compatible with RFC 1490

- mux, the multiplex encapsulation that sets the interface to encapsulate only one protocol

The configuration of setting up the serial interface for ATM-DXI encapsulation is

interface serial [*slot /*] *number*

The ADSU is physically connected to a serial interface on the router so the configuration is done on through an interface command. The above command specifies the serial interface on which the ATM-DXI configuration will be run.

Example: **ip address** 192.168.1.1 255.255.255.0

Like any other interface, the protocol commands define the type of traffic flow. The protocol configured to operate on the serial interface has to be encapsulated to run through the ADSU. The following commands set up the encapsulation:

encapsulation atm-dxi

The type of encapsulation for a serial interface connected to an ADSU is specified in this command. The encapsulation is an ATM data exchange interface. The connection from the serial interface to the ATM cloud at the remote end will be done through a PVC. The PVC will be created and the different protocols will be encapsulated through it. The command for creating a PVC on a serial interface that is connected to the ATM cloud via a ADSU is

dxi pvc *vpi vci* (**snap** | **nlpid** | **mux**)

The type of the PVC is data exchange interface (**dxi pvc**). The PVC is identified by the virtual path identifier (*vpi*) followed by the virtual circuit identifier (*vci*). This enables the devices in the ATM cloud to build a virtual channel from the router serial interface to the end destination through the ATM cloud. The **snap** encapsulation protocols indicate the compatible protocols given in RFC 1483. The **nlpid** protocol is also a multiprotocol encapsulation technique but is compatible with RFC 1490. RFC 1490 is similar to

RFC 1483, but RFC 1490 refers to Frame Relay and RFC 1483 refers to ATM encapsulation. Cisco uses **nlpid** for backward compatibility with older IOS software. Specifying the **mux** indicates that only one protocol will be encapsulated over the PVC.

dxi map *protocol protocol-address vpi vci* [**broadcast**]

The **dxi map** command maps a protocol defined on the serial interface to the PVC created on the interface. The *protocol* followed by the address of the protocol (*protocol-address*) is given to indicate which protocol will flow within the PVC. The PVC created on the interface is identified by a virtual path identifier (*vpi*) and a virtual circuit identifier (*vci*). Specifying the **broadcast** keyword indicates that broadcast traffic will flow over the PVC.

An example of this configuration is

```
interface serial 1
 ip address 192.168.1.1 255.255.255.0
 ipx network C0A80101
 encapsulation atm-dxi
 dxi pvc 0 22 nlpid
 dxi map ip 192.168.1.2 0 22 broadcast
 dxi map ipx C0A80102 broadcast
```

This example demonstrates the use of ATM-DXI encapsulation of IP and IPX over VPI 0 VCI 22. As you can see, the protocol is mapped to the address of the other end of the serial link. The **broadcast** statement enables broadcast packets over the serial link.

Configuring Classical IP

Classical IP over ATM offers the capability to transmit the IP protocol over ATM. The transmission uses an ATM ARP server for address resolution. Each node on the Logical IP Subnet (LIS) registers with the ARP server by including the server address in the nodes configuration. The router can be both a node and ARP server and it can perform routing and ARP services for each LIS with which it participates.

Classical IP does not provide redundancy that includes HSRP. You may want to use Classical IP if a vendor only supports Classical IP or in the event of remote data backup to an external source from a server. Classical IP also offers connectivity at SONET speeds.

An example of a router registering with an ARP server as a node is shown in Figure 21-8. In this example, the router performs the routing for the LIS. Before configuring the router as a node, the ATM NSAP address of the ARP server must be known. An end system identifier (ESI) also must be chosen for the router. This can be the MAC address with a one-byte identifier from 00 to FF. The MTU size for Classical IP is 9180. This will cause a problem if the MTU size of the main ATM interface is less than 9180. If Classical IP is going to be configured on a router, the main ATM interface should be set to 9180. The configuration for the router participating in a Classical IP LIS is

interface atm (slot/**0**.subinterface-number |
slot/port adapter/**0**.subinterface-number | number.subinterface-number)

Similar to LANE, the configuration of Classical IP is usually done as a subinterface. The command above shows the syntax for creating the subinterface for configuring Classical IP. The keywords interface and atm are used to indicate which type of interface. The location is specified by indicating the slot number followed by the subinterface number:

atm esi-address *esi-address*

An ATM device receives an NSAP address through ILMI or the device already has an NSAP address associated with it from the manufacturer. Since Classical IP does not use ILMI, it is good to identify the Classical IP interface with an end system identifier followed by two selector bytes. The *esi-address* value is seven bytes, or 14 hexadecimal digits. A good practice is to define the end-system identifier as the MAC address followed by a selector byte. This provides a unique address since it is MAC-based:

atm arp-server (**self** | **nsap** *server-nsap-address*)

This command specifies where the ARP server is located. If the router is going to act as the ARP server, then the keyword **self** is used. If another device is acting as the ARP server, then the NSAP of that address is given so the router can register with that device. A network configuration example is diagrammed in Figure 21-8.

The following configuration for the router as a registered node, as shown in Figure 21-8, is

```
interface atm8/0.1 multipoint
 ip address 192.168.1.1 255.255.255.0
 atm esi-address 0010A6A5F820.01
 atm arp-server nsap 47.000111111111111111111111111.111111111111.00
```

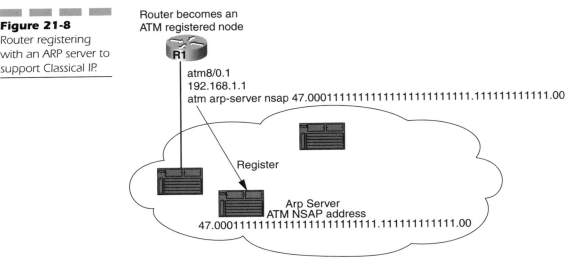

In the example, the router registers with a device that has a different NSAP address specified in the configuration. If the router acts as the ARP server, then the keyword **self** would be used instead.

The router can also act as the ARP server and perform the routing for the LIS. This is shown in Figure 21-9.

The following router configuration is applied to Figure 21-9:

```
interface atm8/0.1 multipoint
 ip address 192.168.1.1 255.255.255.0
 atm esi-address 0010A6A5F820.01
 atm arp-server self
```

These examples assume that Classical IP is configured in an environment with switch virtual circuits (SVC). In an environment where the ATM connections are permanent virtual circuits, the configuration is different. There must be PVCs set up to get reverse ARP datagrams. The default time that reverse ARP datagrams will be sent is every 15 minutes. The configuration for a PVC in this environment is

interface atm (*slot*/**0** | *slot* / *port adapter*/**0** | *number*)

PVCs can only be configured on the main ATM interface of the router. The previous command specifies the interface by giving the interface type and the slot on which the interface resides. There is no subinterface, so 0 or just the number of the interface is used.

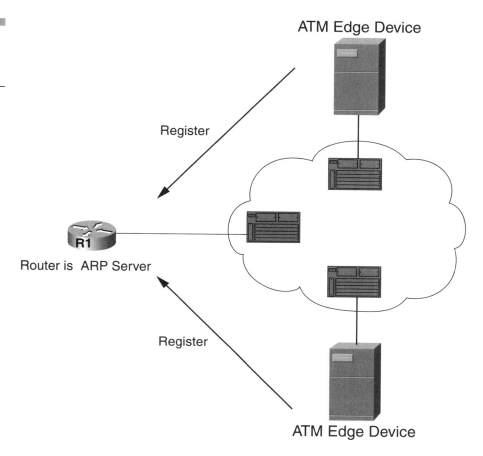

Figure 21-9
Router acting as the ARP server and routing node.

atm pvc *vpi vci* **aal5snap inarp** (*minutes*)

The configuration of the PVC for Classical IP is identified as an ATM PVC. The PVC is then represented by the virtual path identifier (*vpi*) and virtual circuit identifier (*vci*). The type of ATM traffic that will flow over the PVC will be ATM adaptation layer 5 snap (**aal5snap**). The **inarp** keyword enables reverse ARP updates to be received in intervals of so many minutes.

An example configuration for PVC environment is

```
interface atm8/0
 ip address 192.168.1.1 255.255.255.0
 atm pvc 1 0 20 aal5snap inarp 10
 atm pvc 2 0 21 aal5snap inarp
```

This example defines PVC 1 as receiving reverse ARP datagrams every 10 minutes and PVC 2 will respond to reverse ARP datagrams. A map list does not need to be created because this is IP only.

Configuring Multiprotocol over ATM (MPOA)

Why use MPOA in an ATM environment? What MPOA offers is the capability to circumvent the routing device so the edge devices can make the layer 3 decisions using cache entries. The operation of MPOA is simply that MPOA clients in the network query a MPOA server to find a direct connection to another client, circumventing the router. This process is not done without an initial setup. Before explaining the MPOA process, a few terms need to be defined.

MPOA client (MPC):   A multiprotocol over an ATM client (such as an edge device or ATM-attached device that is MPOA-compatible).

MPOA server (MPS):   A multiprotcol over an ATM server (such as a router or ATM switch that contains the information of the MPOA clients).

Ingress edge device: The location in the network where traffic flows into the MPOA system (an MPOA edge device like a Catalyst).

Egress edge device: The location in the network where traffic flows out of the MPOA system (an MPOA edge device like a Catalyst).

Nonbroadcast mulitiaccess (NBMA):   A network that has multiprotocol capabilities but does not have the facility for broadcasts. This is usually a connection-oriented environment.

Next Hop Resolution Protocol (NHRP):   The protocol that routers use to find the device connections in a non-broadcast multi-access (NBMA) environment.

Using these terms, the traffic flow in an MPOA system will be explained. The flow of the MPOA traffic can be seen in Figure 21-10. As shown in the figure, a host would like to communicate with its server. The host is attached to a Catalyst edge device on one end of the network and the server is attached to a Catalyst edge device on the other end of the network. Both

Catalyst devices are MPOA clients (MPC) that have a LEC defined on different ELANS. The Catalyst with the host attached is the ingress edge device because the host is initiating traffic to the server, so the traffic is flowing into the MPOA system. The Catalyst with the server attached is the egress edge device because it is receiving traffic from the MPOA system. The router acts as the MPOA server (MPS), which has the connection information of both clients. As the figure shows, this is an non-broadcast multi-access environment because it is ATM.

Normally, if both Catalysts are defined to join separate ELANs, then a router would have to route the traffic between both ELANs. With MPOA, a direct VCC can be set up between the Catalysts to do the work of layer 3 by the MPS giving the MPCs the connection information. The process is as follows:

1. The MPC of the hosts sends an MPOA request to the MPS.
2. The MPS finds either a different MPS through NHRP or sends a cache-imposition request to the other MPC of the server.

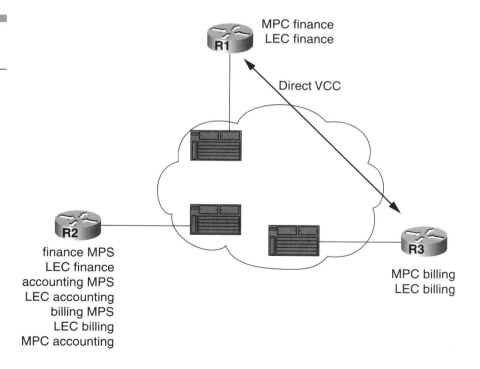

Figure 21-10
An MPOA network configuration.

MPC finance
LEC finance
R1

Direct VCC

R2
finance MPS
LEC finance
accounting MPS
LEC accounting
billing MPS
LEC billing
MPC accounting

R3
MPC billing
LEC billing

3. The cache-imposition reply is then sent back to the MPS.

4. The MPOA resolution is then sent to the MPC of the host.

5. The MPC of the hosts then establishes a direct VCC to the MPC of the server instead of going through the router.

Each time the hosts want to communicate with the server the MPC of the hosts has the direct VCC to the MPC of the server cache for direct communication.

Configuring a MPOA Client (MPC)

Usually a router is not configured to be the MPC. Edge devices servicing end users would be the best candidates for MPCs. If LANE is the existing protocol on the ATM, the router would know of the other router in the network through LANE address resolution protocol. An instance when the router might be a feasible MPC is when a central MPOA server (MPS) is located among many wide area routers, as in Figure 21-10. If the wide area connectivity is SONET, then through the MPS the routers could all be MPCs, which communicate through the wide area via direct cache VCCs. This way the broadcast traffic can be reduced on the wide area.

The configuration for the MPC is listed here. In the LECS database, enter the following:

name *elan-name* **elan-id** *id*

When building the LECS database, the elan name is given, followed by an ELAN *id*. This statement is used after the *elan-name* variable value and the associated LES/BUS server ATM address is indicated. The **elan-id** is used for the MPOA configuration. On the subinterface of the router, the following is used:

lane server-bus ethernet *elan-name* **elan-id** *id*

The LES/BUS server for an ELAN is given the associated elan id that was given in the LECS. The **elan-id** is used for the operation of MPOA:

mpoa client config name *mpc-name*

After the ELANs are identified with ELAN identifiers, the MPOA client is configured under global configuration. The MPOA client is identified by a unique name. Once the MPOA client is identified, it needs to be bound to an interface. This is done with the following two commands:

interface atm (*slot* / **0** | *slot* / *port adapter* / **0** | *number*)

Since the MPOA client has to be bound to a hardware address, the main ATM interface is used. The main interface is identified by slot number followed by 0 or by an interface number:

mpoa client name *mpc-name*

On the main ATM interface, the MPOA is then bound to the hardware address by giving the MPOA client name. These statements associate a physical address with a MPOA client.

Now that the client has a hardware address, the MPOA client will be bound to a LEC. To bind a MPOA client to a LANE client, the following would be done:

interface atm (*slot*/**0**.*subinterface-number* |
slot / *port adapter*/**0**.*subinterface-number* | *number.subinterface-number*)

The LEC definition is usually done on a subinterface, which is identified by slot number followed by subinterface number. This can be seen in earlier sections of this chapter.

lane server-bus ethernet *elan-name*

The LES/BUS definition does not have to be defined on the same interface of the router as the LEC. This statement is shown so it is clear that a LES/BUS is needed for the LEC to function. This statement can be on another router or on an ATM switch. The command indicates that it is a LANE LES/BUS server that emulates Ethernet and is identified by a name. Once the server is set up, the client can be configured:

lane client ethernet *elan-name*

The client configuration is the same in a pure LANE configuration. The client is given with the type of emulation and identified with an *elan-name*. Only one LEC can be defined for each subinterface. The *elan-name* of the LEC has to match what is defined in the LECS database. After the LEC with the associated LES/BUS services is in place, the MPOA client is bound to the LEC client.

lane client mpoa client name *mpc-name*

The MPOA client is bound to the LEC by defining the MPOA client on the same subinterface as the LEC client to which it is being bound. The MPOA client is bound by giving the keywords, **lane client mpoa**. The bound MPOA client is then defined by the MPOA client name bound to the main ATM interface.

Using these configuration commands and Figure 21-10, the following is the example configuration:

The following router configuration are applied to Figure 21-10:

Router R1 configuration applied to Figure 21.10:

```
mpoa client config name widearea1
interface atm8/0
 mpoa client name widearea1
 atm pvc 1 0 5 qsaal
 atm pvc 2 0 16 ilmi
interface atm8/0.1 multipoint
 ip address 192.168.1.1 255.255.255.0
 lane client ethernet finance elan-id 100
 lane server-bus ethernet finance elan-id 100
 lane client mpoa client name widearea1
```

Router R2 configuration applied to Figure 21-10:

```
lane database SONET
name finance server-atm-address 47.000000001111111111111111.111111111111.11
name finance elan-id 100
name accounting server-atm-address 47.000000002222222222222222.222222222222.22
name accounting elan-id 101
name billing server-atm-address 47.000000003333333333333333.333333333333.33
name billing elan-id 102
mpoa client config name widearea2
interface atm8/0
 atm pvc 1 0 5 qsaal
 atm pvc 2 0 16 ilmi
 lane config fixed-config-atm-address
 lane config database SONET
 mpoa client name widearea2
interface atm8/0.1 multipoint
 ip address 192.168.2.1 255.255.255.0
 lane client ethernet accounting elan-id 101
 lane server-bus ethernet accounting elan-id 101
 lane client mpoa client name widearea2
```

Router R3 configuration applied to Figure 21-10:

```
mpoa client config name widearea3
interface atm8/0
 atm 1 0 5 qsaal
 atm 2 0 16 ilmi
 mpoa client name widearea3
interface atm8/0.1 multipoint
 ip address 192.168.3.1 255.255.255.0
 lane client ethernet billing elan-id 102
 lane server-bus ethernet billing elan-id 102
 lane client mpoa client name widearea3
```

This configuration sets up the three MPOA clients. After router R2 is configured to be the MPS, the routers can set up direct VCC between each other via the MPS, instead of being directly connected by one ELAN. This eliminates broadcast traffic among the routers.

Configuring a MPOA Server (MPS)

The MPS does the work of finding the path from end to end through NHRP. The MPS converts MPOA requests and replies from the MPCs in the network. When the path is found, the MPOA sends the resolution to the MPC that initiated the request. The configuration of the MPS is LANE configuration:

name *elan-name* **elan-id** *id*

The same is needed for the MPOA server as the MPOA client. In the LECS database, each ELAN that will participate in MPOA has to be assigned an ELAN identifier. This is done using the previous statement after the definition of the LES/BUS server. The structure of the LECS is given in an earlier section. The ELAN is identified by the same name as the LES/BUS server and the elan-id is assigned by an administrator based on a MPOA design:

lane server-bus (ethernet | tokenring) *elan-name* **elan-id** *id*

It is shown again that a LES/BUS service must be up and running for MPOA to operate with LANE. The LES/BUS configuration defines the server along with the type of ELAN. The ELAN is identified by name and given an identifier for MPOA.
MPS configuration:

mpoa server config name *mps-name*

The MPOA server configuration is similar to the client because it needs a globally defined name. This name is given in global configuration mode using the keyword **mpoa server config name** with the name that will represent the MPOA server in the ATM cloud. Once the MPOA server has been identified by name, it needs to be bound to a hardware address.

interface atm (*slot/0 | slot/port adapter/0 | number*)

The MPOA server is done on the main ATM interface. The main interface has a hardware address associated to it so the MPOA can inherit that address. To bind the MPOA server to the main ATM interface, the interface command is used. This is the main ATM interface, so the subinterface number is eliminated and 0 or the interface number is used.

mpoa server name *mps-name*

Once the configuration mode is created for the main ATM interface, the MPOA server is bound to the interface by identifying the MPOA server that was defined in global mode. The correlation between the two statements is the mps-name. After the MPOA server has a bound hardware address, it can now be bound to a LANE client.

interface atm (*slot* / **0**.*subinterface-number* |
slot / *port adapter* / **0**.*subinterface-number* | *number.subinterface-number*)

The lane client usually resides on a subinterface so the binding of an MPOA server to a lane client is done on a subinterface. The command for getting to an ATM subinterface is as shown above and has been explained in various other sections in this chapter.

lane client mpoa server name *mps-name*

The MPOA server is bound to a LANE client the same way an MPOA client is. The name of the LANE client is not specified and the definition of the MPOA server is placed on the same subinterface as the LANE client. This binds the MPOA server to the LANE client implicitly.

The following is the the additional configuration to finish the example in Figure 21-10.

Additional configuration for router R2 in Figure 21-10:

```
mpoa server config name corporate
interface atm8/0
 mpoa server name corporate
interface atm8/0.1 multipoint
 lane client mpoa server name corporate
interface atm8/0.2 multipoint
 ip address 192.168.1.2 255.255.255.0
 lane client mpoa server name corporate
 lane client ethernet finance elan-id 100
interface atm8/0.3 multipoint
 ip address 192.168.3.2 255.255.255.0
 lane client mpoa server name corporate
 lane client ethernet billing elan-id 102
```

With this configuration, if router R1 wants a connection to router R3, the MPS on router R2 requests and negotiates the connection between the two. This way router R2 does not route between the two routers, but instead a direct VCC is set up between the two for traffic flow.

CHAPTER 22

Defining Frame Relay

Frame Relay has become an integral part of connecting remote locations over a WAN. Its cost-effectiveness and capability to provide traffic shaping using Cisco IOS has proven this technology to be a meaningful backbone infrastructure. In this chapter, the various Frame Relay configurations are discussed in concert with Frame Relay-specific characteristics.

A Simple Frame Relay Configuration

In its simplest form, Frame Relay provides a single circuit from one location to another using a public Frame Relay network. Figure 22-1 diagrams this simple configuration. Frame Relay-connected Cisco routers attach via synchronous line communications to a Frame Relay switch. The Frame Relay provider configures a permanent virtual circuit (PVC) through the Frame Relay public network connecting the two routers. To properly configure the routers, the router administrator must be given some information from the Frame Relay network provider.

First and foremost is the Local Management Interface (LMI) type used by the connecting frame relay switch. The LMI updates passed by the switch to the Cisco router will dynamically update the router to the data link connection identifier (DLCI) being used for the local router PVC connection. The Cisco IOS takes advantage of the Inverse ARP function of the Frame Relay switch to determine the remote IP address of the router on the far-end of the PVC. Using Inverse ARP allows the Cisco IOS to automatically map the local DLCI to the associated remote IP address.

The following router configuration example illustrates the Cisco IOS commands necessary to make the router connection in Figure 22-1.

Router R1 configuration applied to Figure 22-1:

```
interface Serial0
 ip address 172.20.12.2 255.255.255.0
 encapsulation frame-relay
!
router rip
 network 172.20.0.0
```

Router R2 configuration applied to Figure 22-1:

```
interface Serial0
 ip address 172.20.12.3 255.255.255.0
 encapsulation frame-relay
```

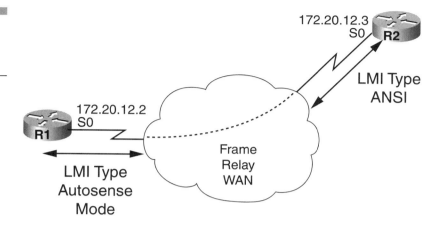

Figure 22-1
A basic Frame Relay network configuration.

```
 frame-relay lmi-type ansi
 !
router rip
 network 172.20.0.0
```

The router configurations for Figure 22-1 take into account that inverse ARP is enabled by default, along with IP split-horizon being enabled by default. The Cisco IOS is made aware that the serial interface being used is a Frame Relay connection from the inclusion of the encapsulation frame-relay command. The format of the command to enable Frame Relay on a serial interface is as follows:

encapsulation frame-relay [cisco | ietf]

The keyword cisco is used by default, should either cisco or ietf not be specified on the command. Using the Cisco keyword causes the Cisco IOS to encapsulate the data using a Cisco proprietary encapsulation technique that includes a four-byte header, which is made up of a two-byte DLCI field and a two-byte field identifying the type of data being encapsulated. The cisco keyword is enabled by default and can only be used with Cisco Systems Frame Relay hardware.

The second keyword ietf is used to allow the Cisco IOS to interact with non-Cisco equipment using the Internet Engineering Task Force (IETF) standard RFC 1490. If the encapsulation type needs to be changed, the serial interface should be modified to a shutdown state prior to changing the encapsulation type. Issuing a no shutdown command after changing the encapsulation type ensures the interface will use the new method. Not performing this scenario causes the router to continue to use the current encapsulation type method. In Figure 22-1, both routers are Cisco routers and therefore the encapsulation default of Cisco is appropriate.

IP split-horizon on Frame Relay interfaces is disabled by default. This allows routing updates to be sent in and out of the same interface for the same destination. IP split-horizon works for the Figure 22-1 scenario because it only involves the use of IP protocol. If bridging or IPX were in use on this connection, split horizon would have to be enabled.

To enable the use of split-horizon on Frame Relay connections, the following command must be entered on the Frame Relay interface definition:

no ip split-horizon

The LMI type is specified on the router R2 configuration. As of Cisco IOS release 11.2, however, the LMI type is automatically determined during initial connectivity to the Frame Relay switch. The autosense capability of Cisco IOS release 11.2 or higher is disabled by explicitly configuring the LMI type on the interface.

frame-relay lmi-type {ansi | cisco | q933a}

The **ansi** keyword is used when the switch utilizes the Annex D ANSI standard T1.617 LMI protocol. The **cisco** keyword is used when communicating with a Cisco switch or any other Frame Relay switch that supports the Cisco LMI type. The **q933a** keyword is specified when the switch supports the ITU-T Q.922 Annex A standard. Not specifying the **frame-relay lmi-type** command on the serial interface definition enables the LMI autosense feature.

Along with the explicit specification of an LMI type, the keepalive command should be entered on the serial line interface to ensure connectivity between the devices. The format for the keepalive command is

keepalive *number*

The number variable is any positive integer that is less than the keepalive timer on the switch. The value is measured in seconds and defaults to 10. The example router configuration for router R2 in Figure 22-1 defaults the keepalive timer to 10 seconds because it is not coded.

Dynamic and Static Addressing

The Cisco router learns of protocol network addresses connecting to the Frame Relay network dynamically through the use of Frame Relay inverse ARP. Using inverse ARP, the router requests the next-hop protocol address connected to the DLCI. The responses received from the inverse ARP are placed in an address-to-DLCI table. Dynamic address mapping and inverse ARP are enabled by default for all supported network protocols. The protocols that are supported by inverse ARP are as follows:

- AppleTalk
- Banyan VINES
- DECnet
- IP
- Novell IPX
- Xerox XNS

Because Inverse ARP is enabled by default, no specific specification is required for dynamic addressing unless Inverse ARP is disabled by entering the following command under the specified interface configuration:

no frame-relay inverse-arp [*protocol*] [*dlci*]

The *protocol* optional variable allows the router administrator to disable inverse ARP for a specific network protocol while still using inverse ARP for the other supported protocols. The value for the *protocol* variable can be one of the following keywords:

- **appletalk**
- **decnet**
- **ip**
- **ipx**
- **vines**
- **xns**

The optional *dlci* variable identifies a specific DLCI to which the **no frame-relay inverse-arp** command applies. The value for the *dlci* variable is a valid DLC number for the interface ranging from 16 to 1007. Specifying both the protocol and dlci variables together targets the protocol of a specific DLCI. This allows another DLCI running the same protocol to continue to use dynamic address mapping. Table 22-1 lists the results of the various combinations of the command.

Table 22-1

The Various Command Format Functional Results of the no frame-relay inverse-arp Interface Command

Entered Command	Result
no frame-relay inverse-arp	All protocols and all DLCIs on the interface are affected.
no frame-relay inverse-arp *protocol*	Only the specified protocol is affected on all the DLCIs used by the interface.
no frame-relay inverse-arp *dlci*	Only the specified DLCI has dynamic address mapping disabled for all the protocols on the DLCI.
no frame-relay inverse-arp *protocol dlci*	Only the specified protocol on the specific DLCI has dynamic address mapping disabled.

Dynamic address mapping is specific to multipoint Frame Relay configurations. In point-to-point configurations, there is only a single destination; hence, there is no need to discover addresses. Inverse ARP should be disabled for a specific protocol and/or DLCI when it is a known fact that the protocol is not being supported on the far end of the PVC.

Static address mapping requires the router administrator to be aware of the next-hop protocol address for each DLCI. Applying a static map is made possible by defining the frame-relay map interface command. Specifying this command automatically disables inverse ARP for any of the affected DLCIs. Static mapping is used when the far-end router does not support inverse ARP or when the specific protocol being used between the routers does not support inverse ARP. The format for specifying static address mapping is

frame-relay map *protocol protocol-address dlci* [broadcast] [ietf | cisco]

[payload-compress {packet-by-packet | frf9 stac [*hardware-options*]}]

The *protocol* variable is the network protocol to which this static address mapping is being applied. The values available for the protocol variable are one of the following:

- **appletalk**
- **decnet**
- **dlsw**
- **ip**

- **ipx**
- **llc2**
- **rsrb**
- **vines**
- **xns**

The *protocol-address* variable value following the *protocol* variable specifies the destination network address of the identified protocol. The value used here must be specified in accordance with the type of protocol being statically mapped.

The *dlci* variable value identifies which DLCI number is being used to connect the *protocol-address* on the Frame Relay interface. The optional keyword **broadcast** is used when the networking protocol functions as a broadcast protocol when multicasting is not applicable. This keyword is particularly important to use when using the OSPF routing protocol for IP networks.

The **ietf** optional keyword instructs the OSPF Frame Relay process to use the IETF Frame Relay RFC 1490 encapsulation method. This is used primarily when the Cisco router is communicating to a non-Cisco hardware platform over the Frame Relay network. The optional **cisco** keyword is used when the router is communicating with another Cisco hardware-based platform. Using either the Cisco or ietf keyword overrides the method specified by the interface configuration command **encapsulation frame-relay** for the interface being defined. Not specifying the **cisco** or **ietf** keywords causes the address mapping to inherit the attributes set by the interface configuration command **encapsulation frame-relay** for the interface being defined.

The optional **payload-compress packet-by-packet** keyword instructs the Cisco IOS to use the stacker method of compressing the payload on a packet-by-packet basis. This method is Cisco proprietary and will not be interoperated with non-Cisco routers. The optional keyword **payload-compress frf9 stac** instructs the IOS to compress using the RFC 1490 FRF.9 compression standard.

Compression of the payload may have performance considerations on the router, depending on the router configuration. If the router includes a compression service adapter (CSA), the compression is performed in the CSA. This is known as hardware compression. If a CSA is not available but the router (7200 series) contains a VIP2 card for the serial Frame Relay connection, the VIP2 software executing on the VIP2 card performs the compression. Using the VIP2 software to compress the payload is called software compression. The final configuration is where neither the CSA nor the VIP2 are available on the router. In this situation, the router performs the compression using the router's main processor (route processor) and is also called software compression.

The *hardware-options* optional parameter of the optional **payload-compress** keyword enables the router administrator to direct which cards are to be used for the compression techniques. Specifying **distribute** as the *hardware-options* value indicates the compression is performed by the software of the VIP2 card. If the **distribute** option is specified but there is no VIP2 card for use, the router performs compression using the router's main processor. This option is specific to the 7500 series routers only. Using the **software** value as the *hardware-options* variable indicates that the router's main processor is to be used for compressing the payload. Specifying the **csa** *csa-number* keyword and variable instructs the IOS to perform the payload compression on a specific CSA card identified by the *csa-number* variable value. This specification applies to only the 7200 series router platform.

Use of the **frame-relay map broadcast** command in conjunction with the **ip ospf network broadcast** interface configuration command negates the need to define each OSPF neighbor. This enables OSPF to treat the non-broadcast multicast access Frame relay network as if it were a broadcast network.

Figure 22-2 diagrams a Frame Relay network connection using static address mapping. The serial interfaces of all the routers involved specify an IP address and identify the network-address-to-DLCI mapping using the frame-relay map command.

The following router configurations apply to Figure 22-2:

Router R1 configuration applied to Figure 22-2:

```
interface Serial0
 ip address 192.168.1.1 255.255.255.0
 encapsulation frame-relay
 frame-relay map 192.168.1.2 30
 frame-relay map 192.168.1.3 31 ietf
!
router rip
 network 192.168.1.0
```

Router R2 configuration applied to Figure 22-2:

```
interface Serial0
 encapsulation frame-relay
 ip address 192.168.1.2 255.255.255.0
 frame-relay map 192.168.1.1 32
 !
router rip
 network 192.168.1.0
```

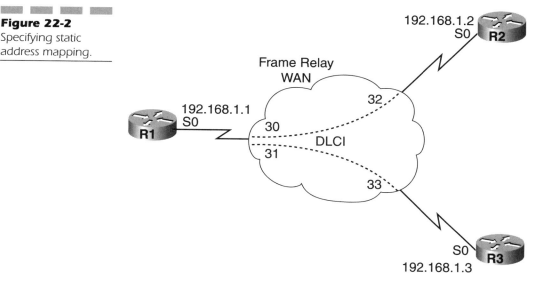

Figure 22-2
Specifying static
address mapping.

Router R3 configuration applied to Figure 22-2:

```
interface Serial0
 ip address 192.168.1.3 255.255.255.0
 encapsulation frame-relay ietf
 frame-relay map 192.168.1.1 33
!
router rip
 network 192.168.1.0
```

The router configuration applying to Figure 22-2 illustrates the use of the frame-relay map command to create static network address mapping. The network address used by the frame-relay map is the IP address of the far-end router that is reached by using the DLCI specified on the command.

For example, router R1 communicates with router R3 using DLCI 31 addressing IP address 192.168.1.3 over this DLCI. Router R3 receives and sends packets to router R1 using the destination IP address 192.168.1.1 over its DLCI number 33. Note that router R2 also specifies the same destination IP address to communicate with router R1 as that used by router R3. However, R2 maps the destination IP address 192.168.1.1 to its DLCI number 32.

Frame Relay Subinterfaces

Subinterfaces are a Cisco IOS feature that enables a single physical interface to be viewed as multiple virtual interfaces. The use of subinterfaces enables a Cisco router to apply physical interface attributes to each virtual interface. For example, instead of having 50 DLCIs assigned to a specific physical interface, each DLCI can be assigned to a given virtual subinterface of the physical interface. This enables the Cisco IOS to apply specific interface requirements to meet the needs of each DLCI.

Point-to-Point Frame Relay Subinterfaces

Subinterfaces were initially created to handle split-horizon on NBMA networks like Frame Relay when using distance-vector routing protocols. Recall that split-horizon infers that routing updates received on an interface cannot be retransmitted back out the same interface. This still holds true for a Frame Relay connection with multiple PVCs defined. This is because the routing protocols use the physical interface as the determining factor in deciding if split-horizon is involved.

In Figure 22-3, router R2 and R3 cannot exchange routing information with each other because their only connection would be out the same physical interface on which they received routing updates about the other router from router R1. This is because router R1 enforces split-horizon for the single physical connection to the Frame Relay network.

Using the notion of subinterfaces for the diagram shown in Figure 22-3, the Cisco router can avoid the split-horizon rule on Frame Relay. Figure 21-4 illustrates this point. Subdividing the single physical interface into two virtual interfaces requires separate network addresses for each virtual interface and hence appears to the routing protocol as distinct interfaces. Because of the use of subinterfaces, routing updates from router 2 on one of the virtual point-to-point subinterface connections can be forwarded to router R3 on the other virtual point-to-point subinterface connection over the same physical link without breaking the split horizon rule.

Multipoint Frame Relay Subinterfaces

Cisco router serial interfaces are considered multipoint connections. The subinterfaces are considered point-to-point only if the point-to-point key-

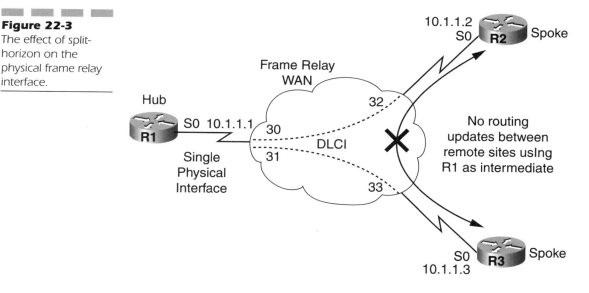

Figure 22-3
The effect of split-horizon on the physical frame relay interface.

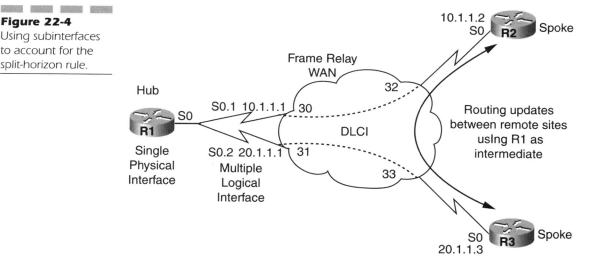

Figure 22-4
Using subinterfaces to account for the split-horizon rule.

word is specified on the interface configuration command. A subinterface can also be defined as a virtual multipoint connection. Although it is a virtual multipoint, it is still bound to the split-horizon rule because all the network resources attached to the virtual multipoint are connected to the same network number. Figure 22-5 illustrates such a configuration.

This type of configuration is most often seen when an existing multipoint frame relay network is being migrated to a subinterface point-to-point network. The virtual multipoint subinterface is utilized to maintain the single network address number for each of the remaining remote locations during the migration process.

Figure 22-5 shows a multipoint subinterface connecting three other remote locations. Each of these remote locations is considered to be connected to the same network number. Router R4 is no longer part of the virtual multipoint network and exists on its own point-to-point subinterface with its own network number. It is important to understand in this scenario that a single physical frame relay connection is still in use to accomplish this configuration.

Specifying a Frame Relay Subinterface

Specifying a Frame Relay subinterface first requires the specification of a physical interface. Once the physical interface is defined, the subinterface(s) can be defined. The order in which the definition is required follows:

interface serial {*number* | *slot/port* | *slot/adapter/port*}

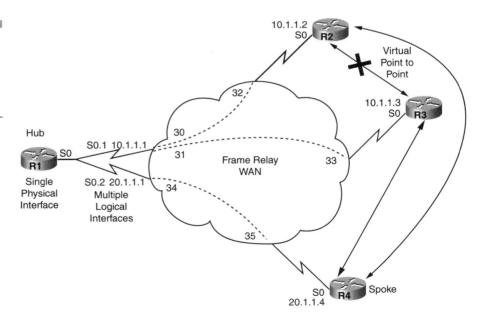

Figure 22-5
A virtual multipoint subinterface and point-to-point subinterface network configuration.

encapsulation frame-relay

interface serial {{*number* | *slot* / *port* |
slot / *adapter* / *port*}.*subinterface-number* {**multipoint** | **point-to-point**}}

The **interface serial** configuration command specifies the physical Frame Relay interface that is to be used by all subsequent subinterfaces. The *number* variable is the value of the port for which this definition is being specified. The *slot* / *port* pair is used on routers that have multiple slots that support a number of ports on which a serial line can be connected. The *slot* / *adapter* / *port* variable is used on routers that support interface cards that have interchangeable adapters with each adapter having a number of ports. The encapsulation frame-relay command must be entered on the physical connection to ensure the appropriate encapsulation technique. The entire encapsulation frame-relay command set is available for use. Following the encapsulation frame-relay command of the physical interface definition, the subinterfaces can now be defined.

The interface serial command is again entered, but the assignment of the definitions to follow the command is applied to the subinterface number of the physical interface through the use of the subinterface-number variable. The subinterface-number variable is the virtual interface number belonging to the physical interface definition. The assignment of the subinterface-number ranges from 1 to 1024. The number, slot/port, or slot/adapter/port variable on the subinterface interface configuration command denotes which interface the subinterface is using. For example, if the following were entered under the interface configuration mode

```
interface serial 1/1
encapsulation frame-relay
interface serial 1/1.1
encapsulation frame-relay
```

the subinterface would be denoted by the 1/1.1 variable of the interface serial command. If serial 1/0.1 were entered following the interface serial 1/1 command, the subinterface being defined is actually the serial interface on slot 1 and port 0, not slot 1 and port 1. Therefore, be careful when making configuration changes to subinterfaces. An innocent typo can cause an invalid configuration by directing changes to a different subinterface than the one desired.

The subinterfaces must also be provided with network addressing. Point-to-point subinterfaces require the use of the **frame-relay interface-dlci** command to identify the network address. Multipoint subinterfaces use inverse ARP and therefore learn that the network addresses also require the use of this command. However, multipoint subinterfaces can be mapped statically when the frame-relay map command is used, as previously discussed. The format of the frame-relay interface-dlci command is

frame-relay interface-dlci *dlci* [**ietf** | **cisco**] [**voice-encap** *size*]

The dlci variable value is the DLCI number used by the Frame Relay provider for connecting the router to a remote location over a PVC. The DLCI and therefore the traffic carried by the DLCI are managed by the configuration commands applied to the subinterface. The **ietf** | **cisco** keywords indicate the type of Frame Relay encapsulation used for the DLCI associated with the subinterface. The voice-encap size optional pairing is strictly used for the Cisco MC3810 Access server to provide the encapsulation of voice over Frame Relay. The value specified for the size variable determines the data segmentation size of the voice message. The value for size varies depending on the Frame Relay port access rate. Table 22-3 lists the recommended size value, as compared to the port access rate.

The recommendation for the size value of the **voice-encap** keyword is based on back-to-back frame relay connection between two MC3810 routers. Extra header bytes may be requiered depending on the type of frame relay switch being used for connection over a public frame relay network.

The command **frame-relay interface-dlci** is required for all point-to-point subinterfaces and multipoint subinterfaces that have inverse ARP enabled. Multipoint subinterfaces using static addressing do not require this command.

Figure 22-6 diagrams a point-to-point subinterface configuration. Router R1 uses a single physical Frame Relay interface and two subinterfaces to connect routers R2 and R3 that are defined for transporting IP traffic. The remote destination address of the point-to-point subinterfaces on router R1

Table 22-3	**Port Access Rate**	**Recommended Data Segmentation Size**
Frame Relay Port Access Rate and the Recommended Size Value for voice-encap Keyword	64 kbps	80 bytes
	128 kbps	160 bytes
	256 kbps	320 bytes
	512 kbps	640 bytes
	1,536 kbps (full T1)	1600 bytes
	2,048 kbps (full E1)	1600 bytes

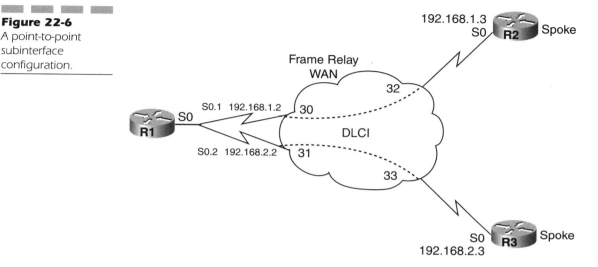

Figure 22-6
A point-to-point
subinterface
configuration.

are learned from the DLCI specification on the frame-relay interface-dlci commands. Since routers R2 and R3 are using the physical interface for connection to the Frame Relay network, the Cisco IOS defaults the interface to a multipoint configuration. Multipoint interfaces automatically use inverse ARP. Therefore, router R2 and R3 will dynamically learn of the network addressing for the Frame Relay network.

The following router configurations apply to Figure 22-6:

Router R1 configuration applied to Figure 22-6:

```
interface Serial0
 no ip address
 encapsulation frame-relay
!
interface Serial0.1 point-to-point
 ip address 192.168.1.2 255.255.255.0
 frame-relay interface-dlci 30
!
interface Serial0.2 point-to-point
 ip address 192.168.2.2 255.255.255.0
 frame-relay interface-dlci 31
!
router rip
 network 192.168.1.0
 network 192.168.2.0
```

Router R2 configuration applied to Figure 22-6:

```
interface Serial0
 ip address 192.168.1.3 255.255.255.0
 encapsulation frame-relay
!
router rip
 network 192.168.1.0
```

Router R3 configuration applied to Figure 22-6:

```
interface Serial0
 ip address 192.168.2.3 255.255.255.0
 encapsulation frame-relay
!
router rip
 network 192.168.2.0
```

In the router configurations for Figure 22-6, the **frame-relay lmi-type** command is not specified. This means that the routers are using Cisco IOS 11.2 or higher and that LMI autosense is enabled.

Hub and Spoke Configurations

In most Frame Relay networks, the configuration is a hub and spoke. In Frame Relay terms, this means a partially meshed network. The advantage of this is the capability to connect multiple remote locations over single communications links by virtue of using multiple PVCs. Using the subinterface feature of Cisco IOS, each PVC can be mapped to a specific subinterface of the physical interface.

Dynamic Addressing for IP-Only Connectivity

Figure 22-7 illustrates the use of Frame Relay subinterfaces in a partially meshed Frame Relay network. The use of subinterfaces in this configuration allows routing updates to be passed from router R2 to R3 and vice versa.

The use of the subinterfaces in the sample router configurations enables the ease of expansions and management of the PVCs. The subinterface assignment to specific PVCs enables a router administrator to selectively shutdown DLCI connections without affecting the entire Frame Relay physical connection. The following router configurations apply to Figure 21-7:

Figure 22-7

A partially meshed network configuration supporting IP traffic only.

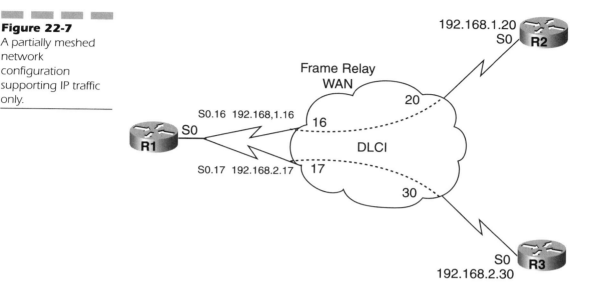

Router R1 configuration applied to Figure 22-7:

```
version 11.2
!
interface Serial0
 no ip address
 encapsulation frame-relay
!
interface Serial0.16 point-to-point
 description Frame Relay to routerR2
 ip address 192.168.1.16 255.255.255.0
 frame-relay interface-dlci 16 broadcast
!
interface Serial0.17 point-to-point
 description Frame Relay to routerR3
 ip 192.168.2.17
 frame-relay interface-dlci 17 broadcast
!
router rip
 version 2
 network 192.168.1.0
 network 192.168.2.0
 no auto-summary
```

Router R2 configuration applied to Figure 22-7:

```
version 11.2
!
interface Serial0
 no ip address
```

```
 encapsulation frame-relay
!
interface Serial0.20 point-to-point
 ip addrs 192.168.1.20 255.255.255.0
 frame-relay interface-dlci 20 broadcast
!
router rip
 version 2
 network 192.168.1.0
 no auto-summary
```

Router R3 configuration applied to Figure 22-7:

```
version 11.2
!
 interface Serial0
 no ip address
 encapsulation frame-relay
!
interface Serial0.30 point-to-point
 ip address 192.168.2.30 255.255.255.0
 frame-relay interface-dlci 30 broadcast
!
router rip
 version 2
 network 192.168.2.0
 no auto-summary
```

In the above router configurations, the router administrator has chosen to match the subinterface number to the DLCI number for the PVC being assigned to the subinterface. This is good practice as it keeps a logical connection between the subinterfaces and the PVCs. The configurations also conserve IP addressing by utilizing the ip unnumbered feature of Cisco IOS.

Static Addressing over a Multipoint Configuration

In Figure 22-8, a single physical router interface is used for connecting router R2 and R3. To ensure connectivity mapping, the router administrator has chosen to use static address mapping by specifying the frame-relay map ip command for the correct address assigned to each of the physical interfaces.

The following router configurations apply to Figure 22-8:

Router R1 configuration applied to Figure 22-8:

```
version 11.2
interface Ethernet0
 ip address 10.1.1.1 255.255.255.0
```

```
!
interface Serial0
 ip address 192.168.1.1 255.255.255.0
 encapsulation frame-relay
 frame-relay map ip 192.168.1.2 16 broadcast
 frame-relay map ip 192.168.1.3 17 broadcast
 !
router rip
 version 2
 network 10.0.0.0
 network 192.168.1.0
 no auto-summary
```

Router R2 configuration applied to Figure 22-8:

```
interface Ehternet0
 ip address 10.2.1.1 255.255.255.0
 !
interface Serial0
 ip address 192.168.1.2 255.255.255.0
 encapsulation frame-relay
 frame-relay map ip 192.168.1.1 20 broadcast
 frame-relay map ip 192.168.1.3 20 broadcast
 !
router rip
 version 2
 network 10.0.0.0
 network 192.168.1.0
 no auto-summary
```

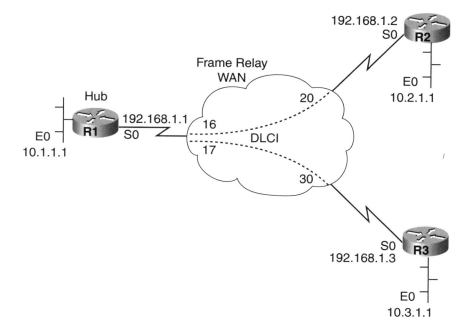

Figure 22-8
Static address
mapping in a
multipoint
configuration.

Router R3 configuration applied to Figure 22-8:

```
version 11.2
!
interface Ethernet0
 ip address 10.3.1.1 255.255.255.0
!
interface Serial0
 ip address 192.168.1.3 255.255.0.0
 encapsulation frame-relay
 frame-relay map ip 192.168.1.1 30 broadcast
 frame-relay map ip 192.168.1.2 30 broadcast
!
router rip
 version 2
 network 10.0.0.0
 network 192.168.1.0
 no auto-summary
```

In the above configurations, routers R2 and R3 map each other's IP address over the DLCI number that is used to reach router R1. This is because inverse ARP is disabled by including the frame-relay map ip command on the physical interface of the routers. In large Frame Relay, partially meshed networks, static address mapping can become an administrative nightmare. It is highly suggested that dynamic address mapping be used whenever possible.

Traffic Shaping on Frame Relay

Version 11.2 of Cisco IOS greatly enhanced the capabilities of Frame Relay on Cisco routers by introducing traffic-shaping features. These features enable the router to perform the following functions:

- *Enforcing traffic rates for each virtual circuit:*   This enables the router to ensure that the peak rate allowed for outbound traffic is available. The peak rate should match that of the CIR for the PVC or a value that provides the service required by the business.

- *The throttling of traffic dynamically for each virtual circuit:*   If the router receives BECN packets, indicating congestion on the network, the outbound rate is reduced to allow congestion to ease. Once the congestion has eased, by virtue of not receiving the BECN packets anymore, the outbound traffic rate is increased.

- *Support for priority and custom queuing for each virtual circuit:* This allows a router administrator to apply custom or priority queuing to a virtual circuit to meet the business requirements.

Traffic-shaping for Frame Relay is enabled by the use of the interface configuration command:

frame-relay traffic-shaping

The traffic-shaping command does not have specific variables in its format. However, the shaping of the traffic for a virtual circuit comes about from the specification of several other frame-relay interface commands.

The following router configuration will be used to explain the various other related commands needed to establish traffic shaping. Let's start with a sample router configuration command employing traffic shaping on a serial interface:

```
interface serial 0
encapsulation frame-relay
bandwidth 64
ip address 10.10.10.1 255.255.255.0
frame-relay traffic-shaping
frame-relay map ip 10.10.10.2 16 broadcast
frame-relay interface-dlci 16
frame-relay class DS1
!
map-class frame-relay DS1
 frame-relay cir 64000
 frame-relay bc 8000
 frame-relay be 0.
 frame-relay mincir 16000.
```

The frame-relay class command in the sample configuration has the following command format:

frame-relay class *name*

This command is used to identify a map-class specification that sets the parameters that apply to shaping the traffic for the associated DLCI. In this case, the map-class providing this information is named DS1. The parameters set by the map-class specification are applied to all the virtual circuits defined to the interface or subinterface on which the frame-relay class command is defined. The parameters are applied to each virtual circuit in the following order:

1. Parameters set by the map-class defined for the virtual circuit
2. Parameters set by the map-class associated with the subinterface

3. Parameters set by the map-class specified on the physical interface

4. The default parameters of the physical interface

The name value identifies a map-class frame-relay global configuration command. The format of the command is

map-class frame-relay *map-class-name*

The *map-class-name* variable value must match the name of a **frame-relay class** *name* variable value in order for the subsequent Frame Relay parameters to affect the virtual circuit. Following a map-class frame-relay global command, the specific traffic shaping commands are encountered.

The first of these traffic shaping commands is the frame-relay cir command. The format of this command is

frame-relay cir {in | out} *bps*

The **in | out** keyword identifies the flow of traffic to which the committed information rate (CIR) is being defined. The default direction of the flow of traffic is in. The *bps* variable is the CIR in bits per second and defaults to 56000. The value chosen here should be the value at which the router will provide the best performance for the applications using the connection without risking poor performance. The rate here is not the provider's CIR. In our example, the frame-relay cir command specifies that 64,000 bits per second (64 Kbps) is being assured for inbound traffic. A second frame-relay cir command can be entered to specify the desired rate for outgoing traffic by using the frame-relay cir out command with a bits-per-second (bps) value specified. The rates defined here are the normal rates assured without network congestion being present.

The frame-relay bc command following the frame-relay cir command in the sample router configuration is used to provide the committed burst rate of incoming and outgoing traffic. The format of this command is

frame-relay bc {in | out} *bits*

The **in | out** keyword restricts the command to the selected flow. If neither in nor out is specified, the committed burst rate is applied to inbound and outbound traffic. The default value for the bits variable is 7000. The rule of thumb is to make the committed burst rate (Bc) one-eighth the rate of the CIR.

Associated with the frame-relay bc command is the frame-relay be command. The frame-relay be command is expressed in the following command format:

frame-relay be {in | out} *bits*

Again the **in | out** keywords restrict the bits value to only one flow. The default, if neither in nor out is defined, is to apply the bits value to inbound and outbound traffic flow. The bits value defaults to 7000 bits per second and defines the excess or extra amount of traffic that can be sent if needed during a given interval. The sample router configuration has the CIR at the port speed, so there is no excess amount of bandwidth to allow extra burst.

The time interval is an important factor in the values used. The time interval (Tc) is equal to the committed burst rate (Bc) divided by the CIR value. In our example, the time interval is equal to

$$Tc = 8K(Bc) / 64K(CIR) = 1/8 \text{ seconds}$$

This means that every eighth of a second the router can send up to the amount defined by the Bc and Be values.

The final command used in our example indicates how the router will respond after receiving BECN responses from the Frame Relay network. Cisco IOS release 11.2 and higher automatically have the BECN response enabled, and it is recommended that you do not disable it. Often the router is set to fall back to the actual CIR provided by the Frame Relay network configuration that is guaranteed for the circuit. This value is defined by using the frame-relay mincir command. The format of the command is

frame-relay mincir {in | out} *bps*

The **in | out** keywords restrict the bps value to only one flow. The default, if neither in nor out is defined, is to apply the bps value to inbound and outbound traffic flow. The bps value defaults to 56000 bits per second and uses the value defined as the rate for when BECN responses are received.

Frame Relay traffic-shaping in Cisco IOS 11.2 or higher can take advantage of the Cisco IOS Quality of Service (QoS) features. For example, the QoS priority queue list can be specified for a Frame Relay interface using the following command:

frame-relay priority-group *list-number*

This command is used in conjunction with a map class to prioritize protocols over the Frame Relay virtual circuit. The list-number variable directs the Cisco IOS to apply the priority-list command set to the traffic on the virtual circuit. For example, the following router configuration assigns a higher priority to IP traffic on the Frame Relay virtual circuit over the other protocols:

```
interface serial 0
 encapsulation frame-relay
 ip address 10.10.10.10 255.255.255.0
 frame-relay interface-dlci 30
 class vc30
!
map-class frame-relay vc30
 frame-relay priority-group 1
!
priority-list 1 protocol ip high
```

In this example, the frame-relay priority-group command points to the priority-list 1. This list indicates that the IP protocol is to receive higher service than other protocols on the DLCI. The example also introduces the class command, which identifies a map-class definition for a specific DLCI. This is juxtaposed to the frame-relay class command, which affects a whole interface or subinterface. The command format for the class virtual circuit configuration command is

class name

in which name is the value of a valid **map-class frame-relay** definition.

The custom queuing feature of Cisco IOS QoS is enabled for frame-relay interfaces much in the same way as priority queuing. The following command is entered on the frame–relay interface or subinterface definition to identify a custom queuing list:

frame-relay custom-queue-list *list-number*

The *list-number* variable value identifies a valid **queue-list** number for which the **map-class frame-relay** command of this **frame-relay custom-queue-list** command is specified. The queues defined in the associated queue-list affect the traffic of the DLCI to which the map-class is applied.

Transparent Bridging

Transparent bridged traffic over Frame Relay is accomplished by applying the bridge-group command to the interface or subinterface for which bridged traffic is to be transmitted. As shown in Figure 22-9 and the associated router configurations, a typical hub and spoke configuration will route IP and IPX traffic and bridge all other traffic. The IP routes are dynamically resolved, in this case using RIP V2. The IPX routers and associated services are resolved dynamically using IPX RIP/SAP protocols. The use of subinterfaces enables the resolution of these routing protocols by avoiding the split-horizon rule.

Router R1 configuration applied to Figure 22-9:

```
version 11.2
 ipx routing 0000.0caa.1111
 !
interface Ethernet0
 ip address 10.1.1.1 255.0.0.0
 ipx network 100 encapsulation SAP
 ipx network 101 encapsulation NOVELL-ETHER secondary
 bridge-group 1
 !
interface Serial0
 no ip address
 encapsulation frame-relay
 !
interface Serial0.16 point-to-point
 description Frame Relay to R2
 ip unnumbered Ethernet0
 ipx network AAAA
 frame-relay interface-dlci 16 broadcast
 bridge-group 1
 !
interface Serial0.17 point-to-point
 description Frame Relay to R3
 ip unnumbered Ethernet0
 ipx network BBBB
 frame-relay interface-dlci 17 broadcast
 bridge-group 1
```

Figure 22-9

The hub and spoke configuration used for routing IP and IPX traffic while bridging all other traffic.

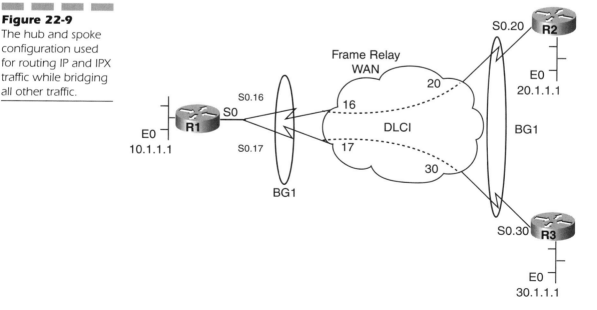

```
!
router rip
 version 2
 network 10.0.0.0
 no auto-summary
!
bridge 1 protocol ieee
```

Router R2 configuration applied to Figure 22-9 :

```
version 11.2
ipx routing 0000.0cbb.2222
!
interface Ethernet0
 ip address 20.1.1.1 255.0.0.0
 ipx network 200
 bridge-group 1
!
interface Serial0
 no ip address
 encapsulation frame-relay
!
interface Serial0.20 point-to-point
 description Frame Relay to R1
 ip unnumbered Ethernet0
 ipx network AAAA
 frame-relay interface-dlci 20 broadcast
 bridge-group 1
!
router rip
 version 2
 network 20.0.0.0
 no auto-summary
!
bridge 1 protocol ieee
```

Router R3 configuration applied to Figure 22-9:

```
version 11.2
ipx routing 0000.0ccc.3333
!
interface Ethernet0
 ip address 30.1.1.1 255.0.0.0
 ipx network 300
 bridge-group 1
!
interface Serial0
 no ip address
 encapsulation frame-relay
!
interface Serial0.30 point-to-point
 description Frame Relay to R1
 ip unnumbered Ethernet0
 ipx network BBBB
 frame-relay interface-dlci 30 broadcast
 bridge-group 1
!
```

```
router rip
 version 2
 network 30.0.0.0
 no auto-summary
!
bridge 1 protocol ieee
```

In these transparent bridge configuration examples, each of the Frame Relay PVCs are grouped into bridge-group 1 and all use the IEEE bridge protocol.

Managing Performance Problems Using the Broadcast Queue

Bandwidth on Frame Relay networks is a valuable commodity. Performance issues may arise in Frame Relay networks that have a large number of DLCIs on a single router interface. These performance issues are caused by the replication of routing and service advertisement updates for each of the DLCIs. These updates not only consume bandwidth, but they end up using interface buffers that would normally be used for end-user traffic. In this type of configuration, high packet rate loss is probable for the Frame Relay interface.

Cisco IOS attempts to resolve this type of Frame Relay performance issue by establishing a special queue that maintains only broadcast traffic. This broadcast queue is managed independently of the normal interface queue. Consequently, the broadcast queue has its own buffers, size, and service rate.

The broadcast queue for Frame Relay is enabled by default. The format of the command is

frame-relay broadcast-queue *size byte-rate packet-rate*

The size variable value determines the total number of packets the broadcast queue will hold. This size value defaults to 64 packets. The byte-rate variable value defaults to 256000 bytes per second and defines the maximum number of bytes that can be transmitted in a second. The final variable is the packet rate. Its value defaults to 36 packets per second and defines the maximum number of packets that can be transmitted in a second. The broadcast queue holds only those packets that have been replicated for transmission over the multiple DLCIs on an interface. The original routing packet and SAP packets are queued on the normal interface queue. Likewise, bridged and spanning-tree packets are sent on the normal queue.

The rule of thumb for setting the byte rate is

Less than n/4 times the minimum remote access rate (bytes/sec)

N is the number of DLCIs that the broadcast is replicated on and the local access rate is bytes/sec.

The packet rate rule of thumb is to set the rate by assuming packets will be 250 bytes.

23

Defining Digital Subscriber Lines (DSL)

In this chapter, we will turn our attention to a technology that is gaining widespread acceptance for use by both businesses and residential users. This technology is known as *digital subscriber lines* (DSLs) and represents a family of products, some of which are more suitable for business use than other members of the DSL family.

Each member of the DSL family of technologies is designed to provide high-speed communication over twisted-wire metallic telephone cable routed from the subscriber's premises to the telephone company's central office that is providing service. In order to obtain an appreciation for the manner by which DSL products permit transmissions at data rates significantly beyond that obtainable by conventional analog modems, one must first examine the telephone channel and the relationship between the normal human audible range and the bandwidth of a telephone channel.

Figure 23-1 compares the approximate range of human hearing to the passband of a telephone channel. Here the term passband represents the range of frequencies that the telephone company central office passes through the use of filters that remove those frequencies below 300 Hz and above 3,300 Hz. The resulting passband of 3,000 Hz actually varies based upon the energy level of a conversation and the fact that filters do not immediately operate at a specified frequency. This fact is illustrated in Figure 23-2, which shows filters being used to create a telephone channel passband. The low-pass filter permits all frequencies up to a cutoff frequency to pass and, in effect, blocks frequencies of and above 3,300 Hz. In comparison, the high-pass filter permits all frequencies above the cutoff frequency of the filter to pass. This explains why the low-pass filter operates at 3,300 Hz while the high-pass filter operates at 300 Hz.

In examining Figure 23-2, it is important to note that the passband is wider at lower dB levels than at higher dB levels. This explains why modern modems can operate at data rates beyond Claud Shannon's computation of 30 Kbps being the maximum operating rate on a voice channel. This is because at a low dB level the passband spreads out beyond 3,000 Hz, pro-

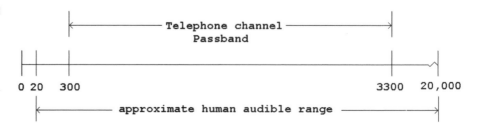

Figure 23-1

The range of human hearing compared to the passband of a telephone channel

Figure 23-2
The creation of a
telephone channel
passband through
the use of low-pass
and high-pass filters

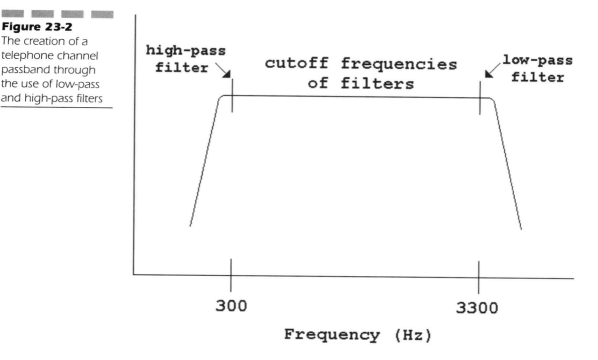

viding modem designers with the ability to develop products that can operate at bidirectional data rates of 33.6 Kbps.

Rationale for Cutoff Frequencies

Author: In the
sentence that
begins, "By lim-
iting the pass-
band . . . ,"
something is
missing from this
sentence. Please
make any neces-
sary corrections
or additions.

The rationale for the creation of a 3,000 Hz passband is based upon the
manner by which humans speak. Both low and high frequencies do not add
much information to a conversation and can be removed without adversely
affecting the ability of a listener to understand the speaker. By limiting the
passband to 3,000 Hz instead of the approximately 20,000 Hz of tones, our
ears recognize it become possible for telephone companies to *frequency division multiplex* (FDM) six conversations onto a trunk linking central offices
using less bandwidth than our ears recognize. Thus, the 3,000 Hz passband
traces its roots to the cost saving goal of phone companies during the establishment of their basic infrastructure.

How DSL Operates

The key to the capability of the various flavors of DSL to operate above a conventional modem's data rate is the removal of filters from the subscriber line. When filters are removed, it becomes possible to use a range of frequencies up to approximately 1.1 MHz on a twisted-wire pair. Because the signaling rate is proportional to bandwidth, the extended bandwidth permits a higher signaling rate to be obtained. Because the use of a modulation technique that packs a set number of bits into each signal change permits a higher data rate, when the signaling rate is increased, this means that the data rate is proportional to bandwidth. Thus, the increase in bandwidth, obtained through the removal of filters, permits a higher data transfer rate to be obtained. Now that you have an appreciation for how to transmit using DSL at higher data rates than obtainable by conventional modems, turn your attention to the DSL family.

The DSL Family

Currently, 10 popular members of the DSL family exist, with each member having certain operating characteristics that distinguish it from other members of the DSL family of products. Those operating characteristics include the operating rate supported, its operating mode (symmetric or asymmetric), and the transmission distance the technology supports between the subscriber and telephone company's central office. This also includes DSL's requirement for special filters to eliminate the effect of maintaining a telephone conversation with the 300 Hz spectrum while using other frequencies up to 1.1 MHz for data. Table 23-1 provides a summary of the operational characteristics of 10 popular members of the DSL family of products.

In the wonderful world of Cisco-based communication, *Asymmetrical Digital Subscriber Line* (ADSL) technology is supported by a large number of Cisco products. Under ADSL, the frequency spectrum of an unloaded copper-pair wire is subdivided into three frequency segments, as shown in Figure 23-3. The first channel represents approximately 4 KHz of bandwidth and is allocated for existing telephone operations. A second segment of frequency that begins at approximately 25 KHz is allocated to an upstream channel from the subscriber toward the central office. A third segment of frequency, as noted in Figure 23-3, is considerably wider than the second segment and is allocated for downstream transmission from the central office towards the subscriber. Because the operating rate of data transmis-

Table 23-1

Members of the
DSL Family

Mnemonic	Meaning	Data Rate	Transmission Mode	Description
HDSL	High-bit-rate DSL	1.544/2048 Mbps	Symmetric	Operates on two or four wires up to 12,000 feet
HDSL2	High-bit-rate DLS	1.544/2.048 Mbps	Symmetric	Operates one wire pair
SDSL	Symmetric DSL	128 Kbps to 2.3 Mbps	Symmetric	Operates on one wire pair
ADSL	Asymmetric DSL	1.5 to 8 Mbps downstream, 16 to 640 Kbps upstream	Asymmetric	Operates on one wire pair at distances up to 18,000 feet and requires splitters
RADSL	Rate Adaptive DSL	1.5 to 8 Mbps downstream, 16 to 640 Kbps upstream	Asymmetric	Operates at adaptive rates on one pair and requires splitters
IDSL	ISDN DSL	128 Kbps	Symmetric	Operates over one wire pair
CDSL	Consumer DSL	Up to 1 Mbps downstream, 16 to 128 Kbps upstream	Asymmetrical	Operates on one wire pair without a splitter and is the forerunner of G.lite
G.lite	Reduced operating rate version of ADSL	Up to 1.5 Mbps downstream, Up to 512 Kbps upstream	Asymmetrical	Operates without splitters
VDSL	Very high data rate DSL	13 to 52 Mbps downstream, 1.5 to 6.0 Mbps upstream	Asymmetric	Operates on a single wire pair for short distances, typically up to 4,500 feet
MVL	Multiple Virtual	128 to 768 Kbps	Asymmetric	Up to 24,000 feet

sion is proportional to bandwidth, Figure 23-3 also explains why the operating rate of ADSL is higher in the downstream direction than the upstream direction.

Figure 23-3
ADSL frequency
utilization

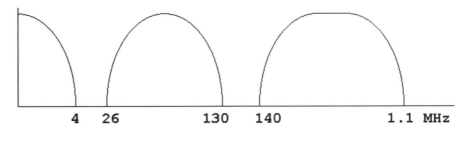

Frequency KHz

Although the exact span distance of ADSL depends upon the quality of the copper cable, communication carriers promote general performance goals. Table 23-2 lists those goals and provides an indication of the downstream data rate you can expect to achieve via an ADSL connection. In examining Table 23-2, note that the term *American Wire Gauge* (AWG) represents a coding scheme that is inversely proportional to the diameter of a metallic conductor. That is, a smaller wire gauge represents a larger wire diameter. Because a larger wire diameter has less resistance to the flow of electrons than a smaller diameter, the transmission distance is greater for a lower AWG than a higher gauge. Both 24 and 26 AWG twisted pair are commonly used by telephone companies, which is why only those two gauges are included in the table.

Although Figure 23-3 indicates that the upstream bandwidth is considerably less than the downstream bandwidth, it is important to note the flow of data in a modern Internet connection environment. In other words, a small amount of data in the form of URLs typically flows from workstations on a LAN to the Internet, while Web pages consisting of significant quantities of data flow in the opposite direction. Thus, ADSL is an ideal technology for organizations that require asymmetric communications and one of the data flows requires the capability of one or more T1 lines. ADSL can provide this capability at a fraction of the cost of T1 lines.

ADSL Modulation

If you are familiar with ADSL, you may be aware of the fact that two different methods of modulation are available that are not compatible with each other. One modulation method, referred to as *Carrierless Amplitude and Phase* (CAP) modulation, was developed by Paradyne when they were

Table 23-2	Data Rate	Wire Gauge	Transmission Distance (feet)
ADSL Performance Goals	1.5/2 Mbps	24	18,000
	1.5/2 Mbps	26	15,000
	6.1 Mbps	24	12,000
	6.1 Mbps	26	9,000

a unit of AT&T. A second modulation method that was standardized by the *International Telecommunications Union* (ITU) is referred to as *Discrete Multitone* (DMT) line coding. Although DMT was also standardized by the *American National Standards Institute* (ANSI), both modulation methods are popular. Recognizing this, Cisco routers can be obtained with port cards that support either CAP or DMT. Thus, you can match the premise router's ADSL modulation method to the method supported by the communication carrier.

Router Connection Considerations

Although most Cisco routers currently support ADSL, it should be noted that support on some Cisco products extend to *Symmetric Digital Subscriber Lines* (SDSL) and *ISDN DSL* (IDSL). Support for SDSL is provided on the Cisco 673 modem, while the Cisco 802 and 804 modems support IDSL. Both SDSL and IDSL are better choices than ADSL when your organization requires an economical T1 substitution and you plan to either perform bidirectional file transfers or host a Web server on your LAN. This is because they provide a symmetric data transfer capability unlike ADSL, which is asymmetric. Because each version of DSL requires a connection to a conventional telephone wire, you simply connect an RJ-11 connector to the applicable DSL card installed in your router. Once this is accomplished, you are ready to configure your router for DSL operation.

Router Configuration

The actual configuration of a Cisco router to support a DSL connection depends upon the operating environment. To understand some of the potential operational environment variations, examine the typical configuration used to provide DSL connectivity. Figure 23-4 illustrates how equipment is used to provide DSL connectivity between a subscriber site and a communication carrier's central office. Note that the router installed at the subscriber site includes a DSL modem and provides connectivity to a *Digital Subscriber Line Access Multiplexer* (DSLAM) located at the telephone company's central office. The DSLAM aggregates communication from multiple subscriber locations that are using a DSL access line and passes the aggregated transmission to a *Universal Access Concentrator* (UAC). To provide an indication of some of the potential operating environments, the operational issues and the configurations required to satisfy those issues will be discussed.

Address Conservation

For the first scenario, assume your organization needs to conserve IP addresses. If the subscriber router and UAC are Cisco 1417 and 6400 devices, respectively, as IOS devices they both support the use of the **ip unnumbered** command. Assume your organization's Ethernet LAN is connected to port E0 on the Cisco 1417 router, and the router's LAN interface has the IP address 198.76.46.1. Also assume that the Cisco 6400 UAC port that connects to the DSLAM has the IP address 192.46.24.2. IP is trans-

Figure 23-4

Using DSL on the subscriber line

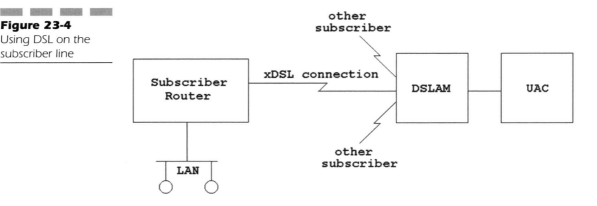

Legend:
    DSLAM   Digital Subscriber Line Access Multiplexer
    UAC   Universal Access Concentrator

ported via ATM because DSL is based upon a cell transport technology, so configure the Cisco router is configured as follows:

```
hostname R1417
!
ip subnet-zero
!
interface E0
 ip address 198.78.46.1 255.255.255.0
!
interface ATM0
 no ip address
 atm vc-per-vp 2048
 atm i|mi-keepalive
!
interface ATM0.1 point-to-point
 ip unnumbered E0
 pvc 1/44
 protocol ip 192.46.24.2
 encapsulation aa|5snap
!
ip classless
ip route 192.46.24.2 255.255.255.255 ATM0.1
no ip http server
!
```

In examining the preceding configuration for the 1417 router, note that the **hostname** command permits a new host name to be assigned to the router. The **ip subnet-zero** command enables the use of subnet zero for interface addressing and routing updates. After defining the IP address to the Ethernet interface, the ATM interface is configured for the WAN connection over the digital subscriber line. The **atm vc-per-vp** command sets the maximum number of VCIs to support per the VPI. In this example, instead of accepting the default of 1,024, 2,048 was configured. After using the **atm-i | mi-keepalive** command, define a point-to-point ATM interface that connects to the 6,400 VAC and support 44 *private virtual channels* (PVCs). Because it is assumed that the 6,400 VAC has the IP address 192.46.24.2, the **protocol ip** command was used with that address followed by the **encapsulation** command to define IP being encapsulated in an *ATM Adaptation Layer* (AAL) 5 *Subnetwork Access protocol* (SNAP).

Using RFC 1483 Bridging

If you maintain the same basic configuration, as previously shown in Figure 23-4, but employ RFC 1483 bridging, bridged packets received on an ATM interface configured in route-bridge mode are routed via an IP header. The rationale for using a route-bridge mode of operation is that it can provide an increased level of performance over integrated routing and bridging. If you assume the same IP addressing, as in the previous example, and use a Cisco 827 router that is capable of supporting routed bridge encapsulation, your router configuration will be as follows:

```
hostname 827 router
!
ip subnet-zero
no ip routing
!
interface E0
 ip address 198.78.46.1 255.255.255.0
!
no ip directed-broadcast
bridge-group 1
!
interface ATM0
 mac-address 0ABC.5F21.13ba
 ip address 198.78.46.1 255.255.255.0
 no ip directed-broadcast
 no ip mroute-cache
 no atm i|mi-keepalive
 pvc 4/100
 encapsulation aal5snap
 bundle-enable
 bridge-group
 hold-queue 244 in
!
ip classless
no ip http server
!
bridge 1 protocol ieee
!
voice-port 1
 timing hookflash-in 0
!
!
voice-port n
 timing hookflash-in 0
!
end
```

Similar to our previous router configuration example, the hostname and ip subnet-zero function as described earlier. Because you use RFC 1483 bridging, turn off ip routing through the use of the **no ip routing** command. Next, assign an IP address to the Ethernet interface and also turn off or disable the translation of directed broadcasts to physical broadcasts. The **no ip directed-broadcast** command prevents a packet with a broadcast address from Layer 3 from being converted into a Layer 2 broadcast. This action is a popular tool used by hackers and other discontented persons, and when directed broadcasts are allowed, it can result in a hacker making a dual attack. That is, a hacker spoofs the IP address of a third party and uses that address to send IP broadcasts to a target network. The result of this action is that the target network converts the Layer 3 broadcast into a Layer 2 broadcast that flows to all stations on the network. All active stations respond, which results in a high level of network utilization. In addition, the responses flow to the spoofed source, thereby permitting a hacker to disrupt two networks at the same time.

Recognizing the previously mentioned problem, Cisco made **no ip directed-broadcast** the default setting under IOS version 12.0. In addition to the directed broadcast problem, it should be mentioned that the two examples covered in this chapter focus upon the configuration required to support a DSL connection and do not include packet filtering that should normally be included in your configuration. For example, it is normally a good procedure to block packets with a source address that equates to stations on your network, RFC 1918 addresses, and the loopback address as those addresses that are popularly used by hackers.

Returning to the configuration example, the **bridge-group** interface configuration command assigns the E0 interface to bridge group number 1. Next, the ATM0 interface is defined. Note that when the router is in a bridge mode of operation, both the Ethernet and ATM interfaces can have the same IP addresses. This is followed by the **mac-address** interface configuration command being used to set the MAC (Layer 2) address of the E0 interface. After disabling three router operations on the ATM interface, you again use the **pvc** and **encapsulation** commands. The **bundle-enable** command associates the bridge-group as a bundle, while the **hold-queue** interface command in this example sets the maximum number of packets in the input queue to 225. Note that the default input hold-queue limit is 75 packets, while the default output hold-queue limit is 40 packets. The **ip classless** command enables the router to forward packets destined to a subnet of a network that has no default router. Thus, this command tells the router to forward such packets to the best supernet router possible.

The command, **no ip http server**, is used to overcome a defect in Cisco IOS software that causes a Cisco router or switch to halt and reload if the IOS HTTP service is enabled and browsing to http://<router-ip>%% is attempted. Hopefully, future releases will correct this problem, rendering the command unnecessary. Last, but not least, the **bridge 1 protocol ieee** global configuration command defines the use of the spanning-tree protocol based upon the *Institute of Electrical and Electronic Engineer's* (IEEE's) Ethernet spanning-tree protocol.

Although a large number of options can be considered when using a DSL, the basic core configuration methods are very similar. That is, a DSL uses

ATM as a transport facility, and you must configure the ATM interface on the router's WAN port. The key differences between configurations are normally based upon a variety of operational environments. In concluding this chapter, the following list outlines some of the operational environments you can consider when using a DSL transmission facility:

- Integrated Routing and Bridging
- RFC 1483 Bridging
- RFC 1483 Bridging with Integrated Routing and Bridging
- RFC 1483 Bridging with Integrated Routing and Bridging and Port Address Translation
- RFC 1483 Routing
- RFC 1483 Routing with Port Address Translation using one allocated IP address
- RFC 1483 Routing with Network Address Translation when assigned a block of IP addresses
- Using PPP over ATM with Internet Protocol Control Protocol

CHAPTER 24

Defining Novell
Networks

Novell networks became the dominant LAN protocol in the early 1990s. Although it could now be classified as a legacy system, as could IP, Novell is given special credence due to its deployment and continued dominance in corporate networks. Internet Packet Exchange (IPX) is actually based on Xerox Network Services (XNS) protocol, but the concept of IPX is akin to IP. Each physical wire on the network is assigned a network number. The hosts on the network, however, are not assigned a Novell networking address. Instead the hosts are addressed by layer 2 of the OSI Reference Model. It is the services of the Novell IPX resources, file and print servers, that utilize the layer 3 network services of IPX.

IPX Processing

Unlike IP routing, IPX processing is not enabled by default in Cisco's IOS. You must manually configure IPX before you can route IPX traffic. In some small designs, you may not find it necessary to route IPX at all. You may, for example, wish to simply bridge two IPX segments together over a WAN connection. In this chapter, we will consider both routing and bridging configurations for IPX.

Configuring for IPX Routing

IPX processing is started using the following global configuration command:

ipx routing

This command assigns a node address for the IPX routing process. The results of this action are displayed when using the show running-config command. The following listing is an example of this display:

```
router# show running-config
Building configuration...

Current configuration:
!
version 11.3
service timestamps debug uptime
service timestamps log uptime
no service password-encryption
service udp-small-servers
```

```
service tcp-small-servers
!
hostname router
!
enable password cisco
!
ipx routing 0010.7b3a.a8b3
!
 —More—
```

Now that IPX processing is initiated, the router is configured to recognize and forward IPX traffic between different IPX networks. This is accomplished by defining unique IPX addresses to each router interface on which IPX is a required network protocol. The IPX address is made up of an IPX network number and node number combination. Cisco IOS assumes the interface's "Burned In Address" (BIA) for the node number when IPX is specified for Ethernet, Token Ring, and FDDI interfaces. For other interfaces, like serial, HSSI, or ATM, Cisco IOS uses the BIA of the lowest available IEEE type interface on the router. If you have a router with only non-IEEE interfaces, Cisco IOS generates a 48-bit quantity to use as the node number for IPX interfaces. Consider this example:

```
router#show interface ethernet0
Ethernet0 is administratively down, line protocol is down
 Hardware is Lance, address is 0010.7b3a.a8b3 (bia 0010.7b3a.a8b3)
```

(additional output omitted)

```
router#config term
router(config)#int e0
router(config-if)#ipx network 10
router(config-if)#end
router#show ipx interface e0
Ethernet0 is up, line protocol is up
 IPX address is 10.0010.7b3a.a8b3, NOVELL-ETHER [up]
```

(additional output omitted)

Examining the output from the **show interface** command, we see that the BIA of Ethernet 0 is the hexadecimal MAC address *0010.7b3a.a8b3*. Likewise, the output of the **show ipx interface** command reveals that Cisco IOS has created an address for our Ethernet 0 interface. The interface uses the 32-bit network number *10* (really 0x00000010—Cisco IOS suppresses leading zeros when displaying network numbers) and the 48-bit node number *0010.7b3a.a8b3* to create an 80-bit IPX address.

In the output above, you will also notice the term NOVELL-ETHER. This refers to the encapsulation chosen for IPX network number *10*. The term describes the OSI Layer 2 protocol that encapsulates the IPX packet before its transmission on the physical network. Novell uses a different term when describing encapsulation formats; the documentation for your NetWare server calls encapsulation "frame type." You have several choices for encapsulation on each interface of your Cisco router. Each Cisco encapsulation option corresponds to a specific Novell frame type. Table 24-1 lists the various frame types.

In order for two directly connected IPX devices to communicate, they must both have addresses on the same IPX network number and they must use the same encapsulation. In Figure 24-1, routers R1 and R2 meet these criteria and are able to communicate. Routers R1 and R3 share the same network number on the link between them, but the administrator has chosen different encapsulations for each router. This misconfiguration will prevent communication between the pair of routers.

Table 24-1

Cisco Encapsulation Type Compared to Novell Frame Type

Cisco Encapsulation	Novell Frame Type
arpa	Ethernet_II
sap	Ethernet_802.2
novell-ether	Ethernet_802.3
snap	Ethernet_SNAP

Figure 24-1

IPX encapsulation misconfiguration.

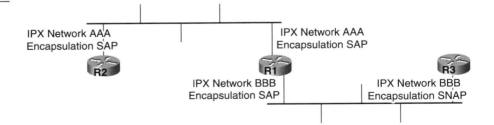

Routing IPX

We have a choice of three dynamic routing protocols for use with IPX. You can also choose to implement static routes in your IPX environment. In this section, we examine the use of three IPX routing protocols:

- RIP
- Netware Link Services Protocol (NLSP)
- Cisco's EIGRP for IPX

We will conclude with a discussion of the use of static routes in an IPX environment.

IPX RIP

When you complete the statements in, "IPX Processing," you also configure IPX RIP routing by default. When you start IPX processing with the **ipx routing** command, Cisco IOS automatically inserts the global configuration command:

```
ipx router rip
```

When you configure IPX network numbers on each of your router's interfaces, IPX also adds commands like

```
router(config-ipx-router)# network 10
router(config-ipx-router)# network 20
```

into the IPX RIP routing section of your running configuration file. As is the case with almost all default commands in IOS, you will not see these commands in the output of the **show running-config** command. You can make the commands visible by inserting a non-default command like

```
router(config-router)# no network 30
```

Observe the result of this configuration using the **show running-config** statement.

Such a configuration will be useful to us when we consider using EIGRP or NLSP to save bandwidth on WAN links. We will choose to disable RIP routing on the WAN interfaces while still running it on the LAN interfaces. The **no network 30** command in IPX RIP routing configuration mode has the effect of stopping IPX RIP broadcasts on the matching interface. In the next two sections, we will see how to replace IPX RIP routing with NLSP and EIGRP on the WAN interface.

You may wonder why we don't dispense with IPX RIP altogether. After all, RIP is relatively bandwidth-intensive and creates a fair amount of processor overhead. Wouldn't it be better to use EIGRP or NLSP to perform all IPX routing? It turns out that this is not a practical approach to improving network performance as devices other than Cisco routers depend on IPX RIP broadcasts for their proper operation. For instance, the process by which a client PC locates and accesses an authentication server requires that a server or Cisco router send it a RIP route.

Consider the network shown in Figure 24-2. We begin our configuration example by enabling IPX processing on each of these routers. We will address each of the interfaces shown in the figure and then examine the IPX RIP routing table that results. Let's begin with router R1:

```
R1(config)#ipx routing
R1(config)#interface e0
R1(config-if)#ipx network 11010
R1(config-if)#no shutdown
R1(config-if)#interface s1
R1(config-if)#ipx network 11020
R1(config-if)#clock rate 64000
R1(config-if)#no shutdown
```

Figure 24-2
IPX internetwork.

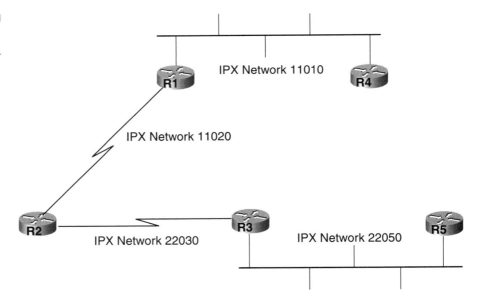

Since we are configuring back-to-back serial connections in the example, it is necessary to supply a clock signal on the DCE-connected interface, **serial 1**. It is unlikely that you will use such a configuration except in a lab environment.

Now we continue our configuration with the remaining routers:

```
R2(config)#ipx routing
R2(config-if)#interface s0
R2(config-if)#ipx network 11020
R2(config-if)#no shutdown
R2(config-if)#interface s1
R2(config-if)#ipx network 22030
R2(config-if)#clock rate 64000
R2(config-if)#no shutdown

R3(config)#ipx routing
R3(config)#interface e0
R3(config-if)#ipx network 22050
R3(config-if)#no shutdown
R3(config-if)#interface s0
R3(config-if)#ipx network 22030
R3(config-if)#no shutdown

R4(config)#ipx routing
R4(config)#interface e0
R4(config-if)#ipx network 11010
R4(config-if)#no shutdown

R5(config)#ipx routing
R5(config)#interface e0
R5(config-if)#ipx network 22050
R5(config-if)#no shutdown
```

We can view the result of our effort by examining the IPX routing table on R5. Use the ***show ipx routes*** command to view the IPX routing table:

```
R5#show ipx route
Codes: C - Connected primary network, c - Connected secondary
network
    S - Static, F - Floating static, L - Local (internal), W - IPXWAN
    R - RIP, E - EIGRP, N - NLSP, X - External, A - Aggregate
    s - Seconds, u - Uses, U - Per-user static

5 Total IPX routes. Up to 1 parallel paths and 16 hops allowed.
```

No default route known.

```
C  22050 (NOVELL-ETHER), Et0
R  11010 [08/02] via 22050.0010.7b3a.d4b3, 16s, Et0
```

```
R   11020  [02/01]  via 22050.0010.7b3a.d4b3, 16s, Et0
R   11030  [08/02]  via 22050.0010.7b3a.d4b3, 16s, Et0
R   22040  [02/01]  via 22050.0010.7b3a.d4b3, 16s, Et0
R5#
```

NLSP Routing

NLSP is the preferred IPX routing protocol for NetWare 4.x servers. It is an IPX implementation of the OSI Intermediate System to Intermediate System (IS-IS) routing protocol. NLSP can be classified as a link-state protocol. That is, NLSP routers establish a neighbor relationship with adjacent devices and then create advertisements of the state of their directly connected networks or links.

NLSP routers use the advertisements to build a database that represents the topology of the IPX internetwork. In order to distribute topology information to distant parts of the internetwork, each NLSP router also forwards each new link state message received from one neighbor to all other neighbors. This process, called flooding, ensures that all routers converge quickly on a new routing solution whenever the internetwork topology changes.

NLSP sends an advertisement, called a Link State Packet (LSP), when the state of a directly connected network changes, such as when a link fails. The router collects LSP's into a link state database. When new LSP's are inserted into the database, a calculation is performed on the entire database, resulting in a table of the best routes to each destination network.

To ensure that routing tables are consistent on all devices in the internetwork, it is essential that neighboring routers have identical databases. NLSP routers synchronize databases with their neighbors using Complete Sequence Number Packets (CSNP) and Partial Sequence Number Packets (PSNP). Every 120 minutes by default, NLSP routers send an advertisement that identifies the LSP's in their link state database. When a router compares the LSP list received from a neighbor with its own table and finds one missing request, it updates its own table.

NLSP creates a hierarchy of routing information within the internetwork. In NLSP, as in its predecessor IS-IS, certain routers share detailed information about destination networks with each other, while other routes only share summarized information. Devices that share detailed information are said to belong to the same NLSP "area."

NLSP routing areas are identified by their area address ranges. Each range is given by an area address and mask. The area address is a 32-bit quantity usually written in hexadecimal digits. The mask, also written in hex characters, identifies the digits that will be common to all networks in the area. A "one" bit in a mask bit position indicates that the position will be common to the networks in the area. A "zero" bit in a mask bit position indicates that the position will be used to differentiate networks that fall within the range (recall that all IPX networks require a unique 32-bit network number). NLSP areas can accommodate from one to three area address ranges.

Three different levels of routing functions are defined for NLSP. In NLSP, routing functions are determined by the neighbor relationship formed between two routers. Any pair of routers can form an NLSP neighbor relationship by exchanging small multicast or broadcast messages called "hello" packets. The messages advertise the area to which a router belongs. Two routers form a Level 1 relationship when they both advertise membership in the same area. A Level 1 router will flood detailed link state information to its Level 1 neighbors. Level 1 routers also belong to the same routing area. Figure 24-3 illustrates Level 1 routers in an area with two address/mask combinations.

A Level 2 neighbor relationship forms between routers that belong to different areas. This relationship is diagrammed in Figure 24-4.

A Level 2 router can also have Level 1 neighbors in its own area. Level 2 routers don't flood LSP's to their Level 2 neighbors. Instead, they send an advertisement of one or more address ranges in the Level 1 area to which they belong. This allows the advertisements of many physical networks to be summarized into only a few area advertisements. Since the size of an internetwork is often limited by the number of networks that show up in each device's routing tables, summarization allows you to design much larger IPX internetworks. In Figure 24-4, we add Level 2 routing to our internetwork.

Level 3 routers further reduce the quantity of routing information maintained throughout the internetwork by allowing you to manually restrict and summarize the advertisements sent between routing domains. NLSP Level 3 routing differs from Level 1 and Level 2 in that it is the IPX implementation of the OSI Inter-Domain Routing Protocol (IDRP). In IOS releases prior to 11.1, Cisco supported only Level 1 routing.

Four tasks are required to configure NLSP routing on your Cisco IOS router:

1. First, you must create an internal network number for the NLSP routing process.

2. Next, you start an NLSP routing process.

Figure 24-3
NLSP Level 1 routing
area.

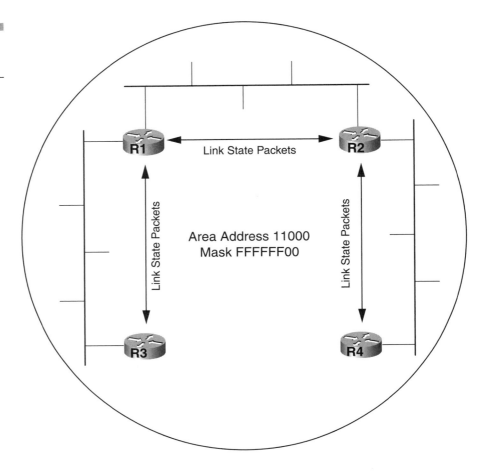

3. Once the process is running, you will specify one or more area addresses for the process.

4. The final step is to specify which physical or virtual interfaces will participate in the NLSP process.

The internal network number represents the routing process to other NLSP routers in the internetwork. It is essential that you choose unique internal network numbers for each NLSP router. If a Cisco IOS router configured for NLSP detects another IPX device with the same internal network number, it will in some circumstances disable its interfaces to prevent corruption of other NLSP databases in the area.

Figure 24-4
NLSP Level 2 routing.

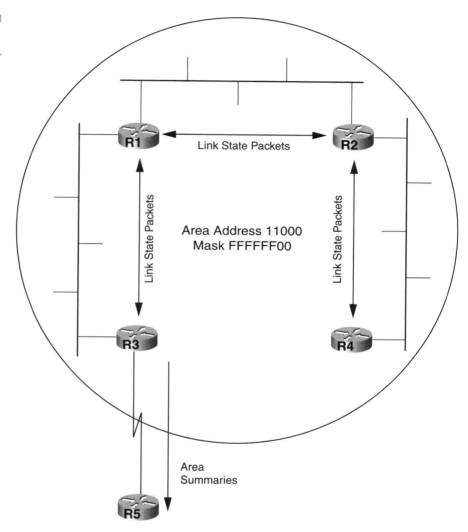

Use the following commands to disable IPX RIP and replace it with NLSP routing on routers 1, 2, and 4, as shown in Figure 24-5:

```
R1(config)#no ipx router rip
R1(config)#ipx internal-network 11001
R1(config)#ipx router nlsp
R1(config-ipx-router)#area-address 11000 FFFFFF00
R1(config-ipx-router)#interface e0
R1(config-if)#ipx nlsp enable
R1(config-if)#interface s0
R1(config-if)#ipx nlsp enable
```

Figure 24-5
NLSP Level 1 routing
example.

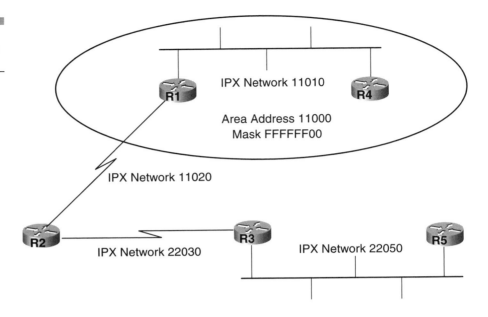

```
R1(config-if)#interface s1
R1(config-if)#ipx nlsp enable


R2(config)#no ipx router rip
R2(config)#ipx internal-network 11002
R2(config)#ipx router nlsp
R2(config-ipx-router)#area-address 11000 FFFFFF00
R2(config-ipx-router)#interface s0
R2(config-if)#ipx nlsp enable
R4(config-if)#interface s1
R4(config-if)#ipx nlsp enable


R4(config)#no ipx router rip
R4(config)#ipx internal-network 11004
R4(config)#ipx router nlsp
R4(config-ipx-router)#area-address 11000 FFFFFF00
R4(config-ipx-router)#interface e0
R4(config-if)#ipx nlsp enable
```

To verify that our NLSP configuration is working, we can examine the
NLSP neighbor list and the ipx routing table. First, let's check the neighbors of R1:

```
R1#
R1#show ipx nlsp neighbor
NLSP Level-1 Neighbors: Tag Identifier = notag

System Id  Interface State Holdtime Priority Cir Adj Circuit Id
R4   Et0    Up 22   64   mc mc R4.01
R2   Se1    Up 55   0    - - 01
R1#
```

As we expected, we see that the R1 has formed relationships with R2 and R4. Now let's see what R4 has learned through NLSP:

```
R4#
R4#show ipx route
Codes: C - Connected primary network, c - Connected secondary
network
    S - Static, F - Floating static, L - Local (internal), W - IPXWAN
    R - RIP, E - EIGRP, N - NLSP, X - External, A - Aggregate
    s - Seconds, u - Uses, U - Per-user static

7 Total IPX routes. Up to 1 parallel paths and 16 hops allowed.
```

No default route known.

```
L   11004 is the internal network
C   11010 (NOVELL-ETHER), Et0
N   11001 [20][02/01] via 11010.0010.7b3a.a8b3, 758s, Et0
N   11002 [47][03/02] via 11010.0010.7b3a.a8b3, 759s, Et0
N   11020 [20][01/01] via 11010.0010.7b3a.a8b3, 759s, Et0
N   22040 [47][02/02] via 11010.0010.7b3a.a8b3, 753s, Et0
NX  22050 [20][08/02][07/01] via 11010.0010.7b3a.a8b3, 759s, Et0
R4#
```

Several items of note show up in the table. First, notice that we see not only the physical networks we configured on the router interfaces, but the internal network numbers as well. We can conclude that our Level 1 routers are functioning properly.

In addition, for the route to IPX network number 20050 in the last line, the type code *NX* appears. This indicates that the route was learned from a source other than an NLSP-level 1 router. In fact, this route was injected into NLSP from the RIP routing process. We will examine the circumstances under which routing information from one protocol is passed into another in the "IPX Route Redistribution" section.

Configuring the NLSP Designated Router   When two or more NLSP routers are connected by a multipoint-capable network such as Ethernet, the potential exists for a large number of relationships to form. Considering the NLSP description to this point, each of n routers connected to the network would form n-1 relationships. The total number of relationships in this arrangement would be given by the formula $n*(n-1)/2$. The relationships would increase exponentially with the number of routers on the network. Obviously, this growth in relationships would consume resources and ultimately limit the number of routers permitted in an NLSP area.

Fortunately, NLSP removes this scalability limitation by defining a special role for one of the routers. A router is "designated" to form a relationship with all other Level 1 routers on the multi-access network. The designated router has extra processing requirements to form and maintain these relationships. It makes sense to select a router with sufficient memory and CPU resources as your designated router.

Designated router selection is based on router priority. Each NLSP router has a default priority of 44. A higher priority router will become the designated router on its multi-access network. To manually configure a router as the designated router, use the **ipx nlsp priority** interface configuration command. To select R1 in Figure 24-4 as the designated router on its ethernet 0 interface, use the following configuration:

```
R1(config)#
R1(config)#interface e0
R1(config-if)#ipx nlsp priority 100
R1(config-if)#
```

You can verify your NLSP configuration using the **show ipx interface** command. First look at R4:

```
R4#show ipx interface e0
Ethernet0 is up, line protocol is up
```

(output omitted)

```
 IPX address is 11010.0010.7b3a.d213, NOVELL-ETHER [up]IPX NLSP is
running on primary network 11010
 RIP compatibility mode is AUTO (ON), last traffic rcvd 16 sec ago
 SAP compatibility mode is AUTO (ON), last traffic rcvd 16 sec ago
 Level 1 Hello interval 20 sec
 Level 1 Designated Router Hello interval 10 sec
 Level 1 CSNP interval 30 sec
 Level 1 LSP retransmit interval 5 sec, LSP (pacing) interval 55
mSec
 Level 1 adjacency count is 1
 Level 1 circuit ID is R1.02
```

```
        Level 1 Designated Router is R1
        R4#
```

On the last line of the show command output, you see that **R1** is the designated router. On the other side of the Ethernet connection, R1 agrees with R4 on the designated router election.

```
R1#show ipx interface e0
Ethernet0 is up, line protocol is up
 IPX address is 11010.0010.7b3a.a8b3, NOVELL-ETHER [up]
```

(output omitted)

```
IPX NLSP is running on primary network 11010
 RIP compatibility mode is AUTO (OFF)
 SAP compatibility mode is AUTO (OFF)
 Level 1 Hello interval 20 sec
 Level 1 Designated Router Hello interval 10 sec
 Level 1 CSNP interval 30 sec
 Level 1 LSP retransmit interval 5 sec, LSP (pacing) interval 55
mSec
 Level 1 adjacency count is 0
 Level 1 circuit ID is R1.02
 Level 1 Designated Router is R1
R1#
```

Configuring NLSP Route Aggregation   In order to implement NLSP Level 2 routing in a Cisco environment, you will configure the NLSP Route Aggregation feature. A Level 2 router will run multiple copies of the NLSP process, one for each Level 1 area to which it belongs. We will use the term "tag" for the NLSP parameter that differentiates each copy of the NLSP process.

An aggregate route contains a 32-bit area address and an eight-bit field that indicates the number of bits common to all the networks in the area range. A router receiving an aggregate route assumes that all network numbers that could fall into the area range are in fact available in the area. For example, if we summarize the routes 22040 and 22050 into an aggregate route, as displayed in Figure 24-6, R4 should see only a single advertised route, 22000, and an indication that the high-order 24-bits are common to all routes in the summary.

If this seems confusing, recall that IPX suppresses leading zeros in network numbers. Thus, network 22040 is represented internally as 0x00022040 and 22050 as 0x00022050. Now consider the left-most 24 bits (six hex digits or 0x000220) as analogous to an IP network number. IPX networks 0x00022040 and 0x00022050 look like two subnets of 0x00022000.

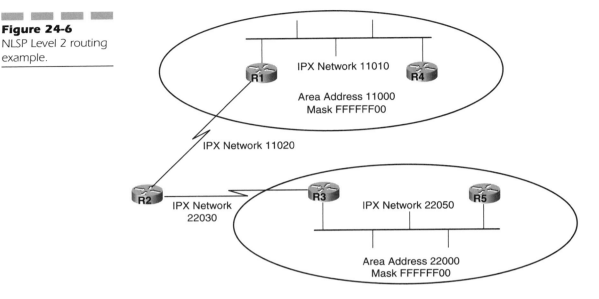

Figure 24-6
NLSP Level 2 routing
example.

Now how might we configure our network to implement the design in Figure 24-6? The syntax below starts an NLSP routing process for area 22000 on R2, R3, and R5:

```
R2(config)#ipx router nlsp Area2
R2(config-ipx-router)#area-address 22000 FFFFFF00
R2(config-ipx-router)#interface s1
R2(config-if)#no ipx nlsp enable
R2(config-if)#ipx nlsp Area2 enable

R3(config)#ipx router nlsp Area2
R3(config-ipx-router)#area-address 22000 FFFFFF00
R3(config-ipx-router)#interface s0
R3(config-if)#no ipx nlsp enable
R3(config-if)#ipx nlsp Area2 enable

R5(config)#ipx routing
R5(config)#ipx router nlsp Area2
R5(config-ipx-router)#area-address 22000 FFFFFF00
R5(config-ipx-router)#interface e0
R5(config-if)#ipx network 22050
R5(config-if)#ipx nlsp Area2 enable
```

Examining the routing tables on R4 and R5 shows interarea routing without aggregate routes.

```
R4#show ipx route
Codes: C - Connected primary network, c - Connected secondary
network
   S - Static, F - Floating static, L - Local (internal), W - IPXWAN
   R - RIP, E - EIGRP, N - NLSP, X - External, A - Aggregate
   s - Seconds, u - Uses, U - Per-user static

10 Total IPX routes. Up to 1 parallel paths and 16 hops allowed.

No default route known.

L   10004 is the internal network
C   11010 (NOVELL-ETHER), Et0
N   11001 [20][02/01] via 11010.0010.7b3a.a8b3, 236s, Et0
N   11002 [47][03/02] via 11010.0010.7b3a.a8b3, 236s, Et0
NX  11020 [47][03/03][01/01] via 11010.0010.7b3a.a8b3, 229s, Et0
NX  11030 [47][03/03][01/01] via 11010.0010.7b3a.a8b3, 236s, Et0
N   22003 [47][03/02]  via 11010.0010.7b3a.a8b3, 236s, Et0
NX  22005 [47][04/03][02/01] via 11010.0010.7b3a.a8b3, 229s, Et0
N   22040 [47][02/02]  via 11010.0010.7b3a.a8b3, 229s, Et0
N   22050 [47][02/02]  via 11010.0010.7b3a.a8b3, 229s, Et0
R4#

R5#show ipx route
Codes: C - Connected primary network, c - Connected secondary
network
   S - Static, F - Floating static, L - Local (internal), W - IPXWAN
   R - RIP, E - EIGRP, N - NLSP, X - External, A - Aggregate
   s - Seconds, u - Uses, U - Per-user static


10 Total IPX routes. Up to 1 parallel paths and 16 hops allowed.

No default route known.

L   22005 is the internal network
C   22050 (NOVELL-ETHER), Et0
NX  10004 [20][04/03][03/02] via 22050.0010.7b3a.d4b3, 179s, Et0
NX  11001 [20][03/02][02/01] via 22050.0010.7b3a.d4b3, 180s, Et0
N   11002 [47][03/02]  via 22050.0010.7b3a.d4b3, 180s, Et0
NX  11010 [20][02/02][01/01] via 22050.0010.7b3a.d4b3, 180s, Et0
N   11020 [20][01/01]  via 22050.0010.7b3a.d4b3, 180s, Et0
N   11030 [47][02/02]  via 22050.0010.7b3a.d4b3, 180s, Et0
N   22003 [20][02/01]  via 22050.0010.7b3a.d4b3, 180s, Et0
R   22040 [02/01]   via 22050.0010.7b3a.d4b3, 187s, Et0
R5#
```

As a final step in implementing Level 2 routing, we must configure the aggregation of individual IPX network numbers. Since R2 is the Level 2 router that interfaces between our two areas, we use this syntax to configure route aggregation:

```
R2(config)#ipx router nlsp
R2(config-ipx-router)#route-aggregation
R2(config-ipx-router)#ipx router nlsp Area2
R2(config-ipx-router)#route-aggregation
```

IPX EIGRP Routing

Cisco's Enhanced Internetwork Gateway Routing Protocol (EIGRP) combines some of the best features of link state protocols with the configuration simplicity of distance-vector protocols. EIGRP has the unique capability to route traffic for three different protocol suites:

- IP
- IPX
- AppleTalk

It isn't necessary to configure all of the protocols, only those of use in your network. In this section, we will examine configuring EIGRP for Novell IPX.

Start EIGRP for IPX   One of the advantages of using EIGRP for IPX is that configuration is trivially simple when compared to NLSP. To enable EIGRP, use the following syntax:

```
router(config)#ipx router eigrp 200
```

This command runs an instance of the EIGRP program on your router. The parameter *200* in this command is called the EIGRP Autonomous System (AS) number. We will see momentarily that the AS number is globally significant and must be configured the same on all routers that you intend to share routing information.

Once the routing process is started, you must specify the router interfaces that you want to participate in EIGRP. Unlike NLSP, we will select EIGRP interfaces while in routing protocol configuration mode, rather than interface configuration mode. Use the *network* command as in the following:

```
router(config-ipx-router)#network 11020
router(config-ipx-router)#network 22040
```

If all the interfaces on your router will process EIGRP, you can simplify the configuration using the keyword **all**:

```
router(config-ipx-router)#network all
```

As soon as you select an interface to participate in EIGRP, a process called "Neighbor Discover" begins. Your router sends a multicast packet on LAN interfaces or a broadcast packet on WAN interfaces to locate other EIGRP routers. These messages are called "hello" packets. EIGRP compiles the results of the discovery process in a data structure called the neighbors table.

When a neighbor is discovered and it belongs to the same EIGRP AS number, our router sends information about the locally configured networks and any networks learned through EIGRP routing. In this sense, EIGRP acts like a distance-vector routing protocol. These advertisements are sent in the form of EIGRP update messages.

When an EIGRP router receives an update message, the information is added to its topology table. The router processes this information to find the best path to each destination network in the topology table. EIGRP uses a metric called Distance to define the best path to each destination. The calculation of the EIGRP metric can include up to five different parameters. By default, only the lowest link bandwidth between your router, the destination network, and the delay encountered by packets passing along the path is taken into account in calculating Distance.

We can examine these details once we configure a sample network. In Figure 24-7, we will configure IPX throughout the network and then configure EIGRP on all the serial links, while leaving RIP active on the Ethernet links. First, starting with R1, we use these commands:

```
R1(config)#ipx routing
R1(config)#interface e0
R1(config-if)#ipx nework 110
R1(config-if)#no shutdown
R1(config-if)#interface s0
R1(config-if)#ipx network 120
R1(config-if)#no shutdown
R1(config-if)#interface s1
R1(config-if)#ipx network 130
R1(config-if)#clock rate 64000
R1(config-if)#no shutdown
```

Figure 24-7
IPX EIGRP routing
example.

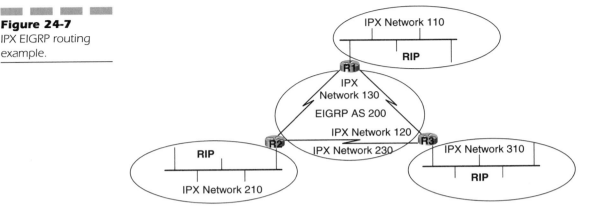

Recall that the *clock rate* statement simply provides the capability to operate two routers in a back-to-back configuration in a lab environment. Continuing with the remaining routers, we use these commands:

```
R2(config)#ipx routing
R2(congif)#interface e0
R2(config-if)#ipx network 210
R2(config-if)#no shutdown
R2(config-if)#interface s0
R2(config-if)#ipx network 130
R2(config-if)#no shutdown
R2(config-if)#interface s1
R2(config-if)#ipx network 230
R2(config-if)#clock rate 64000
R2(config-if)#no shutdown

R3(config)#ipx routing
R3(config)#interface e0
R3(config-if)#ipx network 310
R3(config-if)#no shutdown
R3(config-if)#interface s0
R3(config-if)#ipx network 120
R3(config-if)#no shutdown
R3(config-if)#interface s1
R3(config-if)#ipx network 230
R3(config-if)#clock rate 64000
R3(config-if)#no shutdown
```

With IPX configured on the router, we turn our attention to the routing protocol:

```
R1(config)#ipx router eigrp 200
R1(config-ipx-router)#network 120
R1(config-ipx-router)#network 130
R1(config-ipx-router)#ipx router rip
R1(config-ipx-router)#no network 120
R1(config-ipx-router)#no network 130


R2(config)#ipx router eigrp 200
R2(config-ipx-router)#network 130
R2(config-ipx-router)#network 230
R2(config-ipx-router)#ipx router rip
R2(config-ipx-router)#no network 130
R2(config-ipx-router)#no network 230


R3(config)#ipx router eigrp 200
R3(config-ipx-router)#network 120
R3(config-ipx-router)#network 230
R3(config-ipx-router)#ipx router rip
R3(config-ipx-router)#no network 120
R3(config-ipx-router)#no network 230
```

When this configuration is entered on our small network, the following IPX routing table looks like this on R1:

```
R1#
R1#show ipx route
Codes: C - Connected primary network, c - Connected secondary
network
    S - Static, F - Floating static, L - Local (internal), W - IPXWAN
    R - RIP, E - EIGRP, N - NLSP, X - External, A - Aggregate
    s - Seconds, u - Uses, U - Per-user static

6 Total IPX routes. Up to 1 parallel paths and 16 hops allowed.
```

No default route known.

```
C   110 (NOVELL-ETHER), Et0
C   120 (HDLC),    Se0
C   130 (HDLC),    Se1
E   210 [2195456/1] via  130.0010.7b3a.d4ae, age 00:01:32,
        1u, Se1
E   230 [2681856/0] via  130.0010.7b3a.d4ae, age 00:01:40,
        1u, Se1
```

```
E   310 [2195456/1] via  120.0010.7b3a.d4b3, age 00:01:29,
        1u, Se0
R1#
```

The IPX routing table on R3 looks like this:

```
R3#show ipx route
Codes: C - Connected primary network, c - Connected secondary
network
  S - Static, F - Floating static, L - Local (internal), W - IPXWAN
  R - RIP, E - EIGRP, N - NLSP, X - External, A - Aggregate
  s - Seconds, u - Uses, U - Per-user static

6 Total IPX routes. Up to 1 parallel paths and 16 hops allowed.
```

No default route known.

```
C   120 (HDLC),    Se1
C   230 (HDLC),    Se0
C   310 (NOVELL-ETHER), Et0
E   110 [2195456/1] via  120.0010.7b3a.a8b3, age 00:01:20,
        1u, Se1
E   130 [2681856/0] via  230.0010.7b3a.d4ae, age 00:01:21,
        1u, Se0
E   210 [2195456/1] via  230.0010.7b3a.d4ae, age 00:01:21,
        1u, Se0
R3#
```

With the routing protocol configured, we can examine some of the commands and techniques you will find most useful for troubleshooting your own IPX networks. First, let's look at the EIGRP neighbors table. Use the **show ipx eigrp neighbors** command:

```
R1#sh ipx eigrp neighbors

IPX EIGRP Neighbors for process 200
H Address        Interface Hold Uptime SRTT RTO Q Seq
            (sec)   (ms)  Cnt Num
1 120.0010.7b3a.d4b3  Se0   11 00:05:46 39 234 0 8
0 130.0010.7b3a.d4ae  Se1   14 00:07:21 33 200 0 10
R1#
```

In this display we are looking for the IPX address of our neighboring routers. If a router is missing from this display, we should examine the configuration of both devices to ensure that the same EIGRP AS number is used on both sides of the link. You can also examine details about the EIGRP neighbors discovered on a particular using the **show ipx eigrp interface** command. Here's an example:

```
R3#sh ipx eigrp int s0

IPX EIGRP Interfaces for process 200

      Xmit Queue Mean Pacing Time Multicast Pending
Interface Peers Un/Reliable SRTT Un/Reliable Flow Timer Routes
Se0   1  0/0   257  0/15  1275   0
R3#
```

We see that R3 has discovered R1 on its serial 0 interface.

Besides the ease of configuration, another strong reason for implementing EIGRP is the speed with which it converges after a change in the internetwork topology. Consider, for example, the complete loss of a link, as shown in Figure 24-8.

We can examine the convergence event using IOS debug services. Starting in Privileged Exec mode on R3, issue these debug commands:

```
R3#debug ipx eigrp
IPX EIGRP debugging is on
R3#debug ipx eigrp 200 110
IPX Target enabled on AS 200 for 110
R3#debug ipx eigrp neighbor 200 120.0010.7b3a.a8b3
IPX Neighbor target enabled on AS 200 for 120.0010.7b3a.a8b3
R3#
```

Now it is time to test worst-case convergence in our IPX EIGRP network. We will disable the Ethernet 0 interface on R1 using the **shutdown** interface command to simulate a link failure. Here is the debug output on R3:

Figure 24-8
EIGRP
convergence—loss of
a route.

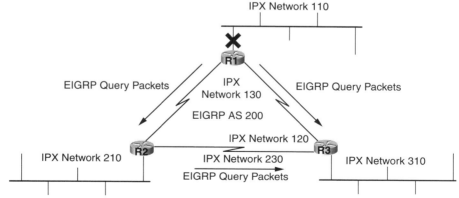

```
00:55:36: IPXEIGRP: 110 via 120.0010.7b3a.a8b3 metric 4294967295
00:55:36: IPXEIGRP: 110 via 230.0010.7b3a.d4ae metric 4294967295
00:55:36: IPXEIGRP: 110 via 120.0010.7b3a.a8b3 metric 4294967295
00:55:36: IPXEIGRP: 110 via 230.0010.7b3a.d4ae metric 4294967295
00:55:36: IPXEIGRP: Received update from 120.0010.7b3a.a8b3 for net
110
00:55:36: IPXEIGRP: worse [0/0/4294967295] route for 110 from
120.0010.7b3a.a8b3, old [65535/255/2195456] route/paths
00:55:36: IPXEIGRP: Received update from 230.0010.7b3a.d4ae for net
110
00:55:36: IPXEIGRP: worse [0/0/4294967295] route for 110 from
230.0010.7b3a.d4ae, old [65535/255/2195456] route/paths
00:55:36: IPXEIGRP: External 110 metric 4294967295 hop 16 delay 44
R3#
```

In the first debug output line, notice that R1 (IPX address **120.0010.7b3a.a8b3**) responds to the link failure by sending an EIGRP update message, setting the metric for network **110** to the maximum value of **4294967295**. The same update message is quickly relayed by R2 in the second line (IPX address **230.0010.7b3a.d4ae**) and the exchange is repeated.

The change in our topology table caused by the loss of R1's Ethernet 0 interface results in a process called the Diffusing Update Algorithm (DUAL). EIGRP routers perform one or two DUAL calculations when the topology changes. If a primary route is lost but an alternate path is available, DUAL performs a "local computation" to determine whether the alternate route can be guaranteed to be loop-free. If the guarantee can't be inferred from the topology table, the router must perform a second "diffusing computation." During this calculation, our router sends an EIGRP query message to the routers listed in the neighbor table asking each one to provide a guaranteed loop-free path to the destination in question. Each neighboring router performs a local computation and, if necessary, a diffusing computation as well. Once the neighbors have made their determinations, they send an EIGRP reply message with information regarding guaranteed loop-free routes.

In our example, we know that there is no alternate path so we are not surprised that both neighbors R2 and R1 send us a reply with Distance still set to the maximum. Notice the time-stamps on the debug message, which is proof of the fast convergence claim. All these events transpired in less than one second. EIGRP is designed to give subsecond convergence in many network designs. In real networks, the actual convergence time is largely governed by the different methods for determining that a given link has failed.

Now let's see what happens when the link returns. Issue the *no shut-down* command on the R1 Ethernet 0 interface. If we were using a distance-vector protocol, we might see several minutes loss of connectivity after the link is restored due to hold-down timers. In the debug output below, we notice subsecond convergence once again.

Now let's look at the case where we do find an alternate path to the destination network. Instead of disabling the Ethernet link on R1, we will fail-out the primary path between network 110 and R3, the R1 serial 0 interface:

```
08:25:43: IPXEIGRP: 110 via 120.0010.7b3a.a8b3 metric 2195456
08:25:43: IPXEIGRP: Received update from 120.0010.7b3a.a8b3 for net
110
08:25:43: IPXEIGRP: create route to 110 via 120.0010.7b3a.a8b3,
metric 2195456
08:25:43: IPXEIGRP: External 110 metric 2195456 hop 1 delay 7
08:25:43: IPXEIGRP: External 110 metric 2195456 hop 1 delay 7
08:25:43: IPXEIGRP: 110 via 230.0010.7b3a.d4ae metric 4294967295
08:25:43: IPXEIGRP: Received update from 120.0010.7b3a.a8b3 for net
110
08:25:43: IPXEIGRP: Received update from 230.0010.7b3a.d4ae for net
110
08:25:43: IPXEIGRP: worse [0/0/4294967295] route for 110 from
230.0010.7b3a.d4ae, old [0/0/2195456] route/paths
08:25:43: IPXEIGRP: External 110 metric 2195456 hop 1 delay 7
08:25:43: IPXEIGRP: 110 via 230.0010.7b3a.d4ae metric 2707456
08:25:43: IPXEIGRP: Received update from 120.0010.7b3a.a8b3 for net
110
08:25:43: IPXEIGRP: Received update from 230.0010.7b3a.d4ae for net
110
08:25:43: IPXEIGRP: worse [0/0/2707456] route for 110 from
230.0010.7b3a.d4ae, old [0/0/2195456] route/paths
R3#
```

Novell NetWare servers before version 4.x software were obligated to advertise all services available on a NetWare internetwork. The protocol used for this process was called the Service Advertisement Protocol (SAP). In a large Novell internetwork, it was common to see many thousands of service advertisements. The SAP protocol required that every SAP-capable device send its entire SAP table as a broadcast onto all networks to which it was connected. The structure of the SAP message allowed seven services to be advertised in each 576-byte IPX packet. Because of this limitation, relatively low-bandwidth links like WAN interfaces could be saturated with repetitive broadcast traffic. This usually resulted in services that disappeared or reappeared from SAP tables at irregular intervals.

Today several alternatives to SAP advertisements are available to Net-Ware administrators. You may choose to use the popular NetWare Directory Service (NDS) or the more recent Service Location Protocol (SLP), for instance. If you must support older 3.x versions of NetWare in your inter-network, you need a way to cope with SAP. Fortunately, EIGRP allows you to stop the periodic broadcast of SAP tables on interfaces with no NetWare servers. EIGRP maintains the SAP table but only sends SAP updates when the table changes. Since traditional SAP devices depend on periodic SAP broadcasts to refresh their SAP table entries, an EIGRP incremental SAP advertisement is only useful on interfaces where our router speaks only to other Cisco routers.

In Figure 24-9, we have a Novell NetWare version 3.2 server connected to the R1 Ethernet0 interface. We can see the advertisement by examining router SAP tables with the **show ipx servers** command:

```
R3#show ipx servers
Codes: S - Static, P - Periodic, E - EIGRP, N - NLSP, H - Holddown,
+ = Detail
U - Per-user static
1 Total IPX Servers
```

Table ordering is based on routing and server info

```
  Type Name        Net  Address Port  Route Hops Itf
  E  4 FileServer_1      110.0000.0c00.1234:0251 2195456/01 2 Se1
  R3#
```

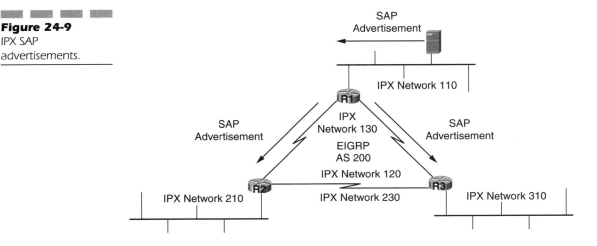

Figure 24-9
IPX SAP
advertisements.

Now we can configure EIGRP on the WAN interfaces to reduce the bandwidth used to advertise our lone server. Use the **ipx sap-incremental eigrp** command on each router's serial interface:

```
R1(config)#interface s0
R1(config-if)#ipx sap-incremental eigrp 200
R1(config-if)#interface s1
R1(config-if)#ipx sap-incremental eigrp 200

R2(config)#interface s0
R2(config-if)#ipx sap-incremental eigrp 200
R2(config-if)#interface s1
R2(config-if)#ipx sap-incremental eigrp 200

R3(config)#interface s0
R3(config-if)#ipx sap-incremental eigrp 200
R3(config-if)#interface s1
R3(config-if)#ipx sap-incremental eigrp 200
```

IPX Static Routes

Static routing is not as easy to implement in an IPX environment as it is with other protocols such as IP. The reason for this is that several services provided by Novell NetWare servers and third-party products require the action of the IPX RIP routing protocol for their functions. One reason for using static routes is to overcome weaknesses of the IPX RIP routing protocol. If you must use IPX RIP, rather than NLSP or EIGRP, perhaps to support another vendor's routers in your IPX internetwork, you can configure static routes and redistribute them into the IPX RIP routing protocol. Redistribution of IPX routing information is the subject of our next section.

The command to create a static IPX RIP route to the network **BADC0FFEE** is

```
R1(config)#ipx route BADC0FFE 110.0000.0c00.1234 6 1
```

In this command, **110.0000.0c00.1234** represents the next-hop gateway for the route, the parameter **6** is the ipx delay or "tick" count associated with the route to **BADC0FFEE,** and **1** is the hop count. You can examine the result of this configuration using the **show ipx route** command:

```
R1#
00:39:51: %SYS-5-CONFIG_I: Configured from console by console
R1#show ipx route
Codes: C - Connected primary network, c - Connected secondary
network
   S - Static, F - Floating static, L - Local (internal), W - IPXWAN
   R - RIP, E - EIGRP, N - NLSP, X - External, A - Aggregate
   s - Seconds, u - Uses, U - Per-user static

7 Total IPX routes. Up to 1 parallel paths and 16 hops allowed.
```

No default route known.

```
C   110 (NOVELL-ETHER), Et0
C   120 (HDLC),    Se0
C   130 (HDLC),    Se1
E   210 [2195456/1] via   130.0010.7b3a.d4ae, age 00:31:54,
         1u, Se1
E   230 [2681856/0] via   130.0010.7b3a.d4ae, age 00:31:54,
         1u, Se1
E   310 [2195456/1] via   120.0010.7b3a.d4b3, age 00:31:54,
         1u, Se0
S BADC0FFE[06/01] via   110.0000.0c00.1234,   Et0
R1#
```

The IPX default route is a special case of a static route. The default route in general represents the path to a device with more complete routing information than our own router. You configure an IPX default route using the **ipx route** statement, as in

```
R1(config)#ipx route default 110.0000.0c00.1234 6 1
```

IPX Route Redistribution

Route redistribution refers to the process by which one routing protocol receives information from another protocol on the same router. In general, IPX routing protocols redistribute information by default. For instance, the two static routes configured on the previous section were automatically redistributed into IPX EIGRP for us. Examining R3's IPX routing table, we see that the default route configured on R1 is now the default route on R3 and the route to network **BADC0FFEE** has likewise been redistributed into IPX EIGRP:

```
R3#show ipx route
Codes: C - Connected primary network, c - Connected secondary
network
    S - Static, F - Floating static, L - Local (internal), W - IPXWAN
    R - RIP, E - EIGRP, N - NLSP, X - External, A - Aggregate
    s - Seconds, u - Uses, U - Per-user static


8 Total IPX routes. Up to 1 parallel paths and 16 hops allowed.
```

Current default route is:

```
E FFFFFFFE [267008000/2] via  120.0010.7b3a.a8b3, age 00:04:37,
        1u, Se1

C   120 (HDLC),   Se1
C   230 (HDLC),   Se0
C   310 (NOVELL-ETHER), Et0
E   110 [2195456/1] via  120.0010.7b3a.a8b3, age 00:45:53,
        7u, Se1
E   130 [2681856/0] via  230.0010.7b3a.d4ae, age 00:45:54,
        1u, Se0
E   210 [2195456/1] via  230.0010.7b3a.d4ae, age 00:45:54,
        1u, Se0
E BADC0FFE [267008000/2] via  120.0010.7b3a.a8b3, age 00:19:57,
        1u, Se1
R3#
```

Virtually the only time you will have to manually configure redistribution in an IPX environment is when you wish to have EIGRP and NLSP share routing information. The command to accomplish this configuration would be

```
router(config)#ipx router eigrp 1
router(config-ipx-router)#redistribute nlsp
router(config-ipx-router)#ipx router nlsp
router(config-ipx-router)#redistribute eigrp 1
```

To reduce the possibility of introducing a routing information loop through redistribution, you will want to ensure that only one device in your IPX internetwork is configured to perform this sort of redistribution.

Bridging IPX

In many simple Novell environments, you may not need to introduce the complexities we have discussed involving the routing of IPX traffic. For instance, if your organization has offices in two buildings with only one Net-Ware 3.11 server, you may consider bridging IPX traffic across a WAN interface. The router will not need to become involved in the IPX SAP process, nor will it send periodic routing updates. In this section, we will discuss the configuration necessary to configure Cisco routers to bridge IPX traffic.

Transparent Bridging

The term "transparent bridging" refers to the process of receiving a link-layer frame of data on one interface and retransmitting it unchanged on another interface of the same type. Except for the buffering delay, the bridging device is invisible or "transparent" to the hosts that are communicating through it. To configure transparent bridging, we must first start an instance of the Spanning-Tree Protocol (STP) to prevent topological loops in our bridged network. Use this syntax to start STP:

```
router(config)#bridge-group 1 protocol ieee
```

Configuring transparent bridging for IPX requires that we identify interfaces that participate in the STP and ensure that the interfaces are not configured to route IPX. Use this syntax to accomplish these tasks:

```
router(config)#interface e 0
router(config-if)#no ipx network
router(config-if)#bridge-group 1
router(config-if)#interface e 1
router(config-if)#no ipx network
router(config-if)#bridge-group 1
```

Encapsulated Bridging

Encapsulated bridging is used when unlike interfaces are configured as part of the same bridge group. When a link-layer frame of data arrives on an interface of one type, such as an Ethernet interface, it is encapsulated in the link-layer protocol appropriate to the outgoing interface, perhaps a serial interface. When the frame is received by another bridge, the serial link header must be removed before the frame is transmitted onto another Ethernet interface in the bridge group. Figure 24-10 illustrates a common encapsulated bridging configuration.

You do not need to specify that encapsulated bridging should be used. It is the default behavior when unlike interface types belong to the same STP. Use these commands to configure the network of Figure 24-10 for encapsulated bridging:

```
R1(config)#interface e 0
R1(config-if)#no ipx network
R1(config-if)#bridge-group 1
R1(config-if)#interface s 0
R1(config-if)#no ipx network
R1(config-if)#bridge-group 1

R2(config)#interface e 0
R2(config-if)#no ipx network
R2(config-if)#bridge-group 1
R2(config-if)#interface s 1
R2(config-if)#clock rate 64000
R2(config-if)#no ipx network
R2(config-if)#bridge-group 1
```

Figure 24-10
IPX encapsulated bridging.

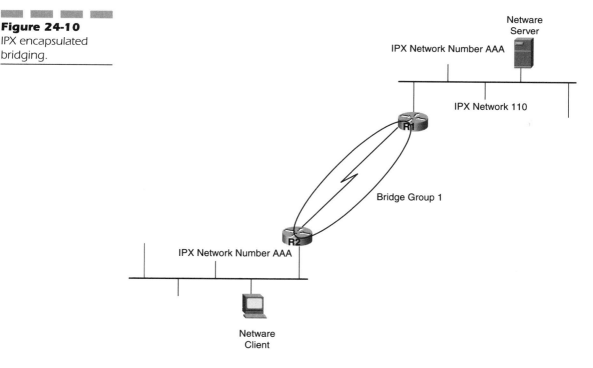

Defining Voice
Networks

This chapter covers the following five VoIP scenarios:

- Simple voice over IP network
- Simple voice over IP network with enhancements
- PBX trunking
- Multipoint Frame Relay configuration
- Additional phone support and management servers

Chapter 25 provides sample configurations for several common voice networking scenarios. Each configuration attempts to provide insight into how the IOS tools set is applied to specific network challenges.

Several configurations are presented beginning with a simple one and quickly progressing to more complex configurations.

Simple Voice over IP Network

The basic configuration represented in Figure 25-1 has been used several times in this book. For the first time, the entire configuration of both routers will be presented. The details are as follows:

- Each site has a Cisco 2610 router, which is used for intersite connectivity over a T1 and for linking two analog phones at each site. An NM-2V with one VIC-2FXS is installed in each of the 2600s. This provides connectivity for the two analog phones and leaves room for an additional two-port VIC to be added later.

Figure 25-1
Simple VoIP network

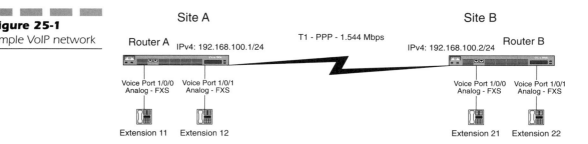

Network Summary

- Routers:
  - Site A: 2610–(1) NM-2V with (1) VIC-2FXS; (1) WIC-2T
  - Site B: 2610–(1) NM-2V with (1) VIC-2FXS; (1) WIC-2T
- Protocols: IP with static routing
- WAN Links: site A to site B–dedicated point-to-point T1
- Management Stations:
  - SNMP: None
  - Syslog: None
- QoS Plan: Weighted Fair Queuing/IP precedence. The T1 provides ample bandwidth to support a maximum of two concurrent calls between sites. Setting the IP precedence to 5 for voice calls ensures that the WFQ scheduler will automatically prioritize voice traffic.

Basic Configurations

The basic configuration for Site A is as follows:

```
Site A-router configuration.
!
version 12.0
service timestamps debug datetime msec
service timestamps log datetime msec
service password-encryption
service tcp-small-servers
!
hostname SiteA2610
!
logging buffered 16384 debugging
enable password xxxx
!
ip subnet-zero
no ip domain-lookup
ip host SiteB2600 192.168.100.2
ip host SB 192.168.100.2
!
voice-port 1/0/0
 description connect to Site A phone 1
!
voice-port 1/0/1
```

```
 description connect to Site A phone 2
!
dial-peer voice 1 pots
 destination-pattern 11
 port 1/0/0
!
dial-peer voice 2 pots
 destination-pattern 12
 port 1/0/1
!
dial-peer voice 3 voip
 destination-pattern 2.
 ip precedence 5
 no vad
session target ipv4:192.168.100.2
!
interface Ethernet0/0
description connection to LAN - SWA port 1/1
 ip address 192.168.1.1 255.255.255.0
 no ip directed-broadcast
!
interface Serial0/0
 description T1 to Site B circuit ID:11104040
 ip address 192.168.100.1 255.255.255.0
 no ip directed-broadcast
 encapsulation ppp
 no ip mroute-cache
!
interface Serial0/1
 description S0/1: not in use
 no ip address
 no ip directed-broadcast
 shutdown
!
ip classless
ip route 192.168.2.0 255.255.255.0 192.168.100.2
no ip http server
!
line con 0
 password 7 104D000A0618
 transport input none
line aux 0
 password 7 060506324F41
 login
 modem Dialin
 flowcontrol hardware
line vty 0 4
 password 7 060506324F41
 login
!
no scheduler allocate
end
```

The basic configuration for Site B is as follows:

```
Site B-router configuration.
!
version 12.0
```

```
service timestamps debug datetime msec
service timestamps log datetime msec
service password-encryption
service tcp-small-servers
!
hostname SiteB2610
!
logging buffered 16384 debugging
enable password xxxx
!
ip subnet-zero
no ip domain-lookup
ip host SiteA2600 192.168.100.1
ip host SA 192.168.100.1
!
voice-port 1/0/0
 description connect to Site B phone 1
!
voice-port 1/0/1
 description connect to Site B phone 2
!
dial-peer voice 1 pots
 destination-pattern 21
 port 1/0/0
!
dial-peer voice 2 pots
 destination-pattern 22
 port 1/0/1
!
dial-peer voice 3 voip
 destination-pattern 1.
 ip precedence 5
no vad
session target ipv4:192.168.100.1
!
interface Ethernet0/0
description connection to LAN- SWB port 1/1
 ip address 192.168.2.1 255.255.255.0
 no ip directed-broadcast
!
interface Serial0/0
 description T1 to Site A circuit ID:11104040
 ip address 192.168.100.2 255.255.255.0
 no ip directed-broadcast
 encapsulation ppp
 no ip mroute-cache
!
interface Serial0/1
 description S0/1 : not in use
 no ip address
 no ip directed-broadcast
 shutdown
!
ip classless
ip route 192.168.1.0 255.255.255.0 192.168.100.1
no ip http server
!
line con 0
 password 7 104D000A0618
```

```
 transport input none
line aux 0
 password 7 060506324F41
 login
 modem Dialin
 flowcontrol hardware
line vty 0 4
 password 7 060506324F41
 login
!
no scheduler allocate
end
```

Configuration Review

The voice port and dial-port defintions are the heart of voice connectivity. The voice ports simply identify the device to which they are connected. Dial peers 1 and 2 assign phone numbers to the physical voice ports. Dial peer 3 defines the VoIP call to Site B and associates the pattern 2 with Site B's router. The IP precedence bits are set to 5, which gives the voice call priority in the weighted-fair-queuing scheduler running on the serial port. Also, because of the abundant bandwidth, voice-activity detection is disabled.

The IP classless command enables the router to forward IP datagrams based upon supernets. The single IP route is for Site B's network (192.168.2.0/24). In this simple scenario, an IP routing protocol is not required.

Simple VoIP Network with Enhancements

Tough times have fallen on the mythical company and the boss doesn't want to pay for the full T1 line charge any more. Not only that, the boss was appalled to find out that no backup was made for the leased line. The solution was to scale the T1 down to a 128 Kbps fractional T1 and to implement ISDN-based dial backup. Figure 25-2 illustrates this new network configuration.

Design Changes

■ Hardware additions:

  ▪ Site A: (1) WIC-1B-U - 1 Port ISDN WIC with integrated NT1
  ▪ Site B: (1) WIC-1B-U - 1 Port ISDN WIC with integrated NT1

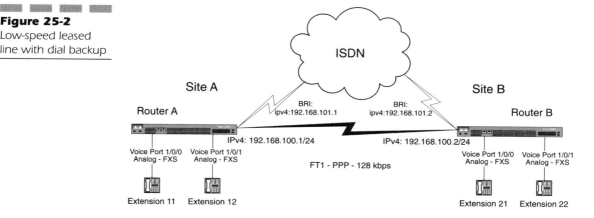

Figure 25-2
Low-speed leased
line with dial backup

- ■ WAN Links:
  - ▪ Site A to Site B: dedicated point-to-point Fractional T1 - 128 Kbps
  - ▪ Site A to Site B: basic rate ISDN dial backup

- ■ Protocols: IP with EIGRP and floating-static routing
- ■ QoS Plan: CRTP, Multilink PPP with LFI, VAD

Configuration Changes The following configuration changes must be made:

1. Configure BRI interface for intersite connectivity.
2. Configure to dial backup over the ISDN link.
3. Configure QoS and link-efficiency techniques for 128 Kbps link.
4. Configure QoS and link-efficiency techniques for dial-backup link.
5. Rework VoIP dial peers to work over primary or backup line.

The first change is to add the BRI interfaces to the routers and configure connectivity over them.

Basic ISDN Configuration Once the BRI interfaces are added, a section will be added into the configuration which looks like the following:

```
interface BRI0/0
 no ip address
 no ip directed-broadcast
 shutdown
```

The basic ISDN configuration is then performed and dialer profiles are used because they are more flexible than legacy backup interface constructs. The resulting configuration is as follows:

```
username SiteB2610 password xxxxx
!
isdn switch-type basic-dms100
!
interface BRI0/0
 description ISDN port: 5554444, 5554445
 no ip address
 no ip mroute-cache
 encapsulation ppp
 bandwidth 128
 isdn spid1 21255544440101 5554444
 isdn spid2 21255544450101 5554445
 dialer pool-member 1
 no cdp enable
!
!
interface Dialer1
 description Dialer-interface to Site B
 ip address 192.168.102.1 255.255.255.0
 no ip mroute-cache
 encapsulation ppp
 dialer remote-name SiteB2610
 dialer idle-timeout 300
 dialer string 5557777
 dialer load-threshold 5 either
 dialer pool 1
 dialer-group 1
 no cdp enable
 ppp authentication chap
 ppp multilink
!
access-list 101 permit ip any any
!
dialer-list 1 protocol ip list 101
!
```

Dial Backup Configuration   To configure dial backup, floating static routes will be used along with EIGRP. While this may be overkill for the small scenario, it is helpful for larger more complex configurations. The plan is to remove the static route for the far site's Ethernet network, and enable the router to learn the route using EIGRP. A new static route for the remote site's Ethernet will be added with a higher administrative distance than that of EIGRP. This route will point to the remote site's dialer interface. In the event of a link failure, the EIGRP-learned route will be removed from the table and the floating static route will be installed, causing traffic to be routed through the dialer interface.

To implement this plan, the following modifications to Router A's configuration are required:

```
!
no ip route 192.168.2.0 255.255.255.0 192.168.100.2
router eigrp 1
 network 192.168.1.0
 network 192.168.100.0
 !
 !
ip route 192.168.2.0 255.255.255.0 192.168.101.2 200
 !
```

Note the administrative distance of 200 assigned to the static route for Site B's Ethernet network.

Configure QoS and Link Efficiency for 128 Kbps Link   The reduction in WAN bandwidth requires that measures be taken to ensure that voice quality does not suffer. To accomplish this, several techniques are applied.

First, the amount of bandwidth required for each call is reduced using compressed RTP. CRTP reduces the bandwidth requirements from 24 Kbps per call to 11.2 Kbps per call.

Second, latency is reduced by implementing multilink PPP with link fragment interleaving. This feature performs Layer 2 fragmentation of packets and provides a mechanism for interleaving priority frames in between fragments of a larger frame. The 20-ms fragment delay causes the router to fragment all frames larger than 320 bytes while the RTP reserve queue ensures that RTP voice frames are interleaved between fragmented packets. This requires that a virtual template be created and used for communication over the serial link.

Third, to further reduce the amount of voice traffic, voice-activity detection is enabled on each VoIP dial peer. With VAD, data are not transmitted when the user is not speaking. VAD can save up to 50 percent of the bandwidth normally consumed.

To implement these changes, the following commands are removed from Serial 0/0 in the router configuration:

```
!
interface Serial0/0
 description T1 to Site B circuit ID:11104040
 ip address 192.168.100.1 255.255.255.0
 !
```

To enable MLPPP with LFI, the following commands are added:

```
!
multilink virtual-template 1
 !
 !
interface Serial0/0
 description FT1 to Site B (128kbps) Circuit ID: 3413413
```

```
 bandwidth 128
 no fair-queue
 ppp multilink
!
!
interface Virtual-Template1
 ip address 192.168.100.1 255.255.255.0
 no ip directed-broadcast
 ip rtp reserve 16384 20
 fair-queue 64 256 1
 ppp multilink
 ppp multilink fragment-delay 20
 ppp multilink interleave
!
```

To enable CRTP, the following commands are added to the router:

```
!
interface Serial0/0
 ip rtp header-compression iphc-format
 ip tcp header-compression iphc-format
!
!
interface Virtual-Template1
 ip rtp header-compression iphc-format
 ip tcp header-compression iphc-format
!
!
```

To enable VAD, the following commands are added to the router:

```
dial-peer voice 3 voip
 vad
```

Note that VAD will not appear in the configuration as its default setting is on.

Configure QoS and Link Efficiency for Dial-Backup Link   For voice calls to receive the same quality of service when the ISDN link is active, the same QoS techniques must be applied. To achieve this, the same commands need to be added to the dialer interface. The necessary additions are presented in the following section:

```
interface Dialer1
 ip rtp reserve 16384 20
 encapsulation ppp
 ip rtp header-compression iphc-format
 ip tcp header-compression iphc-format
 ppp multilink fragment-delay 20
 ppp multilink interleave
!
```

Rework Dial Peers The initial configuration had the VoIP dial peers pointing to the IP address of the remote router's serial port. While this worked well in the limited environment, it will not work when the primary link goes down because the IP address will no longer be reachable. For this reason, it is a good idea to configure dial peers to connect to the IP address of the remote router's Ethernet interface, or if it has one, its loopback interface. The configuration is modified to point the dial peers to the IP address of the remote router's Ethernet interface using the following commands:

```
!
dial-peer voice 3 voip
 session target ipv4:192.168.2.1
!
```

Complete Configurations

The complete configurations for both routers are presented below:

Site A
```
!
version 12.0
service timestamps debug datetime msec
service timestamps log datetime msec
service password-encryption
service tcp-small-servers
!
hostname SiteA2610
!
logging buffered 16384 debugging
enable password xxxx
!
username SiteB2610 password xxxx
ip subnet-zero
no ip domain-lookup
ip host SiteB2600 192.168.100.2
ip host SB 192.168.100.2
!
multilink virtual-template 1
isdn switch-type basic-dms100
!
!
voice-port 1/0/0
 description connect to Site A phone 1
!
voice-port 1/0/1
 description connect to Site A phone 2
!
dial-peer voice 1 pots
 destination-pattern 11
 port 1/0/0
!
```

```
dial-peer voice 2 pots
 destination-pattern 12
 port 1/0/1
!
dial-peer voice 3 voip
 destination-pattern 2.
 ip precedence 5
 session target ipv4:192.168.2.1
!
!
interface Ethernet0/0
description connection to LAN - SWA port 1/1
 ip address 192.168.1.1 255.255.255.0
 no ip directed-broadcast
!
interface Serial0/0
 description FT1 to Site B (128kbps) Circuit ID: 3413413
 bandwidth 128
 no ip address
 no ip directed-broadcast
 encapsulation ppp
 ip rtp header-compression iphc-format
 ip tcp header-compression iphc-format
 no ip mroute-cache
 no fair-queue
 ppp multilink
!
interface BRI0/0
 description ISDN port: 5554444, 5554445
 no ip address
 no ip mroute-cache
 encapsulation ppp
 bandwidth 128
 isdn spid1 21255544440101 5554444
 isdn spid2 21255544450101 5554445
 dialer pool-member 1
 no cdp enable
!
interface Serial0/1
 description S0/1 : not in use
 no ip address
 no ip directed-broadcast
 shutdown
!
interface Virtual-Template1
 ip address 192.168.100.1 255.255.255.0
 no ip directed-broadcast
 ip rtp reserve 16384 20
 ip rtp header-compression iphc-format
 ip tcp header-compression iphc-format
 fair-queue 64 256 1
 ppp multilink
 ppp multilink fragment-delay 20
 ppp multilink interleave
!
interface Dialer1
 ip address 192.168.101.1 255.255.255.0
 no ip directed-broadcast
 ip rtp reserve 16384 20
 encapsulation ppp
```

```
       ip rtp header-compression iphc-format
       ip tcp header-compression iphc-format
       no ip mroute-cache
       dialer remote-name SiteB2610
       dialer idle-timeout 300
       dialer string 5551212
       dialer load-threshold 5 either
       dialer pool 1
       dialer-group 1
       fair-queue 64 256 1
       no cdp enable
       ppp authentication chap
       ppp multilink
       ppp multilink fragment-delay 20
       ppp multilink interleave
      !
      router eigrp 1
       network 192.168.1.0
       network 192.168.100.0
      !
      ip classless
      ip route 192.168.2.0 255.255.255.0 192.168.101.2 200
      no ip http server
      !
      !
      access-list 101 permit ip any any
      dialer-list 1 protocol ip list 101
      !
      line con 0
       password xxxx
       transport input none
      line aux 0
       password xxxx
       login
       modem Dialin
       flowcontrol hardware
      line vty 0 4
       password xxxx
       login
      !
      no scheduler allocate
      end
```

Site B

```
      !
      version 12.0
      service timestamps debug datetime msec
      service timestamps log datetime msec
      service password-encryption
      service tcp-small-servers
      !
      hostname SiteB2610
      !
      logging buffered 16384 debugging
      enable password xxxx
      !
      username SiteA2610 password xxxx
      ip subnet-zero
      no ip domain-lookup
```

```
ip host SiteA2600 192.168.1.1
ip host SB 192.168.1.1
!
multilink virtual-template 1
isdn switch-type basic-dms100
!
!
voice-port 1/0/0
 description connect to Site A phone 1
!
voice-port 1/0/1
 description connect to Site A phone 2
!
dial-peer voice 1 pots
 destination-pattern 11
port 1/0/0
!
dial-peer voice 2 pots
 destination-pattern 12
 port 1/0/1
!
dial-peer voice 3 voip
 destination-pattern 2.
 ip precedence 5
 session target ipv4:192.168.1.1
!
!
interface Ethernet0/0
description connection to LAN - SWB port 1/1
 ip address 192.168.2.1 255.255.255.0
 no ip directed-broadcast
!
interface Serial0/0
 description FT1 to Site A (128kbps) Circuit ID: 3413413
 bandwidth 128
 no ip address
 no ip directed-broadcast
 encapsulation ppp
 ip rtp header-compression iphc-format
 ip tcp header-compression iphc-format
 no ip mroute-cache
 no fair-queue
 ppp multilink
!
interface BRI0/0
 description ISDN port: 5557777, 5557778
 no ip address
 no ip mroute-cache
 encapsulation ppp
 bandwidth 128
 isdn spid1 21255577770101 5557777
 isdn spid2 21255577780101 5557778
 dialer pool-member 1
 no cdp enable
!
interface Serial0/1
 description S0/1 : not in use
 no ip address
 no ip directed-broadcast
```

```
        shutdown
        !
        interface Virtual-Template1
         ip address 192.168.100.2 255.255.255.0
         no ip directed-broadcast
         ip rtp reserve 16384 20
         ip rtp header-compression iphc-format
         ip tcp header-compression iphc-format
         fair-queue 64 256 1
         ppp multilink
         ppp multilink fragment-delay 20
         ppp multilink interleave
        !
        interface Dialer1
         ip address 192.168.101.2 255.255.255.0
         no ip directed-broadcast
         ip rtp reserve 16384 20
         encapsulation ppp
         ip rtp header-compression iphc-format
         ip tcp header-compression iphc-format
         no ip mroute-cache
         dialer remote-name SiteA2610
         dialer idle-timeout 300
         dialer string 5551212
         dialer load-threshold 5 either
         dialer pool 1
         dialer-group 1
         fair-queue 64 256 1
         no cdp enable
         ppp authentication chap
         ppp multilink
         ppp multilink fragment-delay 20
         ppp multilink interleave
        !
        router eigrp 1
         network 192.168.2.0
         network 192.168.100.0
        !
        ip classless
        ip route 192.168.1.0 255.255.255.0 192.168.101.1 200
        no ip http server
        !
        !
        access-list 101 permit ip any any
        dialer-list 1 protocol ip list 101
        !
        line con 0
         password 7 104D000A0618
         transport input none
        line aux 0
         password 7 060506324F41
         login modem Dialin
         flowcontrol hardware
        line vty 0 4
         password 7 060506324F41
         login
        !
        no scheduler allocate
        end
```

PBX Trunking

Proud of your success with a simple VoIP network with enhancements, your boss bragged about it in a meeting and left the meeting with a promise to link the company's newly purchased PBX systems at each site. Four analog E&M trunks are required, so the FXS ports are removed and four E&M ports (2 VIC-2E/Ms) are added to the NM-2V at each site. The new design is depicted in Figure 25-3.

Design Changes

- Hardware additions:
  - Site A: Remove VIC-2FXS and add (2) VIC-2E/M
  - Site B: Remove VIC-2FXS and add (2) VIC-2E/M

- WAN Links: Same as previous
- Protocols: Same as previous
- QoS Plan: Same as previous

Figure 25-3
PBX trunking
scenario

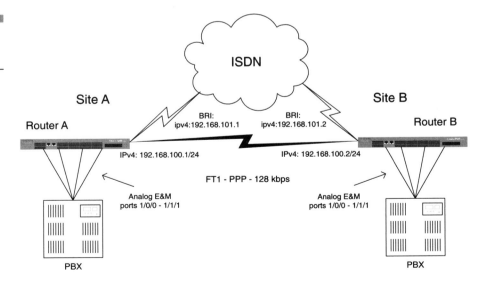

Configuration Changes

1. Configure physical layer parameters.
2. Create virtual trunk between voice ports.

Configure Physical-Layer Parameters   The PBX system's ports are 2-wire E&M type I with wink start. The router commands to support this configuration are as follows:

```
!
voice-port 1/0/0
 description connect to PBX trunk 1
 signal wink-start
 operation 2-wire
 type 1
!
voice-port 1/0/1
 description connect to PBX trunk 2
 signal wink-start
 operation 2-wire
 type 1
!
voice-port 1/1/0
 description connect to PBX trunk 3
 signal wink-start
 operation 2-wire
 type 1
!
voice-port 1/1/1
 description connect to PBX trunk 4
 signal wink-start
 operation 2-wire
 type 1
!
```

The commands for SiteA2610 and SiteB2610 are exactly the same; therefore, only one set of commands is shown.

Create Virtual Trunk between Routers   The first step is to assign destination patterns to the voice ports using dial peers as would normally be done. The following commands achieve this:

Router SiteA2610
```
!
dial-peer voice 1 pots
 destination-pattern 2903001
 port 1/0/0
!
dial-peer voice 2 pots
```

```
 destination-pattern 2903002
 port 1/0/1
!
dial-peer voice 3 pots
 destination-pattern 2903003
 port 1/1/0
!
dial-peer voice 4 pots
 destination-pattern 2903004
 port 1/1/1
!
dial-peer voice 11 voip
 destination-pattern 5561001
 ip precedence 5
 session target ipv4:192.168.2.1
!
dial-peer voice 12 voip
 destination-pattern 5561002
 ip precedence 5
 session target ipv4:192.168.2.1
!
dial-peer voice 13 voip
 destination-pattern 5561003
 ip precedence 5
 session target ipv4:192.168.2.1
!
dial-peer voice 14 voip
 destination-pattern 5561004
 ip precedence 5
 session target ipv4:192.168.2.1
!
```

Router SiteB2610

```
!
dial-peer voice 1 pots
 destination-pattern 5561001
 port 1/0/0
!
dial-peer voice 2 pots
 destination-pattern 5561002
 port 1/0/1
!
dial-peer voice 3 pots
 destination-pattern 5561003
 port 1/1/0
!
dial-peer voice 4 pots
 destination-pattern 5561004
 port 1/1/1
!
dial-peer voice 11 voip
 destination-pattern 2903001
 ip precedence 5
 session target ipv4:192.168.1.1
!
dial-peer voice 12 voip
 destination-pattern 2903002
 ip precedence 5
```

```
  session target ipv4:192.168.1.1
 !
dial-peer voice 13 voip
 destination-pattern 2903003
 ip precedence 5
 session target ipv4:192.168.1.1
 !
dial-peer voice 14 voip
 destination-pattern 2903004
 ip precedence 5
 session target ipv4:192.168.1.1
 !
```

The next step is to configure the virtual trunk between the ports. This is done by applying the connection trunk command to each voice port. The updated voice-port configurations are as follows:

Router SiteA2610
```
voice-port 1/0/0
 description connect to PBX trunk 1
 connection trunk 5561001
 signal wink-start
 operation 2-wire
 type 1
!
voice-port 1/0/1
 description connect to PBX trunk 2
 connection trunk 5561002
 signal wink-start
 operation 2-wire
 type 1
!
voice-port 1/1/0
 description connect to PBX trunk 3
 connection trunk 5561003
 signal wink-start
 operation 2-wire
 type 1
!
voice-port 1/1/1
 description connect to PBX trunk 4
 connection trunk 5561004
 signal wink-start
 operation 2-wire
 type 1
!
```

Router SiteB2610
```
voice-port 1/0/0
 description connect to PBX trunk 1
 connection trunk 2903001
 signal wink-start
 operation 2-wire
 type 1
!
voice-port 1/0/1
```

```
  description connect to PBX trunk 2
  connection trunk 2903002
  signal wink-start
  operation 2-wire
  type 1
 !
voice-port 1/1/0
  description connect to PBX trunk 3
  connection trunk 2903003
  signal wink-start
  operation 2-wire
  type 1
 !
voice-port 1/1/1
  description connect to PBX trunk 4
  connection trunk 2903004
  signal wink-start
  operation 2-wire
  type 1
 !
```

Multipoint Frame Relay Configuration

This scenario shown in Figure 25-4 addresses the challenges of supporting voice connectivity over a multipoint network. A single AS5300 connects to a PBX at the main site, while smaller remote sites use 3620 routers configured with FXS analog ports. WAN connectivity at the central site is facilitated by a single 7206 router, which also supports several local Ethernet segments.

Network Summary

- Routers:

    - AS5300-A: AS5300: (1) 4-port T1 controller card; (2) 24-port voice/fax modules

    - Router A: 3620: (1) NM-2V with (2) VIC-2FXS; 1 2E2W module with (1) WIC-2T installed

    - Router B: 3620: (1) NM-2V with (2) VIC-2FXS; 1 2E2W module with (1) WIC-2T installed

    - Router C: 2610: (1) NM-2V with (1) VIC-2FXS

    - Cisco 7200: 7200: (1) NPE-200 with 64-MB DRAM, 20 MB Flash; (1) PA-4E; (1) PA-4T1

Figure 25-4

Multipoint Frame
Relay network
diagram

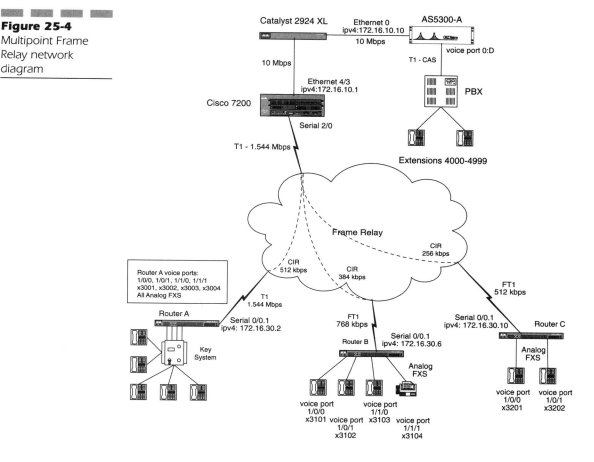

- Protocols: IP with static routing to remote sites
- WAN links:
    - 7200 to Router A: Frame Relay link: 512 Kbps CIR
    - 7200 to Router B: Frame Relay link: 384 Kbps CIR
    - 7200 to Router C: Frame Relay link: 256 Kbps CIR
- Management stations:
    - SNMP: None
    - Syslog: None

■ QoS Plan:

- Frame Relay traffic shaping for bandwidth control
- Reduced mtu for Frame Relay interfaces
- CRTP
- VAD

The dial-peer configuration table is illustrated in Table 25-1.

Table 25-1

Initial Dial-Peer
Configuration Table

Dial-Peer Tag Ext.	Destination Pattern	Type	Voice Port	Session Target	CODEC	QoS
4000	12122904 . . .	POTS	0:D			
3000	161726130..	VoIP		172.16.30.2	G.729	FRTS w/priority queuing (on 7200)
3100	197325731..	VoIP		172.16.30.6	G.729	FRTS w/priority queuing (on 7200)
3200	170344032..	VoIP		172.16.30.10	G.729	FRTS w/priority queuing (on 7200)
1	16172613001	POTS	1/0/0			
2	16172613002	POTS	1/0/1			
3	16172613003	POTS	1/1/0			
4	16172613004	POTS	1/1/1			
4000	12122904 . . .	VoIP		172.16.10.10	G.729	FRTS w/priority queuing
1	19732573101	POTS	1/0/0			
2	19732573102	POTS	1/0/1			
3	19732573103	POTS	1/1/0			
4	19732573104	POTS	1/1/1			
4000	12122904 . . .	VoIP		172.16.10.10	G.729	FRTS w/priority queuing
1	17034403201	POTS	1/0/0			
2	17034403202	POTS	1/0/1			
4000	12122904 . . .	VoIP		172.16.10.10	G.729	FRTS w/priority queuing

Router Configurations

The router configurations for the multipoint network are as follows:

AS5300-A

```
!
service timestamps debug datetime msec
service timestamps log datetime msec
service password-encryption
service tcp-small-servers
!
hostname AS5300-A
!
logging buffered 16384 debugging
enable password xxxx
!
ip subnet-zero
no ip domain-lookup
ip host c7200 172.16.10.1
ip host routera 172.16.30.2
ip host routerb 172.16.30.6
ip host routerc 172.16.30.10
!
!
isdn switch-type primary-5ess
!
!
controller T1 0
 description link to PBX slot 2 port1
 framing esf
 clock source internal
 linecode b8zs
 pri-group timeslots 1-24
!
controller T1 1
 framing esf
 clock source internal
 linecode b8zs
!
controller T1 2
 framing esf
 clock source internal
 linecode b8zs
!
controller T1 3
 framing esf
 clock source internal
 linecode b8zs
!
dial-peer voice 3000 voip
 destination-pattern 161726130..
 ip precedence 5
 session target ipv4:172.16.30.2
!
dial-peer voice 3100 voip
 destination-pattern 197325731..
 fax-rate 9600
```

```
  ip precedence 5
  session target ipv4:172.16.30.6
 !
dial-peer voice 3200 voip
 destination-pattern 170344032..
 ip precedence 5
 session target ipv4:172.16.30.10
 !
dial-peer voice 4000 pots
 destination-pattern 12122904 ...
 direct-inward-dial
 port 0:D
 !
num-exp 4 ...  12122904 ...
num-exp 30.. 161726130..
num-exp 31.. 197325731..
num-exp 32.. 170344032..
 !
voice-port 0:D
 !
voice-port 1:D
 !
voice-port 2:D
 !
interface Ethernet0
 description NY LAN dedicated port to C2924A port 0/10
 ip address 172.16.10.10 255.255.255.0
 no ip directed-brodcast
 !
interface Serial0:23
 no ip address
 no ip mroute-cache
 isdn incoming-voice voice
 no cdp enable
 !
interface Serial1:23
 no ip address
 no ip mroute-cache
 isdn incoming-voice modem
 no cdp enable
 !
interface Serial2:23
 no ip address
 no ip mroute-cache
 isdn incoming-voice modem
 no cdp enable
 !
interface FastEthernet0
 no ip address
 shutdown
 duplex full
 !
 !
no ip classless
ip route 0.0.0.0 0.0.0.0 172.16.10.1
 !
line con 0
 password xxxx
 transport input none
```

```
!
line aux 0
!
line vty 0 4
 password xxxx
 login
!
scheduler interval 1000
end
```

Cisco 7200

```
!
service timestamps debug datetime msec
service timestamps log datetime msec
service password-encryption
service tcp-small-servers
!
hostname 7200
!
logging buffered 16384 debugging
!
boot system flash slot1:c7200-ds-mz_113-8.bin
enable password xxxx
!
ip subnet-zero
no ip domain-lookup
ip host AS5300A 172.16.10.10
ip host routera 172.16.30.2
ip host routerb 172.16.30.6
ip host routerc 172.16.30.10
!
!
interface Serial 2/0
 description FR link to remotes, circuit ID: 5043031
 mtu 640
 no ip address
 no ip directed-broadcast
 encapsulation frame-relay
 no ip mroute-cache
 shutdown
 no fair-queue
 frame-relay traffic-shaping
 frame-relay lmi-type ansi
!
interface Serial2/0.1 point-to-point
 description FR link to routerA - DLCI: 100
 mtu 640
 ip address 172.16.30.1 255.255.255.252
 no ip directed-broadcast
 no ip mroute-cache
 frame-relay interface-dlci 100
  class rtra
 frame-relay ip rtp header-compression
!
interface Serial2/0.2 point-to-point
 description FR link to routerB - DLCI: 101
 mtu 640
 ip address 172.16.30.5 255.255.255.252
```

```
 no ip directed-broadcast
 no ip mroute-cache
 frame-relay interface-dlci 101
  class rtrb
 frame-relay ip rtp header-compression
!
interface Serial2/0.3 point-to-point
 description FR link to routerC - DLCI: 102
 mtu 640
 ip address 172.16.30.9 255.255.255.252
 no ip directed-broadcast
 no ip mroute-cache
 frame-relay interface-dlci 102
  class rtrc
 frame-relay ip rtp header-compression
!
!
interface Ethernet4/0
 description Enet connection to Engineering LAN
 ip address 172.16.1.1 255.255.255.0
 no ip directed-broadcast
 no ip mroute-cache
!
interface Ethernet4/1
 description Enet connection to Sales LAN
 ip address 172.16.2.1 255.255.255.0
 no ip directed-broadcast
 no ip mroute-cache
!
interface Ethernet4/2
 description Enet connection to Admin LAN
 ip address 172.16.3.1 255.255.255.0
 no ip directed-broadcast
 no ip mroute-cache
!
interface Ethernet4/3
 description Enet connection to AS5300 voice gateway LAN
 ip address 172.16.10.1 255.255.255.0
 no ip directed-broadcast
no ip mroute-cache
!
!
ip classless
ip route 172.16.50.0 255.255.255.0 172.16.30.2
ip route 172.16.60.0 255.255.255.0 172.16.30.6
ip route 172.16.70.0 255.255.255.0 172.16.30.10
!
!
map-class frame-relay rtra
 frame-relay cir 512000
 frame-relay bc 32000
 frame-relay be 0
 frame-relay mincir 512000
 no frame-relay adaptive-shaping
 frame-relay fair-queue
!
map-class frame-relay rtrb
 frame-relay cir 384000
 frame-relay bc 24000
```

```
    frame-relay be 0
    frame-relay mincir 384000
    no frame-relay adaptive-shaping
    frame-relay fair-queue
   !
  map-class frame-relay rtrc
   frame-relay cir 256000
   frame-relay bc 16000
   frame-relay be 0
   frame-relay mincir 256000
   no frame-relay adaptive-shaping
   frame-relay fair-queue
  !
  !
  !
  line con 0
   password xxxx
   transport input none
  line aux 0
   password xxxx
   login
   modem Dialin
   flowcontrol hardware
  line vty 0 4
   password xxxx
   login
  !
  end
```

Router A

```
!
version 12.0
service timestamps debug datetime msec
service timestamps log datetime msec
service password-encryption
service tcp-small-servers
!
hostname RouterA
!
logging buffered 16384 debugging
enable password xxxx
!
ip subnet-zero
no ip domain-lookup
ip host AS5300A 172.16.10.10
ip host 7200 172.16.10.1
ip host routerb 172.16.30.6
ip host routerc 172.16.30.10
!
!
!
voice-port 1/0/0
 description Key system port 4
!
voice-port 1/0/1
 description Key system port 5
!
voice-port 1/1/0
```

```
 description Key system port 6
!
voice-port 1/1/1
 description Key system port 7
!
dial-peer voice 1 pots
 destination-pattern 16172613001
 port 1/0/0
!
dial-peer voice 2 pots
 destination-pattern 16172613002
 port 1/0/1
!
dial-peer voice 3 pots
 destination-pattern 16172613003
 port 1/1/0
!
dial-peer voice 4 pots
 destination-pattern 16172613004
 port 1/1/1
!
dial-peer voice 4000 voip
 destination-pattern 12122904 ...
 ip precedence 5
 session target ipv4:172.16.10.10
!
num-exp 3001 16172613001
num-exp 3002 16172613002
num-exp 3003 16172613003
num-exp 3004 16172613004
num-exp 4 ...  12122904 ...
!
interface Ethernet0/0
 description sales and admin LAN
 ip address 172.16.50.1 255.255.255.0
 no ip directed-broadcast
!
interface Ethernet0/1
 no ip address
 no ip directed-broadcast
 shutdown
!
interface Serial0/0
 description FR link 1.544 Mbps circuit id: 3048053
 mtu 640
 no ip address
 no ip directed-broadcast
 encapsulation frame-relay
 no ip mroute-cache
 no fair-queue
 frame-relay traffic-shaping
 frame-relay lmi-type ansi
!
interface Serial0/0 .1 point-to-point
 description PVC to 7200 DLCI 50
 mtu 640
 ip address 172.16.30.2 255.255.255.252
 no ip directed-broadcast
 no ip mroute-cache
```

```
 frame-relay interface-dlci 50
  class rtra
 frame-relay ip rtp header-compression
!
interface Serial0/1
 no ip address
 no ip directed-broadcast
 shutdown
!
!
ip classless
ip route 0.0.0.0 0.0.0.0 172.16.30.1
no ip http server
!
!
map-class frame-relay rtra
 frame-relay cir 512000
 frame-relay bc 64000
 frame-relay be 0
 frame-relay mincir 512000
 no frame-relay adaptive-shaping
 frame-relay fair-queue
!
!
line con 0
 password xxxx
 transport input none
line aux 0
line vty 0 4
 password xxxx
 login
!
no scheduler allocate
end
```

Router B

```
!
version 12.0
service timestamps debug datetime msec
service timestamps log datetime msec
service password-encryption
service tcp-small-servers
!
hostname RouterB
!
logging buffered 16384 debugging
enable password xxxx
!
ip subnet-zero
no ip domain-lookup
ip host AS5300A 172.16.10.10
ip host 7200 172.16.10.1
ip host routera 172.16.30.2
ip host routerc 172.16.30.10
!
!
!
voice-port 1/0/0
```

```
 description phone 1
!
voice-port 1/0/1
 description phone 2
!
voice-port 1/1/0
 description phone 3
!
voice-port 1/1/1
 description fax
!
dial-peer voice 1 pots
 destination-pattern 19732573101
 port 1/0/0
!
dial-peer voice 2 pots
 destination-pattern 19732573102
 port 1/0/1
!
dial-peer voice 3 pots
 destination-pattern 19732573103
 port 1/1/0
!
dial-peer voice 4 pots
 destination-pattern 19732573104
 port 1/1/1
!
dial-peer voice 4000 voip
 destination-pattern 12122904 ...
 ip precedence 5
 session target ipv4:172.16.10.10
!
num-exp 3101 19732573101
num-exp 3102 19732573102
num-exp 3103 19732573103
num-exp 3104 19732573104
num-exp 4 ...  12122904 ...
!
interface Ethernet0/0
 description sales and admin LAN
 ip address 172.16.60.1 255.255.255.0
 no ip directed-broadcast
!
interface Ethernet0/1
 no ip address
 no ip directed-broadcast
 shutdown
!
interface Serial0/0
 description FR link 768Kbps circuit id: 1539349
 mtu 640
 no ip address
 no ip directed-broadcast
 encapsulation frame-relay
 no ip mroute-cache
 no fair-queue
 frame-relay traffic-shaping
 frame-relay lmi-type ansi
!
```

```
interface Serial0/0.1 point-to-point
 description PVC to 7200 DLCI 50
 mtu 640
 ip address 172.16.30.6 255.255.255.252
 no ip directed-broadcast
 no ip mroute-cache
 frame-relay interface-dlci 50
  class rtrb
 frame-relay ip rtp header-compression
!
interface Serial0/1
 no ip address
 no ip directed-broadcast
 shutdown
!
!
ip classless
ip route 0.0.0.0 0.0.0.0 172.16.30.5
no ip http server
!
!
map-class frame-relay rtrb
 frame-relay cir 384000
 frame-relay bc 24000
 frame-relay be 0
 frame-relay mincir 384000
 no frame-relay adaptive-shaping
 frame-relay fair-queue
!
!
line con 0
 password xxxx
 transport input none
line aux 0
line vty 0 4
 password xxxx
 login
!
no scheduler allocate
end
```

Router C

```
!
version 12.0
service timestamps debug datetime msec
service timestamps log datetime msec
service password-encryption
service tcp-small-servers
!
hostname RouterC
!
logging buffered 16384 debugging
enable password xxxx
!
ip subnet-zero
no ip domain-lookup
ip host AS5300A 172.16.10.10
ip host 7200 172.16.10.1
```

```
ip host routera 172.16.30.2
ip host routerb 172.16.30.6
!
!
!
voice-port 1/0/0
 description phone 1
!
voice-port 1/0/1
 description phone 2
!
dial-peer voice 1 pots
 destination-pattern 17034403201
 port 1/0/0
!
dial-peer voice 2 pots
 destination-pattern 17034403202
 port 1/0/1
!
!
dial-peer voice 4000 voip
 destination-pattern 12122904 ...
 ip precedence 5
 session target ipv4:172.16.10.10
!
num-exp 3201 17034403201
num-exp 3202 17034403202
num-exp 4 ...  12122904 ...
!
interface Ethernet0/0
 description sales and admin LAN
 ip address 172.16.70.1 255.255.255.0
 no ip directed-broadcast
!
interface Ethernet0/1
 no ip address
 no ip directed-broadcast
 shutdown
!
interface Serial0/0
 description FR link 512Kbps circuit id: 1539349
 mtu 640
 no ip address
 no ip directed-broadcast
 encapsulation frame-relay
 no ip mroute-cache
 no fair-queue
 frame-relay traffic-shaping
 frame-relay lmi-type ansi
!
interface Serial0/0.1 point-to-point
 description PVC to 7200 DLCI 50
 mtu 640
 ip address 172.16.30.10 255.255.255.252
 no ip directed-broadcast
 no ip mroute-cache
 frame-relay interface-dlci 50
  class rtrb
 frame-relay ip rtp header-compression
```

```
!
interface Serial0/1
 no ip address
 no ip directed-broadcast
 shutdown
!
!
ip classless
ip route 0.0.0.0 0.0.0.0 172.16.30.9
no ip http server
!
!
map-class frame-relay rtrc
 frame-relay cir 256000
 frame-relay bc 16000
 frame-relay be 0
 frame-relay mincir 256000
 no frame-relay adaptive-shaping
 frame-relay fair-queue
!
!
line con 0
 password xxxx
 transport input none
line aux 0
line vty 0 4
 password xxxx
 login
!
no scheduler allocate
end
```

Notes on the Multipoint Frame Relay Configuration

AS5300-A   The AS5300 is configured to speak with all remote sites and the locally connected PBX. All VoIP sessions are set to use IP precedence 5 for added priority. A single default route is configured to forward all traffic to the 7200.

7200   The 7200 is responsible for LAN and WAN routing. Frame Relay traffic shaping is configured to control transmission into the Frame Relay network. A Be of 0 is configured and adaptive shaping is disabled to prevent bursting above CIR. This is done to ensure that all transmitted packets reach their destination. Bursting can be configured, but should be applied carefully as it incurs the potential for lost traffic. Compressed RTP is also configured to reduce the amount of Frame Relay bandwidth consumed by voice traffic. The mtu for the Frame Relay interface is lowered to 640 bytes in order to accommodate latency requirements for the lowest-speed link. The same mtu must be used for all subinterfaces on a Frame Relay interface. Static routes are configured for all of the remote LANs.

Routers A–C   Each of these routers are configured for Frame Relay traffic shaping and compressed RTP to both control traffic rates and reduce the amount of WAN bandwidth consumed by voice traffic. An mtu of 640 bytes is configured to control latency due to serialization delay over the WAN link.

Additional Phone Support and Management Servers

Given the success of the initial voice-over-IP network, a new site has been added in Chicago. It is connected over a T1 link and supports two Ethernet LAN segments, eight analog phones, and four analog links to the PSTN. In addition to the new site, a management station and DNS server have been installed at the main site. The routers should be configured to make use of them as well. Figure 25-5 depicts the new configuration.

Design Changes

- Hardware additions:

  - Router D: 3640–2 NM-2Vs each with (2) VIC-2FXS; (1) NM-2V with (2) VIC-2FXO; 1 2E2W module with (1) WIC-2T installed; DNS Server: IP address 10.1.10.5; NMS/syslog Server: IP address 10.1.10.6

- WAN links: 7200 to Router D: Full T1, 1.544 Mbps
- Protocols: DNS, SNMP, and syslog must be enabled on all of the routers
- QoS plan: RSVP for the new link

Configuration Changes

1. Configure the new link on both the 7200 and Router D.
2. Enable RSVP on the T1 link between Router D and the 7200.

Figure 25-5
Enhanced multipoint
Frame Relay
configuration

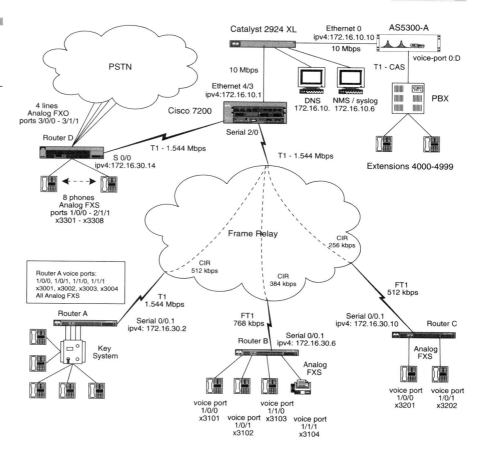

3. Configure FXS and FXO ports on Router D.

4. Configure the AS5300 and Router D to use RSVP when calling the Chicago link.

5. Configure DNS, SNMP, and syslog on all routers.

Configure New Link   To support the new link, the 7200 must allocate another port, and both the 7200 and Router D must be configured with the appropriate IP subnet information. The following commands should be applied to the 7200:

```
!
interface Serial2/1
 description T1 to Chicago-Router D-1.536 Mbps
 bandwidth 1536
```

```
ip address 172.16.30.13 255.255.255.252
no ip directed-broadcast
encapsulation ppp
!
```

Similarly, the 3640 is configured to communicate with the 7200 using the following commands:

```
!
interface Serial0/0
 description T1 to NY-7200-1.536 Mbps
 bandwidth 1536
 ip address 172.16.30.14 255.255.255.252
 no ip directed-broadcast
 encapsulation ppp
!
```

Enable RSVP over the T1 Link   Assuming all 12 phones were active and using the T1 link from Router D to the 7200, 288 Kbps of bandwidth would be required to support the connections. To accommodate this requirement plus that of any other RSVP applications, an upper limit of 640 Kbps reservable bandwidth is set. The upper limit is set to prevent voice and other RSVP applications from taking too much bandwidth from the bandwidth-hungry, non-RSVP applications. To enable RSVP over the T1 link, the following interface command should be added to both routers' serial interfaces:

```
ip rsvp bandwidth 640 192
```

As a result of adding this command, the fair-queuing scheduler for the interface will be updated to reserve queue for the RSVP traffic, and the following command will appear under the serial interface in each router:

```
fair-queue 64 256 20
```

Configure FXS and FXO Ports on Router D   Router D needs to be configured for telephony operation. The same basic techniques are applied to the FXS ports that were applied to the FXS ports in Routers A, B, and C.

The following configuration statements are added to Router D to enable local calling among the FXS ports:

```
!
voice-port 1/0/0
 description phone 1
!
voice-port 1/0/1
 description phone 2
!
voice-port 1/1/0
 description phone 3
```

```
!
voice-port 1/1/1
 description phone 4
!
voice-port 2/0/0
 description phone 5
!
voice-port 2/0/1
 description phone 6
!
voice-port 2/1/0
 description phone 7
!
voice-port 2/1/1
 description phone 8
!
dial-peer voice 1 pots
 destination-pattern 18473183301
 port 1/0/0
!
dial-peer voice 2 pots
 destination-pattern 18473183302
 port 1/0/1
!
dial-peer voice 3 pots
 destination-pattern 18473183303
 port 1/1/0
!
dial-peer voice 4 pots
 destination-pattern 18473183304
 port 1/1/1
!
dial-peer voice 5 pots
 destination-pattern 18473183305
 port 2/0/0
!
dial-peer voice 6 pots
 destination-pattern 18473183306
 port 2/0/1
!
dial-peer voice 7 pots
 destination-pattern 18473183307
 port 2/1/0
!
 dial-peer voice 8 pots
 destination-pattern 18473183308
 port 2/1/1
!
```

The FXO ports present a new challenge. They are used to send calls to the public-switched telephone network. The telephone company has provisioned the links for ground start. To access the PSTN, local users must dial 8, and then they will draw dialtone from the PSTN. The following configuration statements achieve this:

```
!
voice-port 3/0/0
```

```
  description PSTN link 1
  signal groundStart
 !
voice-port 3/0/1
  description PSTN link 2
  signal groundStart
 !
voice-port 3/1/0
  description PSTN link 3
  signal groundStart
 !
voice-port 3/1/1
  description PSTN link 4
  signal groundStart
 !
dial-peer voice 800 pots
  destination-pattern 8
  port 3/0/0
 !
dial-peer voice 801 pots
  destination-pattern 8
  port 3/0/1
 !
dial-peer voice 802 pots
  destination-pattern 8
  port 3/1/0
 !
dial-peer voice 804 pots
  destination-pattern 8
  port 3/1/1
 !
 !
num-exp 33.. 184731833..
 !
```

Router D then needs to be configured to communicate with the main site using voice over IP. As with the other routers, a VoIP dial peer is created referencing the AS5300. The configuration commands are as follows:

```
 !
dial-peer voice 804 voip
  destination-pattern 12122904 ...
  ip precedence 5
  session target 172.16.10.10
 !
 !
num-exp 4 ...  12122904 ...
 !
```

Enable RSVP for Calls over the T1   The serial interface configurations prepared the routers to support RSVP requests from voice and other applications. In order for voice calls to make use of RSVP, they must request reservations on a per-call basis. This function is handled within the IOS by

VoIP dial peers. The following configuration changes are made to Router D to enable RSVP for its calls over the T1 link:

```
!
dial-peer voice 804 voip
 destination-pattern 12122904 ...
 ip precedence 5
 req-qos controlled-load
 session target 172.16.10.10
!
```

The following configuration additions for the AS5300 enable intersite calling to phone extensions in Chicago, the ability to draw dialtone from the Chicago PSTN, and the use of RSVP for these calls:

```
!
dial-peer voice 800 voip
 destination-pattern 184731833..
 ip precedence 5
 req-qos controlled-load
 session target 172.16.30.14
!
dial-peer voice 804 voip
 destination-pattern 8
 ip precedence 5
 req-qos controlled-load
 session target 172.16.20.14
!
!
num-exp 33.. 184731833..
!
```

Configure DNS, SNMP, and Syslog on all Routers   To gain the functionality of the newly installed servers, support must be enabled on the routers. Most of the configuration information is the same for all of the routers and will only be presented once. Exceptions are noted at the end.

```
!
logging buffered 16384 debugging
!
ip domain-name company.com
ip name-server 172.16.10.5
!
!
logging trap debugging
logging source-interface Ethernet0/0
logging 172.16.10.6
access-list 10 permit 172.16.10.6
!
!
snmp-server community public RO 10
snmp-server trap-source Ethernet0/0
snmp-server location NewYork
```

```
snmp-server contact network support: 555-1234
snmp-server chassis-id SHN031400NJ
snmp-server enable traps hsrp
snmp-server enable traps config
snmp-server enable traps envmon
snmp-server enable traps rsvp
snmp-server enable traps frame-relay
snmp-server enable traps voice poor-qov
snmp-server host 172.16.10.6 public
!
```

The exceptions are:

- The contact and location fields should be adjusted to fit each site.

- The trap-source and logging-source should be changed on the 7200 to Ethernet 4/3 and on the AS5300 to Ethernet0.

CHAPTER 26

Defining Security and Firewalls

The Cisco IOS Firewall Feature Set

Cisco has always been a leader in every endeavor they have ever entered. The Cisco *Internetworking Operating System* (IOS) Firewall feature set is a perfect example of this. Most routers are only capable of routing and maybe some standard IP packet-filtering capabilities. The Cisco IOS Firewall option includes features that would normally only be found in dedicated firewalls and application-level gateways. Here are just some examples of its capabilities:

- Context-Based Access Control (CBAC)
- Java blocking
- Denial of Service (DoS) detection and prevention
- Real-time alerts and audit trails
- Dynamic port mapping
- Configurable alerts and audit trails
- Simple Mail Transfer Protocol (SMTP) attack detection and prevention
- MS Netshow support
- Intrusion detection (IDS)
- Dynamic, per-user authentication and authorization or authentication proxy

All these features would constitute a book unto itself. This chapter will cover defining the basic configurations of standard security issues for the routers themselves. Topics will include the following:

- Password protection
- Local and remote access
- Simple Network Management Protocol (SNMP) protection
- Common attack prevention
- DoS prevention
- Anti-spoofing techniques
- Individual host protection techniques
- Context-Based Access Control (CBAC)

So, given that, let's start off with some basic security issues first.

Firewall Design

Cisco has many products that enable multiple security designs, but this handbook deals specifically with the Cisco IOS. The Cisco IOS Firewall feature set is very formidable in and of itself. It can even do the stateful packet filtering we spoke of in the previous chapters. Cisco calls this *Content-Based Access Control* (CBAC). This IOS Firewall feature set also features multiprotocol routing, perimeter security, intrusion detection, *Virtual Private Network* (VPN) functionality, and dynamic, per-user authentication and authorization. It also has provisions for a complete VPN solution based on Cisco IOS *Secure IP* (IPSec) and other CISCO IOS software-based technologies, including *Layer 2 Tunneling Protocol* (L2TP) and *Quality of Service* (QOS). The latest version 12.0.(5) is compatible with almost all the Cisco routers including the 800, 1600, 1720, 2500, 2600, 3600, 7100, and 7200 series.

This section will go over some of the different firewall architectures. Many firewall types have already been discussed, such as packet-filtering, circuit-level, and application-level firewalls or gateways, and any combination of these can be implemented in the following scenarios. The bottom line in firewall design is that you must decide which types of traffic you want to allow. You not only need to consider the types of traffic you let in, but you must also decide on what you will allow to leave. These decisions are critical in any security implementation. It is also very important that you control who can access components such as routers, firewalls, switches, and access servers. Once a person has access to these, he or she can literally allow anything to access the protected information. The architectures that will be covered are the following:

- Screening router or packet-filtering firewall
- Dual-homed firewall
- Screened host firewall
- Screened subnet firewall

Screening Router or Packet-Filtering Firewall

This is the simplest and least expensive firewall design available. Depending on your situation, this might be more than enough. The action a device takes is to selectively control the flow of data to and from a network. The job of a packet-filtering firewall is to either permit or deny packets, depending on their characteristics or content. The most common form of this would be the perimeter router that separates your internal network from that of the Internet or *Internet Service Provider* (ISP). Implementation generally requires that you set up a series of rules for determining which types of packets to permit or deny based on things like IP addresses, protocol types, and their respective destinations. This doesn't have to be a router per se, but even if it is a firewall appliance or individual computer, some form of routing still takes place. The very nature of this design provides a very fast throughput, as screening is done on a hardware level for the most part. An example of this kind of implementation is shown in Figure 26-1.

Dual-Homed Firewall

A dual-homed firewall is essentially a host with two network adapters installed. One adapter is connected to the internal network, while the other is usually connected to the perimeter router that is connected to the public network or Internet, hence the name dual-homed. In this case, the host specifically has its routing capability disabled. Systems on the internal network cannot communicate directly with systems on the public network and vice versa. All communication must happen by proxy through the dual-homed host. This usually happens by running a group of circuit-level proxies or application-level proxies. Additional protection can be provided at the perimeter router by using it as a packet filter. An example of this implementation is shown in Figure 26-2.

Because systems on the Internet cannot route packets directly to the systems on the internal network, you get a much higher degree of security. The host names and IP addresses of the systems on the internal network would be invisible to the Internet because the firewall doesn't pass any *Domain Name System* (DNS) information.

Figure 26-1
A screening router firewall

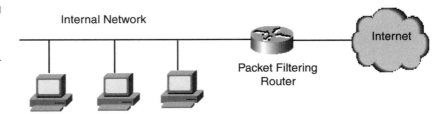

Internal Network

Packet Filtering Router

Internet

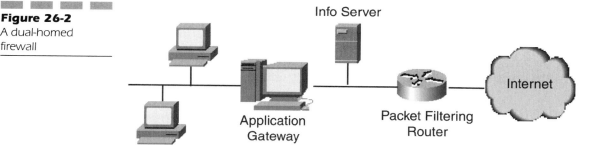

Figure 26-2
A dual-homed
firewall

As you can see, a possible implementation would be to have an information server located on the subnet between the gateway and the router providing proxy services for HTTP, Gopher, and the *File Transfer Protocol* (FTP). Having the information server here adds to the security of the site because, should a malicious hacker penetrate the information server, he or she would still be prevented from reaching internal network systems by the dual-homed firewall. You could even centralize all your email services so that the firewall would accept all site mail and then forward it accordingly.

The only drawback here is that all services to the Internet are blocked, except for those that have been explicitly permitted by the firewall. Any systems that require full access to the Internet would have to be placed on the Internet side of the firewall.

Screened Host Firewall

To solve the issue just mentioned with the dual-homed implementation, you could use a screened host firewall solution. This solves the problem of having all Internet services blocked implicitly. This solution is more flexible but not quite as secure. It is more convenient and still somewhat secure, but it also places more responsibility on the perimeter router. An example of this architecture is shown in Figure 26-3.

This configuration includes a packet-filtering router with an application-level gateway that is on the internal network side of the router. In this case, the application-level gateway needs only one network adapter. This example has the gateway set to enable Telnet, FTP, and any other specific services that have been explicitly permitted by the gateway. The router filters or screens the rest of the traffic before it arrives at the application-level gateway and the rest of the internal network. Now all Internet applications

Figure 26-3
A screened host firewall

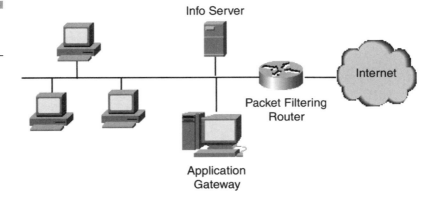

get routed to the gateway and any other traffic is dropped. The perimeter router also prevents all traffic from the internal network from leaving, with the exception of the gateway itself.

Screened Subnet Firewall

The screened subnet firewall adds one more layer of security to the screened host firewall architecture in that it includes a network isolated by two routers. This isolated network is often referred to as the *Demilitarized Zone* (DMZ), an example of which is shown in Figure 26-4.

In this case, you can see that two packet-filtering or screening routers are connected to the DMZ. The first one, the perimeter router, is located between the DMZ and the public network or Internet. The other one is located between the DMZ and the internal network. An attacker would have to first get past the perimeter router, then the firewall, and finally the router on the internal network. This is a very secure setup and many different versions of this design exist, but they pretty much maintain the same idea. When you have a perimeter network, even if someone manages to get past the perimeter router's packet filter and into your application-level gateway, the hacker would only be able to view the traffic on the DMZ. All traffic on the DMZ always should be either to or from the application-level gateway, or to or from the public network or Internet. Because no internal network traffic travels on the DMZ, the internal network traffic is safe from view, even if the application-level gateway were compromised. As you can see, this keeps all application traffic on the DMZ, and the routers on each end filter all other trusted traffic through the DMZ.

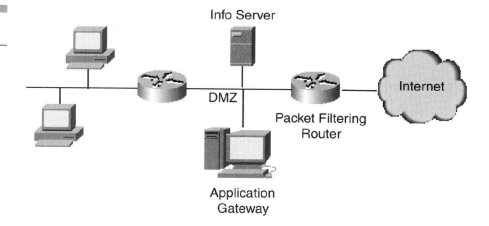

Figure 26-4
The DMZ

First Line of Defense: Router Access

The first line of defense should be applied to the routers themselves. Once a person has access to the router, especially the privileged mode or what is referred to often as enable mode, he or she can take complete control of the router and its behavior. It is essential in a secure environment that access to the enable mode in any router be authenticated and accounted for. The importance of this revolves not only to who can control the behavior of your router, but also to protect the information the router collects from your network. If a person can read the configurations and statistics of the router, he or she can tell a lot about your network's policies, topologies, traffic patterns, routing tables, and protocols. Therefore, controlling who can access a router is more than just protecting one device; it's protecting the topology and integrated operation of all computer systems, configurations, and policies. Cisco routers are accessible in a number of ways, so you should set at least one password for the each of the following four conditions:

- The enable password
- The console password
- The virtual terminal (VTY) line password
- The auxiliary line password

First Things First: Passwords

This section discusses setting up access methods and passwords to the routers themselves, but one quick note is important to mention. For optimal security, the best way to handle passwords is by keeping them on a dedicated *Authentication, Authorization, and Accounting* (AAA) servers such as the *Remote Access Dial-In User Service* (RADIUS) or the *Terminal Access Controller Access Control System+* (TACACS+). That being said, let's move on to setting passwords locally on Cisco routers.

When configuring a router, before you do *anything* else, you should set your passwords. More than a couple of reasons warrant doing this. The first thing to do is to set a password that protects the *enable mode* of the router. This mode, also known as the *privileged* or *privileged EXEC mode*, is the equivalent of an administrator's password that enables you to monitor and configure everything on the router. By default, no password is assigned for the *enable* mode. All that is required is a simple connection to the console port and the **enable** command, as shown in the following code from the *user EXEC mode* (signified by the > symbol after the router name, which in this case is **Router**):

```
Router>enable
Routera
```

To set the enable password, use the **enable secret** global command (once you are in enable mode, the global command mode is achieved by typing the configure terminal command and is signified by the **(config)** after the router name:

```
Router#configure terminal
Enter configuration commands, one per line.  End with CNTL/Z.
Router(config)#enable secret HaRD2GeSs
```

The global command **enable secret HaRD2GeSs** sets the enable password in this example to HaRD2GeSs. Cisco passwords are case-sensitive, and mixing numbers, case, and misspellings while avoiding patterns makes cracking the password with dictionary attacks more difficult. Any attempts to change from user mode to enable mode now require the enable password:

```
Router>enable
Password: <Type the password here. Text is not displayed.>
Router#
```

The following is a list of rules to use when setting passwords:

■ The password must be anywhere from one to 25 upper-case and lower-case alphanumeric characters.

- You cannot use a number as the first character.

- You can have leading spaces, but they will be ignored. However, any and all spaces *after* the first character *are* recognized.

- The password can contain the question mark (?) character if you precede the question mark with the key combination Crtl-V when you create the password. For example, to create the password xyz?123, do the following:

  1. Enter xyz.
  2. Type Crtl-V.
  3. Enter ?123.

- When the system prompts you to enter the enable password, you need not precede the question mark with the Ctrl-V. You can simply enter xyz?123 at the password prompt.

The enable secret command uses the MD5 algorithm (discussed in the "Defining VPN" section), which is a one-way hash function, to store the password. An older command, **enable password**, also sets the enable password but should *not* be used because it uses a simple Vigenere encryption algorithm that can easily be cracked with any modern cracking software available ubiquitously on the Internet.

The algorithm that is used when you enter the enable secret command is irreversible and makes normal password recovery out of the question. However, that is hardly a reason to not use the stronger MD5 algorithm. If you are worried about forgetting the password, just make the password "cisco" and then write it on a post-it note and stick it underneath . . . We're just kidding.

Password Privilege Levels

Cisco IOS supports a total of 16 configurable modes called *privilege levels* numbered from 0 to 15. This hierarchical structure provides more security the higher you go. This means that 0 would have the least privilege and 15 would have the most. By default, a router has two modes: the *user EXEC mode* (upon login) and represents level 1 by default. The *privileged EXEC* or *enable mode* represents the highest level, which is 15. You can configure each privilege level with different command sets and each with different passwords. Then, based on the passwords entered, the person is permitted to execute the commands that you have specified for that level. Table 26-1 displays the commands involved along with some examples. To set the privilege level for a command, use the following commands in global configuration mode:

Table 26-1

Commands

Commands	Purpose
Privilege *command_mode* level *level command*	Specifies the level privilege for a given command.
Enable password level *level* *[encryption-type] password*	Specifies the enable password for that particular level.
privilege level *level*	Specifies a default privilege level for a line.
show privilege	Displays the current privilege level.
enable *level*	Logs in to that specified privilege level.
disable *level*	Exits to that specified privilege level.

Table 26-2

Command mode options

command_mode	Description (prompt)
exec	EXEC mode
configure	Global configuration mode (config)
interface	Interface configuration mode (config-if)
line	Line configuration mode (config-line)
map-class	Map class configuration mode (config-map-clas)
map-list	Map list configuration mode (config-map-list)
null-interface	Null-interface configuration mode (config-if)
route-map	Route map configuration mode (config-route-map)
router	Router configuration mode (config-router)

Table 26-2 is a list of the *command_mode* options listed in the *Commands* column in Table 26-1.

In the following examples, we will use the same **bold** and *italic* structure (in this section only) as in the Commands tables section to help make more sense of the syntax.

The first step in using multiple privilege levels is to configure the passwords for the various privilege levels. Here's an example:

```
enable password level 7 PrIvLvL7
```

In this line, a mid-range level is being specified, level 7, with a password of *PrIvLvL7*. Now that the level and password are set up, go back to EXEC mode. Typing the command from the Table 26-1, **show privilege**, will display our current privilege level, which is 15. Now type in the command **disable 7**, which will take us to privilege level 7. You can confirm this by typing show privilege again. Now, to take you all the way out, type **disable**. Then enter the command, **enable 7**. When you are prompted for the password, enter **PrIvLvL7**. Now if you enter show privilege, you can see that you are right back at privilege level 7.

In order to allow more responsibility to the weight of level 7, use the global configuration command from Table 26-1:

```
Router(config)#privilege command_mode level level command
```

This tells the router which *command_mode* the command fits into, the privilege level, followed by the command with the privilege level that is being adjusted. Let's say you want your level 7 people to be able to do some simple debugging on a few of your Frame Relay operations. Enter configuration mode (at privilege level 15) and configure the following:

```
Router(config)#privilege exec level 7 debug frame-relay autoinstall
Router(config)#privilege exec level 7 debug frame-relay events
Router(config)#privilege exec level 7 debug frame-relay lmi
```

Now anyone you give the level 7 password to can use only the debug commands specified earlier. You should always check the results of these additions prior to releasing the responsibility. To do this, just use the context based help feature (?) to verify your work:

```
Router#disable 7
Router#debug ?
  frame-relay  Frame Relay
Router#debug frame-relay ?
  autoinstall  Autoinstall over Frame Relay
  events       Important Frame Relay packet events
  lmi          LMI packet exchanges with service provider
```

Everything looks fine and now your level 7 people can debug Frame Relay autoinstall, events, and simple *Local Management Interface* (LMI) exchanges. To demonstrate how you can dig even deeper into the *command_mode* structure, let's also do this:

```
Router(config)#privilege exec level 7 ping
Router(config)#privilege exec level 7 trace
Router(config)#privilege exec level 7 configure terminal
Router(config)#privilege configure level 7 interface
Router(config)#privilege interface level 7 ip address
```

Now your level 7 users can use the extended Ping and Trace commands. The third line enables your level 7 people to access configure terminal (global command status) so that they can use the interface command to configure IP addresses. Let's check it again with the context-based help feature to verify your work:

```
Router#disable 7
Router#configure terminal
Configuring from terminal, memory, or network [terminal]?
Enter configuration commands, one per line.  End with CNTL/Z.
Router(config)#?
Configure commands:
  end        Exit from configure mode
  exit       Exit from configure mode
  help       Description of the interactive help system
  interface  Select an interface to configure
  no         Negate a command or set its defaults
Router(config)#int e 0
Router(config-if)#?
Interface configuration commands:
  exit  Exit from interface configuration mode
  help  Description of the interactive help system
  ip    Interface Internet Protocol config commands
  no    Negate a command or set its defaults
Router(config-if)#
```

This ends any further use of the **bold** and *italics* structure that is used to highlight the items in the commands tables. Hopefully now you have some idea as to the granularity and control you can apply through the use of privileges and passwords.

Setting the Console Port Password   Keep in mind that the console port of a Cisco router has special privileges. That is, a hard BREAK signal, sent to the console port during the first few seconds after a reboot, enables one to take complete control of the system. Some password recovery techniques require a terminal to issue a hard BREAK signal. You should find out how your particular terminal or PC terminal emulator issues this hard BREAK signal. For example, in ProComm, the keys Alt+B generate the BREAK signal; in the Windows Terminal program, you can usually press Break or Ctrl+Break; and in Minicom software, it might be Ctrl +A, F. If those don't work, you can always try Ctrl+6, which tends to be pretty universal. Anyway, the point is that anyone who can interrupt power or induce a system crash can initiate a hard boot. If this person has access to the console port by either a hardwired terminal or a modem, he or she can take control of the system, enter a hard BREAK, and have the ability to do as he or she pleases. Still, configuring the console port with a password to discourage the casual intruder is a good idea.

Just in case you don't know what your computer's terminal emulation program settings should be, make sure that you first have the following parameters set:

- VT100 emulation
- 9600 baud
- No parity
- Eight data bits
- One stop bit

When you first get your router, no password, by default, is necessary for console access. You can change this so that even non-privileged people can't log on. To do this, simply enter the following commands during configuration:

```
Router#configure terminal
Enter configuration commands, one per line.  End with CNTL/Z.
Router(config)#line console 0
Router(config-line)#login
Router(config-line)#password HaRD2GeSsCONSOLE
```

You also need to remember that router configurations, by default, do not require passwords on the auxiliary or console lines. If you want to require passwords on these lines, you not only have to set a password on them, but you must *also* configure a **login** command on them. Without the login command, the password prompt does not appear and your password will be ignored.

This sets the non-privileged mode password to HaRD2GeSsCONSOLE. So now when you log into the router, you will see the following:

```
User Access Verification
Password:
```

At which point, you enter HaRD2GeSsCONSOLE, giving you the following prompt:

```
Router>
```

From this point, you can get into global configuration mode (assuming you did the steps in the "First things First: Passwords" section) by typing enable and then entering the original enable secret password, HaRD2GeSs.

Timeout Settings As an added precaution, you can set up a shorter timeout than the default (which is 10 minutes) with the exec-timeout line configuration command using the following syntax:

```
exec-timeout minutes [seconds]
```

Here is how the syntax breaks down:

■ *minutes* is an integer that specifies the number of minutes.

■ *seconds* represents additional time intervals in seconds and is an optional setting. An interval of zero specifies no timeouts.

As an example of what steps you would take, a two-minute, 30-second timeout would be the following:

```
Router#configure terminal
Enter configuration commands, one per line.  End with CNTL/Z.
Router(config)#line console 0
Router(config-line)# exec-timeout 2 30
```

Setting VTY Passwords   This is a very important point. You don't want to find out about the consequences of this at the wrong time. Cisco routers do not have any passwords configured on its VTY ports by default. The point is that, by default, Cisco routers require that you have your passwords set for the VTY lines prior to access by Telnet. If you don't, you will not be permitted into enable mode and will see an error message and be summarily cut loose, as shown in the following code (this would not look good in front of your boss or client, trust me):

```
Your terminal# telnet 10.3.2.1
Trying . . .
Connected to 10.3.2.1.
Escape character is '^]'.

Password required, but none set

Connection closed by remote host.
```

Also, when no enable password exists and you try to connect to the router via Telnet, you will get a very unwelcome response. What will happen is that the message **No password set** is displayed and the prompt returns to user EXEC mode, as indicated by the > character (there's no future in that!):

```
Router>enable
% No password set
Router>
```

To enable Telnet sessions to the router, you must configure a password on the VTY lines. Here is what the configuration looks like:

```
Router#configure terminal
Enter configuration commands, one per line.  End with CNTL/Z.
```

```
Router(config)#line vty 0 4
Router(config-line)#login
Router(config-line)#password HaRD2GeSsVTY
```

This configuration contains the following actions:

- The command line **vty 0 4** tells the router that you want to simultaneously configure all five of the VTY lines numbered 0 through 4. This changes the prompt to line configuration mode, as indicated by the text **(config-line)**.

- The command **login** enables password checking for VTY (Telnet) connections. In VTY's case, this should already be enabled by default, but it is always good practice to enter the command and ensure password checking is on (you won't be sorry you did).

- The last command, **password HaRD2GeSsVTY**, sets the password for the VTY lines to **HaRD2GeSsVTY**.

With passwords on the VTY lines, you can now Telnet to the router and use your password:

```
Your terminal#telnet 10.3.2.1
Trying . . .
Connected to 10.3.2.1.
Escape character is '^]'.

User Access Verification
Password: < Type the password here. Text is not displayed.>
Router>
```

Protecting VTY lines By default, Cisco routers support five simultaneous Telnet sessions, enabling up to five people to log into the router at the same time. The router treats these sessions as logical interfaces called VTY lines. When all the VTYs are in use, no more remote interactive connections can be established. This creates the opportunity for a DoS attack. If an attacker can open remote sessions to all the VTYs on the system, you will not be able to log in. Understand that the attacker doesn't need to actually log in to do this. All that the attacker has to accomplish is to get all of the sessions to be left at a login prompt. You can prevent this by configuring a more restrictive **ip access-class** command on just one of the VTYs in the system (let's say number 4) and just leave the rest alone. You can set this one VTY so that it will only accept connections only from a single workstation or range of IP address. So, if you want to restrict who can Telnet to your router, apply access lists to the logical VTY lines that permit only authorized addresses. Here's an example:

```
access-list 10 permit 10.3.2.0 0.0.0.255
!
line vty 4
 access-class 10 in
```

The command **access-class 10 in** applies access list number 10 to VTY line 4. Only users matching the source criteria **10.3.2.0 0.0.0.255** are allowed to Telnet to the router via that line.

Don't forget about timeouts either. They can be used with VTY line connections as well. So, as an added precaution, set up a shorter timeout than the default (which is 10 minutes) with the exec-timeout line configuration command using the following syntax:

```
exec-timeout minutes [seconds]
```

Adding VTY lines Let's say that you think five simultaneous Telnet sessions are not adequate for your company. Maybe for security reasons you don't want to make it easy to for some attacker to clog up your five VTY lines. However, a means exists for creating more VTY lines. After all, some attackers might assume that once they have clogged up what they think are all of your VTY lines, then they might feel their work is done and move on to greener pastures. To create more VTY lines, all you need to do is enter some **line vty** commands with numbers greater than four. For example, if you were to enter the command **line vty 5 9**, you would create five more VTY lines, numbered 5 through 9. Telnet also uses VTY lines in numerical order, starting with 0 and working up from there. You can just as easily remove the VTY lines by simply using "no" in front of the command, such as the following examples:

- line vty *line-number* increases the number of VTY lines.
- no line vty *line-number* decreases the number of VTY lines.

Setting the Auxiliary Password If you want to access the router remotely via a modem, you will want to perform the same steps as you did earlier. To set the auxiliary password, you just need to enter the following commands:

```
Router#configure terminal
Enter configuration commands, one per line.  End with CNTL/Z.
Router(config)# line aux 0
Router(config-line)#login
Router(config-line)#password HaRD2GeSsAuX
```

Don't forget that router configurations, by default, do not require passwords on auxiliary or console lines. If you want to require passwords on these lines, you not only have to set a password on them, but you must also configure a **login** command on them. Without that command, the password prompt does not appear and your password is ignored.

They same thing goes for the AUX line when it comes to timeouts. They can be used with AUX line connections as well. So, as an added precaution, set up a shorter timeout than the default (which is 10 minutes) with the exec-timeout line configuration command using the following syntax.

```
exec-timeout minutes [seconds]
```

SNMP Security Considerations

This section outlines some guidelines to keep in mind when setting up SNMP security.

Router Access via SNMP

SNMP is simply a protocol that is used to exchange entities called *Management Information Bases* (MIBs) between network devices to help in both management and configuration. SNMP can be used to manage and configure routers. Currently, three versions of the protocol exist: SNMPv1, SNMPv2, and SNMPv3. Version 1 is the most commonly used, yet it presents security problems because of its weak authentication scheme based on a community string, which amounts to a cleartext password transmitted over the network without encryption. Anyone using a network analyzer or sniffer on the network can capture packets and find out the community strings you are using. Once they have the string, they can query or even modify your routers. You can avoid this by using the following command:

```
no snmp-server trap-authentication
```

If you use this command, you can make sure that they can't use trap messages (the messages that SNMP managers and agents use to communicate) to discover these community strings.

Actually, if at all possible, you should always disable SNMP on your perimeter routers. If it turns out that you absolutely have to use SNMP, try to use at least SNMPv2 because it uses the MD5 algorithm. If you must use SNMPv1, make sure you protect it. The means for doing this is discussed later in the chapter.

When using SNMPv1, you should avoid using obvious or default community strings like public or private. You should also avoid using the same community strings on any of your network devices. Be sure to use a different string set for each device or network area. Do not make a *read-only* (RO) string the same as a *read-write* (RW) string. The way to configure community strings on a router is by using the following configuration command:

```
snmp-server community <string> [RO | RW] [access-list]
```

One very important thing should be mentioned here. If you are running SNMPv2 exclusively on your network, you should never use the previous command because doing so automatically enables the weaker SNMPv1 version.

Non-privileged Access

To set up the non-privileged access to your router for SNMP, use the RO keyword of the **snmp-server community** command. Thus, the router agent can only enable the SNMP get-request and get-next-request messages that are sent with the community string, **anynameotherthanpublic**:

```
snmp-server community anynameotherthanpublic RO 1
```

You can also specify a list of IP addresses that are allowed to send messages to the router using the access-list option with the **snmp-server community** command. This way only machines with IP addresses 10.3.2.1 and 10.9.8.7 can access the SNMP non-privileged mode of the router:

```
access-list 1 permit 10.3.2.1
access-list 1 permit 10.9.8.7
snmp-server community anynameotherthanpublic RO 1
```

Privileged Access

To set up the privileged access to your router for SNMP, use the RW keyword of the **snmp-server community** command. This makes it so that the router agent can only enable the SNMP get-request and get-next-request messages that are sent with the community string, anynameotherthanprivate:

```
snmp-server community private RW 1
```

You can also specify a list of IP addresses that are allowed to send messages to the router by using the access-list option of the **snmp-server community** command. This way, only machines with IP addresses 10.3.2.1 and 10.9.8.7 are given access to the SNMP privileged mode of the router:

```
access-list 1 permit 10.3.2.1
access-list 1 permit 10.9.8.7
snmp-server community anynameotherthanprivate RW 1
```

Firewall Configuration Definitions

When defining our firewall configurations, we need to consider the following issues:

- Login banners
- IP source routing
- Controlling ICMP packets
- Disable unnecessary services
- Anti-spoofing techniques
- Avoiding DoS attacks
- Protecting individual machines behind the router

Let's go ahead and get started with login banners.

Login Banners

Login banners are much more important than you might think. In fact, in some states, lack of a warning is an implied invitation for entry. If you want to be able to prosecute anyone who uses your system improperly, the system itself must have a warning banner displayed at all access points. It must warn authorized and unauthorized users of the following:

1. What is considered proper use of the system
2. That the system is being monitored to detect improper use and other illicit activity
3. That there should be no expectation of privacy while using this system

On a Cisco router, to specify a *message-of-the-day* (MOTD) banner, use the **banner motd** global configuration command. To delete the MOTD banner, use the **no** form of this command.

The following is a possible example of the kind of message you might use and how to implement it on a Cisco router. The (**&**) symbol after the **banner** command simply marks the beginning *and* end of the text that should appear in your banner. This is known as the delimiting character. You can use any character you like as long as it is not in the banner message itself:

```
Router(config)#banner motd &
WARNING
This is a private system and is the property of the Unbelievably
Big Company (UBG). It is for authorized use only. Users (authorized
or unauthorized) have no explicit or implicit expectation of
privacy. Any or all uses of this system and all files on this
system may be intercepted, monitored, recorded, copied, audited,
inspected, or disclosed to an authorized site, UBG, law enforcement
personnel, or authorized officials of other agencies, both domestic
and foreign. By using this system, the user consents to such
interception, monitoring, recording, copying, auditing, inspection,
and disclosure at the discretion of authorized site or Department
of Energy personnel. Unauthorized or improper use of this system
may result in administrative disciplinary action and civil and
criminal penalties. By continuing to use this system, you indicate
your awareness of and consent to these terms and conditions of use.
LOG OFF IMMEDIATELY if you do not agree to the conditions stated in
this warning.
```

IP Source Routing

IP has a feature called source routing that permits the sender of an IP datagram to control the route that the datagram takes toward its ultimate destination, as well as the route that the reply will take. This enables a person to send data from one machine and make it look like it came from somewhere else. Many malicious hackers depend on the capability to influence the paths that datagrams take through the network. Once they are in control of the routing path, they can spoof the address of another user's machine and have the return traffic sent to them. They could even intercept and read something intended for someone else or simply use it to create a DoS to the network.

These options are not used very much these days for legitimate purposes in most networks. Some older IP implementations do not process source-routed packets properly, and it may be possible to crash machines running these implementations by sending them datagrams with source-routing options. The command you would use on a Cisco router is as follows:

```
no ip source-route
```

Most modern operating systems can be configured to drop IP packets with source-routing options, but it is always a good idea to drop these packets at the perimeter routers anyway.

Controlling ICMP packets

A lot of attacks take advantage of the ICMP protocol, and you should always limit which types of ICMP messages are allowed. At a minimum, in order to allow for *Path MTU* (PMTU) discovery, you should consider permitting packet-too-big messages. The other types of ICMP messages that are allowed depend upon the local security policy. ICMP is quite different from the *Transmission Control Protocol* (TCP) and the *User Datagram Protocol* (UDP) because no source or destination ports are included in ICMP packets. This presents some interesting challenges when trying to filter certain packets. Malicious hackers know this and are quick to take advantage of these challenges. Fortunately, the packet includes something that can help you out when filtering. That something is the Message Type field, which is used to identify the purpose of the ICMP packet. The most common message types are namely

- 0 or echo reply
- 3 or destination unreachable
- 4 or source quench
- 5 or redirect
- 8 or echo request
- 11 or time exceeded
- 12 or parameter problem

With that in mind, let's go over some possible exceptions you might provide for configuring your router. Remember, depending on your situation, you might have to allow or deny other message types:

```
ip access-list extended ethernet1-in
```

Add the following lines accordingly. To allow fragmentation needed messages (type 3 code 4), use

```
permit icmp any 10.9.8.0 0.0.0.255 packet-too-big
```

To allow outbound ping and MS style traceroute (type 0), use

```
permit icmp any 10.9.8.0 0.0.0.255 echo-reply
```

To allow ping to the inside network (type 8), use

```
permit icmp any 192.168.0.0 0.0.255.255 echo
```

To allow traceroute, use

```
Permit icmp any 10.9.8.0 0.0.0.255 ttl-exceeded
```

Apply the following to inbound packets on the inside Ethernet interface:

```
interface Ethernet1
        ip access-group ethernet1-in in
```

IP unreachables   By default, when an access list drops a packet, the router returns a type 3, code 13 ICMP (administratively prohibited) message. This could enable a malicious hacker to learn that the router implements access-list filters. Most information-gathering attacks, such as UDP scans, also rely on the target sending back unreachable messages. To stop UDP scans, you can prevent the router from sending any ICMP type 3 (unreachable) messages by using the following command on each interface:

```
no ip unreachables
```

IP redirects   Another way that a malicious hacker can penetrate your security is by getting your systems to send data to the wrong address. This technique uses ICMP redirect packets to fool these systems. To turn off this feature, enter the following interface command:

```
no ip redirects
```

Disable Unnecessary Services

The first rule of security is to not allow that which is not needed. It's just one more way into the network. By default, IOS versions 12.0 and above have these small services disabled. However, all versions of IOS starting from 11.3 and down have these small services enabled. Examples of these services would be echo, chargen, and discard.

Let's say that a malicious hacker sends a DNS packet that says its source address is some DNS server that would in normal situations be unreachable and that also says the source port is DNS service port 53. If this packet is sent to the router's UDP echo port, the router would send a DNS packet to this normally unreachable server. The router would then believe that the server had actually generated the packet. This would mean that none of the outgoing access lists would ever be applied to this packet.

Thus, let's disable these unnecessary services, so that this malicious hacker can't get information on your network or perform DoS attacks. You'll use the following commands:

```
no service udp-small-servers
no service tcp-small-servers
no service finger
no ip bootp server
no ip http server
```

Cisco Discovery Protocol The *Cisco Discovery Protocol* (CDP) is designed to enable network management applications to discover any Cisco devices that are neighbors of already known devices. The threat lies in the fact that it enables any system on a directly connected segment to learn that the router is a Cisco device, its model number, and the Cisco IOS software version being run. This information could be used to exploit any weaknesses that may have been discovered for a particular router series. The CDP protocol may be disabled on all your interfaces with the following global configuration command:

```
no cdp running
```

If you want to turn CDP off on a specific interface, you can use the following interface command:

```
no cdp enable
```

Network Time Protocol The *Network Time Protocol* (NTP) isn't all that dangerous in and of itself, but, as we mentioned earlier, any unnecessary service is a possible method of entering your network. If you are going to use NTP, you must make absolutely certain that it is configured to use a trusted time source and authentication scheme. You can actually get around some security protocols by simply corrupting the time base. To disable this service, use the following interface command:

```
no ntp enable
```

The Finger Service Cisco routers provide an implementation for preventing a hacking tool called the finger service. This is a favorite of hackers when running information-gathering attacks, but is rarely used or allowed anymore. The finger service can be disabled with the following command:

```
no service finger
```

Proxy ARP   The router uses proxy ARP to help hosts with no routing knowledge determine the hardware addresses of hosts on other networks or subnets. When the router receives an ARP Request for a host that is not on the same network as the ARP Request sender, and if the router has the best route to that host, then the router sends an ARP Reply packet, providing its own local data link address. The host that sent the ARP Request then sends its packets to the router, which forwards them to the intended host.

That's how proxy ARP was *intended* to be used. Unfortunately, hackers don't quite see it in such a helpful light. They use this to trick packets into being sent where they shouldn't. Cisco enables proxy ARP on all interfaces by default. To disable this, enter the following interface command:

```
no ip proxy-arp
```

Anti-Spoofing Techniques

The idea behind anti-spoofing is that no one from the outside network should be sending packets to you with a source address of either your inside network address or certain well-known and reserved addresses. You will use access lists to drop and log any of these packets:

```
ip access-list extended ethernet1-in
```

The following shows some examples of anti-spoofing. The first one denies packets with a source address that equals our inside net:

```
deny ip 192.168.0.0 0.0.255.255 any log
```

This denies first octet zeros, all ones, and a loopback network:

```
    deny ip 0.0.0.0 0.255.255.255 any log
    deny ip host 255.255.255.255 any log
    deny ip 127.0.0.0 0.255.255.255 any log
```

This denies class D (multicast) and class E (reserved for future use):

```
    deny ip 224.0.0.0 15.255.255.255 any log
    deny ip 240.0.0.0 7.255.255.255 any log
```

This denies RFC 1918 addresses:

```
    deny ip 10.0.0.0 0.255.255.255 any log
    deny ip 172.16.0.0 0.15.255.255 any log
    deny ip 192.168.0.0 0.0.255.255 any log
```

This denies the "test" network addresses. See RFC 1062 if this sounds new. This RFC is actually quite readable and good to know.

```
deny ip 192.0.2.0 0.0.0.255 any log
```

This denies end node autoconfig:

```
deny ip 169.254.0.0 0.0.255.255 any log
```

Apply the following to inbound packets on the inside Ethernet interface:

```
interface Ethernet1
ip access-group ethernet1-in in
```

Using Ingress Filtering to Stop Untrusted Internal Hosts

Suppose your internal network has untrusted hosts or users. You might want to use what is known as *ingress filtering*. When you deny packets with spoofed source addresses, ingress filtering prevents untrusted hosts on your internal network from launching some DoS attacks. To do this, allow your valid inside addresses and then deny all others:

```
ip access-list extended ethernet0-in
 permit ip 10.9.8.0 0.0.0.255 any
 deny ip any any log
```

Now apply this to inbound packets on the inside interface:

```
interface Ethernet0
 ip access-group ethernet0-in in
```

Smurf Attacks

Smurf attacks are continuing to plague the Internet. If you don't take appropriate steps, you can be either a victim or an amplifier in a smurf attack. To prevent your network from being used as a smurf amplifier, you must filter packets sent to the broadcast address of your network:

```
interface Ethernet0
 no ip directed-broadcast

interface Ethernet1
 no ip directed-broadcast
```

Protecting Individual Machines Behind the Router

You can also protect individual machines behind the perimeter router. This could be any host on the DMZ such as Web servers, FTP servers, Exchange servers, and so on. Let's go ahead and do an example involving our Web server. You can apply access lists to filter access to your Web server, which uses the 10.9.8.7 IP address:

```
ip access-list extended ethernet1-in
```

The following code is to allow HTTP packets on your Web server (port 80):

```
permit tcp any host 10.9.8.7 eq www
```

Now apply the following to inbound packets on the inside interface:

```
interface Ethernet1
  ip access-group ethernet1-in in

ip access-list extended ethernet0-in
```

The following configuration enables all established HTTP connections from the Web server:

```
permit tcp host 10.9.8.7 eq www any established

interface Ethernet0
  ip access-group ethernet0-in in
```

Table 26-3 serves as a summary of all the commands.

Table 26-3

Quick Command Summary

Command	Description
enable secret	Sets a password for enable mode.
service password-encryption	Sets a minimum of protection for configured passwords.
no service tcp-small-servers no service udp-small-servers	Turns off unnecessary services for DoS or other attacks.
no service finger	Turns off information-gathering services.

continues

Table 26-3 cont.	Command	Description
Quick Command Summary	no cdp running no cdp enable	Turns off information gathering about routers that are directly connected.
	no ntp enable	Prevents attacks against the NTP service.
	no ip directed-broadcast	Prevents attackers from using the router as a smurf amplifier.
	transport input	Sets the protocols that can be used to connect interactively to the router's VTYs or to access its TTY ports.
	ip access-class	Sets which IP addresses can connect to TTYs or VTYs and reserves a VTY for access from an administrative workstation.
	exec-timeout	Stops idle sessions from tying up a VTY indefinitely.
	service tcp-keepalives-in	Detects and deletes dead interactive sessions, preventing them from tying up VTYs.
	ip access-group *list* in	Drops spoofed IP packets and discards incoming ICMP redirects.
	no ip source-route	Prevents IP source routing options from being used to spoof traffic.
	scheduler-interval scheduler allocate	Prevents fast floods from shutting down important processing.
	snmp-server community something-hard2guess ro list *snmp-server community something-hard2guess rw list*	Enables SNMP v1, configures authentication, and restricts access to certain IP addresses. Use SNMP v1 only if SNMP v2 can't be used. Enable SNMP only if you have to. Do not configure read-write access unless you absolutely need it.
	snmp-server party . . . authentication md5 *secret* . . . authentication with MD-5 encryption.	Configures SNMP version 2
	banner login	Establishes a warning banner to be displayed to users who try to log into the router.

Context-based Access Control (CBAC)

The different kinds of firewalls were covered earlier, as well as packet-filtering gateways. As a rule, most routers do not do stateful packet filtering, but Cisco routers, when using the IOS Firewall Feature Set, have that very capability.

Traditional router security is performed using standard IP filtering, which uses the source address and destination address to determine whether the packet should be forwarded or not. Stateful packet filtering takes this evaluation one step further. It not only evaluates the source address and destination address, but it keeps track of each communication session. Stateful packet filtering also keeps track of the communications that it should receive and drops those that are suspect.

CBAC is Cisco's implementation of stateful packet filtering. It enhances security for TCP and UDP protocols that use well-known ports such as FTP, *Point of Presence* (POP), and SMTP by scrutinizing the source and destination addresses as well as the state of the session. Unlike standard IP filtering, CBAC opens ports that are required, but only for the duration of the session. This prevents unauthorized packets from sneaking into inactive open ports. Previously, in order to support complex applications, you would have to open specific ports for the application to run properly. The problem is that a hole would be created in the security policy. With CBAC, specific ports are opened and closed for each application as needed. Figure 26-5 is an example of what would happen when someone on your internal network initiates a simple Telnet session.

Figure 26-5
The initiation of a Telnet session

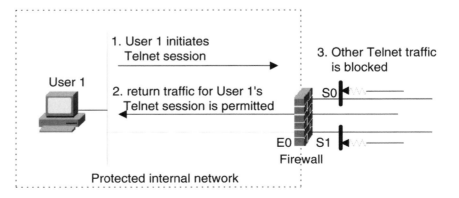

How CBAC Works

You must first decide which protocols you want CBAC to inspect. You then decide on an interface and direction you want the rule applied to. All packets that come in are first filtered through any access lists you might have set for both the incoming and outgoing ports as they relate to, say, the Internet. CBAC inspection doesn't begin until after the packet meets the access list criteria. Once the packet passes this scrutiny, it gets inspected by the CBAC process, which tracks the sequence numbers in all TCP packets, and drops those packets with sequence numbers that are not within expected ranges.

The inspection process can actually recognize application-specific commands. This enables it to take action if it recognizes one of these application-level attacks. Once it does, it can do the following:

- Send an alert.
- Take action to protect any system resources that might affect performance.
- Block the suspect packets.

CBAC also uses timeout and threshold values to manage state information for the session so that it can drop sessions that don't get fully established. You can also set timeout values for these sessions to help avoid any DoS attacks by dropping the session after a given amount of time. Once the session is dropped, a reset message is sent to the devices at both the source and destination end points. To do this, you need to create a CBAC inspection rule and apply that rule to an interface. The inspection rule must include the protocols that you want to monitor against DoS attacks.

Every time a packet gets inspected, it creates a state table. This table is updated with information about the actual state of the session. Any traffic coming back from an initiated session is only permitted through the router if the state table contains information saying that the packet belongs to that same session and it continues to update the state table as long as is necessary.

When any communication involves protocols that use UDP, no sessions or states exist like those with protocols that use TCP. In this case, CBAC approximates these sessions by looking at the information in the UDP packets to see if it is similar to the other UDP packets flowing by. It uses criteria such as the source address, destination address, and port number to make these approximations, and CBAC also makes decisions based on the time between the packets.

CBAC can actually create and delete access-list entries at the firewall interfaces dynamically, based on the information in the state tables. The access-list modifications are applied to the interfaces so that they can examine the traffic flowing back into the internal network. This is where the temporary holes we talked about are located.

Defining a CBAC Configuration

This kind of CBAC configuration definition is an example of the specifics you would add to a configuration for a simple single connection to the Internet using just one router separating your internal network from a connection to your ISP. This provides for both anti-spoofing and traffic filtering on the same access list. Your internal network is connected to the Ethernet 0 interface and your Serial 0 interface is a Frame Relay connection to the ISP.

As an example, your internal network is 200.20.20.0/24. The outside network is 210.21.21.0/24. The /24 represents the bits robbed with a subnet mask of 255.255.255.0.

Let's go ahead and define the inspection list now. Name your list McGrawHill and then list the protocols that you intend to inspect, along with a timeout value:

```
ip inspect name McGrawHill tcp timeout 3600
ip inspect name McGrawHill udp timeout 15
ip inspect name McGrawHill smtp timeout 3600
ip inspect name McGrawHill cuseeme timeout 3600
ip inspect name McGrawHill http timeout 3600
ip inspect name McGrawHill tftp timeout 30
ip inspect name McGrawHill ftp timeout 3600
ip inspect name McGrawHill realaudio timeout 3600
ip inspect name McGrawHill rcmd timeout 3600
!
interface Ethernet0

        description Ethernet network our side
            ip address 200.20.20.1 255.255.255.0
            no ip directed-broadcast
```

You'll define this access list later as 110, but for now go ahead and apply the access list that will permit legitimate traffic from inside your network but at the same time stop any spoofing:

```
        ip access-group 110 in
        no ip proxy-arp
```

Here is where you apply your McGrawHill inspection list to ethernet 0 inbound. Once any communication is initiated from the internal network to the outside, your inspection list creates temporary additions to the traffic permitted by serial interface 0 access list 120 for returning traffic from your initiated communication. From now on, you should be able to recognize all the other lines you see, such as **no cdp enable** and **no ip proxy-arp,** from what we discussed earlier in the "Firewall Configuration Definitions" section:

```
        ip inspect McGrawHill in
        no ip route-cache
        no cdp enable
  !
interface Serial0

        description Frame Relay ISP side
        ip address 210.21.21.1 255.255.255.0
        encapsulation frame-relay IETF
        no ip route-cache
        no arp frame-relay
        bandwidth 56
        service-module 56 clock source line
        service-module 56k network-type dds
        frame-relay lmi-type ansi
```

This access list will be defined later as 120, but go ahead and apply the access list now that some ICMP traffic and administrative Telnet will be permitted, along with taking care of any anti-spoofing. Notice that no inspection list is on Serial 0, but the inspection list you applied on your Ethernet interface list creates temporary additions to this access list when hosts on the internal network initiate any connections through the Frame Relay interface to your ISP:

```
        ip access-group 120 in
        no ip directed-broadcast
        no ip route-cache
        bandwidth 56
        no cdp enable
        frame-relay interface-dlci 10


   ip classless
   ip route 0.0.0.0 0.0.0.0 Serial0
```

Let's go ahead and define access list 10 now. You will apply it later, but, as discussed in the "SNMP Security Considerations" section, it will be used to control which network management station (in this case, 200.20.20.10) can be accessed using SNMP:

```
   access-list 10 permit 200.20.20.10
```

Now define access list 110, which you applied earlier. It permits legitimate traffic from inside your network but doesn't permit any spoofing:

```
access-list 110 permit tcp 200.20.20.0 0.0.0.255 any
access-list 110 permit udp 200.20.20.0 0.0.0.255 any
access-list 110 permit icmp 200.20.20.0 0.0.0.255 any
access-list 110 deny ip any any
```

Now define access list 120, which controls traffic from outside your network but still doesn't permit any spoofing:

```
access-list 120 deny ip 127.0.0.0 0.255.255.255 any
access-list 120 deny ip 200.20.20.0 0.0.0.255 any
```

Here is where you take care of the ICMP considerations discussed earlier in the "Firewall Configuration Definitions" section:

```
access-list 120 permit icmp any 200.20.20.0 0.0.0.255
administratively-prohibited
access-list 120 permit icmp any 200.20.20.0 0.0.0.255 echo
access-list 120 permit icmp any 200.20.20.0 0.0.0.255 echo-reply
access-list 120 permit icmp any 200.20.20.0 0.0.0.255 packet-too-
big
access-list 120 permit icmp any 200.20.20.0 0.0.0.255 time-
exceeded
access-list 120 permit icmp any 200.20.20.0 0.0.0.255 traceroute
access-list 120 permit icmp any 200.20.20.0 0.0.0.255 unreachable
access-list 120 deny ip any any
```

Now apply access-list 10 to your SNMP process as well as some items discussed in the password section:

```
snmp-server community anynameotherthanpublic RO 10
!
line con 0
exec-timeout 5 0
password 7 13271D1444023F8369
login local
line vty 0 4
exec-timeout 5 0
password 7 13271D1444023F8369
login local
length 35
end
```

The examples in this section should now give you a flavor of how to use CBAC and where to apply the inspection lists.

Intrusion Detection and IOS

Intrusion Detection Systems (IDS) monitor packets on a network and try to discover if someone or something is attempting to break into a system or cause a DoS attack. A typical example is a system that watches for a large number of TCP connection requests to many different ports on a target machine. Thus, it can discover if someone is attempting a TCP port scan. An IDS can either run on a target machine, which will monitor its own traffic, or on an independent machine or specialized device that promiscuously watches or sniffs all network traffic. IDSs provide a level of protection beyond the firewall by protecting the network from not only external attacks and threats, but those initiated from within as well. Cisco IOS Firewall IDS technology enhances perimeter firewall protection by taking appropriate action when packets and flows violate security policies or represent malicious network activity.

Cisco IOS Firewall IDS

The Cisco IOS Firewall IDS is designed to identify common attacks by examining a signature, which is a means of identifying a packet, much like a written signature. Looking at signatures can detect patterns of misuse in network traffic. Once an IDS detects any suspicious activity, it takes some form of action before network security can be compromised and then logs the event. The IDS system can be configured to any of the following actions in response to various threats:

- It can send an alarm to a syslog server or a Cisco NetRanger Director, which is just a centralized management interface.
- It can drop the packet.
- It can reset the TCP connection.

An IDS can also be configured to disable any individual signature or group of signatures that under certain network implementations can cause false positives. Although it is preferable to enable both the firewall and the intrusion-detection features of the CBAC security engine to support a network security policy, each of these features may be enabled independently and on different router interfaces. Cisco IOS software-based intrusion detection is part of the Cisco IOS Firewall and is available on the Cisco 2600, 3600, 7100, and 7200 series routers.

Configuring the Router for IDS

In order to implement the Cisco IOS Firewall IDS capabilities, you *must* do the following three steps:

1. Initialize the Cisco IOS IDS feature.
2. Initialize the Post Office feature.
3. Configure and apply audit rules.

As an optional fourth step, you can verify the configuration, but this is highly recommended. Let's go over these steps in more detail so that you can take advantage of these features.

Initialize the Cisco IOS IDS feature

Initializing the IDS feature consists of the following steps:

1. First, log into the router.
2. Enter privileged EXEC mode by typing **enable** and pressing Enter key.
3. Enter the enable password and press the Enter key.
4. Enter global configuration mode by typing **configure terminal** followed by pressing the Enter key.
5. Enter the **ip audit smtp** command in order to set the spamming threshold value with this syntax:

```
ip audit smtp spam recipients
```

   recipients is the value for the maximum number of recipients in an email message. The default for this is 250.
6. Enter the **ip audit po max-events** command to set the value for the cued events that will be dropped and sent to the NetRanger Director.

```
ip audit po max-events number_events
```

   number_events is the value for the number of events in the cue. The default is 100. Note that increasing this number can have an effect on your memory and performance. Each event in the cue consumes 32KB of memory.
7. Leave the global configuration mode by typing **exit**.

Initialize the Post Office feature

This step requires that the following tasks be performed:

1. First, log into the router.
2. Enter privileged EXEC mode by typing **enable** followed by pressing the Enter key.
3. Enter the enable password followed by pressing the Enter key.
4. Enter global configuration mode by typing **configure terminal** and pressing the Enter key.
5. Enter the **ip audit notify** command in order to send event alarms to either a syslog server or NetRanger Director. To send the alarm to the syslog server, enter the following:

   ```
   ip audit notify log
   ```

   To send the alarm to the NetRanger Director, enter the following:

   ```
   ip audit nr-director
   ```

6. If you are sending alarms to a NetRanger Director, you must set the Post Office parameters for both the router using the **ip audit po local** command and the NetRanger Director using the **ip audit po remote** command. First, set the router parameters:

   ```
   ip audit po local hostid host-id orgid org-id
   ```

   host-id must be a unique number between 1 and 65,535 to identify the router. *org-id* must be a unique number in the same range to identify the organization to which the router and Director belong. Now set the NetRanger Director parameters:

   ```
   ip audit po remote hostid host-id orgid org-id rmtaddress
   ip-address localaddress ip-address port port-number
    preference preference-number timeout seconds application
    application-type
   ```

host-id is a unique number between 1 and 65,535 that identifies the Director, while *org-id* is a unique number between 1 and 65,535 that identifies the organization to which the router and Director both belong. **rmtaddress** *ip-address* is the Director's IP address. **localaddress** *ip-address* is the router's interface IP address. *port-number* identifies the UDP port on which the Director is listening for alarms; 45,000 is the default.

preference-number is the relative priority of the route to the Director (1 is the default). If more than one route is used to reach the same Director, then one must be a primary route (preference 1) and the other a secondary route (preference 2).

seconds is the number of seconds the Post Office waits before it determines that a connection has timed out (five is the default). *application-type* is either **director** or **logger**. Note that if you are sending Post Office notifications to a Sensor, use **logger.**

7. When sending alarms to syslog, you have the option of seeing the syslog messages on the router console. In global configuration mode, turn on logging to the console:

```
logging console info
```

To turn off this feature, use the **no logging console info** command.

8. Add the IOS IDS router's Post Office information to the /usr/nr/etc/hosts and /usr/nr/etc/routes files on all NetRanger Sensors and Directors communicating with the router.

9. To leave global configuration mode, type **exit**.

10. To save the configuration, type **write mem**.

11. Reload the router with the **reload** command.

NOTE: *You must reload the router each time you make a Post Office configuration change.*

Configure and Apply Audit Rules

To make configurations to the audit rules, follow these steps:

1. First, log into the router.

2. Enter privileged EXEC mode by typing **enable,** followed by hitting the Enter key.

3. Enter the enable password and then press the Enter key.

4. Enter global configuration mode by typing **configure terminal** and by pressing the Enter key.

5. To set the default actions for info and attack signatures, use the **ip audit info** and **ip audit attack** commands. Both types of signatures will perform any or all of the following actions: alarm, drop, and reset.

   ```
   ip audit info action alarm
   ip audit attack action alarm drop reset
   ```

6. To create the audit rules, use the ip audit name command:

   ```
   ip audit name audit-name info
   ip audit name audit-name attack
   ```

   audit-name is just a user-defined name for an audit rule. Note that you should use the same names when assigning attack and info-type signatures.

7. To attach access control lists to an audit rule, enter the following:

   ```
   ip audit name audit-name {info|attack} list acl-list
   ```

   acl-list is an integer representing the ACL. When attaching an ACL to an audit rule, it too must be defined.

8. As an example, ACL 10 is attached to the audit rule INFO. This does not deny traffic from the 10.3.2.0 network as it would on an interface. The hosts on network 10.3.2.0 won't be filtered through

the audit process because they are trusted. The **permit any** is used to process all the other hosts. ACL 10 is defined as follows:

```
ip audit name INFO info list 10
access-list 10 deny 10.1.1.0 0.0.0.255
access-list 10 permit any
```

9. The ip audit signature command can be used to disable individual signatures. Because this is a global configuration change, it is not included in the audit rules:

```
ip audit signature signature-number disable
```

To reenable a disabled signature, use the **no ip audit signature** command. *signature-number* is the number of the disabled signature.

10. To apply access control lists to individual signatures, use the ip audit signature command:

```
ip audit signature signature-number list acl-list
```

signature-number is the number of the signature and *acl-list* is an integer representing the ACL.

11. To apply the created audit rule, go into interface configuration mode and apply the rule to an interface and direction using the **ip audit** command:

```
int e0
ip audit audit-name direction
```

audit-name is the name of the audit rule and *direction* is either **in** or **out**.

12. Leave the interface configuration mode by typing **exit**.

13. Once you apply the audit rules to the router interfaces, use the **ip audit po protected** command to choose which network to protect:

```
ip audit po protected ip_addr [to ip_addr]
```

ip_addr is an IP address to protect.

14. To leave global configuration mode, type **exit**.

Verify the Configuration

To verify your IDS configurations to see if they are configured properly, you can use the following commands:

```
show ip audit configuration
show ip audit interface
```

The following are two examples of the possible output from these commands:

Example #1:

```
Router#show ip audit configuration
Event notification through syslog is enabled
Event notification through Net Director is enabled
Default action(s) for info signatures is alarm
Default action(s) for attack signatures is alarm drop reset
Default threshold of recipients for spam signature is 25
PostOffice:HostID:55 OrgID:123 Msg dropped:0
   :Curr Event Buf Size:100 Configured:100
HID:14 OID:123 S:1 A:2 H:82 HA:49 DA:0 R:0 Q:0
 ID:1 Dest:10.3.2.99:45000 Loc:172.16.10.99:45000 T:5 S:ESTAB *

Audit Rule Configuration
 Audit name AUDIT.1
    info actions alarm
    attack actions alarm drop reset
```

Example #2:

```
Router#show ip audit interface
Interface Configuration
 Interface Ethernet0
  Inbound IDS audit rule is AUDIT.1
    info actions alarm
    attack actions alarm drop reset
  Outgoing IDS audit rule is not set
 Interface Ethernet1
  Inbound IDS audit rule is AUDIT.1
    info actions alarm attack
    actions alarm drop reset
  Outgoing IDS audit rule is not set
```

CHAPTER 27

Defining Virtual Private Networks

Defining IPSec

What Is IPSec?

Before going into the configurations, we should talk about the underlying technology. The most important ingredient in setting up a VPN is the IPSec protocol. To be more accurate, the IPSec protocol is really a suite of protocols used to protect the data, authenticate the data, control access, and allow for non-repudiation. We will go over the components of this suite of protocols in detail so that the configurations you see later will make more sense. We'll start by discussing the *Authentication Header* (AH) and *Encapsulating Security Payload* (ESP) protocols which can be used by themselves or in combination with one another during an IPSec communication session. Both protocols use encryption keys to protect the data. The difference between AH and ESP is that AH authenticates almost the entire packet including the tunnel header. ESP only authenticates the payload portion:

- **AH:** This protocol defines the authentication methods for IP payloads. It also provides for connectionless integrity, authentication of data origin, and an optional anti-replay feature.
- **ESP:** This protocol defines the encryption methods used for IP payloads. In tunnel mode it also defines encryption methods for part of the IP header. It provides encryption and limited traffic flow confidentiality. It also can provide connectionless integrity, authentication of data origin, and an anti-replay service.

The AH Protocol AH was designed for integrity, authentication, sequence integrity, which serves as the anti-replay feature, and non-repudiation. It was not designed to conceal the data however; that job was left to its cousin, the ESP protocol. AH provides authentication for as much of the IP header as possible. Obvious exceptions exist because parts of the IP header have to change during transmission, so these portions of the IP header cannot be hidden or protected by the authentication header. AH works well in applications where confidentiality is not necessary. Sometimes it is required due to government restrictions on encryption technologies. The AH can be employed to ensure integrity, which in itself can be a powerful foe to potential attackers. This type of implementation does not protect the information from dissemination but enables verification of the integrity of the information and authentication of the originator. AH also provides protection for the IP header preceding it and for selected options. The AH fields are shown in Figure 27-1.

■ **Next Header:** This 8-bit field specifies the next higher layer protocol that is encapsulated such as UDP, TCP, or even ESP.

■ **Length:** This 8-bit field specifies the size of the Authentication Data payload in 32-bit words and can be set to 0.

■ **Security Parameters Index (SPI):** This 32-bit field consists of a pseudo random value used to identify the *security association* (SA) for this datagram. This essentially informs the packet recipient of which security protocols the sender is using. This information includes which algorithms and keys will be used by the sending device. It can be set to 0. If it is set to 0, an SA does not exist. Values in the range of 1 to 255 have been reserved.

■ **Sequence Number:** This 32-bit field specifies the sequence number which tells how many packets with the same parameters have been sent. This number essentially acts as a counter and is incremented each time a packet with the same SPI is sent to the same address. This is the field that guards against a replay attack. A replay attack is when a packet is copied and sent to confuse the sender and receiver of its real origin.

■ **Authentication Data:** This is a variable-length field that must contain a multiple of 32-bit words.

The remainder of the IP header is not used in authentication with AH security protocol. The AH protocol requires the use of keys to verify the integrity of the information in the AH itself. AH requires that implementations support both the Message Digest 5 or HMAC-MD5 algorithm and the Secure Hash Algorithm v1 or HMAC-SHA-1 (both of these were described earlier in the Designing VPN chapter). Other algorithms can still be used. The reason AH uses a keyed hash algorithm as opposed to digital signatures is because it is much faster and provides for better network throughput. The AH protocol does not mandate a specific signature algorithm or *certificate authority* (CA). The two communicating systems must agree on a common authentication protocol during the security negotiation process.

Figure 27-1
The AH Header

0	1	2	3	4	5	6	7	8	9	10	11	12	13	14	15	16	17	18	19	20	21	22	23	24	25	26	27	28	29	30	31
Next header								Length								Reserved - 0															
Security Parameters Index																															
Sequence Number																															
Authentication Data (variable)																															

The ESP Protocol The ESP protocol provides encryption as well as some of the services of the AH protocol. ESP authentication does not cover any IP headers that precede it. ESP authenticating properties are limited compared to the AH due to the fact that none of the IP header information is included in the authentication process. However, ESP is more than sufficient if only the upper layer protocols need to be authenticated. The application of only ESP to provide authentication, integrity, and confidentiality to the upper layers will increase efficiency over the encapsulation of ESP in the AH. Even though authentication and confidentiality are both optional operations, one of the security protocols *must* be used. Another feature of the ESP is payload padding, which conceals the size of the packet being transmitted and further protects the characteristics of the communication. An ESP packet consists of a control header, a data payload, which is an encrypted version of the user's original packet, and an optional authentication trailer. The control header contains a *security protocol identifier* (SPI) and a sequence number field. It may also contain control information needed by some cryptographic algorithms like *Data Encryption Standard* (DES); this optional field is called the *initialization vector* (IV). The authentication trailer contains a digital hash to validate the authenticity of the packet. The ESP header is shown in Figure 27-2.

■ **Security Parameters Index (SPI):** This 32-bit field consists of a pseudo random value used to identify the SA for this datagram. This essentially informs the packet recipient of which security protocols the sender is using. This information includes which algorithms and keys will be used by the sending device. It can be set to 0. If it is set to 0, an SA does not exist. Values in the range of 1 to 255 have been reserved.

■ **Sequence Number:** This 32-bit field specifies the sequence number which tells how many packets with the same parameters have been sent. This number essentially acts as a counter and is incremented

Figure 27-2
The ESP Header

0	2	3	4	5	6	7	8	9	10	11	12	13	14	15	16	17	18	19	20	21	22	23	24	25	26	27	28	29	30	31
Security Parameters Index																														
Sequence number																														
Payload Data (variable)																														
Padding (0-255 bytes)																														
Padding Cont. (0-255 bytes)																		Padded Length						Next Header						
Authentication Data (variable)																														

each time a packet with the same SPI is sent to the same address. This is the field that guards against a replay attack. A replay attack is when a packet is copied and sent to confuse the sender and receiver of its real origin.

- **Payload Data:** Payload Data is a variable-length field containing data described by the Next Header field. The Payload Data field is mandatory and is an integral number of bytes in length.

- **Padding:** This field is a variable in the range of 0 to 255 bytes. Inclusion of the Padding field in an ESP packet is optional.

- **Pad Length:** This 8-bit field indicates the number of pad bytes immediately preceding it. The range of valid values is 0 to 255, where a value of 0 indicates that no Padding bytes are present. The Pad Length field is mandatory.

- **Next Header:** This 8-bit field specifies the next higher layer protocol that is encapsulated such as UDP or TCP.

- **Authentication Data:** This is a variable length field that must contain a multiple of 32-bit words.

ESP encrypts the payload by using one of any number of cryptographic algorithms. The cryptographic algorithms that must be supported by IPSec implementations are as follows:

- DES or 3DES in CBC mode
- HMAC - MD5
- HMAC - SHA -1

Communication Modes

Both the AH and ESP protocols support two modes of operation:

- **Transport mode:** This mode is used to protect upper layer protocols and only affects the data in the IP packet. You generally use this in a host-to-host communication.

- **Tunnel mode:** This method is more involved because it encapsulates the entire IP packet to tunnel the communications in a secured communication. Most likely, this is the mode you will use in setting up a corporate VPN.

Transport mode is established when the endpoint is a host or when communications are terminated at the endpoints. If the gateway in a gateway to host communications uses Transport mode, it acts as a host system, which can be acceptable for direct protocols to that gateway. Otherwise, Tunnel mode is required for gateway services to provide access to internal systems. Packet formats are shown in Figure 27-3.

Transport Mode   In Transport mode, only the IP payload is encrypted, and the original IP headers are left alone. This mode has the advantage of adding only a few bytes to each packet. It also enables devices on the public network to see the final source and destination of the packet. However, because the IP header is being sent unencrypted, it could be subject to eavesdropping. The person eavesdropping would only know that IP packets were being sent; he would not be able to determine what the application was or what was in it.

The Transport mode is designed to provide protection mainly for the upper layer protocols. The source and destination of the data packet are the cryptographic endpoints where the encryption and decryption take place. In IPv4, the Transport mode security protocol header, which could be AH or ESP, appears immediately after the IP header and before the higher layer protocols such as TCP or UDP. Figure 27-3 shows where this is evident.

Figure 27-3
ESP/AH Transport mode

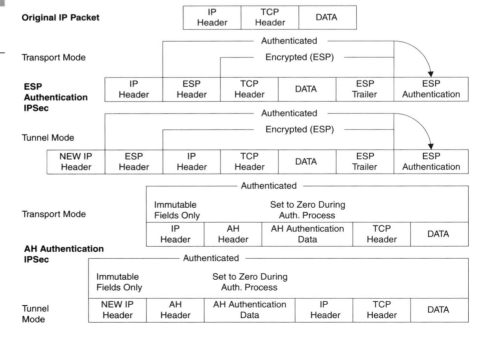

When ESP is utilized for the security protocol, the protection, or hash, is only applied to the upper layer protocols contained in the packet. The IP header information and options are not used in the authentication process, that is, the originating IP address cannot be verified for integrity against the data.

With the use of AH as the security protocol, the protection is extended forward into the IP header. This guarantees the integrity of the entire packet using the static portions of the original IP header in the hashing process. In the case of the AH protocol transport mode, all of the upper layer information is protected, and all fields in the IPv4 header (excluding the fields that are altered during transit.) The fields of the IPv4 header that are *not* included are set to 0 before applying the authentication algorithm. These fields are as follows:

- TOS
- TTL
- Header Checksum
- Header Offset
- Flags

Tunnel Mode Tunnel mode takes the entire original IP datagram, encrypts it, and becomes the payload of the new IP packet. The router performs encryption on behalf of the hosts. The source's router encrypts packets and forwards them along the IPSec tunnel. The destination's router decrypts the original IP datagram and forwards it on to the destination system. The major advantage of Tunnel mode is that the end systems do not need to be modified in order to enjoy the benefits of virtual private networking. Because the traffic is now tunneled, it also protects the packets from eavesdropping completely. They could determine the tunnel endpoints but not the true source and destination of the tunneled packets, even if they are the same as the tunnel endpoints.

Tunnel mode is established for gateway services and is essentially an IP tunnel with authentication and encryption. This is the most common mode of operation. Tunnel mode is required for gateway-to-gateway and host to gateway communications. Tunnel mode communications have two sets of IP headers:

- Outside
- Inside

The outside IP header contains the destination IP address of the VPN gateway. The inside IP header contains the destination IP address of the final system behind the VPN gateway. The security protocol appears after the outer IP header and before the inside IP header. As with Transport mode, extended portions of the IP header are utilized with AH that are not included with ESP authentication, ultimately providing integrity only of the inside IP header and payload.

The inside IP header's *Time To Live* (TTL) is decreased by one by the encapsulating system to represent the hop count as it passes through the router. However, if the router is the encapsulating system, as when NAT is implemented for internal hosts, the inside IP header is not modified. Once the TTL has been modified, the checksum must be recreated by IPSec and used to replace the original in order to reflect the change, maintaining IP packet integrity.

If AH is the protocol being used as the protocol for the Tunnel mode, all of the static portions of the outer IP header are protected as is the tunneled IP packet. In other words, the inner IP header is protected just like the higher layer protocols. If ESP is the one being used, the protection is afforded only to the tunneled packet, not to the outer header.

SA

This brings us to the very foundation upon which IPSec is built. The SA is created from the authentication process of the AH and ESP protocols. In fact the IPSec protocols, AH and ESP, need to carry much more information than just the underlying data. In addition to the packet destination, the protocols need to include information regarding authentication, data integrity, keys used, packet sequence, encryption type, compression, and any other information relating to the set of services employed to secure the packet. In other words, an SA is the method IPSec uses to track a given communication session. It defines how the communicating systems use security services, including information about the traffic security protocol, the authentication algorithm, and the encryption algorithm to be used as well as information on dataflow, TTL, and sequence numbering for anti-replay. Figure 27-4 describes the SA.

Because IPSec services can be provided by both the AH and the ESP protocols independently, each protocol creates its own SA when used. Remember, the concept of an SA is fundamental to IPsec because it describes the relationship between two or more devices and describes how the entities use security services to communicate. The SA includes the following:

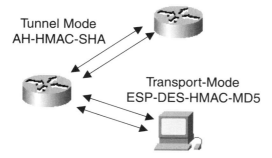

Figure 27-4
IPSec SA-security association

Tunnel Mode
AH-HMAC-SHA

Transport-Mode
ESP-DES-HMAC-MD5

- An encryption algorithm
- An authentication algorithm
- A shared session key

Since an SA is unidirectional, at least two SAs are required for a typical, two-way communication between two devices. The security services associated with an SA can be used for AH or ESP, but not for both. If both AH and ESP protection is applied to a traffic stream, then two or more SAs are created for each direction of travel over the network. This number can quickly increase if a connection includes multiple IPSec protocols and nested tunnels. You will hear terms like "Security Association bundle" or "SA bundle" used to describe a sequence of SAs that are used to satisfy the security policy being used in any given communication.

Each SA is defined by three components:

- **Security Parameter Index (SPI):** The SPI, as described in the protocol format figures, is a 32-bit value used to distinguish different SAs arriving at the same destination and using the same IPSec protocol. This is how the multiplexing of SAs to a single gateway works.

- **Destination IP Address:** The destination IP address can be unicast or even multicast or broadcast and defines the host, gateway, or router that is to receive and process the information in the SA.

- **Security Protocol Identifier (AH or ESP):** The Security Protocol Identifier represents the security protocol being used by this SA. Don't forget that only one security protocol can be used for communication defined by a single SA. If your data needs authentication and confidentiality using both the AH and ESP security protocols in combination, two or more SAs have to be created.

SA Bundles

This brings us to SA bundles. SAs, as you will recall, are a set of security services supplied by using one of the IPSec protocols. SAs can be formed in both the Tunnel mode or Transport mode. A Tunnel mode SA has an "outer" as well as an "inner" IP header. The outer header specifies which system must process the IPSec information, whereas the inner header specifies the actual and final destination of the packet. The AH and ESP protocols support different sets of services, so an SA can only offer the services supported by the IPSec protocol. This means that things like header protection can only be offered by the AH protocol and data encryption can only be handled by the ESP protocol. This is where SA bundling is applied because they are suited for implementing complex security policies.

Bundles can be made in Transport mode, Tunnel mode, and as a combination of both. Tunnel mode implementations offer a wider array of implementation choices and would be the natural choice among VPN implementations that might require services demanding these combined SAs to accomplish the necessary transport. SA bundles basically have two formats:

- **Fine Granularity:** Fine granularity refers to when an SA is assigned to each communication process. Data transmitted over a single SA are protected by a single security protocol, that is, the data can be protected by AH or ESP, but not both, because SAs can have only one security protocol.

- **Coarse Granularity:** Coarse granularity refers to combining services from several applications into an SA bundle. This enables communication with two levels of protection using multiple SAs.

Suppose you have a computer out on the Internet that you want to have establish a Tunnel mode SA with your corporate router and a Transport mode SA to the actual final destination of a computer on the internal network behind the router. This method provides secure communications over an untrusted medium like the Internet and then continues on once it is on the internal network for a secure point to point connection. This requires an SA bundle that terminates at two different destinations. Two kinds of SA bundles exist:

■ **Transport adjacency:** Transport adjacency refers to applying more than one security protocol to the same IP datagram without implementing Tunnel mode for communication. Using both AH and ESP provides a single level of protection and no nesting of communication, because the endpoint of the communication is the final destination. This application of transport adjacency is applied when Transport mode is implemented for communication between two hosts, each behind a gateway as shown in Figure 27-5: Example A.

■ **Iterated tunneling:** Iterated tunneling is the application of multiple layers of security protocols within a Tunnel mode SA. This enables multiple layers of nesting because each SA can originate or terminate at different points in the communication stream. Three occurrences of iterated tunneling are as follows:

   ■ Endpoints of each SA are identical

   ■ One of the endpoints of the SAs is identical

   ■ Neither endpoint of the SAs is identical

Identical endpoints can refer to Tunnel mode communication between two hosts behind a set of gateways. This is where SAs terminate at the hosts, and AH and/or ESP is contained in an ESP providing the tunnel as shown in Figure 27-5: Example B.

With only one of the endpoints being identical, an SA can be established between the host and gateway and between the host and an internal host behind the gateway. This was used earlier as an example of one of the applications of SA bundling as shown in Figure 27-5: Example C.

In the event that neither SA terminates at the same point, an SA can be established between two gateways and between two hosts behind the gateways. This application provides multi-layered nesting and communication protection. An example of this application is a VPN between two gateways that provide Tunnel mode operations for their corresponding networks to communicate. Hosts on each network are provided secured communication based on client-to-client SAs. This provides for several layers of authentication and data protection as shown in Figure 27-5: Example D.

SA Databases

SAs require two different kinds of databases:

■ **Security Policy Database (SPD):** The SPD specifies the security services that are provided for IP packets. This database contains an

Figure 27-5
SA Bundles

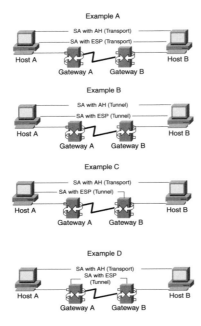

ordered list of policy entries. Each entry includes information about the type of packets to which the policy should apply, such as source and destination address. An IPSec policy entry also includes an SA specification that lists the IPSec protocols, if it is Tunnel mode or Transport mode, and the security algorithms to be used.

■ **Security Association Database (SAD):** The SAD defines the parameters associated with individual SAs. Each SA has an entry in the SAD. For outbound packets, entries are pointed to by entries in the SPD. For inbound processing, each entry in the SAD is indexed by a destination IP address, protocol type, and SPI. Each SA specification in the SPD points to an SA, or a bundle of SAs, in the SAD.

A quick overview of what happens when an IPSec system sends a packet is it first matches the packet against the entries in the SPD to see if an SA for the packet is in the SAD. If an SA does not exist, the IPSec system creates one. It then applies the processing specified, and then puts the SPI from the SA into the IPSec header. When the IPSec peer receives the packet, it looks up the SA in its database by destination address, SPI and security protocol and then processes the packet as required.

SPD The SPD is a security association management database designed to enforce policies in an IPSec environment. One of the most important parts of SA processing is an underlying security policy that specifies what services are offered to IP datagrams and in what fashion they are implemented. The SPD is consulted for all IP and IPSec communication. This applies to inbound and outbound connections which is why it is always associated with an interface. An interface that provides IPSec is referred to as a Black interface. An interface where IPSec is not being performed is referred to as a Red interface, meaning that no data will be encrypted over that interface. The number of SPDs and SADs are directly related to the number of Black and Red interfaces being supported by the router. The SPD must control *both* traffic that is IPSec-based and traffic that is not IPSec related. When a packet is received on an interface, the SPD can do one of three things:

■ Forward and do not apply IPSec
■ Discard packet
■ Forward and apply IPSec

The SPD can be configured so that only the IPSec traffic gets forwarded. This provides a basic firewall function by allowing only IPSec protocol packets into the Black interface. If IPSec is to be applied to the packet, the SPD policy entry specifies an SA or SA bundle to be employed. Within the specification is the IPSec protocols, mode of operation, encryption algorithms, and any nesting requirements.

SPD SA Selectors   The SPD is used to control all traffic through an IPSec system. In order to choose which packets a policy should act upon, the SPD enables the administrator to specify one or several traffic or packet selectors. Selectors or selector values constitute the field or portion of the SPD entry that selects which traffic will be affected by the database policy, which in turn can specify one or many SAs. Some selectors may include things such as ANY host, a specific IP source address, a destination address, a specific user id, a network IP range, the specific protocol used, the high level port number specified in the connection, and so on. Almost any criteria that can be used to identify a packet can be used as an SA selector for the SPD. A selector is used to apply traffic to a policy. A security policy may determine that several SAs be applied for an application in a defined order, and the parameters of this bundled operation must be detailed in the SPD. An example policy entry may specify that all matching traffic be protected by an ESP using DES, nested inside an AH using SHA-1. Each selector is used to associate the policy to SAD entries. The SPD is policy-driven and is concerned with system relationships.

SAD Just like the IPSec standard that specifies a database in order to keep track of the services available and how policies are applied, the standard also specifies a different database that tracks each and every active SA. This database entry contains a record of all the values negotiated at the time each SA was initially created. This database is used by the SPD to quickly link packets to an existing security association in order to process them according to existing policies and conforming to the information contained in the SPI. This database is called the SAD. The SAD is responsible for each SA in the communication defined by the SPD. Each SA has an entry in the SAD. The SA entries in the SAD are indexed by the three SA properties:

- Destination IP Address
- IPSec Protocol
- Security Parameter Index (SPI)

The SAD database contains nine parameters for processing IPSec protocols and the associated SA:

- Sequence number counter for outbound communications.
- Sequence number overflow counter that sets an option flag to prevent further communication utilizing the specific SA.
- A 32-bit anti-replay window that is used to identify the packet that is traversing the SA for that point in time and is used to provide the means to identify that packet for future reference.
- Lifetime of the SA that is determined by a byte count, time frame, or a combination of the two.
- The algorithm used in the AH.
- The algorithm used in the authenticating ESP.
- The algorithm used in the encryption of the ESP.
- IPSec mode of operation, Transport or Tunnel mode.
- Path MTU (PMTU). This is data that is required for ICMP data over an SA.

Each of these parameters is referenced in the SPD for assignment to policies and applications. The SAD maintains a record of all existing security associations for as long as they live, and it is always used in conjunction with the SPD to correctly sort and process all IPSec traffic. Any of the core components of an SA can become a selector parameter for the SAD including destination IP, IPSec protocol (AH or ESP), and SPI.

Key Management and IKE

Key management is an important part of IPSec or any kind of encrypted communication that uses keys for data confidentiality and integrity. Key management is the process used to set up, maintain, and control secure communication for VPN system. In key management, several layers of system insurance exist prior to the establishment of an SA, and several mechanisms are used to accommodate these processes. You will see that SAs are not just for secure VPN communication. Other kinds of SAs are used for initiating key exchanges and the like, which you will see shortly.

Key Management

Key management can be a complex and confusing enterprise. When you start mixing and throwing around acronyms, the confusion only worsens. We will be going over key management as it applies to the IPSec standard. The IPSec standard relies on the *Internet Key Exchange* (IKE). The IKE protocol is actually a mix of other already established protocols. These protocols provide different functions in and of themselves, but when put together, they make a very good hybrid. The three protocols are as follows:

- **Internet Security Association and Key Management Protocol (ISAKMP):** The ISAKMP provides a framework of *phases* for authentication and key exchange but does not define them. ISAKMP is designed to be key-exchange independent; that is, it is designed to support many different key exchanges.

- **Oakley:** This protocol describes a series of key exchanges called *modes,* and it details the services provided by each such as perfect forward secrecy for keys, identity protection, and authentication.

- **Secure Key Exchange Mechanism (SKEME):** The SKEME describes a versatile key exchange technique that provides anonymity, non-repudiation, and quick-key refreshment.

The ISAKMP defines the procedures for authenticating a communicating peer and generating keys. ISAKMP defines payloads for exchanging key and authentication data. This is done to provide a consistent framework independent of the encryption algorithm, authentication mechanism being implemented, and security protocol, such as IPSec.

Public Key Infrastructure (PKI) is a suite of protocols that provide several areas of secure communication based on trust and digital certificates.

PKI combines digital certificates, public-key cryptography, and certificate authorities into a powerful and very scalable network security architecture that may be utilized by IPSec.

IPSec IKE

As mentioned earlier, IKE is a combination of several existing key management protocols that are combined to provide a specific key management system. IKE is rather complicated, and several variations are available in the establishment of trust and providing keying material. Oakley and ISAKMP protocols, which are included in IKE, each define separate methods of establishing an authenticated key exchange between systems. Oakley defines *modes* of operation to build a secure relationship path and ISAKMP defines *phases* to accomplish a similar process in a hierarchical format. The relationship between these two protocols is represented by IKE with different exchanges as modes, which operate in one of two phases.

IKE creates an authenticated, secure tunnel between two entities and then negotiates the security association for IPSec. This is performed in two phases. In phase one, the two ISAKMP peers establish a secure, authenticated channel with which to communicate. This channel is called the *ISAKMP SA*.

These are the attributes used by IKE, and they are negotiated as part of the ISAKMP SA:

- The Encryption algorithm.
- The Hash algorithm.
- The method of authentication.
- Information about the group on which to perform the Diffie-Hellman algorithm.

Both parties must be authenticated to each other as soon as these attributes are negotiated. IKE can use any number of authentication methods. The methods used most commonly are as follows:

- **Pre-shared keys:** The same key is pre-installed on each host. IKE peers authenticate each other by computing and sending a keyed hash of data that includes the pre-shared key. If the receiving peer can independently create the same hash using its pre-shared key, it knows that both parties must share the same secret. Thus, the other party is authenticated.
- **Public key cryptography:** Each party generates a pseudo-random number and encrypts this number and its ID using the other party's

public key. The ability for each party to compute a keyed hash containing the other peer's generated number and ID, decrypted with the local private key, authenticates the parties to each other. This method does not provide non-repudiation; either side of the exchange could plausibly deny taking part in the exchange. The RSA public key algorithm is the one that is supported presently.

- **Digital signature:** Each device digitally signs a set of data and sends it to the other party. This method is similar to public key cryptography, except it also includes non-repudiation. The RSA public key algorithm and the *digital signature standard* (DSS) are both supported.

Both parties must have a shared session key to encrypt the IKE tunnel. The Diffie-Hellman protocol is used to agree on a common session key.

In phase two of the IKE process, SAs are negotiated on behalf of services like IPSec's AH protocol or ESP protocol. IPSec uses a different shared key than IKE does. The IPSec shared key can be produced by using the Diffie-Hellman algorithm again or by simply refreshing the shared secret produced by the original Diffie-Hellman exchange that generated the IKE SA. Once this step is complete, the IPsec SAs have been established so now the data can be exchanged with the negotiated IPSec parameters. Figure 27-6 shows how this works.

Figure 27-6
SA Establishment process

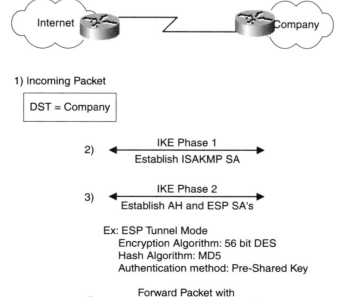

1) Incoming Packet

DST = Company

2) ⟵ IKE Phase 1 ⟶
Establish ISAKMP SA

3) ⟵ IKE Phase 2 ⟶
Establish AH and ESP SA's

Ex: ESP Tunnel Mode
Encryption Algorithm: 56 bit DES
Hash Algorithm: MD5
Authentication method: Pre-Shared Key

4) ⟶
Forward Packet with
Establish ESP SA

Phases and Modes

Phase one takes place when the two ISAKMP peers establish a secure, authenticated communication channel. Each system is verified and authenticated against its peer to enable future communication. Phase two exists to provide information about keys and material to assist in the establishment of SAs for an IPSec communication. Here is how the phases break down:

Within phase one, two modes of operation are defined in IKE:

- Main mode
- Aggressive mode

Each one accomplishes a phase one secure exchange, and these two modes only exist in phase one.

Within phase two, two modes exist:

- Quick mode
- New Group mode

Quick mode is used to establish SAs on behalf of the underlying security protocol. New Group mode is designated as a phase two mode only because it must exist in phase two. The service provided by the New Group mode is to assist phase one operations. As previously mentioned, one of the advantages of a two phased approach is that the second phase can provide additional SAs, eliminating the need to re-authorize the peers.

Phase one is initiated using ISAKMP defined cookies. The *initiator cookie* (I-cookie) and *responder cookie* (R-cookie) are used to establish an SA, which provides end-to-end authenticated communications. ISAKMP communications are bi-directional and once established, either peer may initiate a Quick mode to establish SA communication for the security protocol. The order of the cookies is critical for future second phase operations. A single SA can be used for many of the second phase operations. Each second phase operation can be used for several SAs or SA bundles. Main mode and Aggressive mode each use Diffie-Hellman keying material to provide authentication services (a comprehensive discussion about Diffie-Hellman, and all other key and encryption can be found in Chapter 10, "Designing Cisco VPN Solutions").

Main mode implementation is mandatory, whereas Aggressive mode is not. Main mode provides several messages to authenticate. The first two messages determine a communication policy. The next two messages exchange Diffie-Hellman public data. The last two messages authenticate the Diffie-Hellman exchange. Aggressive mode is an option available to developers that provides much more information with fewer messages and acknowledgements. The first two messages in Aggressive mode determine a communication policy and exchange Diffie-Hellman public data. Then a second message authenticates the responder, and this completes the negotiation process.

Phase two is much easier because it provides keying material for the initiation of SAs for the security protocol. This is where the key management is used to maintain the SAs for IPSec communication. The second phase has one mode, Quick mode, designed to support IPSec. Quick mode verifies and establishes the keying process for the creation of SAs. The New Group mode of operation is used for creating ISAKMP SAs and provides services to phase one for the creation of additional SAs.

System Trust Establishment

The first step in establishing communication is verification of the remote system. Three primary forms of authenticating a remote system are as follows:

■ Shared secret

■ Certificate

■ Public/Private key

Shared secret is widely used. However, it is not scalable and can become unmanageable very quickly due to the fact that there can be a separate secret for each communication.

Certificates are a different process of trust establishment. Each device is issued a certificate from a *Certificate Authority* (CA). When a remote system requests communication establishment, it will present its certificate. The recipient checks with the CA to validate the certificate. The trust is established between the two systems by means of a hierarchical trust relationship with the CA and the authenticating system. Because the certificates can be made public, centrally controlled, and easily accessed, it is not necessary to hash or encrypt the certificate.

Public and private key use is employed in combination with Diffie-Hellman to authenticate and provide keying material. During the system authentication process, hashing algorithms are utilized to protect the authenticating shared secret as it is forwarded over untrusted networks. This process of using hashing to authenticate is nearly identical to the authentication process of an AH security protocol. However, the message, in this case a password, is not sent with the digest. The map previously shared or configured with participating systems contains the necessary data to be compared to the hash.

Key Sharing

Once the two systems are confident of each other's identity, the process of sharing or swapping keys must take place to provide encryption for future communication. The mechanisms that can be utilized to provide keying are related to the type of encryption to be utilized for the ESP. Two basic forms of keys exist:

- Symmetrical
- Asymmetrical

Symmetrical key encryption occurs when the same key is used for the encryption of information into human unintelligible data, or cipher text, and for the decryption of that cipher text into the original information format. If the key used in symmetrical encryption is not carefully shared with the participating individuals, an attacker can obtain the key, decrypt the data, view or alter the information, encrypt the data with the stolen key, and forward it to the final destination. This process is defined as a man-in-the-middle attack. If properly executed, it can affect data confidentiality and integrity, rendering the valid participants in the communication oblivious to the exposure and the possible modification of the information.

Asymmetrical keys consist of a key pair that is mathematically related and generated by a complicated formula. The concept of asymmetry comes from the fact that the encryption is one-way with either of the key pair, and data that is encrypted with one key can only be decrypted with the other key of the pair. Asymmetrical key encryption is incredibly popular and can be used to enhance the process of symmetrical key sharing. Also, with the use of two keys, digital signatures have evolved, and the concept of trust has matured to certificates, which contribute to a more secure relationship.

Configuring CAs

The first step in setting up your VPN is to set up your Cisco equipment to work with a CA. The following list is the order that is recommended to set up a VPN:

1. Configure your CA information.
2. Configure IKE.
3. Configure IPSec.

So now that you're here, let's get started.

Host Name and IP Domain Name Configuration

The router's host name and IP domain name has to be configured prior to doing anything. The reason for this is because the router assigns a *fully qualified domain name* (FQDN) to all keys and certificates. The way the FQDN is determined is by the host name and IP domain name that has been assigned to the router.

Use the following commands in global configuration mode to configure the router's host name:

```
Router(config)#hostname name
```

and IP domain name:

```
Router(config)#ip domain-name name
```

How to Generate an RSA Key Pair

RSA key pairs are used to sign and encrypt IKE key management messages. You must do this before your router can obtain a certificate.

Use the following command in global configuration mode to generate an RSA key pair. The **usage-keys** keyword is used to specify special usage keys, as opposed to general purpose keys.

```
Router(config)#crypto key generate rsa [usage-keys]
```

CA Declaration

You should always declare one CA on your router. Use the following commands in global configuration mode to declare a CA. The first command is used to declare a CA. The name should be the CA's domain name.

```
Router(config)#crypto ca identity name
```

The following command is used to specify the URL name of the CA. If the URL has any non-standard cgi-bin script location, it should be included. This command now puts you into the (ca-identity) configuration mode:

```
Router(ca-identity)#enrollment url url
```

If your CA system provides a *Registration Authority* (RA), then specify RA mode:

```
Router(ca-identity)#enrollment mode ra
```

If your CA system provides an RA and supports the LDAP protocol, then specify the location of the LDAP server:

```
Router(ca-identity)#query url url
```

The following command is optional and is used to specify the retry period. After requesting a certificate, the router waits to receive a certificate from the CA. If the router does not receive a certificate within a given period of time, the router sends another certificate request. The default time is one minute.

```
Router(ca-identity)#enrollment retry period minutes
```

This command is also optional and is used to specify how many times the router will continue to send unsuccessful certificate requests before giving up. The router never gives up trying by default.

```
Router(ca-identity)#enrollment retry count number
```

This command is optional and is used so that the other peers' certificates still can be accepted by your router, even if the appropriate CRL is not accessible to your router:

```
Router(ca-identity)#crl Optional
```

This command takes you out of (ca-identity) configuration mode:

```
Router(ca-identity)#exit
```

The trade-off between security and availability is determined by the **query url** and **crl optional** commands, as shown in Table 27-1.

Table 27-1	**Security and CA Availability**	**Query—Yes**	**Query—No**
Query URL and CRL optional commands	CRL Optional—Yes	Sessions will go through even if the CA is not available, but the certificate might have been revoked.	Sessions will go through even if the CA is not available, but the certificate might have been revoked.
	CRL Optional—No	Certificates will not be accepted if the CA is not available.	Sessions will go through and will be verified against the CRL stored locally.

Authenticating the CA

The router has to authenticate the CA. It can do this by getting the CA's self-signed certificate, which has the CA's public key. Because the CA's certificate is self-signed, their public key should be manually authenticated. You can do this by contacting the CA administrator to compare the CA certificate's fingerprint.

To get the CA's public key, use the following command in global configuration mode:

```
Router(config)#crypto ca authenticate name
```

Obtain the CA's public key. Make sure that you use the same *name* that you used when you were declaring the CA with the `crypto ca identity` command.

How to Request Your Own Certificate

You will have to get a signed certificate from the CA for each of your router's RSA key pairs. To request signed certificates from the CA, use the following command in global configuration mode:

```
Router(config)#crypto ca enroll name
```

This command requests certificates for all of your RSA key pairs. This also causes your router to request as many certificates as there are RSA key pairs, so you only need to perform this command once, even if you have special usage RSA key pairs.

Saving Your Configuration

Always remember to save your work when you make configuration changes. Use the `copy system:running-config nvram:startup-config` command to save your configuration. This command includes saving RSA keys to private NVRAM. WARNING:RSA keys are *not* saved with your configuration when you use a `copy system:running-config rcp:` or `copy system:running-config tftp:` command. (you've been warned . . . .)

Requesting a Certificate Revocation List

You can request a *certificate revocation list* (CRL) only if your CA does not support an RA. Use the following command in global configuration mode to request an immediate download of the latest CRL:

```
Router(config)#crypto ca crl request name
```

Deleting Your Router's RSA Keys

Use the following command in global configuration mode to delete all of your router's RSA keys:

```
Router(config)#crypto key zeroize rsa
```

Deleting Peer's Public Keys

Use the following commands, beginning in global configuration mode to delete a peer's RSA public key. The first command takes you into public key configuration mode:

```
Router(config)#crypto key pubkey-chain
rsa
```

This command is used to delete a remote peer's RSA public key. Specify the peer's fully qualified domain name or the remote peer's IP address.

```
Router(config-pubkey-c)#no named-key key-name [encryption |
signature]
```

or

```
Router(config-pubkey-c)#no addressed-key key-address [encryption |
signature]
```

The following command takes you back to global configuration mode:

```
Router(config-pubkey-c)#exit
```

Deleting Certificates from the Configuration

Use the following commands in global configuration mode to delete your router's certificate or RA certificates from your router's configuration:

```
Router# show crypto ca certificates
```

displays the certificates stored on your router; note (or copy) the serial number of the certificate you wish to delete. The next command takes you into (config-cert-chain) configuration mode:

```
Router(config)#crypto ca certificate chain name
```

The following command deletes the certificate:

```
Router(config-cert-cha)#no certificate certificate-serial-number
```

If you want to delete the CA's certificate, you have to remove the entire CA identity. This removes all certificates associated with the CA including your router's certificate, the CA certificate, and any RA certificates.

Use the following command in global configuration mode to remove a CA identity:

```
Router(config)#no crypto ca identity name
```

This command deletes all CA identity information and all certificates associated with the CA.

Viewing Keys and Certificates

To view keys and certificates, use the following commands in EXEC mode:

```
Router#show crypto key mypubkey rsa
```

displays your router's RSA public keys.

```
Router#show crypto key pubkey-chain rsa
```

displays a list of all the RSA public keys stored on your router. These include the public keys of peers who have sent your router their certificates during peer authentication for IPSec.

```
Router# show crypto key pubkey-chain
rsa [name key-name | address
key-address
```

displays details of a particular RSA public key stored on your router.

```
Router#show crypto ca certificates
```

displays information about your certificate, the CA's certificate, and any RA certificates.

Now . . .

Now that you have completed this, you should move on to the "Configuring IKE" section. After you have done IKE, you need to move on to the "Configuring IPSec" section. Then you are ready to go!

Configuring IKE

Well, good, you made it this far. Now let's begin our second endeavor. (You did do the CA configs first, right? Of course you did, why else would you be here?) You should ALWAYS configure IKE after Certificates and definitely before IPSec. Even if you decide not to use IKE, you must still FIRST disable it before configuring IPSec.

Enabling or Disabling IKE

IKE is always enabled by default. IKE does not have to be enabled for individual interfaces, but it is enabled globally for all interfaces on the router. If you do not want IKE to be used with IPSec, you have to disable it at all IPSec peers. If you decide to do this, you will have to concede the following at all of your IPSec peers:

- All of the IPSec SAs in the crypto maps will have to be set manually.
- IPSec security associations will never time out during an IPSec session.
- The encryption keys will never change during any IPSec sessions between peers.
- No anti-replay services will be available between peers.
- You won't be able to use CA support.

Use the following command in global configuration mode to disable IKE:

```
Router(config)#no crypto isakmp enable
```

Use the following command in global configuration mode if you want to enable IKE:

```
Router(config)#crypto isakmp enable
```

Once you have disabled IKE, you can go directly to the "configuring IPSec" section.

Make Sure Your Access Lists Are Compatible with IKE

IKE negotiation uses UDP port 500. Make sure that your access lists are configured so that UDP port 500 is not blocked at any interfaces being used by IKE and IPSec. Keep in mind that there might be a situation where you might have to add a statement to explicitly permit UDP port 500.

Creating IKE Policies

IKE policies must be created at each peer and a total of five parameters need to be set in each IKE policy. These parameters are displayed in Table 27-2.

Table 27-2

Defining the
Parameters in a
Policy

Parameters	Acceptable Values	Keyword	The Default Value
encryption algorithm	56-bit DES-CBC 168-bit DES	**des** **3des**	56-bit DES-CBC 168-bit DES
hash algorithm	SHA-1 (HMAC variant) MD5 (HMAC variant)	**sha** **md5**	SHA-1
authentication method	RSA signatures RSA encrypted nonces pre-shared keys	**rsa-sig** **rsa-encr** **pre-share**	RSA signatures
Diffie-Hellman group identifier	768-bit Diffie-Hellman or 1,024-bit Diffie-Hellman	**1** **2**	768-bit Diffie-Hellman
security association lifetime	Can specify any number of seconds	—	86,400 seconds (one day)

These are the parameters that will be set for any IKE negotiations once the IKE security association has been set.

Creating Policies

You can create multiple IKE policies, each with a different combination of parameter values. You can assign a unique priority value anywhere from 1 to 10,000 for every policy you create; one is the highest priority. Many policies can be configured on a peer. At a minimum, one of these policies must contain the exact same hash, authentication, encryption, and Diffie-Hellman parameters as one of the policies on the remote peer. Your router will always use the default policy if you do not configure these policies. By default, it is always set to the lowest priority and contains each parameter's default value.

You can configure a policy by entering the following commands starting in global configuration mode. The following identifies the policy you are creating. Policies are uniquely identified by the priority number you assign. Now this puts you in (config-isakmp) command mode:

```
Router(config)#crypto isakmp policy priority
```

This command specifies the encryption algorithm:

```
Router(config-isakmp)#encryption {des | 3des}
```

This command specifies the hash algorithm:

```
Router(config-isakmp)#hash {sha | md5}
```

This command specifies the authentication method:

```
Router(config-isakmp)#authentication {rsa-sig | rsa-encr | pre-
share}
```

This command specifies the Diffie-Hellman group identifier:

```
Router(config-isakmp)#group {1 | 2}
```

This command specifies the security association's lifetime:

```
Router(config-isakmp)#lifetime seconds
```

This exits the (config-isakmp) command mode:

```
Router(config-isakmp)#exit
```

This exits the global configuration mode:

```
Router(config)#exit
```

This EXEC mode command is optional. It displays all of the existing IKE policies:

```
Router#show crypto isakmp policy
```

RSA Key Generation

To generate RSA keys, use the following commands starting in global configuration mode:

```
Router(config)#crypto key generate rsa [usage-keys]
```

This EXEC mode command displays the generated RSA public key:

```
Router#show crypto key mypubkey rsa
```

NOTE: *Always remember to repeat these tasks at* each *peer that doesn't have CA support* and *that uses RSA-encrypted nonces in the IKE policy.*

Setting ISAKMP Identity

For each peer that uses pre-shared keys in an IKE policy, you should set the ISAKMP identity. Each peer sends its identity to the remote peer when two peers use IKE to establish IPSec security associations. The way you have the router's ISAKMP identity set decides when each peer sends either its host name or its IP address. A peer's ISAKMP identity is the peer's IP address by default. If necessary, change the identity to be the peer's host name instead. You should always set all of the peers' identities to be the same.

Use the following commands in global configuration mode to set a peer's ISAKMP identity. The first command specifies the peer's ISAKMP identity by IP address or by host name:

```
Router(config)#crypto isakmp identity {address | hostname}
```

This command maps the peer's host name to its IP address(es) at all the remote peers if the local peer's ISAKMP identity was a host name. If the host name/address is already mapped in the DNS server, this step might not be necessary.

```
Router(config)#ip host hostname address1 [address2 . . . address8]
```

Don't forget to repeat these tasks at each peer that uses pre-shared keys in an IKE policy.

Specifying All the Other Peers' RSA Public Keys

Specify all the other peers' RSA public keys at each local peer by using the following commands starting in global configuration mode. The first command puts you into (config-pubkey-c) mode:

```
Router(config)#crypto key pubkey-chain rsa
```

This command tells which remote peer's RSA public key you are going to specify. If the remote peer uses its host name as its ISAKMP identity, use the **named-key** command and specify the remote peer's fully qualified domain name or FQDN as the *key-name*. If the remote peer uses its IP address as its ISAKMP identity, then you use the **addressed-key** command and specify the remote peer's IP address as the *key-address*.

```
Router(config-pubkey-c)#named-key key-name [encryption | signature]
```

or

```
Router(config-pubkey-c)# addressed-key key-address [encryption |
signature]
```

If you used a fully qualified domain name to name the remote peer using the **named-key** command, you can specify the remote peer's IP address. This is optional.

```
Router(config-pubkey-k)#address ip-address
```

This command specifies the remote peer's RSA public key. This was the key seen by the remote peer's administrator when he generated his router's RSA keys.

```
Router(config-pubkey-k)#key-string key-string
```

returns to public key chain configuration mode:

```
Router(config-pubkey-k)#quit
```

Now, repeat the last four commands to specify the RSA public keys on all of the other IPSec peers that use RSA-encrypted nonces in an IKE policy. This takes you back into global configuration mode:

```
Router(config-pubkey-c)#exit
```

Remember to repeat these tasks at each peer that uses RSA-encrypted nonces in an IKE policy.

Viewing the RSA Public Keys

To view RSA public keys while or after you configure them, use the following command in EXEC mode:

```
Router#show crypto key pubkey-chain rsa {name key-name | address
key-address}
```

This command displays a list of all the RSA public keys stored on your router or displays details of a particular RSA public key stored on your router.

Configuring Pre-Shared Keys

To configure pre-shared keys, perform these next two tasks at each peer that uses pre-shared keys in an IKE policy:

- First, set each peer's ISAKMP identity. Each peer's identity should be set to either its host name or its IP address. By default, a peer's identity is set to its IP address. Setting ISAKMP identities is described previously in the "Setting ISAKMP Identity" section.

- Next, specify the shared keys at each peer. Note that a given pre-shared key is shared between two peers. At a given peer you could specify the same key to share with multiple remote peers; however, a more secure approach is to specify different keys to share between different pairs of peers.

To specify pre-shared keys at a peer, use the following commands in global configuration mode:

```
Router(config)#crypto isakmp key keystring address peer-address
```

or

```
Router(config)#crypto isakmp key keystring hostname peer-hostname
```

At the local peer, the following code specifies the shared key to be used with a particular remote peer. At the remote peer, it specifies their ISAKMP identity with an address. Use the **address** keyword in this step. If you don't want to, then use the **hostname** keyword instead.

At the remote peer, this command specifies the shared key to be used with the local peer. This is the same key you just specified at the local peer. If the local peer specified their ISAKMP identity with an address, use the **address** keyword in this step; otherwise use the **hostname** keyword in this step.

```
Router(config)#crypto isakmp key keystring address peer-address
```

or

```
Router(config)#crypto isakmp key keystring hostname peer-hostname
```

Repeat the previous two commands for each remote peer and don't forget to repeat these tasks at each peer that uses pre-shared keys in an IKE policy.

Configuring IKE Mode Configuration

Configuring IKE Mode Configuration on a router involves two steps:

1. Define the pool of IP addresses.
2. Define which crypto maps should attempt to configure clients.

Use the following commands in global configuration mode to configure IKE Mode Configuration on your Cisco access router:

The existing local address pools are used to define a set of addresses. To define a local address pool, use the existing `ip local pool` command:

```
router(config)#ip local pool pool-name start-addr end-addr
```

The local pool is for referencing the IKE configuration. Use the new `crypto isakmp client configuration address-pool local` command to reference this local address pool in the IKE configuration:

```
router(config)#crypto isakmp client configuration address-pool
local pool-name
```

Use the new `crypto map client configuration address` command to configure IKE Mode Configuration in global crypto map configuration mode:

```
router(config)#crypto map tag client configuration address
[initiate | respond]
```

Tunnel Endpoint Discovery Configuration

This enables IPSec to scale to large networks by reducing multiple encryptions. By doing this, it allows for simple configurations on participating peer routers. Each node has a simple configuration that defines the local network being protected.

Tunnel Endpoint Discovery, however, does have the following restrictions:

■ IKE cannot occur until the peer is identified. You can do this by using the `crypto dynamic-map` command. If you use the `discover` keyword with this command, the receiving router sends out a probe to get a response from the peer router.

■ This feature is only available on dynamic crypto maps. The dynamic crypto map template should cover data from the protected transmission and the receiving router using the **any** keyword. When using the **any** keyword, make sure you include explicit **deny** statements to exempt routing protocol traffic prior to entering the **permit any** command.

To create a dynamic crypto map entry with Tunnel Endpoint Discovery configured, use the following commands, beginning in crypto-map configuration mode:

```
Router(config)#crypto dynamic-map dynamic-map-name dynamic-map-
number
Router(config-crypto-m)#set transform-set transform-set-name1
[transform-set-name2 . . . transform-set-name6]
Router(config-crypto-m)#match address access-list-id
Router(config-crypto-m)#match address access-list-id
Router(config-crypto-m)#set peer {hostname | ip-address}
Router(config-crypto-m)#set security-association lifetime seconds
seconds
```

and/or

```
Router(config-crypto-m)#set security-association lifetime kilobytes
kilobytes
Router(config-crypto-m)#set pfs [group1 | group2]
Router(config-crypto-m)#exit
```

These steps are taken when configuring a dynamic crypto map using the **crypto dynamic-map** command.

The following command is optional. It adds a crypto map set to a static crypto map set. To enable peer discovery, enter the **discover** keyword on the dynamic crypto map. After the dynamic crypto map template permits an outbound packet, peer discovery occurs when the packet reaches an interface configured with the dynamic crypto map.

```
Router (config)# crypto map map-name map-number ipsec-isakmp
dynamic dynamic-map-name [discover]
```

Clearing IKE Connections

Use the following commands in EXEC mode to clear existing IKE connections. This command displays existing IKE connections. Note the connection identifiers for connections you want to clear.

```
Router# show crypto isakmp sa
```

This command clears the IKE connections:

```
Router# clear crypto isakmp [connection-id]
```

Troubleshooting IKE

Use the following commands in EXEC mode when you want to troubleshoot. The first command displays the parameters for each configured IKE policy:

```
Router# show crypto isakmp policy
```

This command displays all current IKE security associations:

```
Router# show crypto isakmp sa
```

This command verifies IKE configuration:

```
Router# show running-config
```

This command displays **debug** messages about IKE events:

```
Router# debug crypto isakmp
```

IPSec Configuration Task List

Now the final step is configuring IPSec and making your crypto map entries. Make sure that you have completed your CAs and IKE prior to this.

Making Sure Your Access Lists Are Compatible with IPSec

IKE uses UDP port 500. The IPSec ESP and AH protocols use protocol numbers 50 and 51. Make sure that your access lists are configured so that protocols 50, 51, and UDP port 500 traffic are not blocked at any interfaces used by IPSec. In some cases you might need to add a statement to your access lists to explicitly permit this traffic.

Setting Global Lifetimes for IPSec SAs

To change a global lifetime for IPSec SAs, use one or more of the following commands in global configuration mode. The following command changes the global "timed" lifetime for IPSec SAs. This command also causes the SA to time out after the specified number of seconds have passed.

```
Router(config)#crypto ipsec security-association lifetime seconds
seconds
```

This command changes the global "traffic-volume" lifetime for IPSec SAs. This command also causes the SA to time out after a specified amount of traffic has passed through the IPSec "tunnel" using the SA.

```
Router(config)#crypto ipsec security-association lifetime kilobytes
kilobytes
```

The following commands are optional; they clear existing SAs. This causes any existing SAs to expire immediately. Future SAs use the new lifetimes. Otherwise, any existing SAs expire according to the previously configured lifetimes.

When you use the `clear crypto sa` command without parameters, it clears out the full SA database, which clears out active security sessions. You may also specify the `peer`, `map`, or `entry` keywords to clear out only a subset of the SA database.

```
Router(config)#clear crypto sa
```

or

```
Router(config)#clear crypto sa peer {ip-address | peer-name}
```

or

```
Router(config)#clear crypto sa map map-name
```

or

```
Router(config)#clear crypto sa entry destination-address protocol
spi
```

How Lifetimes Work

When the router requests new SAs, it specifies its global lifetime values in the request to the peer, and it uses this value as the lifetime of the new SAs. This assumes that the particular crypto map entry does not have lifetime values configured. When the router receives a negotiation request from the peer, it uses the smaller of either the lifetime value proposed by the peer or the locally configured lifetime value as the lifetime of the new SAs.

Either after the number of seconds has passed specified by the `seconds` keyword or after the amount of traffic in kilobytes is passed specified by the `kilobytes` keyword, the SA and corresponding keys expire according to whichever comes sooner. SAs that are established manually using a crypto map entry marked as `ipsec-manual` have an infinite lifetime.

To ensure that a new SA is ready for use when the old one expires, a new SA is negotiated *before* the lifetime threshold of the existing SA is reached. The new SA is negotiated either 30 seconds before the `seconds` lifetime expires or when the volume of traffic through the tunnel reaches 256 kilobytes less than the `kilobytes` lifetime (whichever comes first).

A new SA is not negotiated when the lifetime expires as long as no traffic has passed through the tunnel during the entire life of the SA. Instead, a new SA is negotiated only when IPSec sees another packet that should be protected.

Creating Crypto Access Lists

To define which IP traffic will be protected by crypto and which traffic will not be protected by crypto, you need to use crypto access lists. These access lists are *not* the same as regular access lists. They determine what traffic to forward or block at an interface. Suppose you have access lists created to protect all IP traffic between Subnet A and Subnet Y or Telnet traffic between Host A and Host B. The access lists themselves are not specific to IPSec. It is the crypto map entry referencing the specific access list that defines whether IPSec processing is applied to the traffic matching a `permit` in the access list.

Use the following command in global configuration mode to create crypto access lists:

```
Router(config)#access-list access-list-number {deny | permit}
protocol source source-wildcard destination destination-wildcard
[log]
```

or

```
Router(config)#ip access-list extended name
```

(Follow with `permit` and `deny` statements as appropriate.)

This command specifies conditions to determine which IP packets will be protected. You specify conditions using an IP access list designated by either a number or a name. The `access-list` command designates a numbered extended access list; the `ip access-list extended` command designates a named access list. You will want to enable or disable crypto for traffic that matches these conditions.

Defining Transform Sets

Use the following commands starting in global configuration mode to define a transform set. The first command puts you into the crypto transform configuration mode and defines a transform set. Complex rules define which entries you can use for the transform arguments. These rules are explained in the command description for the `crypto ipsec transform-set` command, and Table 27.3 provides a list of allowed transform combinations.

```
Router(config)#crypto ipsec transform-set transform-set-name
transform1 [transform2 [transform3]]
```

This is an optional command that changes the mode associated with the transform set. The mode setting is only applicable to traffic whose source and destination addresses are the IPSec peer addresses; otherwise, it is ignored for all other traffic.

```
Router(cfg-crypto-tran)#mode [tunnel | transport]
```

This command exits the (cfg-crypto-tran) mode:

```
Router(cfg-crypto-tran)#exit
```

This command clears existing IPSec SAs so that any changes to a transform set take effect on subsequently established SAs. Manually established SAs are reestablished immediately.

Using the `clear crypto sa` command without parameters clears out the full SA database, which clears out active security sessions. You may also specify the `peer`, `map`, or `entry` keywords to clear out only a subset of the SA database.

```
Router(config)#clear crypto sa
```

or

```
Router(config)#clear crypto sa peer {ip-address | peer-name}
```

or

```
Router(config)#clear crypto sa map map-name
```

or

```
Router(config)#clear crypto sa entry destination-address protocol
spi
```

Table 27-3 shows the transform combinations that are allowed.

Crypto Map Entries

Making Crypto Map Entries to Establish Manual SAs   Whenever IKE is not being used to establish the SAs and you need to establish manual SAs, use the following commands starting in global configuration mode to make your crypto map entries. The first command specifies the crypto map entry to make or modify. This command also puts you into the crypto map configuration mode.

```
Router(config)#crypto map map-name seq-num ipsec-manual
```

This command names an IPSec access list. This access list determines which traffic should and should not be protected by IPSec security in the

	Transform Type	Transform	Description
Table 27-3 *Allowed Transform Combinations*	**AH Transform**	**ah-md5-hmac**	AH with the HMAC-MD5 authentication algorithm
		ah-sha-hmac	AH with the HMAC-SHA-1 authentication algorithm
	ESP Encryption Transform	**esp-des**	ESP with the 56-bit DES encryption algorithm
		esp-3des	ESP with the 168-bit DES encryption algorithm (3DES or Triple DES)
		esp-null	Null encryption algorithm
	ESP Authentication Transform	**esp-md5-hmac**	ESP with the HMAC-MD5 authentication algorithm
		esp-sha-hmac	ESP with the HMAC-SHA-1 authentication algorithm
	IP Compression Transform	**comp-lzs**	IP compression with the LZS algorithm

context of this crypto map entry. The access list can specify only one **permit** entry when IKE is not used.

```
Router(config-crypto-m)#match address access-list-id
```

This command sets the remote IPSec peer. This is the peer to which IPSec protected traffic should be forwarded. Only one peer can be specified when IKE is not used.

```
Router(config-crypto-m)#set peer {hostname | ip-address}
```

This command specifies which transform set should be used. This has to be the same transform set that is specified in the remote peer's corresponding crypto map entry. Only one transform set can be specified when IKE is not being used.

```
Router(config-crypto-m)#set transform-set transform-set-name
```

When the specified transform set includes the AH protocol, the AH Security Parameter Indexes and the keys apply to inbound and outbound protected traffic. This manually specifies the AH security association to be used with protected traffic:

```
Router(config-crypto-m)#set session-key inbound ah spi hex-key-
string
```

and

```
Router(config-crypto-m)#set session-key outbound ah spi hex-key-
string
```

This command sets the ESP Security Parameter Indexes and keys to apply to inbound and outbound protected traffic when the specified transform set includes the ESP protocol. Specify the cipher keys if the transform set includes an ESP cipher algorithm. If the transform set includes an ESP authenticator algorithm, specify the authenticator keys. This manually specifies the ESP security association to be used with protected traffic:

```
Router(config-crypto-m)# set session-key inbound esp spi cipher
hex-key-string [authenticator hex-key-string]
```

and

```
Router(config-crypto-m)#set session-key outbound esp spi cipher
hex-key-string [authenticator hex-key-string]
```

This command exits crypto-map configuration mode and returns you to global configuration mode:

```
Router(config-crypto-m)#exit
```

Now, simply do these steps as many times as necessary to make additional crypto map entries.

Making Crypto Map Entries that Use IKE to Establish SAs The IPSec peers can negotiate the settings they will use for the new SAs when IKE is used to establish SAs. This means that you can specify lists such as lists of acceptable transforms within the crypto map entry.

Use the following commands starting in global configuration mode to make crypto map entries that will use IKE to establish the SAs. The following command names the crypto map entry to make or modify. This command also puts you into the crypto map configuration mode.

```
Router(config)#crypto map map-name seq-num ipsec-isakmp
```

This command names the extended access list. This access list determines which traffic should and shouldn't be protected by IPSec security in the context of this crypto map entry.

```
Router(config-crypto-m)#match address access-list-id
```

This command specifies a remote IPSec peer. This is the peer to which IPSec protected traffic can be forwarded. Just repeat for multiple remote peers.

```
Router(config-crypto-m)#set peer {hostname | ip-address}
```

This command specifies which transform sets are allowed for this crypto map entry. List multiple transform sets in order of priority (highest priority first).

```
Router(config-crypto-m)#set transform-set transform-set-name1
[transform-set-name2 . . . transform-set-name6]
```

This command is optional. If you want the SA for this crypto map entry to be negotiated using different IPSec security association lifetimes than the global lifetimes, specify a security association lifetime for the crypto map entry.

```
Router(config-crypto-m)#set security-association lifetime seconds
seconds
```

and/or

```
Router(config-crypto-m)#set security-association lifetime kilobytes
kilobytes
```

This command is optional. It specifies that separate SAs should be established for each source/destination host pair. Without this command, a single IPSec "tunnel" could carry traffic for multiple source hosts and multiple destination hosts. This is used when the router requests new SAs. It establishes one set for traffic between Host A and Host B, and a separate set for traffic between Host A and Host C. Make sure that you use this command with care because multiple streams between given subnets can rapidly consume resources.

```
Router(config-crypto-m)#set security-association level per-host
```

This command is also optional. It specifies that IPSec should ask for perfect forward secrecy when requesting new SAs for this crypto map entry or should demand PFS in requests received from the IPSec peer.

```
Router(config-crypto-m)#set pfs [group1 | group2]
```

This command exits crypto-map configuration mode and returns you to global configuration mode:

```
Router(config-crypto-m)#exit
```

Simply do these steps as many times as necessary to make additional crypto map entries.

Making Dynamic Crypto Maps   When making Dynamic crypto maps, you are going to need IKE. Dynamic crypto maps can make IPSec configuration easier. They are generally recommended for use with networks where the peers are not always predetermined. An example of this is mobile users, who obtain dynamically-assigned IP addresses. First, the mobile clients need to authenticate themselves to the local router's IKE by something other than an IP address, such as a FQDN. Once authenticated, the security association request can be processed against a dynamic crypto map, which is set up to accept requests (matching the specified local policy) from previously unknown peers.

Making a Dynamic Crypto Map Set   Use the following commands starting in global configuration mode to make a dynamic crypto map entry. The following command makes a dynamic crypto map entry.

```
Router(config)#crypto dynamic-map dynamic-map-name dynamic-seq-num
```

This command specifies which transform sets are allowed for the crypto map entry. List multiple transform sets in order of priority (highest priority first). This is the only configuration statement required in dynamic crypto map entries.

```
Router(config-crypto-m)#set transform-set transform-set-name1
[transform-set-name2 . . . transform-set-name6]
```

This is an optional but highly recommended command that accesses a list number or name of an extended access list. This access list determines which traffic should and should not be protected by IPSec security in the context of this crypto map entry. Even though access-lists are optional for dynamic crypto maps, they are *highly* recommended. If this is configured, the data flow identity proposed by the IPSec peer must fall within a **permit** statement for this crypto access list.

```
Router(config-crypto-m)#match address access-list-id
```

If this is not configured, the router accepts any data flow identity proposed by the IPSec peer. However, if this is configured but the specified access list does not exist or is empty, the router will drop all packets. This is similar to static crypto maps because they also require that an access list be specified.

NOTE: *Care must be taken if the **any** keyword is used in the access list, because the access list is used for packet filtering as well as for negotiation.*

This is an optional command that specifies a remote IPSec peer. Repeat the command for multiple remote peers. This is rarely configured in dynamic crypto map entries. Dynamic crypto map entries are often used for unknown remote peers.

This is an optional command used when you want the security associations for this crypto map to be negotiated using shorter IPSec security association lifetimes rather than the globally specified lifetimes. Just specify a key lifetime for the crypto map entry.

```
Router(config-crypto-m)#set peer {hostname | ip-address}
Router(config-crypto-m)#set security-association lifetime seconds
seconds
```

and/or

```
Router(config-crypto-m)#set security-association lifetime kilobytes
kilobytes
```

This is an optional command specifying that IPSec should ask for perfect forward secrecy when requesting new security associations for this crypto map entry or should demand perfect forward secrecy in requests received from the IPSec peer.

```
Router(config-crypto-m)#set pfs [group1 | group2]
```

This command exits crypto-map configuration mode and returns you to global configuration mode.

```
Router(config-crypto-m)#exit
```

Adding the Dynamic Crypto Map Set into a Regular or Static Crypto Map Set   You can add one or more dynamic crypto map sets into a crypto map set, via crypto map entries that reference the dynamic crypto map sets. You should set the crypto map entries referencing dynamic maps to be the lowest priority entries in a crypto map set, meaning the highest sequence numbers.

To add a dynamic crypto map set into a static crypto map set, use the following command in global configuration mode:

```
crypto map map-name seq-num ipsec-isakmp dynamic dynamic-map-name
```

Applying Crypto Map Sets to Interfaces   You need to apply a crypto map set to each interface through which IPSec traffic will flow. Applying the crypto map set to an interface instructs the router to evaluate all the interface's traffic against the crypto map set and to use the specified policy during connection or security association negotiation on behalf of traffic to be protected by crypto.

To apply a crypto map set to an interface, use the following command in interface configuration mode:

```
Router (config-if)# crypto map map-name
```

Monitoring and Maintaining IPSec   Some configuration changes only take effect when negotiating subsequent SAs. If you want the new settings to take immediate effect, you must clear the existing SAs so that they will be re-established with the changed configuration. For manually established SAs, you must clear and reinitialize the SAs or the changes will never take effect. If the router is actively processing IPSec traffic, it is desirable to clear only the portion of the SA database that would be affected by the configuration changes (that is, clear only the SAs established by a given crypto map set). Clearing the full SA database should be reserved for large-scale changes, or for when the router is processing very little other IPSec traffic.

If you want to clear and initialize your IPSec SAs, you use one of the following commands in global configuration mode:

```
Router(config)#clear crypto sa
```

or

```
Router(config)#clear crypto sa peer {ip-address | peer-name}
```

or

```
Router(config)#clear crypto sa map map-name
```

or

```
Router(config)#clear crypto sa entry destination-address protocol
spi
```

When you enter the `clear crypto sa` command without any parameters, it clears out your entire SA database as well as your active security sessions. You can also specify the `map`, `peer`, or `entry` keywords to clear out only a subset of the SA database. For more information, see the `clear crypto sa` command.

Checking Your Configuration   When you want to check your IPSec configuration, use one or more of the following commands in EXEC mode. The following displays your transform set configuration:

```
Router#show crypto ipsec transform-set
```

This displays your crypto map configuration:

```
Router#show crypto map [interface interface | tag map-name]
```

This displays information about IPSec SAs:

```
Router#show crypto ipsec sa [map map-name | address | identity]
[detail]
```

This displays information about dynamic crypto maps:

```
Router#show crypto dynamic-map [tag map-name]
```

This displays global SA lifetime values:

```
Router#show crypto ipsec security-association lifetime
```

Configuring
ISDN

Technologies for remote connectivity were once based on analog systems, yet today it has progressed towards digital operations. Digital technology has become the choice for high-speed, cost-effective telecommunication. The *Integrated Services Digital Network* (ISDN) is a leading digital technology used for providing temporary remote access to corporate networks.

Situations may exist in which a location needs to communicate with another site for only small intervals. A site may need, for instance, to transfer a large file at a specific time every week or use a dialup connection as backup to the dedicated link. Another use for temporary remote connectivity is telecommuting or remote technical support to enterprise networks. In situations like these, ISDN dial connectivity provides a solution.

ISDN eliminates any analog signal conversion in the transmission process. The "call" is digital from end to end. ISDN has two different types of services:

- *Basic Rate Interface* (BRI) service
- *Primary Rate Interface* (PRI) service

BRI service provides two ISDN Bearer (B) channels and one ISDN *Data* (D) channel. The B channels are used for data, voice, video, or fax transmission. The D channel provides out-of-band signaling that sets up and tears down the calls. PRI service provides 23 B channels and one D channel. The transmission of each B channel is either 56 Kbps or 64 Kbps. The transmission rate is dependent on the type of ISDN switch used at the central office of the ISDN provider. Cisco IOS and selected interface processors support both BRI and PRI services.

Configuring BRI Service

BRI is typically used by the remote location, requiring access to the central location of an enterprise or corporate network. Establishing the BRI configuration on Cisco routers is done in two basic steps. The first step is to define the type of ISDN switch connecting the router to the ISDN provider central office. The ISDN switch types supported by Cisco IOS are found in Table 28-1. Specifying the type of ISDN switch used for the connection is done by entering the `isdn switch-type` global configuration command. Here is the format of this command:

```
isdn switch-type bri-switch-type
```

The configuration is for an ISDN circuit, so the `isdn` keyword is used. To specify the exact switch type, the keyword `switch-type` is followed by the *bri-switch-type* variable value. The *bri-switch-type* values available are found in Table 28-1.

There may be some instances where a router has multiple ISDN switch types connected. For instance, in a situation where the temporary access does not warrant a dedicated line, however the information received from the location is vital to business processes, two ISDN providers connect to the same router. The ISDN providers are using a different ISDN switch type. In this case, the `isdn switch-type` interface command can be used on the ISDN interface configuration overriding the global configuration command. The global `isdn switch-type` configuration command must be set prior to configuring the `isdn switch-type` interface command. Allowing the `isdn switch-type` interface command enables the router to connect to multiple switch types concurrently.

NOTE: *The global `isdn switch-type` configuration command takes effect only during the very first initialization of ISDN on the router or when the router is reloaded. Subsequent changes to the global `isdn switch-type` after the initial configuration will not modify the switch type without reloading the router. If the router cannot be reloaded and the switch type must be altered to enable ISDN connectivity, the `isdn switch-type` interface command should be used.*

Associated with defining the ISDN switch type is determining the occurrence of Layer 2 ISDN *terminal endpoint identifier* (TEI) negotiation. The TEI negotiation is the process of negotiating an identifier that is obtained from the ISDN network. This can be done on power up of the router or when the first call is initiated. The default is when the router is powered up. TEI negotiation is done in instances when the switches release layer 1 or 2 when no calls are present. The following command designates TEI negotiation:

```
isdn tei (first-call | powerup)
```

The keyword `isdn` is used to designate the ISDN command set. The `tei` keyword indicates to the IOS that terminal endpoint negotiation is being specified rather than defaulting to `powerup`. Setting the keyword `first-call` is used to say that TEI will be negotiated either at power up of the router or on the first call.

The ISDN provider will provide *Service Profile Identifiers* (SPIDs) for the two B channels on your ISDN circuit. These SPIDs are numbers that usu-

Table 28–1

BRI ISDN Switch
Types and Their
Associated Key-
words

bri-switch-type Variable Value	Switch Names and Their Locations
basic-5ess	AT&T basic rate switch (North America)
basic-dms100	Northern Telecom DMS100 basic rate switch (North America)
basic-ni	National ISDN switches (North America)
basic-ts103	TS013 switch (Australia)
basic-1tr6	1TR6 ISDN switch (Germany)
basic-net3	NET3 ISDN, (Norway and New Zealand)
ntt	NTT ISDN switch (Japan)
vn3	VN3 and VN4 ISDN switches (France)

ally resemble telephone numbers but are not at all related to a phone number. Two SPIDs are provided. Each SPID represents a B channel on the ISDN circuit. Configuring the SPID numbers in the Cisco router configuration is dependent on the type of switch used by the ISDN provider. A DMS-100 or a *National ISDN-1* (NI-1) switch requires the router to have the SPIDs defined. If the ISDN provider is using an AT&T 5ess switch, the router can learn them dynamically and hence are not required.

NOTE: *Even though the AT&T 5ess switch does not require the SPID to be defined in the router, it may be prudent to do as a means of documentation for troubleshooting purposes.*

The SPID numbers are configured under the interface definition for the ISDN port. The format of the command is shown here:

```
isdn spid1 spid-number [ldn]
isdn spid2 spid-number [ldn]
```

The `isdn spid1` and `isdn spid2` interface commands identify the SPID number being defined. The `isdn spid1` interface command defines the SPID number assigned to B channel 1. The `isdn spid2` interface command defines the SPID number assigned to B channel 2. The *spid-number* value must be 10 digits long. A value specified for the optional variable named *ldn* is used as a local directory number. This may be used if the router is going to answer calls to a second directory number. With the SPIDs in place, calls can now be received and initiated by the router, so protocols need to be configured.

Point-to-Point connections are desired in a dial-up environment. By default, the encapsulation of a ISDN B channel is HDLC. Since routing protocols and network layer protocols are the choice, *Point-to-Point protocol* (PPP) encapsulation is the preferred method. To enable PPP encapsulation on a BRI, the following interface configuration command must be issued:

```
encapsulation ppp
```

The `encapsulation` keyword signifies that the interface will do some type of encapsulation of other protocol packets. The `ppp` keyword indicates that packets will be encapsulated in PPP over the ISDN connection.

Now that the desired encapsulation is configured, the protocols that will be encapsulated are configured. For a router to start an ISDN call, it must see interesting packets that will trigger a call. The command that defines interesting packets and who to call is as follows:

```
dialer map protocol next-hop-address name hostname [spc]
[speed 56 | 64] [broadcast] dial-string [:isdn-subaddress]
```

The `dialer map` is what causes the router to do an actual ISDN call. The value of the *protocol* variable identifies the type4 of networking protocol being transported over the connection. The possible values are: `appletalk`, `bridge`, `clns`, `decnet`, `ip`, `ipx`, `novell`, `snapshot`, `vines`, and `xns`. The *next-hop-address* variable value is the protocol address of the partner ISDN device being contacted. Use of the bridge protocol value negates the specification of the next-hop-address variable value. The `name` keyword and its associated hostname variable value identifies and is used as authentication of incoming calls. For ISDN this value is the calling line identification number of the remote ISDN device. The `spc` keyword is useful only in Germany where connections supporting the semipermanent connection feature between the customer premise equipment and the central office switch. The `speed` keyword specifies either `56` Kbps or `64` Kbps transmission rates for each B channel of the ISDN circuit. The default value is 64. The `broadcast` keyword is used if any of the supporting network protocols use broadcasts for communication between resources. Finally, the *dial-string* variable specifies the calling number used to connect to the other ISDN device. The optional *subaddress* variable is used if the router dials into a multipoint ISDN device.

Table 28–2

PRI ISDN Switch
Types and Their
Associated Key-
words

pri-switch-type **Variable Value**	**Switch Names and Their Locations**
pri-4ess	AT&T primary rate switch (United States)
pri-5ess	AT&T primary rate switch (United States)
pri-dms100	Northern Telecom DMS100 primary rate switch (North America)
pri-ntt	NTT ISDN PRI switch (Japan)
pri-net5	European ISDN PRI switch
none	No switch defined

To control who can dial into an interface, a BRI is assigned a dialer-group which associates it to a dialer-list. The dialer-group interface command syntax is as follows:

`dialer-group` *group-number*

The `dialer-group` keyword is used to identify the dialer-list definitions that are assigned to the interface. The *group-number* variable ranges from 1 to 10 and must match a `dialer-list` *group-number*. Using the `dial-group` interface command enables the router administrator to apply the rules of a single dialer-list to any ISDN interface.

The `dialer-list` global configuration command is configured as follows:

`dialer-list` *dialer-group* `list` `access-list-`*number*

The `dialer-group` is associated to an access list so only certain protocols or users can communicate over the BRIs in the specific `dialer-group`. The `dialer-list` keyword is used to configure the dialer list followed by the `dialer-group` being associated to the list. Then the dialer-list is also associated to an access list that is used to enable specific communication for the BRI being configured.

If additional security is wanted, then a screening process can be added for further verification. On the BRI interface configuration mode, the following command can be entered to enable screening of incoming calls:

`isdn caller` *number*

This designates that the `isdn caller` having a *number* that matches the one given on the interface configuration is allowed to connect to the router.

If the number does not match, then the router will not accept the call and disconnect.

These are the basic commands for configuring a BRI. The following section reviews the basic configuration requirements for PRI service.

Configuring Primary Rate Interface (PRI) Service

The PRI service also requires the definition of the ISDN switch type. This was discussed fully under BRI and does not need to be explained again. However, the variable values possible for the PRI interfaces on the router are limited to the ISDN switch types listed in Table 28-2.

The format for the global and interface configuration commands specifying the PRI ISDN switch is shown here:

```
isdn switch-type pri-switch-type
```

The *pri-switch-type* variable value must be one of the values listed in Table 28-2.

The PRI ISDN service uses a full T1/E1 and requires the Cisco router to be able to distinguish the various channels available on the circuit. The Cisco 7x00 series utilizes the MIP interface to provide the functionality of discerning the different channels on the circuit. The instance of the MIP is configured by configuring the global `controller` interface command with the following format:

```
controller {t1 | e1} slot/port | number
```

The `controller` keyword identifies the use of a MIP card to support the ISDN PRI service. The `t1` keyword indicates that the service is using the T1 specifications. Specifying the `e1` keyword indicates the PRI service is using the E1 (European) specifications. The *slot[/port]* variable value identifies the MIP position in the Cisco 7x00 series router. The number variable value identifies the MIP position in the Cisco 4x00 series routers.

Under the controller interface configuration, two subsequent options are usually defined to enable the MIP to properly send and receive data on the T1/E1 connection supporting the ISDN. The first of these is the framing type. The specification of the framing type is accomplished using the framing interface configuration command with the following formats:

```
framing {sf | esf}
framing {crc4 | no-crc4} [australia]
```

The `framing` keyword under the `controller` definition identifies the type of framing being used on the line. The `sf` and `esf` values identify the use of a T1 line. Specifying `sf` indicates that the line is using super frame encoding for the data. The `esf` instructs the MIP to apply extended super frame encoding for the data transmitted on the T1 circuit. The second form of the framing interface configuration command is used for E1 circuits. The use of the `australia` optional value instructs the MIP to use the E1 framing type employed in Australia.

The second option coded on under the controller interface configuration identifies the type of line-coding used on the circuit. The line-code type is specified using the linecode interface configuration command with the following format:

```
linecode {ami | b8zs | hdb3}
```

The values for the `linecode` interface command identify the type of encoding performed on the line. The *alternate mark inversion* (`ami`) is the default for T1 lines but is available for use on the T1 or E1 lines. The *binary 8 zero substitution* (`b8zs)` type is valid only on T1 lines. *High-density bipolar 3* (`hdb3`) is the default for E1 lines and valid only on E1 lines. The `linecode` interface configuration command is used when the T1 or E1 is fractional, using each channel as an individual line, versus using the entire bandwidth. Check with the ISDN PRI service provider on which value to code.

A final optional controller interface configuration subcommand identifies which channels (timeslots) of the T1/E1 circuit will be in use. This is specified using the `pri-group` interface command in the following format:

```
pri-group [timeslots range]
```

The *range* variable value for T1 circuits is anywhere from 1 to 24. E1 circuits may range from 1 to 31. The range defined establishes which channels of the T1 are used for ISDN connections.

The controller definitions must be associated with an interface configuration. The `interface serial` global configuration commands identify how the T1/E1 are channelized in support of ISDN. The format of the `interface serial` global configuration command is as follows:

```
interface serial slot[/port]:timeslot
interface serial number:timeslot)
```

The `interface serial` *slot*[/*port*] command is the format used on Cisco 7x00 series routers. The `interface serial` *number* format is used on the Cisco 4x00 series routers. The *:timeslot* value identifies which channel is acting as the D channel for the PRI service. For T1 circuits, the value must always be :23, and for E1 it must always be :15. Be sure to include the ':' in the timeslot value because it is required.

Dial-On-Demand Routing (DDR) with ISDN

Now that the basics for configuring BRI and PRI ISDN connections have been discussed, we move to implementing ISDN using the Cisco IOS *Dial-on-Demand Routing* (DDR) feature. Figure 28-1 illustrates a typical ISDN solution for telecommuters and remote technical troubleshooting found in many corporations. Router R1, is a Cisco 7500 series router providing PRI service for various remote locations. Router R2 is a telecommuter and router R3 is a remote technical support personnel. The two remote locations are using Cisco 2500 series routers.

The following router configurations apply to Figure 28-1:

Router R1 applied to Figure 28-1:

```
hostname R1-isdn
!
username R2-isdn password 7 68280FDE321
username R3-isdn password 7 879BA478928
isdn switch-type primary-dms100
!
interface ethernet 0
 ip address 10.10.4.1 255.255.255.0
!
controller t1 1/0
 framing esf
 linecode b8zs
 pri-group timeslots 1-24
!
interface serial 1/0:23
 ip address 10.10.9.1 255.255.255.0
 encapsulation ppp
 dialer idle-timeout 300
 dialer map ip 10.10.9.2 name R2-isdn speed 56 2125554040
 dialer map ip 10.10.9.3 name R3-isdn 5411
 dialer-group 1
!
router igrp 10
 network 10.0.0.0
 redistribute static
!
! route to R3-isdn
ip route 10.10.13.0 255.255.255.0 10.10.9.3
! route to R2-isdn
ip route 10.10.14.0 255.255.255.0 10.10.9.2
!
```

Figure 28–1
DDR using ISDN to a
central site router

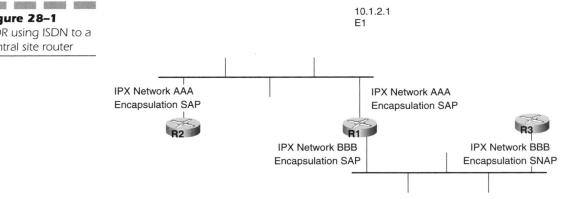

```
access-list 101 deny igrp 0.0.0.0 255.255.255.255 0.0.0.0
255.255.255.255
!NTP
access-list 101 deny udp 0.0.0.0 255.255.255.255 0.0.0.0
255.255.255.255 eq 123
!SNMP
access-list 101 deny udp 0.0.0.0 255.255.255.255 0.0.0.0
255.255.255.255 eq 161
access-list 101 permit ip 0.0.0.0 255.255.255.255 0.0.0.0
255.255.255.255
!
dialer-list 1 list 101
```

The host name of the central site router at the corporate data center is
R1 as denoted by the hostname command in the router configuration of
router R1. The PRI router must have a list of usernames defining what
remote resources can access the router through the ISDN dial-up connection. The username values must be the hostnames of the remote routers
connecting through the ISDN PRI service. The MIP controller card is
installed in slot 1, and port 0 of the MIP is being used for this T1 connection.
This is specified on the controller configuration command. The controller is
to use extended super frame and b8zs line-coding for sending and receiving

data on the T1 circuit. The entire T1 is being used and is denoted by the pri-group timeslot range of 1 to 24. This enables the single T1 line to support up to 23 B channel connections at 64 Kbps each because the R1 router is connected to a DMS-100 ISDN switch. If it were connected to a 5ess switch, it would only support 56 Kbps on each B channel. The PPP encapsulation method is used for the ISDN transport of data. The two dial-map commands of the interface serial 1/0 configuration identify the ISDN connections to router R2 and R3. The R2 router connects to a 5ess switch, hence, you must specify the 56 Kbps speed on the dialer-map definition to router R2. Router R3 in the example connects to the same DMS-100 used by R1. In this case, because they are located on the same switch, only the last four digits of the dial-string are necessary in the dialer-map command representing router R2. The PRI is associated with dialer-group 1, which identifies dialer-list 1, which points to the 101 access list to determine interesting or uninteresting packets used by DDR in determining connectivity to the remote locations. The access list 101 uses an extended access list to deny (mark as uninteresting) IGRP updates, *Network Time Protocol* (NTP) and SNMP packets. All other IP packets, however, are of interest and will case DDR to initiate and ISDN connection to the remote routers R2 and R3 if a connection does not already exist. DDR is made aware of the interesting IP packets by use of static routes configured and distributed to the IGRP routing process within router R1.

Router R3 configuration applied to Figure 28-1:

```
hostname R3-isdn
!
username R1-isdn password 7 98765FEA398
isdn switch-type basic-dms100
!
interface ethernet 0
 ip address 10.10.13.1 255.255.255.0
 no mop enabled
!
interface bri 0
 ip address 10.10.9.3 255.255.255.0
 encapsulation ppp
 no ip route-cache
 isdn spid1 212555541101 5551111
 isdn spid2 212555541102 5551112
 dialer idle-timeout 300
 dialer map ip 10.10.9.1 name R1-isdn 1111
 dialer map ip 10.10.9.1 name R1-isdn 1112
 dialer-group 1
!
ip route 10.10.0.0 255.255.0.0 10.10.9.1
!
access-list 101 deny udp 0.0.0.0 255.255.255.255 0.0.0.0
255.255.255.255 eq 177
```

```
access-list 101 permit ip 0.0.0.0 255.255.255.255 0.0.0.0
255.255.255.255
!
dialer-list 1 list 101
```

Router R3 connects to the DMS-100 and therefore requires the definitions of the SPIDs for the BRI service connection. The username specified is the hostname of router R1. Two numbers are provided on router R3 to contact router R1. If the first `dialer-map` *next-hop-address* connection fails, the second number is used to connect to router R1. The values used in the SPID definitions identify 212 as the area code, 555 as the local exchange and 5411 as the station ID. The last two digits on both SPIDs represent the terminal identifier assigned by the ISDN service provider.

Router R2 configuration applied to Figure 28-1:

```
hostname R2-isdn
!
username R1-isdn password 7 ABE41688
isdn switch-type basic-5ess
!
interface ethernet 0
 ip address 10.10.14.1 255.255.255.0
 no mop enabled
!
interface bri 0
 ip address 10.10.9.2 255.255.255.0
 encapsulation ppp
 no ip route-cache
 bandwidth 56
 dialer map ip 10.10.9.1 name R1-isdn speed 56 12125554442
 dialer-group 1
!
ip route 10.10.0.0 255.255.0.0 10.10.9.1
!
access-list 101 deny udp 0.0.0.0 255.255.255.255 0.0.0.0
255.255.255.255 eq 177
access-list 101 permit ip 0.0.0.0 255.255.255.255 0.0.0.0
255.255.255.255
!
dialer-list 1 list 101
```

Router R2 connects its ISDN BRI line to a different central office and thus uses a different type of ISDN switch. In this case R2 is connected to an AT&T 5ESS ISDN switch. Because R2 connects to a 5ESS, it does not have to have the SPIDs defined in the router configuration. The speed 56 value coded on the dialer-map command sets the ISDN BRI line speed to 56 Kbps.

Using Caller ID

The Cisco IOS can use the *Calling Line Identification* (CLID) number received from an ISDN switch to verify the connecting router. The connection between router R1 and R3 can make use of this because they are connected to the same switch. A slight modification to router R3 and R1 enables the use of the CLID feature. The following configurations apply the CLID feature to router R1 and R3.

Router R1 configuration using the CLID feature:

```
hostname R1-isdn
!
username R2-isdn password 7 68280FDE321
username R3-isdn password 7 879BA478928
isdn switch-type primary-dms100
!
interface Ethernet 0
 ip address 10.10.4.1 255.255.255.0
!
controller t1 1/0
 framing esf
 linecode b8zs
 pri-group timeslots 1-24
!
interface serial 1/0:23
 ip address 10.10.9.1 255.255.255.0
 dialer idle-timeout 300
 dialer map ip 10.10.9.2 name R2-isdn speed 56 2125554040
 dialer map ip 10.10.9.3 name 5555411 1111
 dialer-group 1
!
router igrp 10
 network 10.0.0.0
 redistribute static
!
! route to R3-isdn
ip route 10.10.13.0 255.255.255.0 10.10.9.3
! route to R2-isdn
ip route 10.10.14.0 255.255.255.0 10.10.9.2
!
access-list 101 deny igrp 0.0.0.0 255.255.255.255 0.0.0.0
255.255.255.255
!NTP
access-list 101 deny udp 0.0.0.0 255.255.255.255 0.0.0.0
255.255.255.255 eq 123
!SNMP
access-list 101 deny udp 0.0.0.0 255.255.255.255 0.0.0.0
255.255.255.255 eq 161
access-list 101 permit ip 0.0.0.0 255.255.255.255 0.0.0.0
```

```
255.255.255.255
!
dialer-list 1 list 101
```

The **name** keyword on the dialer-map for R3 specifies the actual calling line identification number returned by the switch.

Router R3 configuration using the CLID feature:

```
hostname R3-isdn
!
username R1-isdn password 7 98765FEA398
isdn switch-type basic-dms100
!
interface Ethernet 0
 ip address 10.10.13.1 255.255.255.0
 no mop enabled
!
interface bri 0
 ip address 10.10.9.3 255.255.255.0
 no ip route-cache
 isdn spid1 212555541101 5551111
 isdn spid2 212555541102 5551112
 dialer idle-timeout 300
 dialer map ip 10.10.9.1 name 5551111 1111
 dialer map ip 10.10.9.1 name 5551112 1112
 dialer-group 1
!
ip route 10.10.0.0 255.255.0.0 10.10.9.1
!
access-list 101 deny udp 0.0.0.0 255.255.255.255 0.0.0.0
255.255.255.255 eq 177
access-list 101 permit ip 0.0.0.0 255.255.255.255 0.0.0.0
255.255.255.255
!
dialer-list 1 list 101
```

Just as in the central site router R1, the router R3 uses the **name** keyword and value to identify the actual number being returned from the switch.

ISDN Callback

The callback feature enables the billing for the ISDN BRI connection to be charged to the central site by having the central site call back the remote location after an initial connection. This assists in managing the billing aspect of ISDN BRI telecommuting and remote technical support.

The following router configurations apply the callback feature to routers R2 and R1.

Router R2 callback configuration:

```
hostname R2-isdn
!
username R1-isdn password 7 ABE41688
isdn switch-type basic-5ess
!
interface ethernet 0
 ip address 10.10.14.1 255.255.255.0
 no mop enabled
!
interface bri 0
 ip address 10.10.9.2 255.255.255.0
 encapsulation ppp
 no ip route-cache
 bandwidth 56
 dialer map ip 10.10.9.1 name R1-isdn speed 56 12125554442
 dialer-group 1
 ppp callback request
 dialer hold-queue 100 timeout 20
!
ip route 10.10.0.0 255.255.0.0 10.10.9.1
!
access-list 101 deny udp 0.0.0.0 255.255.255.255 0.0.0.0
255.255.255.255 eq 177
access-list 101 permit ip 0.0.0.0 255.255.255.255 0.0.0.0
255.255.255.255
!
dialer-list 1 list 101
```

The ppp callback request command indicates to the router that when it contacts the PRI router R1 it will request the R1 call back. The dial-hold-queue command indicates that up to 100 packets of data will be held in the outbound queue while waiting for router R1 to return the call. Any queued packets are dropped after the timeout value of 20 seconds is reached.

Router R1 configuration in support of the callback feature to router R2:

```
hostname R1-isdn
!
username R2-isdn password 7 68280FDE321
username R3-isdn password 7 879BA478928
isdn switch-type primary-dms100
!
map-class dialer class1
 dialer callback-server username
!
interface Ethernet 0
 ip address 10.10.4.1 255.255.255.0
!
interface serial 1/0:23
 ip address 10.10.9.1 255.255.255.0
 dialer idle-timeout 300
 dialer map ip 10.10.9.2 name R2-isdn speed 56 class class1 1
```

```
 dialer map ip 10.10.9.3 name 5555411 1111
 dialer-group 1
 ppp callback accept
 dialer callback-secure
 dialer enable-timeout 1
 dialer hold-queue
!
router igrp 10
 network 10.10.0.0
 redistribute static
!
! route to R3-isdn
ip route 10.10.13.0 255.255.255.0 10.10.9.3
 ! route to R2-isdn
ip route 10.10.14.0 255.255.255.0 10.10.9.2
!
access-list 101 deny igrp 0.0.0.0 255.255.255.255 0.0.0.0
255.255.255.255
!NTP
access-list 101 deny udp 0.0.0.0 255.255.255.255 0.0.0.0
255.255.255.255 eq 123
!SNMP
access-list 101 deny udp 0.0.0.0 255.255.255.255 0.0.0.0
255.255.255.255 eq 161
access-list 101 permit ip 0.0.0.0 255.255.255.255 0.0.0.0
255.255.255.255
!
dialer-list 1 list 101
```

The map-class global configuration command enables the IOS to establish a *Quality of Service* (QoS) for the connection to router R2 by associating a static map. The `dialer` keyword of the map-class command identifies the dialer-map being used. The *class1* value defined on the command is user-defined and maps a class to the dialer-map. The dialer-map interface command now includes a class keyword and the name of the class to which the dialer-map is now associated. The `name` keyword on the dialer-map is used to provide the dial-string to router R1 for the callback. Added security is built into this configuration through the use of the dialer callback-secure interface configuration command. Using this command ensures that the R1 router will only call back R2 if it has a dial-map command with a defined class for router R2 defined. The dialer enable-timeout interface command determines the amount of time in seconds to wait prior to disconnecting the initial call and beginning the callback.

Snapshot Routing with ISDN

Connection time on ISDN networks can become costly especially if bandwidth is being utilized for routing protocols versus the delivery of end user data. A means for reducing routing protocol consumption of valuable ISDN bandwidth is through the use of snapshot routing. Using snapshot routing bandwidth is preserved for an extended period of time for the transmission of end user data without the over head of routing protocols. Snapshot is effective only in connections that use distance-vector routing protocols. The snapshot routing feature is available starting with IOS Release10.2+ and only with the full Enterprise IOS Release 11.0(3) or higher.

Snapshot routing enables distance-vector routing protocols (that is, IP RIP, IP IGRP, IPX RIP/SPX, AppleTalk RTMP and Banyan VINES RTP) to continue to function dynamically for a specified period of time (active period). After the active period, a quiet period (up to 65 days) may be configured to suppress the normal routing updates over the ISDN connection. In essence, the routing tables of the connecting routers using snapshot routing have a "picture" of the routing tables at a specific moment in time. Future routing updates are held until the quiet time has expired and the routers enter into another active period. The configured active period time must be long enough to provide for multiple routing updates to ensure a complete routing table be built in the routers participating in the snapshot routing protocol. Table 28-3 lists the default routing update intervals for the aforementioned distance-vector routing protocols.

The importance of understanding these routing update intervals is because many ISDN connections are based on interesting packets. For example, if IP is defined as an interesting packet for ISDN connectivity, then every 90 seconds the IGRP process within the router will initiate an ISDN call to send the IGRP routing updates. This will occur even if the end user location does not require connectivity. This becomes cost-inefficient. Snapshot routing quiet period enables the router administrator to place controls on the routing update process.

Snapshot routing is recommended only in hub and spoke or temporary point-to-point topologies. Snapshot routing is based on a client-server model. The client (spoke or remote router) sets the quiet period time and the server (hub or central router) is defined to accept incoming snapshot connections from one or more snapshot client routers.

A router is enabled as the client for snapshot routing when the `snapshot client` interface configuration command is specified. The format of the `snapshot client` interface configuration command is as follows:

```
snapshot client active-time quiet-time [suppress-statechange-
updates] [dialer]
```

The `snapshot client` keyword specified on an interface initiates the snapshot routing process on the router. Specifying the `snapshot client` keyword

Table 28–3

Default Routing Update Intervals for Consideration in Defining Snapshot Routing Active Period

Routing Protocol	Default Routing Update Interval
IP RIP	30 seconds
IP IGRP	90 seconds
IPX RIP	60 seconds
IPX SAP	60 seconds
AppleTalk RTMP	10 seconds
Banyan VINES RTP	30 seconds

indicates to the IOS that this router will act as a client connecting to a snapshot server. The *active-time* variable value may range from 5 to 100 and defines the number of minutes the client will exchange routing updates with the snapshot server. The *active-time* variable does not have a default. Typically the value chosen results in the routers exchanging routing tables anywhere from 6 to 10 times during the active period. The value specified as the *active-time* variable in the `snapshot client` interface command must match the *active-time* variable value in the `snapshot server` command. Table 28-4 lists the three time periods used in snapshot routing protocol and their minimum and maximum times to assist in determining the appropriate *active-time* and *quiet-time* values. The *quiet-time* variable value ranges from 8 to 100,000 measured in minutes. The high end results in 65 days for the quiet period. The *quiet-time* variable value does not default. A rule of thumb is to use the *active-time* variable value plus 3 for the *quiet-time* variable value. The `optional suppress-statechange-updates` keyword stops the router from exchanging routing updates whenever the line protocol state changes from down to up or from dialer spoofing to fully up. Using this keyword protects the bandwidth from being overrun with routing update exchanges. The optional `dialer` keyword is useful for directing the client router to contact the server router even though user data is not present to activate the connection.

A router is enabled as the server for snapshot routing when the `snapshot server` interface configuration command is specified. Here is the format of the `snapshot server` interface configuration command:

```
snapshot server active-time [dialer]
```

The `snapshot server` interface command initializes the server function of the snapshot routing protocol process in the router. The *active-time* variable

Table 28–4

Default Routing Update Intervals for Consideration in Defining Snapshot Routing Active Period

Period	Configurable	Minimum Length	Maximum Length
Active	Yes	5 minutes	100 minutes
Quiet	Yes	5 minutes	65 days
Retry	No	8 minutes	8 minutes

value specifies the amount of time routing update exchange will occur between the server and any client. The range is 5 to 100 measured in minutes and follows the same guidelines as given for the *active-time* variable value on the `snapshot client` interface command. The optional `dialer` keyword enables the client router to contact the server even though user data is absent.

Snapshot routing used in conjunction with DDR from a client requires the `dialer map snapshot` interface command:

```
dialer map snapshot sequence-number dial-string
```

A `dialer map snapshot` interface command is required for each snapshot server the client calls during the active period. The *sequence-number* variable value ranges from 1 to 254 providing a unique identifier for the dialer map. The dial-string variable value is the telephone number of the snapshot server to contact during the active period over the ISDN connection.

Using the previous routing configuration example, router R1 (hub) is defined as the server and routers R2 and R3 are defined as the clients (spokes). The following configuration may be applied to the router R1 to enable snapshot routing:

```
hostname R1-isdn
!
username R2-isdn password 7 68280FDE321
username R3-isdn password 7 879BA478928
isdn switch-type primary-dms100
!
interface ethernet 0
 ip address 10.10.4.1 255.255.255.0
!
controller t1 1/0
 framing esf
 linecode b8zs
 pri-group timeslots 1-24
!
interface serial 1/0:23
 ip address 10.10.9.1 255.255.255.0
 encapsulation ppp
```

```
 dialer idle-timeout 300
 dialer map ip 10.10.9.2 name R2-isdn speed 56 2125554040
 dialer map ip 10.10.9.3 name R3-isdn 5411
 dialer-group 1
 snapshot server 5
 ppp authentication chap
!
router igrp 10
 network 10.0.0.0
!
access-list 101 deny igrp 0.0.0.0 255.255.255.255 0.0.0.0
255.255.255.255
!NTP
access-list 101 deny udp 0.0.0.0 255.255.255.255 0.0.0.0
255.255.255.255 eq 123
!SNMP
access-list 101 deny udp 0.0.0.0 255.255.255.255 0.0.0.0
255.255.255.255 eq 161
access-list 101 permit ip 0.0.0.0 255.255.255.255 0.0.0.0
255.255.255.255
!
dialer-list 1 list 101
```

Router R1 no longer needs the static routes to router R2 and R3. The "5" following the snapshot server interface command indicates that the active period is five minutes in length. The following configurations apply to router R2 and R3 in Figure 28-1:

Router R2 configuration using snapshot routing:

```
hostname R2-isdn
!
username R1-isdn password 7 ABE41688
isdn switch-type basic-5ess
!
interface ethernet 0
 ip address 10.10.14.1 255.255.255.0
 no mop enabled
!
interface bri 0
 ip address 10.10.9.2 255.255.255.0
 encapsulation ppp
 no ip route-cache
 bandwidth 56
 dialer map snapshot 1 name R1-isdn 12125554442
 dialer map ip 10.10.9.1 name R1-isdn speed 56 12125554442
 dialer-group 1
 snapshot client 5 43200 suppress-statechange-updates dialer
!
access-list 101 deny udp 0.0.0.0 255.255.255.255 0.0.0.0
255.255.255.255 eq 177
access-list 101 permit ip 0.0.0.0 255.255.255.255 0.0.0.0
255.255.255.255
!
dialer-list 1 list 101
```

Router R3 configuration using snapshot routing:

```
hostname R3-isdn
!
username R1-isdn password 7 98765FEA398
isdn switch-type basic-dms100
!
interface ethernet 0
 ip address 10.10.13.1 255.255.255.0
 no mop enabled
!
interface bri 0
 ip address 10.10.9.3 255.255.255.0
 encapsulation ppp
 no ip route-cache
 isdn spid1 212555541101 5551111
 isdn spid2 212555541102 5551112
 dialer idle-timeout 300
 dialer map snapshot 1 name R1-isdn 1111
 dialer map snapshot 1 name R1-isdn 1112
 dialer map ip 10.10.9.1 name R1-isdn 1111
 dialer map ip 10.10.9.1 name R1-isdn 1112
 dialer-group 1
 snapshot client 5 43200 suppress-statechange-updates dialer
!
access-list 101 deny udp 0.0.0.0 255.255.255.255 0.0.0.0
255.255.255.255 eq 177
access-list 101 permit ip 0.0.0.0 255.255.255.255 0.0.0.0
255.255.255.255
!
dialer-list 1 list 101
```

Because snapshot routing is employed, the static routes for R2 and R3 to reach R1 are no longer required. The dialer map snapshot command on the BRI0 interface of R2 and R3 creates a map using sequence number 1 to connect to router R1 for routing update exchange. The `name` keyword value is used during ppp authentication to verify the name of the connecting router hostname. The active period on the snapshot client command must match the snapshot server active period time in router R1. The snapshot client command also specifies that the quiet period (in this case 43,200 seconds or 12 hours) will pass before a refresh of the routing table. The `dialer` keyword is used in this case to enable the client routers (R2 and R3) to connect to the server router even when end user traffic is absent on the ISDN link to update the routing tables. The `suppress-statechange-updates` keyword is coded to stop the router from exchanging routing updates while end user connections are being used. The coding of this keyword requires the dialer keyword be configured enabling routing updates to flow.

Using ISDN for dial backup

Many topologies involving ISDN utilize the speed of ISDN to provide dial backup to high speed T1, fractional T1, or 56 Kbps dedicated lines. Figure 28-2 illustrates such a configuration.

The dial backup feature is enabled using the `backup interface` interface configuration command on the serial interface definition for which ISDN dial backup is desired:

`backup interface` *interface-name*

The `backup interface` command identifies the dial up interface on the router that is to be used if *data terminal ready* (DTR) drops on the serial interface to which this `backup interface` command is defined. The *interface-name* variable value specifies the interface number, slot/port pair or slot/adapter/port grouping used as the dial backup connection for the serial interface. Routers will only support serial dial up and ISDN as the backup interfaces.

Once in dial backup mode, it is important to mange and control the length of the dial backup connection and when to drop the dial backup connection once the original serial interface no longer drops DTR. This determination is accomplished using the backup delay interface configuration command:

`backup delay` {*enable-delay* | `never`} {*disable-delay* | `never`}

Using the backup delay interface configuration command on the serial interface being backed up enables the router administrator to adjust when to drop the dial backup connection. The *enable-delay* variable value is measured in seconds and determines how long the serial interface DTR signal must be lost (down) prior to initiating dial backup. The *disable-delay* variable value indicates the number of seconds that must pass after the serial interface DTR is high (up) before terminating the dial backup connection. The values chosen for these two variables is important to consider especially in the case of "flapping" serial interfaces. Specifying `never` as the first positional parameter indicates that the dial backup will never occur automatically, forcing manual intervention. Specifying `never` as the second positional parameter forces manual intervention to terminate the dial backup connection. Both of the delay variables default to 0 seconds making it prudent to provide some type of delay for both activation and deactivation. It is advisable to make the activation (enable-delay) a minimum of 0 seconds and the deactivation delay a minimum of six minutes to ensure a stable dedicated connection once again.

NOTE: *Issuing the shutdown EXEC configuration command on the serial interface will not cause the backup process to initiate since this is a controlled shut down. The backup process only takes place when the DTR drops from electrical signal failure.*

The following router configuration applies to Figure 28-2:

Router R1 configuration applied to Figure 28-2:

```
hostname R1
!
username R2 password 7 68280FDE321
isdn switch-type primary-dms100
!
interface ethernet 0
 ip address 10.10.4.1 255.255.255.0
!
controller t1 1/0
 framing esf
 linecode b8zs
 pri-group timeslots 1-24
!
interface serial 1/0:23
 ip address 10.10.9.1 255.255.255.0
 encapsulation ppp
 dialer idle-timeout 300
 dialer map ip 10.10.9.2 name R2-isdn speed 56 2125554040
 dialer-group 1
!
interface serial 2/0
 ip address 10.10.8.1 255.255.255.0
!
router igrp 10
 network 10.0.0.0
 redistribute static
! route to R2
ip route 10.10.14.0 255.255.255.0 10.10.9.2
!
access-list 101 deny igrp 0.0.0.0 255.255.255.255 0.0.0.0
255.255.255.255
!NTP
access-list 101 deny udp 0.0.0.0 255.255.255.255 0.0.0.0
255.255.255.255 eq 123
!SNMP
access-list 101 deny udp 0.0.0.0 255.255.255.255 0.0.0.0
255.255.255.255 eq 161
access-list 101 permit ip 0.0.0.0 255.255.255.255 0.0.0.0
255.255.255.255
!
dialer-list 1 list 101
```

The following router configuration applies to router R2 in Figure 28-2:

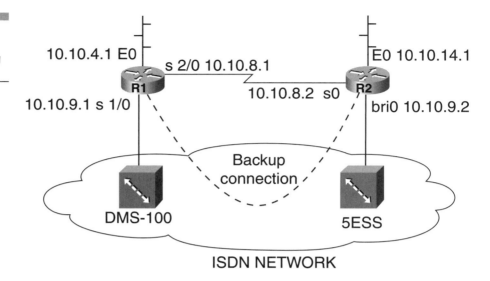

Figure 28–2
Dial backup of a
dedicated line using
ISDN

Router R2 configuration:

```
hostname R2
!
username R1 password 7 ABE41688
isdn switch-type basic-5ess
!
interface ethernet 0
 ip address 10.10.14.1 255.255.255.0
!
interface serial 0
 ip address 10.10.8.2 255.255.255.0
 backup interface bri0
 backup delay 1 360
!
interface bri 0
 ip address 10.10.9.2 255.255.255.0
 encapsulation ppp
 no ip route-cache
 bandwidth 56
 dialer map ip 10.10.9.1 name R1 speed 56 12125554442
 dialer-group 1
!
router igrp 10
 network 10.0.0.0
!
dialer-list 1 list 101
```

Router R2 connects to router R1 using a dedicated serial line. Failure of the dedicated serial line causes router R2 to initiate dial backup to router R1. The dial backup connection on router R2 is terminated only if six minutes passes while DTR is high on serial 0 of router R2. If DTR should drop within the disable-delay value of 360 seconds and then become high again, the disable timer starts again.

Appendix A

Access List Number Ranges for Each Protocol and List Type

Protocols with Access Lists Specified by Numbers

Protocol	Range
IP	1 to 99
Extended IP	100 to 199
Ethernet type code	200 to 299
Ethernet address	700 to 799
Transparent bridging (protocol type)	200 to 299
Transparent bridging (vendor code)	700 to 799
Extended transparent bridging	1100 to 1199
DECnet and extended DECnet	300 to 399
XNS	400 to 499
Extended XNS	500 to 599
AppleTalk	600 to 699
Source-route bridging (protocol type)	200 to 299
Source-route bridging (vendor code)	700 to 799
IPX	800 to 899
Extended IPX	900 to 999
IPX SAP	1000 to 1099
Standard VINES	1 to 100
Extended VINES	101 to 200
Simple VINES	201 to 300

Glossary

AAL—ATM Adaptation Layer. A collection of standardized protocols that provide services to higher layers by adapting user traffic to a cell format. The AAL is divided into the Convergence Sublayer (CS) and the Segmentation and Reassembly (SAR) sublayer.

AAL1—AAL Type 1. Protocol standard used for the transport of Constant Bit Rate (CBR) traffic (audio and video) and for emulating TDM-based circuits (such as DS1 and E1).

AAL2—AAL Type 2. Protocol standard for supporting the time-dependent Variable Bit Rate (VBR-RT) of connection-oriented traffic (packetized video and audio).

AAL3/4—AAL Type 3 and 4. Protocol standard for supporting both connectionless and connection-oriented Variable Bit Rate (VBR) traffic. Used also to support SMDS.

AAL5—AAL Type 5. Protocol standard for supporting the transport of Lightweight Variable Bit Rate (VBR) traffic and signaling messages. Also used to support Frame Relay services.

ABR—Available Bit Rate. One of the two best-effort service types (the other one is UBR) in which the network makes no absolute guarantee of cell delivery, but it guarantees a minimum bit rate for user transmission. An effort is also made to keep cell loss as low as possible.

access control byte—The byte following the start delimiter of a token or frame that is used to control access to the Token Ring network.

access priority—The maximum priority that a token can have for the adapter to use it for transmission.

access rate—The bit per second (bps) rate at which a user can transmit over the network's lines.

access unit—A unit that allows multiple attaching devices access to a Token Ring network at a central point. Sometimes these devices may also be referred to as a concentrator.

ACK—Acknowledgement. A message that acknowledges the reception of a transmitted packet. ACKs can be separate packets or piggybacked on reverse traffic packets.

acknowledgment—In data communications, the transmission of characters from the receiving device, indicating that data sent has been received correctly.

active—(1) Operational. (2) Pertaining to a file, page, or program that is in main storage or memory, as opposed to a file, page, or program that must be retrieved from auxiliary storage. (3) Pertaining to a node or device that is connected or is available for connection to another node or device.

active monitor—A function in a single adapter on a Token Ring network that initiates the transmission of tokens and provides token error recovery facilities. Any active adapter on the ring has the capability to provide the active monitor function if the current active monitor fails.

active program—Any program that is loaded into memory and ready to be executed.

active session— The session in which a user is currently interacting with the computer.

adapter address—Twelve hexadecimal digits that identify a LAN adapter.

adaptive routing—A method of routing packets of data or data messages in which the system's intelligence selects the best path. This path might change with traffic patterns or link failures.

adaptive session-level pacing—A form of session-level pacing in which session components exchange pacing windows that may vary in size during the course of a session. This allows transmission within a network to adapt dynamically to variations in availability and demand of buffers on a session-by-session basis. Session-level pacing occurs within independent stages along the session path according to local congestion at the intermediate nodes.

address—(1) A character or group of characters that identify a data source or destination or a network node. (2) The destination of a message sent through a communications system. In computer network terms, it is a set of numbers that uniquely identify a workstation on a LAN.

adjacent—In a network, pertaining to devices, nodes, or domains that are directly connected by a data link or that share common control.

adjacent link station—A link station directly connected to a given node by a link connection over which network traffic can be carried.

adjusted ring length (ARL)—In a multiple-wiring-closet ring, the sum of all wiring closet-to-wiring closet cables in the main ring path less the length of the shortest of those cables.

Advanced peer-to-peer networking (APPN)—An extension to SNA featuring (a) greater distributed network control that avoids critical hierarchical dependencies, thereby isolating the effects of single points of failure; (b) dynamic exchange of network topology information to foster ease of connections and reconfiguration, adaptive route selection, and simplified network definition; and (c) automated resource registration and directory lookup. APPN extends the LU 6.2 peer orientation for end-user services to network control. It also uses LU 6.2 protocols on its own control point sessions that provide the network control.

Advanced program-to-program communication (APPC)—(1) The general facility characterizing the LU 6.2 architecture and its various implementations in products. (2) Sometimes used to refer to the LU 6.2 architecture and its product implementation as a whole, or an LU 6.2 product feature in particular, such as an APPC application program interface.

AIR—Additive Cell Rate. The cell rate a source can transmit after increasing its rate by the RIF.

AIS—Alarm Indication Signal. One of the OAM function types used for fault management (*see also* CC and RDI).

alert—A message sent to a management services focal point in a network to identify a problem or an impending problem.

algorithm—A prescribed finite set of well-defined rules or processes for the solution of a problem in a finite number of steps. In normal English, it is the mathematical formula for an operation, such as computing the check digits on packets of data that travel via packet-switched networks.

all-routes broadcast frame—A frame that has bits in the routine information field set to indicate the frame is to be sent to all LAN segments in the network. The destination address is not examined and plays no role in bridge routing.

all-stations broadcast frame—A frame whose destination address bits are set to all ones. All stations on any LAN segment that the frame appears on will copy it. It is independent of all-routes broadcasting.

Allowed (or available) cell rate—The available bandwidth in cells.

ANSI—American National Standards Institute. A U.S. technology standards organization.

API—Application Programming Interface. A set of functions used by an application program as a means of providing access to a system's capabilities (operating and communications).

application—A program or set of programs that perform a task.

application program interface (API)—The formally defined programming language interface that allows a programmer to write to the interface.

application transaction program—A program written for or by a user to process the user's application; in an SNA network, an end user of a type 6.2 logical unit.

applications layer—The seventh and highest layer of Systems Network Architecture (SNA) and Open Systems Interconnection (OSI). It supplies functions to applications or nodes, allowing them to communicate with other applications or nodes.

APPN end node—A type 2.1 end node that provides full SNA end-user services and supports sessions between its local control point (CP) and the CP in an adjacent network node to dynamically register its resources with the adjacent CP (its network node server), to send and receive directory search requests, and to obtain management services. It can also attach to a subarea network as a peripheral node.

APPN intermediate routing—The capability of an APPN network node to accept traffic from one adjacent node and pass it on to another with an awareness of session affinities in controlling traffic flow and outage notifications.

APPN intermediate routing network—The portion of an APPN network consisting of the network nodes and their connections.

APPN network—A type 2.1 network having at least one APPN node.

APPN network node—A type 2.1 (T2.1) node that, besides offering full SNA end-user services, provides intermediate routing services within a T2.1 network and network services to its local LU's and attached T2.1 end nodes in its domain. It can also attach to a subarea network as a peripheral node.

APPN node—An APPN network node or an APPN end node.

ARP—Address Resolution Protocol. A TCP/IP protocol used for resolving local network addresses by mapping a physical address (such as a MAC address) to an IP address.

asynchronous—Asynchronous transmission is an approach for acquiring synchronization on a per-byte basis. Start and stop bits are used as delimiters. Asynchronous transfer is an efficient approach for transmitting information where time slots are used on a demand basis (such as in ATDM and ATM) rather than on a periodical one (such as in TDM and STM).

asynchronous transmission—A method of data transmission that allows characters to be sent at irregular intervals by preceding each character with a start bit and following it with a stop bit. No clocking signal is provided. This is in contrast to synchronous transmission.

ATDM—Asynchronous Time-Division Multiplexing. A asynchronous and intelligent TDM in which time slots are allocated to the users on demand (dynamically).

ATM—Asynchronous Transfer Mode. A broadband switching, multiplexing, connection-oriented, high-performance and cost-effective integrated technology for supporting B-ISDN services (multimedia). Since no clock control is necessary, it is called asynchronous (see also STM). Information is transmitted at very high rates (up to hundreds of Mbps) in fixed-size format packets called cells. Traffic streams are distinguished and supported according to different QoS classes.

ATM CSU/DSU—ATM Channel/Data Service Unit. A device that converts information bits (transmitted over the telephony network) or frame-based information into (or from) a stream of ATM cells (*see also* CSU, DSU, and DXI).

ATM forum—Originally founded by a group of vendors and telecommunication companies, this formal standards body is comprised of various committees responsible for making recommendations and producing implementation specifications.

ATM layer—The second layer of the ATM protocol stack model that constructs and processes the ATM cells. Its functions also include a Usage Parameter Control (UPC) and support of QoS classes.

ATM-SAP—ATM-Service Access Point. The physical interface at the boundary between the AAL and the ATM layer (*see also* SAP and PHY-SAP).

AToMMIB—ATM MIB. IETF-defined Management Information Base (MIB) for managing VP/VC links and ATM PVC-supported services and interfaces.

attenuation—A decrease in magnitude of current, voltage, or electrical or optical power of a signal in transmission between points. It can expressed in decibels or nepers.

average cell rate—The mean number of cells that the source can inject into a network over a given virtual connection (VC).

average cell transfer delay—The arithmetic average of a number of cell transfer delays (CTD). See also Mean Cell Transfer Delay.

B-ICI—Broadband Inter-Carrier Interface. An interface that supports service connections (such as CRS, CES, SMDS, and FR) across public ATM networks and/or carriers.

B-ISDN—Broadband Integrated Services Digital Network. An ITU-T protocol platform to support the integrated, high-speed transmission of data, audio, and video in a seamless fashion. ATM emerged as a suitable transport standard.

backup server—A program or device that copies files so at least two up-to-date copies always exist.

backbone—A LAN, a WAN, or a combination of both dedicated to providing connectivity between subnetworks in an enterprise-wide network. Subnetworks are connected to the backbone via bridges and/or routers and the backbone serves as a communications highway for LAN-to-LAN traffic.

backbone LAN segment—In a multisegment LAN configuration, a centrally located LAN segment that other LAN segments are connected to by means of bridges or routers.

backup path—In an IBM Token Ring Network, an alternative path for signal flow through access units and their main ring path cabling.

balun—Balanced/unbalanced. An impedance matching transformer. Baluns are small passive devices that convert the impedance of coaxial cable so that its signal can run on twisted-pair wiring. They are used often so that IBM 3270-type terminals, which traditionally require coaxial cable connection to their host computer, can run on twisted-pair.

bandwidth—The range of electrical frequencies a device can handle.

BASize—Buffer Allocation Size. A one-byte field in the CPCS-PDU header to indicate to the receiving end the buffer space that needs to be reserved for reassembling the CPCS-PDU.

beacon—A Token Ring frame sent by an adapter indicating that it has detected a serious ring problem, such as a broken cable or a multistation access unit. An adapter sending these frames is said to be beaconing.

BEC—Backward Error Correction. An error-correction scheme where the sender retransmits any data to be found in error, based on the feedback from the receiver.

best effort—A QoS class in which no specific traffic parameters and no absolute guarantees are provided. Best effort includes UBR and ABR (see also service types).

bisynchronous transmission—Also called BISYNC. A data character-oriented communications protocol developed by IBM for synchronous transmission of binary-coded data between two devices.

bit—Abbreviation for binary digit. The smallest unit of information (data) and the basic unit in data communications. A bit can have a value of 0 or 1.

bit rate—The number of bits of data transmitted over a communications line each second.

BNC—A bayonet-locking connector for slim coaxial cables.

BOM—Beginning of Message. A PDU that constitutes the beginning of a message.

bps—Bits per second. A measurement of data transmission speeds.

BRI—Basic Rate Interface. An ISDN service specification that provides two 64-kbps data B-channels and one 16-kbps control D-channel, all sharing the same physical medium.

bridge—(1) An interface connecting two similar LANs. (2) A device that connects two LANs. It performs its functions at the data link control (DLC) layer.

bridge ID—The bridge label combined with the adapter address of the adapter connecting the bridge to the LAN segment with the lowest LAN segment number.

bridge label—A two-byte hexadecimal number that the user can assign to each bridge.

bridge number—The bridge identifier that the user specifies in the bridge program configuration file. The bridge number distinguishes between parallel bridges.

broadcast—The simultaneous transmission of data to more than one destination.

broadcast message—A message from one station sent to all other users. On a Token Ring LAN, the destination address is unspecified; thus, all devices receive the message.

brouter—In local area networking, a device that combines the dynamic routing capabilities of an internetwork router with the capability of a bridge to interconnect LANs.

BSC—Binary Synchronous Communication. A set of IBM operating procedures for synchronous transmission used in teleprocessing networks.

BT—Burst Tolerance. Proportional to the MBS, burst tolerance is used as a measure (leaky bucket parameter) for conformance checking of the SCR.

buffer—In data transmission, a buffer is a temporary storage location for information being sent or received. Usually located between two different devices that have different capabilities or speeds for handling the data.

burstiness—A source traffic characteristic that is defined as the ratio of the peak cell rate (PCR) to the average cell rate. It is a measure of the intercell spacing (*see also* MBS).

bus—A network configuration in which nodes are interconnected through a bidirectional transmission medium.

BUS—Broadcast and Unknown Server. A server that forwards multicast, broadcast, and unknown-destination address traffic to the attached LECs.

BW—Bandwidth. Transmission capacity of a communications medium.

byte—A binary character operated upon as a unit and usually shorter than a computer word. It is eight consecutive bits representing a character.

cable loss—The amount of radio frequency signal attenuation caused by a cable.

cable riser—Cable running vertically in a multi-story building to serve the upper floors.

CAC—Connection Admission Control. An ATM function that determines whether a virtual circuit (VC) connection request should be accepted or rejected.

campus—A networking environment in which users (voice, video, and data) are spread out over a broad geographic area, as in a university, hospital, or medical center. There may be several LANs on a campus and they are connected with bridges and/or routers communicating over telephone or fiber-optic cable.

carrier—A wave or pulse train that can be varied by a signal bearing information to be transmitted over a communication system.

CAT-3—Category 3 Unshielded Twisted. A type of UTP commonly used with ATM interfaces for cell transmission at low speeds, 25-50 Mbps, and at distances up to 100 meters.

CAT-5—Category 5 Unshielded Twisted Pair. A type of UTP commonly used with ATM interfaces for higher-speed cell transmission (more than 50 Mbps).

CBR—Constant (or Continuous) Bit Rate. One of the five ATM classes of service that support the transmission of a continuous bit-stream of information where traffic, such as voice and video, needs to meet certain QoS requirements (*see also* QoS Classes).

CC—Continuity Cell. A cell used periodically to check whether a connection is idle or has failed (at the cross-connect nodes) in order to guarantee a continuation in the flow of the information cells. Continuity checking is one of the OAM function types for fault management (*see also* AIS and RDI).

CCITT—Consultative Committee on International Telegraphy and Telephony. A standards and specifications body whose published recommendations cover a wide spectrum of areas that include definition of terms, basic principles and characteristics, protocol design, description of models, and other specifications. Currently known as ITU-T.

CCR—Current Cell Rate. A field in the RM cell header that indicates the current complying cell rate a user can transmit over a virtual connection (VC).

CDV—Cell Delay Variation. A QoS parameter that measures the difference between a single cell's transfer delay (CTD) and the expected transfer delay. It gives a measure of how closely cells are spaced in a Virtual Circuit (VC). CDV can be introduced by ATM multiplexers (MUXs) or switches.

CDVT—Cell Delay Variation Tolerance. Used in CBR traffic, it specifies the acceptable tolerance of the CDV (jitter).

cell—Basic ATM transmission unit. It is a 53-byte packet, comprised of a five-byte header and a 48-byte payload. User traffic is segmented into cells at the source and reassembled at the destination.

cell header—The five-byte ATM cell header contains control information regarding the destination path and flow control. More specifically, it contains the following fields: GFC, VPI, VCI, PT, CLP, and HEC.

cell layer—Same as ATM Layer.

CER—Cell Error Rate. A QoS parameter that measures the fraction of transmitted cells that are erroneous (they have errors when they arrive at the destination).

CES—Circuit Emulation Service. An ATM-provided class of service, where TDM-type, constant-bit-rate (CBR) circuits are emulated by the AAL1.

CI—Congestion Indication. A bit in the RM cell to indicate congestion (it is set by the destination if the last cell received was marked).

CIF—Cell Information Field. The payload (48 bytes) of an ATM cell.

CIR—Committed Information Rate. A term used in Frame Relay, which defines the information rate the network is committed to provide the user with, under any network conditions.

circuit emulation—A virtual-circuit (VC) service offered to end users in which the characteristics of an actual, digital bitstream line (such as video traffic) are emulated (such as a 2-Mbps or 45-Mbps signal).

class of service (COS)—A designation of the transport network characteristics, such as route security, transmission priority, and bandwidth, needed for a particular session. The class of service is derived from a mode name specified by the initiator of a session.

Classical IP—IETF-defined protocols for developing IP over ATM networks (IP support for the QoS classes, ARP over SVC and PVC networks) so that common applications (FTP, Telnet, SMTP, SNMP) can be supported in an ATM environment. The main issues in the transport of IP over ATM are the packet encapsulation and the address resolution.

CLP—Cell Loss Priority. A one-bit field in the ATM cell header that corresponds to the loss priority of a cell. Lower priority (CLP = 1) cells can be discarded under congestion situations.

CLR—Cell Loss Ratio. A QoS parameter that gives the ratio of the lost cells to the total number of transmitted cells.

CMIP—Common Management Information Protocol. An ITU-T-defined management interface standard that can support administration, maintenance, and operation information functions (*see also* OAM&P).

CMIP—Common Management Information Protocol. A protocol formally adapted by the International Standards Organization used for exchanging network management information over OSI. Typically, this information is exchanged between two management stations. It can be used to exchange information between an application and a management station. Although designed for OSI networks, it is transport-independent. Theoretically, it can run across a variety of transports, including IBM's SNA.

CMOT—CMIP over TCP/IP. The use of CMIP over a TCP/IP-based transport.

CMR—Cell Misinsertion Rate. A performance measure that is defined as the number of misinserted cells (those that arrive from the wrong source) per (virtual) connection second.

CO—Central Office. Premises of a carrier service provider where customer lines (telephone lines) are multiplexed and switched to other COs.

coaxial cable—A cable composed of an insulated central conducting wire wrapped in another cylindrical conducting wire. The whole thing is usually wrapped in another insulating layer and an outer protective layer. A coaxial cable has great capacity to carry great quantities of information. It is typically used to carry high-speed data for cable TV.

COM—Continuation of Message. A PDU that is part of a message.

communication—The transmission and reception of data.

communication adapter—A circuit card with associated software that enables a processor, controller, or other device to be connected to a network.

communication network management (CNM)—The process of designing, installing, operating, and managing the distribution of information and control among users of communication systems.

communications line—The physical link (such as wire or a telephone circuit) that connects one or more workstations to a communications control unit or that connects one control unit to another.

Communications Manager—A component of OS/2 Extended Edition that lets a workstation connect to a host computer and use the host resources as well as the resources of other personal computers to which the workstation is attached either directly or through a host.

communications port—(1) An access point for data entry or exit to or from a communication device such as a terminal. (2) On a personal computer or workstation, a synchronous or asynchronous serial port to which a modem can be attached.

composite end node—To a type 2.1 node, a group of nodes that appears to be a single end node.

concurrent—Pertaining to the occurrence of two or more activities within a given interval of time.

CONFIG.SYS—A file that contains configuration options for an OS/2 program or DOS program installed on a workstation or personal computer. It defines the devices, system parameters, and resource options of a workstation or personal computer.

congestion control—A resource and traffic management mechanism to avoid and/or prevent excessive situations (buffer overflow or insufficient bandwidth) that can cause the network to collapse. Various congestion control methods exist (*see also* flow control).

connection-oriented network—A communications service in which an initial connection between the end points (source and destination) has to be set up. Examples are ATM and Frame Relay (*see also* virtual circuit VC).

connection-oriented—See Connection-oriented Network.

connectionless network—Communications service in which packets are transferred from source to destination without the need of a pre-established connection. Examples are IP and SMDS (*see also* datagram).

connectionless service—A networking node in which individual data packets in a LAN traveling from one point to another are directed from one intermediate node to the next until they reach their ultimate destination. The receipt of a transmission is typically acknowledged from the ultimate destination to the point of origin.

control point (CP)—A component of a node that manages resources of that node and optionally provides services to other nodes in the network.

control vector—One of a general class of RU substructures that has variable length, is carried within some enclosing structure, and has a one-byte key used as an identifier.

controller—A unit that controls input/output operations for one or more devices.

conversation—A logical connection between two transaction programs using an IBM LU 6.2 session.

corporate network - A network of networks that connects most or all of a corporation's LANs. Connections between networks and LANs are made with bridges and routers. Also called an internetwork, a WAN, or an enterprise network.

COS—Class of Service. See QoS Classes.

CPCS—Common Part Convergence Sublayer. Part of the AAL convergence sublayer (CS). It must always be present in the AAL implementation. Its task is to pass primitives to the other AAL sublayers (SAR or SSCS). It supports the functions of the standardized Common Part AALs: AAL1, AAL3/4, and AAL5.

CPE—Customer Premises Equipment. Computer and communications equipment (hardware and software) used by a carrier's customer and located at the customer's site (*see also* DTE).

CPI—Common Part Indicator. A one-byte field in the header of the CPCS-PDU in AAL3/4 that indicates the number of bits of which the BASize field consists.

CRC—Cyclic Redundancy Check. A bit-errors detection technique that employs a mathematical algorithm that, based on the transmitted bits, calculates a value attached to the information bits in the same packet. The receiver using the same algorithm recalculates that value and compares it to the one received. If the two values do not agree, the transmitted packet is then considered to be in error.

CRC (Cyclic Redundancy Check)—A process used to check the integrity of a block of data.

CRM—Cell Rate Margin. A measure of the residual useful bandwidth for a given QoS class, after taking into account the SCR.

CRS—Cell Relay Service. A bearer service offered to the end users by an ATM network that delivers (transports and routes) ATM cells.

CS—Convergence Sublayer. The upper half of the AAL, which is divided into two sublayers, the Common Part (CPCS) and the Service Specific (SSCS). It is service-dependent and its functions include manipulation of cell delay variation (CDV), source clock frequency recovery, and forward error correction (FEC). Although each AAL has its own functions, in general the CS describes the services and functions needed for conversion between ATM and non-ATM protocols (*see also* SAR).

CS-PDU—Convergence Sublayer Protocol Data Unit. The PDU used at the CS for passing information between the higher layers and the SAR where they are converted into cells.

CSF—Cell Switch Fabric. See Switch Fabric.

CSR—Cell Missequenced Ratio. A performance measure that is defined as the number of missequenced cells (those that arrive in the wrong order) per (virtual) connection second.

CSU—Channel Service Unit. Equipment at the user end that provides an interface between the user and the communications network. CSU can be combined with DSU in the same device (*see also* DCE).

CTD—Cell Transfer Delay. A QoS parameter that measures the average time for a cell to be transferred from its source to its destination over a virtual connection (VC). It is the sum of any coding, decoding, segmentation, reassembly, processing, and queueing delays.

data circuit-terminating equipment (DCE)—The equipment installed at the user's premises that provides all the functions required to establish, maintain, and terminate a connection for data transmission and the signal conversion and coding between the data terminal equipment device and the line.

data communication—The transmission and reception of data.

data link—A physical link, like a wire, that connects one or more devices or communication controllers.

data link control (DLC)—(1) The physical means of connecting one location to another for the purpose of transmitting and receiving data. (2) In SNA, the second layer of the seven-layer architecture. (3) In OSI, the second layer of the seven-layer architecture.

datagram—A packet transport mode in which packets are routed independently and may follow different paths. Thus, there is no guarantee of sequence delivery (*see also* VC).

datastream—(1) All data transmitted through a data channel in a single read or write operation. (2) A continuous stream of data elements being transmitted, or intended for transmission, in character or binary-digit form, using a defined format.

DCE—Data Circuit-terminating Equipment or Data Communications Equipment. A device at the user end, typically a modem or other communications device, which acts as an access point to the transmission medium.

dependent logical unit (DLU)—An LU controlled by an SNA host system.

destination—In a network, any point or location, such as a node, a station, or a terminal, to which data is sent.

destination address—The part of a message that indicates for whom the message is intended. It's synonymous with an address on an envelope. IBM Token Ring Network addresses are 48 bits in length.

device—(1) An input/output unit such as a terminal, display, or printer. (2) In computers, it can be used for direct access storage (such as the hard disk).

differential Manchester encoding—A transmission encoding scheme in which each bit is encoded as a two-segment signal with a signal transition (polarity change) at either the bit time or half-bit time. Transition at a bit time represents a 0. No transition at a bit time indicates a 1.

diskless workstation—A workstation without a hard disk or diskette drive.

distributed processing—A process within a network of computers in which information is initiated in local computers and the resultant data is sent to a central computer for further processing with the data from other local systems. A LAN is an example of distributed processing.

domain—In IBM's SNA, a host-based systems services control point (SSCP), the physical units (PUs), logical units (LUs), links, link stations, and all the affiliated resources that the host (SSCP) controls.

downloading—The act of receiving data from one computer into another.

downstream physical unit (DSPU)—A controller or a workstation downstream from a gateway that is attached to a host.

DQDB—Distributed Queue Dual Bus. The IEEE 802.6 standard that is a metropoitan area network (MAN) protocol based on 53-byte packets that support connectionless and connection-oriented, isochronous integrated services. It is implemented as two unidirectional buses configured in a physical ring topology.

DS-0—Digital Signal 0. The physical interface for digital transmission at the rate of 64 Kbps.

DS-1—Digital Signal 1. The physical interface for digital transmission at the rate of 1.544 Mbps. Also known as a T-1 standard, it can simultaneously support 24 DS-0 circuits.

DS-2—Digital Signal 2. The physical interface for digital transmission at the rate of 6.312 Mbps.

DS-3—Digital Signal 3. The physical interface for digital transmission at the rate of 44.736 Mbps.

DSU—Data Service Unit. Equipment at the user end that acts as a telephony-based interface between low-rate (56 kbps) services and higher-rate circuits.

DTE—Date Terminal Equipment. The host computer (PC or workstation) to provide the end-user with access to a communications network. The DTE is connected to a DCE that performs the signaling operation (*see also* CPE).

DXI—Data Exchange Interface. A frame-based ATM interface between a DTE (such as a router or a local switch) and a DCE. DXI interfaces to the ATM UNI and has been chosen by the ATM Forum as an affordable solution for providing ATM capabilities over a WAN.

E-1—European Digital Signal 1. The European standard for digital physical interfaces at 2.048 Mbps.

E-3—European Digital Signal 3. The European standard for digital physical interfaces at 34.368 Mbps. It can simultaneously support 16 E-1 circuits.

E-4—European Digital Signal 4. The European standard for digital physical interfaces at 139.264 Mbps.

E.164—An ITU-T-defined eight-byte address format. In ATM, it is typically used in public networks and is provided by the telecommunication carriers, while 20-byte NSAP format addresses are used within private networks.

early token release—This is a method of token passing that allows for two tokens to exist on the network simultaneously. It is used on 16-Mbps Token Ring networks.

EFCI—Explicit Forward Congestion Indication. A one-bit field in the PTI that contains information whether congestion at an intermediate node has been experienced. The EFCI bit is set when a buffer threshold has been exceeded.

ELAN—Emulated LAN. See LAN Emulation.

end user—The ultimate source or destination of application data flowing through a network. An end user can be an application program or a human operator.

end-node domain—An end-node control point, its attached links, and its local LUs.

ENR—Enterprise Network Roundtable. An ATM Forum-associated group of ATM users to provide feedback on ATM-related issues and also present the users with completed interoperable capabilities and functionality.

ER—Explicit Rate. A field in the RM cell header specifying the cell rate a user should use for transmission over a virtual connection (VC) as dictated by the RM (*see also* CCR).

error rate—In data transmission, the ratio of the number of incorrect elements transmitted to the total number of elements transmitted.

ETSI—European Telecommunications Standards Institute. The corresponding body of ANSI in Europe involved in providing and adapting standards for the European telecommunications.

FDDI—Fiber Distributed Data Interface. An ANSI-defined standard for implementing a high-speed (100 Mbps) LAN over fiber.

FDM—Frequency-Division Multiplexing. A technique that allows for the channel bandwidth of a circuit to be subdivided into many little channels (one per traffic stream).

FEC—Forward Error Correction. An error correction technique in which there are no retransmissions and therefore the receiver is responsible for correcting any errors in the packets.

file—A set of related records treated as a unit.

file server—A device that serves as a central location for commonly used files by everyone on a LAN.

flow control—A method used in networking for congestion avoidance and traffic regulation. There are three techniques: window-based control, where a sliding window is used to determine how many cells can be transmitted during a predefined period; rate-based control, where the rate that the source transmits at is monitored and controlled; and credit-based control, where a source can transmit a cell if there is a credit available. CAC is also part of the flow control.

forum—Same as ATM Forum.

FR—Same as Frame Relay.

frame—A group of bits sent serially (one after another). It is a logical transmission unit.

frame check sequence—In a Token Ring LAN, a 32-bit field that follows the data field in every Token Ring frame.

Frame Relay—A packet-switching technology to provide a very reliable packet delivery over virtual circuits (VC). Some of the concepts used in Frame Relay have been incorporated in ATM networks.

FRM—Fast Resource Management. A form of network management for allocating resources (buffers or bandwidth) dynamically.

front-end processor—A processor that offloads line control, message handling, code conversion, error control, and routing of data from the host computer. IBM's 3725 and 3745 are examples of front-end processors. Also known as a communication controller.

FTP—File Transfer Protocol. A protocol used for transferring files between different machines across a network.

functional address—In IBM network adapters, this is a special kind of group address in which the address is bit-significant, each "on" bit representing a function performed by the station (active monitor, ring-error monitor, LAN error monitor, or configuration report server).

gateway—A functional unit that connects two different computer network architectures.

gateway function—(1) The capability of a subarea node to provide protocol support to connect two or more subarea networks. (2) The component that provides this capability.

Gbps—Gigabits per second. Transmission speed or rate of a hundred million bits per second.

GCRA—Generic Cell Rate Algorithm. A reference model proposed by the ATM Forum for defining cell-rate conformance in terms of certain traffic parameters. It is usually referred as the Leaky Bucket algorithm (*see also* traffic shaping).

GFC—Generic Flow Control. A four-bit field in the ATM cell header for supporting multiplexing functions. Its default value is '0000' when the GFC protocol is not enforced. The GFC mechanism is intended to support simple flow control in ATM connections.

group address—In a LAN, a locally administered address assigned to two or more adapters to allow the adapters to copy the same frame.

group SAP—A single address assigned to a group of service access points (SAPs).

half-session—A session-layer component consisting of the combination of data flow control and transmission control components comprising one end of a session.

hard error—An error condition on a network that requires the source of the error to be removed or that the network be reconfigured before the network can resume reliable operation.

header—The portion of a message that contains control information for the message. Usually found at the beginning of a frame.

HEC— Header Error Check or Header Error Control. A one-byte field in the cell header used for the header error correction and detection. Due to the information contained in the header, HEC is quite significant.

hertz (Hz)—A unit of frequency equal to one cycle per second.

hexadecimal—A numbering base in which four bits are used to represent each digit. The digits can have one of 16 values: 0, 1, 2...9, A, B, C, D, E, F.

hierarchical network—A multisegment network configuration providing only one path through intermediate segments between source segments and destination segments.

HOL—Head-of-Line. The head position of a buffer (inside a switch). A blocking phenomenon is associated with the HOL that refers to the fact that cells in the queue have to wait for the HOL cell to depart first.

hop count—The number of ring segments spanned to establish a session between two workstations. In IBM Token Ring networks, the maximum is seven.

hop—In Token Ring networking, the connection between ring segments. The connection is usually made using bridges.

host node—(1) A node at which a host computer is situated. (2) In SNA, a subarea node that contains an SSCP.

host system—(1) A data processing system that is used to prepare programs and the operating environments for use on another computer or controller. (2) The data processing system to which a network is connected and with which the system can communicate.

HSSI—High-Speed Serial Interface. An interface between CSU/DSU and DXI.

ICR—Initial Cell Rate. The rate that a source is allowed to start up at following an idle period. It is established at connection setup and is between the MCR and the PCR.

IEEE—Institute of Electrical and Electronic Engineers. A standards and specification organization with extensive activities in the areas of computers and electronics.

IEEE 802—IEEE committee on LANs.

IEEE 802.1—IEEE standard for overall architecture of LANs and inter-networking.

IEEE 802.2—IEEE data link control layer standard used with IEEE 802.3, 802.4, and 802.5.

IEEE 802.3—IEEE carrier-sense multiple access with collision detection (CSMA/CD). A physical layer standard specifying a LAN with a CSMA/CD access method on a bus topology. Ethernet and Starlan both follow subsets of the 802.3 standard. Typically, they transmit at 10 Mbps.

IEEE 802.4—IEEE physical layer standard specifying a LAN with a token-passing access method on a bus topology. Used with Manufacturing Automation Protocol (MAP) LANs. Typical transmission speed is 10 Mbps.

IEEE 802.5—IEEE physical layer standard specifying a LAN with a token-passing access method on a ring topology. Used by IBM's Token Ring network. Typical transmission rates are four Mbps and 16 Mbps.

IETF—The Internet Engineering Task Force that was initially responsible for developing specifications required for the interoperable implementation of IP. One of the issues IETF has been focusing on is the implementation of Classical IP over ATM.

IISP—Interim Interswitch Signaling Protocol. A protocol that uses UNI-based signaling for switch-to-switch communication (*see also* NNI).

ILMI—Interim Local Management Interface. An ATM forum-defined Network Management System (NMS) based on SNMP that can provide configuration, performance, and fault management information concerning VC connections available at its UNI (public and private). It operates over AAL3/4 and AAL5 and will be eventually replaced once it becomes standardized by ITU-T.

impedance—The combined effect of resistance, inductance, and capacitance on a signal at a particular frequency.

independent logical unit (ILU)—In SNA, a logical unit that does not require assistance from an SSCP to establish a LU-LU session.

Institute of Electrical and Electronic Engineers (IEEE)—A publishing and standards-making body responsible for many standards used in LANs.

International Standards Organization (ISO)—An international standards-making body for creating internationally accepted standards. One such standard is Open Systems Interconnection (OSI).

IP—Internet Protocol. A networking protocol for providing a connectionless (datagram) service to the higher transport protocol. It is responsible for discovering and maintaining topology information and for routing packets across homogeneous or heterogeneous networks. Combined with TCP, it is commonly known as the TCP/IP platform.

IPX—A protocol similar to IP that was developed by Novell.

ISDN—Integrated Services Digital Network. An early, CCITT-adopted protocol reference model intended for providing a ubiquitous, end-to-end, interactive, digital service for data, audio, and video.

isochronous—Refers to the fact that a time slot can be divided into equal-size mini-slots allocated to different channels for the synchronous transmission of information (used in DQDB).

ITU-T—International Telecommunications Union-Telecommunications Standards Sector. A formal international standards, specifications, and recommendations body, formerly known as CCITT. ITU-T is part of the International Telecommunications Union (ITU) founded in 1948 and sponsored by the UN to promote telephone and telegraphy issues.

IXC—Inter-Exchange Carrier. A public switching network carrier that provides connectivity across and between LATAs.

jitter—The Cell Delay Variation (CDV).

jitter—Undesirable variation in the arrival time of a transmitted digital signal.

JPEG—Joint Photographic Experts Group. A standard developed for encoding, transmitting, and decoding still images.

Kbps—Kilobits per second. Transmission speed or rate of 1,000 bits per second.

LAN—Local Area Network. A network that interconnects PCs, terminals, workstations, servers, printers, and other peripherals at a high speed over short distances (usually within the same floor or building). Various LAN standards have been developed, with Ethernet as the most widely used.

LAN adapter—A circuit board installed in workstations that connects the workstation with the LAN media.

LAN Emulation—A technique that specifies the interfaces and protocols needed for providing LAN-supported functionality and connectivity in an ATM environment so that legacy protocols can be interoperable with the ATM protocols, interfaces, and devices.

LAN Emulation Service—An ATM Forum-appointed technical workgroup to address LAN Emulation.

LANE—Same as LAN Emulation.

LATA—Local Access and Transport Area. Geographically defined telecommunication areas, within which a local carrier can provide communications services (*see also* LEC and IXC).

layer—In networking architectures, a collection of network processing functions that together comprise a set of rules and standards for successful data communication.

LE—Same as LAN Emulation.

LE-ARP—LAN Emulation ARP. The ARP used in LAN Emulation for binding a requested ATM address to the MAC address.

leaky bucket—A flow control algorithm in which cells are monitored to check whether they comply with the connection parameters. Non-conforming cells are either tagged (as violators) or dropped from the network. The analogy is taken from a bucket (memory buffer) that loses its contents (cells) due to a leak (*see also* GCRA, traffic contract, and UPC).

leased line—A dedicated communications link usually owned by a telecommunications provider that charges for the use of the line.

LEC—(1) LAN Emulation Client. Typically located in an ATM end system (ATM host or LAN switch), its task is to maintain address resolution tables and forward data traffic. It is uniquely associated with an ATM address. (2) Local Exchange Carrier. An intra-LATA communication services provider.

LECS—LAN Emulation Configuration Server. Its main function is to provide configuration information to a LEC (such as the ELAN it belongs to or its LES).

LENNI—LAN Emulation Network Node Interface. Same as LNNI.

LES—LAN Emulation Server. A server that provides support for the LAN emulation address resolution protocol (LE-ARP). The LECs register their own ATM and MAC addresses with the LES, which is uniquely identified by an ATM address.

LI—Length Indicator. A six-bit field in the AAL3/4 SAR-PDU trailer that indicates the number of bytes in the SAR-PDU that contain CPCS information.

LLC—Logical Link Control. The upper half of the Data Link Layer in LANs which performs error control, broadcasting, multiplexing, and flow control functions (*see also* MAC).

LMI—Local Management Interface. An ITU-T-defined interface that provides an ATM end-system user with network management information (*see also* ILMI).

LNNI—LAN Emulation Network Node Interface. Specifies the NNI operation between the LANE servers (LES, LECS, and BUS).

lobe—A term used to describe the connection from a workstation to a Token Ring concentrator, such as a multistation access unit.

local area network (LAN)—A network of two or more computing units connected to share resources over moderate-sized geographic areas such as an office, a building, or a campus.

locally administered address (LAA)—An adapter address that the user can assign to override the universally administered address (UAA).

logical connection—In a network, devices that can communicate or work with one another because they share the same protocol.

logical link—The conceptual joining of two nodes for direct communications. Several logical links may be able to utilize the same physical hardware.

logical link control (LLC)—A protocol developed by the IEEE 802 committee, common to all of its LAN standards, for data link-level transmission control; the upper sublayer of the IEEE Layer 2 (OSI) protocol that complements the media access control protocol; IEEE standard 802.2.

logical link control protocol (LLC protocol)—In a LAN, the protocol that governs the exchange of frames between data stations independently of how the transmission medium is shared.

logical unit (LU)—An access port for users to gain access to the services of a network.

LU-LU session—In SNA, a session between two logical units in an SNA network. It provides communication between two end users or between an end user and an LU services component.

LUNI—LAN Emulation User Network Interface. Specifies the UNI between a LEC and the network providing the LAN Emulation.

MAC—Medium Access Control. A set of protocols that are (the lower) part of the Data Link Layer and consist of the basis of the IEEE LAN specifications. Generally, MAC determines the way devices can transmit in a broadcast network (*see also* LLC).

MAC frame—Frames used to carry information to maintain the ring protocol and for the exchange of management information.

MAC protocol—The LAN protocol sublayer of the data link control (DLC) protocol that includes functions for adapter address recognition, copying of message units from the physical network, and message unit format recognition, error detection, and routing within the processor.

MAN—Metropolitan Area Network. A term to describe a network that provides regional connectivity within a metropolitan area (such as a city). MANs are classified to be between LANs and WANs.

Mbps—Megabits per second. The transmission speed or rate of one million bits per second.

MBS—Maximum Burst Size. A traffic parameter that specifies the maximum number of cells that can be transmitted at the peak rate (PCR).

MCDV—Maximum Cell Delay Variation. As the name suggests, it is the maximum CDV over a given QoS class.

MCLR—Maximum Cell Loss Ratio. As the name suggests, it is the maximum CTD over a given QoS class, defined for CBR and VBR traffic and for cells with a CLP of 0.

MCR—Minimum Cell Rate. A parameter that gives the minimum rate that cells can be transmitted by over a VC.

MCTD—Maximum Cell Transfer Delay. As the name suggests, it is the maximum CTD over a given QoS class.

mean cell transfer delay—The average of the processing, queueing, and propagation delays.

medium access control (MAC)—A media-specific access control protocol within IEEE 802 specifications. The physical address of a station is often called the MAC address.

mesh network—A multisegment network configuration providing more than one path through intermediate LAN segments between source and destination LAN segments.

MIB—Management Information Base. A data structure that defines objects for referencing variables such as integers and strings. In general, it contains information regarding network's management and performance, such as traffic parameters (*see also* ILMI and AToMMIB).

MID—Multiplex Identification. A 10-bit field in the AAL3/4 SAR-PDU header for identifying the different CPCS-PDUs multiplexed over the same VCC.

MIN—Multistage Interconnection Network. A switch fabric built from switching elements organized in a series and/or in parallel for providing physical connections between the inputs and the outputs of a switch.

mips—Million instructions per second. A measure of computer speed.

modem (modulate/demodulator)—A device that converts digital data from a computer to an analog signal that can be transmitted on a telecommunication line and converts the received analog signal to digital data for the computer.

MPEG—Motion Picture Experts Group. A video technology standard that specifies the digital encoding, transmission, and decoding protocols and is capable of presenting VCR-quality motion video.

MPOA—Multiprotocol Over ATM. A set of standards to support (distributed) routing protocols other than IP. Developed on top of LANE and NHRP, it supports switches, route servers, and hosts all attached to an ATM network.

MR—Mean Rate. Same as Average Cell Rate.

multimedia—A way of presenting a combination of different forms of information such as text, data, images, video, audio, and graphics (such as a videoconference).

multiple-domain network—In SNA, a network with more than one SSCP. In APPN, a network with more than one network node.

multiprotocol encapsulation—Multiprotocol Encapsulation over ATM provides for higher protocols, such as IP, to perform bridging and routing functions over an ATM network.

MUX—Multiplexer. A networking local device in which multiple streams of information are combined so they can share a common physical medium.

N-ISDN—Narrowband Integrated Services Digital Network. Predecessor to the B-ISDN, N-ISDN encompasses the original standards for the ISDN.

native applications—Applications that have been developed for non-ATM environment communications platforms (such as LAN applications).

NAU—In SNA, network addressable unit. In APPN, network accessible unit.

NDIS—Network Driver Interface Specification. Generic name for a device driver for a NIC, which is independent of any hardware or software implementation.

NetBIOS (Network Basic Input/Output System)—Provides an interface to allow programs to operate the Token Ring adapter in a personal computer or workstation.

network—A group of nodes and the links interconnecting them.

network addressable unit (NAU) - The origin or destination of data transmitted by the path control layer. Synonymous with network accessible unit.

network management—The conceptual control element of a station that interfaces with all of the architectural layers of that station and is responsible for the resetting and setting of control parameters, obtaining reports of error conditions, and determining if the station should be connected to or disconnected from the network.

network management vector transport (NMVT)—One of the SNA formats used for the transmission of communications and systems management data.

NHRP—Next-Hop Resolution Protocol. A protocol proposed to be used for ATM address resolution based on Classical IP. In particular, if an address request cannot be served by a node, it is forwarded to the next server-node on the path to the destination until finally the ATM-IP address mapping can be accomplished.

NIC—Network Interface Card or Controller. The hardware communications interface (circuit board) required for the DTE (workstation or PC) to access the network (same as Adapter Card).

NMS—Network Management System. Set of OAM&P functions for setting the required hardware and software parameters used in managing a network.

NNI—Network Node Interface (or Network-to-Network Interface). ITU-T-specified standard interface between nodes within the same network. The ATM Forum distinguishes between two standards, one for private networks called P-NNI and one for public networks known as public NNI.

node—A device connected into a network.

node type—The classification of a network device based on the protocols it supports and the network addressable unit it can contain.

noise—A disturbance that affects a signal and that can distort the information carried by the signal.

non-broadcast frame—A frame containing a specific destination address and that may contain routing information specifying which bridges are to forward it. A bridge will forward a non-broadcast frame only if that bridge is included in the frame's routing information.

NPC—Network Parameter Control. Traffic management mechanism (performed at the NNI) exercised by a network for traffic received by another network.

NSAP—Network Services Access Point. In the OSI environment, it is the SAP between the network and the transport layers, which identifies a DTE by a unique address.

OAM—Operations and Maintenance. A set of administrative and supervisory actions regarding network performance monitoring, failure detection, and system protection. Special-type cells are used to carry OAM-related information.

OAM&P—Operations, Administration, Maintenance, and Provisioning. A set of network management functions and services that interact to provide the necessary network management tools and control.

OC-n—Optical Carrier-n. ITU-T-specified physical interface for transmission over optical fiber at n times 51.84 Mbps (OC-3 is at 155.52 Mbps, OC-12 at 622.08 Mbps, and OC-48 at 2.488 Mbps).

octet—Eight bits or one byte.

Open Systems Interconnection (OSI)—The only internationally accepted framework for communication between two systems made by different vendors. It is a seven-layer architecture developed by ISO.

operating system—A software program that manages the basic operating of a computer system.

OSI—Open Systems Interconnection. The OSI Reference Model introduced by the International Organization for Standardization (ISO) consists of seven layers, each specifying the protocols and functions required for two nodes to communicate using the underlying network infrastructure (physical medium, switches, routers, bridges, multiplexers, and intermediate nodes).

OSIRM—Open Systems Interconnection Reference Model. See OSI.

P-NNI—Private Network Node Interface. The NNI used in private networks.

P-UNI—Private User Network Interface. The UNI used between a user and a private network.

pacing—In data communications, a technique by which receiving the receiving device controls the rate of transmission of a sending device to prevent overrun.

parallel bridge—One of the two or more bridges that connects the same two LAN segments in a network.

payload—Part of the ATM cell, it contains the actual information to be carried. It occupies 48 bytes (*see also* PTI).

PBX—Private Branch Exchange. A circuit switch that relays telephones, terminals, or other equipment and provides access to the public telephone system.

PC—Priority Control. A congestion control function that uses the CLP bit to perform priority queueing and scheduling actions.

PCR—Peak Cell Rate. A traffic parameter that characterizes the source and gives the maximum rate at which cells can be transmitted. It is calculated as the reciprocal of the minimum inter-cell interval (time between two cells) over a given VC. The field in the RM cell header indicates the maximum acceptable ER.

PDH—Plesiochronous Digital Hierarchy. A hierarchy that refers to the DS-0, DS-1, DS-2, and DS-3 interfaces for digital transmission. Originally developed to efficiently carry digitized voice over twisted-pair.

PDU—Protocol Data Unit. Term originally used in the OSI model, also known as message, to describe the primitive passed across different layers and contains header, data, and trailer information.

peak duration—A source traffic characteristic that gives the duration of a transmission at the peak cell rate (PCR). It is equivalent to the burst length (in cells).

permanent virtual circuit—A virtual connection established by the network management between an origin and a destination that can be left up permanently (used in X.25 and FR protocols).

PHY—Physical Layer. The bottom layer of the ATM protocol reference model, it is subdivided into two sublayers, the Transmission Convergence (TC) and the Physical Medium (PM). It provides the ATM cells transmission over the physical interfaces that interconnect the ATM devices.

PHY-SAP—Physical Layer Service Access Point. The physical interface at the boundary between the PHY and the ATM layers (*see also* SAP and ATM-SAP).

physical unit (PU)—The component that manages and monitors the resources of a node.

PL—Physical Layer. See PHY.

PLCP—Physical Layer Convergence Protocol. A protocol that specifies a TC mapping of ATM cells to DS-3 frames.

PM—Physical Medium. One of the two PHY sublayers that provides the bit timing and performs the actual transmission of the bits over the physical medium.

PMD—Physical Medium Dependent. Same as PM.

port—A physical connection to the link hardware. Also referred to as an adapter.

PRI—Primary Rate Interface. An ISDN specification that provides 23 64-kbps B-channels and one 64-kbps D-channel intended for use over a single DS1 or a E-1 line.

print server—A computer or program providing LAN users with access to a centralized printer.

private network—A communications network comprised of dedicated circuits between DTEs and other devices (multiplexers, switches, and routers) where bandwidth is dedicated and network management is much simpler (*see also* PVN and Public Network).

protocol—The set of rules governing the operation of functional units of a communication system that must be followed if communication is to be achieved.

PT—Payload Type. See PTI.

PTI—Payload Type Identifier. A three-bit cell header field for encoding information regarding the AAL and EFCI.

public network—A communications network where users have shared access to the network resources. Network services are usually provided by common carriers, such as telephone companies (*see also* Private Network).

PVC—Permanent (or Provisioned) Virtual Connection. A virtual connection (VPC/VCC) provisioned for indefinite use in an ATM network, established by the network management system (NMS) (*see also* SVC).

Q.2110—ITU-T recommendation for specifying the UNI SSCOP.

Q.2130—ITU-T recommendation for specifying the UNI SSCF.

Q.2931—ITU-T recommendation derived from both Q.931 and Q.933 to provide SVC specifications and standards.

Q.931—ITU-T recommendation for specifying the UNI signaling protocol in N-ISDN.

Q.933—ITU-T recommendation for specifying the UNI signaling protocol in Frame Relay.

Q.93B—Currently called Q.2931.

QoS—Quality of Service. A term that refers to the set of ATM performance parameters that characterize the traffic over a given VC. These parameters include the CLR, CER, CMR, CDV, CTD, and the average cell transfer delay.

QoS classes—Quality of Service Classes. Five service classes are defined by the ATM Forum in terms of the QoS parameters. Class 0 refers to best-effort service. Class 1 specifies the parameters for circuit emulation, CBR (uncompressed) video, and for VPN. AAL1 supports this kind of connection-oriented service. Class 2 specifies the parameters for VBR audio and video. AAL2 supports this delay-dependent, connection-oriented class. Class 3 specifies the parameters for connection-oriented data transfer. AAL3/4 and mostly AAL5 supports this delay-independent class of service.

RBOC—Regional Bell Operating Company. Local service telephone companies that resulted from the break-up of AT&T.

RDF—Rate Decrease Factor. A factor by which a source should decrease its transmission rate if there is congestion (*see also* RIF).

RDI—Remote Defect Indication. One of the OAM function types used for fault management (*see also* AIS and CC).

repeater—A device inserted at intervals along a circuit to boost and amplify a signal being transmitted.

RFC—Request for Comment. Draft documents that contain proposed standards and specifications. RFCs can then be approved or just archived as historical recommendations.

RIF—Rate Increase Factor. A factor by which a source can increase its transmission rate if the RM cell indicates no congestion. This can result in a Additive Cell Rate (ACR) (*see also* RDF).

ring error monitor (REM)—A function that compiles error statistics reported by adapters on a network, analyzes the statistics to determine probable error cause, sends reports to network manager programs, and updates network status conditions. It assists in fault isolation and correction.

ring in (RI)—The receive or input receptacle on an access unit or repeater.

ring out (RO)—The transmit or output receptacle on an access unit or repeater.

RM—Resource Management. The management of critical network resources such as bandwidth and buffers at the node level. A value of six is reserved in the PTI to indicate an RM cell.

route—An ordered sequence between origin and destination stations that represent a path in a network between the stations.

router—An intelligent device that connects two LAN segments that use similar or different architectures at the network layer.

routing—A network management function responsible for forwarding the packets from the source to their destination. Numerous algorithms exist that satisfy various network topologies and requirements.

RSVP—ReSerVation Protocol. A protocol developed for supporting different QoS classes in IP applications (such as in videoconferencing and multimedia).

RTT—Round-Trip Time. The round-trip time between a source and a device, such as a switch, and it is usually measured in number of cells (which depends on the buffering capabilities of the device). It is used as a window in flow control.

SAAL—Signaling AAL Service-specific parts of the AAL protocol responsible for signaling. Its specifications, being developed by ITU-T, were adopted from N-ISDN.

SAP—(1) Service Access Point. The physical interface between the layers in the OSI model through which lower layers provide services to the higher layers passing over the Protocol Data Units (PDUs). (2) Subnetwork Attachment Point. The unique address maintained by a subnetwork for each of the DTEs attached to it.

SAR—Segmentation and Reassembly. The lower half of the AAL. It inserts the data from the information frames into the cell. It adds any necessary header or trailer bits to the data and passes the 48-octet to the ATM layer. Each AAL type has its own SAR format. At the destination, the cell payload is extracted and converted to the appropriate PDU (*see also* CS).

SAR-PDU—Segmentation and Reassembly Protocol Data Unit. The 48-octet PDU that the SAR sublayer exchanges with the ATM layer. It comprises of the SAR-PDU payload and any control information that the SAR sublayer might add.

SCR—Sustainable Cell Rate. A traffic parameter that characterizes a bursty source and specifies the maximum average rate at which cells can be sent over a given VC. It can be defined as the ratio of the MBS to the minimum burst interarrival time.

SDH—Synchronous Digital Hierarchy. A hierarchy that designates signal interfaces for very high-speed digital transmissions over optical fiber links (*see also* SONET).

SEAL—Simple Efficient Adaptation Layer. The original name and recommendation for AAL5.

segment—(1) In an IBM Token Ring network, a portion of a LAN that consists of cables, components, or lobes up to a bridge. (2) An entire ring without bridges.

segment number—The identifier that uniquely distinguishes a LAN segment in a multisegment LAN.

server—A computer providing a service to LAN users. Services may be a shared file.

service access point (SAP)—The point of access to services provided by the layers of a LAN architecture.

service types—There are four service types: CBR, VBR, UBR, and ABR. CBR and VBR are guaranteed services, while UBR and ABR are described as best-effort services.

session—A connection between two stations that allows them to communicate.

SIG—SMDS Interest Group. An industry forum active in producing specifications in the area of SMDS. It has also joined some of the ATM Forum activities.

single-route broadcast—The forwarding of specially designated broadcast frames only by bridges that have single-route broadcast enabled. If the network is configured correctly, a single-route broadcast frame will have exactly one copy delivered to every LAN segment in the network.

SIR—Sustained Information Rate. A flow control mechanism used in SMDS.

SMDS—Switched Multimegabit Digital Service. A connectionless MAN service, based on 53-byte packets, that target the interconnection of different LANs into a switched public network.

SMTP—Simple Mail Transfer Protocol. The protocol standard developed to support e-mail services.

SN—Sequence Number. Part of the header of the SAR-PDU (two bits in AAL1, four bits in AAL3/4), it is used as a sequence counter for detecting lost, out-of-sequence, or misinserted SAR-PDUs.

SNA—Systems Network Architecture. A host-based network architecture introduced by IBM, where logical channels are created between end-points.

SNMP—Simple Network Management Protocol. An IETF-defined standard for handling management information. It is normally found as an application on top of the user datagram protocol (UDP).

SNP—Sequence Number Protection. A four-bit field in the header of the AAL1 SAR-PDU that contains the CRC and the parity bit fields.

soft error—An intermittent error on a network that causes data to be transmitted more than once to be received.

SONET—Synchronous Optical Network. An ANSI-defined standard for high-speed and high-quality digital optical transmission. It has been recognized as the North American standard for SDH.

source routing—A method used by a bridge for moving data between LAN segments. The routing information is embedded in the Token Ring.

source routing transparent (SRT) bridge—A combination bridge utilizing IBM's source-routing mechanism along with a transparent routing mechanism.

SPANS—Simple Protocol for ATM Network Signaling. A protocol supported by FORE Systems switches that provides a SVC tunneling capability over a PVC network.

SPVC—Switched or Semi-Permanent Virtual Connection. A PVC-type connection where SVCs are used for call setup and (automatic) rerouting. It is also called smart PVC.

SS7—Signaling System Number 7. A common channel-signaling standard developed by CCITT. It was designed to provide the internal control and network intelligence needed in ISDNs.

SSCF—Service-Specific Coordination Function. Part of the SSCS portion of the SAAL. Among other functions, it provides a clear interface for relaying user data and providing independence from the underlying sublayers (*see also* SSCOP).

SSCOP—Service-Specific Connection-Oriented Protocol. Part of the SSCS portion of the SAAL. SSCOP is an end-to-end protocol that provides error detection and correction by retransmission and status reporting between the sender and the receiver, while it guarantees delivery integrity (*see also* SSCF).

SSCS—Service-Specific Convergence Sublayer. One of the two components of the Convergence Sublayer (CS) of the AAL that is particular to the traffic service class to be converted. It is developed to support certain user applications such as LAN Emulation, transport of high-quality video, and database management.

SSM—Single Segment Message. A message that constitutes a single PDU.

ST—Segment Type. A two-bit field in the SAR-PDU header that indicates whether the SAR-PDU is a BOM, COM, EOM, or SSM.

station—An input or output device that uses telecommunications facilities.

STDM—Statistical Time-Division Multiplexing. Same as ATDM.

STM—Synchronous Transfer Mode. A packet-switching approach where time is divided in time slots assigned to single channels during which users can transmit periodically. Basically, time slots denote allocated (fixed) parts of the total available bandwidth (*see also* TDM).

STM-1—Synchronous Transport Module-1. An ITU-T-defined SDH physical interface for digital transmission in ATM at the rate of 155.52 Mbps.

STM-n—Synchronous Transport Module-n. An ITU-T-defined SDH physical interface for digital transmission in ATM at n times the basic STM-1 rate. There is a direct equivalence between the STM-n and the SONET STS-3n transmission rates.

STP—Shielded Twisted Pair. Two insulated copper wires twisted together and wrapped by a protective jacket shield (*see also* UTP).

STS-1—Synchronous Transport Signal-1. SONET signal standard for optical transmission at 51.84 Mbps (*see also* OC-1).

STS-n—Synchronous Transport Signal-n. SONET signal format for transmission at n times the basic STS-1 signal (STS-3 is at 155.52 Mbps).

subarea—A portion of an SNA network consisting of the subarea node and any attached resources to that node.

subarea address—A value defined to identify the subarea node and placed in the subarea address field of the network address.

subarea network—The interconnection of subareas.

subarea node—A node that used subarea addressing for routing.

SVC—Switched Virtual Connection. A connection that is set up and taken down dynamically through signaling (*see also* PVC).

switch fabric—The central functional block of the ATM switch, which is responsible for buffering and routing the incoming cells to the appropriate output ports.

switch ATM—An ATM device responsible for switching the cells. Various switch architectures exist that can be classified according to different aspects (buffering, switch matrix, interconnection design, division multiplexing).

switched line—A telecommunications line in which the connection is established by dialing.

switched virtual circuit—A connection in which control signaling is used to establish and tear it down dynamically. Examples are the telephone system, ISDN, and X.25.

symbolic name—A name that can be used instead of an adapter or bridge address to identify an adapter location.

synchronous data link control (SDLC) A bit-oriented synchronous communications protocol developed by IBM.

synchronous time-division multiplexing— A TDM scheme where the interleaved time slots are preassigned to the users.

system services control point (SSCP)—A function within IBM's VTAM that controls and manages an SNA network and its resources.

systems network architecture (SNA)—IBM's seven-layer networking architecture.

T1—A TDM digital channel carrier that operates at a rate of 1.544 Mbps. Known also as a repeater system, it is often referred as DS-1.

T3—A TDM digital channel carrier that operates at 44.736 Mbps. It can multiplex 28 T1 signals and it is often used to refer to DS-3.

TAXI—Transparent Asynchronous Transmitter/Receiver Interface. An interface that provides connectivity over multi-mode fiber links at a speed of 100 Mbps.

TC—Transmission Convergence. One of the two PHY sublayers that is responsible for adapting the ATM cells into a stream of bits to be carried over the physical medium (*see also* PM).

TCP—Transmission Control Protocol. A standardized transport protocol developed for interconnecting IP-based networks. Operating on top of IP (combined known as TCP/IP), it is responsible for multiplexing sessions, error recovery, end-to-end reliable delivery, and flow control.

TCP/IP—A protocol platform, known also as the Internet protocol suite, that combines both TCP and IP. Widely used applications such as Telnet, FTP, and SMTP interface to TCP/IP.

TCS—Transmission Convergence Sublayer. Same as TC.

TDJ—Transfer Delay Jitter. See CDV.

TDM—Time-Division Multiplexing. A technique for splitting the total bandwidth (link capacity) into several channels to allow bit streams to be combined (multiplexed). The bandwidth allocation is done by dividing the time axis into fixed-length slots and a particular channel can then transmit only during a specific time slot.

telephone twisted pair (TTP)—One or more twisted pairs of copper wire in the unshielded voice-grade cable commonly used to connect a telephone to its wall jack. It is also known as unshielded twisted pair (UTP).

Telnet—An asynchronous virtual terminal protocol that allows for remote access.

TM—Traffic Management. A means for providing connection admission (CAC), congestion, and flow control (such as UPC and traffic shaping).

token—A sequence of bits passed from one device to another on the Token Ring network that signifies permission to transmit over the network. It consists of a starting delimiter, an access control field, and an end delimiter.

token passing—In a Token Ring network, the process by which a node captures a token, inserts a message, addresses the token, adds control information, transmits the frame, and then generates another token after the original token has made a complete circuit.

Token Ring—A network with a ring topology that passes tokens from one attaching device to another.

Token Ring interface coupler (TIC)—The hardware interface for connecting front-end processors and controllers to a Token Ring network.

Token Ring network—A network that uses a ring topology in which tokens are passed in a sequence from one node to another.

topology—The physical or logical arrangement of nodes in a computer network.

traffic contract—An agreement between the user and the network management agent regarding the expected QoS provided by the network and the user's compliance with the predetermined traffic parameters (such as PCR, MBS, burstiness, and average cell rate).

traffic descriptors—A set of parameters that characterize the source traffic. These are the PCR, MBS, CDV, and SCR.

traffic shaping—A method for regulating non-complying traffic that violates the traffic parameters, such as PCR, CDV, and MBS, as specified by the traffic contract (*see also* GCRA).

Transmission Control Protocol/Internet Protocol (TCP/IP) - A set of protocols that allows cooperating computers to share resources across a heterogeneous network.

transmission group (TG)—A single link or a group of links between adjacent nodes logically grouped together. In SNA, these nodes are adjacent subarea nodes. In APPN, it is a single link.

transparent routing—A method used by a bridge for moving data between two networks through learning the station addressees on each network.

twisted pair—A transmission medium that consists of two insulated conductors twisted together to reduce noise.

type 2.0 (T2.0) node—A node that attaches to a subarea network as a peripheral node and provides full end-user services but no intermediate routing services.

type 2.1 (T2.1) node—An SNA node that can be configured as an end point or intermediate routing node in a T2.1 network, or as a peripheral node attached to a subarea network. It can act as an end node, network node, or an intermediate node in an APPN network.

type 4 node—An SNA subarea node that provides routing and data link control functions for a type 5 node. Type 5 nodes control type 4 nodes.

type 5 node—An SNA subarea node that contains an SSCP and controls type 4 and type 2 SNA node types.

UBR—Unspecified Bit Rate. One of the best-effort service types (the other one is ABR). Realistically, no traffic parameters are specified by the source, so no actual quality commitment is made by the network management.

UDP—User Datagram Protocol. A connectionless transport protocol without any guarantee of packet sequence or delivery. It functions directly on top of IP.

UME—UNI Management Entity. Software at the UNIs for providing the ILMI functions.

UNI—User-Network Interface. Defined as a set of protocols and traffic characteristics (such as a cell structure), the interface between the CPE (user) and the ATM network (ATM switch). The ATM Forum specifications refer to two standards being developed, one between a user and a public ATM network called public UNI, and one between a user and a private ATM network called P-UNI.

UNI 2.0—An ATM Forum UNI specification for the physical (PHY) and ATM layers, the ILMI, OAM (traffic control), and PVC support.

UNI 3.0—An upgrade of UNI 2.0 with traffic control for PCR and the operation over current transmission systems as some of the additional features.

UNI 3.1—A corrected version of UNI 3.0, this specification also includes SSCOP standards.

UNI 4.0—This UNI specification refers to signaling issues in ABR and VP and QoS negotiation.

universally administered address (UAA)—The address permanently encoded in an adapter at the rime of manufacture. All universally administered addresses are unique.

unnumbered acknowledgment (UA)—A data link control command used in establishing a link and in answering receipt of logical link control frames.

unshielded twisted pair (UTP)—See telephone twisted pair.

UPC—Usage Parameter Control. A form of traffic control that checks and enforces a user's conformance with the traffic contract and the QoS parameters. Commonly known as traffic policing, it is performed at the UNI level.

UTOPIA—Universal Test and Operation Physical Interface. An interface to provide connectivity at the PHY level among ATM entities.

UTP—Unshielded Twisted Pair. A twisted-pair (copper) wire without any protective sheathing, used for short-distance wiring (such as building). Two categories are specified by the ATM Forum for cell transmission: 3 (CAT-3) and 5 (CAT-5).

VBR-NRT—Variable Bit Rate-Non-Real Time. One of the service types for transmitting traffic where timing information is not critical and that is characterized by the average and peak cell rates. It is well-suited for long data packet transfers.

VBR-RT—Variable Bit Rate-Real Time. One of the service types for transmitting traffic that depends on timing information and control. It is characterized by the average and peak cell rates. VBR-RT is suitable for carrying traffic such as packetized (compressed) video and audio.

VC—Virtual Channel. A term to describe the unidirectional flow of ATM cells between connecting (switching or end-user) points that share a common identifier number (VCI).

VCC—Virtual Channel Connection. Defined as a concatenation of virtual channel links.

VCI—Virtual Channel Identifier. A 16-bit value in the ATM cell header that provides a unique identifier for the VC that carries that particular cell.

VF—Variance Factor. It is the CRM normalized by the variance of the total cell rate over a given circuit.

virtual channel—See VC.

virtual circuit—A connection setup across the network between a source and a destination where a fixed route is chosen for the entire session and bandwidth is dynamically allocated (*see also* datagram).

virtual connection—A connection established between end-users (source and destination) where packets are forwarded along the same path and bandwidth is not permanently allocated until it is used.

Virtual Telecommunications Access Method (VTAM)—A set of programs that control communication between nodes and application programs in SNA.

VLAN—Virtual LAN. A networking environment where users on physically independent LANs are interconnected in such a way that it appears as if they are on the same LAN workgroup (*see also* LANE).

VOD—Video on Demand. A technology that enables the customer to remotely select and play a video transmitted over communications links.

VP—Virtual Path. A term to describe a set of VCs grouped together between crosspoints (switches, in other words).

VPC—Virtual Path Connection. Defined as a concatenation of VP links.

VPCI/VCI—Virtual Path Connection Identifier/Virtual Channel Identifier. A combination of two numbers, one for identifying the VP and one for VCI.

VPI—Virtual Path Identifier. An eight-bit value in the cell header that identifies the VP and accordingly the virtual channel to which the cell belongs.

VPN—Virtual Private Network. Network resources provided to users on demand by public carriers such that the users view this partition of the network as a private network. The advantage of the VPNs over the dedicated private networks is that the former allows a dynamic allocation of network resources.

WAN—Wide Area Network. A network that covers long-haul areas and usually utilizes public telephone circuits. The LAN segments are bridged or routed using communication lines, increasing the geographic size of the LAN.

WATM—Wireless ATM. An emerging technology for interfacing wireless and ATM networks.

workstation—A terminal or computer attached to a network.

X.25—One of the first CCITT-standardized public (data) packet-switching network protocols. Originally designed to operate over unreliable communications links, it supports both VC and datagram services.

INDEX